The Market and the *Oikos*

Ideas, History, and Modern China

Edited by

VOLUME 18

The titles published in this series are listed at *brill.com/ihmc*

The Market and the *Oikos*

The Relationship between Religion and Capitalism in Modern China

By

Hans Derks

BRILL

LEIDEN | BOSTON

"The Market and the *Oikos* (here the Royal Palace)," originally published in "Amsterdamse Markten vroeger en nu" (Amsterdam: Kan's katern no. 10).

The Library of Congress Cataloging-in-Publication Data is available online at http://catalog.loc.gov
LC record available at http://lccn.loc.gov/2018031890

Typeface for the Latin, Greek, and Cyrillic scripts: "Brill". See and download: brill.com/brill-typeface.

ISSN 1875-9394
ISBN 978-90-04-38390-6 (hardback)
ISBN 978-90-04-38391-3 (e-book)

This book is printed on acid-free paper and produced in a sustainable manner.

Contents

Preface IX
1 Introduction IX
2 A Mystery Explained X
3 A Famous Debate XVII
4 China XXII
5 Plan of the Book XXIII
Acknowledgements XXVII
Abbreviations and Notes XXIX

PART 1
The Problem

1 Religion, Capitalism and the Rise of Double-Entry Bookkeeping 3
1.1 Introduction 3
1.2 The C in the Relationship 6
1.2.1 *The Origin of Capitalism* 8
1.2.2 *Market versus* Oikos 14
1.2.3 *The Oikoïdal Economy* 17
1.2.4 *"Rechenhaftigkeit"* 25
1.3 Religion and the Rise of Double-Entry Bookkeeping 29
1.3.1 *The Revision* 30
1.3.2 *Business Scruples and All the Rest* 33
1.3.3 *The Catholicism Thesis* 36
1.3.4 *Commenda and Common-law* 37
1.3.5 *A Papal Revolution?* 39
1.4 The Pasts and Future of DEB 41
1.4.1 *The Future of the Present* 42
1.4.2 *The Past of the Present* 43
1.4.3 *The Theory of the Balance* 49
1.4.4 *Political Geometry and Arithmetic* 54
1.5 The Balance of a Theory 60

PART 2
Market and Oikos: *Basics in the West*

2 **How to Bring Cows to Athens** 71
- 2.1 What is a Polis? 71
- 2.2 An *Astu* for a Polis 84
- 2.3 The Southern Greek "Cities" 89
- 2.4 *Astu* Versus *Agros* 93

3 **A Fascinating *Oikos*** 104
- 3.1 Introduction 104
- 3.2 The Basic Concept House-*Oikos* 106
- 3.3 An *Oikos* Controversy 109
- 3.4 The "Whole House" of Otto Brunner 115
- 3.5 The Devil and the Details 119
- 3.6 The End of an Ideology? 125

4 **Oikoïdal Qualities: *Rasse, Volk* and *Nation*** 126
- 4.1 Introduction: Weber and Rasse 126
- 4.2 "Jewish" *Rasse* Theories Now 132
- 4.3 Some "Devastating" Comments in Advance 137
- 4.4 The Future of the Past 142
- 4.5 The Birth of German Anti-Semitism 150
- 4.6 Ignaz Zollschan, 1877–1948 155
  - 4.6.1 Rasse-*theory* 157
  - 4.6.2 *The* Rasse *Categories and Meanings* 163
- 4.7 Arthur Ruppin, 1876–1943 166
- 4.8 Werner Sombart, 1863–1941 172

5 **Market or Oikoïdal Religion: The Case of "Ancient Judaism"** 179
- 5.1 The Problem 179
- 5.2 The Near Eastern Challenge 185
- 5.3 The Many "Signs of Cain" 188
- 5.4 *Amalek*, the Eternal Enemy 195
- 5.5 The Pariah Complex 200
- 5.6 The Crime and Its "*Tatort*" 208
- 5.7 Preliminary Conclusions 212

PART 3
Market and Oikos: *Basics in the East*

6 **Settlers Between East and West** 221
- 6.1 Settlers' Historical Sins 221
- 6.2 Protestants 225
- 6.3 Catholics 227
- 6.4 The Heirs and Heiresses 230
- 6.5 Profiles 234

7 **On the Origin of Market Relations in (Asian) History** 236
- 7.1 Stock Farmers Versus Peasants 236
- 7.2 Weber's Comparative World History 241
- 7.3 Ideology 247
- 7.4 Milk and Meat 249
- 7.5 The Mutual Relationships 255
- 7.6 The Rulers and Their Wars 258
- 7.7 Imperial Oikoïdal Court Rules 261
- 7.8 Market Behavior 263
- 7.9 Ideological Historiography 266
- 7.10 Nomads and Oikoïdal Collectivizations 268
- 7.11 An Evaluation 272

8 **Town and Country in Chinese History: An Overview** 275
- 8.1 Introduction 275
- 8.2 The Pre-Industrial Phase 277
- 8.3 The Roaring 19th Century 285
- 8.4 The Start of Industrialization 291
- 8.5 The Shanghai Westernization 300
- 8.6 Town and Country in the Interbellum 301
- 8.7 A Russian Lesson? 303
- 8.8 The "New Democracy" 305
- 8.9 Land Reform, 1950–1952 307
- 8.10 City Reform, 1950–1955 309
- 8.11 To the Present 310

PART 4
*Toward a Market–*Oikos *Theory*

9 **Old Market-*Oikos* Theories** 317
- 9.1 An Old Debate About New Questions 317
- 9.2 A "Mode of Despotism"? 326
- 9.3 The European Ancestors 331
- 9.4 The Wittfogel Debates 338
- 9.5 From Post-War Modernization to Shock Therapy 340

10 **A Sparring Partner for All Seasons** 348
- 10.1 Introduction 348
- 10.2 Weber in the USA 350
- 10.3 Weber in Europe 354
- 10.4 Weber in China 363

11 **Epilogue** 371
- 11.1 A Favorite Method 371
- 11.2 The Theses 372
- 11.3 The Follow-up 375

Bibliography 377
Name and Subject Index 405

Preface

1 Introduction

In my previous scholarly writings about European history or social and economic experiences, antagonisms between the "city" and the "country," in all possible dramatic "western" and colonial settings, frequently appeared in what were called "developing countries." Much sooner rather than later, they were accompanied by the name of Max Weber and his rather mysterious "market versus *oikos*" concept. It became inevitable to look for theories to answer questions of why things happened as they did in history as well as in daily life.

As usual, there was no straight line from A to Z. At regular intervals, however, the urge to combine or compare individual experiences and studies of possible details in a larger setting became too puzzling: then it was time to take stock and extensive books appeared.

The last of this kind of empirical and theoretical studies was a large socio-economic examination of the opium problem in world history. Militant Dutch merchants and later other—mainly British and French—colonial interests from the 17th century onwards created devastating socio-economic and political problems throughout vast regions of India, China, Indo China and Indonesia. From the middle of the 19th century onwards, these problems were exported ("back") to Europe and the USA, resulting in the present drug trade and its infrastructure and underground aspects, compounding wealth and poverty disparities, contributing to widespread drug addiction and so on.

It is obvious that studies like this triggered, in turn, many theoretical, practical and methodological problems that were more fundamental every time: Who were the perpetrators from the "Western Metropoles"? Why did they appear? Who were the victims in the "Global Countryside"? Why were they susceptible to becoming victims of foreigners? Why did they act as they did? Did this occur only in Asia but not first in Europe itself? Which preconditions had to be fulfilled, for instance, in the "sedentary European households" before European "market households" could be enabled to go to China, thereby creating serious trade or colonial dependencies? And what did those "Chinese results" look like in town and country? And in the colonizers' home countries?

More new questions and unsatisfying or unavailable answers led to the following attempt to combine, compare and systematize things in order to discover the "definitive solution(s)." The subject inevitably concerns a more fundamental level of sophistication, leading to something like the interrelations between "market and *oikos*" (plural) and "town and country" (plural).

How to proceed with such a complicated plan? To make this manageable, the present study is divided into, first, a large empirical part (chapters 1–8) in which the theoretical concepts are briefly defined, and a later theoretical part (chapters 9–11) that uses the practical analysis to create new theory.

So, let's use this preface to contemplate this plan and start with that mysterious *oikos* concept proposed by Max Weber.

2 A Mystery Explained

Half a century ago I discovered and used the *oikos* concept for the first time thanks to a completely trivial reason: I had to explain "ecology" to my students. This was necessary because my colleague (a chemist) and I had to invent a brand new discipline for a new academic activity, defined as "environmental studies" ("milieukunde" in Dutch). These studies had to be multidisciplinary, combining social and natural sciences; among the latter, the biologically oriented ecology had to receive priority.

I wrote in a course book (1975) that like "economy," "ecology" was derived from the Greek *oikos*, normally translated as "house." Some students welcomed this and pointed out some religious guides. At that time some protestant Christians had begun making the deterioration of the environment an instrumental part of their sectarian creed and warning that we should follow God's guidelines for caring for the earth as "God's *oikos*." From this perspective "ecology" had as much to do with biology as with a message of God, which was no party for a humble scholar like me.

Happily I had consulted the *Greek-English Lexicon* of Liddell-Scott and found many other meanings for *oikos*. This became the start of an intellectual trip through history and world-societies that was as unexpected as it was spectacular.

My consultation of this lexicon resulted not only in a much more differentiated translation, but also in quite a different approach to my lessons in "ecology/milieukunde." The reactions of my specialized academic colleagues (religious or not) came as a big surprise: they were not amused, and many of them started quarreling.

In particular, the biologically-oriented ecologists, the natural scientists in general and the religiously-oriented students detested the much more political and economic approach to environmental problems that resulted from my new definition of *oikos*. They favored strict technically, chemically or biologically oriented problems and models, eventually combining them with—in my view at least—primitive (protestant) theological reflections that are typical for technocrats.

Even the academic freedom of speech at the University of Utrecht at the time was so underdeveloped that my colleague and I were dismissed from this institution of learning, victims of my own innocent way of defining concepts and correctly reading Liddell-Scott. Along with the price to be paid for this lesson in academic cooperation aimed at solving together the many problems in the environment, there was a skepticism about multidisciplinary work in universities, let alone the needed interdisciplinary work. These goals, I later learned, could be better achieved in many practical development projects aimed at alleviating direct needs arising from deteriorating living conditions.

But what was written in the student course book, belonging to the "archaeology" of the present study?[1]

> *Oikos* means: house or dwelling, room, apartment, hall, dining-room, tent, form or lair, nest or litter, household, family, fortune or wealth, possession, estate or manor, home or residence, native town, native country. *Oikonomia,* from which our "economy" etc. is derived, means: household government, leadership, division or distribution or partition.

From this one can deduce:

1 that *oikos* is related to spatial elements (house, tent, etc.), and that *oikonomia* is related to the partition of these into rooms, halls, etc.;
2 that *oikos* is related to economic elements (wealth, fortune, etc.), and that *oikonomia* is related to the distribution of these among households, countries, etc.;
3 that *oikos* is related to social elements (family, household, etc.), and that *oikonomia* is related to the division of the labor or leadership of these elements;
4 that *oikos* is related to political elements (native town, native country, etc.), and that *oikonomia* is related to their governance.

This objective way of defining *oikos* and *oikonomia* demonstrates clearly why the ecologists at the time were so angry: it looked nothing like their biological discipline and the other natural scientists, let alone the God-fearing people, also had reasons to be annoyed. The immanent antagonism between the several kinds of sciences was covered in the coursebook (1975): to explain that a functioning *oikos* depends on a fruitful, fertile, prolific environment of town and country in order to satisfy their inhabitants, seems to be too obvious after half a century of hard scholarly labor in universities.

This time, *oikos,* with its spatial, economic, social and political characteristics, shall be analyzed in a more fundamental way, in a specific relationship to

1 Hans Derks, 1975, 2, 3.

the *market.* It may be assumed that this will be a complicated problem or series of problems after the given definition.

The obvious question first: How is *market* defined in dictionaries comparable to the Liddell-Scott, like the Oxford English Dictionary (OED)? It comes from the Latin *mercatus* and the Latin verb *mercari* (to trade), leading to the 15th-century English or French *market* with many related words and meanings like *merchandise, merchant, mercenary, mercantilism, marketing,* etc. Let's see what the OED mentions about *market*:

1 The meeting together of people for the purchase and sale of provisions or live stock, publicly exposed, at a fixed time and place ...
2 *Law*. The privilege granted to the lord of a manor, a municipality or other body, to establish a meeting of persons to buy and sell ...
3 An open space or covered building in which cattle, provisions, etc. are exposed for sale; a market place, market-house ...
4 The action or business of buying and selling; a purchase or sale ... 1525 ... The marketing of a commodity—1680 ...
5 Sale as controlled by supply and demand ... 1684 ...
6 Opportunity of buying or selling 1684.
7 Price in the market, market value. Also *fig.* 1535.
8 A place or seat of trade; a country, district, etc. in which there is a demand for articles of trade; hence, the trade of such a country, etc. 1615.

It looks like as if the definitions of *oikos* and market concern, respectively, a pre-modern and early-modern period in European history; a period in which society was dominated, according to Aristotle, by agricultural "households," families, etc. and a period around 1500–1600 when the classical market-mechanisms were introduced.

This last "market-development" concerns a fundamental transition in European history from "static oikoidal" situations to rather "dynamic market" situations. It was an age when the whole of Europe was constantly at war thanks to the religious reformation and the rise of very aggressive secular states. Globally, the first "Western colonies" were conquered under the cruelest circumstances, which brought the Christian perpetrators not only new lands, but a wealth of previously unknown and very lucrative market products like slaves, pepper, gold or opium.

A new transition to a more modern period arrived, for instance, when the ideologues of the French Revolution like Rousseau appeared on the scene. The first sentences of his *A Discourse on Political Economy* (1754) are:

> The word Economy, or Oeconomy, is derived from *oikos*, a house, and *nomos*, law, and meant originally only the wise and legitimate government

> of the house for the common good of the whole family. The meaning of the term was then extended to the government of thet great family, the State. To distinguish these two senses of the word, the latter is called general or political economy, and the former domestic or particular economy. The first is discussed in the present discourse ... They differ too much in extent to be regulated in the same manner; and there will always be a great difference between domestic government, in which a father can see everything for himself, and civil government, where the chief sees hardly anything save through the eyes of others.[2]

A few years later, around 1764, Voltaire made a similar statement.[3] There is much to say about both writers, the big shots of the Enlightenment, and their theories. Here it's enough to remark that in their age the transition was made from *oikos* as household-family into *oikos* as nation-state. How the modern nation state is constructed as a republic dates from the present. That it was mainly in Protestant countries around the North Sea that the old monarchy could be consolidated is in need of a special explanation about the quality of the indigenous elite.

However, it seems as if some relationship with "market" etc. is still absent in Rousseau's and Voltaire's writings. This is remarkable because neither author comments on the most spectacular happenings in the "financial markets" at the beginning of the 18th century in Amsterdam, London and Paris.[4] Also, both authors comment on the first "household" period without questioning the self-sufficiency (autarky) ideology or doctrine connected with this period. Apparently, the new state-*oikos* should be considered to be as democratic as the romantic *image* of the old *oikos* without a replacement of/for the decapitated monarchs.

Next, the many readers of both authors were immediately confronted with the start of the English "industrial revolution" and brand new phenomena (in the adhered oikos- or oikoidal perspective at least) like private competition related to industrial production on a rather large scale that utilized colonial resources and world-wide markets. For these readers the continental oikoidal mercantilism of the French and other states, and the physiocratic agricultural policy of these states or the "Kameralism" provided the guidelines.[5]

---

2 J.J. Rousseau, 128.

3 Voltaire, vol. 6, 201–218. This edition is a compilation of several of Voltaire's works including the *Philosophical Dictionary,* 1764. He compares an *économie domestique* with an *économie publique,* writes more witty than Rousseau but in content it was the same.

4 Eric S. Schubert, 299–307.

5 See for the details Karl Pribram, vol. 1, Chapters 4, 5 and 7.

In short: Rousseau, Voltaire and the economic experts of their time (Turgot, Colbert, Quesnay, etc.) were busy with the modernization of the state and its bureaucracy, with taxation-systems and "national debt"intended for the general aim to fight wars in Europe and its colonies better and longer. The aberrations resulting in financial speculations around 1700 are perceived by Schubert as similar to London's Big Bang in 1986. This is a mistake.

It cannot be a coincidence that the definitions of *market* are concentrated around 1700, because they concern *new* experiences; the most one can say is that they were the first "finger exercises" for the rather autonomous later financial markets. Although the phenomenon of the *market* existed from time immemorial, that was not the case with the product *money in a market* with which the ancient Greeks or related tribes started to experiment.

The waves of financial speculation around 1700 were ultimately the results of the *private* actions of speculators (who mostly earned their money in the colonies) who gambled on chances provided by the underdeveloped systems of *public* finance and credit.

> The catalyst for closer ties between ... London and Amsterdam [the seat of most speculators, H.D.[6]] was the War of the Spanish Succession (1702–1713), the cost of which forced a huge increase in England's total government debt. The great strains in British finance created large opportunities for the Dutch to invest in the British markets because the British encouraged foreign investment in order to bolster the government's foundering finances.[7]

It took at least half a century before all the features of "market" and *oikos* could be combined with the new industrial elements. But were they combined in, for instance, the work of contemporary heroes of thought like Karl Marx?

Whatever the brilliant innovations Marx made in his work about industrial societies in worldwide relationships, one misses similar analyses about "the new 19th century state" or the oikos-state in general. One reason for this is that Marx did not differ much from Rousseau and his many predecessors in this conceptualization of "the first period" (primitive accumulation; Hausgemeinschaft/household; Greek *oikos*; Aristotle converted into a Christian; and so on). Last but not least, "market-analyses" are not Marx's most popular subject and are not found in Marxist literature.[8]

---

6 How much and why some Dutch earned money is described in my 2015, 163–179.

7 Eric S. Schubert, 300–301.

8 It is remarkable enough that in Iring Fetscher's excellent handbook on nearly all aspects of Marx and Marxism, not even the word "Mark(e)t" appears. Compensation is provided in the sections on "Tausch" or "division of labor."

However, together with several other 18th- and 19th-century Englishmen (from Adam Smith to J.S. Mill), Marx pointed to another, most important dichotomy, that of the *town–country antagonism*.[9] From the abundantly available quotes on this subject, I cite only the following one:

> The basis of all developed division of labor, made possible through the exchange of products, is the separation between town and country. One may say, that the whole economic history of society can be summarized in the movement of this contradiction ...[10]
>
> [Adam Smith is quoted, for instance, in the *Grundrisse* as follows:] The great trade of every civilized society is that which is established between the inhabitants of the town and those of the countryside ... it consists in the exchange of the raw product for the manufactured product ... either directly, or by the intervention of money ... [and so on].[11]

To make the analyses less complicated, we will deal in this book only with this antagonism where it is appropriate and unavoidable. It is already difficult enough to ask today's students to review the 19th-century lessons, as proved by William Roseberry's disenchanting experiences after reading several anthropological market-related essays.[12]

Most anthropologists, he writes, start with a simple definition of "the market" or "the economy" and compare this with "primitive or non-Western societies, where they found the definition inadequate..." Then they move to "economic processes in non-capitalist situations" that seems to reject the original definition of the market, followed by "oppositional models: market vs. non-market societies, Western vs. non-Western, commodity vs. gift exchange and so on ... [where] the basic categories of economic thought remain unexamined."[13] Roseberry did not mention these basic categories and, like most of his colleagues, he was not fond of defining the concepts he used or of combining sometimes impressive findings about markets with oikoidal or town-country features.

That is a pity because it robs the students of the necessary realistic perspectives such as "trifles" found in the Nazi-views on town-country relations, as

9 The writings in which Marx and Engels directly addressed the town-country antagonism are, for instance, the *Frühschriften* (1953), 379; *Grundrisse* (w.y), 20, 363–413, 739, 909; *Grundrisse* (1973), 99, 459–471, 857; *Das Kapital*, vol. 1, 371, 527, 650; vol. 3, 790; *Ausgewählte Briefe*, 105. For this subject see my 1986, 2–50 and *passim*.

10 *Das Kapital*, vol. 1, 373.

11 *Grundrisse der Kritik der politischen Ökonomie* (w.y), 740; *Grundrisse* (Penguin), 857.

12 In: James G. Carrier, ed., 251–260.

13 There are still good exceptions like the essay of Paul Nolte, 1997, 329–360.

stated by a very influential ideologue, Konrad Meyer. They are basic to doctrines leading toward a world war. Meyer writes in 1939:

> Countryside (*Land*) and town (*Stadt*) are the two social and economic bodies (*Wirtschaftskörper*) in which the whole life is lived among every people (*Volk*) with a high culture (*höheren Kulturvölkern*) ...[Meyer also points to features like:] ... The products and services exchanged through buying and selling on the different markets shall receive a valuation in money. The relationships between town and country (*Stadt und Land*) are, therefore, not only characterized by the mutually exchanged kind and quantity of products, but also by a relationship qua value (*Wertverhältnis*). This last exists after the exchange (of the products and services) and their expression in certain price-systems.[14]

It's clear that with Meyer we have arrived in the 20th-century and, while both in the USA and in Germany the swastika flags wave again, we also come to the present. Now that we are confronted in the most popular films and TV programs, from *Lords of the Rings* to *Game of Thrones,* with a world of the classical barbarian, bloody, licentious, medieval *Germanen,* it cannot be surprising that Konrad Meyer as well refers to this world, the first oikoidal period, as that of "primitive accumulation." He also writes:

> The abuses in agriculture start when the old Germanic rules about the soil (*Auffassung vom Boden*) disappear, when the duty-bound (*pflichtgebundenem*) family property is replaced ... by the late-Roman laws of unlimited individual property of mainly the city-soil ...[15]

Indeed, here market–*oikos* and the town–country antagonisms are *combined* in an ideology of a dictatorial nationalist state, an exceptional case that demands further investigations. Thoughts like this about the now well-known *Blut-und-Boden* and *race/Rasse* doctrines were already widespread in the 19th century, but they had to compete with others thanks to different abuses, like an "unbridled capitalism." This led to numerous famous debates and not only in Marxist circles. One of them is highly useful to our aim to analyze the market–*oikos* relationship in all possible details.

14 Konrad Meyer, ed. 1939, 115.
15 Konrad Meyer, ed. 1939, 198 ff.

3 A Famous Debate

One of the best-known and least understood debates in modern sociology is called the *Max Weber Thesis* and concerns the relationship between religion (namely, Calvinism) and the rise of capitalism. The vast literature about this subject has not uncovered how the fundamental market–*oikos* dichotomy formed the nucleus of the whole Weber-argumentation.[16] That is my thesis after discussing old and recent literature about this Weber Thesis; proving this is possible, but will take much space because this case is very complicated and deserves sound historical analyses in the first place.

Earlier I discussed many practical elements of the market-oikos (and town-country) relationship without recourse to the *Max Weber Thesis* and its many consequences. Recently, after a period of relative silence, the debate on the Weber Thesis has started again in the USA, Europe and China.[17] Because it is an old, fundamental, popular subject in every new period of "capitalist crisis" and named after him, Max Weber remains a rather popular "sparring partner." Therefore, a new kind of review of the case is always worthwhile for sociologists, economists, historians and even theologians.

Contrary to recent opinions about Weber's market-option,[18] this book will demonstrate how Weber opted fully for the "oikoïdal ticket." Before starting the "proof of this pudding" with the long Chapter 1, however, it is appropriate to briefly address the question of which kind of debate this was in Weber's time.

For Weber, the "oikoidal choice," already hidden in the title of his *The Protestant Ethic and the Spirit of Capitalism* (*Die Protestantische Ethik und der Geist des Kapitalismus* 1904, 1905, was probably too obvious to mention explicitly; when he referred to a market versus *oikos* antagonism he (or his editor) did not remind the reader of his earlier writings. There is one excuse: his magnum opus *Economy and Society* (*Wirtschaft und Gesellschaft* 1919, 1925) was published after his death and was not as subject to debate as *The Protestant Ethic*.

---

16 See, for instance, Richard Swedberg, in: Mark Granovetter, Richard Swedberg, ed. 77–96. This is, in fact, one of the most interesting readers in economic sociology as it provides a confrontation between the old-fashioned contributions of Polanyi and Collins with the new-fashioned of Granovetter and Swedberg. In my book I reduce theoretical discussions to the bare minimum in favor of the practical historical analyses. See the Preface.

17 See in Mark Granovetter, Richard Swedberg, ed., the article of Gary Hamilton and Nicole Woolsey Biggart. See as well Gary Hamilton in: *International Sociology*, 2, 1987, 289–300. More specific are the writings of Wang Hui on Weber and the Question of Chinese Modernirty, in: Wang Hui and Theodore Huters, ed., 264–308; Dan Zang, 2014, 33–53; Po-Fang Tsai, 2016, 118–133 with interesting further literature. See further Chapter 9.

18 Giacomo Marramao, 2012, 138.

Another reason is more important. When *The Protestant Ethic* was published, Weber was just 40 years old, "an up-and-coming man" while now he is well-known as a choleric debater who first hit below the belt and provoked duels before replying reasonably to the *relevant* criticism. This criticism came, for instance, from the historian Felix Rachfahl.[19]

Rachfahl was the first to point out the main problem of Weber's treatise, the way he handled what he had called the "traditionalistische Bedarfsdeckung" (the traditional satisfaction of demands or human needs) versus the "kapitalistischer Erwerb um des Erwerb willen" (earning money only for the sake of getting more money). In the first chapter this rephrasing of the market-versus-*oikos* concept will be part of our discussion, so I shall not elaborate on it here.

We need only question what "Calvinism" or "religion" has to do with "satisfying demands" and "market" has to do with "capitalism" and how they are defined. The related problems must be addressed as well: referring to fundamental differences inside Germany and its history or—on the largest scale—to antagonisms between a continental European and the Anglo-Saxon cultures, in particular the American one represented by Weber's well-known example of Benjamin Franklin's puritanism. This can be demonstrated rather simply by comparing the available encyclopedic knowledge in both realms.

At the time Weber published *The Protestant Ethic* an excellent and most intriguing, scientific institution existed in Germany, the *Handwörterbuch der Staatswissenschaften* (HdS), edited by *Staatswissenschaftler* like Conrad, Lexis and others.[20] It was the result of multidisciplinary work by the best scholars in sociology, economy, history, constitutional and civil law and jurisprudence, accountancy, etc. aimed at the best possible management of the national state. The HdS was written in the 19th-century liberal mood in which even Friedrich Engels' contribution could be accepted.

As such, the HdS represented the late 19th-century modernization of the 18th-century science of public finance (*Kameralwissenschaften*) which—like French mercantilism—concerned the management of the absolutist state. An important part of it was the *Kameralistik*, the bookkeeping of the state, which is still practiced today.

In their turn, these sciences were a renewal of the much older *household-management* books (for instance, Albertis *Della Famiglia,* 1432), which were reproductions of ancient treatises with the same purpose (Aristotle, Xenophon

19 See among many reports of these highly irritating affairs in relation to his bad health Jürgen Kaube, 2014, 297–302 or Joachim Radkau, 2005, 338–342.

20 The first edition appeared in the years 1890 to 1897; the second in 1898 to 1901; the third in 1909 to 1911 and the last in the years 1923 to 1929.

or Varro). Indeed, there is a direct line between these latter writings and the HdS, between the alleged Greek "household economy" and the modern "theory of state management" as will be discussed further below.

Around 1850 people like Rodbertus started to write about the ancient economy as an "Oikenwirtschaft." Many followed this example, including Weber who began detailing this perspective by using "*oikos*" not only for "house" and "household" (*Hausgemeinschaft*) but for "state" as well, a move with a bright future. Was it an original Weberian innovation?

Although young, compared to the mostly elderly and established authors of the HdS, Max Weber published in its second edition the first version of what later became known as *The Agrarian Sociology of Ancient Civilizations* that would ultimately run to about 280 pages. In 1898, Weber's contribution was not more than 28 pages and it appeared under the heading *Agrargeschichte* (*lit. agrarian history.*) He was adopting the HdS framework and ideology, but looked at historical developments in the tradition of what was called the *Historische Schule*. Furthermore, he joined the politico-economic promotors of a specific oikoïdal continental European way of state-formation or state-management.

In other words, the HdS concentrated many scientific disciplines in the service of contemporary German state-formation (in full swing after the unification of the individual German monarchical *oikoi* in one imperial super-*Oikos* in 1870/71), creating its own historical legitimation through some evolution from the ancient Greeks well into the 20th-century German state. Max Weber became its youngest prophet.

The undisputed leader of these *Staatswissenschaftler*, the economist Gustave (von) Schmoller (1838–1917), got all the space he needed in the HdS to define the main concepts starting with the German word *Wirt* or *Wirtschaft* circumscribed by Schmoller as "the household, like 'economy' is derived from *oikos* = house." It concerns an economy "that is an autarchy that does not work for the market" (ganz auf sich ruhende, nicht für den Markt arbeitende Hauswirtschaft).[21] Such an entity cooperated with its neighbor(s) only when it had to fight against nomads, build common edifices or regulate common use of land.

According to Schmoller, a *Volkswirtschaft*, or national economy, was the next stage in the development of nation-states that developed at the end of the European Middle Ages. This definition is incomplete since he, for instance, does not define *Volk*; the economic side of this national state must be called a "Volkswirtschaft, the political economy, the économie politique ... Just as with

21 HdS, 1900, volume 7, 543.

the family, community and state one could and should perceive [the Volkswirtschaft] as a real totality."

We now have to reveal the other side of the same coin. If we are irritated by the sloppy way of defining terms, our astonishment could better be reserved for the way "market" is treated in this bible for state-bureaucrats, the HdS.[22] It is defined solely as a place (or even a manifestation, *Veranstaltung*) where consumers and producers meet each other to exchange goods. The most remarkable aspect is the near complete absence of any relationship with production, industry, prices or marketing. If this treatment appeared in the ancient oikoïdal writings or in the *Kameralwissenschaft,* I would not be astonished, but this appeared in 1900, and at the time "the best economists of the world" were satisfied with this perspective. This aspect demands an explanation as a subject of this book.

To give the above its proper profile, it is worthwhile looking at it from an Anglo-Saxon point of view, as presented by the comparable American *Encyclopaedia of the Social Sciences* (ESS) by the political economist Edwin Seligman and sociologist Alvin Johnson along with their many associates. ESS was initially published in 1930.

The first thing that is remarkable (for some, even alarming) is the absence in ESS of entries about house, *oikos*, household or something like *Staatswissenschaft* (or equivalents). Of course, the article "market" is used in a few sentences to refer to a geography of markets (village market, etc.), but that is the only aspect of the article comparable to the HdS. The main part of it concerns prices, price theory and problems of continuously changing markets.

It is stipulated that the "classical analysis" concerns a kind of geographical problem only, "the explanation of what takes place in the allocation of *fixed* supplies to potential holders."[23] It is a reference to the organization of a market "from above," as a form of state-intervention. The concepts of "equilibrium," "balance" or "perfect market" used by the economists among the *Staatswissenschaftler,* always looking for balance between supply and demand, are not used (and are even detested) by their American colleagues. A typical quotation demonstrating the stand of the latter is:

> The theory of the perfect market fails to approximate the actual market situation … chiefly because production is more highly specialized than consumption. The conflict between the sellers short run interest

22 HdS, 1900, volume 5, 691–703 an article from Karl Rathgen: "Markten und Messen."

23 I have used the reprint of 1949: ESS, 1949, volume 10, 131. The article is from Charles O. Hardy; my italics.

> in clearing the market and his long run interest in "protecting" it constitutes the problem of "price policy," a concept quite foreign to equilibrium economics.[24]

The above must be enough to demonstrate that a market-*oikos* controversy is not only a highly complex phenomenon within German and European history and economic and political practices of fundamental importance, but that it also concerns the very heart of European–American contradictions.

This is still an interesting "hot issue" in the postwar scholarly debates in "the West."[25] A market-*oikos* controversy can thus be found in the writings of Rodbertus (ca. 1850) and his theory of the *Oikenwirtschaft*. This was transformed by Karl Bücher in his influential economic history to define levels or *Stufen* of economic development. As we will see in Chapter 1, for instance, Max Weber was one of his supporters, who inspired in his turn people like Karl Polanyi and classicist Moses Finley.

After about 1950 the latter became the master of classical economic history. Symbolically or not, at the very moment Finley died, one of the first and certainly one of the most extensive criticisms of his theory of the "ancient economy" was published. This was followed, among others, by a contribution entitled "The 'Ancient Economy': the problem and the fraud."[26]

The result is that at present even the three editors of a reader about Finley (2017) write that, concerning his *Ancient Economy,* much of the scholarly world spent a generation trying "to substantiate the claims that Finley made, before generally concluding that the task was vain and that neither ancient evidence nor coherent argument supported his view."[27] Happily, now a much

---

24 ESS, 1949, volume 10, 132.

25 A controversy of this name was fought as a reaction on the writings of Rodbertus (around 1850) and his theory of the "Oikenwirtschaft" which was transformed by Karl Bücher as one of his *Stufen* of his economic history. This was again accepted by, for instance, Max Weber, who inspired people like Karl Polanyi and classicist Moses Finley. The latter and his many supporters were strongly criticised for the first time in my 1986, 427–456. See further below.

26 In *The European Legacy*, 7, 2002, 701–735. My publication of 1986 lead to a big row including a true lawsuit (!) with several Finley representatives under the leadership of professor Pleket of the University of Leiden (who wrote together with Finley a booklet about sports in the ancient world). Pleket succeeded later to block the publication of my *De Koe van Troje—The Trojan Cow* at the Dutch publisher Contact, Amsterdam, but failed to convince another publisher, Verloren, Hilversum, 1996.

27 Quoted in *Times Literary Supplement,* 24 February 2017, 28 relative to editors like Daniel Jew, Robin Osborne and Michael Scott and their book *M.I. Finley. An ancient historian and his impact.* Cambridge: Cambridge University Press, 2017.

more sophisticated level has been also reached thanks to Chinese scholars like Wang Hui.

4 China

In an earlier version of this text, I had decided to confront the previous typical "Western debate" with a typical non-Western history to create a sound basis under a new market–*oikos* theory in combination with a town-country one. After my recent study on the production, trade, marketing, consumption, etc., of opium in the last three hundred years, it did not take long to choose the modern Chinese context for this purpose. Its modern history and sociology became familiar to me in the perspective of China as a serious victim of the Western assault on the East.

Until recently and for centuries the interest in China always concerned a one-sided affair first and foremost because it was mainly Europeans (Portuguese, Spaniards, Dutch, British, Danes, French, Germans and Russians) and ex-Europeans (Americans), who tried and successfully conquered coastal parts of China from the 16th-century onwards (the Chinese never tried to do the reverse, a subject worth considering today.

The interest in studying Chinese market–*oikos* relations (as well as town–country ones) could have been an old desideratum. Were not many details known thanks to the famous China oriented deliberations like the typically Western theories of the *Asiatic Mode of Production* (AMP) and the *Oriental Despotism* (OD) from the 18th and 19th centuries? They are theories in which the *Max Weber Thesis* in particular came to play an important role. Thanks to this fact we can provide a proper analysis of the East-West relations on a relevant theoretical level.

This is even more revealing now, after I had been confronted with the lively Weber reception in China in which the writings of Wang Hui seem to be the most challenging. Viren Murthy discussed his writing and quotes from him the following on which we will have to comment in the proper context. First Murthy, followed by Wang Hui's quote:

> Unlike many scholars, Wang rejects as spurious the idea that socialism stresses the public/state realm, while capitalism expands the private realm. Following Karl Polanyi, he underscores that, unlike "natural economies" capitalism involved a type of monopoly.
>
> It is not just that market society does not protect the private realm in the manner that contemporary Chinese economists and intellectuals

> hope, on the contrary, the "invisible" relations between the market and controlling power incessantly transform "the private realm" into the "social realm."[28]

It is clear that Wang Hui not only directly addresses the kernel of the following discussions, but that his contributions fit into a longstanding and nearly always hot debate in which no academic tricks are abstained from to reach some private or political goals.

In earlier periods "East" and "West" were fully different worlds in all respects, but today it would be a dangerous intellectual, political, etc. limitation not to treat them as a *relationship* of an increasing intensity that rather automatically decreases the value of all kinds of nationalisms. The following plan of the book must be seen in this light as well.

5 Plan of the Book

To avoid misunderstandings, the reader must first be aware that this book can be technically perceived as one long attempt to discuss *one definition after another,* and next, that every story/chapter aims first and foremost to create another "stone" (or a series of "stones") to build the new market-*oikos* theory to be published in a separate volume. Except for Chapter 1, and whatever their subjects, ancient Greek or modern China, the stories are *not* presented for their own sake.

The stories must be "waterproof," but do *not* form a "theme" through the book! Every time a new *part of the market-oikos* relation problem (with its accompanying dichotomy of the town-country relationship) must come to the fore. It is, therefore, unavoidable that this or that other brilliant expert of some subject might be neglected or placed in the limelight even if he or she is not widely known. Take, for instance Otto Brunner in Chapter 3 or Ignaz Zollschan in Chapter 4: they are only relevant in this book as sparring partners because they make it possible to formulate specific features of our problem in a functional way.

A few "rules of the book" follows directly from this: in the last chapter the available "building blocks" should be collected with the aim of opening up a *vista to the sequel*; in the first chapter, the longest, *the field* is sketched and defined upon which later "building blocks" should be fixed.

28 Viren Murthy, 2006, 137–165. See also the review of Murthy from 2012, 178–180.

The reason for choosing just Max Weber as the major sparring partner in this text should be clear after the previous introduction and Chapter 1. In addition, his oeuvre consists of "building blocks" only, including his so-called magnum opus, *Wirtschaft und Gesellschaft* (Economy and Society), for which his wife and an editor unsystematically collected his writings after his death.

In addition, it is an advantage that I recently published a socio-economic history of a classical format in which, for instance, the Chinese history of Asia plays a pivotal role.

As to the content of this study, the first chapter is, of course, devoted to the *Max Weber Thesis* and his way of defining basic elements concerning his "market versus *oikos*" theory; therefore, features such as religion, capitalism and accountability of the state and companies are discussed in a critical way as well. Together they form the main elements of the *field* of the study.

This study concerns *historical-critical* analyses of basic elements of European and Asian (Chinese) histories, thoughts and practices. They result not only in a new view on the relevancy of Max Weber's work today, but also on phenomena as capitalism and—more important—agriculture, nomadism or urbanism.

Chapter 2 is the first in which the town–country relation is brought into the discussion, not yet having been addressed in the previous chapter. The scene is Greek antiquity; in history and philosophy alike, it provides us with many basic elements of life. In nearly every later period it was re-defined so that today the original and indigenous meanings are largely forgotten. That is a pity: Weber's concepts and of his followers like Polanyi or Finley, etc. were derived from the Greeks (or so they thought).[29]

The next chapter discusses the *oikos*-practice; in particular, I discuss its later and recent use in typical nationalist discourses, whatever its ancient Greek background. Much has already been published about the classical *oikos* controversy; it is therefore interesting to refer to its modern impact.

With the features *Race* (*Rasse*), *Volk and Nation* probably the "most beloved" basic oikoidal qualities are given (chapter 4). It is well known that races do not exist (but, as Guillemin rightly wrote, "... they still kill!"). For this discussion all three belong to the concepts used by an elite group busy with all kinds of aggressive state-*integrating* activities, that immediately concern rather aggressive *expurgating* and *selecting* activities. Within the framework of a market-*oikos* practice it is good to see how they are related to each other. This is to be demonstrated by Ignaz Zollschan's theories, as well as those of his supporters and critics.

29 An Asian reception of these three is of the Iranian Mohammad Nafissi, 2005.

Whether Judaism has any relationship with the secular Zionist settlers/colonists (see also chapter 6) except that a small number of Jews also live/d in Palestine/Israel, is a highly controversial issue. That was, of course, not the case in all centuries before 1948 (in fact before 1918 when the nationalist Zionist arrived in Palestine); it seems, therefore, as if Zionists need Jews to suggest a legitimate stay in the "Holy Land," in which the present 25% of the Jewish inhabitants are only clogged by the 75% secular Zionists. This subject shall not be part of our discussion, but in their difficult relationship not only the "Volk" concept played (plays) a controversial role but so did the concepts of "nation," "language," and "race."

The integrating concept with the best pedigree-papers in the West is *religion* (Chapter 5). It is not for nothing that this was Max Weber's "most beloved" concept and subject, as he seems to have put all his hopes for the future of the world on the integrating potential of a *monotheist* religion. Without doubt, for Weber, that would be Christianity, but it could be one that has much or something in common with other world-religions such as Islam, Confucianism, Taoism, Judaism or Buddhism. In the East-West relation, Christianity was part of both imperialism and colonialism. It seems as if Weber's Christianity was divided between a market and an oikoidal one, respectively (American) Calvinism/Puritanism and the continental, European Lutheranism.[30] Was the one functional in imperialism and the other in colonialism?

Chapter 6 concerns the European settlers in the world. They formed the most uncivilized, militant and cruel machine of conquering and colonizing the East and other parts of the world. It looks as if they are the representatives of the western market par excellence. This subject is chosen as a good intermedium between the previous and the following chapters on the East.

Chapter 7 demonstrates the basic elements of the *market* through Weber's erroneous views on China, but the importance of the chapter is that it presents some very neglected elements in all socio-economic histories, that are too accustomed to describing the "positive features" of agrarian sedentary life and not its dialectical relation with external, mobile, inimical, negative, etc. nomadic, non-sedentary cultural social settings.

After this in-depth analysis of market–*oikos* relations on a large social and economic scale, it is not bad to be confronted again with the Chinese town–country relationship over a long period and a large socio-economic scale. Chapter 8 gives an overview from pre-industrial times until the present. It gives the opportunity to address several controversial issues, for example, the

30 Here a relevant section in WG is entitled "Die Kulturreligionen und die 'Welt,'" 367, with a typical comparison between Jews and Puritans, 372.

relations between the indigenous Chinese modernization and the Western imported one.

The aim of all these exercises is also to come to a new market-*oikos* theory. Thus, it is logical to know the previous theories as well. Chapters 9 and 10 are reserved for introducing this highly complicated task. A rather spectacular example of this is the way the earlier debate raged in the "West" about how to perceive the Chinese and "Eastern" challenges. It concerned the debates about the so-called Asiatic Mode of Production and the Eastern or Oriental Despotism. They are compared here for the first time through the writings of Karl Wittfogel, who first chose a Marxian point of view before World War II and afterwards a Weberian one in his *Oriental Despotism* at the service of the Cold War against China, to which certain corners in the "West" want to return.

Chapter 10 focuses on Max Weber because he was my sparring partner in this book. Typical contexts from the USA, Europe and China are chosen to this purpose. It concerns subjects that might also become important in the development of a new market-*oikos* theory.

The *Epilogue* of the book (Chapter 11) contains a series of theses as a warm-up for the new theory; it is not so much a summary because a new theory deserves a new book rather than a summary.

Hans Derks
October 2017
www.hderks.dds.nl

Acknowledgements

Parts of the texts were published under peer-reviewed conditions in well-known journals or as academic obligations; later this happened again with the whole strongly revised text. The original version of Chapter 1 appeared in *Accounting, Business & Financial History*, 18 (2008), 187–213 and received much attention. It is here thoroughly revised and greatly expanded, because it is the nucleus of the book from which the subjects of the subsequent chapters are derived.

My article in *Geschichte und Gesellschaft*, 22 (1996), 221–243 is used in chapters 2 and 3 together with parts of my book *De Koe van Troje/ The Trojan Cow* (Hilversum: Verloren, 1996), 168–199. An earlier version of Chapter 5 appeared in my book *Jew, Nomad or Pariah. Studies on Hannah Arendt's Choice* (Amsterdam: Aksant, 2004), 79–113. Chapter 7 concerns a new composition of texts that appeared in the journal *Oriens Extremus*, 41 (1999), 7–34 which is expanded with my *De Koe van Troje/ The Trojan Cow* (Hilversum: Verloren, 1996), 3 ff. Chapter 8 and 9 are strongly updated texts originally published for my PhD-study at the Faculty of the Social Sciences of the University of Amsterdam. The rest of the text is published here for the first time.

Too many people to mention here should be thanked for their help, comments and inspiration. Therefore, I have to confine my thanks, first, to the editors of well-known journals that were willing to publish my studies: *Accounting, Business & Financial History*, UK; *Dialogues d'histoire anciennes*, CNRS France; *The European Legacy*, Israel; *German History*, UK, *Geschichte und Gesellschaft*, Germany and *Oriens Extremus*, Germany.

Next, there are the scholars who personally helped me in discussing earlier versions, informed me about new developments, assisted by getting things published, and so on. First, of course, the two anonymous peer-reviewers of this market–*oikos* book with their many interesting comments. Among all whom I owe a large debt of gratitude, I can only point here to John Richard Edwards, UK; Eveline Geny, France; Pierre Leveque, France; Bernhard Slicher van Bath, the Netherlands; Ezra and Sacha Talmor, Israel; Hans-Ulrich Wehler, Germany; Wim Wertheim, the Netherlands and the many peer-reviewers who sometimes shed their anonymity like the eminent UK-scholar Basil Yamey on the bookkeeping issue in Chapter 1.

From the side of the publisher I want only to mention the members of the Brill China Departments (Leiden and Boston): Lauren Bissonette, Kayla Griffin, Albert Hoffstädt, Victoria Menson, Patricia Radder and Wilma de Weert who also greatly assisted in making *The History of the Opium Problem*, 2012 a success. To Marti Huetink I am particularly grateful.

Last but not least, I have to thank my "permanent editor," Alison Fisher, who always corrects my international English, and the special copy-editor, Ms. Wendy Smyer Yu, who transformed the manuscript in the appropriate Brill-Boston format with great skill.

Abbreviations

BHH	Biblisch historisches Handwörterbuch (1962–1966); Dutch transl. (1969 ff.), 6 volumes
DKP	Der Kleine Pauly. Lexikon der Antike in fünf Bänden (1979), 5 volumes.
ES	Max Weber, Economy and Society (1978), 2 volumes.
ESS	Encyclopedia of the Social Sciences (1949), 15 volumes.
HdS	Handwörterbuch der Staatswissenschaften (1898–1900), 2nd edition, 8 volumes.
GARS	Max Weber, Gesammelte Aufsätze zur Religionssoziologie (1923–1924), 3 volumes.
GASS	Max Weber, Gesammelte Aufsätze zur Soziologie und Sozialpolitik (1924).
GASW	Max Weber, Gesammelte Aufsätze zur Sozial- und Wirtschaftsgeschichte (1924).
GPS	Max Weber, Gesammelte Politische Schriften (1971).
MK	Werner Sombart, Der Moderne Kapitalismus (dritte Auflage, 1919–1927), 3 volumes.
OCD	The Oxford Classical Dictionary (third edition, 1996).
WG	Max Weber, Wirtschaft und Gesellschaft (fifth edition, 1976).
Wge	Max Weber, Wirtschaftsgeschichte (1924).

PART 1

The Problem

CHAPTER 1

Religion, Capitalism and the Rise of Double-Entry Bookkeeping

Quod non est in libris, non est in mundo

QUOTED BY WERNER SOMBART, *1919, as bookkeepers' wisdom.*

∵

1.1 Introduction

This book concerns a study about a typical relationship labeled by Max Weber as "market versus *oikos*." It is clear that Max Weber thinks of it as a relationship of a conflicting nature and even the superficial definitions in the preface demonstrate that this conflict concerns the most fundamental issues in society and history. In many unexpected places of Weber's vast oeuvre both "market" and "*oikos*" appear without much analysis or explications.

This made me so curious to learn all the characteristics of this conflicting and fundamental relation that the search for "market versus *oikos*" received priority and "Max Weber" took second place. This decision was also inspired by the fact that no relevant publication exists covering even a part of the problems related to what was suggested in the preface.[31]

Therefore, I proceeded in this case in an experimental, not self-evident and arbitrary way: Weber's most famous debate is used as a vehicle to produce the "practical field" in which I can reveal knowledge about the subject. In other

---

* Although the following text is the much extended version of the one published in *Accounting, Business & Financial History*, 2008, I thank the editor, John Richard Edwards, for his wise patience and, in particular, the two anonymous peer-reviewers for their extensive, critical and highly stimulating comments on an earlier draft of this text.

31 A probably interesting, proposed publication for February 2018, is entitled "*Oikos and Market. Explorations in Self-Sufficiency after Socialism*" about the life of peasants in Eastern Europe. The implied problems of the peasants belong to the other fundamental and conflicting relationship, "Town versus Country." This shall be handled in a specific way, but not on the detailed level of farmlife.

 | DOI:10.1163/9789004383913_002

words: bookkeepers learn that conflicts between market and *oikos* exist only when a book is first written about it!

•••

The remarkable bookkeepers' world outlook ("*What is not in the books, does not exist in the world,*" copied from Roman judges who favored *actis* instead of books) is quoted approvingly by the famous historian of capitalism, Werner Sombart, who is co-responsible for the enduring interest in the relationship given in the title. The problem we have to analyze below is, indeed, partly given in this dictum of the bookkeepers, apparently expressed since the end of the West-European Middle Ages. From then on it is also impossible

> to see boots or shiploads, flour or cotton, as other than only monetary values (*Wertbeträge*), that increase or decrease… the capital concept as such is created… at the same time as the capitalist enterprise of the organization that is aimed at realizing (*verwerten*) a certain capital.[32]

Whatever the relation between a Western European religion, capitalism and double-entry bookkeeping (DEB), all three phenomena seem to match their explicit arrogance to exploit and exercise in an authoritarian way Truth, Money and their Territory.

It is, therefore, not only scholarly curiosity that makes it necessary to contemplate the problems at the root of this typical relationship "religion–capitalism-DEB" in (European) history. This seems obvious in a world in which completely different belief-systems like those of Indian or Chinese cultures successfully strive for dominance and an Islamic culture with its unique and extensive financial system has already operated for over a millennium.

From the Arabs we learned DEB, they say, although the Romans were already skilled bookkeepers according to Minaud.[33] But in our own environment, in which religion largely disappeared in favor of a basically civil and civilized world-outlook, now should be the time to emancipate ourselves from old positions… if possible. Or, in a less moralistic mood: what should be the (historical) basis nowadays for considering the relationship of western religion, capitalism and DEB?

Of course, it is impossible to answer this fundamental question thoroughly here: a few books are necessary. But we can try to give the main outlines of a

32 Werner Sombart, MK, vol. 2, 120–122.

33 One of the peer-reviewers is thanked for this information. See Gerard Minaud, 2005.

relevant answer when limiting the scope more or less to the European medieval historical roots of the relationship and to the Weberian-Sombartian approach. Herewith I follow newly published treatises[34] and can come up with some historical and sociological alternative explanations of the relationship at issue, while pointing to where the suggested emancipation could be found.[35]

First, within this framework the concept "capitalism" will be discussed. The result is, hopefully, a more precise formulation of the *problem* to be tackled here, that can be tested in the second part by means of a discussion of the newest literature on the whole *relationship*. Next follows a discussion about DEB within the given relationship, while the last part sketches some basic features of the root of the relationship.

How to approach the subject of this chapter is, of course, partly fixed by earlier contributions. Indeed, the historical discussion is still throttled in Sombart's and Weber's works and theories. Although the latter also a-historically universalized capitalism as a phenomenon of all times, both describe their "root stories" as only part of a specific medieval (Italian) history with strong religious overtones.

Weber's essay about the role of Calvinism in the rise of capitalism is well-known. His colleague Werner Sombart stressed the relationship of capitalism and religion as well, but referred to scholasticism and, therefore, to Roman Catholicism and, earlier, to Jews, erroneously taken as a non-religious group. Whatever their different approaches, they both gave a pivotal role in the origin of capitalism to the not very popular activity of double-entry bookkeeping, DEB. So, part of the problem to be tackled shall be to scrutinize the relevance of Weber's and Sombart's approaches.

34 James Aho, 2005; Eve Chiapello, 2007; Basil Yamey, 2005.

35 It seems as if the subject has become "hot" since several other related publications are published like Rodney Stark, 2006, which is not worth mentioning thanks to its purely propagandistic aims. However, a quick look in relevant scientific literature presents a rather ambiguous picture: Rosenberg & Birdzell, 1986, repeated largely Weber even inclusive the DEB and Calvinism stories (Ch. 4); David Fischer, 1996, is highly informative but does not mention DEB, Weber, etc.; Fernand Braudel, 1982, vol. 2, 572 is critical about all those "who overstep the mark" in their lyricism about DEB. In the reader of Mark Granovetter & Richard Swedberg, ed., 2001 the latter produced only old-fashioned views on capitalism thanks to an uncritical Weber reception on 77–96. More important are the hot debates in the 1980s and early 1990s like the Brenner-debate, New Left-debates about the writings of Giovanni Arrighi (1937–2009), Perry Anderson, etc. Discussion (if necessary) about these debates will be reserved for the "theoretical" follow-up of this book. Here only this: Arrighi does not define capitalism, but thinks that it is something which originated in the medieval Italian cities!

Another part concerns the problematic present-day reception of these approaches. The most recent American contribution to this debate, the sociologist James Aho's book (2005), is interesting but ambiguous. He is inspired by the writings of Carruthers and Espeland, who stress the legitimating possibilities of DEB and claim to have found a new inroad to Weber's and Sombart's capitalism theories.[36] Aho also follows Weber/Sombart in a rather extreme way. Notwithstanding his exaggeration of the role of DEB, his essay points out major problems in the historiography of capitalism.

To analyze these, recent writings about the subject are helpful as well.[37] Apparently coming from a (neo)Marxian background, these authors try to make a Marx/Weber mix. However, in doing this they became neo-Weberians accepting too easily the Weberian "spirit"-approach, Weber's-Sombart's capitalism theory and *ipso facto* their views on DEB. My main objection to their arguments is that they neglect the very basis of Weber's and Sombart's work, the market-*oikos* dichotomy.

This is of pivotal importance for understanding and interpreting the relationship at hand. Therefore, I shall explain this in some detail below and refrain from commenting on their challenging reshuffle of Marx's thoughts.

In the end, there are the writings of Basil Yamey who is called "Sombart's most hostile commentator."[38] This is not his least quality, but more interesting is his modification of the historical role of DEB and that he was Aho's first critic.[39] His criticism is given from the "inside" of DEB by a life-long student of the subject. Since I am not such an expert, but approach DEB from its context in the market-*oikos* relationship, Yamey's studies are very welcome.

Apart from some clear deviations, I have the impression, that my quite different perception of this relationship, supports most of his criticism. I also see him as a representative of a whole generation of highly competent accounting experts, so that it is not necessary to discuss *in extenso* the writings of people like Raymond de Roover, James Winjum, Yannick Lemarchand and others.

1.2 The C in the Relationship

A prudent conclusion was that Weber's and Sombart's histories locate the "origins of capitalism," in practice in Italy and in medieval times. This is more difficult to ascertain from Weber. Richard Passow, the first to scrutinize how

36 Eve Chiapello, 2007, 272.
37 Including Luc Boltanski & Eve Chiapello, 2005 and R. Bryer, 2000a, b.
38 Eve Chiapello, 2007, 268.
39 Basil Yamey, 2005.

contemporary scholars defined "capitalism," placed Weber and Sombart in particular in the center.

Around 1910 they were exceptional in using the concept of capitalism time and again in their scholarly writings, their journal, the *Archiv für Sozialwissenschaft und Sozialpolitik* (*Archives for Social Sciences and Social Welfare*) or in the well-known *Grundriß der Sozialökonomik* (*Main Features of Socio-Economics*) in which both men had a substantial stake. Nearly no other economists nor economic histories, including the leading lexicons like the famous *Handwörterbuch der Staatswissenschaften,* mentioned it until around 1920, and circumscribed it erroneously mostly as *Geldwirtschaft,* or money-economy. Only a very few referred to "capitalist production."

At the end of the 19th century there was another custom among leading scholars such as the famous classical historian Theodor Mommsen. He often wrote about *Kapital- und Kapitalistenwirtschaft,* the capital-economy and economy of capitalists. Marx's reaction in the third volume of *Das Kapital* is interesting for our subject.

> [It is a mistake] like that of Mr. Mommsen, to discover in every money-economy a capitalist way of production. Mr. Mommsen... understands the word *capitalist* not in accordance with modern economy and modern society, but as popular wisdom, which is not a custom in England or the United States, but only on the continent where old-fashioned traditions are still spread.[40]

One can safely say that Weber and Sombart made the concept socially acceptable in the circles of economists, sociologists and the like. In 1925, however, Sombart could still write that the concept and its meaning were not generally accepted as a *scholarly* concept.[41]

It might be interesting to compare present-day definitions of capitalism, but this is only time-consuming. Instead, I give two popular English examples. A Penguin dictionary defines capitalism as follows:

> The politico-economic system, based on private property and private profit, censured by Karl Marx for its exploitation of labor. There follows a cross-reference to "Free Market Economy."[42]

40 Quoted by Richard Passow, 1927, 3.

41 Richard Passow, 1927, 4.

42 Graham Bannock, 1978, 69.

The other is a contribution by Robert Heilbroner. He first states that "capitalism" refers to the "market system" or "the free enterprise system," which are not identical in my view:

> [It is] the most important mode of economic organization in our time... most unusual... distinguished from all other economic orders, past and present, by three properties... its continuous effort to expand wealth... [its coordination] by a network of markets, rather than by the determinations of kings and local lords... a dual system of power [:] a private sector dominated by... business enterprise and the... consumers... a public sector in which government exercises its traditional powers...[43]

Whatever the many difficulties with these definitions, *market* is still the most crucial concept that is hardly ever explained well or clearly, except as something that is "free," at least defined as "free from a domination by lords."

Let's suppose that *market* is synonymous with the working of supply and demand, which presuppose by definition some relationship of production and consumption. In this case the main difficulty in my view is Heilbroner's third property, that capitalism is a dual system of power. If this is right, how should it be understood? Heilbroner does not explain the existence of something more ambivalent as a "free" market that is, at the same time, a dual system of power.

A view of the origin of this capitalism can possibly help to unravel the obvious contradiction in terms.

1.2.1 *The Origin of Capitalism*

From about 1850—Louis Blanc in France, Rodbertus in Germany, Marx everywhere—until Weber's and Sombart's time, capitalism was nearly always an excellent concept to criticize, to accuse, to judge all deficiencies of economic life.

Passow did not discover it in Marx's *Das Kapital*, and he points ironically to the fact that theologians accepted it directly after Sombart published his first, strongly criticized and severely revised edition of *Der moderne Kapitalismus* in 1902. It is tempting to quote at length from Passow's highly entertaining study.

However, Passow castigated both authors because neither Weber nor Sombart defined the concept properly, giving whatever meaning they wanted to give it and either doing this in the wrong place[44] or in such a vague way that

43 Alan Bullock, ed., 1999, 103.; see also Peter Stearns, 1994, 91–94.

44 As Max Weber in his *Agrarverhältnisse des Altertums*, 1909; translated by R. I. Frank as *The Agrarian Sociology of Ancient Civilizations*, 1976.

developed "money-economy" (*entwickelte Geldwirtschaft*) from time immemorial could be called *Kapitalismus*.[45] As will be explained further below, their capitalism is also projected and perceived negatively as *nearly* identical to *The Market,* trade, commerce, speculation or whatever activity deemed as irregular, uncontrollable, detestable, etc.

What later is called *capitalism* was only semantically related to a phenomenon developed in France and England and some scattered locations elsewhere from around the middle of the 18th to early 19th century. This is, rather, *capitalist production,* the way private property combined different kinds of capital for industrialized, standardized and mechanized mass production to realize mass-consumption and for a certain profit maximization.

The definition of capital is accordingly related to this mode of production, etc., and its other qualities are extensively discussed in earlier literature: Sombart and Weber for the organizational aspects, Marx for the circulation and accumulation of capital, and so on.[46]

Its positive and negative effects were enormous and for a long time irreversible, not the least because of its scale; it could break through all traditional economic, ecological or social barriers. One of the many passages on capitalism in Weber's oeuvre mentions that throughout history there were entrepreneurs who were "capitalist adventurers" and "irrational-speculative characters" eager to catch their prey by violence, war and chronic tax-exploitation of subjects. He called this *Untertanen-Ausplünderung* (*the plundering of subjects*) but I did not know that entrepreneurs had subjects from which taxes could be levied. He continues:

> But only in the West in modern times has one along with it [those "capitalist adventurers" H.D.] a totally different kind of capitalism that was never developed elsewhere: the rational-capitalistic organization of (formal) free labor.[47]

45 Richard Passow, 1927, 73; Werner Fuchs-Heinritz, ed., 1995, 328.

46 Here, of course, I cannot go in detail, while pointing to the usual definitions of fixed, circulating capital and, the day-to-day name of some stock of money (in whatever form) as capital. "Capitalist" is first used in 1792 for somebody "who has capital available for employment in reproductive enterprises" and "capitalism" is used for the first time in 1854 as reported in the *Oxford English Dictionary*. It's clear, however, that a phenomenon can exist before there is a name for it. The new development was that earlier features with their own history were combined into a brand new framework. Apart from a few conceptual problems, Sombart listed its qualities rather appropriately and they are reproduced by Eve Chiapello, 2007, 278–279. But it is, for instance, never proved how "a spirit ... created economic organization."

47 Max Weber, 1934, vol. 1, 7.

In socialist and Marxist circles, one can hear the same opinion about "free labor,"[48] while present Bible Belt representatives still equate capitalism with freedom, although this is historically and conceptually non-sense.[49] For *capitalist production* only the costs and availability of labor matter, not freedom: the same producer who works in England, France or the Netherlands with free-will labor employs slaves in the colonies of his country. In addition, there is the discrepancy that to obtain raw materials, mostly non-free labor or real slavery is used while for the production of end products in the home land, juridically free labor is used.

The intriguing description of big industry in the first volume of Marx's *Das Kapital* is more adequate. It demonstrates the fascination of *capitalist production* that, of course, matches with Engels' classic *The Condition of the Working Class in England* documenting the negative effects of the expansion of this private *capitalist production*. It is not unimportant to remember that the latter was written about twenty years earlier than the former and that Marx did not use *capitalism*.

And, indeed, capitalism had a quite different source. After 1850, as a general trend, the many regional individual instances of *capitalist production* were superseded by a few *networks* of this capitalist production and banks under a mostly victorious leadership and with strong civil and financial support. Thanks to monopoly and cartel positions, these new industrial and financial elites were socially closed to outsiders and economically closed to competitors.

The latter slowly accommodated the defeated traditional feudal classes like the church, aristocracy, monarchy and army that were not defeated in Germany. There, the aim was to counteract the oppositions of socialism, solve the negative effects of the private capitalist production and to start new imperialist

48 Eve Chiapello, 2007, 281.

49 Conceptually: the relevant Marxist distinction between hand- and head labor, must lead to the conclusion that head-labor was socially, philosophically and biologically always free, including that of a slave. Historically: bad enough, but slavery is an exaggerated phenomenon and alone locally and periodically of importance; "free" (only negatively defined as non-slavery) labor was the rule, slavery the exception, but the latter got the most publicity. For the present Bible Belt opinions see Rodney Stark, 2006. His thesis: only devout Christians (medieval monks) brought us capitalism and the scientific revolution that powered it. As usual, that typical product from European soil, Roman Catholicism, has a different opinion. In May 2007 Pope Benedict XVI visited Brazil to fight its main competitor, American Protestantism, but condemning time and again "capitalism and Marxism as systems that marginalize God." Interesting in this kind of discourse, is also the website of the novelist Ayn Rand www.capitalism.org. She propagated an extreme egoism in which one is God himself. A variant of all this is the thesis that capitalism *is* a religion, see Francis Ching-Wah Yip, 2005, and the discussion in the last chapter.

adventures. In my view, it was this marriage of convenience that gave birth to the new-ism, *capitalism*.

As such, this marriage succeeded in England and France much more thoroughly and quickly than elsewhere. Whatever the differences in those two countries this happened because the new industrial elite dominated the traditional one; particularly in France this was accompanied by a heavy anti-clericalism. In Germany the aristocracy and petty monarchies dominated the "marriage," but were reluctant to block a moderate modernization after 1870. And in more eastern and southern countries the traditional part in the "marriage" dominated too much like in Italy and Spain, or conversely, there was a quick "divorce" like in Russia.

A new kind of criticism came to flourish. The traditional criticism of private *capitalist production* was that of the early socialists and utopians from Owen to Saint-Simon who wanted nothing more or less than an alternative factory or (anti-)industrial settlement. After 1850 and certainly after 1870, the new criticism, named *anti-capitalism*, was of a fully different order: all corners preached the New Society-creed. Instead of individual projects, there were a host of projects to reconstruct whole societies coming from adherents as well as critics of capitalism.

Around 1900, everywhere the state (bureaucracy, army, police) and its main supporter, the church, were emancipated from the 19th century status of being "night-watch-men" or from strong anti-clericalism, and had modernized their traditional institutions of repression.

This had nothing to do with capitalist production. Now capitalism had reached the status of organizer of society or even of the world at large that, of course, blurred the concepts involved, exaggerated the importance of capitalist production, and blocked the understanding of their historical roots.[50] The world power-position of capitalism was reached thanks to *national* armies, navies, other *state*-institutions and Christian *missionary activities* as their so-called *scramble for Africa* or the Middle Eastern race for oil demonstrate.

Anyway, this *relationship* between capital and state, which, in the 20th century, had the bloodiest story possible created a *conditio sine qua non* for every new historical research into the roots of capitalism. Around 1900, Max Weber and Werner Sombart were among the first to prove the historical relevance of this relationship, but they failed in a most fundamental way to do this job: as usual in Germany, they were much too state-oriented. If you read *Wirtschaft und Gesellschaft* (*Economy and Society*), you do not get the impression that an

50 Fernand Braudel, 1982, volume 2, 232.

industrial revolution had taken place and a capitalist production had existed with all its consequences.

In addition, Weber's casuistry and methodology, as will be shown below, demonstrate the thoughts of an emphatic follower of the strong *oikos*-state option that was practically a Lutheran requirement, notwithstanding his groundless American liberal image.[51] But this end-result is comparable to Weber's description of the mercantilist patrimonialism with national and foreign, private and public, monopolies.[52]

Sombart is a better historian and in the beginning of his career not yet the rather opportunistic follower of National-Socialism. The fundamental discrepancy of his monumental *Der moderne Kapitalismus* is that while he describes the history of the capitalist production with its positive and negative effects at the proper places, his interpretation of this history is inspired by the German perception of the new capitalism.

To understand the development of capitalist production in the late 19th and early 20th centuries, it is better to choose other sources. Sombart's German background and his methodology were the same as Weber's, but his Roman Catholicism apparently inhibited a much more relevant and non-ideological stand. One symptomatic example: a capitalist entrepreneur was for him

> one hundred percent certain ("*mit voller Sicherheit*") rooted in the following three categories: the heretics ("those who belong not to the State-Church..."), the strangers ("... among which those Christians persecuted for their belief since the 16th century are the most represented..."), and the Jews thanks to their peculiar situation (*Sonderstellung*).[53]

His focus on the non-sedentarians and non-conformists was relative to the dominant church! In his view, that such kind of folk ruthlessly cheated all other good-willed, God-fearing people in order to gather and expand their financial wealth must be accepted as self-evident.

Last but not least, both Sombart and Weber, each in his own way, became rather sharp critics of what was then called Manchester-capitalism. That was

---

51 See Hans Derks, 1989, 282–297. Weber's conservatism can be proved, because he defends the oikoïdal position in most principal matters as demonstrated below. His liberal image in the USA is established by Talcott Parsons, Edward Shills or Reinhard Bendix who created Max Weber as the anti-Marx. In Germany in a reaction upon the "Roaring Sixties," the same image is established by the writings of Wolfgang Schluchter, Guenther Roth, or Wolfgang Mommsen, which revived and strengthened the Parsons-tradition in the USA.

52 WG, 645–648; ES, 1102.

53 MK, volume 1, 840.

not an original stand because it was broadly condemned by mainly continental Europeans from all political corners as the most detested form of *free market-capitalism*.[54]

However, this so-called Manchester capitalism concerned in fact nothing but the real market struggle of capitalist production and had nothing to do with the later (anti-)capitalism. Ideological positions of -isms are always in need of enemies; in short: *capitalist production was one of the main enemies of capitalism*. Why? Because in a "free market" the forces of "supply and demand are allowed to operate unhampered by government regulation…"[55]

More precise and in conclusion: contrary to capitalist production, capitalism is used as an ideological construction once a combination or relationship of the state and capitalist elite—at one time or place state-dominated, at another time or place capitalist elite-dominated—is realized that intentionally *undermines* the normal workings of supply and demand in order to get and sustain a kind of monopoly position: for the state a "monopoly of force" (*Monopol der Gewalt*; Max Weber's beloved thesis[56]), for the capitalist elite a monopoly-position in all (if possible) product- and/or consumer markets. While the latter can make the workings of supply and demand of its customers practically zero or only virtual, the former can limit the individual *and* collective freedom of its clients/subjects so that only a (theoretical) alternative to flee remains.

In other words: thanks to the given cooperation, *capitalism became the concept of a "system" in order to dominate societies*.[57] Thanks to this reformulation,

54 The criticism of supporters of a radical liberalism and free-trade since Richard Cobden (Corn Laws, etc.) was concentrated in Germany since Friedrich List and supported by a large part of the conservative feudal lords with an extensive grain trade, Marxists of all corners like Lasalle, "normal" conservatives (including Bismarck) who feared for a total undermining of the society through free and uncontrollable trade. In England used Disraeli "Manchester capitalism" in a pejorative sense. At the moment, the term "Manchester -Liberalism" is used as synonymous for "predator capitalism" ("Raubtierkapitalismus"). Anti-Semitic circles used it as synonymous for "Jewish capitalism" since about 1870. See Doering, 2004.

55 Graham Bannock. 1978, 190.

56 WG, 98, 388, 397, 418.

57 The definition of "system" is given in the previous paragraph and it has nothing to do with a "mode of production" in the Marxist sense, eventually with "Produktionsverhältnisse." There are, of course, many kinds of monopolies in earlier times. Jean-François Bergier, 1979, 123–125. wrote interestingly about the differences of the Italian and German business organizations of the 15th and 16th centuries. He concluded, first, that the Italian firms were organized in a decentralized way (main firm + autonomous branches), while the German firms were centralized. Next, as a structural innovation the Germans emphatically formed cartels and monopolies. A few were also known in Italy (like the monopoly of papal alum held by the Medici), but in Germany they became a structural

anti-capitalism flourished everywhere and was mainly directed to the strongest enemies, the big money men in the USA, England, and was often mixed up with anti-Semitic reactions. Socialism, Fascism, Nazism, Communism, Roman Catholicism, Lutheranism... they all supported anti-capitalism, not the least as a means to propagate their own *New Society* projects. Although it did not exist as such, they consequently had to take capitalism as a whole, as a logical, comprehensive system covering the whole society. This ideological construction received a realistic socio-political and economic basis thanks to two hot and one cold world wars.

Historians can date its origin in the period 1850–1900. Where this capitalism is state-dominated like in Weber's Germany, it is in need of a historical legitimation, as provided for the first time by Weber and Sombart. That is a reason for their continuing popularity. As usual with probably all other -isms, the history of origin is projected as far back as possible. Happily, there are positive features of their historical and socio-economic analyses as well. To this belongs their oikoïdal theory.

1.2.2 *Market Versus* Oikos

There is room for the thesis that the capitalism as described above did not live long. The economist Lester Thurow stated in 1941 that the USA and Great Britain were the only capitalist countries left on earth: "The capitalism that now seems irresistible could, with just a few missteps, have vanished."[58]

Indeed, the 20th century capitalism as a means to organize society or the world at large seemed to be buried thanks to the combined efforts of mainly European continental activities and those of Japan: radical nationalism, socialism/ communism, all Christian adherents of a strong state and, generally, all enemies of *"the market,"* all supporters of *"the oikos"* as the Household of the State. But in the 1990s, capitalism arose from its grave. It is defended and attacked now with all the traits of its heyday a century earlier and thanks to the many new information and communication technologies.

---

element in the hands of merchant bankers: "... a new concept in business strategy: they expressed the capitalist mentality of their members." These monopolies were the result of deals between the state (emperor) and privileged bankers. Bergier also mentions that these monopolies were "the object of violent criticism and of suits ... conducted by business circles ... which had not absorbed the modern capitalist spirit." The undermining of the market by means of monopolies, was felt very well as an aberration. That this should be typical for a "capitalist spirit" is only true for capitalism as defined in the main text. See also WG, 648; ES, 1102 in which Weber showed a better view on the anti-market effects of monopolies in the oikoïdal patrimonialism as Bergier.

58 Lester Thurow, 1996, 5.

Capitalism again comes to us in the classic imperialist form from the USA and Europe with economic wars in its periphery, and is explicitly supported by many religious sects and denominations. It appears also in not very new forms from relatively isolated areas within the former communist realms of China and the Soviet Union.

As in the 19th century it is accompanied by the most rigorous forms of speculation, deterioration of the environment, child labor, glamorous consumerism in the highest echelons of society, and stunning poverty in the lowest.

In my view, a new contradiction between capitalist production and capitalism is at stake on a global scale and, therefore, at the level of the historical or political-economical research as well. For instance, if you want to discover the roots of capitalism in contemporary China, you should not consult Weber's chapters on China in his sociology of religion,[59] nor his root history of European capitalism. And what about DEB? Is there a direct line between its invention and present forms of capitalism? The basic contradictions of market-*oikos*, Weber and Sombart analyzed, can be very helpful in answering these questions.

However, it is also impossible to negate that brand new, powerful means of production used even by the poor in the Third World, the personal computer and its derivatives. Here the classical characteristics of capitalist production are demonstrated relative to the information technology and the "anarchistic Internet," a world that is not yet dominated by oikoi, but that still seems to be the most typical market possible.[60]

The famous economist Hernando de Soto disturbed, without knowing it, Weber's universalism and Wallerstein's thesis about the integration of the world economy into one system. He states that the "lifeblood of capitalism is not the Internet or fast-food franchises. It is capital." But the reality is that capitalism "is viewed outside the West with increasing hostility, as an apartheid regime most cannot enter."[61] A contradiction between capitalist production and capitalism is well demonstrated here. De Soto and his colleagues tell us nowadays about the poor in the world:

> Why then are these people so underdeveloped? Why can't they turn their assets into liquid capital, the kind that generates new wealth by increasing production and productivity? For a very simple reason: To be useful in an expanded market, capital must first be represented in a property

59 See below Chapter 4; Hans Derks, 2004, 49–79.

60 Will Hutton and Anthony Giddens, 2000.

61 Hernando de Soto, 2000, 209.

> document where it can then be assigned a status that allows it to produce additional value. What most people possess outside the West is not "paperized" in such a way as to produce capital. When you step into an airplane in New York to fly to Jakarta, what you are leaving behind is not the high-tech world of fax machines and ice makers, television and antibiotics; many people in the Third World also have those. What you are leaving behind is the world of enforceable legal representations.[62]

De Soto puts all his eggs in the state bureaucracy's basket and comes up with typical oikoïdal solutions. For anyone who has *worked* for some time in Third World countries (and not walked around as tourist, scholar or politician), this looks self-evident. Corrupted governments and bureaucrats, including police and soldiers, are a source of daily sorrow in Third World states; they show up in the USA or Europe as well, and the poor in the Third World do not want to wait until their states cater for those "enforceable legal representations."

Another solution is put forward by the economist Michael Perelman who sketched such a gloomy perspective of the destructive working of market-competition that his proposal—an industrial structure that is not too competitive, nor too concentrated—sounds as hypocritical as nonsensical: why not say directly that the corrupt states avoid every competition or that one normally cannot be a little bit pregnant.[63]

Many top-down and bottom-up activities demonstrate that, happily, there are also numerous initiatives in India, China or South America to transform a nearly non-existent local consumer-power of the poor into production-power based on group-solidarity in villages and city-quarters. But also on the demand side of, for instance, purchasing-cooperatives initiatives add to the necessary restoration and democratization of the markets of the poor and other classes as well! This is far from abandoning market-opportunities.

Therefore, if one has to look into the problem of the historical roots of capitalist production as well as capitalism, one should consider, first and foremost, De Soto-like findings *plus* production-consumption activities of those who have to work together from a *tabula rasa* situation. For a historian this presupposes that he or she has to look for the roots of the critical and dramatic *relationship* between *oikos* and market, not the market or the *oikos* alone, but the relationship between both.

Whatever his motivation, Max Weber was the first to point to this fundamental antagonism, but his remarks are so scattered and preliminary that until

62 Hernando de Soto, 2000, 159 and see also Hernando de Soto, 2001.

63 Michael Perelman, 1999.

now they were paid only superficial attention and could not be used in a proper way. Still, this remains strange because it will not be difficult to demonstrate that the market-*oikos* antagonism is of pivotal importance to the understanding of his theories; it provides comprehensiveness to a crumbled oeuvre.

More importantly, it helps to explain basic processes in history including those that are significant for our subject. Only a tip of the veil can be lifted in the following paragraph, after which my specific treatment of the whole relationship religion-capitalism-DEB will be understood better.[64]

1.2.3 *The Oikoïdal Economy*

As told earlier, the Greek word *oikos* (plural: *oikoi*) has several meanings and translations: house, household, family, manor, etc. In the socio-political literature it indicates not only the authoritarian way of rule in the house/family, but also the economic self-sufficiency or autarky of a household. Aristotle introduced these words for all generations to come in his *Politics* and added the *polis-oikos* relationship.

Nearly all later political philosophers and theologians translated *polis* not as "community," but as "city" or "state," most often "city-state." However, of the approximately 2000 ancient Greek *poleis,* only about ten can be reasonably called cities (*astu*) and none a state in whatever definition. In the ancient Greek culture *polis* can only mean the "public community" and *oikos* the "private community" with both, of course, political, economic or social characteristics as discussed in the chapters 2 and 3.

The *polis* as city-state is a result of the medieval Christianization of Aristotelian concepts. *Oikos* received a similar treatment. Max Weber accepted all of this, inspired by political economists like Carl Rodbertus and Karl Bücher. Rodbertus coined the concept *Oikenwirtschaft,* an economy of oikoi or an oikoïdal economy rather than the economy of one *oikos*; Bücher created very influential concepts like the *geschlossene Hauswirtschaft,* or closed household economy. This was perceived as the first in a chain of phases or levels (*Stufen*) that formed for decennia the last word in economic history and theory.

The most reasonable definition of an *oikos* given by Weber, in my translation, is:

---

64 The market-*oikos* mechanism is analyzed in my thesis, 1986, 42–101, 413–456, 479–488, 640–654. It is followed by several other studies. See www.hderks.dds.nl. To study Weber's oikoïdal analyses one can best start with chapter three of WG, 212–233 or the chapters three and four of ES, 356–385. The translation in the American edition is not very well (see below); for further study it is unavoidable to use the German original. One of the best introductions to Max Weber's theories and ambiguous language is Veit Bader and others, 1976. For the next discussion see his 261–308.

> An *oikos* in a technical sense is not simply any extended family [*Hausgemeinschaft*] or a household that produces a mixture of products, for instance, industrial and agricultural ones; an *oikos* is the large household of a prince, manorial lord or patrician, that is managed in an authoritarian way not, in the end, for capitalistic acquisition of money but to organize the satisfaction in kind of the lord's needs [*naturale Deckung des Bedarfs des Herrn*]. ... It remains decisive for the lord to exploit his inherited fortune [*Vermögensnutzung*] of land, etc. and not to invest [money] capital. The principle of the *oikos* is organization of the satisfaction of needs [*organisierte Bedarfsdeckung*], even if it uses individual production companies [*erwerbswirtschaftliche Einzelbetriebe*] in its realm for this purpose.[65]

This definition refers to many dichotomies that are explained and discussed somewhere in Weber's oeuvre. For instance: household [*Haus*] versus market; landed capital as inherited fortune versus money capital; consumption versus production; agriculture versus industry; authoritarian family father versus other family members as his subjects; natural economy [*Naturalwirtschaft*] versus money economy [*Geldwirtschaft*]; closed versus open societies or economies, and so on.[66]

The dichotomy of the German concepts *Bedarfsdeckung* versus *Erwerb,* which are crucial here are difficult to translate, because they are embedded within an intensive debate between German economists, economic historians, philosophers and sociologists from ca. 1870 onwards. It is impossible here to resolve that debate that not only concerned the origin, characteristics and criticisms of capitalism, but also items from *Grenznutzenlehre,* the marginal utility doctrine, to the possibility and implication of value-free scholarly activities.[67]

In my view, it ultimately concerned the simple question: what is more important in economic life, the "subjective" satisfaction of personal needs of people or the "objective" workings of supply and demand in the market? And beyond this question lurked the existential anxiety of the traditional German pillars of the state like church, aristocracy, monarchy, state-bureaucracy and army (the *staatstragenden Kräfte*) losing their power-positions and their grip

---

65 WG, 230–231; ES, 381.

66 Remarkable as well in this context is the concept "Rasse" which is a typical feature of an oikoïdal or closed society.

67 Karl Pribram, 1998, 401–467 and 521–546; Jan Drukker, 2006, 39–54.

on society to this fascinating but uncontrollable, highly mobile capitalist industry and its money- and product- markets within civil class societies.

Anyway, Weber definitely choose the first answer as did most supporters of the Historic School of German economists including Schmoller, Sombart, Von Wieser, and Brentano, with followers in England like Cliffe, Thorold Rogers or in France, for instance, Le Play, Sée, etc. It resulted also in his criticism of an "objective spirit" inherent in capitalism, conceived of, in several passages, as the drive to accumulate (*rationalisierte Erwerbsstreben*), as the most important value in a capitalist society. Weber's criteria for criticizing capitalism were, therefore, derived from the "spirit of the *oikos*" with its roots in ancient Greece.

In its pure form, one that does not frequently exist, the *oikos* refrains from any exchange and operates in a self-sufficient way as an economic autarchy (*tauschlose Eigenwirtschaft*). According to Weber the following are the main need-satisfaction economies rather than production-for-a-market economies: Oriental monarchical economies like those of the Egyptian pharaohs; the properties of Homeric so-called aristocrats and kings; the large manorial powers in the Roman Empire that, according to Rodbertus and Weber, became more self-sufficient thanks to increasing state-bureaucratic and tax-related limitations of their "market production" (*Erwerb*); the monarchies of the medieval Franks. The manorial properties of the latter gradually emancipated from their autarkic existence thanks to the influence of urbanization, developing money markets or money-need of monarchies to finance their mutual wars.

In Eastern Europe there existed large *oikoi* until the beginning of the 20th century in which several companies, producers for markets, were often incorporated and compulsory labor was exploited. Typical for all *oikoi* is this kind of unfree labor, while they were all first and foremost organizations engaged in a predominance of grain-growing agriculture and not animal husbandry, or pastoral and nomadic activities.

The basic element of the household power is the *patria potestas*, the "monarchical" power of the father over the life and death of wife, children and other (non-)free members of the family and self-sufficient, peasant households. In the political theology of the Middle Ages and early-modern Europe, Aristotle's *oikos* model was not only Christianized, but it received a highly significant extension as well. The *oikos* with its authoritarian father was now augmented with the meaning and practice of o*ikos-as-State* (hereafter referred to as *Oikos*) in which an absolutist monarchy with a state-household ruled as a self-sufficient *patrimonium*.

Sombart described it well: Louis XIV's absolutist monarchy with its new taxation and mercantilist system and endless wars became the relevant modern model of the *Oikos*.[68] The rules of the authoritarian but "Good Father" went top-down, often with lethal results for his subjects if they did not stick to his rules; all possible wealth went upwards to satisfy the needs of the clerical or worldly lords, courts and armies.

To the outside world this *Oikos* was very aggressive; the inside world of its territories was—at least theoretically—systematically divided along the classical grid-iron or checkerboard model in an increasingly detailed way within a power-hierarchy with, at the bottom, no power, and at the top all power. This geometry of power seems to me a clue to discover the origins of DEB as will be demonstrated below.

Weber also sketches the transformation of the *Oikos* into patrimonial powers (*patrimoniale Herrschaft*). We have arrived then not only at the large "international" clerical economies, the absolutist monarchies after the Middle Ages, but also in the widespread family banking network of the Rothschilds in the 19th century.[69] Medieval Venice, for instance, is seen as a patrimonial state in which patricians acted as if they together formed a monarchical government (*patrimonialstaatlichen Tyrannis des Stadtadels*).[70]

An oikoïdal economic science was, first and foremost, directed to the management of this oikoïdal state; it was called *oikonomia politika* or *Staatshaushaltskunde* in Germany, *staathuishoudkunde* in the Netherlands, etc. "Economy" or "economics" was quite a *different* discipline that was practiced only in Anglo-Saxon countries. The latter was seen as a "market-science" opposed to the "state-science," *Staatswissenschaft*.

For Weber, Sombart and their followers the purest form of oikoïdal management literature must have been the so-called *Hausvaterliteratur* like Leon Battista Alberti's *I Libri della Famiglia* and many other similar publications in the Italian 15th century of Dominici, Vergerios, Barbaros, Palmieris, etc.[71]

68 MK, volume 1, 142.

69 WG, 215; ES, 360.

70 WG, 760; ES, 1271.

71 That Weber and Sombart often disagreed is demonstrated in a quarrel about exactly the interpretation of Alberti's "Famiglia." See the very long note in Weber's "Protestant Ethic and the Spirit of Capitalism" in Max Weber, 1934, volume 1, 38–41. One is confronted here also with all the given dichotomies in a comparison between the Catholic Alberti and the Puritan Benjamin Franklin. Luc Boltanski and Eve Chiapello, 2005, 59 state that their view of a "spirit of capitalism" is "consistent with that of Werner Sombart or Max Weber. Sombart refers to ... Alberti ... 'family government' ... Weber supplies a preliminary

They mostly concern the management of an estate or a city with its surrounding country. At a modern state level, mercantilism, physiocratism and cameralism of the 17th to 19th centuries belong to similar oikoïdal theories and practices.[72]

But we now know how the economic policy of the Nazi's largely belonged to the same category thanks to its dominant autarkic political economy.[73] It is logical that Weber subsumed all planned economies under the heading *Haushalten*.[74] Altogether, this history from the Ancients up to the Rothchilds and the new realities of the early 20th century form Weber's *Evolution der Hausgemeinschaft*, which he describes in all possible detail scattered all over his works and which is, principally, not very different from Karl Bücher's *Stufen*-theory.[75]

In a socio-economic theoretical framework, this *Evolution* is derived (or is it the other way around?) from his model of the two kinds of economies: commodity-supply/household (*Bedarfsdeckung/Haushalt*) versus acquisition (*Erwerb*). This model forms the very basis of the whole edifice of Weber's casuistry. This is important for our analysis here and can be detailed in the following way.

The explanation given in *Wirtschaft und Gesellschaft*, of this basic dichotomy defines:

> economy with the aim to satisfy one's own needs/wants versus the economy *zum Erwerb*... [is]... the exploitation of the scarcity of... goods in order to obtain one's own profit, because you are in the possession of these goods.

It is symptomatic that the latter is derived from the former in this relationship and is *not* developed in its own right.[76]

Without these two different concepts and their relationship, one cannot understand anything of Weber's theories and descriptions. Probably more important: if one does not accept the validity of this conceptual relationship as such

description of the spirit of capitalism by citing ... Franklin." Apparently "business" and "family economy" are for them identical. In the same book (100 note 4), however, they tell about differences between Sombart and Weber concerning Alberti.

72 David Lindenfeld, 1997.

73 Hans Derks, 1996.

74 WG, 59; ES, 109.

75 WG, 64; ES, 118.

76 For Weber's technical casuistry about "Haushalten" versus "Erwerben" see WG, 46–62 and ES, 85–114. For Sombart's treatment of the "Bedarfdeckungsprinzip" see MK, volume 1, 49, 63, 183 and for his "Erwerbsprinzip," MK, volume 2, 12, 102, 119.

and its fundamental relevance for the explanation of all economic historical facts and phenomena, one has to refute all of Max Weber's and a substantial part of Werner Sombart's works.

However, Weber's fascination with this relationship with its Aristotelian background is understandable: it has a substantial heuristic value; "house, household" are indeed fundamental elements of societies from time immemorial; the same is true of "production and consumption"; the multipurpose of the concepts involved and their multi-faceted meanings are substantial and intriguing. Notwithstanding this, the (*supposed*) *interrelationship* of these concepts provides us with serious difficulties that can be demonstrated with the way it is handled in the translation from an "oikoïdal language" (German) into a "market language" (English).

Whatever historical economic facts confronted his readers, Weber advised them to first ask "Are they used relative to a household or a production for a market?"[77] In *Economy and Society*, however, celebrities like Talcott Parsons, Edward Shils, Günther Roth, Hans Gerth or Max Rheinstein, and all American Germanophiles, translate this as: "... one must ask... whether they are used in a context of budgetary administration or of profit-making enterprise."[78] They are not very certain of their case and add a justification by explaining what Weber meant with *Haushalt*

> essentially what Aristotle meant by the "management of a household" ... It is a question of rational allocation of resources in providing for a given set of needs. The concept of budget and budgetary management seems to be the closest English equivalent in common use.[79]

If we leave aside mistakes like the use of "rational" and the "making of a profit" in this context, the following remarks can be made.

The translators are right to refer to Aristotle, but they read his relevant writings as clumsily as they read Weber's. To place in this context an "administration" against a "production" is incorrect, where even Weber points clearly to something of a similar and comparable economic nature. Rather strange is the identification of an "administration" with a "management" of a household: the former is, in my view, nearly synonymous with bookkeeping or DEB and the latter with the organization of all activities that have to result, among

77 My translation from: "... handelt es sich um haushaltsmäßige oder um erwerbsmäßige Verwendung?" WG, 63.

78 ES, 114.

79 ES, 207 note 14–16.

other things, in DEB, but also in providing the daily food on the tables, bringing children to school, repairing the house or planting the garden.

In addition, in German and other languages, *Haushalt* received another meaning, one which *oikos* never had and Aristotle never envisaged, namely, a *budget* of a person, a family or even a state. Two different meanings for budget are at stake. First, it can be an *estimate* of income and expenditure for a future period, and, second, it can be a *real* amount of money available to satisfy the needs of the one in the possession or use of this budget.

In the given translation and its justification, there is no sensitivity for these two meanings, and apparently no idea of the use of "budget" in the sense of a "budgetary administration" or a totally different "budgetary management." If we are talking about a state budget, then the latter is the concern of a Minister of Finance who, for instance, has to fill the budget deficit by means of government borrowing on financial markets; the former is work for the clerks of this ministry to count the spending and compare these with the taxes raised or invent new taxes as the deficit becomes alarming.

This kind of misunderstandings increases for the counter-concept *Erwerb*. *Economy and Society* always translates this in the main text as "profit making." One should have been warned in advance because "profit" does not show up in the highly detailed register of *Wirtschaft und Gesellschaft*, and the more general term *Gewinn* appears only four times by accident! In a note *Economy and Society* explains that "the term *Erwerben* would perhaps best be translated as 'acquisition'...", but because Weber used it as antithesis of *Haushalten* they prefer "profit-making." This is a strange argument for several reasons.

First of all, profit is the result hoped for of *Erwerb*. Somebody who is *erwerbslos* does not have a job and/or money with which he can earn a living. "Acquisition" is not bad and a genuine Sombartian qualification,[80] because it reflects the literal meaning of *erwerben*, to get something, but that refers only to the first link in the whole supply-demand chain.

So the best and, in fact, only possible meaning in Weber's oeuvre is: "to get something in order to earn something in the market." If the last "something" would be "money," Weber adds *kapitalistischer Erwerb*[81] and not a meaning like "capitalistic profit."[82] It is obvious to make the connection with *Haushalten*, but apparently it is not understood that this is related to personal activities while *Erwerb*, is related to exchange relations with others which can be made in gifts,

80 Eve Chiapello, 2007, 278.

81 WG, 432.

82 ES, 719.

barter, etc., and also in money. That Weber uses a primitive capital-concept cannot be a reason to provide American students with new wrong ideas.

Next factor: how to get something must inevitably refer to something that is produced, not necessarily to the producer, but to his products. Another factor: normally the costs of getting something must be less than the result of selling it; the difference could be called *profit*. Weber, contrary to the very detailed and positive considerations about *Haushalt* or *haushalten*, refrains from defining *Erwerb* or *erwerben* properly.

Whatever is discussed in *Wirtschaft und Gesellschaft*, one cannot find anything about profit-making, next to nothing about prices and markets, while trade is mentioned only because he had to discuss the exchange between households (*haushaltsmäßig*) as, for instance, between states; only a few remarks are made about something like *erwerbsmäßige* exchange as, for instance, the money or product exchange between individuals or companies and the same about capitalistic production or its costs patterns.

This seems to me an unforgivable mistake for a scholar whatever his political position. The only reason I can imagine for this is that there is no contradiction between a *Haushalt/oikos* and a (capitalist) *company* in Weber's mind; one has only to stress that they are both *manageable* enterprises. Apart from this there is the suggestion in *Wirtschaft und Gesellschaft* and *Economy and Society* that a *Betrieb* (enterprise, works, undertaking, etc.) is derived from the *Haushalt* in the sense that the latter "works" for itself and a *Betrieb* is a *Haushalt* that works for others, the shortest definition of "market."[83]

In other words: here all stress is laid on the organization, the oikoïdal part of the enterprise, and much less on its relation with the outside world of production output to market-relations or consumers. The further development is seen as one of a capitalistic Betrieb/Erwerb to a *erwerbsmäßige Kapitalismus* in which stress could be laid on the outside money-world only. We shall return to this below.

All this demonstrates that Weber's oikoïdal nature was too deeply ingrained, having an overly fundamental impact on his historical and socio-economic analyses. He tells us with some exaggeration: the world was always organized along the "household principle" (*Haushaltsprinzip*), which is a *political* concept from which an economic practice is derived. In the future this must be the case as well if only to avoid anew that terrible historical aberration, that *erwerbsmäßige Kapitalismus* (here in particular "Manchester capitalism"), as a purely economic and therefore unbridled, chaotic reign of uncontrolled money-makers in which a political leadership becomes entangled.

83 WG, 229. In English: "The capitalist enterprise, created by the household …" ES, 379.

Parsons, Shils, Roth and the other American Weberians opt for a less stringent interpretation of Weber's work that I cannot support because of the very dominant impact of the *Haus-Oikos* background. It is purely anti-Marxism, but also an a-historical, anti-economical and therefore ideological point of view as Weber declares in the ES translation:

> Domestic authority and household are relatively independent of economic conditions, in spite of the latters' great importance, and appear "irrational" from an economic point of view; in fact, they often shape economic relationships because of their own historic structure.[84]

Sombart largely took the same stand as an economist and economic historian and therefore he was politically consistent with Nazi authoritarianism. Although Weber died in 1920, for many observers including his wife, Marianne, there was little doubt about which direction German politics would have taken if Weber's political aspiration to become a German political leader had materialized.[85]

1.2.4 *"Rechenhaftigkeit"*

At a principal level there remains the question of how DEB can be situated within Weber's casuistry. This is possible through his discussion of what he called *Rechenhaftigkeit*. The most likely meaning is "the ability to count," but accountability seems to be a good translation relative to the DEB problem. It should be a more Weberian attitude to use a circumscription like "the ability to transform things into numbers" upon which one becomes answerable to them or dependent on counting.[86] Weber, however, never explained it properly.

The first time he used it in *Wirtschaft und Gesellschaft* was in the framework of an analysis of the primitive *Hausgemeinschaft* at the moment a means of exchange is introduced, therefore something with a money-function like shells or cattle.

The second time he describes the effects of dowries and the differentiation between legitimate children and bastards relative to heritage rules. He

84 ES, 377; WG, 227–228.

85 Rainer Baum, 1981, 110.

86 "Rechenhaftigkeit" is a word which one cannot be found in a present German dictionary (at least not in my "Mackensen"). "Haft" means among others "arrest"; somebody can be "haftbar," in which case he has to give security for another, is "accountable." See for the following WG, 41. In English one translates "economic calculations" although it concerns here the *general* ability to reckon: ES, 79; WG, 225, 227–230. It is already better translated with "sense of calculation." ES, 374, 376–381.

concludes that "the dowry... in fact... tends to be set aside as a "special account." The "counting" starts to interfere in the internal relations of the [Haus]communities." Apparently, the *Rechenhaftigkeit* was still too primitive.

Whereas Weber is referring here to Roman times, *Economy and Society* suggests that the "calculating spirit enters" the household, as if for the first time in history people started to make considerations in quantitative terms.[87] As in the earlier period the dowry was later not an "oikoïdal asset" as Weber supposed, but always both a means to get the highest price on the available *marriage market* and a way to make a (foreign) household capital available for the *capital market*.[88]

In the third instance we arrive in medieval Italy of the 12th or 13th century and are confronted with the internal and external impulses to disintegrate households. In short: the dissociation of "house" and "job" (*Beruf*) and, therefore, of "house" and "work" (*Betrieb*); the creation of new needs in the outside world specifically of the cities and mainly of a cultural nature; limitations of the communities (*Haus*) are slowly broken down, and the household is "no longer a place of common production, but of common consumption" (*nicht mehr Stätte gemeinsamer Produktion, sondern Ort gemeinsamen Konsums*). In the agricultural areas there is the tendency of enlarging the large property-holdings (cloisters and secular manors) and of further partitioning of the small peasant households: the first are better able to uphold the traditional *Hausgemeinschafts*-ideals and practices.

A few sentences later Weber suddenly writes about "large capitalistic households of medieval cities" and projects within his *Evolution der Hausgemeinschaft* the origin of capitalist enterprises as a consequence of the separation of household and *Betrieb*. This was deemed as "uniquely Occidental."[89] "What is crucial is the separation of household and business for accounting and legal purposes, and the development of a suitable body of laws..."[90]

Here is the place and time to discuss DEB within Weber's/Sombart's works and minds, realizing that Yamey is against any notion that DEB is in some sense necessary for this separation.[91] One can say that for Weber and Sombart DEB must be located not only in this medieval and renaissance Italy and in their *evolution of the household*, but more precisely, in the transformation of

87 Gérard Minaud, 2005, 351–353. For the same line of reasoning, see R. Bryer, 2000a and b; Luc Boltansky and Eve Chiapello, 2005, Eve Chiapello, 2007.

88 Hans Derks, 1995, 55–58 for antiquity; Iris Origo, 1986, 192 for late-medieval Italy; Richard Goldthwaite, 2009, passim.

89 WG, 49.

90 ES, 379.

91 Eve Chiapello, 2007, 269.

enlarged households into money-oriented enterprises, of self-sufficiency, into relations with the outside world.

In short: it is embedded in the monetization of northern Italian enterprises and institutions, in an economy that is oriented to become a full-fledged money economy. This has nothing to do with capitalism as defined above, but with what Passow supposed to be the only meaning of capitalism for Weber and Sombart, namely *Geldwirtschaft* or money-economy. Let's call it only this, which is good enough.

It is self-evident that in hindsight a new step, a highly important one, is taken. To this end, Weber uses the ambiguous transformation "towards rationalization," a word that can easily be mistaken here for the *Rechenhaftigkeit* as accountability in money. Here Weber also starts using the concept *Kapitalrechnung,* which is translated in *Economy and Society* as *capital account.* This English concept, however, cannot have the same meaning as *Kapitalrechnung*, neither in the private nor in the public use. What does Weber mean by this?[92]

It is difficult to go into detail here, but it concerns one of the most extreme demonstrations of the market-*oikos* antagonism. The *Kapitalrechnung* is namely perceived as contrary to the *Haushaltsrechnung* (translated in *Economy and Society* as: "calculations appropriate to a budgetary unit") which has an orientation to the marginal utility (*Grenznutzen*), whereas the former account is oriented to *Rentabilität* (incorrectly translated as "profitability").[93]

Weber refers here once more to *Bedarfsdeckung* and *Erwerb* and to the economic theory of his time. He clearly announces what nobody has said about a capital account, that the *Kapitalrechnung* in DEB

> presupposes *the battle of man with man*... and further implies that the outcome of the economic process is decisively influenced... thanks to rich consumers who can outbid (*Überbieten*) and influential producers who can underbid (*Unterbieten*).

92 For the following see Veit Bader, ed. 1976, 211, 264–265.

93 WG, 49; ES, 92; Veit Bader, ed. 1976, 265–269. The translators of ES (in this part Talcott Parsons himself) do not inform readers about the typical German background or ideological intentions of these concepts. For a private firm it concerns something like an account stating the amount of funds and assets invested by the owner(s) or stockholders, including retained earnings. "Rentabilität" like rentability concerns the measured result of the *relationship* between the net-profit ("Reingewinn") and the invested or original capital of a venture: a ratio of profit to capital, therefore, and not the profit itself. The other concept discussed here, "capital account," is normally seen as part of the balance of payments of a country, the net result of public and private international investments flowing in/out a country.

> (In *Wirtschaft und Gesellschaft*: ... *setzt... den Kampf des Menschen mit dem Menschen voraus... weiter auch die entscheidende Beeinflussung des Resultates* ...) [94]

This is a most fundamental statement in Weber's oeuvre: to my knowledge he never used such strong wording for other situations.

This formulation demonstrates Weber's negative attitudes to and limited appreciation of supply-demand practices. He, however, is also attacking the most basic element of *any* economic activity, namely, that there is in principal always a *peaceful* relation between supply and demand.[95] It is exceptional if this relation leads to the (mutual) negation of human experiences: after all, if somebody gives and another asks, they have to reach an *agreement* on the value of their deal, to make the negotiation perfect.

This does not change if money is used within these exchanges; it does not change either if somebody under- or outbids in the negotiation, for which it is unnecessary to be rich or influential. Of course, if you possess this quality, you have the chance to take a larger share. The billions of people all over the world who from time immemorial do their daily dealings in their local markets and shops shall not understand Weber's exclamation.

Things change, of course, if from either side somebody or some institution *orders* the buying or selling of something against a zero-value or a fixed value without any negotiation, while threatening with some punishment. In this case Weber's dictum is appropriate, *but this concerns only the exceptional oikoïdal situation and not the normal market relationship.*

This authoritarian element is always given in Weber's and Sombart's writings. Their DEB concept *Kapitalrechnung* deriving from *their* enterprise aims as *kapitalrechnungsmäßiges Erwerben,* oriented to money profit, represents at the same time an exchange of personal labor for money. It is this perception of DEB that must be the background for Weber's exclamation.

It is, therefore, not surprising that Weber perceives the monetary price of products not as innocent indication, but as weapon in the struggle of interests and as products of struggle and compromises.[96] Furthermore, this demonstrates how Weber takes a moralistic stand, which is normally inappropriate in the majority of market deals.

In the meantime, the consequences of Weber's and Sombart's attitudes are rather serious. It is the source of their immanent anti-Semitism or anti-Judaism

94 WG, 49 his italics; ES, 93.

95 See in my 2012, 141–143 how the Arabian and Chinese trade before the 16th century was largely peaceful.

96 WG, 58.

as they, for instance, disqualify the alleged general attitude of Jews for "feilschen" (to chaffer, haggle) or abuses the English in the First World War by calling them "Krämer" (hagglers) with a "Krämerkultur" (hagglers-culture) and "Krämerideale" (hagglers-ideals).[97]

An opinion like the following is also clear enough, namely: "... that the maximum of formal rationality in capital accounting is possible only where the workers are subjected to domination by entrepreneurs...."[98] They claimed that "capitalism without double-entry bookkeeping is simply inconceivable": we now know why. However, the best historian of DEB has serious problems with this, since he states that DEB:

> ... does not itself define the scope and detail of the [accounting] information... it does not prescribe which occurrences or changes that do not involve external transactions should be recorded... it does not prescribe whether changes in the value of the firm's assets should be recorded... Double entry neither generates nor requires any particular set of valuation rules or profit concepts... it is concerned with arrangement and organization rather than with scope and content.[99]

This is a world apart from what Weber and Sombart perceived as their DEB. Let's now discuss this DEB through the eyes of its recent supporters.

1.3 Religion and the Rise of Double-Entry Bookkeeping

Notwithstanding the above critical analysis, there can be no doubt that Weber and Sombart wrote highly influential works. Sombart may be dated and old-fashioned or wrong in his interpretations, but social and economic historians still find many reasons to consult his *Der Moderne Kapitalismus*. It is more difficult to say this of Weber's works and particularly of *Wirtschaft und Gesellschaft*. But what to do with James Aho's aim to revive their theories at this time, apart from the fact that now an opportunity is given to reach our subject from another viewpoint?

For the earlier period of European history Weber and Sombart invented the tradition of DEB as the trigger for the birth of capitalism. Now we know that we have to say, for many reasons, that *their* capitalism was something very

97 Hans Derks, 2004, 100–104.
98 ES, 138; WG, 78.
99 Basil Yamey, 1987, 918.

different from handling industrial production for the market. In addition, they were dealing with a *Geist,* a capitalist spirit and with a chimerical subject like Calvinism and the Capitalist Spirit.[100]

At least in non-theological circles there is nothing worthwhile left after this analysis. It was a fate that Weber had to share with Sombart, the analysis of the role of Jews in the establishment or development of capitalism. Notwithstanding this they strongly contributed to the stigmatization of American Puritans and European Jews as the alleged sources of (a misunderstood) capitalism.

1.3.1 *The Revision*[101]

The sociologist James Aho, who studied DEB as the root of capitalism through Weber and Sombart, can support the given verdict about Weber by using even stronger words.[102] He thinks of Sombart's *Der Moderne Kapitalismus* (1902 ff.) as challenging despite much unreliable information about and confrontations with dangerous liaisons.

The purpose of his book, however, "is to expand on and enrich Sombart's proposition... As for the errors in Weber's history of DEB, these are not just dangerous (as they are with Sombart); they are deadly." Why? Because of the "basis of his entire argument that within the Christian cosmos only Protestantism could have sired modern capitalism."

Immediately follows Aho's central thesis:

> ... far from being a product of the Calvinist spirit, DEB emerged from the culture of the high Middle Ages, when through her sacramental regulation of the total life course of the individual, Roman Catholicism dominated the European psyche as never before.[103]

---

100 What is left from that debate is not only Aho's essay, but are also profound discussions about the tiniest details of Weber's biography by life-long Weber researchers like Wolfgang Schluchter, Günther Roth, etc. Furthermore, there are hesitating considerations of desperate theologians about the dark future of Christianity and Christian culture as given in Wolfgang Schluchter and Fr. Graf, ed., 2005. Here you can find near to nothing about capitalism, nor about a capitalist production or the *Haushalt-Erwerb* dichotomy, let alone about DEB, while it was a 100-year commemoration of the publication of Weber's *Geist des modernen Kapitalismus*, 1904–5. written by the best German Weber-experts to date.

101 The best historian of DEB gave a sharp criticism of an earlier article of Aho. See Basil Yamey, 2005. My comments below follow a different argument, but I agree with Yamey's views. The article reviewed by him is largely similar to Aho's Chapter 7 in his new book; it concerns the alleged rhetorical and aesthetic qualities of DEB. To save space, therefore, it is not necessary to deal with that chapter again.

102 James Aho, 2005, 9–10.

103 James Aho, 2005, 10.

Several conclusions can be drawn immediately: Aho remains within the "spirit"-discourse; he does not refer in some way or other to the real 18th–19th century capitalist production. It is, furthermore, clear that within his "spirit"-discourse he missed the interesting earlier Catholicism versus Protestantism debate.[104] Next, I am not aware that DEB had anything to do with the origins of that 18th–19th century capitalist production, while one must realize that even the Rothschild banks did not use DEB before the 20th century.

Yet, promising insights arise from a "Catholic Spirit" as the new source. It is, anyway, a brave attempt of Aho to enrich Sombart's stand and, notwithstanding Weber's "deadly" errors, to correct Weber as well.[105] We are anxious to know, therefore, whether he can prove that DEB as a pivotal feature of capitalism

> emerged from the moral milieu of the late Middle Ages, how Roman Catholic moral theology insinuated itself into commerce via sacramental confession; and how both commerce and morality were changed as a result: morality becoming, as it were, commercialized... and commerce "Christianized."[106]

Based on the discussions so far, one must conclude that Aho is playing on two chessboards. The first concerns the question of whether a Weberian/Sombartian capitalism theory (including its DEB chapter) is still appropriate to explain the late-medieval economic developments in northern Italian regions with their far-reaching monetization of the urban and rural households, trades and industries and a resulting money-mentality.

The other concerns the question of whether a DEB theory, including improved Weberian/Sombartian capitalism theory, is still appropriate to support the spiritual control of the medieval church over the economy or to accept that this church tried to counteract, to convert and/or to encapsulate these activities for its own economic interests and, therefore, to look for an alternative DEB theory. At least for most medievalists, the view that this church energetically pursued its economic interests is standard knowledge.[107] Whether Aho is playing hopeless games on both boards is still to be seen.

---

104 Amintore Fanfani, 1939; Michael Novak, 1993; Raymond de Roover, 1976, 345; Julius Kirshner, 1976, 16.

105 James Aho, 2005, 11.

106 James Aho, 2005, 1.

107 Josef Kulischer, 1928/1971, volume 1, 89–91; Alfred Doren, 1934, Chapter 1.3; Roberto Lopez, 1980, 451–453; Roberto Lopez and Raymond de Roover, 1990, Chapter 24; George Duby, 1968, 233–235; George Duby, 1974, 213–214; George Fourquin, 1969, 252–254; Jean Favier,

One must stress, first, the words "as it were" in the above quotation. There is, indeed, a large difference between fact and fiction in this case. The church, master definition-maker of what is good/evil and wholesale cashier of the penalty, vehemently attacked usury, the use of false scales, the asking of interests on loans, etc. Aristotle was often its main resource although he was not as rigid as claimed. But the main target, the interest verdict, was seriously mitigated during the council of Lateran (1139), a wide opening was provided for the *commenda* (see below) and other incorporated societies, while theories also circulated in which the merchant's money was perceived as bearing fruit in the manner of the sower's seed.[108]

Accusations with often far-reaching effects were only used against Jews, but even here there were remarkable exceptions as in Venice which "resigned herself to admitting the first *condotta* (consortium) of Jewish usurers (1382–87) who lent money to small borrowers and even on occasion to patricians."[109] Not only a secular government but also the church was too often a strong competitor in the land, luxury, consumption and production, loan and credit markets. Venice was the scene of the harshest struggle of the Franciscan bankers against the Jewish competitors around 1500 with the establishment of the Venetian ghetto as a direct consequence.[110]

Two main voices at issue in the 13th and 14th century, Thomas of Aquinas and Nicolas Oresme, were critical of some mercantile activities, but in the end supported trade and profit-making as a necessity to people who brought goods from places with a supply (surplus) to places with a demand.[111] Also the Franciscan monk Lucas Pacioli, the author of one of the first treatises about DEB, stated: "The purpose of every merchant is to make a lawful and reasonable profit so as to keep up his business." And, of course, Pacioli writes that the good merchant is also charitable while attending religious meditation every morning.[112]

Delumeau's conclusion must be appropriate:

> The skillful cover-ups of the bankers, coupled with the theologians' disagreements, allow the continuation and growth of practices that were indisputably opposed to the spirit of canon law regarding usury. As the

1987, Chapter 18; Jacques Le Goff and Jean-Claude Schmitt, 1999; Peter Spufford, 2002, Chapter 1.

108 Jean Delumeau, 1990, 220–228; Joel Kaye, 1998, 79–78, 120.

109 Fernand Braudel, 1982, volume 3, 129.

110 Hans Derks, 2004, 136–140; Lester Little, 1978, 42–57.

111 See Raymond De Roover's stand in Julius Kirshner, 1976.

112 John Geijsbeek, 1914, 33, 37.

> Dominican de Soto observed in the mid-sixteenth century: This question of exchange, already abstruse enough in itself, is made increasingly obscure by both merchants and the contradictory opinions of church doctors.[113]

In short: the church's moral verdict policy was too well known as highly ambiguous for aristocracy, monarchy and merchants. The "spirit"-discourse should be settled within a very earth-bound practice.[114] Therefore, it would be great if Aho could shed light on the relationship between the *Oikos* (represented by church and state) and the market (here, for instance, the combined merchants and bankers with their activities).

1.3.2 *Business Scruples and All the Rest*

The first chapter of Aho's book concerns the origin and procedure of Roman Catholic penance. It discusses practices that are still alive in a few Western countries in very specific circles and in underdeveloped regions. Aho only says

> that the influence of the penitential legislation... was hardly limited to ecclesiastical circles. On the contrary, through its ceremonial procedures, etc. [it got a serious grip on society]. The consequences for commercial record-keeping... were immense.[115]

What commercial record keeping has to do with this is not substantiated, nor is the immensity of this influence specified.

In the paragraph "Confession and Accounting" Aho starts with: as "the personal account of their spiritual development was to the medieval poet and mystic, the financial account was to their more worldly counterparts, the urban merchant and the rural estate manager."[116] He perfectly knows that this is difficult to appreciate and that this cannot be more than an allegorical comparison.

To convince the reader, Aho presents three considerations:

> Business records can be preserved in convoluted longhand; moral ledgers... can be tabulated and quantified. [Next, he states that commerce is an] inherently moral enterprise... This being so, commerce naturally and

113 Jean Delumeau, 1990, 225.
114 James Aho, 2005, 47.
115 James Aho, 2005, 22.
116 James Aho, 2005, 22.

> easily fell under the jurisdiction of the medieval Church's confessional regime. [Last but not least, Aho points to what he calls] a species of moral obsession regarding private business dealings... [According to Aho, it is in this context that] the moral-psychological significance of double-entry bookkeeping is best understood.[117]

The first consideration is a new allegory, and like the second, it is not substantiated in some way or another. Cases of moral obsession (see below) can be found, but it must be difficult, if not impossible, to prove that they should be representative of the mercantile professions or of only the rich and extravagant merchants.

The next chapter about business scruples should provide the proof of the pudding. The start is not very convincing. One of the first books on DEB by Luca Pacioli (1494) is seen as "behind the Bible, one of the most influential" publications![118] Pacioli wrote about DEB in a small part of a book about mathematics some 150 years after the first DEB *practices* can be registered in several northern Italian cities and then, eventually, in southern Germany and Flanders. DEB practices proliferate outside these cities and regions at a very slow pace.

Aho does not mention that the bulk of the merchants and craftsmen businesses were small, often itinerant, and never practiced DEB; one may be surprised if they practiced something like single-entry bookkeeping. This, however, is not the case in northern Italian cities of the 14th century. They do not use DEB, but they do register the relevant petty loans and credit transactions in their books, and many other facts that demonstrate a substantial complexity of economic life as recorded in Datini's Prato.[119]

A few other points are necessary to give our historical analysis some body. Foundations for DEB were laid in the 12th and 13th centuries: scribes-bookkeepers on 12th century galleys were the most important people after the captains; merchants at the Champagne fairs took many interesting notes. However, it was only around 1300 that something like DEB could start after the

117 James Aho, 2005, 29.

118 James Aho, 2005, 31.

119 For Datini see now Richard Goldthwaite, 2009, 88 and Chapter 1 about the complicated mercantile networks in cities as Prato, Florence, etc. He also writes that the entrepreneurs responsible for the industrial revolution "managed their affairs quite satisfactorily without recourse to double entry ..."(93). This accounting technique was widely used but Goldthwaite reminds us about " ... its utter simplicity: the rules could hardly be simpler and clearer, and they do not rest on difficult intellectual premises." Therefore, Goldthwaite is not a fan of Weber nor of Sombart, see his xii, 463.

"sedentarization" of long-distance traders and in the cities like Siena or Florence in which they dominated. Mercantile book-keeping did not reach full maturity until 1400 after the famous Medici banking house was founded in 1397.[120]

It is, furthermore, not unimportant to note that the development of monetization in Western Europe around the year 1200, reached a level that did not exacerbate general fraudulent practices, with remarkable exceptions like England. In the north of Europe the situation was better than in the south. The production and distribution of coins were at that time already an exclusive business of monarchies, princes and some important merchant-dominated cities. It was only at the end of the Middle Ages that money regained the full public functions that it had in Roman times:

> This return was inevitable, because money is by nature inimical to a feudal system—i.e. the execution of a private power by the possessive class. That was well understood by Aristotle in his political theory of public benefit which inspired the West of the 13th century.[121]

It was the Norman bishop Nicolas Oresme, inspired by Aristotle's remarks about *chrematistics*, who insisted that the power over money does not belong to a monarch, but to the people. This does not mean that money totally lost its feudal bonds: it remained the best means to collect taxes, while it generally still bears its classical symbols, the cross and crown. Bisson's conclusion demonstrates this well: "With money, the power is in the hands of the rich. With coins, the power is a transcendent authority—hidden or spoiled—but impossible to abolish in a highly dynamic exchange."[122]

The obsessive accumulation of money is not only the aberration of the later capitalists, but also of the early taxing powers and their tax collectors. It is only by instrumentalizing a God as the ultimate manager of money/coins that medieval theologians could legitimize the organized theft of money, needed for court, church, army, bureaucracy and their luxury. It would have been more realistic if Aho had pointed to the very one-sided judgments of these theologians and the small scale of the intellectual environment.[123]

Anyway, for Aho, until late in the 18th century the bookkeeper's satisfaction of an "obsession ... with precision and comprehensiveness for themselves" is the most important objective of bookkeeping; not the aid that partnerships

120 Raymond de Roover, 1971; Charles Verlinden, 1971; Herman van der Wee, 1977.

121 Jacques Le Goff and Jean-Claude Schmitt, 1999, 768.

122 Jacques Le Goff and Jean-Claude Schmitt, 1999, 769.

123 James Aho, 2005, 45, 46; Joel Kaye,1998, 52–53.

had from DEB, nor the maximization of profit or the calculation of expenditures and gains.

To demonstrate this obsession Aho points to two figures, Alberti and Pacioli, from whom he himself accepts "that it is unfair to generalize from their outlook to that of the typical merchant." With the third example of Francesco Datini, the wool merchant of Prato, a really obsessed person is introduced who cannot be representative for the extensive merchant class in Italy, let alone for that in southern Germany and the Netherlands: all three together must be considered when talking about the influence and effects of DEB. But Aho witnesses in the case of Datini

> some of the very qualities of the capitalist spirit enumerated by Weber: sobriety, deliberation, the "avoidance of sleep and sloth" and above all vigilant record keeping. To be sure, we are still some distance from Weber's full-blown inner-worldly ascetic...[124]

A Calvinist in 14th century Italy? For Weber everything was possible in this respect. He compared the puritan spirit of Franklin, his "tabular-statistical bookkeeping" with attitudes of medieval monks and a "moral bookkeeping," the "bookkeeping of God" as shopkeeper, etc. Once one receives a loan from this shopkeeper, one is happy to pay the interest by means of all one's good deeds, but one is never able to return the total sum.[125]

It is a pity that Weber had no feeling for historical paradoxes, otherwise he would have discovered which policy medieval monks followed in these matters. The Datini case provides the answer, probably because, as a conspicuous consumer, he demonstrated non-Calvinist behavior.[126]

1.3.3 *The Catholicism Thesis*

After committing all possible major sins in his life, Datini gave a large part of his substantial fortune to the Franciscan monks on his deathbed in 1410: in an economical sense he blocked herewith economic development by pouring it in an unsatisfiable oikoïdal economy while provoking the notorious "poverty" policy and other ambiguous attitudes of these monks. In the meantime, however, the message is clear: not Calvinism but Catholicism was responsible for capitalism; "it definitely provided the model for it, down to the kinds of

124 James Aho, 2005, 40.
125 Max Weber, 1934, volume 1, 123.
126 Iris Origo, 1986, 261–276.

information bookkeepers were urged to write down."[127] This is a one-sided view, to say the least.

In the following three chapters the author tries to substantiate this Catholicism thesis, but demonstrates only conflicting money-interests of Church institutions and mercantile ventures. Using many Latin words,[128] suggesting the direct influence of the Church with her Roman law, and using Weber quotations at will, a strange cocktail of facts and fiction is produced. A few examples will do to substantiate this.

According to Aho, Weber held that many forms of cooperation among merchants "were based on the ancient Roman law of partnership."[129] This is impossible to conclude from Weber's essay or from the later *Wirtschaft und Gesellschaft* and *Economy and Society*, where he writes about the victory of the English common law over the clerical Roman law.[130]

The subject of this essay is the *conflict* between the urban medieval family and labor bonds and the inability of the Roman law jurists to grasp the *commenda practice* within Roman law formulas. Weber even sometimes uses a term like "nonsense" (*Unsinn*) for the jurists' work. He concludes, however, that the jurists ultimately assisted in dividing the oikos (house; household) of the *commenda* participants from their work (company), indicating as well that DEB has nothing to do with this separation.

In Weber's whole oeuvre this is the first indication of a principal form of the *oikos* (*Haus, household*) development and its contradiction to the market-oriented company (*Erwerbsbetrieb*), but also of the difficult relationships within a hierarchy of small and big *oikoi*.

1.3.4 *Commenda and Common-law*

First, notwithstanding its Latin name, the *commenda* of Genoa had nothing to do with Roman law, let alone with a Roman church. It is an *original* form of a *self-evident* organization of merchants and merchant-families developed in order to avoid the many risks of the sea-trade and to create opportunities for

127 James Aho, 2005, 40.

128 The author is inaccurate and clearly unfamiliar with foreign languages: he seldom attaches an *ä* where it is necessary in German language (Aho, 9, 52, etc.); the Latin formula on page 42 must be "ego te absolvo"; the citation from Berman's book on page 84 is at least on three places wrong; the title of Simon Stevin's book is nothing but "Verrechting van Domeine" (90); Aho mentions Alberti's work "Del Governo della Famiglia" which seems to be written in 1443 in-stead of about ten years earlier (6,7), etc.

129 James Aho, 2005, 48.

130 Max Weber, 1889, 45, 151; WG, 563, 564; ES, 977.

many kinds of little companies to participate in sea-trade, shipbuilding, and so on.[131]

Later this form of cooperation and its *common law* were extended to land-trade and banking activities and a bit later it allowed the reinvestment of family fortunes instead of giving them to the church as Datini had done. Therefore, in the *commenda* original urban bonds and their answer to the new circumstances can be studied in which, of course, the incorporation of all kinds of professionals like jurists, notaries or bookkeepers is also at issue.[132] This division of labor is only possible after long-lasting substantial profits in rather large companies of participants at social levels in which literacy and commercial arithmetic were commonplace. There is no reason to underestimate the literacy of the merchants as Sombart did.[133]

So, in defense of his Catholicism thesis, Aho opts for a *commenda* as a result of the strictest oikoïdal idea and organization with Church and Roman law. Weber introduced a Germanic-Romanic dichotomy. This concerned the (juridical) *conflict* between the little versus the big *oikoi* and the (socio-economic) *conflict* between a household economy versus a market-oriented economy. *In abstracto* the conclusions of Aho and Weber do not seem to differ much: both incorporate elements from the other.

In fact, however, there is from the beginning a (large) gap between the *practical* activities/ organization, customs, aims, and rules of the merchants, who accumulated practical and experimental knowledge, and the largely *abstract* activities of the church with its substantial theoretical and for a large part juridical knowledge by which it served as the source of most power claims. It is a gap that was never closed, but was widened and institutionalized.

The merchants normally do not object to the existence of a church (but see the Reformation and the rather murderous north Italian practices), because religion belongs to their household. They fight and neglect the church as a moral authority and compete with it as an economic power if necessary, for instance, where its institutions try to intervene in their work (company) or in the very basis of their activities (the market). The institutionalization of these attitudes follows at the moment that the household and business of the merchants become separated, church/religion are perceived as something of "the other," and the businesses of the church and its monasteries are simply treated like competitors as, for instance, in the banking business of those quasi-poor Franciscan friars or of the Vatican.[134]

131 Raymond de Roover, 1971, 49, 75–77.

132 Alfred Doren, 1934, 429–430; Jean Favier, 1987, 184–186; Peter Spufford, 2002, 23, 43.

133 Raymond de Roover, 1971, 89.

134 David Fischer, 1996, 11–12.

It is, however, necessary to point to differences among large and small merchants, both itinerant and settled, and long-distance traders and local shopkeepers and artisans. For the latter there was no place in the famous studies of Melis and de Roover. Marshall could contrast the great Datini of Prato with a substantial number of petty shopkeepers in the same city and period.

Among the latter there were partnerships as well. However, they concern activities like the sharing of "administrative tasks such as supervising and paying employees and acquiring building materials from suppliers and haulers."[135] Each partner also worked on the job as a skilled artisan, but there does not exist a formal *compagnia* with a fixed capital. There is occasionally a capital fund (*corpo*), but one of the partners who is asked to fulfill his financial duties to this fund "paid this not in cash but in work over the next two months..."[136]

Such a *corpo* exists mostly to pay for raw materials in advance like building material for masons, while at the same time their unpaid wages accumulated as credits on the capital account. Wages did not differ very much: unskilled soldo 10 per day on average, skilled soldo 13 and top wage for the partners of soldo 15.

The conclusion, then, is that below the level of the risk-avoiding *commenda* (common law) and far below contractual constructions based on Roman law, there existed the many practical, rather short-lived market deals.[137] The main reason for this is that there is a large market of money, but it is divided into small amounts; a large market of labor is divided into small wages; undoubtedly the largest market of all kinds of products is divided into relatively small amounts; and so on. All in all, it is a rather free exchange with nearly no juridical interventions from outside to limit its movements. All levels indicated above had their own bookkeeping methods. What about DEB?

1.3.5 *A Papal Revolution?*

The next example of the way Aho operates is the following. In his last chapter he makes much of the immense influence of a Papal Revolution of the 12th and 13th centuries, a concept he borrowed from a highly interesting book by Harold Berman. Aho:

> The Papal Revolution also effected the modernization of medieval commerce. This, in two ways. First, it provided (an admittedly porous) moral and legal umbrella under which merchants could ply their trade with

135 Richard Marshall, 1999, 37.

136 Richard Marshall, 1999, 37.

137 Harold Berman, 1963, 352–353.

> some security. Second, it inspired the practice of modern bookkeeping, without which capitalism as we know it today would not be possible.[138]

In his chapter "Mercantile law" Berman supports, in fact, my socio-economical argument in the previous paragraph. He states that the

> mercantile community had its own law, the *lex mercatoria*, just as the church had its own law, the *jus canonicum*... When the two bodies of law conflicted, it might not be clear which of the two should prevail... Only time could mediate the conflict... The merchants constituted a self-governing community... From that historical fact are derived all the characteristics of the new system of mercantile law...[139]

There were separate courts, with separate procedures that "sharply distinguished commercial law from the formalistic procedure of urban and royal courts and also from the written procedure of the canon law in ordinary cases."[140] Berman also extensively describes how this mercantile law, belonging to *common laws* and not to Roman law, spread over Western Europe.

Furthermore, he does not support the thesis that the Pope was responsible for DEB. On the contrary, he rightly points to the autonomous development of mercantile law, including its own professionalization, and that in addition "to notarial records, bank ledgers and cartularies of ships also had legal force, and even merchants' accounts were admissible in evidence."[141] I could not find some direct remark about DEB in his study, but this does not mean that the invention or even development of DEB must be found in mercantile circles.

The following conclusion can be drawn from this Part B. No relationship of cause and effect between DEB and a capitalist production could be seen in medieval Italy, as was the case as well in the later "Industrial Revolution." Aho did not even try to foster this illusion, otherwise he would have discussed medieval production, technology, labor relations, consumption patterns, class conflicts, and so on.[142]

The same is true for capitalism as normally perceived. But it is, indeed, quite significant that no literature exists, to my knowledge, about the subject "of religion, the industrial revolution and the rise of DEB." This is primarily because the bond between the last two items in this relationship is very weak.[143]

138 James Aho, 2005, 84.
139 Harold Berman, 1963, 346.
140 Harold Berman, 1963, 347.
141 Harold Berman, 1963, 355.
142 Compare with Michael Mann, 1987, volume 1, 373.
143 Jürgen Kocka, 1978, 543–544; Alfred Chandler, 1978, 83–84.

Of course, accounting techniques arising from management practices of the Industrial Revolution and comparable practices in northern Italy in the 14th or 15th century are well attested.[144]

This supports the mitigation of the importance of DEB by scholars like Braudel, Yamey, and others. Yamey's nearly classic suspicion of Sombart is supported as well. Do we have to conclude also that the study of double entry bookkeeping within a broader context is not interesting anymore? Is there any perspective on the rise of DEB?

What Aho studied, in fact, concerns the roots of the relationship of the *oikos* and the market in Western Europe. To shed light on this is, in my view, much more relevant than all talk about "the origin of capitalism" in this period. The question remains whether DEB, which was given a fundamental role in the development of a capitalist spirit, even in something like a "Catholic capitalism," can play a role in the development of a market-*oikos* relationship?

This is not an easy question, and can be answered below only in a preliminary way. A few superficial things are certain such as the Pope was *not* responsible for DEB. Has the element "religion" any relation with DEB?

1.4 The Pasts and Future of DEB

To start with, I still assume that DEB is a merchant's creation, as is common wisdom, although now a pope is put in the foreground. It seems as if Weber and Sombart never took DEB for what it was. Relative to the *content* it is a way of organizing, arranging, and registering accounting data from relatively large ventures (public and private) to discover gain or loss, the amount of debt. It is used to remember past activities, to achieve, "a greater control or surveillance of transactions internal and external to the firm"[145] or other institutions. It looks as if Weber and Sombart are only fascinated by the form in which the given data is molded. Yamey pointed to this view with his Wremark:

> Teachers and professional bookkeepers were attracted to double-entry by the elegance and mathematical precision and symmetry of the method. The development of the 'art' owes a good deal to the interest of mathematicians and arithmeticians from Pacioli onwards. The fact that the "art" was regarded as a "mystery" by many merchants probably helped to make it popular with professional bookkeepers.[146]

144 Fleischman and Parker, 1997; Richard Goldthwaite, 2009, 90–93.

145 Barry Supple, 1977, 412.

146 Basil Yamey, 1949, 113 note 2.

As we will see below, symmetry, equivalence or equilibrium are form concepts well-known before Pacioli, which must have played a substantial role in the development of DEB. This mathematical form and the given content are, indeed, easier to discover in medieval Italy than at present.

1.4.1 *The Future of the Present*

Today, with the development and possibilities of the computer, the need to use this form for that content seems to be definitely undermined. On the Internet one easily finds expressions like DEB "is becoming the Latin of business schools" or that it "is not in demand in everyday practice" as well as the alternative "in defense of DEB." This happens when one tries to *introduce* DEB in a country where it existed many centuries ago (Belgium-Flanders), or that thanks to computer technology, people assert, "the concept of debits is archaic and is used by few computerized accounting systems."[147] So, is there reason for pessimism about the future of DEB? In that case the relationship signaled in the title of this chapter must have a very short life.

A professor in enterprise information systems (EIS), material requirements planning (MRP, with the nickname "bookkeeping of the future") and enterprise requirements planning (ERP) recently came up with a surprising evaluation when he retired:

> It was long after the end of my student period... that I realized how immensely important the invention of modern double-entry bookkeeping, about which one, unjustly, often has disdain, has been... it reproduces a relatively clear amount of data related to each other in a model, which are comparable because they are expressed in similar values, namely in financial values.[148]

But this expert continues with a look into the (near) future in which combinations of ERP with office automation

> ...signify, that the information systems no longer represent a *model* of reality—no, they start partly to coincide with that reality... Earlier, an order or contract was made first and afterwards brought into the information system, but the combination of ERP with office automation shall make an end to this division: an order only exists if it is entered into the information system; an activity is executed if it is executed in

147 David Fischer, 1997.

148 Johan Wortmann, 2003, 6.

> the information system; a supply is accepted, if this is accepted by the information system, and so on.[149]

This development shall also make (or has already made) an end to paper documents, ledgers, etc. in favor of electronic forms. In short: an integration of many aspect-systems into one integrated information system has been realized, as is the case for the most important "streams" like money, goods and work.

Information technology is transformed from a marginal phenomenon into the nucleus of companies and bureaucracies. In addition, for Wortmann the Internet is of pivotal importance in this process. This Internet, a global market in the most ideal form, is given a proper place in his super-oikoïdal design of the (near) future. Here the struggle between *oikos* and market is decided in favor of the former; a certain *balance of power within capitalism,* as defined above, is broken down.

All this looks like the most perfect translation of *Quod non est in libris, non est in mundo*; the total fulfillment of the DEB creed seems to be at stake: the double-entry bookkeeping of reality! Total arrogance? Totalitarian dream? In any case: technologically and partly politically (thanks to events like "9/11"), this reality is apparent in only the most advanced western countries. Here I have to remember De Soto's advice to the poor in the Third World countries: "capital must first be represented in a property document," it must be "pauperized," and one is in need of "enforceable legal representations."

This points to the same development and, according to Littleton, to bookkeeping logic that lay in "proprietorship."[150] De Soto, however, did not consider the Internet, let alone "open source" information technology, to be the best available alternative to centralized IT systems for a period in which not capitalism, as defined, but the traditional capitalist production must be nearly an anachronism.

With this perspective of future developments in mind, one can ask: as Wortmann makes a direct link to the invention of DEB, what did DEB look like in that remote past, and how could it be a precursor of present technological systems?

1.4.2 *The Past of the Present*

In the first centuries of its existence, DEB was not a matter of life and death to the economies of the northern Italian cities, cloisters, and manors, nor to the large companies or large households: if adopted, their management was

149 Johan Wortmann, 2003, 12–13.

150 Ananias Littleton, 1961, 15.

only facilitated with this powerful tool. It was, however, still an exceptional phenomenon among the late-medieval households. Sombart, Weber and others troubled our minds with their erroneous views about DEB as a kind of soul of a social and spiritual system of a whole era, an invention à la Newton and Galileo, as the very "forceps of Capitalism."

When Pacioli published his treatise on DEB, the northern Italian societies were fully monetized, and there were many good bookkeeping practices, often "in advance of Paciolo's simple explanations of bookkeeping mechanics."[151]

Apart from the fact that an inventor of DEB cannot be found, the highest priority here should be given to the development of such a thing as a new theory of the balance and struggle between Oikos, oikoi and market in which DEB could be a tool to concentrate as much fundamental information about "households" and the available supply and demand mechanisms as possible. To do this, one should consider this balance/struggle in a different way than did Weber, Sombart and their supporters, although they did point to some basic contradictions that are at stake here in the northern Italian merchant cities. Let's enter the battlefield, which is not the internal one indicated by Weber.

Whatever DEB is, it is also a double-edged sword, because *external* powers (tax-collectors, clerks of the municipalities, bankers, police or the higher institution in a hierarchy) are eventually allowed to peep into the very details of a company or institution in order to control it, and eventually to sue or plunder it much more effectively than was possible before DEB.

In absolutist France, the first orders from above to use DEB appeared in 1673 (Colbert, Savary), creating what seem to be the first elements of what later became capitalism as defined above.[152] The *Code de Commerce* of Napoleon (1807) with the same obligation was the model for a large part of Europe. In the second part of the 19th century in Western Europe and the USA, regular auditing practices were introduced in most levels of society (including public auditing), and around 1900 they were a rather self-evident affair.[153] In the USA, however, it was not until the Depression that several Securities Acts were accepted with far-reaching public regulations of private accounting practices.[154]

In Germany the *Handelsgesetzbuch* already established rather strict orders around 1870, but one could just avoid the fact "that every merchant was obliged to keep those books, which allowed examination at any time of his commercial

151 Ananias Littleton, 1961, 22.

152 Gérard Minaud, 2005, 18, 35 note 28.

153 Ananias Littleton, 1961, 95–108.

154 Ananias Littleton, 1961, 136.

activities and situation of his fortune."[155] This happened a bit later. During the Nazi regime the planning and making uniform of all private books within the framework of the planning of the whole economy was ordered and executed through "Directions to the Organization of the Bookkeeping" (1937). The government control of private enterprise is still rather strong today.

Also in the public sector the control of the lower echelons of the hierarchy by the highest is remarkable, particularly in periods of cutting expenses. The most recent example comes from Belgium where the central government had a budget deficit of around 3 billion euro in 2007, whereupon the Office of National Budget Control urged the *introduction* of DEB.[156] Its president remarked that this was the only way to discover fraudulent accounts: "... credit and debit must be always equal... The United Kingdom, France and Germany are already using this system and the European Commission will follow." In Belgium a law passed in 2003 required the introduction of DEB, but it had not yet been put into effect.

The reason for the introduction of DEB is, therefore, solely the control and punishment of fraudulent budgets of local and lower government institutions. However, the direct effect of all this is that "Belgium delays the introduction of double-entry bookkeeping until 2008, but we probably have to wait until 2010..." To which degree was this development apparent in the period of the invention of DEB?

One must realize that life in these northern Italian cities was not as glamorous as tourists experience today: the utmost cruelty was often employed to eliminate competitors, whether secular or clerical. Members of coalitions changed time and again, and one was never certain when and by whom lethal actions were undertaken: to know your enemy meant that you had already won half the war.

Lucas Pacioli, the Franciscan monk who wrote the model textbook in 1494 about the Venetian DEB, was aware of this problem. In Chapter 6 he rightly says, for instance, about the memorandum:

> Many are accustomed to enter their inventory in this book, but it is not wise to let people see and know what you possess. It is not wise to enter all your personal property and real property in this book.[157]

155 E.L. Jäger, 1874, XII.

156 For the following see Erik Pompen, 2007.

157 John Geijsbeek, 1914, 39.

But earlier he emphatically urged merchants to not be lazy and to write down in an inventory every kind of property in every detail, from gold and silver to feather beds, fine skins and real estate. And, to mark every page so that no one can do "something crooked… tear out one of the pages… [such that] fraud could not be discovered."[158] That was good to know, and not only for the present historian. This was copied time and again starting with "city-dweller Dominicus Manzoni" in 1554.[159]

Pacioli himself mentions apparently serious antagonists who can fine, dismiss and punish people if the books are not well kept: the representatives of offices like the *Camera de L'Impresti* (municipal loan bank), *Monte de La Dote* in Genoa or, in Venice, the office of the *Messetaria* (market master or exchange) and the *Chiamans*.[160]

Was DEB, therefore, also a tool in the contemporary power-play, one to uphold the political balance of power between Oikos and market at several levels? Or only at the highest level? The differences between these possibilities are immense.

The claim that for Datini there "are more business records… than for all other entrepreneurs of Florence together throughout the fourteenth century and the first decade of the fifteenth" is good enough to illustrate the difference, but foreword-writer Spallanzani even adds that this claim "could probably be extended to include the rest of Italy, if not also all of Europe…"[161]

It would be better if we knew how many merchants, banks or church institutions used DEB in North Italy of the 14th–16th century and, further, "all of Europe." I am afraid that it was only a small proportion within an elite of the business, political or cultural world and this until far into the 19th century, but who can prove this? If it is correct, it does not mean that accounting was unpopular.

The approximately 30 account books Marshall found concern people from "the middling class" of Prato society with incomes well above subsistence level, but far below the Datini's. Although they do not constitute a homogeneous group because the existing assets and way of life varied widely, they are in the position to supply most consumer needs at all levels of society. The oldest books date from 1285, most concern the period 1340–1415. Like Datini's papers these survived from legacies to charitable institutions for the poor, which had a golden period in the 14th–15th century.

158 John Geijsbeek, 1914, 39.
159 E.L. Jäger, 1874, 9–23.
160 John Geijsbeek, 1914, 53.
161 Richard Marshall, 1999, xii.

These shopkeepers and artisans did not invent their bookkeeping, but their work in the marketplace and its financial consequences, prescribed the content and form of their accounts. That these written testimonies were found is also exceptional in the sense that these shopkeepers must have normally used the blackboard (*tavola gesata*) still familiar to me in the neighborhood shops of my youth before super-markets took over.[162]

First, because many customers bought on credit, a relevant identification of the debtor with much circumstantial information was necessary according to the local customs. It is surprising to find that all these tradesmen extended credit to men and women on all rungs of the social ladder, while these sales constituted a very large portion of their business. Happily for them, nearly all debts were paid. At the upper level of society, the credit operations were much riskier, in absolute terms incomparably larger, and, therefore, bankruptcies became rather normal events.[163]

The small traders were not interested in ascertaining their financial health by means of a balance sheet or an income statement showing profit or loss. It is, therefore, not surprising that Marshall confesses about the surviving accounts that their disparate content prevents any meaningful classification.[164] Still some similarity in format and terminology of all the books is found, suggesting that these petty shopkeepers had "some formal training in accounting procedures or had learned traditional practices as assistants or apprentices."[165]

From whom did they learn even this meager knowledge? From the guilds, answers Marshall,[166] but there were also practical manuals with simple instructions, and practical training in the service of a merchant.[167] It would be interesting to compare Marshall's results with those of Yamey, De Roover or Melis. This is not our aim here, but one thing is certain: DEB is not something for these representatives of a middle class.[168]

The situation is very different, indeed, for what must be called the DEB stratum to which we have to confine ourselves now. It is the level of the prominent

162 Richard Marshall, 1999, 69.
163 Jacques Bernard, 1973, 324–329.
164 Richard Marshall, 1999, 63.
165 Richard Marshall, 1999, 64, 65.
166 Richard Marshall, 1999, 116.
167 Jacques Bernard, 1973, 328.
168 For instance, Yamey's conclusions that the merchants in this early period did not use their bookkeeping "to keep a regular and accurate check on their capital and profits" or that accounting practice does not suggest "the quantification of possessions, the comparison of profits and invested capital" seem to be still valid sixty years later. See Basil Yamey, 1949, 110.

merchants, the large and rich households of a regular and secular nature for whom specific textbooks are modeled with extensive similarity to Pacioli's or Manzoni's. The obvious question is: Who devised the rules of how to organize these books?

It seems a crucial question, but it presupposes a person, an inventor with a Newtonian spirit instead of some impersonal oikoïdal institution(s). In my view we have to look for an institution that accumulated knowledge by trial and error in a business-like banking, which could be of a regular as well as a secular nature. Institutions able to transform specific abstract knowledge into specific practical knowledge, and vice versa. In short, we should look for intermediary institutions within the elite. Some considerations must be stated here: first, the trial-and-error question.

It arises comparable to the present state of the Internet: for a relatively long time it developed in an anarchistic way, out of the control of oikoïdal institutions (municipality, church institutions, national bureaucracies or secret services). That time seems to be over: the bureaucracies mentioned soon discovered both the tool and the playground that also gave them *un*controllable power over the private lives of the citizens in most developed democratic societies, *not* in the so-called Third World, and *not yet* (?) in China or India as the new superstars.

With DEB in use in the northern Italian city-states, at that time comprising the richest and most developed societies, a tool was created by which the most uncontrollable counter-power of the Church, aristocracy and monarchy with their armies, could be trapped. The nomadic merchants and itinerant traders became sedentary and started slowly to become bureaucrats and, thereby, competitors of the classical bureaucrats, who were already writing the textbooks. It was not yet true that laws could force merchants and entrepreneurs to use DEB on penalty of punishment.

Still, pressure "from above" to do so could be very strong in medieval Italy, starting with a threat of violation of the usury doctrine of the Church, of the obligatory payment of salt and other taxes, and, thanks to court practices, "entries in account books had been recognized as prima facie evidence of debt since early in the Trecento."[169] The latter privilege, however, was gained only after legalization and registration of the journal and the ledger, but not the memorial, in specific public offices.[170]

Apart from all this, there must have been the indirect pressure of, for example, organized religion, as the patronage of numerous religious institutions

169 Richard Marshall, 1999, 76, 97–99.

170 Pieter de Waal, 1927, 54–56.

was deemed "essential to business success. Without this clientele, some shopkeepers [in Prato] would have found their sales cut in half."[171] However, the systematic violation of religious, guild and municipality rules by the tradesmen relative to closing hours/ days of their shops (even on Christmas Day), demonstrates the other side of this coin. The usury verdict, "the laws and statutes of God... [that] no interest should be taken on a loan of money" or heavy taxation, could also be evaded rather easily.[172]

The language used in Pacioli's treatise is, first and foremost, authoritative. There is no explanation of *why* some act would be *financially* favorable to one's business, but these texts are nearly written as orders with a strong reliance on personal moral and civil duties. God as the main overseer is omnipotent in DEB textbooks as well as in the accounts of the petty traders of Prato.[173] Pacioli's balance is first and foremost a "means to control" the equation of debit and credit amounts.[174] Let's look a bit closer at this question.

1.4.3 *The Theory of the Balance*

The origin of account books and of DEB is much debated among accounting professionals since Pacioli, but the evolution of its techniques has hardly been discussed.[175] A non-professional like me is therefore excused from doing this only piecemeal in the following reflection on the balance in and of the ledger (Italian, *el bilancio del libro*), which has led to the most remarkable comments.

According to the *Oxford English Dictionary* (OED) the word *balance* enters the post-Latin period around 1600, but it clearly missed Pacioli, who used it as a well-known word in his time. But from the beginning of the 17th century, it broke through with torrential power: the policy of the *balance of power* lead to a permanent state of the cruelest wars still going on today.

Comparable to Sombart's exclamation about DEB, its theorists described it as "the political counterpart of Newton's physics." Its practitioners sold it as "the central 'realist' concept for the preservation of international order," while an American Secretary of State had already coined its successor as early as 1955 with the "balance of terror."[176]

With the *balance of payments* between nations and the *balance of trade,* a more "realist" relation with DEB is laid, but they are also rooted in the intellectual climate and nationalistic practices of the 17th century, the world of a

171 Richard Marshall, 1999, 28.
172 Iris Origo, 1986, 151–157.
173 Eve Chiapello, 2007, 272.
174 Pieter de Waal, 1927, 58.
175 Basil Yamey, 1980.
176 Alan Bullock, ed., 1999, 65.

William Petty, Gregory King and Pierre Boisguillebert.[177] In these heydays of the oikoïdal mercantilists the taxable capacity of the nation-state, the redistribution issues associated with it, the possession of as much gold as possible, and so on, were of much interest.[178]

This was much so that it became the first time in which anyone tried to combine all the given balance-policies in absolutist France, and thus the first orders came from above to practice DEB. That the DEB-balancing was the inspiration of all these difficult balancing acts seems obvious, but I haven't seen any proof of this. Otherwise Weber's dictum about the struggle of man against man presupposed in the *Kapitalrechnung* could have had some justification. Anyway, the nature of the difference of both sides and the reason(s) for entering it in the account are in fact the most important aspects, and not only in DEB.[179] Without it there is no *equilibrium* or *equality*, which are also the key-concepts of the balance of power, etc.

The *form* of the bookkeepers' balance seems to be nothing but an *equation*: the addition of sums on the right side of the ledger equals the addition of the sums on the left side. The very large proportion of the deals on *credit* in medieval northern Italy leads to the obvious consideration that the blackboard is reproduced on paper: the long list of debtors was equated if notices were added when somebody paid their *debt*. If it was paid, one simply struck out the name and debt of the customer, not only on the blackboard but also later in the books.[180]

Whenever someone has to pay for deliveries, the creditor usually makes up a list of goods and amounts, and again one or two lists appear. There is, furthermore, the supply–demand mechanism: goods against other goods, goods against money. This has been known to the most simple-minded from time immemorial, and it easily leads to mutual opposite lists, particularly if the value of the currency used in the deal is included. This was a serious problem for merchants who visited international fairs. All this points directly to the practical background of the bilateral character of DEB. Is this science?

Only in Germany has DEB been upgraded into a science; Weber and Sombart did their utmost to support this. De Waal perceives the question of whether DEB is a science as non-sense. A science aims to study problems in order to discover a logical coherence in its elements, or an origin, an explanation, a solution; it is an abstract undertaking. According to him this is not the case with

177 Fernand Braudel, 1982, volume 2, 204–206.
178 Joel Mokyr, 2003, volume 4, 33–34.
179 John Geijsbeek, 1914, 14.
180 Pieter de Waal, 1927, 33–36.

DEB, which is "a perception of concrete phenomena." DEB enables us to follow the changes of a certain capital and to provide a proper overview of these changes. The basis for, in particular, the financial policy of an enterprise is laid by this: "A summary, a judgment, an explanation is not given. It [DEB] provides an analysis of what happened, but it is impossible to give a synthesis."[181] Here I refer to the long quotation of Yamey at the end of Part 1.

The balance-concept, however, should be understood as a medieval scientific concept. If Aho uses the analogy of the blindfolded judge who "sits full-faced in bilateral equilibrium... precisely positioned between two comparably sized columns... harmony, and balance," he misses the main element: this scale is never in balance.[182] Whatever the Good, it must always be heavier than the Bad; only an inattentive interpreter perceives the judge's scale as something in balance. In other words: if the scale of the blindfolded judge should be the model for DEB, there could be never a ledger with similar columns. Indeed, the problem is the difference, the *resto*.

It is not a play of words when Aho combines his idea of a bookkeeper's balance with ideas about justice and morality or equating "good and evil" with "credits and debits."[183] Remarks about "good" and "evil" may sometimes appear in a *kind* of forerunner of DEB, the memorials, but never in DEB because the memorials belonged to the *un*divided phase of the *oikos*—the household or company of the merchant.[184]

One should, furthermore, consider scholastic theologians, famous for arguing about questions like whether an angel could sit on the head of a pin. In a serious matter of "good" and "evil," they must have problems if a loss or a non-payment of a debt has to be registered. Was this an evil or a sin: were dirty tricks with non-payments a reality?[185] Not for the bookkeeper or his boss, but for the third party; this was a circumstance that cannot result in a *personal* sin/evil of the bookkeeper or his boss within this strictly *personalized system.* Where "good" and "evil" come into the picture, "guilt" and "punishment" are also at stake.

In addition, it is suggested that this is all a matter of "the chicken" or "the egg." However, at least in economics *both* credit and debit are of the utmost importance or are morally good for the functioning of "capitalist society," and for the management of the state since Louis XIV. For most economists since

181 Pieter de Waal, 1927, 279.

182 James Aho, 2005, 72.

183 James Aho, 2005, 72.

184 Basil Yamey, 2005, 79.

185 Jean Delumeau, 1990, 225.

Keynes, a substantial state budget deficit seems to be preferred. In other words: the *relationship and its value* are important, not whether one is "good" or "evil." Aho's equation leads to rather unsolvable problems for old scholastics and present readers.

Jean Favier, in his chapter on the origins of bookkeeping, convincingly explains how the several parts of DEB (memorial/ledger, profit-loss account, cashbook, stock-book) had their *own* history, that was always based on *practices* and not on theories.[186] Indeed, one can say that the *relationship* between these parts, the combination of them, constituted DEB and because these parts did not know their destiny, it was important to find them.

Marshall discovered, for instance, that it was the overriding practice among the petty traders and shopkeepers to give credit to their customers, while they had the sound *fiducia* (trust) that the customers would later pay their debts. This "later" could extend to six years between close relations.[187] As shown above at the upper level of the northern Italian societies and in Europe, it was normal to give substantial loans as well. In short, from the point of view of the credit-givers, these were acts in which the most money-capital and goods in account-capital were pushed into circulation.

So, one can deduce from the historical reality that in this *loan-economy* the first and simplest thing people on all levels will do (from shopkeepers on their blackboards to the highest levels in their books), is to make a list of their debtors accompanied by remarks if the loans are paid back later. That is not DEB, but still the formal backbone of it.

It is not possible to go into further detail to discuss, for instance, the widespread extension of credit in Prato, the paying of interest on debts, the periodical scarcity of specific coins, etc. Anyway, in Pacioli's or Manzoni's and Simon Stevin's writings, these practices cannot be uncovered. Part of the explanation is found in the question of the personification they used.

It is said that from the beginning of the 13th century, in the pre-DEB period, the custom among Italian merchants was to place oneself *in the position of the customer* to which the account was presented: a demand on Giovanni was, *from the point of view of Giovanni*, noted as a debt. This is not a strange custom in a loan economy.[188] That the same principle must be used in DEB books is not self-evident in my view.

In Favier's example, consider the cashier in a municipality, or in a large church with its many lands, buildings, etc. or, a bit later, in any large company.

186 Jean Favier, 1987, 301–326.

187 Richard Marshall, 1999, 82.

188 Jean Favier, 1987, 313–314.

He was responsible for all notations in the cashbook, which was seen as the account of the cashier, who owes money to his boss, the owner. It is only for this reason that the cashier writes as a debt the amounts he receives and *therefore* as a credit what he pays. The cashier must be well aware that there could not be any difference between the debit and credit side of his cashbook.

This again seems to me to be self-evident. Not for a loan-economy (in which Giovanni's debt is an asset for the boss booked in DEB on the debt side), but for a full-fledged money economy in which a cashier is dealing daily with cash money. At the end of the day, his boss will be unhappy if there is a difference between debit and credit and the cashier has to compensate, as he is responsible for *his* accounts.

This also has nothing to do with striking a balance, but with making an *equation* between credit and debt, always assuming that where there is a creditor there is a debtor or vice versa. This is less obvious for a payer-receiver, a supplier–"demander" and quite difficult for the good-bad dichotomy. In a theological discourse one must say in Roman Catholicism that the one who is always good cannot be bad, while in Calvinism one must say: you are always bad, which means that you cannot be good!

But apart from this, one has to realize also the following about the use of "debtor" and "creditor." Here is Littleton:

> The first bookkeeping texts did not generalize upon transaction analysis to the extent of stating rules for resolving transactions into debits and credits. And it is doubtful whether the early authors resorted to personification of impersonal accounts.[189]

This personification and ruling seems to belong to the strategy of the authoritarian oikoïdal DEB and not of market-bookkeeping. This is, unintentionally, also the implication of Littleton's statement: "Impersonal accounts in an early day would undoubtedly have been hard to teach as abstractions."[190]

If the first bookkeepers (before the DEB period) had the same opinion, they would have immediately used personification, but they did not! They simply wrote matters down to remember who owed them money, etc. One may also ask how abstract were these early accounts, for instance those discovered by Marshall? However, those who stood *outside practice* in the later teacher/authority–pupil/subject situation had to rely on this method. If these teachers

189 Ananias Littleton, 1961, 46.

190 Ananias Littleton, 1961, 47; see also John Geijsbeek, 1914, 15 about Simon Stevin's personification.

were clerics one may even compare this personification with the personal guilt they are obliged to *create* in order to execute their professional and lucrative absolution practices (Datini's heritage!).

Against this background, the "*Quod non est in libris…*" should be appropriate, if one combines this with Pacioli's classical conservative motif, "Where there is no order there is confusion."[191]

1.4.4 *Political Geometry and Arithmetic*

Quite different elements of the elite position of DEB can be found if one poses two innocent questions: 1. Why did an original and professional outsider like Pacioli have such an intimate knowledge of the daily dealings of merchants and shopkeepers? 2. What is the meaning of the many other professions of Simon Stevin as an acknowledged expert in DEB? This latter question is relatively easy to answer, but requires first the answer to the former question, which can lead to complex explanations that must be dealt with rather superficially. However, I think that these both answers touch on the very intellectual, social and political background of DEB and arrive at the heart of the subject of this chapter.

The clue is that Pacioli wrote the pages about DEB as a Franciscan monk in a period in which his order, famous for its claim of eternal poverty, was one of the richest institutions in Europe. It possessed, for instance, many banks that were fighting for the financial souls of Venetian shopkeepers and bigger fishes, while succeeding in driving out or ghettoizing their strongest competitors, the Jewish bankers.

It must have been a great advantage for these "holy" banks, which already had detailed insight into the financial and social position of their customers, to receive Pacioli's instructions as a means to transform the rather confusing bookkeeping into an orderly and, particularly, controllable overview of the changes of the customer's capital and their households. The risks of their loan-activities could be mitigated and, probably more importantly, the Franciscans would be given an enormous advantage in the permanent competition between the several spiritual orders in their respective heritage, real estate or indulgence and miracle policies.

There are, however, other reasons why Pacioli and his book *Summa de Arithmetica, Geometria, Proportioni et Proportionalita* is of an "ideal-typical nature." This not for its DEB instructions, which cover only the brief Part 1, Section 9, treatise 11 of his book. Rather, Pacioli combines his status as a well-known Franciscan monk with that of an outstanding mathematician within a remarkable Franciscan tradition that goes back at least to the 13th century.

191 John Geijsbeek, 1914, 17, 27.

It is a tradition of theologian-mathematicians who all had a strong interest in ethics, economic exchange, and in some theory of money, and who often worked as radical thinkers in the margins of (and sometimes strongly opposed to) mainstream theology and the Roman Catholic Church.[192] Let's look first into some mathematical features. Notwithstanding that the parallels are striking with the present status and institutional effectiveness of algorithm steered calculations and data processing performance, only the following is relevant to characterize the mathematical tradition.

It is nearly impossible to doubt that Pacioli must have been strongly influenced by the scholastic-Aristotelian ethics that conceptualized justice in a highly mathematical way. Without going into any mathematical detail, I only want to point to the following.

Aristotle writes for instance in his *Nicomachean Ethics,*

> The just, then, is a species of the proportionate (proportion being not a property only of the kind of number that consists of abstract units, but of number in general).[193]

Herewith Pacioli's book is provided with a remarkable classical background formed by a main work by the arch-father of any *oikos*-theory. In addition, its gist encouraged the use of numbers as a practical aid in the description, analysis, and measurement of real phenomena.

Aristotle separated justice into two forms: a distributive and a corrective or directive one. The former concerns "the distribution of common goods by a central authority in proportion as the recipient had proved himself worthy of reward through service."[194] The quality of service and virtue is inherently unequal, and, therefore, distributive reward must be unequal as well. In this mathematical way of thinking, this kind of justice asks for a *geometrical equivalence*: greater service receives proportionally greater reward.

It is possibly with this in mind that the Franciscans gave a numerical definition of the communities in which they settled in order to know whether a community could bear a parasitic friars community.[195] The corrective-directive justice, however, is determined by an *arithmetical equivalence.* Kaye says,

192 For backgrounds see Lester Little, 1978; Dirk Noordman, 1996.

193 Quoted by Joel Kaye, 1998, 40.

194 Joel Kaye, 1998, 41.

195 Lester Little, 1978, 25, 150–152.

> The intermediate point between gain and loss is found through the arithmetical process of addition or subtraction to an imaginary line of gain and loss. Directive justice is also called "rectificatory" and "corrective" because it applies to those cases in which balance is restored by a judge or intervening orderer.[196]

Aristotle is, furthermore, busy with something like *equalizing unequal lines*: real, existing problems were perceived as representing numbers and lines and solved mathematically. After his exposé about the distributive and directive justice, Aristotle introduces the concept of *reciprocity*. In this context he discusses economic exchange, which leads to an immense and continuing debate about the status of the "ancient economy."[197]

This should be substantiated further, but in my view Pacioli's work *including his DEB-instructions* is a perfect demonstration of these scholastic-Aristotelian thoughts on ethical-mathematical subjects. In other words: DEB is used as a demonstration of proportionality, but the question is which one.

Now, to the economic tradition. The mainstream theology of Thomas Aquinas and others was largely characterized by its oikoïdal and Christianized Aristotelianism, taking a middle-of-the-road position relative to profit, trade, etc. But, for instance, the Franciscan Peter Olivi (1248–1298) positively accepted contemporary mercantile practices and criticized both Aquinas and Aristotle, despite being a leader of the rigorous party of Franciscans—sworn to poverty and opposed to Franciscan ownership of property.[198]

Olivi used a concept of *capitale* that allowed him to accept interest on invested money if an "equivalence" with a lost profit was at stake. He was concerned with looking for an "explanation of how the productive labor of the merchant is transferred to money itself, turning sterile coin into fruitful *capitale*." A major question was also the way he brought his dynamic capital-concept "into a scholastic scheme still preoccupied with the ideal of equality (not profit) as a governing principle of exchange." Olivi saw "the market as a *mechanism of equalization*, that ordered itself independently of the intention of its individual participants."[199]

The old and the new became connected with the strongest stress on the latter. There were no limits on market-determined behavior as Aquinas preached, because this was rational and constructive. So, this view approved of high

196 Joel Kaye, 1998, 42.
197 Hans Derks, 1986; Hans Derks, 2002; now also Gérard Minaud , 2005.
198 For the following see Joel Kaye, 1998, 42.
199 Joel Kaye, 1998, 126 italics of Kaye.

prices for grain during famine, because possessors of grain could sell it more quickly and thereby avoid suffering; an opinion that was in accordance with many practices of city governments.

People like Olivi, with a high level of market understanding, were no exception in Franciscan circles, but it is difficult to gauge his influence. One year after his death, a number of his works were condemned and burnt; later everything was forbidden. Raymond De Roover's hero, Bernardino of Siena ("one of the greatest economists of all time," 1380–1440), popularized Olivi's ideas while simply copying his statements on value and price determinations, notwithstanding the condemnation.[200]

Franciscans like Duns Scotus (1266–1308) and Odonis (1290–1349), secular masters like the very influential Jean Buridan (1295–1358) and Nicole Oresme (1323–1382) and others further developed Olivi's economic theories using the equalization concept that was more clearly now a process of supply and demand and mutual agreement between the parties on a just value of the things exchanged.

Their denial of the intervention of a judge "in the equalization of gain and loss" as Aristotle and Aquinas prescribed was also important. If an agreement is made voluntarily and mutually and despite an uneven gain and loss, no subjective orderer is needed. The market has to do its work. This led to the highly principal debate among Franciscans about whether a society has to rest more "on the virtuous activity of men or on the strength and enforcement of positive law."[201]

The answer of Odonis was clear: the good man is more rational, just, divine and to be prized than the good law. Odonis was also the one who recognized that parties sought from the other a benefit proportional to the benefit offered. And Buridan added that a "just" exchange has taken place even in cases where one party has gained an unequal advantage; personal advantage is the natural condition of just exchange.[202] A conception of a market system was formulated in full opposition to the Christianized-Aristotelian *oikos*-model: a self-ordering market in which equality could result as a product of willed inequalities.

On the above question of why Pacioli had such detailed knowledge of the market, several answers can now be given: because the daily banking activities of the Franciscan order in Pacioli's time provided him with that data; because in order to serve the interests of the banks, he had to personalize his instructions as a matter of customer-binding and to translate abstract geometrical

200 Julius Kirshner, 1976, 28; see for another Bernardino in James Aho, 2005, 6, 46.

201 Joel Kaye, 1998, 130.

202 Joel Kaye, 1998, 132.

principles into comprehensible language; because he knew the alternative Franciscan geometric-economic writings in which many of these daily details were discussed. One may expect that in Pacioli's time one could be more open in assessing the necessity of profit (as he did), while not deviating too much from the Aristotelian-scholastic principles. Therefore, how influential a "Franciscan market economics" was, along with its dominant *oikos*-household economics is interesting.[203]

Important here is the clear *oikos* versus market debate at a theoretical level as opposition against the hegemonic position of the oikoïdal powers. That its supporters were persecuted and their books burnt and that these persecutors focused on *equilibrium* and the establishment of *equivalence* as the proper motive and end of exchange (not profit and the desire for gain) belongs to the medieval balancing act.

DEB was one of Pacioli's examples to demonstrate simple balancing, proportionality, equivalence between gain and loss, credit and debit;[204] as such it "equals" an economic-theological statement on oikoïdal geometry. Pacioli's room to maneuver intellectually was not that large. One cannot forget that at the time he wrote his treatise, the Contra-Reformation and the economic shift from the Mediterranean to the North Sea region were underway.

Literally along the coast of this last sea, the other "ideal-typical spirit" in this history of DEB, the Flemish-Dutch mathematician Simon Stevin (1548–1620), acted as inventor of a sail-car running with a substantial speed over the beaches. Stevin is, indeed, a man of all markets and his influence in many fields is much larger than that of the Italian.[205]

It seems as if a world as antagonistic as *oikos* and market separated both DEB promoters. Stevin supported the market position in many ways: his writing is highly communicative in place of Pacioli's authoritarianism; he published for everybody interest tables that were intended as bank secrets only; he stressed private property, capital account, separation of company and household capital, separation of state (public) and merchants (private) bookkeeping, and so on.

His way of reasoning and acting starts from practice and moves to theory and not the reverse; his non-theological, mechanical way of thinking led to the abandonment of all pious headings or references to God in DEB. Pacioli is still a medieval man, Stevin a modern one; the former is a theorist, the latter was a professional cashier and bookkeeper in Antwerp for at least a decade.

203 Dirk Noordman, 1996, 11–15.

204 Pieter de Waal, 1927, 58.

205 Pieter de Waal, 1927, 259–277; Gérard Minaud, 2005, 20, 33–35.

This Flemish-Dutch practical scholar is even so modern that he was far ahead of *present* Flemish-Belgian attempts to introduce DEB in government administrations (see above), which he had already proposed in his *Wisconstighe Ghedachtenissen* (Arithmetical Considerations, 1608).

However, there are also some similarities apart from the fact that they both introduced DEB. Both were mathematicians, both dedicated much of their work to mighty princes (the Duke of Urbino and Prince Maurits of Nassau, leader of the successful Dutch army), and both served oikoïdal interests with their knowledge. If one studies the details, these similarities disappear as well: the rather familiar dialogues Stevin held and published with Prince Maurits, anyway an army leader of European stature, was impossible in Pacioli's Italy.

A more important point is that the latter is a geometrical mathematician and Stevin, an arithmetical one. For Pacioli, therefore, DEB is a demonstration of or even derived from his theory of proportionality, equality and equivalence. De Waal characterizes Stevin as follows:

> ... he is more an engineer than mathematician; for him it is not enough to describe the technics, but he explains as well the principles on which these are based, in order to come to as simple an explanation as possible and to develop this technics to a higher level.[206]

DEB is for him an algebraic task that must be done very precisely and be controlled by means of a balance not once, but twice. He would be very glad about the present-day definition of the accounting equation as "assets = liabilities + shareholders equity."

In terms of the former paragraph, it is Pacioli who could perfectly support a balance of power and equilibrium policy with his apriori thinking. Therefore, I should not be very surprised if one day somebody makes an even better link between his "geometric DEB" and the classical balance of power policy of the 16th–20th century, as I have suggested.

Stevin, however, was, in the most literal sense, one of the main designers of the new Dutch civil society; the title of one of his many popular works was, *Het burgerlick Leven* (*The Civilian Life*),

> ... the overriding need for order and discipline... also deemed it useful to propagate applied science among the people, publishing several of his scientific works in Dutch... stressed the usefulness of decimals...

206 Pieter de Waal, 1927, 262.

> deferential to patrician authority, not involved in politics, and submissive in the face of the bewildering state of church affairs.[207]

Arithmetic, including arithmetic DEB, was the main tool to reach these aims that would result in a fully mechanized society, one equalized to the utmost like his grid-designs for fortifications and in which religion was only another tool for maintaining order. Stevin was cynical enough to advise his readers to start no religious quarrels, to accept one superficial kind of Protestantism even if they did not believe anything, just to support order and discipline. It could be argued that his thought was along the lines of: our common enemy is Spain, we cannot have any internal problem if we want to conquer this enemy; in short, balance of power arguments favored by his Prince Maurits.

1.5 The Balance of a Theory

Now I have to end this discussion about the complex relationship between religion, capitalism (à la Weber and Sombart), and DEB with a few conclusions in which overlaps are intended, because things have to come together from different sides at the end of the day.

1. From the discussion of the definition and meaning of capital*ism* and its fundamental differences from capitalist production, it must inevitably follow that this capital*ism* cannot have existed in the northern Italian medieval cities and regions or elsewhere.[208]

Some elements of this capital*ism* may be discovered in an earlier period, but there was never the *combining* of these elements, nor the quality of the whole. And it is still possible that *locally* a capitalist production could flourish (for instance in the Luccan and Florentine silk industry, the Venetian "Arsenal" and other places like Flanders' textile industry or the German Ravensburg), but it was never on a relevant scale or with the capacities shown later in the so-called "Industrial Revolution," and then, only after the monetization of the northern Italian societies was completed (around 1400).

It is also possible that *periodically* capitalism as defined could flourish during long periods of war in Renaissance Italy and more certain during the Thirty Years War (1618–1648), with De Geer's iron monopoly serving all warring parties.

207 Jonathan Israel, 1995, 567–568.

208 This is also the consequence of the way capitalism is defined or the origin of capitalism is discussed as in the newest dictionary at issue: Joel Mokyr, ed. 2003, volume 1, 319–325.

Directly referring to Max Weber, the economic historian Joel Mokyr acknowledged that there were numerous precedents, but "that the Industrial Revolution meant the ever-growing physical separation of the unit of consumption (the household) from the unit of production (the plant)."[209]

This means, of course, that the *relationship* between religion, capital*ism,* and DEB could not develop in another period than after 1850 and only in Western Europe or in the USA after the Civil War, from which it spread around the world through destructive imperialist and World Wars, demonstrating the "*Quod non est in libris"* arrogance *in extremis*. In other words: the relationship is only feasible within a political-economic "unit," a religiously oriented state that can organize its territory according to oikoïdal principles under which capitalist productions are subsumed.

Therefore, another periodization than, for instance, the very popular one of Sombart (early, high and late capitalism) is necessary. My proposal is the following. After the so-called "fall of the Roman Empire" or end of the "ancient economy": West European monetization (ca. 500–1500), West European oikoïdalization (ca. 1500–1750), West European capitalist production (ca. 1750–1850), West European capital*ism* (ca. 1850–present). For eastern parts of Europe everything takes longer.

These periods do *not* represent an evolution as was given in Sombart's periodization (and all other competing periodizations), which is scientifically obsolete: they represent the *dominant feature* of a period (money, state, production, world domination) that was developed and learned by trial and (t)error, and this in the sense that *all former periods were incorporated and further developed within the following ones.*

2. After 1850, the best example of the relationship given in the title of this chapter with a dominant *religious* orientation is the state now called the Vatican. From 1859 to 1870 it fought one military battle after another to remain in power in its large Italian territory. It lost, but transformed the mini-state that remained into the basis of the largest multinational political-economic monopoly, the "ideal-typical" and self-sufficient Oikos.

This included the normal oikoïdal imperialistic policies against the main competitors Judaism, Islam, Greek-Orthodox Christianity and American sectarian Protestantism that are still around today. This Oikos can easily exist economically without any believer in its worldwide network of branches and settlements ruled by an autocratic monarchy or can eventually launch another product for the world service-market.

209 Joel Mokyr, 2002, 120; see also Luc Boltanski and Eve Chiapello, 2005, 154–156. In his latest book, Joel Mokyr, 2017, 230–234, Calvinism and Weber are discussed in a few sentences but "capitalism" even disappeared from the index!

Germany, which, from after unification in 1870, was Weber's and Sombart's Germany, provides the "ideal-typical" example of this capitalism with a *secular* orientation: an always belligerent Oikos-state with political monopoly claims, legitimated in an extreme way by Lutheranism and Roman Catholicism and in close cooperation with the big industries and banks (Krupp, Deutsche Bank, IG Farben, etc.) with economic monopoly claims.

The Oikos-state overrules its subjects with clear directions, for instance, to use DEB, or provides "enforceable legal representations" (De Soto), while the big industries overrule their competitors by placing the capitalist productions in economic dependency relations. The very German capitalism theories of Weber and Sombart are intended to legitimate this German "marriage of convenience" called capital*ism*, while their critical content is aimed at pushing the economic partner in an oikoïdal direction (against money-making as an aim in itself).

3. About the content of Sombart's theory one can be brief. Only a few people, definitely not Chiapello,[210] discovered the serious discrepancies between Sombart's spectacular comparisons of DEB "and the systems of Galileo and Newton... modern physics and chemical science... the cosmic world of the stars or the blood-cells... the idea of gravity, circulation of the blood..."[211] at the beginning of his monumental *Der Moderne Kapitalismus,* and the less than disappointing near silence in the last volume, written a quarter of a century later.[212]

Apparently for Sombart, DEB now exists in only a small corner, but capitalist production has been in full swing for about one and a half centuries and capital*ism* had shown its formidable strength during spectacular imperialistic adventures and into the First World War. To make this discrepancy larger: for Sombart capital*ism* and DEB were "connected as intimately as form and contents" as Aho reminded us.[213]

With this "state of capitalism" theory (let alone with Weber's/Sombart's theological "spirit-exercises"), transplanting a first, second, etc. "spirit of capitalism" yet again into present discourses like those of Boltansky and Chiapello, does nothing but create mysteries and provide at best an air of harmony for the outside world in a "marriage of convenience" among very differently oriented partners.

---

210 Eve Chiapello, 2007, 265–266.

211 MK, volume. 2, 119.

212 MK, volume 3, 889. Here, in a few sentences DEB is seen ¨as a beginning¨ which is the start of a serious modification: DEB is ¨a small island in the vast ocean of the empirical. When, how and where the other parts of the industrial management will have a scientific character is difficult to forecast ...¨ etc. That's all what is left from DEB.

213 James Aho, 2005, 8.

There is, however, still room for a capital*ism* theory. If one wants to rely on Weber and/or Sombart, then one should base it on their *Haushalt*(*en*)-*Erwerb*(*en*) exercises and not on their socio-theological analyses of Calvinism, Catholicism or Judaism.[214] The household concept and its inseparable production-consumption relations are, for example, also used time and again by Mokyr, sometimes even without a relevant meaning.[215]

4. Weber's and Sombart's work is, therefore, only interesting in so far it provides us with numerous theoretical elements and historical analyses to make a modernized Aristotelian theory of the market-*oikos* contradictions.

It has only been possible to provide an outline of this modern market-*oikos* theory, that in truth could be expanded in another book with much profit. From the discussion so far, one may conclude that *the market* is not only an attractive location for most people in the world, but in its basic supply-demand mechanism also the fundamental precondition for people to become *zoon politikon,* that are human beings fit to live in some public or private community (*polis* or *oikos*) with others.[216]

Next, one may conclude that for this basic level, if that market mechanism is negated (self-sufficiency or autarky!) in some government or some socio-economic setting, it sets up trouble in social and family relations, particularly if (as in capitalism) *polis* and *oikos* combine their substantial powers to undermine the basics of market-life. That is, however, a blind alley at the end of the day, a losing option, as two World Wars and several regional wars have now proven convincingly.

To defend a concept of *market* against the wave of criticism of blind consumerism is not easy, because this consumerism exists everywhere. It concerns, of course, a very one-sided view of to what a market is or could be related; it is quite as one-sided as the concept of capital*ism* as "money-economy" (*Geldwirtschaft*) that is accepted in most anti-capitalism criticism, including by Weber and Sombart.

As such it is still a consequence of the ancient Christianized-Aristotelian anti-money attitudes. Therefore, it is not as obvious as it should be to say that

214 Hans Derks, 2004, 79–149.

215 "'Production' should be taken to include household activities such as cooking, cleaning, childcare, and so forth, which equally require the manipulation of natural phenomena and regularities." See Joel Mokyr, 2002, 10 note 12 ; besides "capitalism" in Joel Mokyr, 2017 also "production" and "household" fully disappeared.

216 Highly interesting is Michael McKeon, 2005, who from page 7 onwards uses the *polis-oikos* relationship and Aristotelian theory to develop a much more complex household concept and practice including the state as family/household. This voluminous study of nearly 1000 pages concerns mainly the English 17th and 18th centuries.

the *market* concerns not only money or products in the supermarket, but also labor (manual and spiritual), resources, production, services… in short: everything and all that is understandable concerning supply and demand. Is there anything left outside of this? The shortest way to define *market* is "peaceful communication"; a market–*oikos* relationship is seldom a peaceful affair.

5. It is, furthermore, necessary to perceive Weber's *Evolution der Hausgemeinschaft* with its ideological *Bedarfsdeckung-Erwerb* dichotomy only as a heuristic tool to study why and how things can become related to each other. It is not a realistic economic-historical model. To receive that status it should be combined with a famous largely non-ideological relationship, that of *town versus country*.

Most great 19th century thinkers, including Marx, though not Weber, perceived the change of this relation not only as a developing antagonism but also as one in which the "whole of the economic history of society" is summarized.[217] Notwithstanding this, the changing fate of the combination of market-*oikos* with town-country remains of decisive importance for the historical, economic or political practice, which cannot be a question of an evolutionary change alone.

Also, Chiapello supports the idea that the one phase follows from the other.[218] The most extreme is Bryer's DEB theory in which a farmers' mentality and merchant's mentality are mixed, giving rise to a modern capitalistic mentality, whatever that may be.[219] This may seem a rather unfair judgment, where Bryer defines a capitalist mentality explicitly as "the maximisation of return on capital employed in production."

What is done here is quite the same as in the Weberian-Sombartian "spirit"-stories, namely to confuse a mentality or spirit (as a certain state of mind) with the *goal* of any market oriented (capitalist) venture (maximization, etc.), that must be fulfilled under pain of stopping this venture sooner or later. The farmer's and merchant's goal must be similar if they bring their products to the market and both have to make that return, while their mentality must be very different to live continuously on a farm, grow crops, etc. or to choose being in the city working in a factory or on the road to reach their goal. In my view, these mentalities cannot, by definition, be mixed.

These evolutionary schemes are too primitive to explain the course of history: there are things that follow each other, but *most of the phenomena discussed above exist together*, like capitalist production and capitalism; capitalist

217 Hans Derks, 1986, 11–50.
218 Eve Chiapello, 2007, 265.
219 R. Bryer, 2000b, 328.

production industry and non-capitalist agriculture; monetized parts of the economy along with non-monetized parts; barter and gift exchange together with valuations in money or bitcoins; and so on and so forth.

The question is which "form" has a hegemonic or dominant position, what is the degree of negation of the market elements at stake, or under which conditions did this negation take place. So, it does not help, but is logically more satisfying, to combine that evolution with an "evolution of the market" and a "(r)evolution of the *relationship* of market-oikos." Here one must remember that "*oikos* against market" is the rule in (European) history and therefore one can understand how exceptional it was that at the end of the 19th century a "marriage of convenience" between these arch-enemies developed in capital*ism*.

6. Therefore, many levels of doing bookkeeping must be seen as *existing together*, often changing in mutual relationship: household scrapbook; middle-class shopkeepers (using the blackboard along with something like single-entry bookkeeping), bailiff accounts and traders' bookkeeping; DEB for the elite, which also has cameralistic bookkeeping available, or state budget accounting.[220] There is a class differentiation in accounting practices.

Viewed socio-historically and economically, DEB is a *combination of accounting elements* from different and rather contradictory corners. There are the elements of a market and household (*oikos*) nature; the theoretical and practical elements; those from sedentary and nomadic sources; the elements that have been developed in the practices of trading activities in the broadest sense of the word (from small shopkeepers to itinerant merchants), and in production enterprises or intermediary institutions like banks and money-lenders.

But DEB as such, which developed in late medieval and early modern times in northern Italy, the Netherlands and Spain,[221] is first and foremost a tool for the political-economic elite *including* specific church institutions. It is a representative model of elitist political aspirations, and their *combination* is made by the scholars of the day, often belonging to the Franciscan order. However, it

220 R. Bryer, 2000b, 329, 330; Eve Chiapello, 2007, 271; Bernard Slicher van Bath, 1963, 176–178; Bernard Slicher van Bath, 1978.

221 I have to thank an anonymous reviewer from which I received much information about the Spanish performance which should be combined with my story. Because they were difficult to obtain and could not be used by me, I can only mention some titles. Hernandez Borreguero, J. (2003), The Accounting System in the Cathedral Council's Accounting Office ('Majordomia') throughout the Seventeenth Century, in: *26th Annual Congress of the European Accounting Association* (Sevilla); Rivera Fernandez, D. et al (2004), A Historical Antecedent of Accounting Regulation; the Form in the Cistercian Order, in: 27th *Annual Congress of the European Accounting Association* (Prague); Villaluenga de Gracia, S. (2004) La catedral de Toledo en la primera mitad del siglo XVI: organizacion administrativa, rentas y contabilidad (diss. University of Castilla-La Mancha).

must be denied that DEB has any relation with western European religions as belief systems and their core rituals like the sacrament of confession.

I have a strong impression that DEB was not spread widely among the relevant institutions and enterprises until late in the 19th century. And even then it is not spread under some capitalist pressure, but thanks to state legislation that has been rather selective until today. It will probably receive its definitive breakthrough in information systems prescribed by technocrats, at which point, it will likely no longer be called DEB.

The fascination with DEB, which is irrational within a Weberian- Sombartian historical religion-capitalism context, is understandable within the context of the described "marriage of convenience." Here DEB received its Janus face: a tool to manage its own company or institution and a tool to control society, the competitor(s), in the hands of the state bureaucracy.

7. The use of dichotomies for methodological or ideological purposes in the evolution/revolution debates is of an ambiguous nature. What was said above about the moralistic-religious good-bad/credit-debit dichotomies as the nucleus of some exchange should be formulated in a better way, since we are often dealing with a *representation* of original exchange-activities. This was a point of view still held by several 16th century Italian and Dutch authors writing about bookkeeping.[222] Which *real* exchange?

Goods and *services* are exchanged for *money* which means that the one is in debt to goods/services and the other is in debt with money while, of course, both debtors must accept the *same value* to make a deal: supply and demand are in need of a value intermediary. It must be for some the logic behind the *similar* notation on the debit and credit side of the ledger, but that is only the case for scholastic-Aristotelian equivalence seekers. At least the original practice was more precise: herein money is seen as another commodity since the merchant was confronted with many kinds, weights and qualities of coins.[223]

This *goods-money-value* mechanism could and had to be improved along all three elements at the moment credit was given or if the payment and delivery of goods took time (long-distance trade; bill of exchange). In the 14th and in the 15th century a clear division of labor represents this mechanism in the northern Italian cities, in which the one became specialized in goods (producers),

222 Pieter de Waal, 1927, 22–25.

223 This is illustrated also by the so-called "bullion or money famine," the hunger for coins, which was stilled by selling all the precious gadgets one had at home, in the church or where-ever. Furthermore, there are the differences between the "money of exchange" (real money) and the "money of account" (imaginary bookkeepers money). "Value" was determined "by weight of gold or silver, measured in grains and later in grams of precious metal." David Fischer, 1996, 282–285.

the other in services (notaries, lawyers, etc.), in trades (merchants) or transports (ship-owners, captains, etc.), payments (banker) or in values (money-changer), and so forth.

But where the reflection on this process leads to something like DEB, this goods-money-value mechanism is reduced and fixed: the immanent movement and dialectic from practice disappeared in a rather sterile grid made to overrule instead of inspire and activate that mechanism, more a tool in power plays than an improvement project. The *goods-money-value* mechanism disappeared in the most extended household economy ever seen, misleadingly called "capitalism," but probably it can be simulated at a much higher level through the use of information technology.

8. The *Household* economy (oikoïdal economy) as an autocratically ruled and regulated self-sufficient economy from an absolutist state, church, monastery, feudal property or monarchy is always raging a serious battle against its main target, the outside world, the *market*. From the point of view of the household, the market is irregular, uncontrollable, immoral, inimical or foreign. The households' very aim is to negate the market forces. At the same time, however, there is a clear and sometimes strong mutual dependency, a mutual fascination as well. It is, therefore, in some sense a utopian battle that in the end is always lost by the household.

For instance, in the period in which the Italian medieval cities fully accepted all the opportunities of the market and improved their abilities to master these opportunities, the bloody battle with the several oikoïdal economies (from emperors, kings, popes) raged as well. We are not dealing with a universalism, Weber's "*battle from man to man*," but a periodically raging battle from sedentarized, institutionalized ruling groups against nomadic, nonconformist newcomers embedded in town-country antagonisms.[224] Mutual learning processes developing to win such struggles, in which the development of DEB should be placed in a kind of hierarchy with other forms.

The individual life cannot escape this environment. Here one can quote appropriately from Friedrich Engels who wrote to his friend Karl Marx (April 3, 1851) in what Chiapello called "accounting language":

> In commerce, the merchant as a firm, as a producer of profits, and the same merchant as a consumer are two entirely different people who confront one another as antagonists. The merchant as a firm means capital account and/or profit and loss account. The merchant as a guzzler, toper, householder and procreator means household expense account.

224 Hans Derks, 1986.

> Hence the capital account debits the household expense account with every centime that makes its way from the commercial to the private purse.[225]

It is, indeed, a process that can also be studied in the northern Italian regions in the period when nomadic merchants became sedentary, and one of the main checkerboard-designers and oikos-theoreticians, Leon Battista Alberti, could write that the merchant had "the duty... to write everything down... and to check everything so often that it seems, he is always with pen in hand... the merchant should always have his fingers stained with ink."[226]

Some of the new market powers transformed themselves on a large scale in the 18th–19th centuries into autonomous capitalist industrial enterprises which happened. Whatever their technological characteristics or specific relationship with a free stock of laborers, their common element was that they tried to be self-sufficient and regulate "their" part of the market through monopolies (syndicates, oligopolies, etc.) that were nothing but new oikoïdal economic forms; a kind of copy of the old guild practices including their political power, as the Flemish guilds demonstrated perfectly in their struggle against the French king and aristocracy.

Again a utopian ("Master of the Universe"), bloody, as well as, in the end, useless undertaking: if a monopoly is achieved, the game is over; internal as well as external powers will try to crush this oikoïdal economy in order to reestablish and accept anew the rules of the market game: the interrelationship of supply and demand presupposes a free decision of the parties involved because of an agreement on the matter of value; if from the supply or demand side an organized oikoïdal attack is launched, this most fundamental freedom is lost.

For oikoïdal powers, including churches and sects (probably mainly in this case), "value" is here in the end not only an earthly quality and quantity, but an other-worldly or geometrical/arithmetical quality. The impossibility to measure the first by means of the latter forms the very source of the conflict between religion, capitalism and DEB.

225 Quoted by Eve Chiapello, 2007, 289.

226 James Aho, 2005, 36; Roberto Lopez,1952, 325–326.

PART 2

Market and Oikos: *Basics in the West*

CHAPTER 2

How to Bring Cows to Athens

2.1 What is a Polis?

With this question we enter the hard core of classical studies: the *polis,* whatever it is, laid the basis for nothing less than for European civilization. Easy question, easy answer: Is the *polis* the Greek city(-state) and does its history go back to the dark ages? Weber wrote about it many times as a city, a settlement with at least a local market in which craftsmen, merchants and peasants could exchange products and services. It could be likened to something like a self-sufficient latifundia or manor. In doing so Weber combined a market–*oikos* approach with some view on the town versus country problem.[228]

The common meaning of *polis* with the status of a public opinion, is often shared by academics, who should know better, as the following short overview reveals.[229] First, a well-known architectural historian wrote in the best handbook:

> The Greek city was a creation of the Archaic period, in architectural form as in political, religious and social life.[230]

In the same year is written:

> ... the world of Greece and Rome was essentially a world of cities. At times, the countryside attracted... but more usually the countryside was a

228 WG, 1976, 732, a "Gegenbild ... gegen die auf planmäßig umgelegten Arbeits- und Abgabenleistungen spezialisierten abhängigen Wirtschaften, in Verbindung mit dem auf Kumulation und Kooperation von Arbeit im Herrenhof ruhenden, im Inneren tauschlosen *Oikos*, und daß die *Regulierung* der Tausch und Produktionsverhältnisse in der Stadt das Gegenbild darstellt für die *Organisation* der Leistungen der im Oikos vereinigten Wirtschaften." italics from Max Weber. This is a good example of *half* a sentence in which Weber points to the title of our book.

229 The most nuanced discussion of the *polis*-problem at present is by Jonathan Hall in: H.A. Shapiro, ed., 2007, 40–61. There are still so many difficulties with it that I choose not to argue about/against this inspiring text but to develop my own arguments. For the usual definition, in this case of Oswyn Murray, see OCD, 1996, 1205. A typical example of a poor treatment of the problem is Ian Morris' article in: John Rich and Andrew Wallace-Hadrill, ed., 1991, 25–57.

230 Robert Wycherley in John Boardman, ed., 1992, 184.

 | DOI:10.1163/9789004383913_003

> place of menace and danger... For the Greeks, the city—the *polis*—was... the only acceptable (natural) way of life for normal human beings... All this reflects the historical realities...[231]

A bit earlier Finley tried to support public opinion with:

> ... the true city in classical antiquity encompassed both the *chora,* the rural hinterland, and an urban center, where the best people resided, where the community had its administration and its public cults.[232] ... Ancient cities in the great majority counted farmers... as the core of their citizenry.[233]

From the "excavating fields" assessed a well-known archaeologist the polis problem in a most classical way. It concerns John Nicholas Coldstream, specialist in settlement and demographic problems in what is called "Geometric Greece":

> To confront the archaeological record, let Aristotle be our chief witness. From his *Politics* we learn that a *polis* must be a completely self-sufficient and autonomous state consisting of a single central settlement and its surrounding countryside.[234]

Another well-known archaeologist, John Bintliff, made the "guesstimate" of 625–1000 inhabitants pro polis in Bronze-Iron Age Karphi on Crete as follows:

> When one considers this range of population we can note that such a large community has a quite different set of political and economic parameters to a village of say 200 people... In effect such a large community contains the potential to behave like an introverted city state... what I have termed a "proto-polis."[235]

A *polis* seems to be not only a state, but also a settlement of at least more than 625 inhabitants; below this range we are dealing, anyway, with a village and

231 Richard Tomlinson, 1992, XI and 1.
232 Moses Finley, 1975, 123.
233 Moses Finley, 1975, 131.
234 John N. Coldstream, 1984, 7.
235 John Bintliff, 1997, 2. See also Scheidel's remarkably outdated demographic contribution in *The Cambridge Economic History of the Greco-Roman World,* 2007, 42 ff., apart from the usual definition of *polis* as city.

not with a town or city. Still, this is apparently not understood at present by a German historian, Winfried Schmitz, who could write without one bit of suspicion: "The Greek society was in the archaic period (700–500 BC) an agrarian one, notwithstanding the widespread urban settlement patterns."[236]

Another example, this time from a translator of numerous Greek philosophical texts, who also tried to write a vivid history of Athens for the visitors of the Olympic games in 2004. A compilation of ideal-typical and classical opinions about the Greek *polis* (plural: *poleis*) is the result:

> The topographical isolation of each city led over the years to a common civic culture... Each community was economically and politically independent of its neighbors... The ideal of self-sufficiency meant that a polis had to be small to work, small both in extent and in overall population, including the inhabitants of the outlying villages.[237] ... in Classical times over 90 percent of the Attic population were still peasant farmers, living in the countryside rather than in the city, and in the mid- fifth-century population of perhaps 350,000, only 50,000 were adult males with full citizen rights. There were about 100,000 slaves and 30,000 resident aliens.[238]

A small *polis* as city of 350,000 inhabitants, around 400 BCE, but nearly all farmers living in a countryside?! Recent, popular handbooks or rather useful source books point to the other traditional characteristic of *poleis* as a Greek City State. Pomeroy even defined:

> The city-state form of government came into existence during the eight century... The *polis*, as the Greeks called it... As an ideal, the polis has had enormous significance in the history of later nations... What is a city-state? A simplified definition is: a geographical area comprising a city and its adjacent territory, which together make up a single, self-governing political unit... The capital cities of what became city-states existed all through the Dark Age...[239]

Finley called the use of *city-state* simply "an English convention in rendering the Greek word polis" and rightly suggested, that it was a translation of

236 Winfried Schmitz, 2007, 9.
237 Robin Waterfield, 2004, 41.
238 Robin Waterfield, 2004, 149.
239 Sarah B. Pomeroy, ed., 1999, 84. In the last print of 2007 this text nearly did not change.

the German *Stadtstaat*.[240] According to him it was designed to get around a terminological mess, apparently not realizing how he himself contributed to an untenable intellectual and scholarly confusion. The main excuse for this is probably the acceptance as historical reality the many sayings of intellectual heroes such as Aristotle and Plato.[241]

Also Rhodes' book makes people walk in a blind alley. It starts with the translation of one of the most quoted and misused Aristotelian sentences:

> The Greek philosopher Aristotle wrote that "man is by nature a political animal," that is, one for whom life can best be lived in *poleis*, or city-states (*Politics*, I. 1253 A 2–3, III. 1278 B 19). The purpose of this book is to present the world of the Greek city states... how the various states were governed...[242]

The popular textbook of Austin and Vidal-Naquet also spread the state-concept with the highly ambiguous formula:

> The first distinction which must be made is that between *ethnos* (people, tribe) and *polis* (city) which is best rendered as "state without an urban center" and "state with an urban center." Athens was here a perfectly typical *polis* state: her territory... included the whole of Attica... but the city of Athens... was its political center. In an *ethnos* state... the population lived scattered about in villages over a more or less wide area... The *ethnos* type of state represents a much less developed stage than the *polis* and chronologically it precedes it.[243]

240 Moses Finley, 1981, 4. He left it to this right announcement, where he had to assess the consequences.

241 Finley demonstrates this as well as his status as Cambridge Don, who easily can afford it to joke around with another hardcore concept in the debate: "It is self-evident that *autarky* is a nonsensical idea for a town. Plato and Aristotle did not write nonsense: they took city and hinterland ... as a unit ..." Moses Finley, 1981, 5. And that remained Finley's point of view in his whole work and not only from that page onward: an opposition between town and country did not exist; the peasants were by definition autarkic (128); the towns/cities at least practically, because export remained fully underdeveloped, etc. See also his, 1975, 133–136.

242 Peter Rhodes, 2007, IX; italics by Rhodes.

243 M. Austin, Pierre Vidal Naquet,ed. 1977, 78, 79. They uncritically lend it from authors like Ernst Kornemann, 1934, 30 who opposed Wilamowitz formula and accepted Victor Ehrenberg's formula of a city + adjacent land = "Stadtstaat ... im Gegensatz zum Stammstaat, griechisch *ethnos*, dem Staat ohne städtischen Mittelpunkt."

More or less a variant of this statement is Paul Cartledge's formulation in his popular book on the Spartans. It nears, at least in the first nine words, the necessary insight:

> A Greek *polis* was not just a physical space, though it connoted a physical unit combining rural territory with an administrative center. Nor was it a state in our modern sense... Rather, a *polis* was a citizen-state, a state where "the Spartans" were the city, as it were.[244]

Not a settlement, nor a state, but still a state that was a city "as it were." For a relevant definition of a state one can consult Kenneth Minogue's text, which rightly points specifically to the form of centralized civil rule developed in Europe since the sixteenth century as the source of our state-concept. Generally, however, he states:

> [The state] ... is a territorial unit ordered by a sovereign power, and involves officeholders, a home territory, soldiers distinctively equipped to distinguish them from others, ambassadors, flags, and so on. Since the 1880s, the inhabitable land of the world has been parceled up into such units; before that, quite large areas had been either unclaimed and uninhabited, or inhabited by nomadic and wandering peoples who were not organized as states.[245]

It is difficult to discover herein any settlement or community in Greek antiquity. The reference to a nomadic way of life is quite relevant, because it is this that has a much more important role to play in the formation of Greek societies, which were *stateless societies*. This does not mean that *poleis* were

244 Paul Cartledge, 2002, 36. This "definition" is the wrong reproduction of the sociologist Runciman's definition: "But what is a *polis*? For my purpose, a *polis* is a type of society for which the proper label is not 'city-state' but 'citizen-state'. It does not have to have an urban center dominating a rural hinterland (which would exclude Sparta for a start)." etc. Runciman, in: Oswin Murray and Simon Price, ed., 1990, 348. For his definition Runciman is largely influenced by Max Weber's "monopoly of the means of coercion" as a prerequisite of a state. He is not supporting Cartledge while mixing up all kinds of considerations. Weber also lead him to conclusions like for instance: "The *poleis* which survived and indeed flourished in the Hellenistic and even Roman periods were, therefore, *poleis* in name only: they were urban communities with a life of their own, but not "citizen-states" in the sociological sense." (348). Weber is a very ambiguous source which is used by most historians in a breathtaking way like, for example, in the same volume Oswyn Murray in his introduction (5–7).

245 Kenneth Minogue, "State," in: Adam and Jessica Kuper, ed., 1999, 835.

without relations to any internal or external organization or to *some form* of settlement.

I end this *summa errorum* with Mogens Herman Hansen, a man who wrote some interesting things about Athenian democracy, but who as the leader of a true "Polis center" in Copenhagen proliferated a wild conceptualization around *polis* that seriously aggravated the *polis* problem.[246]

After a study of ten years and many publications and translations that haunted the scholarly world, this center closed down in 2005. I can imagine why this happened. The end conclusion of all this scholarly activity, the most perfect circular reasoning, and the profit of this big investment is the following:

> Now, if *polis*, in the sense of town and in the sense of state was often used to denote essentially different objects, it would be a waste of time to draw up an inventory of all *poleis*... The validity of the Polis center's enterprise depends on our observation that the different meanings are connected through the reference: with very few exceptions—if any at all—every *polis* town was the urban center of a *polis* state, and conversely: every *polis* state had an urban center called a *polis* in the sense of town.[247]

Truly, a symptomatic end to the *polis* story. The beginning is located in the time that enigmas were roaring around in Europe, Karl Marx had already said that "Antiquity" was based on the city, while "The Middle Ages" were based on the countryside. With this dictum, he was far from original; he reproduced the current opinion of largely German historians and philosophers, who borrowed this point of view, in the end, on medieval theologians who translated and transplanted Aristotle and Plato into a Christian framework.

It is therefore, that this "Greek City" looked so similar to a medieval walled and towered city in which aristocratic clans played a rather bloody powergame, although at least 90% of the settlements never had walls at all, including Sparta in its heyday. The course of such a history was predictable: a Great Leader with a still Greater Son, who died at the age of 33, should end these endless quarrels in favor of an empire. Since this overruling in the battle of Chaeronea in 338 BCE these *poleis* disappeared from history until Olympic Games should be played in 1896 AD. That was again similar to the overruling of powerful cities by the absolutist monarchical European nation states.

246 A recent example how a true desperation seized researchers when working with Hansen's concepts is Gocha Tsetskhladze's introduction to his, 2006, xxiii and in particular xxxviii–xlii.

247 Mogens H. Hansen, ed., 2007, 11. It is in fact the end-report of the whole enterprise in which most Hansen's publications at stake are enclosed.

Most of the time this historiography is accompanied with sayings responding to guilt of a decadent democracy, of a heathen polytheism or of the "obvious" impossibility to oppose a Great Leader or even a *Flächen–und Großstaat*.[248]

Austin and Vidal-Naquet dared to complain about the many errors of German historians and economists of the 19th century, but they rightly concluded:

> Clearly the discussion had been wrongly approached and so made a bad start. One may even say that it has never quite overcome this false start... in imposing a view of the Greek economy that is surely untenable.[249]

What is left from this insight? As demonstrated above, the identification of *polis* with city retains has a mythical sound in the academic literature, that equates the identification of *polis* with state. For their own untenable view on "Greek States," Austin and Vidal-Naquet did nothing but reproduce the thought of Victor Ehrenberg, who was as pupil of Eduard Meyer one of those brilliant creators of the classical basis of the German Ideology. The intellectual background of Finley cannot be understood without this very tradition.

About the *polis* = state model, it is sufficient to point at last to the results of Ruschenbusch's investigation.[250] As he tries to estimate the total population of Hellas in classical times, he writes in earnest about "750 states in the Greek motherland" while providing a good bookkeeping starting with "103 states had each 265... inhabitants; 166 states had each 530... inhabitants...," etc. He continues with this list until he gathered three million people "in the motherland and islands together"! That not only old established even young scholars, who are critical of many aspects of present classical studies, reproduce this non-sense thus demonstrate a general "other worldliness" of these studies.[251]

Things are more complicated concerning the *polis* = city and/or state model. Eminent scholars depart from it hesitatingly. De Ste. Croix, a much more inspiring scholar than Finley, accepts only the most minimal meaning of *polis*: for him it concerns a "political entity" at the moment "if it is recognized

248 For many examples see my 1986, 537–538 note 61 or Peter Green's Alexander biography (1992). See Ernst Kornemann, 1934, 30 and 49. Sparta is for Kornemann the "true example of a Flächenstaat."

249 M. Austin and Pierre Vidal-Naquet, ed., 1977, 5.

250 Eberhard Ruschenbusch, 1984, 55–57. Only believers cannot be convinced. See for them Robin Osborne, 1985, 218 note 34 to whom, again, Ehrenberg, is a source.

251 See the old John Bintliff, 1997 and the young Armin Eich, 2006. See my review of this last book: Hans Derks, 2008 in *The European Legacy*.

as such."[252] This is not very satisfying (a cow is a cow, if she is called a cow by another cow!), but it points to a basic uncertainty about the official meanings as given above. Another eminent scholar, the archaeologist Anthony Snodgrass, partner of the straight model-adept John Bintliff, confesses while criticizing Osborne:

> Most studies of the *polis* at least play lip service to the axiom that it formed an indissoluble union between town and countryside but, when and if they move from the abstract level to the physical, they find that they have embarrassingly little to say about the second element in this partnership... we can... comfort ourselves by laying a good part of the responsibility on the ancient Greeks, first for using such an infuriatingly ambivalent term as *polis*, and secondly because their surviving authors do in fact show an almost exclusive preoccupation with the urban component of the physical make-up of the *polis*, at the expense of the rural.[253]

But what about the responsibility of the ancient Greeks and their alleged urban bias, if a *polis* was/is not at all a city: about which bias can we speak in this case?

That question was the subject of Wilfried Gawantka's highly relevant in-depth study, *Die sogennannte Polis* (The so-called Polis, 1985), which referred to and was a devastating criticism of the "*Deutsche Wissenschaft*" (German science) of the 19th century. These German historians and philosophers from Böckh and Hegel to Weber, which were at that time the most influential in Europe, explicitly created the modern version of both *polis*-myths. In short: the bias we have to consider is one of the modern classicists and their supporters and, in particular, of the translators of the ancient texts.

My own studies, starting as a sociological criticism of people like Max Weber, followed, anyway, the same path as Gawantka, but stressed- apart from the given German Ideology with both *polis*-myths- also the related *oikos* concept of course, not for the Greeks.[254] As a result I developed the thesis, that in principle a *polis* can never be a city in a strict sense, nor a state, let alone a city-state.[255] It is clear from the above, that it takes a while before the obvious is acknowledged as such.

252 Geoffrey de Ste. Croix, 1981, 9.

253 Antony Snodgrass. 1990, 113.

254 Hans Derks, 1986, 413–456.

255 For the first time I pointed in this direction in an extensive study, 1973. Next came a better analysis of the case in Hans Derks, 1986, 51–78 in a continuous debate with Max Weber, Werner Sombart and its supporters among classicists like Moses Finley, etc. Later, among

Thanks to further studies this thesis can now be adjusted in the following sense: a *polis* is not a city, nor a state but the *public community* of specific groups of Greek men and the *oikos* is the *private community* of Greek extended family and/or household-members. *Polis-oikos* are as contradictory as public and private and men and women, but in many situations they adjust and support each other.

The location of this *polis* and *oikos* is not the physical city as opposed to the countryside, but can be found in- and outside both and is independent of the size of the settlement. Besides this, they can be found in the mobile setting of nomadic and pastoralist societies. Therefore, *polis* and *oikos* can be related but never identified with (parts of) settlements: the (male) representatives of the (private) *oikoi* make an alliance in the (public) *poleis* to do something together, called "politics."

This view has, of course, its own complexities, but helps in solving many traditional problems for which one now has to lift one's hands in despair, as De Ste. Croix and Snodgrass, above, did or as Finley when writing:

> The *origin* of pseudo-kinship-groups within the *polis* and of the major role of the family, nuclear or more extended, within the community is probably beyond us except in an abstract, speculative analysis.[256]

It helps if one starts reading the ancient texts and their translators or interpreters in a much more critical way: not as if we do not suffer from ideological prejudices or as if the writings of the ancients must be accepted at face value. Let's take a simple example for close reading from William Hutton's sophisticated analysis of Pausanias' highly stimulating texts. They will provide us with some relevant material to discuss the concrete sides of the *polis* problem.

Hutton intends to demonstrate how Pausanias approaches the business of describing a city while assuming himself that a *polis* = city and translating accordingly.[257] This notwithstanding the following interesting description about an insignificant location:

---

others in my. 1996, I refined that thesis—which is now again the case—without altering the direction: to discover the ins and outs of an oikos-market antagonism in history. I "suffered" not for nothing because in this year Finley's vision is fully refuted. See Daniel Jew, ed., 2017.

256 Moses Finley, 1985, 92 italics from Finley. This appears in the failed attempt of Finley to come to terms with Max Weber's thinking. The advantage, however, of this—in itself courageous attempt—is, that this confrontation with a real socio-economic way of analyzing history quickly demonstrates the shallow ground on which most classicists opinions are based.

257 Will Hutton, 2005, 127.

> It is twenty stadia from Chaironeia to Panopeus, a city of the Phocians, if, that is, anyone would give the name of city to those for whom there are no government buildings, no gymnasium, who have no theater, no market-place, no water conducted into a fountain, and who live in hollow shelters, quite similar to the huts used in the mountains, right at the edge of a ravine. Still, they at least maintain boundaries of their land with their neighbors and they even send representatives to the Phocian assembly.[258]

Hutton reminds the reader that Pausanias is not in the least impressed "by the formidable city walls that are still visible."[259] This is an astonishing information since Pausanias says nothing more than that a king in Homeric times was "using Panopeus as a fortress" (X, 4,1), but that the place was "razed to the ground" (X, 3,2) by Philip of Macedon. This occurred at least 500 years later. Small wonder that Pausanias, visiting the region again ca. 400 years later, was "not in the least impressed."

It is also exaggerated relative to the other famous ancient source, Strabo (9, 2, 42), who apparently had no reason to mention more than Panopeus' name as a *polis* about a century earlier than Pausanias. Where Hutton has seen his "formidable city walls" remains strange, apart from the problem of choosing from which period to date his city wall.

It was the famous British antiquarian and topographer William Martin Leake (1777–1860) who not only disagreed with Pausanias' measurements (the distance between Panopeus and Daulis is not 7 but 27 stadia, etc.), but also concluded from own observation that Panopeus "having been placed between two cities... [was]... a frontier fortress of Phocis."[260] He sketched a plan of this fortress "with towers at the most prominent angles... in some places still 30 feet high."

258 Will Hutton, 2005, 130. It is always necessary to compare translations, in this case with, for instance, the one of Peter Levi (Penguin Classics, volume 1, 410) or with a well-known German one of Ernst Meyer (Artemis Verlag, 479). The latter apparently also accepted the *polis*-state myth, while he translates Hutton's "boundaries" with "Landesgrenzen" (= national or state boundary). Levi is closest to the original and actual situation as he translates the Greek "stadia" with "two and a half miles" and the Greek "horoi" with "boundary stones" which are erected even to indicate the end of agricultural fields. This is far from national boundaries which are suggested by Meyer. He and Levi make of "Panopeas polin Phokeoov" respectively "Panopeis, einer phokischen Stadt" and "the city of Panopeus in Phokis". This is not the same; not in the least because Pausanias explicitly tells that its inhabitants were *no* Phokians; X, 4,1.

259 Will Hutton, 2005, 130 note 12.

260 William M. Leake, 1835, volume 2, 109–110.

Leake saw this, therefore, around 1830. Lionel Casson's history of ancient tourism remembers the name Panopeus only because of a local legend known until the 6th century that the available clay was the same as that with which Prometheus created the first man.[261] Leake also tells this story, but distrusted it in a very humorous way: "I can never perceive the smell of human flesh in them, which Pausanias recognised..."[262] Anyway, the tourists apparently bought so much of this stuff, that the "formidable city walls" were gone already in Pausanias' time.

Another 19th century geographer, Heinrich Kiepert, mentions Panopeus only in passing as an *Ort* (place) in a mountainous region only suitable for pastoralists with their flocks; it is a region in which the names of many *Orte* refer to the kinds of trees in the environment and the rest has non-Greek names. These *Orte* are also unsuitable for traffic, but 22 of them made a political alliance "which, of course, had to remain unimportant."[263]

In most present lexicons Panopeus is not mentioned at all; it is clearly too unimportant. Only the DKP explicitly writes about "... a city of Phocis, important for trade and transport... with a well conserved wall of 1200 m from the 4th century BCE....[264] The Swiss author, Ernst Meyer, is only suspicious about the "remarkable" use of the name in the literature, but not about his own contradicting information concerning the many times that Panopeus, whatever its meaning, was destroyed (in total I count seven times including the long Roman period!) and that Pausanias only saw "only a miserable village of huts." His main source, Ernst Kirsten, does not reveal anything in his well-known *Griechenlandkunde* about formidable city walls but only of something like "a remarkable ruin of a castle." Unfortunately Kirsten does not mention the period of its construction.[265]

According to an Internet-picture of the site we are dealing with here, in my view at least, with the ruins of a stronghold of the Venetian imperialist traders (and eventually the later crusaders of about the 12th century), the first people who could afford and were interested in constructing a castle on a site like this mountainous region after the ruinous Roman period.

261 Lionel Casson, 1978, 272.

262 William M. Leake, 1835, 111. A bit later William Hazlitt, 1851, 260 only mentions Panopeus as a town "destroyed by Xerxes."

263 Heinrich Kiepert, 1878, 286. Kiepert must have referred here to the long-lasting conflicts of this region against Delphi and its allies. A Dutch colleague of Kiepert, Johan Schlimmer, 1879, 50–54 tells the story of these conflicts (the three "Holy Wars"), but mentions only the name of Panopeus, without any indication of its role in these conflicts.

264 DKP, volume 4, 464; this lemma is mainly based on several writings of Ernst Kirsten.

265 Ernst Kirsten and Wilhelm Kraiker, 1967, 785.

What does we learn about our *polis*-problem from this short philological and geographical analysis? First and foremost, that in the relevant literature interpretations about even rather simple and unimportant situations can be diametrically opposed. Also the people, who claim to be personally familiar with that situation, can *see* different things (a city versus a castle), and others *read* different things in the same simple texts (an important city versus a miserable village), apart from their opposed interpretations (a city of the 4th century BCE versus a castle of the 12th century CE), definitions (*polis* = city, settlement versus *polis* = public, political community) and so on. It is necessary, therefore, to consult data from different sources and periods, because an (alleged) authority can never be trusted. Next, however, a choice should be made in all these details to which the following is helpful.

After all this, it is as interesting as unexpected that Hutton remarks how Pausanias perceives Panopeus as a *polis* only because of its political position (it sends people to an assembly) and he starts doubting what a *polis* for Pausanias could be, while ending up with the following conclusion:

> While size, physical attributes, or numerous attractive buildings can help to determine whether or not he [Pausanias.H.D.] will use the term [*polis*.H.D.], the most consistent criterion would seem to be one of political status; a *polis* is an autonomous community in control of itself and its borders... This definition is consistent with almost all the evidence, but... Pausanias does, infrequently, use the word to designate communities that were not... autonomous, large, or well appointed...[266]

This "definition" demonstrates in the best way the intellectual struggle with the *polis*-concept. It must be clear from the given short tour through the available "Panopeus"—and other literature which false *polis*-idea Hutton is working into his interpretation and how this idea even blocks the seeing in the field or the reading of a text.

However, notwithstanding this, Hutton discovered the beginning of the solution: a *polis* is not a physical settlement but a political community plus borders (which could be translated from Hutton's background to: not a city but a state), while the reference to Pausanias here defines this community-idea further as referring also to non-autonomous communities, leaving also the *polis* = state idea behind, knowing that borders of a community normally have a metaphorical meaning only.

266 Will Hutton, 2005, 132 and note 14 on this page.

With, for instance, the translator Waterfield the same process of "enlightenment" could be demonstrated. Notwithstanding his pre-fab opinions quoted above, he also gave the following *additional* characterization of the "Hutton definition" with:

> An ancient Greek *polis* was its citizens: the name "Athens" referred only to the physical city with its buildings and open spaces; as a political unit, the name was "the Athenians." The Spartans, then, did not make war on "Athens," but on "The Athenians."[267]

Indeed, the *polis* concerns the members of a public and not the members of a private community, the *oikos*.

Below, however, *not* this *polis,* nor this *polis-oikos* relationship is the subject, but it is confined to the phenomenon of the city in ancient Greece, to the settlements as such and their inhabitants; more to the geography than to the sociology of the *polis* problem. In Greek terms: we have to look at the physical *agros* Attica, the Athenian countryside, as opposed to the physical *astu* Athens and related town-country problems.

From the above, one thing must be clear: of the ca. 2000 settlements that can be counted around the year 400 BCE in the whole Greek realm, only a very few can be called a city (and, therefore, there are only a few urban communities) and not one is a state; we have to deal with stateless societies.

From the statements given, another thing must be clear as well: far from being a semantic game the abandoning of the formula "polis=city=state" concerns the heart of the interpretation or explanation of the Greek culture as such, including therefore, the very basis of the European civilization. It is, therefore, necessary to look at this problem from different sides as well, answering the question whether there were real cities in ancient Greek society and how they looked like? That will be the subject of the rest of this chapter.

To conclude this paragraph and introduce the next as well, I will quote the fabulous Strabo to substantiate again my argument about the meaning of *polis*:

> It suffices, then, to add this much: According to Philochorus, when the country was being devastated, both from the sea by the Carians, and from the land by the Boeotians... Cecrops first settled the multitude in twelve *poleis* [*Kekropa proton eis dodeka poleis sunoikisai to pleithos*], the name of which were Cecropia, Tetrapolis, Epacria, Deceleia, Eleusis, Aphidna ...,

267 Robin Waterfield, 2004, 42.

> Thoricus, Brauron, Cytherus, Sphettus, Cephisia. And at a later time Theseus is said to have united the twelve into one *polis*, that of today. (IX, 1, 20)[268]

2.2 An *Astu* for a Polis

Settlements presuppose also an unsettled population: living outside settlements in other specimen of the "built environment," permanently or periodically roaming around in tents, ships and "mobile houses" or migrating from elsewhere. If settled, the inhabitants not only have their mobile history, but also cannot do without new relations with lands abroad. This apart from the fact that "abroad" also wants several (un)pleasant contacts with the settled.

Already in the first sentences of his history, Thucydides (I, 2) points to this constellation: open settlements without walls, in fact camps of tents for migrating peoples, fishermen, nomads, pastoralists; regular quarrels about pastures; pirates of the Aegean (like the Carians) were as famous far into Roman times as later were their colleagues of the Caribbean. He more or less gave a catalogue of elements mentioned in the first chapter in opposition to a settled agricultural way of life. Thucydides story can be read only as one about the rise of commerce and commercial settlements. It is obvious that his text uses *polis* independent of a settled life, which is negated by most readers.

There are, as in every society, many settlement forms in Greek life that must be stressed here in advance: isolated farms (*monagria*); several kinds of clusters of farms and other buildings in villages (*komai, katoikia, komion, deimoi, epoikos, sunoikia, oiei*, etc.); suburbs (*proastion*, which means also estate or manor), and *oikos* which is not only related to a house but, eventually, also to a tent.

In this series belongs also *astu* or city. Where this is used it concerns concrete situations; the city with which the acting person has a close relation. It has much more emotional value than *polis* and also a much more distinguished sound. *Polis* is nearly always vague and general.

268 In the Loeb translation of Horace Leonard Jones, 1927, volume IV, 267, of course, *polis* was translated with "city" resulting—by implication—in the untenable proposition that the whole of Attica, including the *polis* of the Athenians became one single city. Jones not even changed this after his note to this quotation: "Thus only eleven names are given ... But it seems best to assume that Strabo either actually included Athens in his list or left us to infer that he meant Athens as one of the twelve." *Polis* cannot be different from a political association, bond or *public community* as I called a *polis* to differentiate it with the private community, the *oikos*.

Opposite this *astu* exists *agros,* the countryside. Symbolically, derivations like *asteios* mean elegant, refined, clean, fine, civilized, distinguished or witty; *agroikos*, however, is related to clumsy, rude, cruel, boorish, etc. Both kinds of qualifications are typical for an urban elite. It is symptomatic that *astu* also means simply "Athens," expressing the conviction that there is only one city in Greece or in the world. It is sometimes profitable to spell all the possible semantic relations at issue, but we have now to get some insight in the urban situation in ancient Hellas.

Earlier I made an overview of the regional division of *new* settlements in the whole of the Mediterranean in the period 1300 BCE until 260 CE.[269] Hellas was the starting point for this complex analysis; until about 800 BCE the count was made per century, after this date per half century. Results gave a good overview of the settlements in the Mycenaean and Minoan regions, and of the Greek colonization activities, etc. One cannot make oneself too many illusions about the reliability of these figures, but a good impression is given of the proportion and extension of settlement-activities in antiquity.

Around 700 BCE, in Hesiod's time, in Greece inclusive of the islands there existed a *minimum* of 309 settlements; on Crete, Cyprus and Rhodos together 74; until that year Mycenaeans and Greeks established 76 so-called "colonies."[270] That is to say: After this period in Greece south of Thessaly or on the islands no new settlements were founded. Only outside that area did urbanizing activities continue: until 300 no less than 121 new settlements can be registered. The obvious questions are: what is the value of these figures? Are we dealing here with cities or with a different kind of settlements?

That I stressed, only a minimum is grasped, must be taken seriously: most parts of the whole settlement pattern remains nearly invisible because, by necessity, we have to count now one *polis* for only one settlement. This, notwithstanding many *poleis* as political (public) communities consisted of an alliance of more settlements as was the case in, for example, Panopeus, that belonged to a *polis* of about 22 settlements!

This outcome is probably compensated for to a certain extent, because in one settlement several *poleis* can also exist. Only if archaeologists make (infra-red) aerial close-ups does the density of a settlement pattern becomes visible.[271] Where this has happened many small villages and hamlets can be

269 Hans Derks, 1986, 264–266 and 630–631.

270 From these 459 new settlements 224 were established before 1200 and, therefore, 235 between 1200 and 700.

271 Whatever merit, I do not mean books like R. Schoder, *Ancient Greece from the air,* 1974.

seen and, once the 459 new settlements are incorporated, there is a good chance that they become (in)visible as well.

Generalizations for the whole of Hellas are also difficult to make, because every region is first of all, in need of specific clarifications concerning the economic, ecologic and agricultural data including the many exchange developments, without which *relevant* comparison is not possible.[272] Apart from this, for most areas the rather rich sources of Attica are absent. However, whatever their stubbornness, it is clear from the investigations so far: for the largest majority of the 2000 settlements, a population of more than ca. 100–500 persons (all-in) cannot be envisaged before Hellenistic times.[273] For the later period it must be the same for long periods, but data are even less reliable or insufficient until about 1900 CE.[274]

272 That was not the case in an overview made by the influential excavator John Bintliff, 1997. Bintliff is, for example, unconvinced of exchange-centered and commercial considerations. Apart from what is said before, there is the fact that the archaeological "sites" are quantified and qualified in an irritatingly insufficient way; the technical quality of many survey teams was less than sufficient: very young and very inexperienced peoples without proper guidance; the Attica-surveys mentioned by Bintliff considered only a limited amount of agricultural activities using an agricultural definition of "carrying capacity" as if Athens and Attica had not many other sources of income or food; the language used is as abstract as possible. Whatever their extension, excavations result nearly always in useful and interesting data, but "sites" are only in a (very) limited way representative for a settlement (pattern) or population (changes). The usual mistakes of *polis* = city, etc. are made and what signifies here "urban" is not explained; a meaningless broad geo-political differentiation is made between North and South of (present!) Greece; it is difficult to find some relativity concerning the results like: that the differences between the periods and locations are largely due to the money and labor investments in "sites." The difficulties to come up with explanations are mostly sublimated by the excessive use of models from "abroad" instead of Greek realities; models from which one too often gets the impression that the (ideological) background and implications of these models are not understood. And so on ....

273 See above for different figures. Also Bintliff refers to the strongly speculating Eberhard Ruschenbusch, 1985, 262 who counts 750 "states" on the Greek mainland from which 103 have less than 66 citizens, 166 have less than 33 citizens, 160 have less than 400 citizens, 160 have less than 800 citizens, 44 have less than 1200 citizens and the last 113 "states" have more than 1200 citizens.

274 See, for instance, the four articles of Lock, Kiel, Roller and Papadopoulos about the post-Roman period of Boeotia in John Bintliff, ed., 1997, 305–377. Kiel provides population figures of four villages in fertile Boeotia over a period of four centuries (1466–1879) as follows: from 84 to 189 *households* with a maximum of 256 for all villages *together*, which are often of the same size (page 338). Bintliff himself in ed., 1997, 231–252 gives a good example of how he and his colleagues worked in assessing populations in Boeotia by means of their ambiguous *central place model*.

Other sources urge us to speculate with different population figures. The so-called Athenian tribute lists, which give a specific insight into the financial and other support for the war against the Persians, are such a source. At least Ruschenbusch's calculation is as follows: from the 238 *poleis* listed in the year 431 there are 36% with less than 500 inhabitants, 43% have between 500 and 3000 and the remaining 21% would have had more than 3000.[275]

There is also another division to make, as Thucydides made the relevant differentiation between coastal and inland settlements (I, 7). Thanks to the existence of tribute lists of the Delian League (predecessors of the former lists), an alliance formed in 478 against the Persians, something can be said about this differentiation. The number of members of this league changed between 343 and 205 *poleis,* that were mainly located at the coasts.[276]

In the last case the regional division of the settlements is approximately: 60 settlements at the southern coast of Asia Minor and neighboring islands like Rhode and Kos; 31 settlements at the same coast North of Milete until the island Lesbos; the region around the Sea of Marmara and Hellespont with 39 places; 51 on the three promontories of Chalcidice with the adjacent Macedonian and Thracian coast; and last, about 24 settlements on Euboa, the Cyclades and Sporades. From the first 60 places, for instance, about 25 are real coastal settlements and the rest are located in the inland. One must realize that the distance between both is seldom more than twenty kilometers.

I will end these quantifications with Bintliff's conclusions, so that some comparable figures are available for my own analysis below. Starting from Ruschenbusch's speculations, he ends up at a far more optimistic level:

> The "normal" city-state had an average of 2000–3000 citizens crammed into a territorial radius of around 5 km (Ruschenbusch 1991) ... As for the abnormally large city-state of Athens... estimates of maximum Classical population are of the order of 200,000–250,000 people...[277]

---

275 Eberhard Ruschenbusch, 1984, 55; Ruschenbusch calls them already here consequently "Staaten"; for criticism of Ruschenbusch' approach and figures see Lucia Nixon and Simon Price, in: Oswyn Murray and Simon Price, ed., 1990, 146, 165. The assumption of "a direct relationship between tribute and population does not work." Here, again, the correct meaning of *poleis* is demonstrated: the adult (male!) inhabitants of settlements gathering together *publicly* forming as such the *polis,* decide whether they will make some alliance, a new *polis,* with others.

276 See map in Norman Pounds, 1973, volume 1, 29.

277 John Bintliff, 1997, 26.

No differentiation is made between Athens and Attica and if he should be right with his estimate of *citizen's*, then the total population of his alleged "normal" so-called "city-state" must be four or five times this 2,000–3,000 range, i.e. 8,000–15,000 peoples! Some pages earlier Bintliff gave, only for Attica, a population of "around 180,000 by 480 B.C., well above Garnsey's recent estimates... of 120,000–150,000 for Attica's carrying capacity."[278]

Let's suppose, that if he writes Attica, he also means Attica (and not Athens + Attica) and if he writes population, that he also means population (and not citizens), we still arrive at unbelievable figures.

Well, based on all the above data with their own stories, the following classification can be made of the types of settlements in classical Hellas:

1. settlements with only a pastoralist orientation;
2. settlements with husbandry + agriculture (resp. 75 and 25%);
3. settlements with agriculture + husbandry (resp. 75 and 25%);
4. settlements with only agriculture;
5. trade settlements;
6. *astea*.

The first four concern types of (semi-permanent) villages with respectively an estimated average population of 150 (1), 300 (2), 500 (3) and 700 (4); trade settlements are small towns (1,000–3,000 population) and *astea* (plural of *astu*) are cities.

What and which are the latter are questions not to be answered with the confusion of tongues as around *polis, poleis.* That will be the consequence as we follow the example of Snodgrass by calling settlements like the villages Haliartos or Thespiai an *astu.* He characterizes Thespiai as "a cluster of small village-sized settlements": these villages probably formed a *polis,* but never were an *astu.*[279]

The classical authority in demographic matters, Julius Beloch (1886), called the 5th century Greek settlements Athens, Thebes, Corinth, Sparta, Argos, Elis and Corcyra (on the island Corfu) cities, because they stick to the criterion of 10,000 inhabitants or more. In the 4th century this very select group is adjusted with Megalopolis, Messenia and Olynthos. On the Asiatic coast there are, in this century, a maximum of three places that could be called a settlement of this magnitude.[280] If one accepts the 10,000 criterion, there is no difficulty

278 John Bintliff, 1997, 8.

279 Anthony Snodgrass, in: John Rich and Andrew Wallace-Hadrill, ed., 13–14.

280 Hans Derks, 1986, 575 note 438.

calling them "cities,"[281] but for all the others, there are serious objections to be made, as will be revealed below.

2.3 The Southern Greek "Cities"

Take for example Elis, which is mentioned as a "rather odd city" by Osborne, but that is, anyway a city. The following description challenges every perception of a city:

> It had the pan-hellenic sanctuary at Olympia in its territory, and this was a source of local strife within the city. Elis was made up of the distinct regions Hollow Elis, Pisatis, and Triphylia... The formation of a new city in the fifth century seems to have had little major effect on settlement... What happened was a change at the organizational level... The settlement pattern reflects the strength of the village centers and the wide variety of services that the villages were able to provide... The loose political organization and strong villages of Elis show one way in which city organization could be carried on while respecting the integrity of the countryside.[282]

Ruschenbusch estimates that "the state" Elis had 130,000 inhabitants.[283] On the given map of Elis one can see what happened here and what consequences follow from the erroneous use of *polis* to equal city.[284] This must be, anyway,

281 Even this is stated with some reservation. Without any doubt, Bintliff and his colleagues did the most thorough excavations and archaeological surveys in Boeotia. However, in the assessment of their findings of, for instance, the "super-city status of Classical Thebes" Bintliff is highly naive. He suggests that Thebes and Athens "were in the peak Classical era seen as approximately as populous as each other"; John Bintliff, 1997, 232. The only reason for this suggestion is "the enormous scale of the Theban outer wall", while there is no answer on the question: How much of the 350 ha is then likely to be genuine densely-settled land?, let alone that one could imagine for what reasons such a large field was necessary except for agriculture/ horticulture. The differences, furthermore, between Athens and Thebes are "compromised by giving a range of 211–350 ha for Thebes, and taken a figure in the middle of this range (281 ha) for the calculations which follow"!

282 Robin Osborne, 1987, 124–127.

283 Eberhard Ruschenbusch, 1984, 56 reproduces here "the realistic estimates of Beloch".

284 The map is from Robin Osborne, 1987, 127. The difficulty with this map is the word "sites" which refers to archaeological sites, which are not necessarily settlements. Also the word "fortification" could be misleading: it refers to a settlement, a castle but also to simple edifices (watchtowers) customary in the animal culture. In the case of Elis the latter possibility seems rather obvious (see main text). See for archaeological site-maps also Robin

the only explanation for descriptions like the above. Osborne also talks about the "foreign policy" of Elis, therefore supposing as well, that this *polis* equals state. The description of Elis given by Polybios (second century ACE) and quoted by Osborne approvingly, adds in an astonishing way to this:

> Some of the inhabitants were so enamoured of country life that they, being sufficiently prosperous, had not taken any part in politics for two or three generations.[285]

Further confusion can be credited to the fact that "Elis" in its physical constitution is largely "a city" with *poleis* (?) such as Arcadia and Achaea.

Conclusion: many village-like settlements together made a public political community through an alliance called the *polis Elis* to which not everybody among the rich was attracted for generations. As a regional alliance, Elis was established in 471 BCE in relation with the Persian menace and, therefore, so was an occasional bond (*polis*), a mutual agreement to help each other in battle, etc. This is not a matter of any regular "foreign policy"; in fact there was established a new *polis* at the moment "those of Kylene, Pylos etc. as members of the former *polis* Elis" had to choose between Sparta or Athens in the Peloponnesian War, half a century later.

Next conclusion: that scholars from Beloch to Osborne put this "Elis" as a regional paper-construction on the exclusive list of large cities, leads to the demand that scholars should stop writing in this way; their logic must be largely Greek to us!

They, however, refrained from pointing to Elis' highly pronounced character as an important center of animal husbandry thanks to its wet moist, fertile low hilly land that made such practice possible on a big scale. In 209, Philip V of Macedon captured, in one location in the region of Elis an enormous herd of 20,000 animals.[286] That could even stand the centuries, because in 1960 the whole plain lodged no less than 360,000 animals (cattle, sheep and goats) excluding 150,000 within a pastoralist setting.[287]

This region, furthermore, was in antiquity particularly famous for its democratic behavior and institutions, which is a structural characteristic of husbandry-based culture. Thucydides gave the impression (to translators,

---

Osborne, 1996, 72–73; in this text "sites", "villages" and "cities" are used without any differentiation, forgetting everything what young Robin Osborne once wrote (see below).

285 Robin Osborne, 1987, 126.

286 Stephen Hodkinson, in C.R. Witthaker, ed. 1988, 62.

287 Adriaan de Vooys, 1962, 212.

anyway!) that Elis had nearly no relations to ships etc., another such structural element. This seems to be a remark inspired by the less than spectacular performance by Elis as compared to those of the main antagonists in the civil war like Corcyra, Corinth, Athens or Sparta.[288]

The next example is Sparta, which is always imagined as a big city, in whatever story, with as many as 230,000 inhabitants in the classical period. However, notwithstanding its status, something like relevant population figures are absent. The OCD gives the present result of all investigations: around 480 BCE it had "8,000 potential soldiers… By Aristotle's time Sparta probably had fewer than 1,000 citizens."

If here the usual Greek exaggeration should be neglected and soldiers should be similar to citizens (which is often not the case: mercenaries are used in abundance) than we could estimate with these figures a Spartan *population* development from about 60,000–80,000 to 4,000 inhabitants in a period of about 150 years. Scholars, who accepted this as realistic, considered every kind of disaster to explain this development. That is not relevant here: anyway, the latter figure cannot be related to a city, but this is the case with the first, although it is far from Ruschenbusch's 230,000.

But what do we know about the settlement of ancient Spartans? From Thucydides' translators one can learn about early Sparta:

> Since, however, the city is not regularly planned and contains no temples or monuments of great magnificence, but is simply a collection of villages, in the ancient Hellenic way, its appearance would not come up to expectation (I, 10).[289]

288 See DKP, volume 2, 249–251, but compare this with Thucydides, II, 25; I, 27–30 and II, 84. Ruschenbusch gave Corcyra 100,000 inhabitants, Corinth about 70,000 and Sparta even 230,000 which is 60,000 more than Athens. Eberhard Ruschenbusch, 1984, 56.

289 This translation is from Rex Warner, introduced by Moses Finley (Penguin Classics, 1976). As usual translations differ seriously. Other examples are: Jowett (1900) "But their city is not built continuously, and has no splendid temples or other edifices; it rather resembles a group of villages like the ancient towns of Hellas, and would therefore make a poor show." The older Crawley translation (1876, reprint 1934) is more fluently: "Still, as the city is neither built in a compact form nor adorned with magnificent temples and public edifices, but composed of villages after the old fashion of Hellas, there would be an impression of inadequacy." Indeed, the Greek language allows in principle these remarkable variations, but it should be more realistic to translate: "But the Spartans developed their community after the old fashion of Hellas: they were spread over a group of villages and lived not in one concentrated settlement; they had no splendid temples or other edifices. For us, all this makes a poor show."

As is the case elsewhere, no single translator, nor a man like Finley, asks himself while reproducing this text, whether one can actually talk about a city. Again it is a proof of the real meaning of *polis* as nothing but a public-political community at different levels of settled and unsettled life; from the private *oikos*-level to the alliance of villages (*synoecism*).

Until the year 188 BCE Sparta also remained *without ramparts*, because it was feared and famous for its creed that its fighters were the walls. In this year, however, Sparta was not Sparta anymore: original Spartans were already an exception. Here it is important that until now nobody wrote an interesting study about the four or five Spartan villages, its population changes and so on, let alone that one considered the many anthropological elements of a Spartan nomadic society.[290]

The third example concerns Megalopolis, even a "Very Large City" from which Pausanias reports (in the translation):

> Great City (Megalopolis) is the youngest city not only in Arkadia but in Greece... The Arkadians gathered here to mass their strength, because they knew that long ago the Argives had been in almost literally daily danger of being defeated and overrun by Lakonia, but than Argos had increased its numbers by breaking up Tiryns and Hysiai, Orneai, Mycenae and Mideia, and every other insignificant town in the Argolid, and at once Lakonian pressure decreased... Arkadia made a combined settlement with the same idea... (VIII, 27, 1).

This was closely after the year 370, after the Spartans lost a devastating battle (Leuktra) against the Thebans and *poleis* in the north dared to talk big against the loser. It was Thebes as well which took the initiative to form something like Megalopolis as a buffer against Sparta.[291]

Out of enthusiasm for this *synoikismos* (an alliance between two or more *poleis*, related settlements or groups) or out of hostility and fear, forty *poleis* accepted

> to abandon their native places... [a few changed their minds and] withdrew their consent to abandon their ancient cities, and some of them were forced into the Great City against their will... (VIII, 27, 2–6).

290 Eduard Lévy, 2003 is one of the best comparable to Stephen Hodkinson, 2000. However, no one produces a relevant sociological-demographic analysis. See the review of this last book in Hans Derks, 2002, 725–735.

291 See the map in Ernst Kirsten, 1984, 230.

Did they really destroy their own settlements in order to establish a mega-*polis*, so that Thebes could be buffered against Sparta? And has some Harrison Ford discovered already the mysterious ruins of the lost city of Megalopolis with its 75,000 or so inhabitants?

There is, anyway, an interesting scenario available: Pausanias tells how 130 (!) years later the Spartans conquered Megalopolis and (tried to) destroy with a "powerful machine" its walls and a tower. However, a storm destroyed this machine and—Spartans never gave up, as you know—it is again twelve (!) years later that Cleomenes led the Spartans to victory over the Great City: so long did it take to bridge a distance as far as an easy day's walk from Sparta. The reports mention the usual suspects: although everybody was "massacred" most people escaped to Messenia, which was formed in 369 in the same way as Megalopolis. Soon they could return to this Great City, whereupon the original forty *poleis* were allowed to rule their own business again.[292] The whole Theban paper construction of Megalopolis falls apart.

Again, if this Great City is perceived by accident, still, as a real city there arises a serious problem: how to understand the rebuilding of a Great City if the original 40 "cities" become autonomous again? Answer: the only possibility is to perceive this *synoikismos* (synoecism) not as the founding of a real city, but as a political alliance (a *polis* of 40 communities could be a large one if, however, these communities were populous, which is far from certain) that had some central buildings for religious meetings or political negotiations. The same must be said about many other, if not all, similar synoecisms like Tegea, Mantinea, Heraia, etc.[293]

A further conclusion concerning "Beloch's list" is, that Sparta, Elis, Messenia, Argos and Megalopolis can be deleted from this list: on the Peloponnese there existed no *astu;* Athens is one (for some the only one) that will be analyzed now in some detail.

2.4 *Astu* Versus *Agros*

A city such as Athens must have given an overcrowded impression in its heyday. The streets were narrow, never straight; no house or housing block was the same; public buildings were spread at random among workshops and housing blocks. Something such as piped waters or sewerage in houses is absent

292 DKP, volume 3, 1140–41.; see also OCD, 1996, 950–951.

293 OCD, 1996, 1463 the lemma *synoecism* must, therefore, use a wrong idea that in the case of Megalopolis "a migration of citizens to the new city" took place.

in favor of public sources and for an aquaduct one had to wait for emperor Hadrianus. The course of the main roads, which start at the southwest corner of the *agora,* is determined by the qualities of the environment and not by "the will of the designer"; one circumventes the lowest parts of the valleys to avoid the regular inundations. In the outskirts of the city, where enough space is available, one will not find the famous Hippodamian grid as in Piraeus.[294]

As is wellknown, Athens is the successful result of a *synoecism* of several villages, which can still be seen in several city quarters. Whatever its urban concentration, rural bonds are always apparent. How real town-country relations and antagonisms can be perceived in an adult city, will be demonstrated by means of a table.

This table, however, should be seen as the conclusion of all the discussions and calculations in this and the previous paragraphs. It is, therefore, a conclusion with far-reaching consequences. To show this, I will give a last quotation from what should be considered a compilation of standard knowledge at stake.

Here, Lin Foxhall refers, in fact, to all available authorities like Garnsey, Jameson, Hansen, Burford-Cooper, De Ste Croix, and so on. Whatever their mutual differences they all have in common the fact, that they support in one way or another the "tillage paradigm," the idea that the ancient Greek economy and society, including the one from Athens and Attica, is based on the so-called self-sufficient small peasant landholders, who have to earn their living with grain-growing, assisted by an army of slaves. From this background comes the following conclusion:

> The population of Athens is notoriously problematic, but the most recent estimates suggest that it normally fluctuated in the range of 20,000–30,000 citizen males. I have used Jameson's estimate of around 22,000, in preference to Hansen's higher estimate on the grounds that a number of young citizen males will not have been heads of their own households, and therefore would not have owned and worked independently of their fathers and brothers. My working total of 22,000 then, really refers to numbers of households, rather than adult males. Of these households, perhaps 5000 owned no land at all... Perhaps another 5000 owned less than the so-called "subsistence portion" of 60 plethra (5.5 ha). At the other end of the scale, Davies has identified nearly 800 wealthy men... It is

294 Beautifully illustrated books like the one of Peter Connolly and Hazel Dodge, 1998 provide an excellent impression of old Athens.

> clear that there was no sharp divide between large and small landholders in ancient Athens...[295]

Which additional criteria are used here apart from those discussed above? For the sector agriculture it is supposed that the Pedion plain, which surrounds Athens (22% of the total agricultural area) is wholly managed from *astu* Athens and that, therefore, a large part of the Pedion peasants and farmers lived in the city.

From Finley and others we learn that in ancient Greek culture, peasants are city dwellers, but it is necessary to be as precise as possible about the object of their work: this was not agriculture proper, but *horticulture* for which there was a good market in *astu* Athens and even an opening to the Mediterranean market (perfumes from flowers, etc.). One has to consider as well, that for the poorer people, vegetables comprised the main part of the diet. Whether the sophisticated Athenian market-gardeners should call themselves "peasant" is another question. I am afraid they should not.[296] Concerning the horticultural activities in the *agros,* I suppose that they are incorporated in the agricultural figures.

The modest activities in the city concerning animal husbandry are related to the substantial transport activities with oxen, to horse breeding and trade, etc. In the *agros* one is, of course, confronted with the large-scale herding of

295 Lin Foxhall, 1992, 156. Foxhall's variant is in the end: 1000 "citizen households" of 20–50ha; 1000 of 10–20ha; 10,000 of 5.5–10 ha; 5000 of less than 5.5ha and the last 5,000 households are landless. Together they occupy an "area of Attika ... for agricultural activities of some kind: something over 1000 km^2." The tables 2–4 in Hans Derks, 1996, show an estimate of 405 km^2 with strictly about 10,000 farms. Most mistakes I discussed earlier are available in the quotation: no difference between *astu* Athens and *agros* Attica; the value of numbers is not known, when you simple change a number for adult males for one of households (this means, in fact, that no figure is properly argued: for instance, Foxhall's ca. 20,000 households result by definition in 4–5,000 adult citizen males for both Athens and Attica?!) ; no difference is made between land for agriculture and land for all forms of husbandry, let alone for other activities; there is, furthermore, the usual reduction of many activities in a landscape to only one, grain growing; a population estimate is consequently based on only an agricultural surface; there is considered only something like "citizen households" as if non-citizens (*metics* and even slaves) could not occupy or use land and as if every citizen was a landholder/ farmer, and so on. All this apart from "minor" questions as to whether property should be defined in our modern (in fact Roman) way or that it should not be necessary to differentiate between use rights, common or public rights and property rights? This, among others, to determine what is the meaning of something like "control of the Attic landscape."

296 For horticulture DKP, volume 2, 698, 737 for fruit and vegetables; DKP, volume 4, 1580; OCD, 624; Georg Busolt, ed., 1887, 468a ; Elisabeth Welskopf, 1974, volume 4, 1795–1800.

cattle, sheep, goats, horses, pigs, and mules including the slaughtering, skinning, etc. of these animals.

An Athenian and Attic middle class to which Murray correctly points, cannot count more than 10,000 to 15,000 persons.[297] They belong to the sector "Crafts and Services" of the many kinds of shopkeepers, bureaucrats, laborers in factories, and in shipbuilding and construction industries. They are, of course, more concentrated in Athens and Piraeus than in the *demes* (a kind of municipality) of the *agros,* although in quarries and mines more peoples could have worked than envisaged here. Periodically this will be the case as, for instance, a new mine or quarry is opened.

According to Hansen one has to reckon with 10,000 *metics* (plural, metoikoi), Athenians with a foreign (meaning non-Athenian, often Greek) background, from which a substantial part has a family.[298] Late in the 4th century they formed "half the size of the (reduced) citizen body."[299] So, an estimate of 30,000 persons cannot be far from the mark.

Metics lived mostly permanently in the *astu* in which they strongly contributed to the colorful life of this center of the Mediterranean, and not in the least to the wealth of the city thanks to their sometimes-fabulous richness as bankers, shipowners, merchants, etc. They had no full citizenship and payed extra taxes. Additionally. A large trade center such as Athens always has a group of other permanently present foreigners like mercenaries, sailors, prostitutes, merchants, students and so on: say 5000 persons.[300]

Then there are the slaves. Based on earlier studies, I concluded that there are no more than maximum 5000 for Athens and Attica together.[301] In the city they were mostly domestic servants in the few rich households; in the *agros* they were workers in quarries, silver mines and large farms. My much lower estimates than others (many state out of the blue that every Athenian had one slave and that, therefore, there were much more than 100,000 slaves[302]) are in principle based on the thesis that, generally, Greeks were slave-*traders* and not

297 Oswyn Murray, 1991, 256–258.

298 Mogens Hansen, 2001, 93.

299 OCD, 969.

300 Without any substantiation Finley wrote about the "constant coming and going of tens of thousands of 'foreigners,' Greeks and others …" in Moses Finley, 1975, 134. During special occasions this could be possible as, for instance, the greater *Panathenaea* festival. Still one has to know how in an already overcrowded city they should be lodged other than in tents outside the city.

301 Hans Derks, 1986, 288–293; Hans Derks, 1996, 259–263 criticizing in particular Geoffrey De Ste. Croix.

302 Moses Finley, 1975, 71 apparently based on a ridiculous *plan* of Xenophon (*Poroi,* 4, 17). A highly ambiguous census of the Athenian population, attributed to Demetrius of

slave-*holders* as the Romans. This was one of the elements of an animal rearing culture (see Chapter 7). Besides this, the absence of relevant proofs of substantial slave holding is not unimportant.

The present general desperation vis à vis this subject is reproduced in the following quotations:

> Difficult to identify in the streets of ancient Athens where citizens were often mistaken for slaves—who were therefore protected from assault, lest a citizen be struck in error and bring a lawsuit—he or she was even harder to distinguish in his or her archaeological afterlife. [And Jameson's dictum:] If we have trouble identifying "agricultural slaves" in Athens it may be in part because they are everywhere.[303]

Last but not least is the translation of the many names for those who are doing manual or less favored work, which is misleading as if it concerned slaves. Among the arrogant Athenian elite there is a general disdain for those who are doing manual work in factories and in the fields or service work in households. The eating of barley, instead of the more expensive wheat was perceived as eating "slave food," although most Athenians in and outside the city regularly had to eat the former.[304] Indeed, the *talk* about slaves was "everywhere."

Regarding the table as such, it is interesting that this is my third version (previous versions in 1986 and 1996) and always accompanied with a warning that, based on new literature relevant for a revision, the resulting estimates were too optimistic. Not only are the new results again lower, but I think as well that we have to deal with maximum estimates. The practical reason for this is that I was more keen on the inter-cropping and "inter-peopling" policies and practices.

Archaeology revealed also that the 139 Attic *demes* were not as populous as estimated earlier: with an average of 500 persons we arrive at the top, which is also the case with the estimate of the adult males in the population.[305]

Phaleron (ca. 317 BCE), reported even about 400,000 slaves in Attica and a citizen population of only 21,000 and 10,000 metics.

303 Sarah Morris and John Papadopulos, 2005, 185 and Jameson's quotation. In this excellent article most sources about ancient slaves are discussed again.

304 This is controlled the best in the Marxist literature which is fully based on the thesis that the whole Greek or ancient economy/society were backward because of its basis in slavery. And the best of this literature is still the impressive Geoffrey de Ste. Croix, 1981. See now Armin Eich, 2006, 75–76, 257–353, particularly, 274.

305 Robin Osborne, 1985, 43–44. made estimates with the help of the UN model life tables for persons from under-developed and pre-industrial countries. He used it to estimate

TABLE 1 Population model per sector in Athens and Attica, ca. 430–330 BCE

Sector	ASTU-Athens				AGROS-Attica				Totals	
	5*x*	%	4*x*	%	5*x*	%	4*x*	%	5*x*	%
Agriculture	–	–	–	–	40,150	51	32,120	47	40,150	31
Horticulture	11,325	22	9,060	20	–	–	–	–	11,325	9
Animal husbandry	1,950	4	1,950	4	17,550	22	17,550	25	19,500	15
Forestry	–	–	–	–	3,000	4	3,000	4	3,000	2
Crafts + services	11,250	22	7,500	17	3,750	5	2,500	4	15,000	12
Total citizen	*24,525*	*48*	*18,510*	*41*	*64,450*	*82*	*55,170*	*80*	*88,975*	*69*
(Adult males)	4,905	10	4,628	10	12,890	16	13,793	20	17,795	14
Metics	22,500	45	22,500	50	7,500	10	7,500	11	30,000	23
Foreigners	2,500	5	2,500	6	2,500	3	2,500	4	5,000	4
Slaves	1,250	2	1,250	3	3,750	5	3,750	5	5,000	4
TOTALS	50,775	100	44,760	100	78,200	100	68,920	100	128,975	100
% Town-country		39		39		61		61	–	100

With the given systematic analysis of the soils, ecology, landscapes, land use and so on, it is anyway remarkable that the result for the *agros* is nearly the same. More basic is, of course, the refinement of the whole approach with its starting point not in the grain-growing agriculture, but in the traditionally and in its consequences more dominant animal husbandry. In other words: the 19th century ideology with its backgrounds and its many present supporters, is given a clear farewell.

A serious problem is hidden behind 39 and 61 percent representing the relationship between *astu* and *agros*. As told, Finley and many others perceived town and country as a "unit" based on a specific interpretation of Aristotle and Plato. The nearly existential problem that arises among (young!) scholars who cope with it, is expressed by Osborne in his first book. He confessed about his own study:

> The dangers inherent in the use of "city" in a Greek context are indeed great, greater than is generally admitted, and perhaps greatest of all in the case of Athens, where it may be totally unclear whether "the city of Athens" refers to the *astu* or to the polis as a whole. It is part of the burden of this work that the polis is a unity, that "Athenians" live all over Attica, and that talk of the loyalty of the villages to Athens radically misconceives the nature of the polis. It is, however, a further burden of this work that potentially the "state" element of "city-state" is no less misleading.[306]

That the author soon after forgot his principal doubts about the concepts at issue and did not accept its consequences in his next books, is not my problem here. I only can refer to the first paragraph of this chapter and point to a note connected to the "generally admitted" factor in the quotation which says: "E.g. it seriously obscures the fact that the majority of Athenians lived outside the *astu*, and that it was important that they did so."[307] Cambridge-Junior Fellow

the adult male population and arrived at figures as 15,300 or 16,000 for *astu* and *agros* together. I am glad that something in the same order could be gained based on original ancient Greek "models." As a "minimum population of a deme" he also proposed 65 males (45). Note that Osborne used the data of 127 *demes*—his table 1- and I reckoned with the traditional Cleisthenes' figure of 139 *demes*. Note also that Osborne uses the word *deme*, which is of course the local *polis*, the public political realm at local level, to which, for instance, no women belonged. I had to use here the name of settlements in the *agros*, but the correct way must be reserved for a more complicated analysis of the whole situation.

306 Robin Osborne, 1985, 8. At that time Osborne was only a "Junior Unofficial Fellow, King's College, Cambridge."

307 Robin Osborne, 1985, 218 note 32.

Osborne, furthermore, was one of the first to criticize Cambridge Don Finley as writing "absurd" things as a consequence of the adapted town-country unit model ("ancient Athens-including Attica-was the model of a face to face society") and the uncritical acceptance of Aristotle's view, that in Athens the whole people exercised power.[308]

Osborne rightly points to the large differences between theory and practice relative to the political decision-making, wealth or the occupation of influential jobs as general, etc. There are many plans, proposals and theories in ancient Greek writings, but were they realized in one form or another? He, furthermore, proved how the wealthy people of the *astu* and the *astu* as such were privileged and that the *demes* near the *astu* (Pedion) came second. Extreme exploitation of the *agros* by the *astu*, however, was not discovered by Osborne. What does this extreme exploitation mean? It is not explained. The following aspects of their relationship, anyway, are important enough to undermine the idea of a "harmonious unit."

Historically the periods of Solon, Cleisthenes, Peisistratos and others cannot be interpreted other than as stages with strong antagonisms between *astu* and *agros*, in which the *astu* could gain from the antagonisms inside the *agros* between coast and inland. It is a complicated and long history that cannot be described here. Anyway, these struggles led, in the end to certain compromises. From this, mainly from the 5–4th centuries, can be reported the following elements of town-country antagonisms.

Referred to above are the pejorative connotations of several words (*asteios* positive, *agroikos* negative) that directly refer to discriminatory potentials. They did not remain limited to the daily language, but had important political effects. There was, for instance, a council (*boule*) for both *astu* and *agros* for which nearly 500 *bouleutai* were to be chosen. It is, first, remarkable that the division of 61% *bouleutai* from the *agros* and 39% from the *astu* is similar to what was found through my calculations above.[309] This division is quantitatively correct, but the practice behind it is quite different.

For the *deme*-politicians and representatives in the *boule* it is, of course, important to stay as close to their own electorate as possible, but to function well in the *boule* they had to stay as long as possible in the *astu*. Doing this, there was a good chance that the representative would be kicked out of local

308 Robin Osborne, 1985, 65 which was immediately remarked in the obligatory review of the *Classical Review*, 36, 1986, 265–266. It is symptomatic that at the moment Osborne himself became a "Don" his pupil Kirsty Shipton seriously attacked his and in particular Finley's point of views in 2000 with the thesis I defended already in 1986.

309 Robin Osborne, 1985, 196 table 2.

networks. Only the rich can afford it to negate this dilemma and this had serious and negative consequences for the functioning of the democracy in the *astu* as well as in the *agros*.

This concerns the men. For the other half of the population, the women, things were quite different and not only because they had no public-political rights. As told above, all Athenians were called *Atheinaioi,* which is a clear reference to the *astu* and the *polis.* However, the Athenian women, including those of Sounion, Hagnous or Marathon, were called *Atticai gunaikes* (women of Attica). In addition, as they had no rights in the *polis,* they could not participate in the local *polis,* the *deme*: their *oikos* is only related to a settlement. Here it is demonstrated how the *polis–oikos* (public–private, etc.) can be intimately related to an existing town-country antagonism.[310]

That, also from an economic point of view, the *astu-agros* relationships were far from harmonious, is denied by Osborne, although he himself points to rather sharp rich-poor relations between city and country. From his data and the table, one can deduce remarkable differences in the professional populations.

In the *agros* lived and worked mainly tillers of the soil and several kinds of actors involved in the animal culture, together comprising three quarters of the population. In the city, however, the "green front" occupies only a quarter of the population. Thanks to this division of the professionals from the quite different production elements (in the country this included most cash crop and "cash animal" production, silver, stone, wood and the related crafts) a very remarkable situation exists: the "green producers" of the city largely find their market in the city and in export and are able, therefore, to remain *independent of the agros.* In its turn the *agros* does not need Athens at all to have a decent existence with strong negotiation power thanks to its good economic basis.

For both "parties" there is a snag somewhere: both are in need of wheat (there is enough barley!) that must be largely imported if it is necessary; this is only seldom the case apart from a regular transit trade of the *astu.* If that wheat is in demand the *agros* has large quantities of other products available to deal with, but no means to transport it abroad or extensive capital to finance its export. For the latter two, one has to rely fully on the rich *astu* with famous middle-class resources like pottery etc. In other words: city and country do deal with each other in an economic sense by way of the circuitous route of the

310 Here one can find a fundamental political background for the typical man—woman (and *oikos*—*polis*) relationships in the Greek animal culture. See Hans Derks, 2001, "Un Mal Splendide" about the emancipated Greek women, which was denied by the 20th century feminists.

great "international" market. It is not only the rich, but also the clever people who are able to exploit *both* city and country.

There is, next, also a military side of the given town-country contradictions. As the table shows there are in the *agros* more than twice as many adult citizens as in Athens, thanks to which the latter is strongly dependent of the *agros*. Metics and mercenaries can help fill this gap, but only if Athens can provide some advantages like giving metics more rights or privileges and paying mercenaries more money.

We know from Thucydides how Athens forced the peoples of Attica to leave their homes to help the defense of the city, where they fell victim to the plague and later to the Spartans. Thucydides gave another intriguing example of the troubled relationship between Athens and the country.

This time it concerns the Acharnians, the largest *deme* in the northwest of Attica. In the summer of 431 BCE, the Spartans under the leadership of Archidamus, stayed in Acharnae considering what they could do to provoke Athenians to start an open battle. Thucydides continues with:

> Acharnae itself seemed to him a good position for a camp, and at the same time he thought it likely that the Acharnians, who, with their 3000 *hoplites* [infantry.H.D.] ... would not allow their own property to be destroyed, but would force all the others as well to come out and fight for it. If, on the other hand, the Athenians did not come out and fight during this invasion, the Peloponnesians would in future invasions have all the more confidence in laying waste the plain and advancing right up to the walls of Athens. By that time the Acharnians would have lost their own property and would be much less willing to risk their lives for the property of other people; consequently there would be a lack of unity in the counsels of Athens. This was the policy of Archidamus that accounted for his remaining at Acharnae (II, 20).

Archidamus was playing for time, as did Pericles in Athens as well. The latter went even so far as to eliminate the workings of the *polis* by manipulating the time the *polis* had to meet. The Spartans were not able to attack the *astu*, while Athens was not able to defeat the Spartans in an open battle. Whatever the details, the *astu* played its own game and left the *agros* at the mercy of the Spartans and their allies: it had to look for its own fate.

The Peloponnesian War proved in my view, that the "life threads" of *astu* Athens are connected with its own sea trade market relationships and not at all with "its own" *agros*. The absence of the other connection is probably the reason why it lost and why the *agros* lost as well: it sent its greatest asset, its cattle, to Euboa; most of men and women went to *astu* Athens to perish with this city, and their fields were devastated. But the Athenian Xenophon remained optimistic, saying: where "there is land that yields no fruit if sown, and yet, with quarries, feeds many times the number it could support if it grew corn." (*Poroi*, 1, 5).

CHAPTER 3

A Fascinating *Oikos*

3.1 Introduction

In the several controversies related to the market-*oikos* debate, one thing is crystal-clear: "*oikos*" rather than "market" was the subject of the discussions. Why this is the case in modern discussions in the post-Weber period as well is rather complicated and will be investigated now in a special chapter. Some overlap with the preface or Chapter 1 is in fact quite functional.

To stress this aim, we tried to look at it from its use in historiography and under the critical circumstances of the Second World War. Let us turn, therefore, to the historian Otto Brunner (1898–1982). He started before the war as an important German-Austrian historian, remained one during the war as a more or less fanatic Nazi and was still influential in the postwar period.

Brunner coined a new *oikos*-concept in his "das Ganze Haus" ("Whole House") writings. Other reasons why this man is interesting is that he has been "forgotten" in the postwar *oikos*-controversy that mainly occurred in UK and USA. This was not unavoidable because Otto Brunner's main book was available in translation. Besides this, typical German elements of the *oikos* discussions cannot be "forgotten" since their roots are to be found in 19th century Germany.[311]

An impression of the complexity of Brunner's concept and its background can be grasped rather quickly. Whether it relies on historical practice or not, Brunner's *oikos*, dressed in its translation *Das Ganze Haus,* was still relevant to 20th-century socio-economic historiography, *Verfassungs*-historiography and sociology.[312] As such it was conceived by Wilhelm Riehl (1823–1897), probably the most influential German ideologue of the 19th century, and led to the dominating state-supporting German tradition.

Otto Brunner wrote about older traditions of the concept, saying:

311 See for the modern oikos controversies Mohammad Nafissi, 2005, who seldom refers to German literature.

312 For the meaning of *Verfassungsgeschichte,* see below. This historiography by Brunner and colleagues was created before and after 1945 in an attempt to block the existing more liberal (German meaning) legal historiography. See Karl Kroeschell, 1983, 47–49. Another concept is found in Hans Boldt, 1990, volume 1, 10–17.

 | DOI:10.1163/9789004383913_004

> The old European Oikonomic [model] appears in our modern view as a complex of doctrines that belong to ethics, sociology, pedagogy, medicine and the several technologies incorporated in the science of the household and agriculture. It is either economics or managerial science and it is no pure doctrine of the household or consumption.[313] To this "Doctrine of the Oikos" belongs in short "... the whole of human relationships and activities in the house."[314]

The important source of the aristocratic and church-related *Hausvater Literatur* is now quite near. It is found in particular in the 17th and 18th century but much more widespread. Not only did Luther contribute much to it,[315] but the early modern start can be discovered, also, in the influential *I Libri della Famiglia* (1428) by Leon Battista Alberti and in other writings.[316] Like Brunner, Alberti derived his concepts from ancient Greek sources such as Aristotle, Xenophon and Hesiod.

Alberti's basic concept house-*oikos* was later used in different fields like historiography, anthropology, economics, sociology, political science/political economy (*Staatswissenschaft*), philosophy and, particularly, theology. The theory and practice of the Mercantilists and Physiocrats cannot be understood without this ancient background. For two thousand years Aristotle's differentiation of the "three statusgroups in the house" was obligatory for all European social philosophy.[317] Brunner stresses also how until 1800

> the religious historical views, the Christian historical theology, fully dominates, in which since Tertullian, an *Oeconomia* of the Christian Dogmatics was incorporated, producing the divine world-government, the "salvation plan" (Heilsplan), which determined history.[318]

In other words: the legitimation for the most far-reaching imperialistic adventure in history, the Christian one, is to be found in this concept.

A not superficial analysis of Brunner's reception of the *oikos* concept, not only receives a specific meaning and fascination thanks to Brunner's national-socialistic choice, but a fundamental one thanks to the profound backgrounds. Its fascination is, therefore, a mixture of a particular historicity, a rather strong

313 Otto Brunner, 1956, 36.
314 Otto Brunner, 1956, 35.
315 Gotthardt Frühsorge, 1976.
316 Hans Derks, 1986, 596.
317 See the excellent overview of Hannah Rabe, 1974.
318 Otto Brunner, 1956, 60.

ideological emanation, a broad scholarly application and a strong metaphorical expression.

3.2 The Basic Concept House-*Oikos*

If we look into this matter a bit more closely in the relevant texts, we easily see how different and complicated this concept, used by the ancient Greeks, is. In the next section I will report on this after some background information is provided about the areas in which it is used. In other words: how does one start a "house" problem-definition?

The following complexity is derived from ancient Greek meanings.[319] As mentioned in the preface we have to deal with: 1. The spatial elements of house/*oikos* like dwelling, building, tent, residence, temple, town, etc.; 2. The economic elements of house/*oikos* like property, fortune, household, manor, etc.; 3. Its social elements like family, servants, *Heimat*, nativity, kinship, etc.; 4. The political elements of house/*oikos* like master of the family, landlord, state, fatherland, etc.

This division can, of course, be refined if necessary: cultural characteristics of the house (*oikos, domus, maison, huis*, or *Haus*) could be perceived as qualities of the former elements. For our aim, there is no need to do so. An insight into certain connections and antagonisms between elementary social phenomena, can be enhanced. Together, these elements can function as a kind of checklist for historians, sociologists, economists or political scientists: where, for instance, "house" is only used as social element, a certain one-sidedness becomes directly apparent.[320]

Although Brunner often used the word "economy" (*Wirtschaft*), he never carried out an economic analysis of his "Ganze Haus," let alone an agronomic one like that of Alexander Tschajanow.[321] His interest was only connected to politics from which he derived social elements. A simple meaning of the term "house as tent" immediately opens vistas on mobile and wandering ways of life (pastoralism, nomadism) and related production methods. Such a world, as that of animal husbandry for example, is never envisaged by the traditional *oikos*-house scholars.

319 Hans Derks, 1986, 60–70 and the lemma "Oikos" in: *Pauly's Realencyclopädie*. One can find nothing in DKP, München, 1979. See furthermore Hannah Rabe, 1977, 14, 15 and, of course, the several editions of the *Greek-English Lexicon* of Liddell & Scott.

320 Karl Kroeschell, 1968, 48–53 writes short and effective about the early derailment of the conceptualization within the group of "House" scholars.

321 Alexander Tschajanow, 1923.

As to the *oikos*-house pair, combinations of these elements are often used. Take, for instance, simple examples as "the House of Windsor," "my home is my castle," or quite complex one's like the following two theses:

> ... The house forms a social body of the order of Creation, in which the individual each in the role of house-father, -mother... servant... shall find its place in daily life to enhance his personal development, to act up to one's duty, to satisfy his needs.
> [or]
> The house as part and analogon of the State is... juridically deeply connected to the aims of the political body (*Gemeinwesen*).[322]

Differences between the current ideologies are clearly shown, if one brings the four elements into a hierarchical order. The very act of doing this is already ideologically as the former and the next two examples demonstrate. The first tells something about interconnections, the second about contradictions.

If house-*oikos* as political element dominates, overrules or determines the other elements, it is highly probable that an authoritarian male-dominated power constellation is planned or established. In this case, the first element could always represent its claims of some eternal existence or divine ancestry: changes of such a power constellation are deemed to be principally unnecessary and only thinkable as an extension of its *Lebensraum*. The important representative architecture of the worldly or spiritual authority is to be seen in this light.[323]

Within such a model the second element characterizes an economy based on a one-sided exploitation of the dominated resources such as foreign labor, foreign land, and incomes by means of tributes, taxes or plain theft. The third element within such authoritarian political domination is the basis of biological reproduction and the socialization of the own family-members and kin; eventually such a family will become part and parcel of the state itself.

Here the fatherly element provides the identity whereas the motherly functions as something "other," to be exploited. The authoritarian fatherly power could be softened only into patriarchalism if a higher—in the end divine—power can be constructed.

Against this combination of the four elements another traditional one can be posed that takes its start from the second element. Where "house" as

322 Dieter Schwab, 1975.

323 Martin Warnke, ed., 1984. With Oikos-architecture deals the interesting Reinhard Bentmann and Michael Müller, 1970.

economic element is fixed in an absolute way, a specific *chrematistical* market constellation appears. Aristotle and Plato condemned this energetically.

A "natural" exchange of goods in an oikoïdal economy based only on the satisfaction of needs (*Bedarfsdeckungswirtschaft*) is sharply distinguished from an "unnatural" money exchange and money market. Whatever different interpretation can be gleaned from Aristotle's texts, in the end for the whole of Christianity and its ideologues "Aristotle's market" pointed (and still points) to the highest forms of evil in society, such that it became the absolute counter-power of an autarky, a self-sufficient or closed individual household or state economy. Until far into the 19th century theologians energetically attacked activities like money exchange, loans by interest, price-fixations, purchase contracts and many other commercial practices.[324] The later socialist and national-socialist rhetoric repeated these religious hymns.

Therefore, this market-model was historically fixed as the negation of ideals, if not of utopia. A long list of dichotomies is the result of such a procedure. That is to say, that one seriously has to question whether what is subsumed under this ideological market-concept has anything to do with market relationships, mobile ways of life, supply and demand in prices and wages, with the circulation of goods and money or fluctuations on labor-markets. Mostly this is not the case.

Furthermore, one has to consider the following: House-*Oikos* is nearly always only related to large ownership, agrarian and country relations, while the market appeared mostly in connection with industry or urban and commercial phenomena. Herewith the dominant town-country antagonisms are addressed in which, as could be expected from the above, the *house* position is not only connected with the land and its inhabitants, but also with a third position, that of the state overarching the town and country. And this state position in its turn can have a specific relationship with one city, the capital. This state as super-Oikos became the main point of reference in the theory of the consumptive city of Werner Sombart and Max Weber, with which Moses Finley in his turn constructed his ideal- type of "city in antiquity."

Other parameters must be considered as well. In several periods and at least in the European history the use of house-*oikos* is strongly class and/or status determined. Mostly one can seriously doubt whether the lower classes used "house" in other than the daily, banal, sense. In higher classes and status-groups, however, the motives behind its popularity and fascination are seldom not inspired by authoritarian and patriarchal power-aims. Variables for this

324 See, for instance, Alois A. Waibel, 1839–1844, volume 8, 181–451.

behavior can be found if one differentiates between urban and rural or aristocratic (including high ranked clerical) and bourgeois writers.

At last, one can stress how important for the study of the concept it is whether house–*oikos* is posed in defense of the top of some socio-political hierarchy, in particular of a state or church. For historians it is sufficient to remark here: in the making of a problem-definition at least the given four elements of the concept should be considered in their theoretical and practical implications and in relation to changes in time and place. Only then can the factual existing or ideologically intended interdependencies be determined and analyzed. Just after this is completed, it becomes methodologically unproblematic to limit a certain study to, for instance, the social element.

3.3 An *Oikos* Controversy

Here I will briefly mention only two important stages of this controversy. The first is related to the debates about the classical *oikos* concept and the second concerns Max Weber's involvement in the question.[325]

In Greek antiquity the plural, *oikoi*, was used to circumscribe the concrete appearances of the Greek social and other relations in particular of the production, consumption and reproduction. The singular, *oikos*, was used as basic category in Aristotle's political theory and was, as such, a symptom of a clearer differentiation of a social hierarchy. From this was the neologism super-*Oikos* derived that concerns the state (state-power, state-household), territory or *patrimonium* as legitimated (more or less) by the Aristotelian creed or its variants in the works of Thomas of Aquinas, Jean Bodin, and many others until the present time.[326]

Small wonder that this complicated concept, which is at least the metaphor of the whole monarchical and state hierarchy, is also the subject of the about 150 years long *oikos* controversy, to the end-phase of which this book eventually belongs. It all began with detailed studies from the political-economist Rodbertus (1805–1875) on taxations in the Roman empire.

Based on the classical interpretations and false translations of Aristotle's *oikos*-theory, he interpreted the ancient economy as oikos-economy (*Oikenwirtschaft*). This concept, and its alleged meaning, was incorporated within the

325 Further details can be found in Mohammad Nafissi, 2006, Part 2 about Max Weber (57–127) and Chapter 10 "The battle of the ancient economy."

326 Hans Derks, 1986, 228 and 648–649.

economic-historical development theories (*Stufen Theorien*) of highly influential German historians and economists.

The internationally most important of them, Karl Bücher (1847–1930), successfully launched his theory of a historical sequence of house-economy (*Hauswirtschaft*), city-economy (*Stadtwirtschaft*) and national economy (*Volkswirtschaft*), in which all phases are perceived as closed (*geschlossen*), autarkic, and self-sufficient phases.

Until about 1930, Karl Bücher and historians, economists and sociologists such as Eduard Meyer, Julius Beloch, Michael Rostovtzeff, Max Weber, Werner Sombart, Robert Pöhlmann, Felix Oertel and Johannes Hasebroek, along with their pupils, supporters and networks fought their battles during the first phase of the *oikos* controversy. This debate interfered with several other scholarly ventures of this kind like the bloody debates on the "(German) State of the Middle Ages," "the *Grundherrschaft*" [manorial system], or the "Transition from Antiquity to Middle Ages," all of which had substantial international repercussions.

In the Nazi-period it seems quiet at this front, but elsewhere the knives were sharpened anew. Karl Polanyi and Moses Finley spent their time in the United States to study the *oikos*-problem without knowing hardly anything about the complexity described above. They used, in particular, the relevant writings of Max Weber, Werner Sombart and Karl Bücher, while giving the debate the name of *Bücher-Meyer controversy*. From then on, the debate raged in particular between English, American and French scholars, without the Germans but about the Germans.[327]

Thanks to a strong Marxist and structuralist influence from several directions received the debate an interesting interdisciplinary character. The controversy is also known as the debate between the primitivists (Finley c.s.) and modernists (Meyer c.s.), which is a rather artificial difference, hiding more than elucidating. Moses Finley fully dominated the discussions until his death at the end of 1986. It was the sign for the third and present phase.

This present constellation can be sketched only by means of the change of directions in the debate. The attempt to replace the age-old perception of the self-sufficient grain growers' economy and authoritarian state (in short: the "oikoïdal option") by a market and animal-cultural orientation and democratic

327 So between Moses Finley, Eduard Will, Karl Polanyi, Arnaldo Momigliano, Sally Humphreys, Pierre Vidal-Naquet, etc. I only mention here some programmatic writings like Eduard Will, 1954; Moses Finley, 1981 and Sally Humphreys, 1978 with chapters on Polanyi, Momigliano and others. Recently a certain revival of Karl Polanyi is organized thanks to the biography of Gareth Dale (2017). See for this biography the review of Robert Kuttner in the *New York Review of Books*, 21 December 2017, 55–57.

polity (in short: the "market option"[328]) implied a strong criticism not only of Finley and his many supporters, but also of Max Weber, Werner Sombart and their sources.

Such a shorthand formula does not pay tribute to the fact that the real problems are hit here only at the surface. It will take many years before the highly necessary transformation of the ancient studies into a modern and relevant scholarly activity is realized. Precondition to this is a new and clear problem-definition.

Part of the *oikos*-controversy always was, for instance, the primitiveness or modernity of the Greek banking activities. It seems to be the wrong starting-point because *both* positions use modern criteria to prove their thesis. The former urges that they are "not yet," while the latter sticks to "already modern."

However, this is not to deny that Athens in the classical period harbored adequate and complex "international" networks for insurance, mortgages, money-lending or money-exchange activities as attendant circumstances of an extensive trade in persons and goods, as Edward Cohen rightly argued against Paul Millett. Moreover, it can be proved that not a few women occupied leading positions in these activities, undermining not only the perception of the authoritarian male as head of the *oikos* and "*oikos*-as-state," but also the oikoïdal feminist historiography that is in need of a primitive past in order to point to a bright new female future.

An important subject of the oikoïdal historiography concerns the hotly defended thesis of the ancient consumption-city by Sombart, Weber or Finley.

328 Nowadays some "Market Option" is more or less supported by Oswyn Murray, Robin Osborne (after 1991), Hans Derks, Edward Cohen, 1992. Still Germany is also able to show some innovations in this respect as there is Wilfried Gawantka's excellent ideology-criticism, 1985. Further started unobtrusively the journal *Münstersche Beiträge zur antiken Handelsgeschichte*, which slowly abandoned the oikoïdal option of the Cambridge School without—on the other hand—be incapsulated by the dominant German Ideology from Brunner and his colleagues. The most important animal husbandry, pastoralism etc. aspects of the problem are discovered by Bernard Slicher van Bath, 1944, 1963, 1978 in his brilliant attack on the classical medieval studies which he extended in his post-war work till about 1960. It concerns, in short, the far reaching relationship between an animal culture, democratic decision-making processes and a money-market which he found in the Dutch coastal provinces in the early Middle Ages. He also formulated the outline of a general theory of this problem-network. Small wonder that I, as his pupil, now extended and successfully tested this "animal option" in ancient Greece which resulted in a profound new interpretation of its history and big quarrels in Holland with the "Dutch Finley," Harry Pleket (with his pupils like Hans van Wee, Teitler, etc.). See my, 2002, note 12. It is more serious, that the opportunity to renew the economic history of ancient Greece and to liberate it from the old orthodoxy, is not taken; on the contrary! See Walter Scheidel ed., 2007.

Criticism of it leads directly to the heart of the matter, the interpretation of ancient town-country relationships. In Roman times, not to mention classical Hellas, they say, nearly only peasants lived in cities and, therefore, cities depended only on the produce from the nearby land. The large landowners (*Oikenwirtschaft*), therefore, forced town and country into an isolating autarky.

Finley derived this image of "the ancient city" from his study of the eternal city, Rome. Thanks to this the totalitarian and imperial power became intertwined with his model that he, imperialistically, spread over the whole of antiquity. Pupils like Jongman quasi-renewed even this by using sophisticated modern research-methods. It did not help much because even for the grain-feeding of the ancient Romans, let alone of the whole empire, it has been proved, in the meantime, that at least 70% of the food was provided through the markets of private producers and merchants;[329] that the production, distribution and consumption of wine was 100% a marketing matter;[330] that in classical Hellas large landowners were so rare that they as such could not play any role of importance, whereas relatively small farmers and merchants sometimes played an impressive role in the "international" market with cash-crops like olives, wine and grain or with cash-resources like stone, metals, wood and animal products (wool, textiles, leather) apart from their substantial trade in "cash-people" (slaves and mercenaries) and cash-money.[331]

At last there occurred in this third phase a rather spectacular renewal, the confrontation of the traditional grain-growers theory and ideology with the different forms of an animal-raising culture, i.e. from pure nomadism over pastoralism to animal husbandry. Bernard Slicher van Bath discovered the importance of this animal-rearing culture for Dutch and other European coastal regions in particular for the development of mobile ways of production, a strong orientation to money, flexible labor-markets and a democratic decision-making process.[332]

The effects of all these rather fundamental changes of direction of the oikos-controversy on the historiography of other periods, must be as unavoidable as was in earlier times the change into an oikoïdal direction. It seems as if the second height in the conceptual history of *oikos* belongs to another world, but this semblance is false: it will appear to be the very heart of the house-*oikos* debate in modern times.

329 Boudewijn Sirks, 1984.

330 Tchernia, A, 1986.

331 Oswyn Murray in Oswyn Murray and Simon Price, ed., 1990, 1–29.

332 Hans Derks, 1995, 3–33. See Chapter 7.

Here we have to consider, first, the transformation of the house-ideology inspired by Immanuel Kant. Aristotle limited a personal property-relationship to masters and slaves, but Kant and his predecessors like Walch (1726) extended this to "*real objects* that clever people in their own interest have at their disposal."[333]

Kant perceived the marriage-, parents- and house-master-laws as objective personal right, as a *right of mine and thine*. From now on and thanks to this transformation, in the elite women and children were seen as a property that could be received through an act of acquirement (Erwerb; could be a form of buying and selling): "The man gets a wife; the couple gets children and the family gets servants."

Now was created an at least theoretical relationship between household and acquirement (*Erwerb*) with a very special content and particular connotations. The house-being, or household (*Hauswesen*) became something like the whole of a society of members in which people, mostly based upon a contract, possess and acquire each other. The consequences of this strange and controversial transformation of the Aristotelian *oikos*-theory have not been overcome even until today, either in theory or in a practical social policy.

In the reception of Max Weber, many aspects of his work have been neglected as demonstrated in Chapter 1.[334] Here I recall only the fundamental statement that one can act economically only in two ways: *haushalten* (manage a household) or *erwerben* (something like "acquire a living").[335] Under the direct influence of Bücher and Rodbertus, Weber builds on this dichotomy his whole casuistic.[336]

Many contradictions arise from these constructions. The oikoïdal Weber, who until recently was not discovered, is determined by both sides of the dichotomy: he often ideologically chooses the household-side and uses authoritarian language (*Herrschaftssprache*[337]) in descriptions of the other side in which market subjects or real market relations are very difficult to discover.

333 Quoted in Hannah Rabe, 1974, 1012 and also for the following quotations.

334 Hans Derks, 1989, 282–296.

335 WG, 61–71 and 257–258.

336 In the original language these are, for instance: Bedarfsdeckungs- versus Erwerbswirtschaft; Vermögen versus Kapital; Haushaltsrechnung versus Kapitalrechnung; Selbstversorgung versus Markttausch; Staats- und Kommunale Haushaltung versus einem auf Kapitalrechnung basierenden und marktgängigen Unternehmen; geschlossene versus offene Beziehungen," and so on.

337 As, for instance, *Verfügungsgewalt* or *Verfügungsmacht* over goods.

Also the definition of his central concept, *Herrschaft* (authoritarian domination), is derived from the market-*oikos* dichotomy.[338]

The leading thread running through his historical analyses is his perception of an evolution of the house-community: "The original carrier of all bureaucracy (*Verwaltung*)... the *Hausherrschaft*... the principally absolute power of the *Hausherr*"[339] stands at the start to be continued at present in "the dominating bureaucracy of the state (*staatlichen Herrschaftsbetrieb*"[340]); somewhere in between the patriarchal and patrimonial *Herrschaft* are located.[341] It is a history in which often a market is played against an *oikos*, and an oikoïdal domination always succeeds in the end.[342]

In the analysis of another famous Weber category, charisma, you will find not only confrontation with a medieval Frankisch charismatic *Hausherr*, but one can also read:

> But in the realm of the specific capitalistic economy one finds the antagonism of charisma versus daily life, in the sense that now not charisma and house are placed against each other, but charisma and company.[343]

The German-American translators and editors of *Wirtschaft und Gesellschaft* are probably right as they circumscribe the meaning of household for Weber as "what Aristotle meant by management of a household."[344] There they were not able to show the interconnection between this household, the specific "chrematistic-market" and the oikos concept, either within Max Weber's own methodology and historical theory or within the conceptual history briefly sketched here. It is here that the concept as used by Otto Brunner can receive its proper place.

338 WG, 691. An *Oikosherrschaft* is based on authority, a *Marktherrschaft* is based on some constellation of interests. Weber uses only "the concept Herrschaft in the limited sense... identical... with authoritarian power to command (*autoritärer Befehlsgewalt*)." See also 695.

339 WG, 498; see also 277–278.

340 WG, 1047.

341 WG, 742.

342 WG, 1007–1008.

343 WG, 838.

344 As told earlier, the editors Talcott Parsons, Guenther Roth and Claus Wittich in ES, 1978, 207 choose for the current use "budget and budgetary management" as synonymous for "Staatshaushalt(sführung)."

3.4 The "Whole House" of Otto Brunner

First, some remarks about the man, Brunner (1898–1982) and his scholarly performance. His career shows perfectly well how easily one can negate the National-Socialist past in the guild of historians, while even demonstrating a remarkable benevolence for a man "whose normative and basic explications express what we as citizens of the Federal Republic of Germany feel if confronted with the deepest corners of our not yet disappeared past."[345]

During his lifetime, criticism of his writings was "not done." The legal historian Karl Kroeschell, one of the very few and the most important of his opponents, wrote a devastating criticism of the *Hausherrschaft*,[346] but his work was only mentioned dutifully in some footnote to "the developed theories from Otto Brunner and Walter Schlesinger that are until today in force."[347]

345 Ludwig Deike in a speech at the occasion of the 80th anniversary of Otto Brunner at the University of Hamburg, 1978. Quoted by Robert Jütte, 1984, 237. Four years later could Brunner "now and in the future serve as guide and stimulator" (Jürgen Deininger), while his successor did not find a word about Brunner's active war-years during the academic commemoration. L. Buisson, *Zum Gedenken an Otto Brunner, 1898–1982*. Hamburg, 1983, 10, 22.

346 Karl Kroeschell, 1968, 46 for example: "The concepts 'House' and 'Houselord' [Hausherrschaft]… changed … [from the point of view of social and legal reality]… into general concepts. The increasing ideological use of 'House' is to prove through the line of influence from Justus Möser to Wilhelm Heinrich Riehl unto the new 'House and Fireside' mysticism [*Haus- und Herdflammen Mystik*]. What concerns 'Herrschaft' you may think, first, of the old French theory of the feudal order as the 'Herrschaft' based on conquering… second, of the meaning given by Gierke of the whole history of laws as derived from the dialectics of 'Herrschaft' and 'Genossenschaft.'"

347 Hans-Werner Goetz, 1987, 35; Hans-Werner Goetz, 1999, 176 reported quite content that Kroeschell's theory had no effect and that the traditional point of view "auch bis heute geltender Forschungsstand geblieben (ist)." Hans K. Schulze, 1985, volume 1, 155 tells, that "seldom there was a criticism" and he regrets this a bit relative to Kroeschell's work. Even this footnote fails in the highly uncritical Brunner-adaptation of Hans Medick, ed., 1981, 38–74. It is yet clear that Hans Boldt, 1990, distances himself from Brunner, but this is done quite ambiguous as in his volume 1, 94–99. The most ridiculous Brunner-servility is not the expurgated USA-translation of *Land und Herrschaft*, but what is demonstrated by the Dutch editors of the medieval parts of the "official" Dutch general history (editors/ authors like Blok, Van Caenegem, Jansen, Prevenier, Verhulst and Weiler) in: *Algemene Geschiedenis der Nederlanden*. Haarlem, 1981, volume 1, 17–20. They admit that concepts like "Hausherrschaft," "Gefolgschaft," etc. cannot be found at all in medieval sources, that they are difficult to translate and that they are invented one day by German medievalists. However, "we" only use them as "typical *termini technici*"! The fundamental criticism of Karl Kroeschell was known to these scholars, but did not matter.

After his death a revival started, not only in West Germany (FRG), but in Italy and the USA as well, and it ran in parallel with those of Carl Schmitt and Max Weber, persons who historically and in terms of their scholarship have much in common.[348] Even a lucid historian such as Hans-Ulrich Wehler concluded that Brunner, like Theodor Schieder and Werner Conze, could become "one of the great initiators of the modern... social history."[349] This must be only valid for the FRG.

Anyway, it is difficult to deny that Brunner never withdrew one word of his National-Socialist writings, while he only gave them a simple cosmetic treatment after the war. He even started a redevelopment and extension of his controversial thoughts and he succeeded to institutionalize these. Brunner wrote mostly programmatic books and essays; no one consults his few empirical investigations anymore. Now, thanks to his FRG-career and his own stubborn performance a " Brunner Affair" was initiated with the publications of Robert Jütte and Otto Oexle[350] where, for the first time Brunner's Nazi-writings became known to contemporary Germany although they could and have been consulted rather easily. New, and for him, unpleasant, results of investigations into his Nazi-activities cannot remain unmentioned in the near future. This will occur in Germany and abroad within the framework of research into "die Vordenker der Vernichtung" (Preparers of the Holocaust).[351]

Let's start with some remarks concerning methodological aspects of Brunner's political commitment. The most well-known historian from after World War II, Fernand Braudel, has stressed these in his devastating criticism of "the extreme abstractions... of Max Weber" [l'immense abstractions webérienne... de Max Weber bien sûr]" and "the authoritarian dichotomy of Otto Brunner"

348 Reinhard Blänkner, 1987, 559–564.

349 Hans-Ulrich Wehler, 1988, 105.

350 Robert Jütte, 1984; Otto Oexle, 1984, 304–342.

351 Michael Burleigh, 1989; Götz Aly and Susanne Heim, 1993. In the *Deutsche Ostforschung* historians like Aubin, Conze, Schieder, Oberländer, Brunner—to mention only some who got also important positions after the war—played an important role. Otto Brunner, who—as Mitteis was able to tell already during the war in *Historische Zeitschrift*, 163, 1941, 255—for the history of the "east-German Danube region... was well-known as first authority," happened to join the core-group of the *Ostforscher* already in March 1940; see Michael Burleigh, 1989, 240. With this, Brunner belonged to the top of the "Vordenker." For the post-war period of these Ostforscher, see Michael Burleigh, 1989, 300–321. The so-called "structural historiography" is to be seen as a heritage of this Ostforschung and its parallel-institution, the "German Westforschung" from historians like Franz Petri or Franz Steinbach and their Belgian and Dutch followers. The outline of a concept as "structure" including its historiography is to be found in Brunner's articles about problems concerning socio-economic history and the "Verfassungs"-concept in 1936 and 1939.

[l'autoritaire dichtomie d'Otto Brunner].[352] After this, Brunner's general historical theses can be considered and, in particular, his family-historical and -sociological thoughts. Specialized historians who want to behave like sociologists or political philosophers will meet their limits rather soon.

Also historisist oriented scholars such as Brunner constructed politically motivated ideal-types à la Weber, and after 1933 the slow and sure incorporation of a more technical methodology came on top of this. Brunner and his colleagues and pupils tried, after 1945, to construct a series of interrelated concepts in order to categorize and then to explain European history once and for all. They were, furthermore, historians who capitulated to their fascination with Max Weber and Carl Schmitt because they did *not* have (or did *not* want to have) the critical capabilities to come to terms with these brilliant but also highly controversial figures.[353]

As a case in point to demonstrate this behavior some remarks about the way these people dealt with the concept of *Strukturgeschichte* (something like: a historiography based on historical structures). Together with the concept *Landesgeschichte* (historiography of the regions of Germany known as *Länder*) and its practices, the aim should be achieved to create a pure oikoïdal German historiography.

For Brunner, Conze and colleagues "the political" was the very object of their *Strukturgeschichte* by which they copied the political theologian Carl Schmitt. It is difficult to see Max Weber's political studies as an alternative for Schmitt's.[354] This "political" is only related to the political action of families, villages, whole states, nations and peoples (*Völker*). All these "fight for their existence, and defend themselves"; they are social forms in which a legally ordered power relation exists and permanently power-fights rage as in earlier times among the ancient Greeks in their *poleis*.

Most important to Brunner in this constellation is the state ("... it is therefore that the political has the priority here..."). He suggests that to understand this one must have a profound "knowledge of the inner composition, the social structures and the spiritual attitudes." Therefore, "this Strukturgeschichte... cannot be executed without a continuous look at what happens with the political. In its construction it is determined by the political." The very heart of this politicization constitutes the state's own survival (*Selbstbehauptung*) relative

352 Fernand Braudel, 1969, 175–191.

353 In: Helmut Quaritsch, ed., 1991, 22, 33, 78; sie also the preface in Karl Bosl, 1966.

354 The following quotations are from Otto Brunner, 1959, 23–25. See also for the sake of comparison Otto Brunner, 1943, 1–5. These passages of the *Rektoratsrede* are nearly quotations from Otto Brunner, 1936, 676 and 677.

to external circumstances and "the fight for mastery and power" in the inner structure of the state.

As if this ideological speculation is not enough, a remarkable coldblooded Brunner made the connection here between this Strukturgeschichte and the

> totalitarian claim of the historical discipline. [This pretension arises if the historian] as political historian [not only circumscribes the external sequence of the political actions] but if he with the help of the Strukturgeschichte, tries to discover the backgrounds of the ideas and institutions.[355]

In this way, fifteen years after the war, Brunner announced the potentialities of the *Strukturgeschichte* in his oration at the University of Hamburg. A scandal did not occur.

The aims of Brunner and his colleagues are difficult to compare to those of Braudel's structuralism or the *Annales*-group as Oexle supposed.[356] Whatever one may say about these French scholars, they never wanted to discover an a-historical model of political mastery in medieval or modern history. For them *structures* are always connected to real historical developments, i.e. to what they called *a longue durée*, a quasi-immobile geological, ecological, etc. sequence of events. Together with a cyclical-conjunctional and development of events, they are intertwined in a three-fold conjuncture called *temps de l'histoire*. This is far from an ideological construction, but a scientific one, and therefore always target for critics.

One consequence of this constellation should be stressed here: interdisciplinarity in the *Strukturgeschichte* does not mean more than that auxiliary troops come to help the Central Command; in the *Annales*-case, however, the part-whole dichotomy disappeared in favor of a more or less functional use of geological to political data within a *temps de l'istoire*. Braudel rightly states that the problems arising from Brunner's actions "in the end undermine the whole methodology and even the sense of the historical sciences."[357]

It is also symptomatic that the themes and views of Brunner are largely unknown in France. For Oexle this is "unbelievable," because in his attempt to compare modern with pre-modern societies Marcel Mauss had yet also used "total social phenomena."[358] However, the Sanskrit researcher and historian of

355 See previous note.

356 Otto Oexle, 1984, 321.

357 Fernand Braudel, 1969, 175. See also Jacques Le Goff, ed., 1978, 316–343 and 528–553.

358 Otto Oexle, 1984, 323 note 87.

religions, Mauss, learned from his extensive ethnological studies on exchange in archaic societies just how far this phenomenon was "a total social activity."[359] With this he wanted to tell that this exchange was not only an economical or juridical phenomenon, but a moral, aesthetic, religious, mythological and socio-morphological as well. This is graspable, Mauss wrote, "if we see it in its concrete, complex reality";[360] a totality, indeed, that we cannot understand if we are not prepared to abandon our usual, abstract way of thinking.

This is, therefore, miles away from Brunner's methodological premises derived from Aristotle's abstract *oikos*-theory, politicized with Carl Schmitt's abstract "doctrine of the state legitimation" [*Verfassungs Doktrin*] and modernized with Max Weber's abstract ideal-typology. Although Brunner knew how complicated, for instance, a "doctrine of the old-European Oikonomic" was, he never took as *starting point* for historical analysis social activities in all their complexities.

In fact, there came into existence only one single conceptual grid in which Brunner's *Struktur* after 1945 functioned in its political cosmetic.[361] How far Brunner's and the *Annales*-group's theoretical products differentiate from each other, was apparent in the Italian Brunner revival. Here Brunner was used as an alternative to the *Annales*.[362]

3.5 The Devil and the Details

It's time to go into more detail about characteristics of Brunner's *oikos* concept. Opitz tried to criticize these by using the newest social-historical and sociological family-research of Rosenbaum, Mitterauer, etc. According to Opitz, the latter must have demonstrated that there is nothing like a unity of production

359 Marcel Mauss, 1968.

360 Marcel Mauss, 1968, 10.

361 Otto Brunner, 1943, 4: "Nicht darum geht es, nach den geistigen, wirtschaftlichen, sozialen, rechtlichen "Voraussetzungen" zu fragen, sondern die Struktur der politischen Gebilde in ihrer Ganzheit darzulegen." In 1965 became *Struktur* in this programmatic declaration *Strukturen*.

362 Reinhard Blänkner, 1987, 560. It is characteristic for the level of Oexle's criticism, that he Braudel of all peoples *accused* of launching suspicions against Brunner. Objectively, Oexle has no single point against Braudel, which is a historian with a five year prison-history in German concentration camps. Besides this, Oexle could have read that it was Braudel, 1969, 190 who regretted the loss of communication between French and German historians and that he even created the possibilities to come to terms "laissant à Otto Brunner l'initiative de ce débat."! Brunner refused even this generous offer and Oexle legitimated this afterwards.

and consumption in such a family-house as has been theoretically predicted; only the position of the father in the house was articulated and while that of the house-mother minimized.[363]

Based on writings of Hans-Ulrich Wehler, who was a declared Max Weber proponent, Opitz also liked to get rid of "the legend of the economically autarkic Whole House." She rightly shows how Brunner's theory of the pre-modern social and economic forms of life rested more on Aristotle and conservative historians of the 19th century than on sources. Therefore, the theory or the Whole House Model should be to a large degree demystified as a-historical. Brunner, furthermore uses this model in an ideological sense in order to support his own patriarchal-authoritarian, anti-feminist, anti-modernistic and cultural pessimistic way of thinking.

What is there to say about this strong criticism? From Wehler's *Deutsche Gesellschaftsgeschichte* it is not possible to derive arguments for Opitz' views. Wehler talks "with Max Weber" about a "quasi-autarkic House-economy," which in reality, so obviously to Max Weber, was only a phenomenon of late antiquity. What such a quasi-case is in reality nobody can know, and with Max Weber such a legend cannot be told.

But my stance is contrary to this. Weber's text tells about a bottle-neck in the slave trade to which the large landowners reacted with attempts to make themselves independent of the market by using their own labor potentials (*Bedarfsdeckung*). He continues with:

> Rodbertus believed that this autarky of the *oikos* was an original characteristic of the whole of antiquity, but it is only a phenomenon of late antiquity and it arises to its zenith in the period of the Carolingians.[364]

Therefore, it does not concern here a quasi-case or a legend, but a real development in the period of about 200 BCE–1000 ACE. Whether this Weberian opinion is right or not, is quite another case. Max Weber, furthermore, does not tell here about autarky in general, but only about labor problems related to the Oikos (as state). So, for what reason are Opitz and Wehler in need of a legend?

Wehler often uses, in a positive sense, the concept *Whole House*. Take for instance the following:

> From this so-called "Whole House" should be developed in a process of continuing differentiation of functions and division of labor the pure

363 For Opitz see my *Geschichte und Gesellschaft*, 1996, 221 ff.

364 Wg, 1924, 124.

> agricultural undertaking, the pure industrial plant, the pure market gardeners, the pure commercial business always with their own laborforce. Only under these preconditions can the agricultural economy be perceived as its own, proper complex.[365]

Which other economic-historical phenomenon has such a nearly legendary meaning?

Another example: at the end of the 18th century, a minority of businesses gradually develops an agrarian capitalism, namely in the commercialized agricultural sector that depends on export. The so realized market-relations have "dissolved the 'Whole House' into the general economy, but for local needs and a local market... small agrarian units represent for many their orbit of economic activities."[366]

It is, in fact, only necessary to read the first sentences of the introduction to the first volume of Wehler's monumental *Deutsche Gesellschaftsgeschichte.* Here one sees the profound influence Brunner's thesis of the bipartite partition of European history had, with its division into an "old European part" and a "modern part," with a transformation at the end of the 18th century. If Opitz, therefore, with Wehler (and implicitly, Max Weber) tries to prove how obsolete the concept *Whole House* is, her aim cannot be fulfilled.

At the moment she tries to criticize Brunner's *oikos*-model by reference to recent socio-historical and sociological family-research, Opitz disappoints again. Heidi Rosenbaum's or Michael Mitterauer's work contain some minor criticism but mostly they produce nothing but support for Brunner's theory. In a reader Rosenbaum reproduced Brunner's most relevant text with some very prudent critical remarks in the introduction, but six years later even this disappeared.[367]

As Rosenbaum looks for the reasons why farmers/ peasants have absolute dominance as house-father, she accepts Brunner's dictum: "The house (*oikos*) is thus a whole, based on the inequality of its parts, that transform into a unity by the leading spirit of the lord." The concept house-father receives its logic only through the power to dominate. Therefore, Mitterauer calls the house

365 Hans-Ulrich Wehler, 1989, volume 1, 71.

366 Hans-Ulrich Wehler, 1989, volume 1, 119. Compare also Idem, volume 2, 413, 422. See also the highly remarkable universal unchangeabilities in a 2000 year period in Hermann Kellenbenz, 1981, volume 2, 31: "The old society from the basis goes back into Greek antiquity ... had its center of gravity in the 'economy within the house.' This old society started to crumble with the industrialization, so that new structures could take their place."

367 Heidi Rosenbaum, ed., 1978.

"a social form organized through a dominant lord" (*dominant herrschaftlich organisierte Sozialform*). From this is derived the sole political and juridical ability of the man, or house-father, to act.[368]

Knowing all the well-known ideological backgrounds, Rosenbaum, notwithstanding this, declares without any hesitation:

> Whatever its ideological content, in my opinion Brunner's proposed concept of the "Whole House" is better able to analyze traditional peasant ways of life. The social form "Whole House" is characterized by the unity of production and household; the unpaid labor from members of the family; the servants who live within the house-community; the domination of the house-father over everybody else in the house.... In such an understanding of the concept "Whole House" are central characteristics of peasant way of life and labor-relations demonstrated.... In my view this analytically sharper and more useful concept is to be preferred.[369]

It is no surprise that Rosenbaum also relies on Brunner's model and this leads for the dissolution of the Whole House, of course, to the negation of this model: so, not unity, but separation from household and business, etc.[370] It is clear that this current family research provides nearly no basis for criticism of Brunner's *oikos*-theory.

However, Brunner's most important influence is not yet mentioned. It concerns the realm that in German is called *Verfassungsgeschichte* (not so much the history of constitutions or laws, but more particularly that of state-organizations and their legitimations) with its German structural-historical tradition. Apart from Brunner this tradition is supported by influential historians like W. Schlesinger, Th. Mayer, H. Dannenbauer, K. Bosl. H.K. Schulze or H. Hirsch and their pupils; many other "old Comrades" ("Alte Kameraden") like Franz Petri or Franz Steinbach found their spiritual *oikos* here.[371] They form

---

368 Heidi Rosenbaum, 1982, 85. Richard J. Evans provides an interesting profile from Riehl und his popular works as *Die Familie*, 1858. This book "was a romantic hymn of praise for the patriarchal peasant family, though perhaps as he portrayed it it was to a great extent the product of his imagination." Richard J. Evans and W. Lee, ed., 1981, 260.

369 Heidi Rosenbaum, 1982, 116; see 176 as well.

370 Heidi Rosenbaum in: Michael Mitterauer and Reinhard Sieder, ed., 1982, 57–59. It concerns a text from 1977.

371 For the influential Nazi historian, Franz Petri, see my forthcoming *Victims and Perpetrators*, 2018 Chapter 6.

a quite aggressive and closed group of medievalists and other historians, for which Brunner played a leading, if not the most important role.[372]

In particular, thanks to the indefatigable but lonely fight of the legal historian Karl Kroeschell, a detailed picture of this—euphemistically labeled—anachronistic group, that dominated long after 1945 the scene, is sketched.

The group's activities resulted in the development of many other concepts around Brunner's house-oikos; in a more or less systematic way arose a network of concepts that covered a series of important phenomena. So stand, along house-*oikos*, for example, country-, house-, land-authority (*Grundherrschaft*), retinue-Herrschaft (*Gefolgsherrschaft*) or something like "the German State in the Middle Ages."

Inside these concepts new one's with a smaller area of influence were located like *Schutz* (protection from the man, head of the family or Lord), *Schirm* (certain compensations from the Lord, etc.), *Gewere* (the power of the man, etc. to dispose over life and goods of other family-members, etc.), *Munt* (=*Schutzherrschaft* of the man, head of the family, etc.), or the interesting *Geblütsheil* (charisma received from God that gives good luck in battle, or other difficult acts), etc., etc.

Anyway, Karl Kroeschell has given a detailed and uncontradicted criticism of this conceptual rain and its alleged reality covered by sound sources. Of course, his main attack concerned the cornerstone of all this, the *Hausherrschaft*, i.e. the authority in/of the house-*oikos*. His conclusion is crystal-clear:

> In the Middle Ages the abstract idea of the "'Herrschaft" was alien. (Dem Mittelalter war [aber] die abstrakte Vorstellung von "der Herrschaft" fremd.)[373]

For historians and sociologists the studies supported by these "sound sources" on concrete social situations in town and country are not the last basis on which one has to rely.

Take, for instance, the relevant studies of D.W. Sabean.[374] He researched 8,000 documents in Neckarhausen but only twice found the singular "house," rather often, however, he did find the verb "hausen." He criticized Brunner

372 For examples see Karl Kroeschell, 1983, 102.

373 Karl Kroeschell, 1980, volume 2, 158. This legal history is, by the way, a goldmine for realistic interpretations of old legal and juridical practices.

374 David W. Sabean, 1990. In particular, "The ideology of the house," 88–124. Here he mentions the "oikos controversy" in which also Brunner is rightly placed, 95.

> because he thought of the house as a single, substantial entity... he did not understand the representational character of "*Haus*" for state and church officials bent on hegemonic control through the construction of moral hierarchies.[375]

Probably more important is his conclusion that reminds us of Mauss' exchange-studies or of the many subtle relations in life:

> We have come to think of a household as a place where various exchanges took place, where one and the same act might have different meanings for a particular couple, their respective kin, and for the administrative agents of the wider polity.[376]

Herewith the sharpest contradictions with the above house-*oikos* ideologues are expressed: in fact, Sabean comes to the fore with real market-relationships, which I also discovered in ancient Greece and situations in the early Middle Ages.

The results of Sabean's highly revealing Neckarhausen-studies are underpinned by the research of Rainer Beck on the Bavarian village Underfinning.[377] Here the concrete interdependencies between individual "Houses," communal resources and "collective" ways of economizing in the village are demonstrated very well. It is good to see that here animal husbandry is seen as fundamental.[378]

However, the large discrepancy between the German conceptual means and the historical realities are demonstrated as well. Beck still works with a market-definition as negation of the *oikos*[379] and nothing more, although his clear performance shows abundantly how not only money and prices, but also ecology, labor, divisions of labor, animals and men, town and country do have altering exchange-relations with each other, while these have the ability to further develop slowly or quickly. Thanks to these sketches of concrete relationships, we can conclude autarkic, authoritarian-male "Whole Houses" simply do not and cannot exist.

375 David W. Sabean, 1990, 91 ff.

376 David W. Sabean, 1990, 122.

377 Rainer Beck, 1993.

378 Rainer Beck, 1993, 56–57, 86, 107, 139–140.

379 Rainer Beck, 1993, 20 for example uses here also the concept "naturale Ökonomie" for a, at least, for 80% by people created environment; on 617, note 6 he refers as self-evident to pure oikoïdal theories of Polanyi, Cajanov and Medick.

3.6 The End of an Ideology?

At the end of this problem-definition, tensions between ideology and reality are nearly unbearable, but there are possibilities to diminish them. Opitz, for instance, could have asked why concepts like "house-*oikos*" or "whole house" had and have such a enormous fascination for historians and sociologists leading to questions in several directions; which historical practice in which period must have been covered? With which political aims and by whom were these concepts used?

For a historian, "ideology" is part of reality, but this does not mean that it refrains from bringing an ideology, but rather that it receives a realistic place within our complex existence and its history. This means that historians should always execute an ideology-criticism, an activity for which they are in need of strong cooperation with, in particular, sociologists.

The more important task, however, is to prove that an ideological concept or model can be found elsewhere in the historical practice. From Aristotle onwards until today the house-*oikos* concept is used by parts of the elite as a metaphor for the whole of society, as political model for the ordering of the economy or the relations between men and women. It seems no exaggeration to state that in a European history of political thought there is no concept with a longer tradition and differentiated meaning. It is, therefore, not a good idea to throw Brunner's Whole House away, because it seems to be the German Herrschafts-model *par excellence.*

It is the task to analyze how and why a certain society in a specific period reacted to the attempt to mold it into the Procrustean-bed of the *oikos*-model. It is no lesser task to demonstrate market practices in all possible areas and situations that have left behind the ideological "market" as pure negation of the house-*oikos* model. For German historians and sociologists, for instance, it could mean a quite important way to come to grips with its dark past.

At last, a problem-definition of the notion of the "whole house" could be perceived as a "network of historical concepts" that originated in phases spread over many scientific disciplines. If a historian or sociologist wants to spin that he or she has to know how the network is conceived in order to produce adequate preconditions for relevant histories and sociological analyses.

CHAPTER 4

Oikoïdal Qualities: *Rasse, Volk* and *Nation*

4.1 Introduction: Weber and Rasse

There are several occasions on which Max Weber implicitly or explicitly wrote about *Rasse* (race), using the concept in an affirmative way, sometimes critically as well, but never in an outspokenly negative way like "races do not exist," etc.[380] In a later chapter on ancient Judaism, a demonstration of an implicit anti-Semitism is given. From this, it could be concluded that this cannot be defined as racism although the latter often implies anti-Semitism as well or is accompanied by it.

In the famous introduction to Weber's *The Protestant Ethic and the Spirit of Capitalism* (1904–1905) its author

> confesses how he, personally and subjectively, perceives biological hereditary as very important... [in this specific dossier, however, he cannot use the results of]... the important achievements of anthropological work.[381]

Notwithstanding this, in contrast to a dominant trend in Germany and Europe, Weber was hesitating to fully accept the Rasse-rhetoric of his days, and the pseudo-scientific support for its theories: his nationalism was already as wild as necessary for the very near future in Germany.[382]

Weber died too early to make the next step to a full National-Socialist position possible; he could not evolve beyond being more than member of a

380 In the first period of his public life, he delivered his very nationalistic *Antrittsrede* (1895), *Der Nationalstaat und die Volkswirtschaftspolitik;* see GPS, 1–25. Here the practical, political interrelations between the German *Ostpolitik* and the Polish *Westpolitik* is at stake and Weber behaves often as a bad-tempered political agitator, labelling the influx of Polish immigrants as "wild animals." Another time the race-issue comes to the fore in a large study entitled *Zur Psychophysik der industriellen Arbeit* (1908). See GASS, 61–255. Probably the most explicit non-political attention paid to the concept is his reaction on a contribution of Alfred Ploetz, one of the main "rassenhygienischen" propagandists in Germany (1910). See GASS, 456–462.

381 GARS, 15.

382 Here "scientific" support can be only defined as "support by people with some scientific background." In hindsight it concerned always "pseudo" (today: "nep") knowledge. Before the Second World War still few people doubted its sound scientific content, certainly when it was demonstrated by peoples "in white coats."

 | DOI:10.1163/9789004383913_005

benevolent, nationalist and overly anti-Semitic elite. Still, in the first pages of *Wirtschaft und Gesellschaft* (WG), he declares that the results of the classical Rasse-research (with its skull- and skin-color measurements) are acceptable once more statistical evidence is provided.[383]

It is no accident that his discussion is combined here with explainations with the typical oikoidal concepts like *Vergemeinschaftung* (making communal relations) or *Auslese* (selection of members of the community) as antagonists in "the struggle (Kampf)" of the market and in the *Vergesellschaftung* (making association, communication) between partners in the exchange (competition).[384] It seems to be no accident either, that he refers here explicitly to Jews in the sense that they chose for *Vergemeinschaftung* "to a very limited extent"; this in contrast to Zionists.

It is important to stress here the background for Weber's "preliminary position" in a few remarks since it is a reproduction of the fundamental intellectual and political changes in Europe around 1900. They do not concern so much an autonomous *Rasse*-discourse, which has seldom been demonstrated in serious scholarly work to date. However, rather dangerous confusions arose and still arise about the *combination* Nation(alism)–*Rasse*–*Volk*–Language, its consequences for imperialistic and colonial adventures against the East, etc. The rest of this chapter presents a detailed analysis of how this combination developed in Europe in a concrete setting of stubborn nationalism and colonialism from which we are still suffering.

Remember that this combination was known in 19th century USA as well as being practically the main source of the genocide of the so-called Indians, mass slavery of the "negroes" and general discrimination against the "colored," all three by the civilized European "white settlers." Here also an alternative was available and it is good to refer to it at the start of this chapter.

It is Thorstein Veblen who demonstrated this to date in of all books his famous *Imperial Germany and the Industrial Revolution* (1915). This was unknown to Weber or Sombart. They did not know of other books by Veblen either, though he is still known as "the most creative mind American social thought had produced" (Max Lerner).[385]

383 WG, 3.

384 WG, 22, 23.

385 *The Portable Veblen,* 1948, 2. Sombart and Weber not even knew Veblen's famous *The Theory of the Leisure Class,* 1899. This is rather unbelievable because of their visits to the USA (Weber) or publications on USA-socialism (Sombart). This neglect could be even called "a German neglect and arrogance" when one consults the post-war German sociological handbooks. In Hartfiel-Hillmann's sociological lexicon, 1972. is even stated that Veblen is inspired by the *Historische Schule*; in Veit Bader, ed. 1976, an introduction to Marx and

What can be learned from him for our subject must be indicated in a few words while knowing that Veblen did not refuted a race-concept *as such* but avoided its use. Veblen complains that "painstaking historians" are not free from confusing matters. In their and others'

> ... colloquial use of "race" this concept is taken without a relation to "nation" and "people" [*Volk*]. Whatever else it may be taken to convey, "race" always implies a solidarity of inheritance within the group so designated... "Race" is a biological concept... "nation" or "people" do not necessarily imply such a biological solidarity... recourse is usually had [to] the community of language [as well]... [these confusions occur] in cases where there is in fact ground for nothing more substantial than a discriminating comparison between divergent schemes of use and wont.... A meticulous discrimination between the two concepts—of habit and heredity—is the beginning of wisdom in all inquiry into human behavior... [the confusion of both is more serious]... the larger the burden of chauvinism ... the more spectacular and sweeping has been its output of systematic blunders. ... *das deutsche Volk*... is in no defensible sense... a distinct race, even after all allowance has been made for intrusive elements in the population, such as the Jews or the Germanised Poles and Danes. The German people are not a distinct race either as against the non-German populations of Europe or within itself. ... [only]... the divergence in the cultural type may yet be serious enough.[386] (italics from Veblen.)

This is the cultural framework of Thorstein Veblen's social, economic and historical thought; the biological elements of European civilization have not changed much since "its Neolithic source." It's clear that people like Weber and Sombart did not received this level of sophistication about the concepts at issue.

Thanks to several UNESCO declarations it is no longer possible to accept a race-concept, but it remains an historical fact that in some form or another the *combination* with nation etc. was exploited and still is exploited under some circumstances. The "blunders" Veblen referred to could not be avoided.[387]

Weber, no discussion on the relevant thoughts of Veblen is given; these are as well absent in Kreber's sociological lexicon, 1984; in Dirk Kaesler's *Klassiker der Soziologie,* 1999 an article concerns a fully overrated Norbert Elias, but a Veblen is negated. At last, this happened as well in the newest *Soziologiegeschichte,* 2015 of 600 pages.

386 *The Portable Veblen,* 1948, 297–305 which are a series of quotations from the introduction to his *Imperial Germany,* 1915.

387 Remarkable expectations still exist in the USA: several recent publications (Steve Garner, George Yancy, Linda M. Alcoff) report not only that "white European Americans" are set

Therefore, Christian Geulen could recently write a highly relevant analysis about how Germany at the end of the 19th century there developed a brand-new "biopolitical project" with the substantial help of new natural sciences—in particular physical anthropology, biology and medicine—so that some "national community" became defined as *Volkskörper* ("body of the people") or *Volksgemeinschaft*.[388]

The rhetoric and terminology of the social descriptions changed accordingly, for instance, as the "heart" of the city; the traffic in the streets as the "blood in the arteries" and consequently a "heart attack" for a traffic-jam; a park as "the lungs"; and thus, the "health" and "hygiene" of a *Volk* became hot political items. The radical state interventions into city and other life were consequently called "surgical operations" as though by a medical doctor who cannot be stopped or criticised. In this framework the Rasse-thinking fit perfectly well with all consequences.

A famous physical anthropologist and politician like Rudolf Virchow (1821–1902) was inspired by the German unification of the 1870s and formulated a "rational religion" in substitution for the "old" church confessions. This consisted of a population theory for a *Volk* supported by, among others, extensive investigations into the division of blond and brown people in the German population as the two "Urrassen" (Jews were definitely subsumed under the less worthwhile brown people, although about 11% of them were blond and from a "bodily point of view" there were no differences between "German" and "Jewish" peoples).[389]

---

to become a minority within a quarter of a century. In particular after Obama's election "the number of racial hate group sharply increased" (*Times Literary Supplement*, 8-1-2016 review of Alcoff's *The Future of Whiteness*). Alcoff criticizes left-wing scholars who separate class and race because "they are deeply integrated in structures of oppression." That seems clear enough thanks to the rather epidemic killings of (unarmed) black boys by white police officers, but it is far from clear. Ta-Nehisi Coates' attack (2017) on *white supremacy* is understandable and necessary notwithstanding black victim's like criticisms of peoplle like Cornell West.

But let's leave it here to "American Facts": that it concerns as well black police officers who kill blacks; among the American poor colored people are in the majority; that the USA has the highest crime rate and most expanded *prison- and weapon industry* as nowhere in the world; the USA lost its "war on drugs" as it lost all other wars after 1945 (except the one against the small rather unarmed island Grenada) and is left with an extensive culture of fear and violence; this seems to become its main export article: see Obama's only innovation, the world wide drones-war backed by world-wide operating secret services, or, the enormous amounts of money Obama and Trump exchanged for weapons in the Middle East to start new wars or the vulgar threatening language used by "atomic mammoth" Trump against "rocket mice" North Corea.

388 WG, 242.

389 Cristian Geulen, 2004, 113–115.

Together with the then virulent Rasse-theories and anti-Semitism, the perception of a nation as *Volkskörper* created nearly automatically a radical enmity against "the other": the racial struggle became synonymous with the struggle between nations as *Volkskörper.* A basic notion was that a *Volk* could prove its racial superiority externally only by waging war and gaining *Lebensraum* and internally only by making everybody eugenically and racially pure while disposing of the non-pure.

Before 1800 *Rasse* (race, razza, etc.) was something external to civilized "white" European peoples and part of a superficial imperialistic stance with mythical connotations about strange foreign peoples, animals and plants. However, around 1900, it was a common perception in this civilized Europe that (parts of) its own population itself belonged to a *Rasse* (etc.) and, therefore, could be ethnically defined in some tribal and *völkisch* way.

This *new* definition was not so much a cultural or xenophobic matter but first and foremost a biological, linguistic, psychological and physical-anthropological nature; it also covered a social-Darwinian *valuation* and every form of belligerent European *nationalism.* All this was strongly supported by scholars from many disciplines; at that time this kind of support covered scholarly content as well. It took about sixty years before it was officially acknowledged that races did not exist at all, but even until today the conclusion that, *therefore* no *combination* of *Nation-Volk-Language-Rasse* can exist, is not officially drawn.

On the contrary: directly from 1900 onwards until today, there appear the terrible consequences of this *combination* as one genocide after the other is performed, all originating from European (colonial) sources. The end of this misery cannot be seen now that the strata responsible for it once again hold strong political positions in the USA and Europe.

The present troubles in the whole of the Middle East, for instance, have their sources in the former and present European (neo)colonial practices. If one should want to counteract the widespread attempts to "take revenge on the West" one has to abandon all (traits of) the former "surgical" colonial interventions including its territorial presence through wars and occupations.

The preparations to arrive at this situation started about two centuries earlier. The impulses came from the Enlightenment and French Revolution. Many *separate* activities with their own histories, now called scientific disciplines (from state administration, political-economic practices to agronomical sciences), and ways of thinking aimed at *combining* fields of knowledge (mechanicism and the alternative organicism) merged slowly in the 19th century.[390]

390 An inspiring analysis of this proces is David F. Lindenfeld's history, 1997, of the German sciences of state (*Staatswissenschaften*) which is not used by Geulen. See from the latter 25–26.

At the end the social-Darwinist and nationalist oriented natural sciences dominated; the other sciences like history and social sciences eventually had to accommodate to them.

Max Weber and certainly Werner Sombart soon became important German scholars and young leaders of the *Historical School*. Confident of their own social scientific and historical abilities, they did not want to surrender to the natural scientific domination. Their response to it was quite different.

They both were struggling against the old conservative feudal interests like the *Junkers* and churches and supported the modernization of Germany that would making it an industrial society; both accepted the inevitability of capitalism and imperialism, while they later fanatically supported the German World War (1914–1918). Both had a peculiar, rather anti-Semitic, relationship with Jewish religion (Weber) and history (Sombart), but the former was not interested in actual Zionism while the latter was a rather strong supporter albeit for more or less opportunistic reasons (see below).[391]

However, they were quite different personalities. For instance, Weber was much more interested in religious and abstract-theoretical problems; politically he showed time and again a strong attraction to problems of nationalistic state-organizations. Sombart was in everything a much more down-to earth man and interested more in social politics and activism, while thanks to his easy life-style he could tell his colleagues in 1899, that "to want to be moral at the cost of economic progress is the beginning of the end of the whole development of civilization."[392]

Whatever their other differences, Sombart wrote several bestsellers and quickly became "world-known," while this only happened to Weber long after his death. Strong nationalism (Weber) and social activism (Sombart) urged them to mitigate the devastating effects of "capitalism" (see chapter 1), but they pointed to different solutions.

In the end, Weber accepted a "rational state nationalism" in a rather mechanistic framework. At the end of their lives Sombart accepted National Socialism, but Weber died too early for us to define his choice with certainty. However, in my view, Weber would have made the same choice, but for a different reason: the nationalist one was the "better" organization of the state. Sombart was typically *völkisch* and opted for an "organic" National Socialism for a "better" life for the *Volk*. The racial element did not fit perfectly in the

391 For the general anti-Semitic attitudes among German intellectualls see Joachim Radkau, 2005, 678–698 with, among others, a rather old-fashioned perception of the "Ancient Judaism" problem.

392 Quoted in David Lindenfeld, 1997, 301.

former "rational choice" contrary to the other more "emotional and sentimental choice."

Still, there was a lacuna in both their works. From the given combination of Nation-Volk-Rasse-Language, none of the two paid much attention to language notwithstanding that this theme was very popular in all "Aryan" discourses, focusing on the developments of Indo-German languages and so on. The more or less official definition of *Volk* was clear enough:

> Eine durch Rasse und gemeinsamen Volksboden geprägte naturhafte Gemeinschaft von gemeinsamer Abstamming, Geschichte, Sprache und Kultur, die einer starken Führung und steter Erziehung und Ausrichtung bedarf.[393] (*Volk* is a natural community characterized by race, common land, common descent, history, language and culture; this community is in need of a strong leadership, education and indoctrination.)

The above must be enough as introduction to the main text of this chapter. The subject concerns a detailed analysis of how the national-socialist Rasse-propaganda played a much larger role in thought after the end of W.W.II: even those who suffered in Europe most from Rasse (race, etc.) politics were not only used by the main colonial powers to create or sustain colonies, but to spread the most simple and influential European nationalistic doctrine, to date, abroad. This is as well the last existing example of all those new western colonial ventures established in the period 1800–1948, which a few years later had to be abandonned wholesale, though not yet in the Middle East with all possible consequences.

Therefore, the subject of the following chapter is a very curious and interesting case to which people like Werner Sombart and Max Weber contributed much of their scholarly attention and positive support. The subject concerns basic "oikoidal qualities" because their common characteristic was that they were all directed to the *internal* conditions of the *oikos*-as-state and society, to the means to define, select and integrate the "pure" and allies, and to expurgate the "impure" and those defined as enemies.

4.2 "Jewish" *Rasse* Theories Now

Thanks to a big brouhaha in Israel about Shlomo Sand's *The Invention of the Jewish People* (2009), Rasse theories are receiving a renewed attention. In this "holy" land these theories constitute an *internal* Jewish and Zionist struggle

393 Cornelia Schmitz-Berning, 2000, 642.

about their antagonistic identities. Its background was/is the profound doubts about whether Jews and Zionists rightly occupy the land of the indigenous peoples, the Palestinians.[394]

At least indirectly, the struggle also concerns the earlier "inventions" of people like Maurice Fishberg, Paul Kaznelson, Arthur Ruppin, Redcliffe Nathan Salaman, Aron Sandler or Ignaz Zollschan before the war and Patai, Falk or Sand himself after 1948, and can be summed up by the tensions of a "Jewish Rasse, not a Zionist Rasse."[395]

It is good to know beforehand that in a proto-Zionist way of thinking all principal elements of it are demonstrated. In a speech titled *Der Nationaljude* (May 1892) somebody told a Berlin meeting:

> We can be and must be proud to belong to a Semitic race and a Jewish Volk that made and developed a large part of modern culture in many ways. We have to consider that we should be the most cultivated and most intelligent element of all human races if we could live today in *one* state and *one* country. It is not necessary to deny a honourable national history of many thousand years, nor to deny the blood-relationship with many thousands of martyrs (Blutzeugen) of the Jewish Volk...[396]

The vehemence with which the debate was carried on after 1948 proved that a still open vein was hit. As so often in Israel, it led to names calling, while the subject matter was not discussed at all, let alone did it not lead to a policy change. The particular subject, the uneasy conscience for occupying a foreign country, remains unresolved and emerges again anew.

394 Ilan Pappe, 2017, 23–50. We do not intend to discuss the many problems between Palestinians and Israelis or other actors in the realm. Pappe's booklet is a relevant introduction to them.

395 It is useless to refer as well to the shocking experience of the famous anthology of Yiddish *Witze,* and see how the "Jüdische Rasse" concept is defended anew in the full conscience of the Nazi use of it in Salcia Landmann, 1974, 38–65. It goes without saying that Landmann provides us with the usual mix of most non-sensical reasonings, half-truths, so-called scientific facts and approved opinions. Three typical 19th century authorities like Disraeli, Marx and Freud are enough for her to believe that "die Rassenlehre sei überhaupt der Schlüssel zur gesamten Weltgeschichte" (64). It remains interesting that Landmann time and again relies on nomadic-Bedouin analyses to make her point: see, for example, 14 or 144.

396 Quoted in Jehuda Reinharz, ed., 1981, 31. The speech was given in 1892 which is five years before the first Zionist Congress. The speaker is Heinrich Loewe, 1869–1951, among other editor of the influential *Jüdischen Rundschau.* The speech is also an example of the extreme minority feelings basic to the given exaggerations about some Jewish or Zionist influence, which were at the time very limited or non-existent in the West.

The most important orthodox Jewish theologian, Yeshayahu Leibowitz (1903–1994), gave the healthiest and most relevant answers for these cases. It is well known that Leibowitz denied that the state of Israel had any Jewish religious significance and therefore defended the complete separation between religion and state.[397] This was a most serious criticism of current Zionism, which is—whatever its secular background—always in need of a religious Jewish cloak that is eagerly provided by some rabbis in exchange for financial and other privileges.

Leibowitz was among the first Israeli intellectuals who stated, immediately after the Six Day War in 1967, that if Israel held on to the occupied territories, this would lead to the decline of Israel's moral stature. And that happened in an overwhelming and fully underestimated way, while the USA was carried away as well by this tremendous loss of prestige in the world. Leibowitz demonstrated this himself by accusing Israeli soldiers of a "Judeo-Nazi" mentality, a sentiment recently repeated by the famous novelist Amos Oz, intellectual spirit of the Israeli *Peace Now* movement.

Notwithstanding these outspoken opinions, in 2005, Leibowitz was chosen by the general public participating in an Israeli poll as "the 20th greatest Israeli of all time." Concerning our subject he stated the following in an interview:

> The historical Jewish people is not defined as a race and not as the people of a particular land or of a specific political framework, nor even of a particular language, but as the people of the Torah and religious prescriptions…

The journalist Boaz Evron, who is obliged to live from the "empirical facts" and managed to become a sparring partner of Leibowitz, adds to this:

> If we give the state the operational definition of "the Jewish state," a state that has to be Jewish, we are immediately confronted with the question "Who is a Jew?" I do not want to, nor can I, decide who is a Jew. Nobody is able to do that.

And again Leibowitz:

---

397 For the opinions quoted below, it is important to know that Leibowitz was not only a theologian, but that he taught biochemistry and neurophysiology for nearly six decades, disciplines quite important in the development of a race-concept; see *Wikipedia* under "Yeshayahu Leibowitz." He is not mentioned in Ilan Pappe, 2017.

> Our problem cannot be "Where to go with the state of Israel?" ... but "The present Jewish people: what is this?" And again, it is a question which I cannot answer empirically; there is no human being and no institution allowed to pose this question from a normative point of view and to answer it.[398]

Indeed, a theologian is by definition unable to answer something empirically; they must keep their God always available. Still, in the present situation real Jews should be guided by this man and his writings, while the secular Israelis could profitably use them against the rigorous, mostly American colonists who haunt the country, giving the occupation the character of a true Christian crusade against the pagans.

Leibowitz's opinions can be discerned in the USA as well, in for instance, the *Jews for Peace* movement and even among the few Jews known as Zionists like the novelist of Romanian origin, Maurice Samuel (1895–1972). He, who is also called a rabbi, extends Leibowitz's argumentation. In an essay about "Rasse and Nation in the Jewish Bible," published after the Six Day War, he came to the following conclusion:

> The belief that war is an innate necessity of man, with the implication that powerful warrior states are born to rule other states, falls away. War is something that is learned. It is not in the genes, in the blood. It is a vice that man has picked up... rationalising it with the belief that rivalry is more creative than cooperation... This belief is in essence racial, since it subordinates man to an unchangeable psychological make-up; and it is therefore natural that the most warlike peoples should be the most prone to racist illusions. Such illusions find no countenance in the Jewish Bible...[399]

398 The quotations are from Yeshayahu Leibowitz, 1993, 25, 117 and 171 respectively. Shlomo Sand, 2009, 284 also referred to him, but clearly did not read his book. That is strange. This booklet is the translation of the important discussion between Leibowitz, Zimmermann, Galnor, Burg, Evron and Naor, mostly from the Hebrew University of Jerusalem. It was originally published as *Am, Erets, Medina* (Jerusalem: Shorashim Institute, 1992). It is selfevident that Leibowitz denies the importance of race in this respect; see for the combination race-nation in Shlomo Sand, 2009 and in particular the important Ernest Renan as given in Shlomo Sand, 2014. If one is looking for strange definitions of Jews, compare a Protestant view in Paul Achtemeier, ed., 1996, 525 with a Catholic one in Xavier Léon-Dufour, ed., 1962, 512–513.

399 Maurice Samuel in: A. Leland Jamison, ed., 1978, 45 and he reminds the Israeli a page earlier to the famous dictum repeated several times in this Bible: "they shall beat their swords

Now, the importance of the Sand controversy was that a secular "Jew-insider," or Zionist, questioned the Israeli legitimation of being in Palestine. Against a similar opinion of about 98% of the world, including almost all international legal institutions, people are secured inside secular Israel by the largest wall around "their" land and mind.

In Sand's book the ambiguous Bible is not used as the source of his arguments. Nor did he discuss my Hannah Arendt book of four years earlier, giving the strong impression that he was poorly copying it, starting with the main thesis, that something like a "Jewish *Volk*" does not exist.[400]

Sand provided many opportunities to avoid discussing a few highly important questions about the residence of Zionists and/or Jews in that corner of the Middle East.[401] There could have been a discussion of Zionist interests to exploit Judaism; or the possible invention of Jews by Christians in late antiquity; or the possible invention of a "Jewish *Volk*" in the 19th century; or why people started to talk and write about some "Jewish race (Rasse)" in the 19th century; or why no Zionists *as such* arrived in Auschwitz, which happened only after they were defined *as Jews* through the available German *Rasse* theories and practices; and so on. If Sand was hired to make these debates impossible, then he has done a wonderful job.

Outside Israeli or Zionist circles, a new literature is developing, that is not halting for sacred cows, most of which have been slaughtered by all sorts of international institutions and thanks to their own rude behavior.[402] The old concepts from around 1918, when Zionism started its conquest of Palestine, is subject of this literature now, including the Rasse and Volk theories. One cannot

into ploughshares and their spears into pruning hooks; nation shall not lift up swords against nation, neither shall they learn any more war." Isa. 2:2–4; Mic. 4:1–3. How utopian this was Samuel probably knew as he decided to join the Zionists, early in his life. This was shortly after the first belligerent Zionists in 1917 entered Palestine openly aiming to expel all the indigenous inhabitants from their homes and country by force.

400 See Hans Derks, 2004, 150, 248–251, 316–317.

401 This thanks to his ambiguous "Khazars solution"; his poor knowledge about ancient history; his poor knowledge about the performance of Zionism in Palestine since 1917; his promising start with a "Jewish race" discussion and rudimentary continuation with it; the indefensible "post-Zionism" thesis; etc. A rather devastating review of his book was published by the classical historian and Zionist, Martin Goodman, in *Times Literary Supplement*, 26-2-2010, 7. Notwithstanding this: if Shlomo Sand did not existed, he must have been invented; a spoilsport as him was needed after the Peace movement and people like Avishai Margalit or Amos Oz were silent or converted and ideologues as Martin van Creveld or Benny Morris could continue threatening with genocide and atomic bombs. See furthermore the excellent Shlomo Sand, 2010 and 2014 or Ilan Pappe, 2017, 11 and 21.

402 The most recent is the 2017 affront concerning Trump's and Netanyahu's plan to replace the USA Ambassy to Jerusalem, which was perceived by *all* other countries in the world as a violation of international law and a provocation to start a new war.

forget how these theories are closely connected to Western colonial exploitation and racism; the mandatory settlement of the British was the last colonial activity ever of its kind by the Western world at large.[403]

This said, we could continue the discussion about the interwar years, the period in which the later Shoah and Holocaust victims were growing up in Germany, Poland or the Netherlands or were busy fighting for a colonial future in Palestine, often quite optimistically. Shlomo Sand did not discover their interesting publications.

The theories of the Zionist Ignaz Zollschan are chosen as a good vehicle to demonstrate the ins and outs of Zionist, "Jewish" or Israeli Rasse thoughts. After 1945 he is still discussed in Israel on a small scale, as will be revealed below. Zollschan is not only the most discussed author from before the war, he represents the new Zionist discourse around the end of World War I when the Palestine adventure of the British-Zionists started. That is the constellation in which his Rasse theory should be considered.

4.3 Some "Devastating" Comments in Advance

An opinion like the one by Sander Gilman seems the best to start with:

> The tone is set in what is without a doubt the most important Viennese contribution by a Jew to the question of the racial identity of the Jews, a study by Ignaz Zollschan, that first appeared in Vienna in 1912. Zollschan, a physician whose strong support of political Zionism made him an opponent of Nazi racial anthropology, redirects the Jewish question in two specific ways… determining the racial value of the Jews… [and]… whether it is possible to speak of a discrete Jewish race…[404]

The status of this quote is remarkable, because a few sentences earlier an excellent scholar like Gilman mentions names like Sigmund Freud, Otto Weininger and Ludwig Wittgenstein in this Viennese environment.

The question is, of course, which tone is set by Zollschan. That it concerns a controversial figure was already clear in 1912 as Zionism was only supported

403 For the following discussion I used Ellis Cashmore, ed., 1994, 64–68; Tim Ingold, ed.,1997, passim; Adam and Jessica Kuper, ed., 1999, articles "race" and "racism"; interesting are also the lemmas "race" (Boas), "race conflict" (Kohn) and "race mixture" (Herskovits) in ESS, volume XIII. For the colonial expansion of the British in the Middle East after World War I, see the excellent James Renton (2007).

404 Sander Gilman, 1996, 104.

by a very tiny minority among Jews, let alone by people outside this religion. In this perspective, the first thing one should remark about a Zionist like Zollschan is that he has been largely forgotten in the present official Zionist historiography.[405]

Apart from the fact that Zionism is no longer what it once was, there is a clear reason for this and it says as much about this historiography as about Zollschan. He is politically considered a Zionist, but not one of the power-political nationalists arriving in 1917 with the British army. The earlier European settlers with a Jewish background or the Oriental Jews (*Sephardim*), who had lived for centuries in the region, soon became enemies of the newly arrived Zionists (*Ashkenazim*) because the latter came to conquer, while the other had lived for centuries in peace among the Palestinians.[406]

The militant post-1918 Zionist pioneers (the so called "sabra's), succeeded only thanks to the help of the British, their own ruthless anti-Arab activities and European/USA money to drive the indigenous population out of their country. They acted like the Dutch Boers in South Africa or French colons in Algeria with the same kind of devastating consequences, except that in this case there was no Nelson Mandela or Charles de Gaulle to finish off the "masquerade."[407]

I do not know whether Zollschan was a Jew at all. From his writings it seems unlikely because no Jewish theological argument or reasoning is ever used. Zollschan was not a friend of aggressive Zionist activities, but was also not explicitly against them. There are also quite different and probably better reasons

405 Among those who fully negate this politically active Jewish Zionist and gifted writer are: Georges Bensoussan, Walter Laqueur, David Vital or Bernard Wasserstein, let alone the radical political Zionist writers like Benny Morris, etc. What is, in fact, astonishing is that even young German researchers like Veronika Lipphardt, 2008 or Dirk Rupnow, 2011, do not know Zollschan at all. Today Zionism has no clever defenders and that seems to be the case as well with Israel. The top-executors of its well-known pre-emptive strikes and disproportional measures were "clever" enough to show up in Dror Moreh's film *The Gatekeepers*, 2012. Its cast is formed by six unbelievable arrogant heads of Israeli security agencies talking about their dirty work as if they were consuming cakes in a lunchroom.

406 Jeff Halper, 1991 shows how this antagonism between Sephardim and Ashkenazim in Palestine became more complicated around 1850: an old and ultra-orthodox group of the latter from Eastern Europe started to live in Jerusalem as inexperienced newcomers in the environment of about 40–50% of all Sephardim called "Oriental Jews." These were fully integrated in the Muslim society and dressed in the indigenous clothes. In the text, we address the new Polish and Russian Ashkenazim, die-hard Zionists who immigrated after about 1925. Raphael Patai, 1975, 49 concludes as a consequence of the *present* situation, that he can negate Sephardim even in the distant past.

407 It is the title of one of the best analyses of the formative years of the Zionists in Palestine, James Renton, 2007.

for Zollschan's negation than that he did not suit some military tasks. The historian Joachim Doron concluded in 1980 that

> based on the very rich sources... it is to state without any doubt: in the Zionist ideology there is no authoritarian claim based on racist superiority.[408]

But as early as 1969 another historian, Egmont Zechlin, wrote quite the opposite:

> In fact, both the Rasse—anti-Semitism... and the Jewish nationalism worked largely with the same conceptual system, the same thinking—models and value-criteria... Both the Rasse—anti-Semitism and this völkische Zionism stated that they had an inextricable binding to a "Community of the Blood" ...[409]

Faced with these contradictory opinions, Bacharach tried to answer the questions of whether something like a "Jewish Rasse-theory" existed and whether Zollschan was a Rasse-theoretician. These tasks were too difficult for Bacharach because he supposed that ethnology as well as

> Rassenkunde is a science that tried to look for empirical proof of their theses, while Rasse-theory is nothing but a Weltanschauung... no science, but an ideology like the Nazistic racism. The greatest enemy of this ideology was exactly scientific proof, which aimed at showing how untenable this ideology was.[410]

Bacharach presupposes the highly controversial existence of Rasse, while he had an overly optimistic idea of science as a non-ideological activity; in the language of the day: as a value-free phenomenon. And to perceive something like *Rassenkunde* as value-free in Israel (and elsewhere) just a few years after the Eichmann trial and its following controversy is simply stubborn.

The optimism about the possibilities of science could be a reflection of the Jewish minority position that—as Lipphardt concluded, is characterized by a longing for acknowledgement from science. It is a tricky attitude which made the debate about a, or the, "Jewish race/Rasse" deteriorate into a verbal dispute

408 Quoted by Zwi Bacharach, 1984, 179 note 1.

409 Quoted by Zwi Bacharach, 1984, 179.

410 Zwi Bacharach, 1984, 181.

about what was or was not scientific.[411] Science was part of the problem and not a neutral judge or something "above all parties."

A typical example is the published discussion about Bacharach's contribution after which he confesses that Zollschan as a person is "not interesting" and that his answer to the anti-Semitism of his time "was irrelevant and wrong (*ungeschickt und verfehlt*)" and, of course, we must consider that "nationalistic Zionism does not have racist tendencies."[412]

In the following debate, people like Zuckermann, Funkenstein, Doron or Schoeps—to mention only a few participants—were silent as well about the questions mentioned above. No one doubted whether it was wise to make from Darwin's theory an -ism. What is remarkable is what they said despite this.

Margarita Pazi uttered the defensive opinion, heard from several participants, without any argumentation, that

> Zollschans theory cannot be taken seriously… Robert Weltsch was already right in acknowledging that Zollschan went the wrong way. Therefore, he cannot be seen as a Rasse—theoretician or as a scientist. There are no racist authoritarian claims among the Jews (*Herrschaftsanspruch*).[413]

For Funkenstein, Zollschan was also a grumbler. He was suspicious of Zollschan's opinion that Darwinism was characterized by its unchangeable and constant Rasse—concept, but while social-Darwinism used concepts alien to biological Darwinism. Zollschan, furthermore, did not acknowledge superior and inferior races, but accepted instead that *Rasse* mixtures were inferior. Zollschan is dishonest towards his own kin and his own country (*seinem eigenen Boden*; emphasized by Funkenstein): "in Judaism from ancient times there was already a tendency to stress ethnic purity… it is possible to perceive these ideas as a naive racism or as purposefully bad."

Doron mentions how Zollschan went to Eugen Fischer in Germany, a top Rasse scientist of the Nazis, to discuss his Rasse-theory with him. This behavior was comparable to that of Arthur Ruppin, the top ideologue of Zionism, who not only visited Fischer (according to Doron), but also discussed his case with Hans Günther (nickname: *Rasse-Günther*).

Typically enough, Doron concludes from this: "Here one finds the proof that thoughts with a Rasse orientation are not always located in the radical right-wing corner" as if it was or is possible to see Zionist nationalism as a left-wing phenomenon. That belongs to the successful "masquerade" to stress

411 Veronika Lipphardt, 2008, 305.
412 Veronika Lipphardt, 2008, 196–197.
413 Veronika Lipphardt, 2008, 191, 192.

sometimes the first, another time the second concept of "National Socialism," but not both.

How then should we call people like Weizmann, Ben Gurion, Jabotinsky, let alone full-time terrorists like Begin or Shamir? The only alternative for them is "violent anarchists," but such is too far beyond the achieved political goal to fight for "an honest case."

A strange aspect is provided by Zuckermann, known as a left-wing Israeli (whatever this means), who is surprised "that there were Jews who supported the Rasse-theory" as if he had heard this for the first time. This is a good demonstration of Doron's conclusion.

The most realistic reaction to Bacharach's analysis comes from Josef Karniel. He told that the Zionist movement developed "parallel to the anti-Semitism in Germany and Austria, but came not to the fore with a struggle against such anti-Semitism." Zionist clubs invited the anti-Semite Werner Sombart (for many commentators something like "a hard-core Jew") to hear from him about similarities in Socialism and Nationalism. Jewish Nationalists only wanted to return to "the Heimat der Urväter," or land of the forefathers:

> The parallels between the völkischen movements, which intended to extradite the Jews, and the Zionist movement, which intended as well to move the Jews abroad, are obvious.[414]

For post-war scholars of other disciplines and nationalities, Zollschan is interesting for different reasons.[415] They are apparent in remarkable judgments like the following from Elazar Barkan:

> One of the first and most energetic antiracist activists in Europe, Zollschan, had begun publishing on the Jewish "racial" question in 1910, when he opposed the racist theories of Houston Stewart Chamberlain… Following the Nazi seizure of power, Zollschan began to rally support for an international inquiry into the question of race.[416]

In particular, the suggestion that Zollschan was an "antiracist activist" from 1910 onwards must lead to misunderstandings.[417] There are alternatives to

414 Veronika Lipphardt, 2008, 192.

415 For Zollschan see also Stefan Kühl, 1997, 146 and the highly relevant analysis of John Efron, 1994, 153–166.

416 Elazar Barkan, 1988, 191.

417 It looks like the "mistake" on the website of the *Center for Jewish History,* where the dates of Zollschan are given as "1877–1944," as if he perished in Auschwitz or some similar place. Zollschan died quietly in London in 1948.

these political suggestions. John Efron not only corrects the reference to Chamberlain and provides a view on Zollschan's anti-Semitic Vienna, but begins his analysis of the author's *Rasse*-theory with the sentence:

> The clearest and most unambiguous expression of the purpose of Jewish race science was made by the Austrian physician Ignaz Zollschan.[418]

As the world was arming itself (1914), Zollschan wrote on how to attack anti-Semitism: to employ the same weapons as his opponents, namely, anthropology, sociology and natural science. There were many military tacticians around at the time who could have told him that this use of the same weapons always ends in a draw, in no solution at all. In this case, it could mean as fanatic a pro-Zionist/Jewish *Rasse* option as the racist anti-Semites had with Jews. That will be investigated below.

4.4 The Future of the Past

At the beginning of his main work, Zollschan writes that if the Jews had as many faults as the anti-Semites ascribed to them, *so wäre der Untergang der Rasse wünschenswert* (italics by I.Z; "in that case it should be desirable if the Rasse perished.")[419] He is pointing here to a, or the *Jewish Rasse* and nothing else, whether he is being ironic or not.

Benoit Massin also called Zollschan an "antiracist," but put this between inverted commas. In addition, he explained the term more or less by stipulating that it concerns the scientific battle between (neo)Lamarckism and (neo) Darwinism. Zollschan rallied for the former case, however both -isms used and propagated race/*Rasse* concepts, albeit based on a different reasoning and with different consequences. For instance, neo-Lamarckism accused its opponents of supporting

> the theory of "permanent racial characteristics," preventing any racial progress through social change, and leading to "racial hatred" and "racial chauvinism" ... [which also had]... theoretical and methodological implications for craniometry...[420]

418 John Efron, 1994, 153. For Chamberlain see 155.

419 Ignaz Zollschan, 1912, 4.

420 Benoit Massin, 1996, 124, 125.

Anyway, in Zollschan's case the misleading qualification "antiracist" should have been replaced by *anti-(neo)Darwinist.* For both directions the political issue of the *Rasse*-question depended on the outcome of debates over the question of heredity. So, it is appropriate that in the end the pot calls the kettle black.[421]

An example of how the Darwin-Lamarck question became politicized comes from a top-Nazi *Rasse* scholar, Lenz. He wrote:

> The inclination of the Jews towards Lamarckism is obviously an expression of the wish that there should be no unbridgeable racial distinctions. For instance, it is extremely characteristic that Kammerer, who was himself both a Jew and a Lamarckian, should write that "the denial of the racial importance of acquired characteristics favors race hatred." ... If acquired characters could be inherited, then, by living in a Teutonic environment and by adopting a Teutonic culture, the Jews could become transformed into genuine Teutons... But this, of course, can make no difference to the fact that the Lamarckian doctrine is an illusion... Jews do not transform themselves into Germans by writing books on Goethe...[422]

Paul Weindling perceives Zollschan as an anti-Houston S. Chamberlain, while Francis R. Nicosia has suggested the reverse.[423] Many misunderstandings about the man could arise from Weindling's description. To point to Zollschan's Lamarckism and mention only three sentences later that he "defined Jews according to Darwinist precepts..." is not enlightening. Also ambiguous is the characterization that he made

> ... the transition from an advocate of Jewish race purity... before the First World War to taking the lead in an international coalition against Nazi racism during the 1930s. By this time, Zollschan had to radically revise his scientific ideas about the Jewish race, and moderate his Lamarckism.[424]

421 In a science-historic publication, 1978, I published an extensive comparison between the positions of the Lamarckists and Darwinists in the 19th and 20th centuries resulting in 18 main antagonisms. On this basis quite different systems—theories were later developed after about 1950. It would take up too much space to discuss this subject here again and it is not very relevant for the rest of the book.

422 Quoted by Robert Proctor in George Stocking, ed., 1988, 147, 148.

423 Paul J. Weindling, 2007, 267–268. For Francis Nicosia see *Metapedia* (German) under "Zollschan, Ignaz," Juli, 2012.

424 Paul J. Weindling, 2007, 268.

This points to the framework in which we have to place Zollschan, but Weindling's conclusion that Zollschan was an] early opponent of racism and its stranglehold on German hygiene accords him a bit too much honor as we will see below.

A commentator who studied her subject in a highly interesting and thorough way is Veronika Lipphardt in her *Biologie der Juden* (2008). For a German scholar to write a book like this must have been a temptation. Indeed, one of her first words is "*Ratlosigkeit*" (desperation) when she first read relevant texts that were for her *völlig inakzeptabel* (fully unacceptable). Her first impression of the subject was that it was concerned "with *Rasse*—biology fighting against racism" by scholars with a Jewish background and that their texts were "grotesque."[425]

From the many "Jewish" *Rasse*—theoreticians she studied, Arthur Ruppin and Felix Theilhaber were famous, but it was Ignaz Zollschan who published "the most famous" book, *Das Rassenproblem* in 1909.[426] The top-Zionist Ruppin was a fervent supporter of the "Jewish *Rasse*" concept in which a *Rasse* was a genealogical homogeneous group; people who descended from this group were part of this *Rasse*.

This concerned German-speaking scholars, and it is remarkable enough that the Jewish-American Fishberg was not a fan of Zionism.[427] At least until about the 1930s, there was a general and sometimes active anti-Zionism in the USA among the Jewish elite. During the Peace Conference in Paris (1919), a specific address circulated to the representatives of the deliberating nations that did not support the establishment of some British-Zionist colony in Palestine. It was an action by the most important Jewish leaders in the USA.

However, thanks to the influence of Zollschan's publications and his support for the idea of a "Jewish Rasse" (theory), a certain contra-movement developed: a clear "Rassebewusstsein" among German-speaking Jews. Fishberg attacked this vehemently and succesfully: Zollschan did not got much support for his ideas during a visit to the USA.[428]

Non-Jewish German scholars used Zollschan's book to support their own theory of Jews as "inbreeding people" (*Inzuchtvolk*), who isolate themselves in "guest-nations." One of their outstanding propagandists, the Nazi Fritz Lenz,

425 Veronika Lipphardt, 2008, 9.
426 Veronika Lipphardt, 2008, 70.
427 Maurice Fishberg, 1911, 498–503.
428 Veronika Lipphardt, 2008, 253, 254.

wrote that the Jews were not a uniform *Rasse*, but one composed from several *Rassen* and, in any respects, alien.[429] That was also how Fishberg argued:

> Many of the most competent new anthropologists are of the opinion, that in the Jews, as in all civilized *Rassen* and *Völker*, several kinds of *Rasse*-elements are concentrated, and that the only thing in common is their religion.[430]

It was immediately clear around World War I that there were two directions in the "Jewish *Rasse*" question. The one in which Americans like Fishberg ("anthropologically one cannot speak of a homogeneous Jewish race," etc.) supported the *assimilation* policy and a Darwinian approach. The opponents, mainly Zionists, promoted a Lamarckian approach and the concentration of some group, called "Volk" in a *Rasse*-unit, called "State."[431] The first "perennial problem" for the "assimilationists" was

> ...whether it is possible to assimilate the vast number of Southern and Eastern immigrants to the United States and British colonies... [that]... has been applied more to the Jews than to any other white people. It has even been questioned whether there is ever a probability of incorporating the Jews into the body politic of Anglo-Saxon communities.[432]

The first problem for the "white" Zionists (whatever their motivation to be a Zionist) was to find the most relevant combination of "*Rasse*," "*Volk*," "*State*." The second problem was to determine the qualities of these three concepts in theory (and in practice). Concerning the motivation at stake, it was quite important to know whether one was inspired by some vague feeling of being "Jewish," "Socialist" or "Nationalist" or a combination. It is not surprising, therefore, that in the two directions their most outspoken "Jewish" ideologues were put on a pedestal: Fishberg (or Luschan) and Zollschan (or Kahn).[433]

The next author I want to refer to is an American-Zionist cultural anthropologist, folklorist, etc., Raphael Patai 1910–1996, clearly a representative of the "Fishberg direction." Although he wrote several books and articles, he was not well known until the star journalist Seymour Hersh connected a Patai book to

429 Veronika Lipphardt, 2008, 81.

430 Quoted in Veronika Lipphardt, 2008, 166.

431 Maurice Fishberg, 1911, 466–504 titled: "Assimilation *versus* Zionism," (italics from M.F.; see also Veronika Lipphardt 2008, 164–165.

432 Maurice Fishberg, 1911, V.

433 Veronika Lipphardt (2008), 181.

the Abu Ghraib prison scandal. The CIA and American military praised Patai's book as a textbook for military training in relation to Arab terrorism. Then, Brian Whitaker of *The Guardian* viewed it "as a doorstop," and a controversy was born.[434]

I refer here to another Patai book, *The Myth of the Jewish Race,* which he wrote together with Jennifer Patai Wing in 1975,[435] first, because I do not want to be distracted by the intricacies of Zionist, CIA or military propaganda and, second, because Patai in *The Myth* provided useful encyclopedic knowledge about *Rasse*-theories and how they could still be exploited in today's arguments and practices.

Patai's basic stimulus for writing *The Myth of the Jewish Race* was the absence of modern *Rasse* publications in English after Maurice Fishberg's study. Since this book, a "new science of genetics" had developed as well as "a new understanding of the genetic relationship between the Jews and their non-Jewish neighbours." Furthermore, the study of Jewish history had intensified.

Next came the question of whether Jews constitute a race, given the labeling of Jews as an inferior and evil race in World War II. Last but not least, in 1948, Israel was founded such that different Jewish "ethnic groups" came together forcing the thought of "One Jewish Race" to immediately become a myth. These "ethnic groups" also started with serious mutual quarrels "bearing many of the hallmarks of 'racial' friction." This "racism within their own ranks" was tragic for people who had just escaped the German menace.

In the 1950s and 1960s the UNESCO declared several times that races do not exist. Thanks to the above use of *race* and *racism* by Patai, we can experience how he coped with this serious and complicated situation. He wrote in 1975:

> This work attempts to approach the question of the Jewish race from every angle which might contribute to its understanding. After a brief review of the several... views, the first chapters present historical data... of the Jewish-Gentile race mixture in the course of more than three

434 See: Seymour Hersh, "The Gray Zone," in: *The New Yorker*, 24th of May, 2004; Brian Whitaker in *The Guardian*, 24th of May, 2004; an American military voice, N.B. Atkine, in: *The Middle East Quarterly*, Summer 2004,. 47–55. This quarterly states that it could discover only one example of military praise of Patai, which it immediately published again. It did not know that there was, for instance, an early understanding and CIA praise by Lloyd F. Jordan in: *CIA Historical Review Program*, 2 July, 1996; etc. It is symptomatic that the CIA man connects Patai to what he called "the national character research," which is very useful for the CIA and intelligence in general, knowing that this kind of "research" originates from the beginning of the 20th-century European nationalist (including Fascism and Nazism) scenes.

435 Raphael Patai, 1975.

> thousand years... consider... the extent and probable effects on the Jews as a genetic entity of Jewish proselytism, Jewish-Gentile intermarriage, concubinage... extramarital sexual intercourse, and slavery...[436]

Patai accepts, therefore, the existence of something like a Jewish race, but something more as well. The use of a phrase like "Jews as a genetic entity" could make readers suspicious, and this suspicion will not be allayed when reading Patai's basic thought that the "racial identity of *any* human group has not only a physical but also a psychological dimension" (emphasis added, H.D.). Therefore, according to Patai, it becomes necessary to discuss as well whether there exists such a thing as a "Jewish mind" different from a "Gentile mind."

In the biological-genetic part of his study, Patai aims to present "all the available serological, medical, and anthropometric data that bear on the topic." These data "supply the concrete evidence as to the present-day 'racial' composition of Jewish communities all over the world." So, contrary to what the title promises, Patai in fact constructs through a suggestive listing and accumulation of data, all the requisites of a new (modern?) "Jewish *Rasse*." He definitely does not want to abandon the whole *Rasse*-concept. This is strange for a person who also wrote:

> It would be tragic indeed if the Jews, after having been reduced to almost one-half their number by the Nazi racist madness, now encountered the spectre of racism within their own ranks in Israel.

What Patai is doing is "modernizing" the concept by defining and using it as a genetic concept, and referring to people like Cavalli-Sforza.[437] Whether this is more than a cosmetic change is not evident from the three hundred pages of the well-known *Rasse*-data. From Zollschan, Patai reserves only half a page containing one very long, inexpressive quotation.[438]

The above documents the fatal heritage in post-war Zionist and Israeli history and that experience will deepen after the confrontation with the last author in this paragraph. Under the same title, *Das unselige Erbe,* Rakefet Zalashik, a historian from Tel Aviv, published a history of psychiatry in Palestine and Israel.[439] What could be "a Jewish Mind" is well illustrated by Zalashik.

---

436 Raphael Patai, 1975, 2.

437 Raphael Patai, 1975, 14–17.

438 Raphael Patai, 1975, 24, 25.

439 At first, I used and quoted from Jutta Faehndrich, Rezension zu Rakefet Zalashik *Das unselige Erbe,* in: *H-Soz-u-Kult*, 28.08.2013. Later I bought Zalashik's book and used it, but I found no reason to change this passage.

Zalashik's book concerns a study of the treatments administered to psychiatric patients in 19th-century Palestine by immigrating Zionists from Europe and concerning new knowledge later brought to Israel from 1948 onwards. In this latter period, immigrating Shoah-victims were often psychologically traumatized. This last problem was addressed in particular.

Apart from this history of psychiatric treatments, Zalashik was confronted on a methodological level with the European eugenic views, *Rasse*-psychology and -psychiatry, and how they were used in the new colony on their own *Volk* and on the indigenous Palestinians.

European psychiatrists were educated in the German-Austrian tradition (Freud, etc.). They dreamt of creating a "New Jew" without the attitudes of the European Diaspora. In Palestine, however, they were also confronted with "abject" personalities: both the indigenous Arabs and the oriental Jews (Mizrahi), who had lived there for centuries in relative peace with the Palestinians. They were seen as primitive and racially deficient.

It was a perception that was also based on the fact that new immigrants from Europe committed suicide more often than indigenous peoples. This was explained as a reaction of the confrontation with an uncivilized world. In addition, the *Jewish Agency* (the Zionist bureaucracy in the British colony) had developed specific selection criteria for immigrants to be implemented in Europe, so that only "healthy" persons, according to eugenic criteria, would arrive in the Holy Land. This led to remarkable situations as the review explains:

> The close connection between the German-Austrian psychiatry with the later Israeli one leads to the paradoxical phenomenon, that the German actors of euthanasia and *Rasse*—hygiene [the same as *eugenics*, H.D.] had studied at the same universities as their colleagues, who had immigrated to Palestine. In the German Reich eugenics immediately led to mass-murder of psychiatrist's patients and disabled persons… and to the Shoah or Holocaust, while in Palestine psychiatric patients were sent back to Germany [where they were killed, H.D.], because one needed for the New Jewish State only healthy "human material."

This gave Zalashik's study its title of "Fatal Heritage." The author easily combined this pre-war situation with the post-war arrivals of the "Holocaust" survivors in Israel. She concludes from her perspective as Tom Segev or Idith Zertal had earlier: the treatment of this "unhealthy human material" ("human dust" in the words of President Weizmann) was similar to that around 1933 and following years. Auschwitz survivor Hajo Meyer mostly introduced himself to his lecture audience by saying: "The one before you was called 'unfit human material' once I started to live among the living in 1945."

Eugenic reasoning still prevailed (also in the USA at the time); the survivors were first denied immigration under the supposition that the present "sickness" of the survivors was due to psychiatric problems from before 1940 that were therefore, equated with a genetic heritage. Besides this, the authorities looked at the survivors as costing Israel too much before they would be able to function as sturdy warriors and peasants. Result: these helpless former camp-inmates were fully negated and had to fend for themselves in an alien and chaotic country, in which the Zionists fought their way against the other "racially disabled/ primitives," the Arabs, to establish their "white colony."

In Israel, this last colony of the West, we are confronted with most of the characteristic elements of all colonial systems of the West, in which the imported "white" elite represses the "primitive" indigenous population with their superior weaponry.[440] There is a special aspect: this elite could *successfully* legitimate this common repression by boasting of its non-existent "Holocaust performance" and create in this way its identity as victim instead of as perpetrator.

This is not only the background of the work of the medical doctor Zollschan and of his many supporters, but also the background of his future. His past is modeled, like so many others, by his German origins. "Without Germans, no Jews," one can hear in an exaggerated form, but the suggested relationship between perpetrator and victims is evident. This dramatic relationship was also formed in modern times. A few words about it are most appropriate here.

440 But also the details with the pre-war situation were more similar than Zalashik could imagine. After 1933 and a profitable treaty with the Nazis, the *Jewish Agency* established eugenic selection offices in Europe with the "output" that those who did not meet the Zionist selection criteria were left in Germany to the whims of the Nazi regime. Still, some "sick people" could slip through the selection nets (thanks to the criterion "capitalist," I suppose). Now, after the Second World War the Zionists opened selection offices again with their eugenic criteria, and again many ex-camp inmates were refused admittance to the new Israel. That is only a very small difference from the policy of the British to capture ships with immigrants and send them back to the former concentration camps, leaving them to the whims of post-war chaotic Europe. See for this whole problematic the excellent books of Tom Segev, 1993 and Idith Zertall, 1998.

4.5 The Birth of German Anti-Semitism

Two years after Zollschan was born near Vienna, the Treitschke-Mommsen row started in Berlin. Now better known as the *Berliner Antisemitismus Streit,* 1879–1881, it was the first and immediately a rather spectacular, nearly nationwide confrontation between Germans and Jews. Of course, since the time of Martin Luther anti-Jewish writings or activities had been a common phenomenon in the German culture. It could be expected that since the emancipation of Jews around 1800, things had developed in a favorable direction. Also, in hindsight, the ridiculous anti-Jewish smear campaigns of Lutheran and Catholic priests and their learned supporters had never been seen before and were shocking in their impact and elite-context, only comparable with Greek Orthodox actions in the underdeveloped East.

To understand its impact within the roaring 1870s, it's necessary to look into the broad panorama of political, economic and cultural conflicts sketched by Hans-Ulrich Wehler.[441] In such a sketch, this *Streit* was not very important for ordinary Germans, but for the cultural and political habitus of the German elite and its offspring it was of pivotal importance.

The perspective in which Wehler himself saw it, is best given by the following exclamation mark. It is used after the reaction of one of the main targets of the anti-Semitic smear-campaigns of the Protestant clergy-man Stoecker, against the financial advisor of Chancellor Bismarck, the banker Bleichröder with a Jewish background. In June 1880 the latter even protested in a letter to Bismarck in which he gave

> the symbolic forecast, that such a cynical power-game very easily could escalate into "the beginning of an unhappy terrible social revolution"![442]

That was an exaggeration at the time, about a bad habit that haunted every party in the actual conflicts, but in hindsight of the future Nazi performance, was apparently no exaggeration at all. Still, in every respect they were astonishing years; only a few impressions can be given here.[443]

---

441 Hans-Ulrich Wehler, 1995, volume 3. The "Innenpolitische Krisenherde," 889–1000, should be consulted in particular.

442 Hans-Ulrich Wehler, 1995, volume 3, 922. About the German origins of the relationship "Nation-Volk-Rasse" see now the excellent study of Peter Walkenhorst, 2007.

443 A most important and nearly complete source is the two-volume study of Karsten Krieger, 2003 in which many further data are given. The *Antisemiten-Spiegel,* 1900, first edition

First, this time it was clear to everyone how the elite was the nucleus of the anti-Jewish agitation, while "the street" followed long after the "parties" (and their supporters and journals) within the elite had taken up appropriate positions. The representatives of the perpetrators belonged to the political-cultural scene of the Lutheran and Catholic church, proponents of science, and their conservative political parties and means of publicity.

Among them belonged the well-known historian Heinrich von Treitschke, 1834–1896, who triggered the row with an anti-Jewish article; the Lutheran court-priest Adolf Stoecker, 1835–1909, who perceived himself as a new Martin Luther; the economist Adolph Wagner, 1835–1917, who "discovered" the massive immigration of Jews from the East. The last two were leading figures in the influential Christian-Social Party, an antidote to the Socialists, to which the younger members of the Max Weber family had strong ties.

From the Jewish victims' side, the most important were the Kantian philosopher Hermann Cohen, 1842–1918, the historian Heinrich Graetz, 1817–1891, and the philosopher Moritz Lazarus, 1824–1903. The first two were no match for the anti-Semites and were attacked in the Jewish press as well; the last was the only one who organized a Jewish counter-attack, but the first and last meeting with his compatriots ended in strong animosity.

This was also the fate of the attempt by Ludwig Philippson, 1811–1899, a liberal rabbi who established the *Allgemeine Zeitung des Judentums* (General Newspaper for Judaism) that published many charges on the anti-Semites. In fact, the most effective attack on them came from a man with a Jewish background, the statistician and medical doctor for the Berlin poor, Salomon Neumann, 1819–1908. He published *Fabel von der Jüdischen Masseneinwanderung* (Fable of the Jewish Mass Immigration). In this booklet he fully undermined the main complaint and attack of the anti-Semites, that there was a "massive immigration of Jews from the East that undermined the economy," as Wagner suggested.

However, apart from Neumann's publication, it was the non-Jewish "bystanders" who were the main defenders of the German-Jewish position. The most important was the world-famous historian Theodor Mommsen, 1817–1903, but others were well-know as well like medical scientist Rudolf Virchow, 1821–1902, the philosopher Heinrich Rickert, 1833–1902, father of the other philosopher with the same name; the historian Johann Gustav Droysen, 1808–1886, etc. They issued together, in November 1880, a kind of manifesto ("Erklärung") of 75 Berlin notables against anti-Semitism.

1890 is in my view excellent. It is published anonymously, but somewhere I read that the famous philosopher Heinrich Rickert was the editor.

This made a strong impression since nationally important figures in the economy, politics and cultural life now expressed their support.[444] This was worded as follows:

> ... the unity of our fatherland is reached, because of our... victory over tribal and religious antagonisms. To express these [antagonisms] anew, directed to individual members, ... is not just and without honor and only those are affected, who seriously and honorable try... to get rid of their special position (*die Sonderart abzuwerfen*) ... The aim is and must remain: the negation of all contradictions in the German nation. In an unexpected and seriously humiliating way the racial hatred (*der Racenhaß*) and fanaticism of the Middle Ages came to life in several locations, among which are the biggest cities of the Reich. These were directed against our Jewish fellow-citizen... [in] a breach... of the law as well as the honor, that [states that] all Germans in rights and duties are equal.

The message of this "manifesto" was double. To the anti-Semites: stop your hate campaigns, that disturbs a necessary unity in a country in (economic) crisis; to the Jews: assimilate fully as soon as possible, so that you become "normal" Germans.

The last one was, in fact, not very different from the demand of Treitschke if one reduces his poisoned language to its essentials. He attacked the writings of the popular Jewish historian Graetz, because this historian still stressed the Jewish position as a sworn enemy of Christianity, while this should have been stopped after the emancipation of the Jews.[445]

The fear was expressed that now that emancipation was realized Bismarck's appointment of the banker Bleichröder, was "the first finger," and that Jews would next grab "the whole hand" of "government in the whole of Germany or even the world." Bleichröder's position as Bismarck's financial advisor was "clear proof" enough for most people who did not want detailed explanations.

Treitschke and his supporters distrusted the will or ability of German Jews to follow the given logic of emancipation:

---

444 Karsten Krieger, 2003, 551–554. Among the supporters were not only Mommsen, Droysen, Rickert or Virchoff, but also the brothers Werner and Georg Siemens, the mayor of Berlin, Duncker, three of the main Berlin Jewish (?) merchants, several of the highest bureaucrats, or Max Weber, father of the sociologist of the same name. For the "manifesto" (in fact nothing more than an *Erklärung von 12. November 1880*) see also Walter Boehlich, ed., 204–206.

445 Karsten Krieger, 2003, 14; a return to a period before emancipation would be ridiculous.

> ... with the realization of the emancipation, the old claim of the Jews creating a nation for themselves should have been fully negated as well. In this century of the formation of national states, the Jews can play a peaceful... role only, if they decide... to integrate in those cultures of which they speak the language.[446] ... [if not] ... there appears again this racial arrogance... to demand of acknowledging a Jewish nationality, and then the basis under the law on which this emancipation rests will collapse. In order to fulfil such wishes, there is only one solution: emigration, establishing some Jewish state somewhere abroad... in Germany there is no place for a double-nation.[447]

We cannot take texts like this lightly. Involved in the *Streit* was Hermann Cohen who, as the worthiest boy in the classroom, tried to convince the Germans how willing the Jews were to assimilate. Ludwig Philippson, the editor of the *Allgemeine Zeitung des Judentums*, was clearly irritated by this.[448]

He asked whether this is only demanded of Jews and not of the Germans themselves: a large part of the population belongs to religions "which places the Church above the Nation and another part has its point of gravitation beyond the mountains" [in Rome, therefore]. Then there are not a few who glorify tribes like the Welfen, Sachsen, Bojaren, Austrians, so that their *Deutschtum* is very shallow! Cohen should have remarked that there was no single difference between the ways jobs and firms were managed by Christians and Jews.

The next remark is as effective as the first:

> ...if we have to assimilate, why, Cohen, do you remain silent about "*what* they [the Germans. H.D.] should do? *What* they, to this aim, have to do and *what* to avoid... Those Jews now come from German schools, have a pure German education in all its details... Yes, we have to develop ourselves in this spirit..., but we do not need to develop it more than all other non-Jewish Germans. We do not acknowledge in all these moments whatever difference there is between Jews and Christians (italics from Philippson).

Cohen will probably accept this second remark, but for the editor this again went wrong where Cohen made Jewish monotheism similar to the

446 Karsten Krieger, 2003, 121.

447 Karsten Krieger, 2003, 126.

448 Karsten Krieger, 2003, 432.

Christian one. That is not of interest here, but see the next chapter.[449] In the purely anti-Semitic turmoil, it is anyway unwise to introduce anti-Judaist themes to quarrel about.

It is less than a formality to say that this controversy about anti-Semitism ended with a victory for the Mommsen group. It can only be called a Pyrrhic victory. However, in sociologically terms, it proved how isolated all of the groups/participants were in relation to each other and that they continue on their own road, undisturbed by what the others were doing; in fact, all failed in the end.

In other words: this *Streit* was basically an occasionally passionate fight between those German groups modernizing in several respects (modernizing in terms of a strong state, industry, banking, imperial policies or big cities with scientific supporters) and those groups that stuck to and ruthlessly defended the traditional tribal and Christian interests in the recently united parts of the Reich (the two big churches, large parts of the aristocracy, agricultural or middle class interests with their scientific supporters).

Optimistically one can argue that the just established German Reich tried to integrate and that this controversy was a major symptom of it; the resulting void was gradually occupied by the most aggressive interests from the two antagonistic blocs: the military, aristocracy and the militant factions in the churches and middle class who were given substantial publicity under the heading of a war-like (and for some lunatic) Kaiser.

Whatever served Jewish interests at the time, apart from individual power positions, it was, in my view, already now crushed between these large antagonistic blocs. Philippson sketched their impossible dilemma in dealing with the devil and Beelzebub, without being already organized in a way that could demand something in return.

A remarkable aspect of the Treitschke as well as the Mommsen supporters was that nobody used in the public debates *Rasse*-theory or *Rasse*-jargon or *Rasse*-accusations of any kind; not yet. The Mommsen group argued against the usual xenophobic creeds and demands by characterizing Jews as normal hard-working German citizens, who obey the Law. The position of Rudolf Virchov in this respect was typical.

Virchov strongly opted for the liberal pro-Jewish position, but later he became one of the important scientific supporters of the *Rasse*-approach. This new approach succeeded as soon as the new power filled the void and demanded new challenges for science, the elite-producer of the *Rasse*-theories.

449 See for the close relationship between the ideas of Hermann Cohen and Treitschke in the *Streit*, Georg Geismann, 1993.

The Treitschke bloc, however, had opened a Pandora's Box. It seems that no decision-making committee in either of the two fronts had seen it, let alone considered some way to close that box. Treitschke himself loved polemics against many things, but always Jews appear as the real sinners.[450]

Thanks to the Treitschke activities, a real army of writers entered the publicity market with only one theme: Jews. Hundreds of brochures, pamphlets, books and thousands of speeches all over the place brought the seed of anti-Semitism.[451] Even in a city like Berlin this army gave the impulse to pogrom-like activities. Nobody in the two blocs was alarmed or prepared to look for sound compromises: this was probably the most drastic situation, one that later could not be repaired in Germany, and things unavoidably went from bad to worse.

One idea of Treitschke's had, however, such success that after two world wars we still suffer under its impact: the best that Jews could do was to go abroad and establish their own state. More than a decade later, Theodor Herzl copied the idea in the other "German" capital, Vienna. Ignace Zollschan quickly worked hard to realize it and modernized the idea to the extent that now everybody can perceive the idea in "real *Rasse*-terms." Who was he?

4.6 Ignaz Zollschan, 1877–1948

For him and, eventually, other "Jewish" scholars the theoretical work of the (neo)lamarckian Richard Semon, 1859–1918, was of pivotal importance. Zollschan and Semon knew each other from correspondence. The latter was not only an inventive zoologist and evolutionary biologist, he was a remarkable figure as well. He perceived himself not as a Jew, although he had a partly Jewish background. Semon and his closest friend, Otto Lubarsch, demonstrated that they were "fanatic German patriots": wrapped in a German flag he committed suicide apparently because Germany had lost the war.

Semon's relevant scientific achievements concerned a theory of the abilities of human memory and the relationships between the psychological state and

450 Hans-Ulrich Wehler, 1995, volume 3, 925–926.

451 To mention some of opinion-makers in the anti-Semitic movement: Hermann Ahlwardt, Moritz Bush, Eugen Düring, Otto Glagau, Paul de la Garde, Wilhelm Marr, Theodor Fritsch and so on. They got their chance to earn a living in times of crisis with many bestsellers. Sometimes petitions to Bismarck with nearly 300,000 signatures were gathered (Jews Go Home To the East! Juden raus! No Jews in Public Functions! No Jews as teachers for our schoolkids!). They acted outside everybody's control, and none of the Treitschke people, the Mommsen professors or the Jewish clever elite had the faintest idea what to do against the spreading poison.

physiological phenomena: his theory says, in short, that stimuli produce some record upon cellular material; this record is called an *engramm* of which there are billions; the more often a certain stimulus is given to the body, the more certain such an *engramm* is fixed in the cells; this could result even in a hereditary quality and not only in the brain. In Semon's theory, the whole of all these *engramms* forms the memory, the *Mneme*.[452]

This is a typical (neo)Lamarckian way of reasoning. Zollschan and others applied the *engramm* thesis to the question of a "Jewish" *Rasse*: the permanent repression of Jews through the centuries must have fixed their behavior in specific directions so that hereditary characteristics develop.

He added that negative influences lead to degenerative nervous diseases, that are specific for Jews. Since many knew that the heredity research on the principles of Mendel could not explain how hereditary characteristics originated, Semon's and Zollschan's ideas *could* provide the explanation required.

However, they did not consider that there was a profound check on all this natural-scientific *Rasse*-puzzling: was it not a matter of traditional *historical* research concerning the question of whether Jews were indeed repressed since antiquity? And about which kind of Jews were being spoken and written about here? Is is not an advantage to create a mystery by avoiding answering the question "who is a Jew?" that is so easy for the other monotheists? The only thing that is relevant here is that, according to Zollschan, Fishberg in his *The Jews*

> still sticks to his old views that differences in skulls and pigments… can be explained only by the difference in descent. He denies that the Jews from the different corners of the globe are still identical of blood [*blutsidentisch*] and also, that they are identical of blood with the Jews in antiquity.[453]

Here a new priority problem arises: if the historical record of "Jewish" repression is dubious, can we ignore the biological one as well?

452 Veronika Lipphardt, 2008, 97; Sander Gilman, 1996, 105. Of course, this theory and its further development cannot be followed here. See *Wikipedia* under "Engramm," "Semon," "Mneme," etc. An engramm is the physiological spur which is left in the brain (but never seen!) or elsewhere after some stimulus. Semon called it a memory-spur; others found already in Aristotle a good picture of it: it looks like the imprint of a seal-ring in (weak) wax. Whether all this concerns non-sense seems obvious, but is far beyond my understanding!

453 Ignaz Zollschan, 1912, XII, XIII. See, for instance, interestingly Maurice Fishberg, 1911, 475 the long note 2 with several references to Roman authors pointing to the fact that there was criticism of the nature of the Jewish religion, but not the usual argument of anti-Semites about unfair business dealings, etc. Those kinds of sounds were only heard from the Middle Ages onward.

From his initiatives to establish scientific institutes, we can ascertain Zollschan's other intellectual backgrounds. As a reaction to the establishment of the Nazi regime in Germany, he proposed founding an anthropological research center in Jerusalem (1933). It had to be an institute for "pure science" and would not be active in the fight against anti-Semitism (another kind of institute should be established for that aim). In this scientific institution

> ...the following research disciplines and methods had to be part of it: anthropometry, statistics; "X-ray methods," blood group and twin research, heredity analyses and "biological experiments." This produced an "exact basis" not only for "questions of *Rasse*-biology" but also for *Rasse*-hygiene and eugenics... Its main task was the study of "the change of human body types"... and its laws... the proof of these changes was the definite undermining of the *Rasse*-principle... which was similar to an "eternal continuity... of the spiritual condition...; and so on.[454]

Zollschan's initiatives all failed, but this kind of research institute was established by others in many places and supported by representatives of the Jewish elite.[455] Let's now take a look into the writings of the author.

4.6.1 Rasse-*theory*

Zollschan was indeed an activist, but for the Zionist case, i.e. the establishment of a good *Rasse*-nation in Palestine. In a Western pre-war society, nearly everybody understood what this meant. He was a colonist-activist also in the sense that he struggled against anti-Semitism as the main trigger to establish that kind of "colonial nation" creating new waves of anti-Zionism or anti-colonialism; erroneously called anti-Semitism, even today.

The political side of Zollschan's biological thinking can be best found in his *Revision des jüdischen Nationalismus*, 1919. It was written directly after the publication of the so-called Balfour Declaration and the Peace Conference in Paris. He starts the preface with the sentence:

> The Zionist movement has reached its goal. The Peace Conference has accepted all Zionist proposals relative to Palestine with an unanimous vote.

---

454 For Zollschan's initiatives to establish scientific institutes, see Veronika Lipphardt, 2008, 252–258. The quotation is from 255, 256.

455 Veronika Lipphardt, 2008, 296. for an initiative of Wilhelm Nussbaum supported by Leo Baeck in 1935.

An utopian "Dreamland" could be colonized, and Zollschan was one of those who provided an extensive answer to the questions of "what to do now and why?" Obviously that we cannot discuss this whole program; "ethnic unity as the basis of the organization" is the only aspect of interest here. First, however, some strategically important definitions he and others used at the time.

A *Volk,* implying more than a *Nation,* is determined by the political unity (*politischen Zusammengehörigkeit*) and hereditary community [*Abstammungsgemeinschaft*]. A *Volk* is, therefore, at once *Sprachvolk, Staatsvolk, Blutsvolk;* literally: a "language-, state- and blood-Volk."[456] A quick and not very logical conclusion was drawn: "We are able to work with a concept as *jüdisches Volk...*"

For *nation,* matters are much more difficult: the few hundred freshly imported real Zionists in Palestine in 1917 could not colonize the territory of nearly a million Palestinians or Arabs. That would only be possible by the armed English colonizers, the Zionist's overlords.

Zollschan defines, however, that for his nation it is sufficient that the non-English colonizers have: the same descent, tradition and religion, leading to a society with a common fate [*Schicksalsgemeinschaft*], and who have a "blood-community" [*Blutsgemeinschaft*]. Defining elements of both are not, for example, common feast days and funeral rituals, but a common enemy and common repression. It is in this framework that a Jewish religion erects

> a wall around the Jewish community against the outside world and which kept every alien influence outside while inside a Jewish mini-state was established.[457]

This tradition could be the start of the new Nation, but there are *dangers*: it is a custom in the West that Church and State must be separate, and in particular among the Western Jews, religion is no binding force at all so that the given state-tradition is only applicable to the Eastern European Jews (Ostjuden). It is therefore urgent that "the last cell of Jewish identity [*Eigenlebens*]," the religious community, does not loose its present legal basis now that a listing in the land registry is at stake. The only juridical basis on which they can continue to exist concerns the acknowledgement of "the fact that the Jews

---

456 Ignaz Zollschan, 1919, 45, 46 including for next citation.

457 Ignaz Zollschan, 1919, 47. This idea of a wall around the new Zionist society predates the famous one of the national Israeli hero, the radical right-wing Jabotinsky, about fifteen years later and, of course, the present concrete wall around large parts of Israel/Palestine.

are not only a religious community, but also a national political community [*Nationsgemeinschaft*]."[458]

The disadvantage of this is that, internally, Jews will be divided, and a mass exodus from the religion will take place. And, indeed, that the antagonism between the secular majority and the religious minority remained one of the main cleavages until today in the Israeli society. To exorcise this serious danger, Zollschan produced, with long quotations of Klatzkin, a long exchange of abuse against all those assimilated Jews: the un-Jewish traitors, "they live in the spirit of non-Jewish traditions, of non-Jewish history...," and so on.[459]

Here he stressed that, "his views about the Jewish *Rasse*-question , as I formulated them earlier, did not change them at all." Therefore, he had to invent a *Rasse* policy circumscribed as follows:

> Mixed marriages and racial mixture are the more serious enemy of the continuity of Judaism than the acknowledgement of a foreign nation.[460]

In this perspective, political realities remain pressing, including the unfortunate reality that many Zionist leaders had mixed marriages!

Anyway, language and territory are the most important elements for differentiating nations. Zollschan mentions how a psychological element was recently added to this, a purely subjective one. It concerns the *will power to suffer collectively*, to stay together now and in the future. But, for Zollschan it is also a subjective element: the Nation must be established on "*Rasse, Raum, Kultur, Staat*" [Race, Space, Culture, State].[461]

Notwithstanding this, the "bio-psychological" element is stressed in particular in the chapter entitled "Ethnic Unity as Basis for the Organization," where Zollschan points to an "over-individual binding" [*überindividuellen Bindung*] of a Jewish "descent-community" *Abstammungsgemeinschaft*]. Here the concepts Tribe, *Volk*, Nation, Blood or Organism are stumbling over each other.

---

458 Ignaz Zollschan, 1919, 85.

459 Ignaz Zollschan, 1919, 49; another long quotation from Klatzkin about the same question appears on 87, 88. Jakob Klatzkin (1882–1948) is an influential Zionist philosopher born in Russia.

460 Ignaz Zollschan, 1919, 87. It is a conclusion which is drawn time and again. At the moment rabbis never are shy to use big words: assimilation and all its related "dangers" (abortions, etc.) are simply described as the *Silent Holocaust* (see under this term in *Wikipedia!*). Zollschan also quotes Klatzkin at length in this item.

461 Ignaz Zollschan, 1919, 52 and as the main characteristic of this combination, Zollschan sees according to the German discourse at issue: *Autarkie* (self-sufficiency; economic *Selbstbestimmung*) and *Autonomie* (political independence, *Selbstverwaltung*).

We learn how something like a "Jewish *Volk*" is *invented in biological terms*, that later became a political *tradition*. Zollschan writes quite frankly:

> A word like "*jüdischnational*" can be only used as identification for the ideal political programmatic direction of Zionism and not relative to a present reality... There are, therefore, no difficulties in using a term like "Jewish People" [*jüdisches Volk*]. When, indeed, the demand for acknowledgement of an unavailable nationality is wrong, the further exploitation of a concept "jüdischnational"... and the concept "jüdisches Volk" is quite in order.[462]

However, he tries to be a benevolent realist and accepts, for the time being, the presence of the largest possible majority of Arabs. He supposes that there will be a "State constituted of several nationalities," and in that case it is ridiculous to mention "Jewish nationality" behind the name of Jews in the national registry. This must lead to many internal and external conflicts, but it remains possible that people *feel* themselves *privately* "Jewish national," for the time being.

The same insoluble problem arises with the language. Zollschan supposes quite logically that in such an ethnically differentiated country, Jews will speak, as a "national" language, what their tribe and tradition prescribes: the "*Jüdisch-Deutsch*" (Yiddisch). Hardly anyone suggested Hebrew at the time.

After all this, Zollschan arrives in his last chapter at the biological conditions under which his ideal has to be realized. Again with Klatzkin he acknowledges that "land" and "language" are of paramount importance:

> Still, he [Klatzkin] neglects... the physical Jew, the ethnic body of Jewry as a biological, as an anthropological, prerequisite of the Jewish nationality. Also without their own language and land—which can later be added—this ethnic body incorporates the Nation as long as these *Volk*-bodies [*Volkskörper*] are not undermined by a too high percentage of mixed marriages and *Rasse*-mixture. This given *Rasse*-body is the condition we can never neglect.[463]

462 Ignaz Zollschan, 1919, 82. It is remarkable that not long ago a local dispute about Shlomo Sand's book *The Invention of the Jewish People* was extended into an international row thanks to the publication of this book in English (2009). Sand did not mention Zollschan, who is one of the inventors, but not the only Zionist. Sand's book as well as the unbelievable reactions to it, are all testimony to the limited historical knowledge among present-day Zionists and Israeli, as well as of a rather underdeveloped political understanding.

463 Ignaz Zollschan, 1919, 152.

Zollschan sketches the situation of a tribe of black men settling in Palestine with adoration for the Holy Land and command of the Hebrew language: how could this be a Jewish Nationality? It serves as the relevant support for his thesis in the quotation. Herewith he starts the explanation of his *Rasse*-theory. The basis is that for the civilized people,

> ...the *Rasse* characters are not any more of an unchangeable continuity, but fit to be formed and to be influenced by external impulses. In addition, located between the inherited instinct and the instinctive action is the reasoning mind... under its modifying influence the instinct becomes only a predisposition... on a high level of civilization there is, furthermore, education and a differentiated system of regulations on ethical ground... In principle, man has the ability to emancipate from his instincts... which one can perceive as *Rasse*-energies.[464]

The elementary differences between *Rassen* are not negated in this theory, but the direction of their development is given under the constant influences of the environment. The immutability of *Rassen* must be denied categorically.

For Jews and Zionism this theory has far-reaching consequences, if accepted:

> ... whatever the viewpoint chosen, we always had to conclude that the attempt to obtain a national autonomy, that their whole political nationalism is something nonsensical and that this movement, whatever the ideal motives of their supporters, follows a false direction... To be a Jew does not mean only something religious and not always something ethical; anyway, it does not mean a political commitment; however, in all instances it indicates an ethnic fact... Diaspora Jews [therefore] do not form a nation... [but]... a mass of people as only an ethnological unity, not a political one.[465]

Zollschan strongly criticizes the current Zionist thesis of the "Jewish Nationality" of people like Weizmann and the given nationality as a non-truth, as was demonstrated in World War I. It is quite modern when Zollschan raises his demand to "melt swords into ploughshares."[466]

When all this nationalistic misery seems to be over, with the end of the war and the Peace Conference of 1919, it is exactly at this moment that the Zionist

464 Ignaz Zollschan, 1919, 156, 157.
465 Ignaz Zollschan, 1919, 165.
466 Ignaz Zollschan, 1919, 168.

Party starts "to create a new 'nationalism'". There is no single precondition fulfilled for any type of Jewish nationality, let alone a Jewish state.

Zollschan reminds us that at that moment of Zionist history, many people like him did not envisage a "Jewish Nationality" in Palestine, but they tried to look at *all Diaspora Jews as a Nation, as a Volk*. Therefore, he exclaims in his writing: "We struggle against the proclamation of Nationality as basis for the organization of the Diaspora Jews."[467] Possibly for the *Ostjuden* this nationality topic could be discussed, but for the *Westjuden* (Western European Jews) it is pure fiction. The only reasonable basis for an organization is the *Rasse* or ethnic unity. The whole Diaspora must be divided up into these kinds of ethnic units, eventually perceived even as "Zwangsgenossenschaften," or compulsory communities.[468]

One has to doubt whether this will be a democratic organization. The first thing Zollschan demands is a rigorous centralization [*Zentralinstanz*] "which has in all directions authoritative, representative competence… represented by a National Council" and so on and so forth until "in the future the full Nation [*Vollnation*] in Palastine is realized"[469] and a "continuous stream of taxmoney… went from here to Palestine."[470] Then, a Hebrew University, Academy or Museum can be established to glorify a real ethnically based Jewish Nation.

Two pages further the crown is put on this *Zentralinstanz*: "In the hand of the Zionist leader [*Führer*] it is given to determine the future road of the Jewry also in the Diaspora… to the full happiness of the Nation…"[471] It seems as if the model of the future *Rasse*-world had received its definite shape.

Zollschan demonstrated a typically European way of intellectual development: critical of the existing political and/or scientific ways of thinking and acting and their consequences (here: nationalism, capitalism combined with mechanical Darwinistic thinking), creating an alternative (here: other nationalism, socialism combined with biological Lamarckistic thinking), laying the intellectual basis for an even more repressive regime than the one being criticized (here: a purely *Rasse*-based national-socialist form of Zionism).[472]

467 Ignaz Zollschan, 1919, 170.

468 Ignaz Zollschan, 1919, 171.

469 Ignaz Zollschan, 1919, 173.

470 Ignaz Zollschan, 1919, 174.

471 Ignaz Zollschan, 1919, 176.

472 It is about 15 years later that such a centralization within Palestine took place (not in the Diaspora) under the direct influence of Jabotinsky and Ben-Gurion. It resulted in an organization capable of widespread anti-English and anti-Palestinian terrorist actions never seen in Europe (invention of letter-bombs, destruction of large buildings like 9–11 *avant la détonation*—a large hotel in Jerusalem with several hundred deaths, etc.).

4.6.2 *The* Rasse *Categories and Meanings*

A *Rasse*-theoretician also has to elaborate on the technical-biological (anthropological, etc.) means that could be used. Do these also fit into the political ideas of medical-doctor Ignaz Zollschan? Unlike other Jewish *Rasse*-theoreticians, he criticized the anthropological preconditions used in order to arrive at a new Jewish *Rasse*-theory.

Around 1900 *Rasse*-science had several kinds of elements: the case of the Aryan language; the case of the German (here: the Germanic) tribe; the measurement methods with the most popular skull-index (craniology, phrenology); the case of the *Rasse*-history from pre-historical times, including the differences between *Rassen* among animals, plants and humans. In all these fields Zollschan had to come up with new views, because he had to explain why and how Jews were treated as *Rasse* and why and how they were discriminated as *Rasse*.

His *Das Rassenproblem* is probably the only study of the Zionist creed that tried to address *all* these questions; an impossible task. Happily for him he regarded many theories as hypotheses

> that concern very remote pre-historical times and that it is obvious that they cannot be proved and cannot be used for sound anthropological conclusions, which must be derived from very different sources.[473]

It was customary among scholars with a Jewish background who discussed the Jewish Question, to be silent about the anthropological discourse: the Jew-hatred could be substantiated by it on natural scientific grounds, they said. As a medical doctor, Zollschan felt he was well equipped to accept the challenges.

Therefore, he came up with an alternative categorization of *Rassen*. As *first* and basic considerations in this discourse about Jews, Zollschan presents the following:[474]

1. Contrary to the dominant views, there is “no anthropological difference between Aschkenazim and Sephardim”;
2. “The Jewish *Rasse* incorporates no fundamental mixture of other ethnical elements”;
3. This *Rasse*, therefore, “represents everywhere the same, uniform *Rasse*-body, which has been pure for at least the last 2,500 years; in the genealogical sense it is a homogeneous unity.”

473 Ignaz Zollschan, 1912, 142.

474 Ignaz Zollschan, 1912, 144.

4. "Based on craniological criteria it is false to view Jews as types of the Homo Alpinus... [which is]... impossible, because this species does not exist at all."
5. The brachycephalic skull "from people with which Jews are identified is the consequence of life in the mountains, while [this kind of skull] from Jews is a consequence of the intensive intellectual activity. Jews are, indeed, part of the melanochroi *Rasse*-group."[475]
6. Because the *Rasse*-qualities of the Germanic *Rasse* [seen as: xanthochroi group] are compared with the Jewish *Rasse* and perceived as superior to it, I, Zollschan, have to make in my turn "a comparison... between the cultural achievements of the melanochroi and of the xanthochroi.";
7. The performance of the melanochroi are: "The cultures of the Sumer-Accadians, the late Babylonians and Assyrians, the Persians, the Hittites, the Phoenicians, the Jews, the Egyptians, the Greeks, the Romans, the Arabs and the largest part of the Renaissance culture."
8. The performance of the xanthochroi is: "... largely the creative results of the modern culture, in which only the Romans and the Jews from the melanochroi cooperated."

About this last comparison, in 6–8, Zollschan writes that he is not yet prepared to make it, because he is not convinced of the importance of the *Rasse*-moments for the history of cultures; this apart from the availability of many uncertainties in the *Rasse*-categorization given.

Does he also have reservations about the *pièce de résistance* of every *Rasse*-theory, the craniological skull index? In the long chapter devoted to this subject, Zollschan recapitulates all possible available results from craniological exercises.[476]

He has great sympathy for several of them, for instance Nyström's experiments with deforming children's skulls or Ranke's environment theory, which says that dolichocephalicy skulls transform into brachycephalicy ones during life in the mountains. This last skull-form is also a result of "intense spiritual

475 Based on ideas of Thomas H. Huxley, 1870, Zollschan accepts the Rasse-type of the *Leukodermes* (= Greeks, Italians, Spaniards, Portuguese, etc.). It is a type which is sub-divided into two types, the Xanthochroe (light-colored) and Melanochroe (brown-colored). Zollschan, 120–121, writes -chroe, where all other should write -chroi. In *Wikipedia* under "White People," however, *xanthochroi* is defined as "light whites of North Europe" and *melanochroi* as "dark whites of the Mediterranean" and in the popular press "dirty whites/ vuil blank/ etc." A small demonstration how *Rasse*-classifications are defined even from the same source.

476 Ignaz Zollschan, 1912, 80–96.

labor" during several generations, and it leads, of course, to larger brains.[477] According to Zollschan (based on Nyström's opinions) this is the reason, rather than life in the mountains, why the Jewish *Rasse* has brachycephalic skulls. And in a typical Lamarckian sense, he adds in italics: "With increased use the organ used also enlarges; the brain is no exception in this respect."[478]

His final conclusion is, however, not in favor of craniology and its skull indices. There is no single proof that different indices represent different *Rassen*, and similar indices represent similar *Rassen*. There is, furthermore, no proof that a typical skull shall remain unchanged for thousands of years in some *Volk*:

> The conclusions of craniology that are of interest to us only tell us that the spiritual value of a *Rasse* according to the presently available scientific results does not depend on the type of skull. *If one still wants to come up with a judgment, than it would be that it is remarkable how among the specific Rassen there is always a tendency to enhance their cultural value and in the same time there is a tendency of a slow transformation from dolichocephaly to brachicephaly.* All categories of *Rasse* based on the form of skull or hair are unusable… (italics from Z.)[479]

This conclusion is most of all in favor of the future: the most extensive and highly dangerous use of these craniological myths was still to come. Even after the Shoah and long after 1945, there are still many biologist, biological anthropologists and medical doctors who try by all means to uphold these myths.

Jewish people like Zollschan and their supporters were still too ambiguous, however. They are too opportunistic in accepting or rejecting some skull theory, the importance given to a dolichocephalic or brachycephalic skull. The only reason why he is against these skull games is because the dominant trend in it does not support his Jewish Rasse-position. That the change to brachycephalic skulls is identified with increasing intellectual capacities (for Jews) is as nonsensical as the Germans identifying the dolichocephalic skull with a blonde, blue-eyed Aryan *Rasse*.

Because his aim was to disarm anti-Semitism with studies about the outstanding capacities of a *Jewish Rasse*, if not the superiority of Jews, this

477 Even today one is regularly confronted with otherwise very clever people who defend this reasoning of why "Jews" are such clever people. The former Israeli Ambassador in the Netherlands, Arad, always send messages to the newspapers to point to a "Jewish winner of a Nobelprize," whereupon the question was posed: "Are you sure: *as Jew* and from which sect?"

478 Ignaz Zollschan, 1912, 91.

479 Ignaz Zollschan, 1912, 95, 96.

craniological discourse demonstrates its effect. It is a good demonstration of the result of fighting the enemies with the same weapons.[480]

4.7 Arthur Ruppin, 1876–1943

A few remarks about Ruppin are appropriate because of his highly important position in Palestine and its Zionist organization.[481] Ruppin also belonged to the group of well-known *Rasse*-authors, and they often agreed in important respects.

He received the position of "the only intellectual" in the Zionist leadership in Palestine but is only mentioned here to demonstrate the nasty consequences of the *Rasse*-discourse as demonstrated by the Zionist psychiatrists (Zalashik) in the new British colony. The scholar Ruppin was fully German-oriented like most scholars in Palestine. His two-volume *Soziologie der Juden* (1930–31) is still an important source of practical information about the position of Jews in the world after 1900 (vol. 1) and their struggle for emancipation, including the internal changes (vol. 2).

Indeed, Ruppin was a gifted sociologist, but he was also a Zionist organizer. Much more than any other Zionist leader, he shaped the basis of the Zionist settlement policy and practice and, therefore, the practical basis of an independent Zionist colonial state in Palestine. However, because of being a *yekkes*, a German-born, German speaking and -writing Zionist, so although he was one of the very few intellectuals of the time, he was considered to be less important than the well-known bullies like the Polish-Russian Weizmann, Ben-Gurion, Jabotinsky, etc.

That Ruppin, like Zollschan, was a fanatic *Rasse*-theoretician is symptomatic for the nature of the Zionist movement at the time. He wrote in 1913:

> The Jews have not only preserved their great natural gifts, but through a long process of selection these gifts have strengthened. The result is that, in the Jew of today, we have what is in some respects a particularly valuable human type. Other nations may have other points of superiority, but

480 See for this constellation also John Efron, 1994, 71 ff. about the aims of the physical anthropological work of Joseph Jacobs. Zollschan used Jacobs' studies several times. See Ignaz Zollschan, 1912, 48 and 91.

481 It should be necessary to come up with a longer story about Ruppin to demonstrate the untenable position of Götz Aly, 2011 who time and again relies on Ruppin to answer the dramatic question of why the Germans killed millions of people only because they were Jews. This leads directly to a racist judgment.

> in respect to intellectual gifts the Jews can scarcely be surpassed by any nation. For this fact alone the Jews may well claim their right to a separate existence and resist any attempt to absorb them.[482]

Several mistakes are made here in one quote. First, "the Jews" are used as if they were a *Volk,* before the Zionists called them that, and not as members of rather small religious sects. It deserves, at least, a very complicated *theological* analysis to demonstrate the mysterious source of the "natural gifts" of these religious peoples (supposing that they all held the same beliefs), what a "process of selection" of a religion looks like, and how the "natural gifts are strengthened over" the course of many centuries (see further Leibowitz).[483]

Second, with Ruppin, that nearly unavoidable propaganda-item that "Jews" were/are intellectually superior to all other people was initiated. However, sociologically Judaism, is not only a sectarian mini-religion of a social minority compared to the other monotheistic religions, but its customs are at least as anachronistic as several Islamic and Christian sects, while theologically and organizationally it is by definition less developed than the large churches.[484]

Third, at the time Ruppin wrote this (1913), there were small pockets of people known as Jews in several Western nations, comprising a purely religious group; they were separate from much smaller political groups with Jews (or people with a Jewish background), that nurtured Socialist, Anarchist, Communist, Zionist or other ideas. They never formed a nation, *Volk* or a state.

Fourth, *claiming* rights derived from the ideas arising out of this many colored political-sectarian landscape must be by definition without any foundation. It was, therefore, not this kind of "claim" that impressed, but the last attempt four years later of the British Empire to colonize a little corner of the world with white colonists instigating the conquest of Palestine.

In Ruppin's discussion of the relationship between anti-Semitism and *Rasse*-theory, he starts by quoting the well-known German classical historian

482 Quoted in Marius Turda, Paul Weindling, ed., 2007, in the article of Kamila Uzarczyk, 284. The same kind of boasting can be found in Arthur Ruppin, 1931, volume 2, 256, 257 and 305–319.

483 Recently, an old and clever physicist told me that his sound learning of theoretical physics was due to properly reciting the Torah; this notwithstanding he was an agnostic, although his parents had some Jewish background.

484 See the older study of Will Herberg, 1960, 84–89 and chapter XI concerning the distinctions of sects versus churches and USA versus Europe. In that period, scholars like Herberg still believed that man must be *homo religiosus,* who needs a faith as much as he needs food. Already a few years later, in the world-wide cultural revolution of "the sixties," this opinion became undermined and never recovered except among pious people in several remote corners of the USA or in popular dictums for all purposes like: "Oh, My God!."

Eduard Meyer who wrote: "The popular opinion that… anti-Semitism is a matter of *Rasse*-antagonism, is fully nonsense."[485] Ruppin adds that in the whole of the Orient or in Islam, *Rasse* is fully absent, a factor that changed immediately after Ruppin and his Zionist colonists entered this foreign country: Zionists needed an enemy that was still absent for asking military support and money from abroad and for creating a legitimation to attack their guest people.

In order to create a motive of the "enemy" Ruppin apparently agrees with Fritz Lenz, who sees anti-Semitism as a consequence of envy of the have-nots and that the economic superiority of Jews is the real reason for it. To support this, he provides a remarkable example: in Turkey the Armenians, who dominated all trades, were massacred, while in the same period Jews lived in Turkey in peace. Ruppin also points to the fact that anti-Semitism as a *Rasse*-question "is only a phenomenon of the last decades… glorification of the Aryans… by Gobineau… Chamberlain."[486]

It cannot be right to make one *Rasse* criterion for all: it is then too simple to judge others as "less valued" (*minderwertig*) than one's own *Rasse*. He immediately forgets this reasonable point of view as he is boasting about what the "Jewish Rasse" has achieved: only a few sentences later, we can read about the "Kulturleistungen der Juden" [cultural achievements of the Jews] and their influence on the world culture and that these are "inordinately great" ["ausserordentlich gross"]:

> Of the *Rassen* living today or, better, *Rassen*-mixtures, three do have a particularly high value (for culture): the Jewish, the German and the Roman ones. In particular, the first of these has proved in history its high cultural ability [Kulturfähigkeit]… the Jewish spirit is along with the Germanic one the main driving force of modern Western culture…[487]

Where can we find the source of this absurd opinion? Ruppin himself refers to a book about *Soziale Pathologie* and to Lenz's *Menschliche Erblichkeitslehre*, but the main source—as of Zollschan's similar opinions—is without doubt Werner Sombart. Before discussing this source, it is appropriate to mention Ruppin's practical work in Palestine and that of his supporters and successors, the psychiatrists.

Beginning in 1908, Ruppin was the leader of the Zionist colonisation movement inside Palestine, mainly busy with the emigration and settlement office.

485 Arthur Ruppin, 1931, volume 2, 39.
486 Arthur Ruppin, 1931, volume 2, 41.
487 Arthur Ruppin, 1931, volume 2, 42.

He personally started the controversial buy-up of land from indigenous clans.[488] A decade later he published a programmatic essay on the "selection of human material," [*Auslese des Menschenmaterials für Palästina*]. Talking and writing about "human material" became the usual manner of the Zionist leadership until long after 1948; this custom was borrowed by Ruppin from natural scientists in Germany and the USA.

Until 1917 anybody could come into Palestine without much difficulty, but together with the British colonial (mandatory) government, the Zionists introduced selection criteria and practices in accordance with the new modern eugenic trends, as if Palestine was already their "property."[489]

Only the best persons, healthy in body and mind, were allowed to enter the country so that the new generation in Palestine could be healthy, sturdy and have a relevant hereditary capacity [*Vererbungskapazität*]:

> Therefore, we have to limit the health selection of the emigrants and to avoid letting people emigrate… with syphilis, … tuberculosis… mentally disorders, those who are unfit for work, epileptics… who all shall be a ballast for the Palestinian society… [and in *Haaretz* somebody wrote:]… In an eugenic respect we have to look for the establishment of the new immigrants as a healthy kernel from which a healthy and brave Volk can grow as we envisage the Jews in Palestine in the future.[490]

In Europe, offices were established for carrying out medical selections, but still "wrong human material" did arrive in Palestine. However, officials were not afraid to kick them out of the country and back to Europe, even after the 1930s. This was organized by the *Jewish Agency,* the bureaucratic head office of the Zionists. They used this opportunity to get rid of the chronically sick and disabled. Zalashik:

488 Hillel Cohen, 2008, 78. Cohen wrote a remarkable book about the large scale policy to filch the land from the Arab owners "used… to undermine Palestinian society from within and then betrayed them…" This is a text of the cover which has another surprise: a highly illustrative cover picture of two strongly gesticulating men well dressed in European clothes (certainly no settlers!) with in between two very intimidated Arab landowners. Later these Arabs are accused of collaboration with the occupying enemy, while these junk-dealers were congratualed with their results. The latter may be "the paid agronoms" described in a settlement study as "from western Europe… unfamiliar with the psyche of the eastern Europeans" therefore, a large part of the farmer-settlers, and not with the Arab customs. See the illustrative pro-Zionist settlement analysis of Henrik Infield, 1946, 14–15.

489 Rakefet Zalashik, 2012, 33–34.

490 Rakefet Zalashik, 2012, 34, 35.

> Precise data are not known about the number of those sent back to Europe by the Zionist leadership, but it is certain that among the candidates for this kind of emigration there were also mentally ill people whose psychiatric treatment practically (lack of beds) or financially (payment of the stay in psychiatric clinics) was a ballast for the Jishuw [name of Zionist *Volk*]. In 1930 the labor leader Berl Katznelson wrote to the leader of the financial office of the Jewish Agency, "I am not bothered about sending back sick people, who are already more than a year in Palestine. On the contrary: everybody must have the possibility to leave the country. The 240 sick peoples who are returned... saved us great expense."[491]

Zalashik demonstrates almost the same story and mentality in her analysis of the fate of the Shoah survivors in Israel around 1948, but this can be compared with the astonishingly similar attitudes of the psychiatrists in Germany after the First World War.

This cannot be a coincidence because the psychiatrists in Palestine before the Second World War were nearly all imported Germans. The brutal reaction of Berl Katznelson, Zionist pioneer and Russian, avoids the counter-reaction that "those *yekkes'* (nickname for Germans) are all alike."

Indeed, the psychiatrists who sent only their incurable patients back to a very inimical country in Europe had the same warped ideas as their colleagues in Germany. Not only were they, like Ruppin, a main source of the ridiculous superiority feelings about "Jews," they also nurtured the classical widespread racist animosities between "Jews" and Arabs. The way they demonstrated this is symptomatic enough.

Zionist pioneers like Ruppin or Max Nordau (later Ben-Gurion would repeat the "argument" in 1948) stressed that they, the newly imported "Jews," formed the "New Men" in a totally underdeveloped oriental environment; they were the avant-garde of European civilization, etc. A serious difficulty with this arose when the British concluded in a census (1931) among Arabs, Christians and Jews that mental illness was noted in 65, 109 and 141 per 100,000 persons, respectively.

These spectacular differences were explained away by means of the argument that this concerned "civilization sicknesses," defined as the mental damage received by the accommodation of newly immigrated Jews to the modern urban life in Palestine.[492]

491 Rakefet Zalashik, 2012, 36, 37.

492 Rakefet Zalashik, 2012, 41.

It was known that there existed an anti-Semitic accusation in civilized Europe and that Jews evidenced much more mental illness than "normal" Europeans because they represented a degenerated *Rasse*. In that respect, the civilization argument was, therefore, an innovation. This remarkable explanation was adjusted in 1935 by Herrmann, chairman of the psychiatric club, who called himself "President" of some five members. He wrote:

> Here is the opportunity… to compare between the several *Rassen*. The 126 schizophrenic Arabs of a total 659 schizophrenics provides me with the right to point to this side of the problem… I have the impression that the [number of] mentally ill among the Arabs is more or less the same as among the oriental Jewish part of the settled population and also as among the Ashkenazim…[493]

This seems utterly nonsense: those 126 belong to a population of about 850,000 (1935) Arabs and the remaining 533 to a "Jewish" population of only 200,000; there are thus, relatively, twenty times more schizophrenics among "Jews" as among Arabs! This must be again a blow for a Jewish identity in Palestine.

Therefore, the current "civilization argument" was not enough here. A solution had to be found for the Jews who had lived for centuries in Palestine/ the Ottoman Empire. They were, first, defined as Old Jishuw (the old Jewish *Volk*) and, second, as "oriental Jews" who not only looked like the Arabs, spoke Arabic (Hebrew was nearly unknown) and were as "underdeveloped" and "less civilized" than the Arabs, but had indeed less schizophrenia (and other mental illnesses) than the *New Jews* or *New Jishuw,* who were only Europeans. The "civilization argument" was only used for the civilized Europeans who had to accommodate themselves, and all the indigenous people could be defined as people with a "simple mental structure" [*einfachen Geistesstruktur*].[494]

This white lie for classical racism was even aggravated into a complete intellectual and practical chaos. The European psychiatrists, whom the New Men in Palestine were clones, also differentiated in the normal German way between the *Westjuden* (or German Jews) and the *Ostjuden* (Poles, Russians).

The latter were perceived by the *Westjuden* as fully underdeveloped, if not degenerated. This was again complicated by the differentiation between the Ashkenazim and Sephardim or Portuguese Jews. The latter perceived

493 Rakefet Zalashik, 2012, 46. These arguments were also related to neuroses, suicides, etc.

494 There existed, of course, other solutions, because psychiatrists differ. One of them, Blumenthal, claimed that he could cure Jewish schizophrenics and that was a substantial advantage in the mutual competition. See Rakefet Zalashik, 2012, 90–91.

themselves to be much more civilized than the former. Alas, the Oriental Jews in Palestine were closely related to these Sephardim, while the Ashkenazim (as Zionists) were imported to dominate everybody else.[495]

This racist superiority feeling of the secular Zionists is the usual behavior of "white colonists" from Europe and is also in this case based on nothing ("*Race does not exist, but it does kill people*," wrote Colette Guillaumin, 1972). The majority of the newly imported Zionists, mainly from Poland, Russia and other East European countries, came from very underdeveloped agricultural regions and not from big cities as was claimed by "civilization" apostles. The "intelligent people" all came from Germany and were "*Westjuden*."

Furthermore, the Palestinian society itself (with the largest majority being Arabs), into which all these Europeans arrived, was already a modernizing society with a small but active Arab progressive bourgeoisie and nationalist aspirations.[496]

Many decades of indoctrination with this fully chaotic and nonsensical *Rasse*/civilization talk has definitely prevented any rapprochement between Zionists, Jews and Palestinians. On top of this, and with the same background, the conflicts between secular Zionists and Orthodox Jews persisted from long before 1948. And as if it is not enough to become chronically schizophrenic, many (Israeli) Jews and Zionists still think of themselves as far superior to everybody else, including Europeans. It is a remark that brings us back to a main source for these quasi-superiority games, namely Werner Sombart.

4.8 Werner Sombart, 1863–1941

Most Zionist and Jewish *Rasse*-theoreticians extensively discussed the work of the non-Jewish historian Werner Sombart, without doubt their most beloved sparring partner. He praised Jews in as ridiculous a way as he criticized them.[497] It resulted in a highly effective combination of glorification with

495 For this relations see now my forthcoming *Victims and Perpetrators*, 2018, passim.

496 Rakefet Zalashik, 2012, 44. Zalashik rightly points to these circumstances as a critique of the Zionist psychiatrists. There are also at the time reports of research group who analysed the Palestinian economic situation independently from the Zionists and arrived at very different results; the Zionists only boasted of their own performances. See, for instance, Sa'id B. Himadeh, ed., 1938.

497 It is, therefore, interesting to compare defenses of Sombart's Jewish writings. The first is from 1911 and extensively quoted in Jehuda Reinharz (Ed., 1981), 100 ff. It is published in the influential *Jüdische Rundschau* (15-12-1911) and the author writes that Sombart came "to the very similar results as the founders of modern Zionism." The editor remarks how

demonization, and this led to disproportionate praise for the normal, largely mediocre people.

This is a most pernicious tactic of clever anti-Semites. It gives the impression that secular people (with a Jewish background) are much more vulnerable to its influence than pious Jews. It did not help that in all these debates, pious Jews hardly ever participated. People like Martin Buber were very exceptional and already too secularized for the majority of rabbis of whatever sectarian direction, let alone for their flocks.[498]

The typical anachronistic character of the Jewish religion creates a healthy (in this respect) distance to intellectual anti-Semitism, and probably to all secular intellectual (rational) debates. Therefore, we conclude that real Jews were largely the victim of the secular Zionists from the beginning of this political movement, which hijacked Judaism and modern Rasse-theories to complete in its own emptiness.

To discuss the intellectual anti-Semitism of Werner Sombart has not been a priority in Israel or elsewhere after 1948.[499] In my Hannah Arendt study I already presented a criticism of his immanent anti-Semitism and that of his partner, Max Weber.[500] Sander Gilman positioned him rightly with Leroy-Beaulieu in the intellectual anti-Semitic corner, and he stressed as well Sombart's strange euphoria for "The Jewish Genius."[501]

---

the non-Zionists, anti-Zionists and Jewish liberals accused Sombart of anti-Semitsm, etc. The second defense is by the top-Nazi historian Ernst Kelter (*Abhandlungen zur Rechts- und Wirtschaftsgeschichte—Festschrift für Adolf Zycha*, 1941, 551–588) starting with exclamations as: "... Sombart nowhere better proves his ability to discover and explain important problems as through his Judenbuch." The rest of this contribution is not uncritical. Probably the main Nazi—sociologist Peter Seraphim used Sombart in a very positive way in a programmatic piece of work: passim, in particular in 1940, 9–11.

498 It is not my subject in this book, nor do I intend to study it later, but in my 2004 and elsewhere I touched several times on the subject of a comparison between the theological methods and theories of the Jewish sects and of, for instance, the Roman Catholics or Lutherans. They (Marten Luther, Council of Lateran) are only studied—and rightly—as important sources of anti-Semitism, but that is not enough. The Roman Catholic theologian Hans Küng started with it, but non-religious scholars should take over this task.

499 In Israel not even by Shmuel Eisenstadt or Kimmerling, to mention two of the very few interesting sociologists. Even Patai did not mention him.

500 See Hans Derks, 2004, 123 and passim; Veronika Lipphardt, 2008, 84 wrote how Maurice Fishberg perceived Sombart as "Judenfreund," but in his *The Jews*, 1911, 543 he was critical about a crucial characteristic of Jews in anti-Semitic propaganda: "All successful business of today is conducted on these principles [to undersell another; to push out competitors; to create a demand; etc.]. To call this the "Jewish capitalistic method" as Sombart does, and ascribe it to race characteristics of the Jews is not justified. ... the English, and especially the Americans, have outdone them during the last fifty years."

501 Sander Gilman, 1996, 47–50 and 73.

Therefore, I give here only an impression of what Ignaz Zollschan remarked about Sombart. It also demonstrates important features of the *Rasse*-discussion, while supporting another comparison between Sombart and Auerbach. The:

> ... aims and methodologies of Auerbach and Sombart were totally at odds. The former was trying to prove a biological point by recourse to economics, and the latter was attempting to create an economic theory by recourse to a biological or racial argument. Yet the two drew from the same well of explanations to make their points. How often the arguments of Zionists and anti-Semites, as the early Jewish opponents of Zionism declared, sounded uncomfortably similar.[502]

First, it is necessary to mention that it was only from the third edition of his *Rassenproblem* (1912) onward that Zollschan expressed an almost wild enthusiasm for Sombart, in particular for his book *Die Juden und das Wirtschaftsleben* (1911). In the previous edition only one small note with Sombart's name appeared, without mentioning any source; a year later, Zollschan devoted thirty pages to Sombart's book.[503]

Sombart had stressed the role of Jews in the economy and according to him they were the original money-capitalists. Zollschan, like Ruppin, immediately exaggerated this with his fully nonsensical notion of Jews as the "Creators of Modern Europe" and "where they appear, there is economic expansion; where they depart, there is depression." Zionists were highly enthusiastic, no single Jew reacted. Zollschan continued: "... for many decades Jews never heard such positive stories from Christians..."

This mood lasted until they started reading Sombart's book, and Zollschan soon discovered that Sombart was a critic of capitalism; Sombart also criticized the unlimited hunt for money in capitalism and its cold impersonal calculations and rationalizations! And, therefore:

> The proliferation of this capitalist economic drive [*Wirtschaftsgesinnung*], this individualistic treatment of the whole of the economy, that was the role of the Jews.[504]

502 Ignaz Zollschan, 1912, Xiii; see also John Efron, 1994, 130–135.

503 Ignaz Zollschan, 1912, XIII–XLII.

504 Ignaz Zollschan, 1912, XIV.

What could be done now? Sombart supported his view with extensive sources and asked himself what makes Jews able to do what they did? He never asked himself, nor did many others: did they do this *as Jews* or simply as clever people exploiting the chances of their minority position; see chapter 1?

There are the self-evident, "objective" reasons like knowledge of languages and foreign cultures, living in big cities, average wealth or limitation to specific kinds of professions. There are specific "subjective" reasons as well. Most of all the influence of the Jewish religion with the same ideas which make up the hardcore of capitalism: there is no mysterious drive to an overriding God as in Christianity, it is the construction of stubborn rabbis who propagate the denaturalization of life, the repression of lust and spontaneity, and who support a drive to efficiency:

> By means of this it [the Jewish religion] robs all impulses of their originality and tries to incorporate them into a clear mechanical end-means mechanism, to rationalize them... these basic features of the Jewish religion also refer to capitalism... it is this which results in the creation of the *homo capitalisticus* who realizes the reversion of all valuations of life at present...[505]

Sombart was, in fact, the first non-Jewish scientific authority to ascribe *unfounded* typical controversial characteristics to Jews *as Jews, as religious people,* and this in the exalting way so well known in the Rasse-discourse. What impact this creation of a dangerous illusion had on a very small minority (in practice, restricted to a few thousand members of a Jewish or Zionist elite) that was too often used as a scapegoat for failures of the Christian elite, is clearly demonstrated by Zollschan. He wrote:

> Notwithstanding this [what Sombart said about the Jewish religion, H.D.] the Jew is not just a product of this religion, which did not make him a Jew. This religion was not made possible in its entire specificity, if it was not grounded in a previous racial identity. Therefore, from this characteristic one can hark back to the *Volk*-identity of Jews.[506]

505 Ignaz Zollschan, 1912, XV, XVI. See also first chapter.

506 Ignaz Zollschan, 1912, XVI. Literally: "Aber doch ist der Jude nicht einfach ein Erzeugnis dieser Religion, wurde er nicht erst durch sie zum "Juden" gemacht. Vielmehr wäre diese Religion selber in ihrer ganzen Absonderlichkeit nicht möglich gewesen, wenn nicht eine bestimmte, vor vornherein rassenmäßig gegebene Eigenart sie getragen hätte. Aus der Eigenart der jüdischen Religion kann man daher auf die volkliche Eigenart der Juden zurückschließen."

After he elevated *Rasse* above religion in this way, he overruled even Sombart in exaltations about the "world-historical importance" of his own *Rasse*, apparently not very different from *Volk*. Only one example of this kind of language of a clever "Jew" will suffice:

> But that a *Volk* with such attributes is able to create such dynamic effects as the Creation of the Whole Modern World–Economy, to this should be added yet the historical fact, that this so peculiarly equipped Volk, was a Volk from the desert being driven off one's course by chilly, melancholic, sedentary [*bodenständigen*] people of the North. Only in cooperation with these, did the Jew develop all his capacities… Desert and Woods are the great antagonisms between the countries and the people who are born there… from the eternal desert, from the economy of the herd develops the response to that old Nordic economic order, bound to the soil: capitalism… Only here, as happened with the nephews of the Desert in the modern big city with its continuous hurry and hunting, could be discovered the idea, that the abstract quantity of goods and not the use-quality had to be the dominant category of economic life…[507]

Therefore, Efron is not right when he states that Zollschan like Aron Sandler, warns about or even refutes a theory of racial superiority.[508] Sombart played with all these concepts and antagonisms in a dazzling speculation; brilliant nonsense is interchanged with reasonable insights. Zollschan, not equipped to discover the difference between fact and fiction, reproduced the end result of Sombart's exercise, an inextricable web of interesting thoughts and half-truths. He then attached a *Rasse*-concept to this to help "the Oriental *Volk* of the Jews" to its "world-historical significance" thanks to its "cultural cohabitation" [*Kulturpaarung*] with the Nordic peoples.[509]

And Sander Gilman quoted what Zollschan wrote from another source:

> Character, quality of genius and the quantity of genius is determined by race. While the character and the quality of genius may be determined and modified by the environment and eventually through free will, the *quantity of genius* is the single constant in all environments (Zollschan's

507 Ignaz Zollschan, 1912, XVII, XVIII.
508 John Efron, 1994, 157.
509 Ignaz Zollschan, 1912, XX.

> emphasis). [Above all, one is born, not educated, to genius. Whereas] talent can be cultivated, genius arises with the power of a drive or instinct.[510]

Zollschan even claims that the two "pure races," Germans and Jews, do have this innate intellectual ability, leaving all other nations in the cold of stupidity and stubbornness.

Zollschan later tones down Sombart's and his own world-panorama a bit. However, the idea of the remarkable "cultural cohabitation" between victims and perpetrators remains what he calls "the general theoretical basis of the Jewish Question and the *Rasse*-problem."[511]

It is, furthermore, symptomatic that he fully negates the clever warnings of Fishberg against the exaggerations of Sombart about "Jewish" business abilities. Fishberg attacks them, first, with the traditional proverb (with many variations) about fraudulent Oriental businessmen:

> One Greek is as bad as two Jews, one Armenian is as bad as two Greeks and two Armenians are as bad as the devil… [he adds] … The Russians, Poles, and others cannot successfully compete with the Jews, simply because the latter never drink to excess, and assiduously attend their affairs. When they meet, however, with Greeks, Armenians, and others, who are equally sober… they do not excel at all, while with the Chinese they cannot even compare as traders… To call this the Jewish capitalistic method" as Sombart does, and ascribe it to race characteristics of the Jews is not justified. The most that can be said is that, being the first merchants in Europe with international connections, … they were ahead of their time. Even at this game the English, and especially the Americans, have outdone them during the last fifty years.[512]

We cannot forget that using language like "The" Jews, Russians, Chinese, etc. as still too many academic writers do and that is nearly unavoidable in *Rasse* literature and propaganda, is already a guarantee for writing non-sense or fostering prejudices.

Whether Gilman's excuses for Zollschan's behavior and that of his many followers are appropriate remains to be seen (even today, one often hears "Were not Marx, Einstein and Freud Jews?" and every year anew "Do you know how many Jews have received a Noble Prize?" and even without a "#Me Too" action:

510 Sander Gilman, 1996, 105.

511 Ignaz Zollschan, 1912, XXVIII.

512 Maurice Fishberg, 1911, 542–544. See also Sander Gilman, 1996, 79–80.

"Is not every Jewish leader a rapist like Straus Kahn or that Israeli President?"). He thinks, namely, that every time we are confronted with refutations "of the charge of Jewish unoriginality and parasitism" and that we have to understand "the self-doubt not only of the Jew but especially of the mixed-race writers at the turn of the century."[513]

Again, we have to consider that "Jew" is the name for a religious people, like "Catholic" or "Protestant," and nothing else. If we then ask whether a Jewish person is superior, more intelligent, etc. than a Catholic, or whether a Roman Catholic or Calvinist race exists, every discussion on these points is immediately stopped, as we realize we are wasting time with nonsense. This should be added to Gilman's attractive and successful attempts to dismantle the myth of the "Smart Jew."

513 Sander Gilman, 1996, 106 and 143.

CHAPTER 5

Market or Oikoïdal Religion: The Case of "Ancient Judaism"

5.1 The Problem

When this chapter was nearly finished, I glanced at the recently published correspondence of Max Horkheimer. I was struck dumb by the word "Nomadentum" and the passage in which it appeared. After an intensive study, I had come to conclusions that seemed quite similar to opinions written nearly 80 years ago! Although my astonishment partly faded away after studying the whole letter and its context, the content is perfectly suitable for circumscribing the problems to be discussed in this chapter.[514]

On the 18th of September 1940, "Teddie" Adorno wrote a letter to Max Horkheimer who was on a business tour in Hollywood. Both were coping with the problem of how to get money for new scientific projects. An unsuccessful *German Project* on German history from 1900–1933 had been proposed in which they had invested a lot of time and money. In this letter Adorno wrote about another project, the *Antisemitismusprojekt*, which had to result in a new anti-Semitism theory and not in a "commentary of a law-sociological nature."

In a postscript to the short letter, he confidentially formulated provisional thoughts on this theory. With these, Adorno felt, he should arrive at a "unified and non-rationalistic explanation of anti-Semitism." Therefore, he proposed for Horkheimer to direct activities along those lines. This never happened. In fact, the start was made with what later became the famous *Studies in Prejudice* like *The Authoritarian Personality*. But what did Adorno propose in vain about nine years earlier?

Anti-Semitism, he stated, dates back far beyond the period in which liberalism and capitalism triumphed. It has certain archaic traits and relies on motives "that are very old and already second nature." According to Adorno, we are in need of a history of the origins of anti-Semitism [*Urgeschichte des Antisemitismus*]. "This *Urgeschichte* cannot be understood as a psychological one as Freud supposed but has to search for the origin within archaic but real

514 Max Horkheimer, 1995, volume 16, 760–765 and 748. These pages are also the source of the following quotations.

 | DOI:10.1163/9789004383913_006

social movements." That was a clear statement which obviously could not earn Horkheimer's approval.

Like the historian Geremek later,[515] Adorno points to specific connotations for Jews in the German folklore: their old age and *Wanderschaft* (roaming around) or their perception as *Schnorrer* (beggar). Probably, this last image is related to "a rich beggar's shoulder-bag filled with *taler*."[516] For Adorno, this situation could not be explained from the history of the Jewish diaspora, let alone from a specific Jewish characteristic.

> I, however, want to point to the following explanation. In a very early stage of the history of mankind, the Jews despised the transition from nomadism to sedentarity and remained nomads, or they only made an incomplete and fake transition, a kind of pseudomorphosis.

Biblical history should be analyzed from this perspective. In contrast with Momigliano[517] Adorno stressed that the period of the Patriarchs, the history of the "promised land of milk and honey" and the short period of the weak monarchy should be studied.

Also monotheism had to be seen in the light of this fixation to nomadism. In Adorno's view, Jews are from before matriarchy. This made Jewish patriarchalism so fully incompatible with modern society and with developed society in antiquity. "The reasons why the Jews refused to accept some partial or local gods could be discovered in connection with their refusal to accept a single and isolated home." The editor of the correspondence remarks that Horkheimer wrote at this place in the margin: "very true." Political miscalculations of the Jews could be explained, according to Adorno, by this fixation of their prehistorical past:

> In any case, this explains that typical ex-territoriality of the Jews vis-à-vis the whole European [*abendländischen*] history. In both anti-Semitism and in Jewish reactions to this, one can find it expressed nowadays. The revival of nomadism among the Jews cannot be the explanation for only the Jewish condition but also, and even more, for anti-Semitism.
>
> It seems as if in history the abandonment of nomadism was one of the severest sacrifices imposed on humanity. The European concept of labor and all the instinctual negations [*Triebverzicht*] connected to it must have precisely coincided with sedentarization.

515 Bronislaw Geremek, 1988.

516 Note 515, 762. A *taler* is an old German silver coin.

517 See my HA, 32–40.

> The image of the Jews represents a condition of humanity without labor, and all the later attacks on the parasitic, greedy Jewish character are only rationalizations. The Jews are those who did not want to be "civilized" or submitted to the primacy of labor.... They did not want to be kicked out of the Paradise or wanted to leave it only against their will. Moses' description of the "promised land of milk and honey" is still a sketch of Paradise.
>
> This clinging to the oldest image of happiness is the Jewish utopia. Here, it is unimportant whether the nomadic way of life was indeed the condition of ultimate happiness. In all probability, it was not. But the longer the world reproduced sedentarity as repressing labor, the more the older condition had to appear like the ultimate happiness. It was a forbidden longing; even thinking about it must be forbidden as well. This prohibition is the origin of anti-Semitism...[518]

In this way Theodor Adorno provided a historical and socio-economical framework for a highly topical and complicated problem. In the end, we can only guess why this promising perspective disappeared from the agenda. Horkheimer's quick reaction (24th of September) is reserved in two ways.

Of course, Adorno's analysis is to the point but only as far as anti-Semitism is concerned and not so much for the

> explanation ... of *Judentum*. At present, this *Judentum* is only to be understood in a negative sense, from the negation of its God [*aus dem Abfall von seinem God*] ... they are lost for the false Gods.... Even in England they are thrown in concentration camps. [Horkheimer wanted to use the Antisemitismusprojekt as a] discussion with Freud, the maker of the latest anti-Semitism theory.[519]

This was the far-reaching decision that paved the way for the famous post-war *Authoritarian Personality* studies. At the same time, however, Horkheimer rejected, in my view, a more relevant historical and socio-economical study.

518 Note 515, 763 and 764.

519 Max Horkheimer, 1995, volume 16, 765: letter of the 24th of September 1940. He added: "Ich bin davon überzeugt, daß die Judenfrage die Frage der gegenwärtigen Gesellschaft ist—da sind wir mit Marx und Hitler einig, sonst aber hierin so wenig wie mit Freud." As far as I know, Adorno or Horkheimer did not use Adorno's socio-historical thoughts elsewhere. Not in Max Horkheimer and Theodor Adorno, 1944, 199–245, nor in the chapter on anti-Semitism in Theodor Adorno, 1971, 105–134. In the last text, it seems as if anti-Semitism is reduced to a matter of educational and psychological concern.

Another reasonable guess seems to be that the financier of the *Prejudice* project, the American Jewish Committee, was not victim- but perpetrator-directed. The question of how to avoid new right-wing racial crimes brought about a strong interest in oikoïdal strata within the American population.

This project pragmatically focused on "the socialisation practices of the middle-class patriarchal family ... in which the father's authority could not rely anymore on an independent civil existence."[520] In fact, one was interested in a socio-psychology of (the most sedentarized!) white middle-class city-dwellers, the so-called potential future enemies.

At the same time, Horkheimer's psychological and philosophical approach almost guaranteed an inoffensive attitude against (American) government agencies and private interests. In particular, Adorno's stress on the labor side of the problem must have worried Horkheimer and later members of the *Prejudice* project like Löwenthal. It was not necessary to fear social consequences or fundamental policy changes from a psychological project, apart from the fact that the political temperature had already decreased substantially in the first years of the Cold War.

Concerning the definition of the problem, however, Adorno pointed to important elements. First, nomadism and Judaism are mutually related, but the characteristics of this relationship must be analyzed. Second, a historical and socio-economical study of biblical circumstances is preferable in order to find the data about the former relationship. Next, the antagonisms between sedentarism and nomadism are highly responsible for phenomena as different as anti-Semitism and the utopia of a happy paradise. Finally, then the Jews are typified as "*the secret gypsies of history*" who made a "*fake transition*" from nomadism to a sedentary way of life.

These qualifications tell as much about Jews as about gypsies (Sinti or Roma) and their position *vis-à-vis* tensions from a sedentary lifestyle. At the same time, they question the real meaning of a transition between these two antagonistic social and economic ways of existence.

The unexpected acquaintance with Adorno's view on the *Jewish Question* led to a renewed confrontation with my own search for a historical definition of the *Nomadic Question* in Max Weber's relevant studies. Using Weber's sociology of religion for the sake of the study of nomadism, some serious ideological problems arose. Those, concerning the alleged *nomadic menace*, are discussed in Chapter 7. Other are elucidated by the following essential statements.

520 Theodor Adorno, 1976, XI.

In the first sentences of *Das antike Judentum*, Weber uses the concept that hints at the main characteristics of his ideological position, his sociological theory as well as his stand on the *Nomadic Question*:

> From a standpoint of the history and sociology of religion, the best way of understanding the original problem of Judaism is to compare it with the Indian caste system. In fact, what were Jews in a sociological sense? A pariah people. This means as we know from India: a guest-people formally or factually separated from the social environment but also in a ritual sense … one can derive from this the essence of the dualism between an internal and external morale and its way of life in the ghetto, voluntarily chosen long before it existed as an enforced internment.[521]

In a historical perspective, Weber's choice to look into Indian social relations is rather obvious as is demonstrated elsewhere.[522] However, the background for Weber's pariah concept must be grasped from the following part of Weber's Hinduism analysis. I quote extensively to show how Weber developed his concept, because there are many, even dangerous misunderstandings (see end of the chapter) about it:

> Everywhere there existed (and still exists) within the Hindu communities the social phenomenon of 'guest-peoples.' We know these still today … as the gypsies, a typical old Indian … guest-people … This phenomenon does not exist only in the form of a wandering people living completely without any dwelling place.
>
> More often one can see it in tribes with their own village settlements, who interlocally sell their own homemade products … or their casual labor … or who monopolize the interlocal trade in a specific product … or a service that is considered as religiously unclean by the sedentary population … in its most developed form, sedentary guest-work of a specific and very skilled nature is in the hands of people who are considered as aliens [*Ungenossen*] … and who have to live outside the settlement without any

521 GAR, volume 3, 1–5. The difficulties with this pariah-concept are legion. See for a good introduction Wolfgang Schluchter, ed., 1981 with the excellent essays by Eugène Fleischmann (263–289) and Freddy Raphaël (224–263). My way of analysing the whole question is so different that I want to develop my argumentation first instead of debating the problematic opinions of Schluchter anew. See for Schluchter's models my 1986, 54–59 and 635–638.

522 HA, 23–25.

> rights … other than a guest-right partly religiously sanctioned and partly sanctioned by a king…
>
> Where a guest-people are liable to such ritual limits, we want to speak … of a pariah-people. A pariah people … is not everybody who is considered by a local community to be an alien, barbaric or "magical unclean" group of workers. (It can get this qualification only) if it is for a substantial part or on the whole, a guest-people. This type is shown in the clearest way if it has completely lost its own binding to the land and is fully incorporated within the satisfaction of economic needs [*Bedarfsdeckung*] of other sedentary people. This is the case with the gypsies or … with the Jews in the Middle Ages.[523]

Here I conclude, first, that this concept is or became a kind of *trait d'union* between the East Asian, Near Eastern and European world. Most important, the pariah concept seems to be an universal concept directly related to nomadic peoples.

Furthermore, Weber first and foremost tries to circumscribe and classify what is going on in the non-sedentary sectors of societies strictly from the *sedentary point of view*. This is the main antagonism from which negative valuations of specific Jews or Jews in general could be derived. Here the Jewish Question becomes a real *Nomadic Challenge* receiving the very nasty undertones referred to even by Schluchter as he stated: "Between Weber and us existed the National Socialism."[524] In between, in 1940, Adorno also conquered his *locus operandi* as he connected in one stroke the unbearable fate of the Jews in World War II with nomadism.

Along with Adorno and Weber, I define a highly complex problem, the interrelations between a Jewish and a Nomadic Question. Indeed, both Adorno's suggestions and Weber's option urge the need for a comparative world historical analysis of these interrelations, but we have to know first what we have to look for in history.

Adorno seems to have a positive idea about the relationship between nomadism and Jews as a result of a victim-oriented point of view. Thanks to the

523 GAR, volume 2, 11–12. Other misunderstandings are created by the master in this profession. In a note to this last page, Weber rightly announces that his pariah concept has nothing to do with the Hinduistic realities. He adds to this announcement (and, for many, to the confusion): "We use the expression 'pariah' here just as there it is in the usual European way, comparable to the expression 'Kadi' in 'Kadi-Law.'" See also WG, 300; EC, 493. The problem is, of course, that by using the Hinduistic concept Weber perceives the concept in a pejorative, Muslim and European-Christian way. The inevitable next series of problems is the subject of the following and many other analyses!

524 Wolfgang Schluchter, ed., 1981, 9.

development of his pariah concept, one can expect that Weber had a negative perception of the nomads-Jews relationship. If true, one could deduce that Weber's point of view implies a perpetrators' orientation as well, whereas it is part of a classical oikoïdal defense mechanism against (alleged) enemies from the outside.

My thesis concerning Weber's point of view is that he defended not only a radical anti-Judaistic position (erroneously for many peoples synonymous with anti-Semitism) but also a radical sedentarist stand. Both are mutually related. If true, this outcome is a relevant substantiation of Adorno's argument.

This leads to the following procedure in this chapter. First, we need a better understanding of the Near Eastern setting of Adorno's "secret gypsy" or Weber's nomadic (pastoralist or non-sedentary) *ideal-type*. Second, we have to analyze both Adorno's and Weber's ideological position concerning the *Nomadic Question*, that both points to the need for an analysis of Old Testament sources. Adorno's case, however, remained too abstract to derive other guidelines for this chapter. Therefore, I shall mainly concentrate on Weber's biblical performance and confrontation with the nomadic way of life in the Near Eastern region.

5.2 The Near Eastern Challenge

Only the first question is obvious: What does Weber's nomadic ideal-type look like in the Near Eastern context? In *Das antike Judentum* Weber starts with a description of Palestinian geography. He describes old Egyptian or Mesopotamian political developments in the area.[525]

In about the 8th century Palestine became independent. At the time, her neighbors were Phoenician cities and Philistines in the South, Aramaeans in Lebanon, and the Bedouin tribes in the eastern desert. From the earliest times one could find grain in the central and northern plains along with cattle husbandry. In the desert oases dates were grown. The peasants and pastoralists did not like the "sterile desert" in the south and east where demons lived. In the steppe regions one could find camel, sheep, and other animal husbandry by steppe-nomads [*Hirten*] and shifting cultivation [*nomadisierenden Gelegenheidsanbau*].

In fact, Weber sketches a highly mobile situation with all forms of animal culture including so-called *transhumance*: in the winter with the flocks at the coast, in summertime in the mountains. He also notes

525 GAR, volume 3, 8. Here he discovers in old Babylon already "frühkapitalistischen Geschäftsformen."

> that times of sedentarization in villages changed with times of nomadism ... peasants in their mountain-villages of Judaea live in tents during ... half the year.... The strictest binding at the soil and the tent-nomadism are connected by all possible transitions ...[526] [Especially for the steppe-nomads,] Palestine is mostly no land of milk and honey.

After this geographical description, he constructed a scale to give some order to the main elements of Palestinian life. A few strategic citations are necessary to understand his position on the Nomadic Question:

> At one end of the scale stood and stand the Bedouin of the desert. The original *bedu*, who differed strongly from the sedentary Arab also in North Arabia, always detested agriculture and living in houses or castles; nourished himself with camel milk and dates; had no knowledge about wine; did not need or accept some form of state organization.[527] ...At the other end of the scale stood and stand the city, *gir* ... Its early forms were ... castles of military leaders with their personal followers [*Gefolgschaft*] or refuges for animals and peoples.... The city was quite different in an economical and political sense: a small market town with ramparts inhabited by peasants [*Ackerbürgergemeinde mit Markt*]. ...In a fully developed stage, the city was not only a marketplace, but, in particular, a fortress and as such the habitation of the armed forces, of the local deity with its priests, and of the monarchical, subsequently oligarchical, power. This equals clearly ... the polis in the Mediterranean area.[528] ...[In between City and Bedouin Weber placed two other elements on his scale] Against the city-patricians and the Bedouin stood both the peasants and pastoralists in the same kind of opposition. For this reason they had the same interests.[529]

526 GAR, volume 3, 11. He bases this rather flexible opinion on present descriptions found in the *Zeitschrift* and *Mitteilungen* of the (political) influential *Deutschen Palästina Verein;* GAR, volume 3, 10 note.

527 GAR, volume 3, 13. For nearly the same text see also WG, 519 and EC, 909, 910. A remarkable difference between GAR and WG/ EC is that Weber talks about Arabs ("*heidnischen Zeit der Araber*/Arabs during their pagan age") in WG/ EC. Apart from the fact that this indication does not fit very well with the Bedouin, Weber refers in both publications to his main source in Judaism questions, the theologian Julius Wellhausen.

528 GAR, volume 3, 16–17. In this chapter I do not analyse or criticize Weber's 'stadt' -ideal-type. This is already done in Christa Schäfer in Wolfgang Schluchter, ed. 1981, 78–110. More detailed is Christa Schäfer-Lichtenberger, 1983 and Hans Derks, 1996, 168–199.

529 GAR, volume 3, 62, 63.

For our discussion Weber's profile of the Bedouin is most interesting. After listing the characteristics, he continued to describe these nomads in an almost aggressively negative way. This description is dominated by strong language like "adventurous," "blood vengeance," "war," "(street)robbing," etc.

He suggests that their political organization is highly unstable because they usually do not have strong top leaders. "From an economic point of view, the present Bedouin is seen as a traditionalist without any creativity and as someone who is not in for peaceful work."[530] For Weber, there is only one reason not to generalize this judgment, namely, the Bedouin's interests in trade relations.

Still, for him there is no difference between intermediate trade and street-robbing: "The foreign merchant was and will be robbed," if he is not protected by militaries. His conclusion concerning the relationship of nomads versus "Israel" is not unexpected after these hostile judgments. Still, it is an astonishing verdict, a biblical ordeal:

> ...traditionally the Bedouin is the mortal enemy of Israel. Eternal struggle exists between Yahweh and Amalek. The ancestor of the Kenites tribe, Cain, marked with "Cain's sign," the tribal tattoo, is the murderer of God and as such he is damned to be on the move forever. The terrible harshness of the blood vengeance is his only privilege. Also in other respects, traces of the Bedouin within Israeli customs are nearly completely missing. Only one important trace is known: the painting of doorposts with blood to keep off the demons...[531]

---

530 GAR, GAR, volume 3, 15. For the interpretation of Weber's point of view see my 1986, 531–533 note 20 and 546–547 note 123.

531 GAR, volume 3, 16 and 46 for the same text. A transformation into present language is, for example, Wolfgang Keller's 1964, 83 and 168 description of Abraham's Palestine: "The nomads are there suddenly and without any warning, they kill everybody, capture the cattle and steal the harvest. Just as suddenly they disappear, and it is impossibile to find them in the wide deserts of the South and the East. The struggle of the sedentary peasants and stock-farmers rages permanently with the robbing tribes who does not know a fixed house, which is only a tent from goat-hair somewhere outside in the wide deserts." To demonstrate the typical use of *Amalek*, I refer to the famous Shoah-historian Raul Hilberg who wrote having seen a book about the Shoah-perpetrators named *Out of the Whirlwind*: "In the last resort this attitude is a consequence of a warning in the *Second Book Moses*: '...I will utterly blot out the remembrance of Amalek from under heaven.' [text from *Exodus*, 17-14].... As their ancestors the present Jews know of the danger to provide the perpetrators with a face...." Raul Hilberg, 1994, 114.

Understanding and explaining Weber's Near Eastern nomadic ideal-type, a remarkable mixture of ideology and historical "fact," is a complex affair; a step-by-step strategy seems most appropriate here.

"Weber's Challenge" can be defined as *Weber's provocation by the nomadic phenomenon.* The question then is how he handled this attack from reality on his theoretical model? If I can provide a reasonable answer to this question, the second can be answered as well: Why did he "attack" reality with his harsh ideological point of view? He answered the first question in his conclusion, given in the last quotation.

Weber, like many others before and after him, confronts us here with the single most important myth, legitimating legend or ancestor-history in our culture. As is suggested above and will be substantiated below, it also became a decisive story in the case of the *Nomadic Challenge.* A Weber case is rather unimportant compared to that. In addition, I shall take the opportunity to develop, step by step, an alternative way of thinking about the subject. Therefore, a close reading of these few lines is worthwhile. This is necessary but not very pleasant reading.

5.3 The Many "Signs of Cain"

The wording of the last citation is rather similar to a passage in Meyer's *Israeliten*,[532] but there are important differences. Whereas Weber speaks about an "eternal" enmity, Meyer quotes *Exodus* 17:16, "war with Amalek from generation to generation," and 1 *Samuel* 30:26 that talks about Amalekites as "enemies of Yahweh"; not more, nor less.

Since in the Bible nearly everybody and everything seems inimical to Yahweh (and vice versa), this is not a very disturbing announcement. Apart from this, the Israelites, whoever they were, fought holy wars against many other tribes. And in the end, Meyer showed how there are different Yahwehs for several landscapes.

Weber, however, tells the story to stigmatize the Bedouin (Amalek; Kenites; etc.), a *general* name for -say- camel driving nomads in the Near East, whereas Meyer does not exaggerate and points at the Bedouin as an "older brotherhood." This can refer positively to a love relation between biological brothers as, for instance, Cain (Qain, for Meyer) and Abel. Weber, however, wants to

532 Eduard Meyer and Bernhard Luther, 1906, 391 and 394. See also Roland de Vaux, 1961, Chapter 5.

create nasty phenomena such as blood vengeance. He forgets that this is nearly as common as addressing people as "brother"!

In principle, this activity is not a Bedouin prerogative but a privilege for everybody and every culture in the Near East or Mediterranean region. Weber should have known as well how the Bible favored blood vengeance. In *Deuteronomy* (19:11-13) one can read:

> But if any man hates his neighbor, and lies in wait for him, and attacks him, and wounds him mortally so that he dies, and the man flees into one of these cities, then the elders of his city shall send and fetch him from there, and hand him over to the avenger of blood, so that he may die. Your eye shall not pity him...

Weber even forgot another well-known fact because, for some reason or other, he denied the existence of a Bedouin law. In, for instance, the wording of De Vaux:

> In contrast with Bedouin law, however, Israelite legislation does not allow compensation in money, alleging for this a religious motive: blood which is shed defiles the land in which Yahweh dwells, and must be expiated by the blood of him who shed it (Nb 35: 31-34).[533]

Nowadays, it is still the case that premeditated murder in Bedouin and rural Arab societies may be settled through payment of *diyya* (blood money) or through mediation rather than through revenge.[534] Depending on the membership of some co-liable group, cases can become rather complicated.

533 Roland de Vaux, 1961, 12. Weber's omission is rather serious. Eduard Westermarck's (1862–1939) famous encyclopaedical socio-anthropological works like *The Origin and Development of Moral Ideas* (1906–1908) were available in Germany. His 1907, volume 1, Chapter 16 provides many interesting facts about blood-vengeance, 397–411. Due to a four-year stay in Morocco to study Bedouin and Berber life, Westermarck was one of the few scholars with first-hand knowledge about nomadic life. Nowadays, nobody will support his theory on the importance of emotions, but there is no reason to reject his wide-ranging research. In the case of blood-vengeance, he sometimes referred to biblical sources but more often to other customs. Among the Algerian Kabyles the dialectic of vengeance/ indemnification is even solved by replacing the son-victim with the murderer as a new son, 402. Moroccan Berber tribes also have several kinds of peaceful indemnification rules. For Bedouin Law see Frank H. Stewart, 1988–1990; for more complex information on present nomads see the excellent reader of Dawn Chatty, ed., 2006.

534 Joseph Ginat, 1987, 22–24. Differences between unintentional and premeditated killing are not always clear. In some Arab countries there are legal rates for *diyya*; in Oman, a

> It is customary, however, for every male member of the group who is not of the co-liable group to give the family of the murdered man a camel or its value in money. This payment is called *be'ir al-nom* (camel of sleep) and once it is accepted the giver can sleep in his tent without fear. The payment is really an "insurance policy," a wise precaution…[535]

Remarkable conclusions could be drawn from this. First, blood vengeance is, for settled (Christian) peoples and, obviously, for peasants in particular, a much harsher affair than for the most nomads.

Weber's "terrible harshness of the blood vengeance," therefore, seems pure sedentary prejudice. Furthermore, in the acceptance or not of money compensation in matters of life and death, one can detect a specific characteristic of the market-*oikos* contradictions.

But it is, in particular, the common character of blood vengeance that worries me, as Weber uses an expression like *Cain: murderer-of-God,* which cries for vengeance! And who was accused of the same crime? Exactly: the Jews. Are these victims of the largest act of theologically legitimated blood vengeance, indeed, comparable to nomads? In the last paragraph, I will try to answer this question.

As theologians in Weber's time and normal historians like Redford nowadays have stated: Yahweh is a *nomadic* god.[536] I am not familiar with theological concepts, but it seems to me that Weber's expression *Cain: murderer-of-God,* is ambiguous, to say the least. The only possible option I can imagine in this case is: If this is true, then God and Abel, a true nomad, are equal. That is not Weber's intention but near to a historical truth *if it is assumed that only Abel is a nomad.*

This brings me immediately to the next bloody practice, *fratricide*. The prelude to such an act could be Jacob's cheating his brother Esau, Judah's selling of

---

person who unintentionally kills somebody has to pay $14,500 to the injured family (half of this for a woman !). If family honor is violated (through illicit sexual relations, for instance) the judge prescribes a penalty for murder of between six months to two years in Jordan. In Lebanon, however, with its strong Christian influences, in cases of illicit sexual relations of wives or daughters, the husband-murderer will not be punished.

535 Joseph Ginat, 1987, 41. These affairs are always managed through mediators who will receive a share in the payments. This "market-situation" makes it interesting for all kinds of persons to become involved in settling activities. The effect is, of course, that the chances for peace are larger.

536 Donald Redford, 1993, 272, 273 on the basis of Egyptian sources from the 19th and 20th dynasties.

his brother Joseph as an Egyptian slave and other ignoble deeds. Not only the Bible has the privilege of repeatedly reporting about brother murder.

Pierre Oberling talks proudly about the subject of his studies, the influential Iranian Qashqa'i nomadic tribe with its long history lasting into the last century. There were sometimes violent quarrels between brothers, but they never resulted

> in the death of any member of the Quasqa'i ruling family. This is in sharp contrast to the practices of other tribal ruling families in Persia, where fratricide was a common occurrence.[537]

Fratricide was not uncommon but still was an exception among, for instance, the Greek pastoral nomads, the Sarakatsani.[538] This was *not* a consequence of inheritance rules. After the dowries were spent, in principle, parents and children had an equal share of the flock, but the youngest brother got an extra portion because of his duty to look after the aging parents.

No, fratricide occurred in relation to the competition between brothers (and do not forget the sisters) for all kinds of external favors, e.g. the praise of the world outside the family. If in large constellations like the Iranian Quasqa'i (in Weber's time about 300,000 members and ca. 5 million animals) or Khamsé[539] the social differentiation was great enough to give rise to ruling families, the external favors and praise weighed much heavier on the shoulders of its brothers. Only in these families can fratricide become a rather common phenomenon.

In the case of Cain and Abel, there was an external force/praise with a divine status. Suppose: *both* biological brothers *were nomads,* in fact, the most self-evident situation. They made antagonistic decisions in a crucial situation. Young Abel wanted to remain a nomad, while older brother Cain decided to quit the nomadic way of life in favor of a peasant existence. The end is known: the nomadic God Yahweh did not applaud this last idea whereupon Cain, immediately losing his honor and *raison d'etre,* killed his brother.

He got the usual nomadic punishment: if he had killed somebody of another tribe or family, he would have been killed also by blood vengeance if he could not pay compensation. In this case, that of an internal family affair, he was sent into the desert in the expectation that he would die. As everybody knows, the man survived, and by this "act" he received a new identity.

537 Pierre Oberling, 1974, 217.

538 John K. Campbell, 1964, 172–179.

539 Victor Monteil, 1956, 15–17.

This interpretation has the *dis*advantage of its logical consistency within a nomadic context. In concentrating on the reasons why a Cain-Abel story is told in the Bible, Weber's position can also be seen in another light, because a second interpretation can be offered.

The Cain problem, located directly at the start of all histories, concerns what can be called *the sin of the second stage*. It is a really serious case with a highly symbolic meaning. Only one thing seems to be equal to real homicide cases: nobody cares about the victim![540] Many different groups had an interest in rewriting (Biblical) history and accused their alleged enemies, of course, of rewriting history.[541]

Furthermore, it is assumed that the Hebrew *qain*, the word from which *Cain* is derived, equals "blacksmith."[542] Probably in vulgar Marxist writings this laborer can be found at the very beginning of human history. There also seems to be a contradiction between this most sedentary profession and Cain's status as nomad. In another context, however, things become clearer.

In Paradise, Adam and Eve were collectors of what was available. When they wanted more than this (or when the plenty was over), they had *no other choice* (a good definition for a divine ordeal) than to leave and *collect* new opportunities and products.

With Abel and Cain, the second stage came in which an answer had to be given to the more fundamental question: now that we clearly have *to produce* food ourselves, how should we continue? There were only two options (otherwise more brothers would have been introduced!): we fundamentally improve our way of roaming around (Abel), or we stay in a place, build a house and grow food (Cain).

Both answers were judged by Yahweh, and he, without any hesitation and in the clearest possible way, decided in favor of the nomad Abel and a mobile way

540 The exception to the rule is the article "Abel" in *The Anchor Bible Dictionary*, 1992, volume 1, 9 and subsequently Hess' article "Cain," 806–807. Compare this with the articles "Abel" and "Cain" in *The Harper Collins Bible Dictionary*, 1996, 3 and 163. See BHH, volume 1, 12 and BHH, volume 3, 3.

541 Weber, for instance, accused a "politische Tendenzlegende" which "redigierte die Überlieferung um" in GAR, volume 3, 123. In this case Weber decided that Goliath was not killed by David, but by "einer der Ritter Davids" and the "Tendenzlegende" came up with a "unbekannten und ungepanzerten Hirtenknaben David" who killed the colossus "nach Bauernart." BHH, volume 1, 500 did not want to decide on the question of whether Elchanan, Weber's "Ritter Davids," was the same as David. In BHH, volume 2, 207–208, however, the identity of the oldest and youngest "tradition" is implied. Roland de Vaux, 1961, 108 clearly states that "Elhanan" was the birthname of David and, therefore, the "original killer of Goliath."

542 See, for instance, Norman Gottwald, 1979, 578, 579.

of life. Cain was a digger of the soil, the first peasant and sedentary because he was the one who sacrificed to Yahweh the first fruits of the fields. In Yahwist tradition there is also this picture of Cain: "The building of the first cities and the invention of the first arts are attributed to the cursed race of Cain."[543] Therefore, he seems to be the ideal-typical sedentarist.

Cain, the metaphor, also happened to have very nasty and jealous qualities: for "the first time in history," aggressiveness against a nomad was expressed through an act of killing. The story continues with Yahweh's remarkable verdict: as the most serious punishment for an aggressive sedentarist, He rightly chose to send Cain into the desert. This means, however, first, that *sedentary life was sentenced again* and, second, that *within the nomadic way of life a division of labor was announced between those who cater to animals and those who have to do more or less sedentary "services" occupying lower status.*

At this point, Cain as a blacksmith becomes historically possible. A realistic example of this constellation can be found in the division of labor between the Tuareg of the Central Sahara and "their" *sedentary* Inadan/Ikalan who supply the work of the blacksmith.[544] (Here we see the difference from what Rost, the editor of the Biblical *Handwörterbuch,* BHH, told us about an alleged hierarchy *within* the Bedouin: the lowest level should be occupied by "the pariah-tribes of blacksmiths and musicians"[545]).

In fact, this reading of the case works out as a variant of my first interpretation. Both deviate from the existing stories that never look at Biblical documents as historical sources written very long after Adam, Eve and their two sons lived. First, they were looked at as tools to legitimate political-religious positions not only in about 1000 BC but right up to 2018 AD and every period in between.

Theologically inspired Bible exegesis mostly defends a strong sedentarist solution but has a serious problem with explaining *the sin of the second stage.* Which solutions are given? Weber and his sources gave the simplest one by making Cain a proto-Bedouin as a consequence of God's punishment. Weber's Cain-like aversion against nomads made him forget the Bible.

From the standpoint of Genesis, it is not only impossible but also too strange to view Yahweh or "Israel" as an eternal enemy of nomads. Apart from what was said before, one can ask: What to do, for instance, with the god-chosen patriarch Abraham, undoubtedly a pastoral nomad on a large scale, or with

543 *Genesis* 4:17. See J. Flight, 1923, 213. Flight wrote in the important tradition of the alternative German theologist Karl Budde, 1896, 57–79.

544 Hans Derks, 1995, 17–21.

545 BHH, volume 1, 197.

Moses the Lawgiver who lived with his tribe in the desert. Here, in fact, the whole covenant scenario was constructed that gave these Bedouin their world-historical role in the formation of Christendom, Judaism and Islam? Who was responsible for *the sin of the second stage*?

Quite wild answers come from Mendenhall and Gottwald. For them, the Cain and Abel story presupposes, as a matter of course, "that the shepherd and the farmer were brothers, just as most references ... presuppose that the shepherd is a member of a city or village community..." The Bedouin of the Bronze Age as well as the modern Bedouin "can be safely regarded as statistically and historically negligible"![546] Here, "brothers" cannot refer to biological brothers. Such a close relationship is incompatible with a division of labor between farmers and nomads.

The pastoral nomadism with sheep, goats or cattle to which Mendenhall could point has at least three forms that are never considered. Spending summertime in the mountains and the winter along the coast or in the valleys (with two important variations: long or short distance nomadism); steppe-nomadism; and, third, the nomadism that uses the desert oases in wintertime and coastal regions in summer.

Camel-nomadism is often mixed with the last two forms (see below). Therefore, "brothers" can be found first and foremost *between* the several kinds of nomads. Mendenhall's exclamation sounds similar to Weber's failure to detect any "traces of Bedouin within Israeli customs." Gottwald specifies Weber's most popular Cain trick. From the whole story he isolates Cain as "a fugitive and a wanderer" and, therefore, as a nomad ("a tent-dwelling cattle breeder").[547]

As shown elsewhere, the monk Roland de Vaux occupies a slightly different position. First, he accepts that Cain was a farmer.[548] The desert behavior of Cain, however, is for him the ultimate proof of "the condemnation of outright nomadism." Even the desert self shares in the burden because she becomes synonymous for Hell. This seems true for the reasoning as well. De Vaux: "Before his crime, Cain was a farmer (Gn 4:2). So, in this story, the real desert is presented as the refuge of disgraced settlers and outlaws..."

What can be criticized here, in my opinion, is the lack of imagination for giving "So" no meaning at all. The next example was related to no less a

546 George Mendenhall, 1962, 69. Apart from this, it is worthwile mentioning the meaning of *fields* in the Old Testament "which make up much of the hill-country, and can never have been cultivated even for vines" says George A. Smith, 1966, 72. As a general statement, Mendenhall is right to point to some interrelation between farmers and nomads, but in this region this can never have had much impact.

547 Norman Gottwald, 1979, 578.

548 Roland de Vaux, 1961, 14.

historian than Arnold Toynbee. It is told that he did not study his history very well because he gave Abel the peasant and Cain the nomad role in the story.[549] This message is communicated to Iraqi peasants and uncritical scholars who immediately discovered "the terrible truth" about their own Bedouin. The struggle between *these* Iraqi Cains and Abels is fixed as permanent and used as a pretext to support the strongest possible State.[550]

5.4 *Amalek*, the Eternal Enemy

Until now, I could show serious problems with Weber's use of blood vengeance, fratricide, the *Cain, murderer-of-God* option and with the specific negation of *Cain-the-peasant*. Weber did not stop creating problems in his conclusive text, quoted above.

He also said that there was an "eternal struggle between Yahweh and Amalek." Who or what is Amalek, and what does Cain have to do with this Amalek? Apparently this is a simple question but one who reads the following information, is confronted with nothing less than the Shoah evil:

> In the city of The Hague, where Jews were rounded up in 1943 and children abused them with their cries of "Desert nomads!" there is an unobtrusive monument near the Gedempte Gracht with the text: "Remember what Amalek did to you. Never forget it."[551]

Whether we like it or not, after reading the above and what follows, this warning will become a different one.

Amalek[552] seems to be the name of a "nomadic tribe classified as part of the Esau tribe" (*Gen.* 36:12). Esau (lit. savage, hairy), son of Isaac and Rebecca

549 This "solution" is still defended in feminist Bible exegesis. See Eilaine Pagel, 1989, 209. And what can be said about somebody who cannot see a nomad-peasant contradiction *at all*, as happens with Hess in his article "Abel," note 519 above?

550 Arnold Toynbee, 1946, volume 1, 58–74. This *false* story is used by quite a famous Iraqi sociologist, Ali Al-Wardi, 1972, 45–49. A worthwhile study about real interrelations between nomads and peasants is still J. Weulersse, 1946; for the situation in Iraq see 302–314.

551 The Dutch children yelling "Woestijnnomaden! Woestijnnomaden!" ("Desertnomads! Desertnomads!") were mentioned in a radio-broadcast (VPRO, 4-5-1995).

552 For this part see in BHH in particular the lemma's *Amalek, Bedoeienen, Esau, Hebreeën, Herder, Nomaden, Kain, Kenieten* and *Woestijn(reis)*; Eduard Meyer and Bernhard Luther, 1906, 389–400; Isreal Finkelstein, 1988, 27, 38, 45; Roland De Vaux, 1961, 215, 256–261; Donald Redford, 1993, 296, 349; John Bright, 1979, 122.; Martin Noth, 1966, 57–59. Around Weber's use of the *Kenites* it is perfectly possible to come up with the same kind of

and older brother of Jacob, is supposed to be a representative of a hunting culture, while Jacob represents pastoral culture. Who can imagine a nomadic tribe and a pastoral one within a hunters' tribe? In *Genesis*, the Esau-Jacob story seems to be told as a metaphor for the interrelations between hunters and shepherds and for the slow development into a domination of shepherds over hunters.

Weber again has his own interpretation of the professions of Esau and Jacob:

> As Abel is opposed to the peasant Cain, so is the soft Jacob as pious shepherd living in tents opposed to the raw peasant Esau. On the other hand, in the way that Cain becomes a Bedouin, Esau changes into a greedy hunter.[553]

In the Old Testament, descendants of Esau, the Edomites, are seen as undifferentiated and rash people. For some reason, they are also considered especially wise people, in contradiction to the first characteristics. In the New Testament, however, the people of Edom are considered symbolic of (materialist) Jewry.

Gottwald et al. identified Amalekites (and Amorites, Shosu, Midianites, etc.) as "transhumant nomadic peoples who were predecessors or contemporaries of Israel."[554] Other information shows that Amalek and the Amalekites lived only in the Negev desert. Sometimes they raided southern Palestinian areas and during the long march through the desert, a Jewish defeat by the Amalekites could be avoided because of Moses' request for divine intervention (*Exodus* 17:8-16). This battle seems to be the very reason why Weber could talk about the eternal struggle between Yahweh and Amalek.

Also later (1 *Samuel,* 15:6), Saul and David fought and won against these desert nomads. The first went to war against the Amalekites who cooperated with the Ammonites, Midianites and the Qainites as well (Qain=Cain). Saul, however, asked the Cainites to leave the Amalekites before his attack because Cainites (Qain) had done him a favor in the past. And, indeed, Cain disappeared from the battlefield.

Elsewhere (*Judges* 1:16), one can read "C(Q)ain dwells with Amalek" or "C(Q)ain, the father-in-law of Moses." In 1 *Samuel* 15:5-8 there is also some information about a town and a king of the Amalekites. Without any hesitation,

analysis as with *Amalek*. Somebody else should look into such a bunch of irrationalities if this would be interesting enough.

553 GAR, volume 3, 58 note 3 and 4. Weber does not see any contradiction here.

554 Norman Gottwald, 1979, 231.

archaeologists concluded from this "fact" (created by the translation) that sedentarization had developed.[555] Furthermore, the Biblical *Handwörterbuch* (BHH) announces that this "definitely broke their power." With this, the aim of all sedentary governments is defined in their policies against nomads. Theoretically, in this way a serious problem disappears from the table.

What can be understood from this strange and contradictory information from the giants in the profession? Before entangling ourselves in more details, it is necessary to get closer to the heart of the matter.

One of Weber's main sources, the eminent historian Eduard Meyer, can probably help with this.[556] He is certain that the small tribe of the C(Q)ainites were part of the Amalekites,[557] and he believes that this was confirmed by the C(Q)ain-Abel story: "Because here is Qain the wild tribe of the desert, that did not have a fixed dwelling place…" This circular argumentation does not bring us very far. What else does he offer? First he states:

> Abel, in fact, as Wellhausen already knew, is identical with Jabal[558] the ancestor of all animal breeders, and he is the representative of the sheep breeders from the Negev desert. [A few lines further he also confesses] that the idea, that Qainites were originally peasants and then changed into Bedouin, is most unbelievable … [Next, Meyer says:] In Gen. 4 Qain plays exactly the same role as Amalek in the later stories … [and] … the

555 Take the example of Tel Masos in the south near Bersheba; oldest part around 1225 BC. This site was excavated in 1972–1979 and was considered the showpiece of the Israelite Settlement. The earliest phase of this settlement, therefore, "marked the first phase of sedentarization by a group of semi-nomads." Quoted by Israel Finkelstein, 1988, 41. Finkelstein makes it perfectly clear that on many grounds Tel Masos cannot be an Israelite Settlement site. His teacher Moshe Kochavi already identified the place as the "*city of Amalek*," 1982!

556 In particular Eduard Meyer and Bernhard Luther, 1906, 394–396. Meyer's sources are Julius Wellhausen and Stade's analysis of the so-called *Cain's sign*. Meyer mostly writes about "Qain" (Qainiter) but he also uses "Kain."

557 This should correspond to Martin Noth, 1966, 162 who looks at the Amalekites as a "Nomadenstämmeverband in der südlichen Wüste" who lived "more or less in a permanent enmity" with Israel. Earlier, 149 note 2 Noth remembered that the Amalekites or Midianites in *Judges* 6:3-33 and 7:12 appeared with "*the Sons of the East*," i.e. the most general expression for the inhabitants of the eastern deserts. For the equation nomads = barbarians see Klaus E. Müller, 1997, *passim*, for example, 57–58 and 171.

558 As usual, finding an absolutely contradictory opinion is rather easy. In BHH, volume 2, 433 one can read about Jabal: "1. The son of Lamech and Ada in the pedigree of Cain according to J. He was the father of all shepherds (Gen. 4:20). Etymologically this name could be connected to the Arab *abbalun* = camel-driver." Jabal's brother, Jubal, was the father of all musicians; Jabal's step-brother was according to *Gen.* 4:22 a blacksmith.

> Rechabites are the only ones left from the Qainites...[559] [Weber, in the end, made Cain] the ancestor of the Kenites tribe [and that these Kenites or Qenites were mostly identified with Midianites; except by De Vaux].[560]

If both Abel and Cain are seen as ancestors of nomads who, in some way or other, are all related to Amalek, an expression such as "eternal struggle between Yahweh and Amalek" is utter nonsense (and sheep are no animals of the desert!). The exaggerated language is also dangerous, using religious tracts to fundamentally discriminate against some party. This is the case despite the logical possibility of talking about an "eternal struggle between Yahweh and the father-in-law of Moses." Other conclusions are more important.

The authorities cited did not have many problems with nomads in a positive or negative ideological sense, but rather with Cain's peasanthood in particular and with the act of sedentarization. For all these *sedentarized* ideologists/theologians, a peasant can never be the bad guy in a story, let alone "an eternal enemy of Yahweh/God himself." Such a basis for a religion would have deprived them of their most persistent followers.

Furthermore, the peasant-agrarian component of an oikoïdal economy is of pivotal importance because an animal-based economy is *by definition* market-oriented. From the start, i.e. the Cain-Abel story, the very purpose of Biblical history is sedentarization, evolving into a solid agrarian economy and society. The Israelite Settlement (in capitals) is as such an ideological and not a historical model. *Within this model*, in my opinion, only the following variants can be constructed with Biblical data:

a. "In the end," agriculture must be established with a monarchy, etc. (the *Oikos model*). This supposes that somewhere "in the middle" a transformation of nomads into peasants has to take place; the sedentarization must come from "transhumant semi-nomads (shepherds)" and not from camel nomads from the desert; therefore, a good and bad (camel) nomad

559 Eduard Meyer and Bernhard Luther, 1906, 399.

560 John Bright, 1979, 125 note 46. BHH, volume 3, 28 states that they belonged to the Amalekites till the beginning of the monarchy. At that time they divorced the Amalekites and "joined the Juda-tribe and transformed into peasants." To blur the story again, BHH states that some Kenites (or Qenites) stayed nomads and, in any case, the nomadic Rechabites looked upon Kenites as their ancestors; see Roland de Vaux, 1961, 15. Martin Noth, 1966, 56–58 tells the same story and also points to other southern tribes, although he knows of Kenites in the northern Galilee as well! First of all Judah, but also the Kalibbites (or Calebites, the inhabitants of Hebron) who are related to Kenizzites and Edomites. Furthermore, there lived Othnielites, Kenites, Jerachmelites and the Simeon tribe. See also G.A. Smith's story of the Kenites invasion of Palestine, 187.

can be substituted at in the start of the development. The end result is: Cain and Abel were both nomads.

b. "In the end," agriculture must be established with a monarchy, etc. (the *Oikos model*). This supposes that somewhere "in the middle" a transformation of nomads into peasants has to take place; the sedentarization must come from "transhumant semi-nomads (shepherds)" *but also from "nomadic agriculture"* (see Weber[561]); therefore, a good nomad and a still bad peasant (who only has to become a real peasant in a later stage) can be substituted at the start of the development. The end result is: Abel was the only nomad and Cain, the peasant.

Both models are not from this world. Ideologically motivated students will not be bothered by this judgment. Christians have always known that there was a fundamental antagonism between the *civitas Dei* and *terrena civitas*. The two other ideologies with interests in the Holy Land, Judaism and Islam, are both strongly divided by the fundamentalists. The pivotal Cain-Abel story will divide them, too.

I am not familiar with their theological debates, but I would guess that the Jews choose the second alternative and the Islamic theologians, the first.[562] The nomad Abraham is, in fact, the father of both religions; Jerusalem and Hebron are Holy Cities for Jews and Muslims. Mohammed himself experienced strong Jewish influences in the first years of his ascendancy and so on.[563] It must be clear that both models have everything to do with the (mis)understanding of a sedentarization phenomenon.

Back to *Antike Judentum*. Some general questions on this phenomenon can be posed at this junction. If a from-nomad-to-peasant sedentarization is "most unbelievable" (Meyer), what could be the alternatives in the history of this part of the Near East? First, of course, no sedentarization at all. This, however, can only be an academic question because every nomadic lifestyle has its peculiar elements of sedentarization.

Far more realistic for this area is the next alternative: nomadic sedentarization as *market urbanization*. Recent anthropological or sociological studies can be combined with the latest archaeological results (Finkelstein, Redford, Zarin, etc.). These have to be related to each other and also expanded in a somewhat

561 Even nowadays this nonsensical concept is used in *Anchor Bible Dictionary* (note 520), volume 1, 634.

562 At a basic technical level see Geert Cohen Stuart, 1984; Karel van der Toorn, 1985 and 2007. Directly related to Weber's involvement is one of the many readers of Wolfgang Schluchter, ed., 1987. The essays from Rudolph Peters, 217–242, Patricia Crone, 294–334 and Michael Cook, 334–342 are relevant here.

563 Albert Hourani, 1991.

more complex framework. That is not my task here, but elsewhere I will provide an alternative along these *market lines* (see Chapter 7).

I do not intend to show in further detail what was good or bad in Weber's "practical" analysis. The question I posed at the end of Section 5.2 (how he handled the "*attack*" from reality on his theoretical model) can be easily answered now: Weber fled from nearly all Palestinian realities and did not reply to any attack.

Instead, it seems as if he was constructing a solution out of the blue to win a theoretical battle that was practically lost. He acted as an Icarus searching for the definite explanation of Judaism in World History, not content with only becoming a better Wellhausen, the most up-to-date (Lutheran) Bible scholar.

Therefore, the second question posed (Why did Max Weber attack reality with his strong ideological point of view) could be more revealing in discovering the real content of his or any other *Nomadic Challenge*.

5.5 The Pariah Complex

Again the Cain-Abel story can serve perfectly well to provide insight into a seemingly very different discourse. Why? Because the Bible, in fact, did *not* say that the peasant Cain became a *bedu* but only that he became a vagabond and, in any case, a *wanderer always in danger of being slain*!

> And the Lord said, "What have you done? The voice of your brother's blood is crying to me from the ground. And now you are cursed from the ground, which has opened its mouth to receive your brother's blood from your hand. When you till the ground, it shall no longer yield to you its strength; you shall be a fugitive and a wanderer on the earth." Cain said to the Lord, "My punishment is greater than I can bear. Behold, thou hast driven me this day away from the ground; and from thy face I shall be hidden; and I shall be a fugitive and a wanderer on the earth, and whoever finds me will slay me." Then the Lord said to him, "Not so! If any one slays Cain, vengeance shall be taken on him sevenfold." And the Lord put a mark on Cain, lest any who came upon him should kill him. Then Cain went away … and dwelt in the land of Nod, east of Eden.
>
> *GENESIS* 4: 10-17

This text can be easily rationalized as a metaphor for the highly common migration of *peasants* following the loss of yields due to droughts, earthquakes, war or repression. These facts could be symbolized in Yahweh's refusal of Cain's offer! That they sometimes have to flee through the desert in an area with deserts around every corner is not so strange. But with this, one can change the subject of the discussion from the *nomad versus peasant* part of the story to the more abstract *mobile versus sedentary* way of life. The last dichotomy has other connotations than the former. The following example will show what I mean.

One of the interesting and valuable books by the historian Bronislaw Geremek has the title *La Stirpe di Caino*, Cain's sign, understood by Weber as "a tribal tattoo" for a "murderer on the move forever."[564] The English writer Thomas Nash (1567–1601) already saw Cain as "the first vagabond in world history."[565]

His Scottish contemporary, John Cleveland, however, introduced other dimensions in his *The Rebel Scot*: "Had Cain been Scot, God would have changed his doom, / Nor forced him wander, but confined him home." The Scots were strongly discriminated against by the English in every sense and consequently had to flee the country or to migrate. For Cleveland there seems to be only one difficulty with Cain: he was not Scottish enough, although Cain was already a rebellious wanderer with a good cause! Nash's remark states:

> On one hand the concept [Cain] marks the nomadic existence the poor had to live while … at the same time, a criminal connotation is added: this wandering is not of one's own free will but a matter of fugitivity caused by a crime.

In the Middle Ages, this double meaning was well known in the stories about "werewolves with Cain's sign" for vagabonds living in the woods as symbols for hypocrisy and fraud. But beggars who tried to get their alms by fraud were also seen as descendants of Adam's eldest son.

When going back in time, from the late Roman Empire beggars or vagabonds played a large role in plays from Lucianus of Samosata, to Petronius and Apuleius. Here, marginal figures, in fact, were only perceived as criminal demi-gods busy with defrauding and cheating to get money for alcohol and prostitutes.

With Roman Christianity, indeed, there was a break with this perception: *poverty was praised as a virtue*, although nothing else gave rise to more hypocrisy. The reason why poverty became a virtue is simple. According to the Fathers, it is only a matter of God's grace whether you will become rich or poor and receive a high or low social position. So, you have to accept your destiny in all humbleness. What He has given to you is a virtue. Amen.

---

564 Bronislaw Geremek, 1988. In Kipling's *Jungle book* Shirkan the tiger, the Ultimate Evil, was provided with "Cain's stripes."

565 Bronislaw Geremek, 1988, 9 also for the next quotations.

Furthermore, Christianity later developed an institutionalization of *eternal poverty* to organize real poverty and related phenomena by means of rural and urban cloisters, beggar communities or public *charitas* institutions. This became a most lucrative means of transmitting money and riches to the Churches. With care for the sick and education, this trinity formed very effective instruments to creep into all corners of society.

When the urban heir of beggars expanded too quickly and the rich started fearing for their position, hard repression by law, church and army was exercised. In particular, from the beginning of the 16th century on, this repression became systematized, large scale and often very cruel. Then the stories about the "richness" of the poor, their laziness and refusal to work, their cleverness in simulating illness and, in the end, their descent from Cain also started to be told.

Last but not least, the place where all those sinful wanderers and beggars concentrated, the city, could be rather easily incorporated by something that became the absolutist (patrimonial) state, the super-*Oikos*. It is surely no accident that Cain also became responsible for building The City As Place of Sin (see *Genesis* 4:17).[566]

There is a poor legitimation for poverty-as-a-virtue in the Old Testament. In a nomadic tribal society, there are differences in individual prosperity but only "collective" poverty due to droughts or pests. Contrary to sedentary Christianity, here richness is a virtue. It is expressed first and foremost in the number of animals one has.[567]

Everybody accepts that the rich are the most pious, clever, etc. and the poor (the ones with fewer animals) are those with bad luck, who are not very clever and, therefore, are a kind of sinner. But sharp distinctions cannot be made because all participants in this society know very well how relative richness is, how everybody has to rely somehow on each other, and what the minimum

566 Indispensable for the period concerned is Robert Muchembled, 1988.

567 One example from Near Eastern nomads demonstrates present realities in the area. In a study of the famous Yörük of Southeastern Turkey, of the 168 nomadic families studied only six "owned shares in fields or urban property from which they derived a predictable income. Variation in herd size therefore is an accurate measure of a family's economic standing." Daniel Bates, 1973, 161. Among this Yörük, with an average herd of about 250 sheep per family, there is "a strong ideology which calls for supportive behavior among agnates, particularly in dealings across close descent lines." The richness of people is generally demonstrated by acquiring second wives at high bride prices, by devoting much wealth to hospitality and charity and by interacting with kinsmen in a preferential way, 168. In my view, this means a high levelling rate of income distribution and, subsequently, a rather comfortable position for poor members.

number of animals for a good poor life is. Also, a poor man remains independent and free.

Real (unfree) poverty arises *in oikoïdally organized urban and rural societies*. For a substantial part, the very hierarchy of that society rests on the existence of a relatively large real poverty and, therefore, on the (legitimation of) institutional dependency of "the top."

Some prophets learned about this society for the first time in exile (*Isaiah* 14:32; 25:4; 49:13) and started to give poor people a profile as "the poor from Yahweh." In the New Testament and in apocryphal writings (*Tobias* for instance), there is already more talk about poverty in the Christian sense. Jesus, far from being a social reformer, used the poor as the first receivers of the richness of faith. Still, it is typical enough that Gottwald, who must have a strong interest in making his revolution theory acceptable, could not mention any *substantial* fact about poverty.[568] This is clearly related to the obvious difficulties of coming up with a reliable picture of agriculture (Cain's work).

All this has provided *sedentary* people within Western Culture with one of the strongest prejudicial notions: *wandering peoples are criminals, uncontrollable scum.* The authorities and the ideologues did everything to foster these prejudices because they adhere to the hard core of sedentary legitimation.[569] How is this non-conformist (Cain) behavior treated in Weber's writings? And what about "criminal wandering" behavior?

How Weber perceived the Bedouin is clearly stated above. The two serious mistakes he (also) made can now be concluded from the discussion so far. First, he makes the overly strong suggestion that the so-called sign or mark of Cain indicates that the bearer is a criminal. From the *Genesis* text quoted, I can only conclude that this sign *protects the bearer from being slain.* The example of the *Yellow Star* is obvious here: this clearly had the first function.

Second, here (again) it is proven that Cain is not damned "*to be on the move forever.*" Although *Genesis* in this case is not specific enough, the safest

568 It is also typical that Martin Noth or John Bright and even Ronald de Vaux do not mention the phenomenon at all. The latter provides some facts about oikoïdal towns and cities; Ronald de Vaux, 1961, 72–74. If poor people (*ebjonim*) can be found, Weber points to two possibilities: GAR, volume 3, 55. In post-exilic times, the poor could be found only within the city-demos of petty traders, craftsmen etc. In pre-exilic times, however, Weber finds them only within the small peasantry exploited by town patricians. But a few pages later, he notes from a source "aber es sollte eigentlich keine israelitischen Bettler geben," 73.

569 The whole literature about the way gypsies are treated in police and other bureaucratic reports through the ages (to this day), or people who live in caravans, is illuminating. See, for instance, Leo Lucassen, ed. 1998. For an interesting comparison between Jews and Gypsies see Wolfgang Wippermann, 1997.

conclusion is that the peasant Cain had to wander until he settled in the land of Nod, where he built a "city" for his son Enoch. Therefore, *Cain is a sedentarian temporarily on the move because he committed a crime.*

Now, quite a different type of people come to the fore. They are no doubt wanderers but also "in between" people: those engaged in small-animal husbandry or pastoral nomadism and the patriarchs. In the entire passage, Weber gave the impression that the breeding of small animals equals a socially and politically impotent constellation. Clans or tribes, however, can have enormous herds of sheep and goats. Only the power of numbers gave them substantial political power.

I cannot imagine that patriarchs were people with only a few sheep. Sometimes pastoral-nomads were for Weber synonymous with "half-nomads" (*Halbnomade*) and another time with shepherds (*Hirten*). A *Halbnomade* is comparable with "a woman who is only a little bit pregnant"; a shepherd is only a short-distance manager of a flock. Weber's poor conceptualization in this respect is a fact with which I cannot deal further.

What about the criminal record of such husbandmen and their patriarchs? In fact, Weber looked into the *perception* of these peoples in the common opinion of the so-called monarchy (the Patriarch legend). In connection with this legend, Weber reached the nucleus of the Pariah question, announced above as the core of his ideological position.

According to Weber, the legend provided a profile of patriarchs.[570] They were isolated house-fathers of large families who did not cooperate politically. They were pastoral-nomads, *metics* (as in the Greek sense) and true believers in a peaceful God. They received land for animal breeding from the sedentary population in a peaceful way and subdivided this peacefully among their family members. They did not have the charisma of heroes.

Still, one has the impression that Weber is reproducing coolly, as stated, the *perception* of the patriarchs. However, in telling the last element of this Patriarch legend, this honorable Wilhelminian scholar inexplicably produces an emotional exclamation lasting a full page. In Weber's work one will never read another passage containing so much sarcasm, distaste, wrath and indignation. After displaying that incriminatory "last element," I will quote the first and last sentences of the passage and in between the emotional keywords. Here, again, one regrets providing a translation because it is necessary to read the German original to understand all the connotations.

570 GAR, volume 3, 58. The following long quotation is compiled from Idem, 58 and 59. Sometimes the German translation is added.

First then the "last element" of the profile: the patriarch is willing to provide his patron [*Schutzherr*] with the most beautiful women, even his own wife. He then asks God to liberate her by means of plagues, although it had not crossed his mind to defend her honor [*Frauenehre*]. Weber continues with:

> To them it seems quite laudable to get rid of their own daughters instead of their guests so as not to injure the holiness of the law of hospitality. One has to distrust the ethic guiding their manners [*Verkehrsethik ist fragwürdig*]. For years an amusing play full of blackmail was performed between Jacob and his grandfather. In it they haggled [*Feilschen*] about desired women or the cattle gained from the grandson's work as a lad. In the end, the Ancestor of Israel sneaks off from his grandfather's Lord while stealing the Lord's house-idol to assure himself a quiet retreat. [Weber continues with a catalogue of abuses from which I only quote keywords:]
>
> Jacob's fraud (is) absolutely in order ... a pious pastoral nomad out-haggled his brother[571] pictured as a thoughtless peasant[572] and hunter ... (Jacob) cheats the father with the mother's help ... prays a very miserable prayer in fear ... to kill his brother or sell him as a slave ... this Joseph shows fiscal qualities in exploiting Pharaoh's subjects ... [Weber compares the patriarchal behavior with] the ethic of a pirate and merchant ... or (with) Odysseus' excessive complaints [*maßloses Jammern*] ... (this remains) for us beyond the virtues of a hero [*Heldenwürde*] ... These are the characteristics of the ethic of a pariah-people [*Pariavolksethik*]. Its impact on the external morals [*Außenmoral*] of the Jews in the period of their dispersion as an international guest-people cannot be underestimated. With the very articulated pious obedience, they form the whole of the inner stature of this kind of people ... without any doubt, this stratum is, like powerless *metics*, the same as pastoral nomads living among free citizens [*wehrhaften Bürgern*].

The vision like that given by Weber on the *Exodus*, when not mixed up with the pariah option, could reveal a healthy relativism or sarcasm about those

571 Weber's note: "In the same way that Abel is confronted with Cain, so is the soft Jacob confronted with the wild peasant Esau as if he is 'the pious nomad who lives in a tent.' On the other hand, as Cain becomes a Bedouin, so Esau is seen as a fanatic hunter": GAR, volume 3, 58–59 note 4.

572 Weber's note: "Because in this way one has to translate 'isch sadeh' ('Man of the field,' Gen. 25, 27) and not as is done at present: 'Man who wanders over the steppe' which is not the meaning of 'sadeh.'" GAR, volume 3, 58 note 3.

patriarch stories. It could be the same mood in which Donald Redford wrote about the ironies of the *Exodus* events and the curious use in modern religion

> ...as a symbolic tale of freedom from tyranny ... namely that of Pharaoh, (which) was mild indeed in comparison to the tyranny of Yahweh to which they were about to submit themselves. As a story of freedom the Exodus is distasteful in the extreme ... and in an age when thinking men are prepared to shape their prejudice on the basis of a 3000-year-old precedent, it is highly dangerous.[573]

Of course, Redford's modern (democratic) English contrasts sharply with Weber's class-bound elite German from around 1900. The main difference, however, is that scholars like Redford try to work on a 1:1 relationship with reality.

It looks like as if Weber is taking "blood vengeance" because reality cannot be manipulated in the direction of his own *Geist*. In the previous compiled quotation, Weber used Wilhelminian bourgeois-aristocratic values as positive criteria. Who else worries in this way about *Frauenehre*? What to think about a *Kriegs-Held* with its *Heldenwürde* for whom/which it is utterly impossible to make a difference between *Außen- und Innen-Moral* or to accept a *würdelose Erniedrigung*? And who else shall judge everything except 100% fidelity to the Master as fraudulent behavior?

The (in his eyes) negative values Weber expresses to characterize Pariahs are indicated here with the verb *feilschen* (to barter or haggle) as the ultimate market behavior and that to do so with *maßloses Jammern* (excessive complaining) is something like "to barter with emotions." Therefore, he could conclude that their *Verkehrsethik* is *fragwürdig*, they demonstrate an abject way of communication with foreigners; a conclusion that could follow the classical (and false) complaint about the Jews asking foreigners but not fellow Jews for interest on loans (which was *inter alia* a normal Mediterranean custom as old as the ancient Greeks).

In this passage Weber, therefore, displays the moral and sexual indignation of the Wilhelminian elite and the strong (religious) disappointment about the fact that the ancestor of Israel (which must be, in his eyes, his own ancestor) is only a fraudulent, sexually perverted, dishonorable and criminal pastoral-nomad. At least, he reproduces the 1914–1918 German elite thought about *Helden versus Händler* (heroes versus merchants) in his Judaism analysis of

573 Donald Redford, 1993, 422. For his profile of Yahweh see his 275, 276.

the same period. At the time, this was the usual talk in his own circle to be demonstrated by his friend and co-editor Werner Sombart.[574]

In his *Die Juden* Sombart gave a profile of the Jews as *Händler*. Only a few years later he wrote one of the most poisoned, nationalistic pamphlets in favor of the German war efforts under the title *Händler und Helden. Patriotische Besinnungen,* 1915.[575] Here he abused not only the English and England as *der Feind des deutschen Wesens* (the enemy of the German spirit), but he also tried to eliminate, on paper, the race of *Händler* as such. This race Sombart had adored in *Die Juden.* Now he ridiculed *der englische Seeräuber* with their *ewigen Handeln und Feilschen* (eternal hawking and haggling), which could be only fought in a religious war. This had to be a war between "two ideologies: a commercial ideology versus a militant heroic with their corresponding cultures" [*händlerische und heldische Weltanschauung und dementsprechende Kultur.*] Sombart added, so that we might not forget it, that this dichotomy, "*Händler und Held* forms the largest contradiction … the two poles of all human behavior in the world"! The relevancy of a book entitled *The Market and the Oikos* could not be demonstrated better.

Later in his Nazi book,[576] Sombart reproduced these texts. There, he openly adored Mussolini as a typical Hero, found it quite reasonable to deny—"without any reason" [*ohne jede Begründung*]—Jews from commanding and responsible positions (no army officers, lawyers or university professors) and he gave the highest priority to getting rid of a "Jewish Spirit."

In 1914, most Germans, in particular those in academic circles, saw the English as *Krämer* (peddlers, hawkers). They constantly used words like *Krämerkultur, Krämerideale*, etc. Weber connected these words with sexual connotations to violence as he wrote about the English with their "*rapes and the immoral hatred* [*of their*] *'krämerhaften' economic war.*"[577] This was the mood in which he at the same time wrote about Judaism.

It seems furthermore striking that the key concept "guest people" is already used in Weber's above-mentioned text. Weber knew that he was dealing with a legend. Indeed, at the moment[578] it is still clear that no single relevant Bible passage fits into a *historically* verifiable chronology of Israelite or Hebrew, let alone Jewish history, history.

574 Compare Werner Sombart, 1911, 332–334.

575 The citations come from VI, 16, 21, 4, 64 in that order.

576 Werner Sombart, 1934, 76–77, 192.

577 GPS, 117.

578 Donald Redford, 1993, 258–263, 422–429.

Strangely enough, Weber provided the legend as the *first historical setting* in which all negative (also positive?) elements of Jews popped up. In other words, in a legendary birthplace of a concept, Weber comprehensively located the reasons why *later* people/Jews had to become a guest people. In this way it became the *Tatort*, the crime scene, the place where Cain committed his crime and where an *eternal enmity* could be created.

It seems, therefore, appropriate to give a detailed reconstruction of "the crime." A further aim is to show the mutual connection of a bunch of Weberian concepts. It does not matter which concept one chooses as an example. Still, there is a particular reason to take the following step. Thanks to Weber, the discussion is politicized to the utmost. To counterbalance this situation, I shall take the least ideologically loaded concept Weber used in this context.

5.6 The Crime and Its "*Tatort*"

The shortest description of *Pariavolk* Weber used here is "metics on sufferance between armed civilians" ["*geduldete Metöken zwischen wehrhaften Bürgern*"]. As usual with Weber, this definition is also highly ambiguous if seen as a historically correct comparison.

In the Greek classical period, metics (*metoikoi*) were privileged foreigners without civil rights in the settlement where they lived. *Met-oikoi* means literally "the dwelling together" (*metoikion* is the name of the fee they had to pay). They were often Greeks but also came from other parts of the Mediterranean. Some became very influential due to their money capital (ca. 400 BC the Athenian metics Pasion and Phormion belonged to "the richest people in the world") or to specific talents such as the orator Lysias.[579] Some stayed poor, and most of them occupied small and marginal jobs in commercial, service or handicraft activities.

Contrary to Weber's suggestion, they could serve in the army in separate divisions and could become normal oarsmen in the Athenian fleet. They could get several dispensations and receive the same protection from the courts as citizens, but could not contract legal marriages with citizens or own real-estate property. They even had their own god of a high status, *Metoikios Zeus*. In short: apart from some political and legal restraints, they had practically the same social position as a citizen.

Therefore, they were not "on sufferance" or merely tolerated, but had a definite status distinguishing them from all other foreigners (*xenoi*); they were

579 Hans Derks, 1995, 257–259.

wehrhaft[580] as Weber knew perfectly well from Thucydides (II, 31). To call them "*machtlose Metöken*" (powerless metics) is, to say the least, a contradiction in terms also within his own ideology.

A historical parallel with the patriarchs, furthermore, is not possible because they were nomads, and not sedentarized foreigners, from the moment they arrived in Israel, according to the stories. This was the case, despite the fact that there was no such thing as Greek citizen-rights in the area until Hellenistic times. The question remains of why Weber made the comparison between pariahs and metics.

Weber's text discussed here was a *conclusion* for him. He prepared his opinion on the issue carefully. In the introduction to the second section, I provided the whole framework of his model, which stood at the start of his argumentation: the largest contradictions exist between city (patricians) and the Bedouin, *bedu*; pastoral-nomads (defined as *Kleinviehzüchter*) cooperate with peasants against both the city and the *bedu*. There he already talks about the *Wehrverband* (military formation) and he made the early settlements in the region similar to the Greek *poleis*. Due to this comparison, he already operates on an extra-reality level suggesting that most settlements were real cities.

In enhancing this model by detailing the *Kleinviehzüchter*, he again referred to the Cain constellation.[581] Weber, of course, saw the transition from the Bedouin to semi-nomads, peasants and "city" as the phases to pass through successively in an inevitable sedentarization. The effect here is that the main differences between pastoral-nomads and shepherds (mostly caring for the animals of some proprietor in the neighborhood) are blurred. With this, the semi-nomads automatically get an (ideal-typical) intermediate position: "… they were *gerim* (foreigner, aliens, guest worker, etc.) … could easily receive full citizenship in the cities [of residence] for their economically best achieving clans by means of contracts or through violent conflicts."[582]

580 "Wehrhaft" refers to the possibility of bearing and using arms. As usual, Weber has something different in mind when he uses this word. For example: "Die volle Wehrhaftigkeit und also: politische Macht lag aber in vorexilischer Zeit in erster Linie bei den stadtsässigen Sippen." in GAR, volume 3, 32. For Weber, political power is *by definition* the property and use of arms, nothing more or less. This is probably the hard core of his ideology but also of his mentality. In the meantime, the citation demonstrates once again his heavy reductionism.

581 GAR, volume 3, 44–51. If one reads 16–17, 44–45 and 58 (the conclusion) one right after the other, one has a good example of how a Weberian ideal-type is constructed. It is not a discussion of several alternatives and situations ending in a well argued conclusion (the model), but an *a priori* statement from which the details (i.e. the pivotal concepts within the model) are repeated to a large extent in slightly different configurations.

582 GAR, volume 3, 46.

Who or what were *gerim*? In answering this question, Weber used all the keywords already discussed in intermediate passages.[583] They were related to craftsmen, merchants, were "ritually unclean," or suffered "ritual alienation from the tribe," were "guest craftsmen," "pariah caste," "Dan tribe" and "Cain." In addition, he referred to Kammalar craftsmen in the south of India as being similar.

Surprisingly, after the return from exile, *gerim* are also identified with a "typical urban *demos*" (Greek civilians). In the same sentence Weber also identified *gerim* with a "plebeian stratum," as if *demos* and *plebs* could be compared here. To make this opportunistic name-dropping fully indigestible, only one page later he confessed that there were differences between "a real '*Demos*' in a technical sense" and "a '*popolo*' … as used in medieval times."[584] He denies that the *ger* or *toschab* from the sources, translated with *Metöken* by Meyer, were free men who did not belong to the highly valued clans [*vollwertigen Sippen*].[585]

To illustrate his case, Weber gave as an ideal-typical example the Danites, a quite promising choice. According to him, the members of the Dan tribe were *Wanderhirten* (pastoral nomads, I guess) who could not obtain fixed places within Israel/Judea till they could conquer the city Lajisch in the north. He must have known from Meyer[586] that this is half of the Biblical truth, let alone the real truth.

First, they were settled in the hills west of Jerusalem in the cities Sora or Estaol but had to leave these places because of the pressure of Amorites. The Dan people were known because they produced well-known artists. They had great commercial talents and had services to perform in the harbours. Their adherence to sectarian religious beliefs, however, made the authorities afraid and suspicious.

This must be the reason that much later it was predicted that the Antichrist would come from the tribe of Dan. (There is, however, no reason to be afraid according to Donald Redford.[587] As is the case with Amalek, there is no extra-Biblical evidence for a Dan settlement in the north, and it seems wise to reserve judgment also for the rest.) Of course, Weber knew the relevant Meyer passages about the Dan tribe as he himself reproduced many particulars, and it is, therefore, unbelievable that he was unaware of their very negative image.

583 GAR, volume 3, 34, 35.

584 GAR, volume 3, 36.

585 GAR, volume 3, 32 and note 1.

586 Eduard Meyer and Bernhard Luther, 1906, 524; see for the following also BHH, volume 1, 351. See also GAR, volume 3, 34 where Weber used the Dan tribe in relation to Cain and the *gerim* for the first time.

587 Donald Redford, 1993, 296.

But what did the Biblical sources really say about the *gerim*? Roland de Vaux provides the clue:

> Nomad life also gives rise, invariably, to a law of asylum. In this type of society it is impossible and inconceivable that an individual could live isolated, unattached to any tribe. Hence, if a man is expelled from his tribe after a murder or some serious offence, or if, for any reason whatever, he leaves it of his own free will, he has to seek the protection of another tribe. There he becomes what modern Arabs call a *dahilc*, 'he who has come in,' and what their forefathers called a *jâr*. The tribe undertakes to protect him, to defend him against his enemies and to avenge his blood, if necessary. These customs are reflected in two Old Testament institutions, that of the *ger* (which is the same word as the Arabic *jâr*) and that of cities of refuge.[588]

The old texts consider, therefore, a *gerim* as one who stays for some time in another tribe, clan or place. Patriarch Abraham became a *gerim* in Hebron to bury his wife Sarah on land with a cave given to him by the Hittites, *Genesis* 23:4. Moses fled to Midian, helped the seven daughters of Reü'el was allowed to stay and had a son with Zipporah: "…he called his name Ger'shom; for he said, I have been a sojourner [*ger*] in a foreign land," *Exodus* 2:22. *Ger*(*im*) could be used as part of the characterization of the Rechabites.[589] The family of the patriarch Jacob comprises three generations. Included were the servants, the resident aliens or *gerim* and the "stateless persons," widows and orphans, who lived under the protection of the head of the family.[590]

All these meanings suggest a peaceful attitude against foreigners and a far-reaching hospitality. I cannot see any reason for Weber's denigrating opinion about nomadic hospitality and the marrying of daughters. Furthermore, no patriarch can be put into the constellation Weber sketched as typical for *gerim*/pariah in any context.

The use of *gerim* underwent changes.[591] After settling in/conquering Canaan, the Israelites considered themselves "owners" of the country and the former inhabitants as *gerim* unless they were assimilated by marriage or reduced to slavery. In the beginning, the *gerim*, as free people, had to hire out

588 Roland de Vaux, 1961, 10.

589 Roland de Vaux, 1961, 15: "…you are to dwell in tents all your life, so that your days may be long in the land where you live as aliens (*gerim*)." Is this the beginning of the Ahasverus legend which is a well-known feature in anti-Semitic literature?

590 Roland de Vaux, 1961, 20.

591 See for the following Roland de Vaux, 1961, 74–76.

their services like the Levites with their own profession. *Resident alien* became an inferior position compared by the Israelites themselves to their own *gerim* situation in Egypt. De Vaux discovers, therefore, a similarity with the Spartan *perioikoi*, the suppressed original population of the Peloponnese. The only comparison to be made is that *metoikoi* is also a Greek word.

Apparently shortly before the Exile, however, a series of new provisions were made for the gerim to reduce their differences with the Israelites, to enhance the assimilation of their own (Israelite) *gerim*, and to pave the way for the assimilation of foreign gerim. They came to share in the social and religious advantages and obligations. They were entitled to justice and liable to the same penalties, while in everyday life they experienced no difficulties whatsoever. They had to observe the Sabbath, fasting on the day of Atonement or celebrate Passover with the Israelites, provided that they were circumcised. They were subject to the same laws of cleanliness and so on. If one likes comparing, this *gerim* could be seen as *metoikoi* in the same way I sketched the Greek position.[592]

5.7 Preliminary Conclusions

At the end of this chapter, some conclusions can be directly scrutinized thanks to a publication about the pariah problem by Hyam Maccoby, emeritus fellow of the Leo Baeck College in London.[593] One citation is enough to reveal the problems he raises. Maccoby writes:

> Max Weber never put forward an explicit theory of anti-Semitism, but his concept of the Jews as a pariah people has obvious implications for the study of anti-Semitism ... Since in this book, which is chiefly about anti-Semitism, I also put forward a theory of the Jews as a pariah people, it is important to state at once how my theory differs from that of Weber. The basic difference is that Weber argues that the Jews made themselves into

592 Weber criticized Eduard Meyer in GAR, volume 3, 32 note 1 for making a difference between *ger* and *tôshab* (for Meyer resp. "Metöken" and "Klient") while he himself did not see any difference. Roland De Vaux, 1961, 75,76, concludes that a *tôshab* seems less assimilated (socially and religiously), less firmly rooted in the land and also less independent than a *ger*.

593 Hyam Maccoby, 1996. The negative opinion I have of this book is only the result of reading "Weber passages." In passing I read many interesting things on which I cannot elaborate here. In particular, I fully agree with his thesis (last chapter) that the Holocaust is no mystery, although I probably have a different argumentation for this. The citation is from 20.

> a pariah people by their adoption of a separatist religion; while I argue … that the Jews became pariahs only because they were cast in that role by Christians…

In this last section, I will comment on this theory, first, indirectly by starting with some simple logical conclusions regarding the repeated use of *Metöken/ guests/pariahs* by Weber. Afterwards I shall return to Adorno and, now, Maccoby as well.

It is perfectly clear from the last part of my analysis that the three possible *gerim* meanings from Biblical texts do not correspond with Weber's pariah model for several reasons, while the real *metic* position is not appropriate either. Furthermore, it could be shown how the nomadic elements (hospitality, etc.) are denied in a fundamental and even hostile way. Now it is easy to verify Weber's firm universalistic statements in *Wirtschaft und Gesellschaft* and to see the very weak basis of his argumentation.[594]

Next, it seems obvious that Weber's use of the pariah concept does not refer to any historical reality nor does it refer to the perception of historical patriarchs but to the *negative perception of Jews and their 20th century position.* This perception is transformed into an *ideal-type* and a universal truth suitable for all times and all corners of the world. Apparently, this is made possible through the immanent and original *anti-nomadic moment* (Cain-Abel syndrome) and, therefore, the general sedentarians' aversion to non-conformism. Therefore, one can better speak of a *pariah complex.*

For all fundamentalist sedentarians, this complex serves as the historical legitimation to *stigmatize and discredit* nomads, all wanderers as such, and irregular, uncontrollable market peoples or the ones who are regarded as such, like the Jews. Furthermore, there is envisaged a negatively loaded *guest* position in order to keep the "guests" only temporarily within your reach and *to avoid any form of assimilation.* At last one can conclude: in Weber's time, as the many given examples have shown, the *Nomadic Question* and the *Jewish Question* are strongly intertwined in the sense that the *former is the general and the latter the specific question.*

These results confirm Adorno's opinion that there is a mutual relationship, first, between nomadism and Jewishness and, second, that this relationship must be connected in a profound way to the nomadism-sedentarism antagonism.

This opens a new avenue of fundamental research. From the above analysis it also follows that Adorno's notion of a prehistory of anti-Semitism can be

594 See WG, 748 and EC, 1247.

reconstructed through a study of the prehistory of the Patriarchs. Paradoxically enough, this leads to confrontation not with a real history of so-called "patriarchs" in old Palestine, but with 19th and 20th century anti-Judaism (Meyer, Sombart, Wellhausen, Weber, etc.).

From this follows, next, that it is highly preferable to make the distinction between *anti-Semitism* (racially oriented -ism from the 19th and 20th centuries in many European countries, the USA, etc.), *anti-Judaism* (religiously oriented -ism originating in the West-European Middle Ages and still active today), and *anti-Jewish measures* (secular measures from a social, cultural and economic nature taken against some Jews sometimes in antiquity but mainly from the Middle Ages onwards).[595]

So, only in the 19th and 20th centuries could all three phenomena be active *together*, but they have their own history and are in need of their own explanation. In my view, many misunderstandings about the un-mysterious Holocaust could be avoided by adopting the given distinction.

In this way of defining problems it is easier to see why, for example, Weber is a diehard anti-Judaist in his studies of the Bible. Because he universalized and secularized his *pariah* concept while making it also a "secular" concept, Weber contributed to anti-Semitism and to anti-Jewish measures, which are not very different from anti-foreigner measures.

He, furthermore, "confessed that, personally and subjectively, I am inclined to value highly the meaning of the biological heritage,"[596] because of "highly rewarding" racial studies that probably shall be significant in the future!

Apparently for this reason, Weber thinks a racial determination [*rassenmäßige Mitbedingtheit*] of Jews as *Fremdvolk* to be "certainly available" although it was yet unproven.[597] That was never historically the case, not even thanks to an intellectual hero like Max Weber. Apart from this, Weber adopted the erroneous and highly ambiguous general thesis: that "wherever the Jews appeared, they were the agents of the money economy."[598] That practically makes him an anti-Semite as well.

Maccoby documents another, quite serious problem, namely the stigmatization and criminalization of the victims. He is rather critical of Weber's *Antike*

595 Of course, there are also anti-Israel measures or critique which are erroneously considered by some as "typical anti-Semitism." They belong to the species anti-americanism, anti-arabism and all down the alphabet of the day-to-day political discourses.

596 GAR, volume 1, 15.

597 WG, 720 and EC, 1202 with a remarkable translation. Instead of Weber's certainty appears "probably exist in one sense or another" Weber's use of a word like *Blutsfremd* in this context is not very innocent either.

598 WG, 721 and EC, 1203.

Judentum and sometimes comes to the same conclusions I do. However, as a responsible and critical Jew, he accepts that all Jews are pariahs because they are named so by Weber and others. This is not just Maccoby's problem.

In 1944, Hannah Arendt wrote an article about *The Jew as Pariah,* which is, strangely enough, unknown to Maccoby. Arendt created the same problem: uncritically accepting Weber's concept as representative for her own position. Furthermore, Maccoby did study Weber and his circle through the writings of, in particular, Arnaldo Momigliano who displays curious attitudes.[599]

The latter stressed that "the Patriarchs lived before the Hebrews received their God-given law and God-given land" and, therefore, there is no need to define Jewish status; exit pariah-problem. In other words, once sedentarized (The Settlement), one is liberated from the primitive, inimical nomad who may be a pariah, too. Thanks to this ostrich policy, we come across a fundamental aspect of the pariah complex, the denial of one's own ancestral history. Furthermore, here one can find the source of the discrimination of the Diaspora in favor of Jerusalem and-in secular terms-the source of the Zionist creed.

Whatever the difficulties with Max Weber's *Antike Judentum* or his sociology of religion in general, a world historical panorama could be unrolled in his defense of theological and ideological positions against historical or social realities. The dimensions of the most profound antagonism between the nomadic and the sedentary modes of life or production have been shown in this part of the study.

Weber's biased analysis of the Chinese and Central Asian realities revealed in particular the weak empirical basis of his work, and now his weak ideological basis can be demonstrated (see Chapter 7). However, without Weber's extensive and wide-ranging studies, it would have been more difficult to discover the world historical dimensions of the nomadic-sedentarian antagonisms *and* interdependencies. Furthermore, it must be clear that the *Nomadic Question* and the *Jewish Question* are inseparable.

How biased Weber was can be demonstrated also by asking which definition of "Jew" he used? The answer is short: he did not have one! Apparently, he was too obsessed with his paria-theory and resentment as an element in Jewish ideas about redemption.[600]

The definition of the eminent Jewish theologian Yeshayahu Leibowitz is the only reasonable one here and the most relevant one in relation to the previous deliberations:

599 Hans Derks, 2004, 32–47.

600 WG, 300–301.

> The historical Jewish people is not defined as a race and not as the people [Volk. H.D.] of a particular land or of a specific political framework, nor even of a particular language, but as the people of the Torah and religious prescriptions…[601]

A secular person of any kind, including a Zionist, cannot be a Jew and that is purposefully forgotten by too many people. For these secular people, there is also a non-religious and accessible source for the right definition.

In the well-known *Philo Lexikon, Handbuch des jüdischen Wissens* (1935), probably the last book that Jews published in Nazi Germany, there is a picture of twelve representatives of the Jewish faith under the heading *Rasse*. It includes men from China, Jemen, Buchara, an African-American in New York, and four European rabbis in their typical folk dress: the only possible conclusion to be drawn is, that these very different people (according to "race," "ethnic descent," "Volk") have only *one thing in common* and that is their belief.[602]

The money-price paid for hitching (orthodox) Jews to the secular Zionist car of Ben-Gurion or Weizmann in 1948 was almost unbearably high and led recently to a substantial counter-movement of secular Israelis, ca. 75% of the population. Reason: all (orthodox) Jews with their fertile families are paid by the tax-payer to do nothing but pray; they do not need to fight and are not conscripted in the army; they have their own city-quarters closed off to others; they do not pay taxes, etc.

Apart from the above, defining who is a Jew or what is Jewish remains a difficult and political job. Rabbi Shalom Cohen, a member of the Council of Torah

601 The quotation is from Yeshayahu Leibowitz, 1993, 25; see also his 117 and 171. The first Dutch demographic—statistical analysis of a Jewish part of the population, Emanuel Boekman, 1936, 11–15 strictly defines Jews (officially "Israelites") as *religious* people, similar to Protestants or Roman Catholics. Boekman, himself with a Jewish background, compares Jews in every feature with these two last religions. Only thanks to Zionism or race-theories one started to define "Jews" in a different way for obvious reasons, but statistically there is no framework for this. Apparently "Volk" or "Race/Rasse" were too difficult as categories for statisticians. Also Boekman, 96, acknowledges the impossibility to prove statisticially racial features.

602 *Philo Lexikon*, pictures between 575 and 576. This *Lexikon* with a preface by Leo Baeck is a most remarkable product: all anti-Jewish Nazi laws are reproduced without any comment like *Ariergesetzgebung*, 41–43; non-Jewish writers are indicated with a Δ, like a "J" is used with a Jewish author in anti-Semitic literature (like "Adolf Δ Hitler," 486); its strong anti-communist bent is evident as well as its strong German patriotic—attitudes (see, for instance, *Kriegsstatistik*, 387–389) and under *Nationalsozialismus* a rule from a 1920 program of the Nazis is reproduced which states: "Volksgenosse kann nur sein, ohne Rücksicht auf Konfession, wer deutschen Blutes ist. Kein Jude kann daher Volksgenosse sein." And so on…

Sages and Shas leader, solemnly announced that "national religious Jews aren't Jewish" (*The Times of Israel*, 14th of July 2013). As he delivered his sermon, he stood next to rabbi Ovadia Yosef, who is Shas's spiritual leader. He is perceived by many "as the most influential living rabbi" (whatever that may be).

Zionist politicians, such as minister Bennett were furious: the old and fundamental antagonism was again stressed that orthodox Jews do not acknowledge some "Jewish state." These Jews are simply "Amalek … who must be wiped off the face of the earth" (Bennett)! For this politician, even a Holocaust was not sufficient.

Answering, at last, the question "correctly" of whether Judaism is a market or an oikoidal religion, I have to produce a "Judgment of Solomon": a "Jewish state" (a theocracy) must be the most oikoidal construction as it fixes the behavior and minds of its citizens completely; whoever negates such a construction must be the most market-oriented person!

In addition, we can point to the important global diamond market with its central organization in Antwerp (turnover of about 3 billion dollars annually): a substantial part of it is run by orthodox Jews, who indeed are the strongest enemies of the Zionist state of Israel and publicly demonstrate as such.

Stanislav Andreski, reviewing the result of Weber's sociology of religions for the question of "the rise of capitalism," came to the conclusion:

> Weber was partly right: Judaism was not a crucial factor in the rise of capitalism; but he was wrong in imputing this to its economic ethics. This ethic was extremely favorable to capitalism but its influence as always severely limited by the non-proselytic character of Judaism.[603]

Alas, Andreski remarked only a few lines earlier about the situation in Eastern Europe that "their presence in large numbers acted … as a brake upon commercial development because as soon as trade came to be monopolized by the Jews it became a depressed occupation." Let's leave it, that whether many or a few Jews were active, capitalism did not rise!

Besides the fact that the logic has disappeared in these statements, it is difficult to discover their meaning or impact because too many scholars refuse to define the concepts they are using. In Eastern Europe, too, several kinds of "Jews" dwell in cities or their "shtetl," as very poor proletarians or rich landowners.

However, it is important sociologically that Judaism (whatever the definition) concerns not a church organization (by definition oikoidal) but is

603 In S.N. Eisenstadt, ed. 1968, 60.

dispersed over different *sects*, divided into several mutually competing "*sub-sects*," and it concerns a small *minority* compared to all the other religions or large USA sects.

Furthermore, Judaism depends largely on the behavior of *individual rabbis* who act largely *autonomously* in all relevant Jewish matters, leading to different consequences. Leibowitz's definition implies that Judaism does *not concern a settled -ism*. Thanks to these four qualities, one must have a large social flexibility and a "natural" market orientation. In addition, one has to ask why all oikoidal powers fear such a minority.

PART 3

Market and Oikos: *Basics in the East*

CHAPTER 6

Settlers Between East and West

6.1 Settlers' Historical Sins

If one thing relates the West to all other "points of the compass," it is the phenomenon of the settler-relations. In Weber's *Wirtschaft und Gesellschaft* this is addressed only superficially within deliberations about the expansion of "Worldpowers" (*Großmächte*) and the usual consequences of this expansion, the "direct theft of the land after eradication of the existing indigenous propulation." It is considered to be "the way of nature"![604] Because it represents the market–*oikos* (and town–country) relations in the most extreme way, a short chapter must be devoted to it at this juncture of the book.

Let's start with an extensive quotation by the eminent historian Jürgen Osterhammel to define the problems at stake:

> The early Canadian frontier was an undemarcated zone of contact between Indians and white fur hunters and traders, all highly mobile people poles apart from settlers, and the Amazonian frontier was never anything more than a space of plunder and overexploitation. Frontier *colonization* is therefore a subcategory of frontier *expansion*, a phenomenon known in most civilizations, that denotes a push into the "wilderness" beyond the existing cultivation boundary to develop land for agriculture or mineral extraction.
>
> Such colonization is by its very nature coupled with settlement; the economic objective is to bring the mobile production factors—labor and capital—closer to location-dependent natural resources. It does not necessarily have to involve a new political entity, since the colony is often founded at the edge of an existing area of settlement: for instance, the gradual extension of the Han Chinese agricultural zone at the expense of the pastoralist economy of Central Asia … (see next chapter. H.D.)
>
> Settler colonies are a special form of frontier colonization that first appeared in Europe in Greek antiquity … a city would plant offshoots across the sea, in regions where only a relatively small commitment of military power was possible and necessary … this involved a decisive logistical difference with other kinds of frontier colonization. The sea, but also

604 WG, 520–527.

 DOI:10.1163/9789004383913_007

> forbidding distances on terra firma (Gulja in Xinjiang, in preindustrial times, took longer to reach from Beijing than Philadelphia did from London), stood in the way of the regular links that alone permit social continuity.[605] (italics by J.O.)

The settler phenomenon belongs to expansionisms within the *Empire–State–Nation–Volk* chain. In European history it was very often the settlers who stood at the forefront of the extensions of space, power and production. That seems already to have been the case in antiquity and in the European Middle Ages, but this must be qualified: in Greek antiquity with its many "colonizations" a very different form of expansionism was experienced than in imperial Roman antiquity.

Gocha Tsetskhladze, the expert in this dossier, writes how Greek newcomers and local peoples seldom clashed:

> In many cases, Greeks and locals lived alongside each other in a Greek settlement, whether in the western Mediterranean or in the eastern Black Sea.... Many colonies were established in territory either occupied by a local population or with one close to hand.... Sometimes the land for settlement and agriculture was given to the Greeks by local rulers, either by special agreement or in return for payment of a moderate tribute.... The relationship between the newcomers and the locals was often pacific, to their mutual benefit.[606]

In other periods as well, settler activities on the *Volk* level nearly always concerned private actions, from peasants, eventually together with their local leaders, and included not only "colonizations" but also all sorts of reclamations and rural works, and new settlements.

Only when Athens, Sparta or foreign intruders suffered from too much "hubris" was something like a "civilizing mission," an "elimination of a (commercial) competitor" or "the (temporary) holding of slaves on a large scale" at stake.

Real colonies as defined later were in fact non-existent: one settled somewhere else after life "at home" became impossible for some reason or another (from famines to earthquakes or military conquest), and in the new location one tried to be friendly as possible (from intermarriage with locals to the avoidance of "racial" tensions) while being active in the existing production or production relations. In short: the transfers of labor, skills and technology

605 Jürgen Osterhammel, 2014, 370–375.

606 Gocha R. Tsetskhladze, ed., 2006, vol. 1, LII–LIII.

occurred mostly under non-military, "non-state" market relations after mutually satisfactory negotiations. Violence occurred sometimes if circumstances had already reached a critical point.

The Roman emperors operated on a very different level. Their imperialism was often accompanied or directly followed by large-scale and *real* colonizations in the conquered areas (Gaul, North Africa, etc.): military state violence achieved the elimination of everybody and everything blocking the occupation, re-population and (re)settlement (town and country) of foreigners. The latter could now accumulate land as "property," the basis for the later feudal system, and so forth.

The first who demonstrated this with all the accompanying "collateral damage" was the famous Julius Caesar, well-known writer of an interesting book for innocent high-school students: during his expeditions into foreign environments, more than a million people of Gaul were killed, a number that was between the 60 and 80 per cent of the population at the time; and the rest was enslaved. Who else could/can compete with this Roman hero, now celebrated as a saint? All later Christian emperors and kings read his book and followed this example.

In antiquity, autonomous nations and states did not exist despite the actions of some "monarchies." Thus, only the two ends of the whole chain were "established," and the main lethal struggles happened in the long periods of the formation of the "in between" states and nations.

The Roman Empire was an unorganized whole without citizens, formed by an important symbol plus environment, the empire and the city of Rome (Urbi et Orbi), plus the most violent weapons, the Roman army. In short: a self-sufficient super-*Oikos* without any competitor except itself.

From the 15th century onwards, the entire chain started to function, and the expansion of military, commercial and settler interests reached outer-European realms. A new kind of confrontation occurred between the European chain with non-European *Volk* and eventually their own chain relations.

Giovanni Arrighi pointed to the next phase as the French and British newcomers in the colonial "business" started to compete with the Dutch, Portuguese and Spaniards. The former two not only had to overtake the latter but also to restructure the political geography of world commerce:

> This had three major and closely interrelated components: settler colonialism, capitalist slavery, and economic nationalism. All three components were essential to the reorganization of world political—economic space, but settler colonialism was probably the leading element in the combination. British rulers in particular relied heavily on the private

> initiative of their subjects.... Capitalist slavery was partly a condition and partly a result of the success of settler colonialism.[607]

This had fundamental consequences for both "parties": global perpetrator–victim relations were established, of which the two most spectacular were the disposal of colored *bodies* through slavery and the enslavement of colored *minds* through the opium.[608] These relations were accompanied over the course of time by one genocide after another committed by the representatives of the European/Western "chain." Apparently, this cannot be said of, for instance, the Chinese imperial settlement activities as described by Belich.[609]

Several types of settler activities can be seen in modern history.[610] First the "New England" type corresponding to an "individualist market logic" (according to Adam Smith, 1776) in which newly arrived white settlers take the best lands after elimination of the colored indigenous owners (Canada, Northern America, etc.).

Second, the type indicated by Weber above, where a "politically dominant minority with the help of the colonial state" ("Pied Noirs" in Algeria, Zionists in Palestine, Rhodesian Frontiers, etc.) drives the indigenous population "into the sea" or exploits its labor force. Third, the type where the intruders import a new colored labor force as slaves after the eradication of the indigenous colored population (Southern USA, Caribbean region, etc.).

Last but not least, those settlers who did all the above and started afterwards to establish their own state or autonomous settlement mostly inimical

607 Giovanni Arrighi, 1994, 49.

608 For the first time there is now a handbook available about this last global development: Hans Derks, 2012.

609 James Belich, 2011, 21–22, 38–39, 442. See also Giovanni Arrighi, 1994, 34–35 who underscores colleagues like Abu-Lughod in a very strange reaction on the question, of why Ming China decided to withdrew its fleet, restricted maritime trade and terminate relations with foreign powers after the successful expeditions of its admiral (around 1400 AD): close to world domination, but the Chinese stopped and went back to China! This "has perplexed—indeed caused despair among—serious scholars for at least the past one hundred years." Arrighi did not discover the typical Western arrogance and aggressiveness, and could not imagine that different ways of decision-making exist in other cultures. He supposed that the Chinese emperor decided as he did after calculating the costs and advantages to proceed to world domination, which could never be the case. This way of reasoning is alien to "the Chinese", and if those "serious scholars during the past hundred years" had done their job, they would not be surprised! See my 2012, 467–470 and for another background 141–142. In the context of the present book, the shortest way of explaining "the mystery" is: at that time Chinese decision-makers followed the market-customs and "market-logic," the Western "serious scholars" the oikoidal.

610 See Jürgen Osterhammel, 2014, 371.

to the original colonial state (Rhodesia, white South Africa, Israel, Hong Kong, Chinese extraterritorial settlements, etc.).

From these types one can subsume the first under "market" but the others under "*oikos*"; the first certainly to "country," some of the others to "temporary country," but the rest to "city/settlement." Notwithstanding Max Weber's preoccupation with religion, the association between the settlers and their religion is not made which is important relative to the market–*oikos* relations. So, let's compensate for this omission.

6.2 Protestants

It is true that the North Americans (Protestant European settlers from England, Germany, Holland, etc.) did an effective genocidal job by eliminating the native North Americans (the so called "Indians") and, as the second classical settler's achievement, by turning another people "from elsewhere" into its slave labor force.[611]

The Calvinist Puritans among them believed they were predestined from the time of setting foot ashore to win against all "foreign" elements in the "New Jerusalem" they had captured from the original inhabitants. They were the new bosses and became very practical: profit must be made under all circumstances. They started double-entry bookkeeping on their victims, making a good business from killing, using the following market prices:

> Those hard-headed virtuosi of Protestantism, the Puritans of New England, in 1703, by decrees of their assembly set a premium of £40 on every Indian scalp and every captured redskin: in 1720 a premium of £100 on every scalp; in 1744, after Massachusetts Bay had proclaimed a certain tribe as rebels, the following prices: for a male scalp of 12 years and upwards £100 (new currency), for a male prisoner £105, for women and children prisoners £50, for scalps of women and children £50.... The British Parliament declared bloodhounds and scalping for "God-given and natural means."[612]

611 William T. Vollmann, 2003, is the most effective North American reproducer of the USA and Western bad conscience in his six volumes plus a volume MC.

612 Karl Marx, 1971, volume 1, 781. A famous German Lutheran theologian, Helmut Gollwitzer (1908–1993), who was Marxist-oriented and prominently involved in the political debates ensuing in the late 1960s and 1970s (e.g. pastor to the RAF-terrorist Ulrike Meinhof), referred to this same period and location. He, however, wanted to prove that "the church had with the gospel the weapon at hand against class society, which those discovered

This is quoted by Karl Marx in his famous analysis of the Christian character of the so-called "original accumulation" in which he tells one terrible story after another about Dutch or English colonization and conversion practices. The Dutch Calvinists had already ruthlessly decimated the populations of East Indian islands in a genocidal way; their American fellow-believers made a profitable business out of it.

Belich stresses recent and impressive scholarship, "It emphasizes that the Anglos were more Protestant, more individualist, more democratic, and more capitalist than the competition; and that their colonies were more decentralized."[613] The meaning of this remains largely in the dark; for whom, for instance, is "democracy" interesting in all these settler activities?

Anyway, the English Anglicans demonstrated several times how mass-exterminations could be organized by causing and/or exploiting severe famines. For instance, they forcefully requisitioned rice several times in order to sell it for fabulous prices, a practice that cost the lives of a million Hindus in the Indian province of Orissa in 1866 alone.[614] This was a typical example of a monopoly trade, that was only possible in Western colonies.

About half a century later, the last British settlers, the Zionists, started their 100 years' war in Palestine with the slogan: *the land without people, for a people without land.* It was a request for genocide and permanent ethnic cleansing similar to the usual practice of all white, Protestant-Christian colonialists. Even today no compromise is possible with the indigenous population, not even a profitable one (for the Zionists) like the so-called "two-state solution" in a country in which they are "juridical guests."

---

who wanted to avoid that the slaves and the subjected by colonial powers could receive the Christian message and education". Gollwitzer added in a note: "This was forbidden in several North American states until the end of the 18th century. In 1708 the missionary ... Ziegenbalg was imprisoned for several months by the commander of the Danish East Indian Company.... Also the English in India were as inimical...". See Helmut Gollwitzer, 1974, 117, 118 and 131. It is a pity that this pastor did not read his Karl Marx. To get the whole picture clear, it almost suffices to read a review about present-day Indian problems in the USA and the reasons why the reviewer is disappointed: Christopher Vecsey. "Review of Huston Smith, *A Seat at the Table: Huston Smith in Conversation with Native Americans on Religious Freedom,*" H-AmIndian, H-Net Reviews, March, 2007.

613 James Belich, 2011, 28, 29. This characterisation was similar for the Dutch, although they were not as active as settlers like the Protestant English. For Protestantism see further 60 and *passim.*

614 See the still prudent formulations in the history of these disasters in David Northrup, in: Andrew Porter, ed., 93; see also his 406–407. For another interpretation of Marx's Orissa story, see Vincent A. Smith, 1928, 740 and Dharma Kumar, ed., 1984, volume 2, 528–529. "The Orissa Famine of 1866" and "Famine in India", in *Wikipedia.* Prabhat Mukherjee, 1958 for 1957, 69–95; David Hall-Matthews, 2007.

6.3 Catholics

Did Roman Catholicism, which operated earlier, have the same influence on colonialism and settler's policies in the world? In the first days of Christian imperialism after Columbus's discovery of "Indians" (1492), the basic imperial constellation was formed *without* divine legitimation. The Emperor (Charles V, etc.) and the Pope (Alexander VI, *Bulls of Donation,* 1493), not God or the Bible, ordered and allowed the imperialism.

Roman Catholic imperialism developed imperialistic theories as legitimation *a posteriori.* Compared to the Protestant legitimation—including the Zionist one—Catholics are the very picture of flexibility. This does not refer to the Catholic colonialists' reactions to the many accusations of cruelty against the indigenous population with simple counter-accusations: it concerns gross exaggerations from non-Catholic sources ("leyenda negra," Black Legends). I refer to the judgments of the remarkably similar sociological and economic elements as in Protestant colonialism. A short excursion into the history of international law will demonstrate this.[615]

The famous tract of Fray Bartolomé de Las Casas (1474–1566), glorified as the first defender of the indigenous population against the cruel foreign settler-conquistadors, has been unmasked as written in defens e of the interests of the Emperor, Charles V/Philip II (of "Madrid") against his own Spanish settlers, who achieved autonomy with the loss of the gold colonies as the main effect. It was this gold that was desperately needed to avoid bankruptcy of the constantly warring Spanish state in Europe.

De Las Casas had, therefore, to paint the settlers' behavior in the darkest colors and to formulate serious accusations, while the Emperor and the Roman Catholic religion had to be pictured, at least implicitly, as the friendliest protectors and saviours of the "Indians." He also designed new laws to outlaw the settlers, and undermined all criticism of his own story so effectively that it is, even nowadays, rather difficult to check the truth of these cruel stories, although nobody doubts their realism.

However, it is telling that the Emperor also promoted a second legitimation for repressing the "Indians" if the settlers could be eliminated or replaced by "Madrid"-friendly colonists. This was based on the famous Aristotelian theory of the "natural slavery of barbarians" (that is to say: the *Christian* perception of a principal part of Aristotle's *oikos* theory). It was the result of the work of de Las Casas's opponent, the Dominican Juan Ginés de Sepúlveda (1494–1573).

615 The following is based on Henry Kamen, 2003.

But the settler-conquistadors also obtained their theological legitimation thanks to the Franciscans: they developed an anti-European, anti-urban theory to promote the evolution of the societies of the "Indians" in the sense that they designed a purely patriarchal society needed to cultivate and convert those "poor, childish creatures," a society that stood under the military and economic guidance of the new settlers.

The next line of reasoning is the most sophisticated one. It was designed by the modernizing Spanish and Portuguese scholars of the School of Salamanca, the Dominicans (Francisco de Vitoria, Domingo de Soto, etc.) and Jesuits (Luis de Molina, Francisco Suarez, etc.). A few remarks must be sufficient here.[616]

Vitoria tended to think of an empire as a commonwealth and not a dominion, so that the subjected indigenous peoples retained their rights and property. Negotiation was favored above war, which was only legitimate in specific cases: for instance, expansionist wars, wars for glory, and wars to convert infidels or pagans were unjust.

A broad framework of new rights had to be invented. All members of this School supported for the first time, some form of separation of church and state, of limitation on the legitimate powers of government (contractual power that made popular government possible), private property, the free use of money, etc.

Vitoria's task was also to find legitimate claims on foreign (discovered) lands, of which he listed eight. I mention only the universal right to travel and do commerce (if "Indians" should refuse this, the "aggrieved" party could eventually start a war of self-defense); the right to preach ("Indians" could refuse conversion, but not stop the Christian religion being preached; if this right was violated, a "just war" could also be waged); the right of a sufficient number of Christians in the new land to receive a Christian government together with the prohibition to use force against converts returning to the pagan customs secured the position of settlers.

Also here a "just war" could be started if there was a lack of just laws, magistrates, agricultural techniques, etc. Although the Europeans received enough "legitimate rights" to conquer foreign lands in this way, Charles V was

616 It is not possible to give a satisfactory explanation of their work, which concerns not only imperialist juridical theories (natural law, sovereignty, just war, etc.), but also economics (private property, money, etc.) and theology (the existence of evil, etc.), which are related to one another. In addition, Henri Kamen, 492, may be right that their theories of empire "served to guide legislators (such as Philip II in his *Ordinance* of 1573)," but "had little influence on the real world." Of course, the practical rule became: when slavery was essential for some reason or another, it was used.

not satisfied. He expected exclusive rights for Spain or for him, but not universal possibilities for every foreigner.[617]

Thanks to the activities of all these intellectual initiators of colonialism, the Catholic approach was quite different from the Protestant one. After a relatively short but severe conquering start, the colonial efforts of the former were characterized by far-reaching integration in many respects with the indigenous populations.

The aim was to make a new Catholic *society and state* abroad as part of the mother country, *including* the indigenous population as the lowest echelon of a detailed racial, labor, etc. hierarchy. The Spanish and Portuguese governments and their autonomous settlers, and later the French, did not continue with a program of *permanent ethnic cleansing* as the Protestant colonists did until the last "natives" were eliminated, but integrated them through intermarriage, conversion or language programs.

The most far-reaching effort to create a European Catholic *colored* society abroad was conducted by the Portuguese in Brazil and Mozambique.[618] The most far-reaching results of creating a *white* Protestant European society abroad were the USA and Australia, while the Zionist one is nothing but an abortive Protestant model (and, therefore, always bound to fail in its original "white" aims).

The characteristics of the two European conquering and settlement strategies are, therefore, very different. The "white, Western State" and its settlers terrorized every part of the globe from 1492 onward and executed one genocide after another on largely unarmed foreign people without any form of legitimation. For the Catholics this largely involved the initial assault; for the Protestants it took the form of a permanent ethnic cleansing.

617 In the different positions of the empire, the settlers, Fransciscans (who played a double game and took advantage of both the emperor and the settlers) and Dominicans, the beginning of the development of the chain in the period 1500–1600 can be easily reconstructed.

618 It ultimately resulted in the luso-tropicalism, the rather mythical or utopian doctrine about the Portuguese ability of miscegenation to the benefit of slaves and masters alike. The label dates from the writings of Gilberto Freyre (1930 onwards) and the activities of dictators like Salazar, but the practices and its consequences date from much earlier. See Hans Derks, ed., 1989, 63–68. The Portuguese colonization in South America and Africa provides the best examples of the integration of masters and slaves within a strict oikoidal form of the domains (*prazo*). For Spain see Kamen's analysis of the mestizos in colonial society and the role of the missionaries in the consolidation of the colonies/ settler societies, a role which is much more influential than that of the Protestant clergy. See for the latter's racism and sexuality, Ronald Hyam, 1990, 37–49.

The lack of legitimation created a permanent bad conscience in "white Western Culture" vis-à-vis the other part of the globe: for the Protestants it was an *exclusive* bad conscience related to largely invented enemies, for the Catholics it was an *inclusive* bad conscience related to the lowest in the newly created hierarchy. The "white, Western Christian scholars," including those who tried to represent the case of the victims, are only a few individuals who were never followed by their churches or other representative institutions.

The bad conscience felt by well-informed Christian and secular circles, from the beginning of the "white Western expansion" never affected the soldiers who usually had to execute this lethal expansion on all continents.

The main method to silence this bad conscience was and is *racism* as the most basic and permanent *element* of the white Western perpetrator culture, including the implicit arrogance to think of this culture as highly superior compared to all other cultures, a claim based only on military brutality.

6.4 The Heirs and Heiresses

The most "positive" outcome of what has happened so far in this terrible dossier is that some heirs and heiresses of those who were eliminated wholesale have been "rehabilitated" and accepted as tourist attractions or export articles. They have far fewer economic, political and cultural possibilities than the heirs and heiresses of the conquerors. This happened because they are fully surrounded by their enemies or "made harmless" like *Anatevka* Eastern Jews in the Pale of Settlement, the so-called alcoholic "Indians" in North American reservations, or the always "dreaming" aboriginals in Australia.

These racist constellations remain preconditions for further racism and repression. The white Protestant racism is, therefore, an exclusive one; some compromise with the "colored other" is only possible if it suits a "white (money) deal"; the last possibility is to emancipate as a "white", never as a "colored".

From the start in 1917/18, the nationalist Zionist policy in Palestine was to create their own state (territory, land), their own population with their own weapons: the secular settlers' ideal and utopia. Like all their "colleagues" in the past, the formation of this settlers' society was guided by rigorous chauvinism (state-nationalism), rigorous inimical attitudes to *any* outside world, a rigorous military uniformity inside ("socialism"). Using the *Empire–state–nation–Volk* chain, this can be demonstrated with a few examples (see also Chapter 4).

The liberal Zionist *Haaretz* star-journalist, Ari Shavit, also described as "a scion of Zionist aristocracy," describes in his recent book his well-to-do British ancestor, a colonist in Palestine, and his relationship with the indigenous population. As was typical for too many of the first Zionists and Western imperialists and colonists in general, he had a typical blind spot regarding the indigenous population:

> My great-grandfather does not see because he is motivated by the need not to see.... He does not see because if he does see, he will have to turn back.[619]

Not only British but also American Zionists at the time were similarly blind: they knew next to nothing about Arab Palestine. One of their leaders, Brandeis, wrote in 1929 about Palestine:

> The situation reminds me of that in America, when the settlers who founded the Massachusetts Bay Colony had to protect themselves against the Indians.[620]

These examples are related to the first link in the *Empire–state–nation–Volk* chain. Ten years earlier the second and third links were addressed as well, in a nearly forgotten way. In addition, once again the strong differences between (organized) Jews and Zionists are demonstrated.

During the *Peace Conference* (1919) the British and French made their definite imperialist deals concerning the Middle East, the very basis of the *present* conflicts in Palestine. A statement was published by "the majority of American Jews" strongly attacking British Zionists, who combined British imperialism with their own nationalism.[621] A few quotations:

> ...the undersigned citizens of the United States ... setting forth our objection to the organization of a Jewish State in Palestine as proposed by the Zionist Societies ... and to the segregation of the Jews as a nationalistic

619 Quoted in Jonathan Freedland, 2014, 22.

620 Jonathan Freedland, 2014, 22.

621 The full text of this *A Statement to the Peace Conference March 4th 1919* was found on www.al-bushra.org but see also *The New York Times*, 5th of March 1919. Italics added by the authors. However, I did not found anything on the quoted document in the well-known histories of Zionism of Laqueur, Bensoussan, Pappe, Segev (2001), Morris (1999) or Vital. Some simply used their fantasy only by constructing a perfect unity between Zionists and American Jews during the conference. Interesting are other reports to the Paris *Peace Conference* in which the Arabs in Palestine, Lebanon and Syria overwhelmingly petitioned against Zionists, or those of the King-Crane Commission of the *Peace Conference* advising against accepting the Zionist plans. Now, not even James Renton referred to this text, but gave relevant additional information on 2007, 138–148.

> unit in any country.... The American Zionists represent only a small proportion of the Jews..., about one hundred fifty thousand out of three and a half million.... We raise our voices in warning and protest against the demand ... for the reorganization of the Jews as a national unit ... now or in the future.... The fundamental principles of democracy ... assert equal rights for all citizens of a state, irrespective of creed or ethnic descent ... [They should be applied] as to exclude segregation of any kind.... *Any such plan of segregation is necessarily reactionary in its tendency, undemocratic in spirit and totally contrary to the practices of free government.... We therefore strongly urge the abandonment of such a basis for the reorganization of any state.*

The full text of this document was published on March 5, 1919 in *The New York Times* under the headline "Protest to Wilson against Zionist State: Representative Jews Ask Him to Present It to the Peace Conferences."

Among the 31 signatures affixed to the document and the 300 signatories of an attached memorandum there were Congressmen (for example, Julius Kahn), the US Ambassador to Turkey (the famous Henri Morgenthau), an Attorney General (Simon Rosendale), a Chief Justice of the Supreme Court (Horace Stern), many rabbis, professors of universities, etc. This demonstration of the fundamental character of the current antagonisms should be remembered.

About thirty years and many upheavals in Palestine later, an American President played a tricky game, as revealed recently in John Judis' book.[622] It was President Truman himself who could have easily used American might to impose a binational solution on Palestine in 1947, which is still the "official proposal" for present USA and EU politicians attempting to solve the conflict. It could have been the fulfilment of older optimistic Zionist thoughts from Ahad Ha'am to Judah Magnes, let alone of the American Jewish majority behind the 1919 petition.

It was, however, the muscular pressure and extreme nationalism of American Zionists like rabbi Silver or Stephen Wise that altered Truman's decision to

622 John Judis, 2015. His first chapter provides a reasonable historical introduction to the origins of Zionism with the following concluding end. After mentioning the many rationalizations "by which the early Zionists justified their conquest of the lands on which another people lived," Judis continues with: "They laid the basis for a Zionism that, while justifiable in the abstract, committed in practice many of the sins that Western European countries had visited upon native populations and that led to national rebellions." That concerned the situation around 1918. The rest of Judis story concerns the many ways the anti-Britisch Americans helped to repress these anti-Zionist rebellions in favor of their oil and military interests during the following 100 year of civil war in Palestine.

favoring the Zionist case over the Palestinian. Neither Truman nor his successors altered their decision after they were confronted with the fate of nearly a million Palestinians in the *Nakba* (1948).

This did not change even after the strong criticism by Americans with a Jewish background like Albert Einstein, Hannah Arendt, most orthodox Jews and many others against the Zionist massacres around 1948, against the establishment of a "Jewish State" by secular Zionists, and all the rest. Therefore, all post-1948 troubles until today can be characterized as directed against the Zionist settler's society with their disappearing support in the world but also as against American imperialism in the Middle East. Who are so stubborn on the Zionist side?

The Israeli philosopher, Avishai Margalit, recently wrote a remarkable *In Memoriam* on the very prolonged death of one of the best known Zionist soldier-settlers, Ariel Scheinermann Sharon, 1928–2014.[623] His fate seems highly symbolic for that of his colony. He was nicknamed the "Caucasian," not only because his parents met there (although he was born in Belarus), but also because this word evoked

> ...a strongly built agrarian tribal chieftain—a man fiercely loyal to his family and his people, while ferociously mean and vindictive toward his enemies, namely, the rest of the world.

With this profile of the prototypical settler, we are back at the Volk-corner of the *Empire-state-nation-Volk* chain with all the basic primitive characteristics of it "unmediated and uncluttered by ideological superstructures" and troubled with that settler's stubbornness that made him—as general and prime minister—buy "the largest ranch in Israel with money ... from a wealthy friend..."

The poor Palestinian victims of this bully danced with joy when they heard that at last "the real butcher of Sabra and Shatila" (1982), "the builder of the Wall" who hated the Arabs "when they were strong" and despised them "when they were weak," was dead.

The death of Sharon, which took eight years, may be a symptom of his extraordinary power, but more closely represented the fate of his settler country. The final struggle takes its time, but Margalit is right: Sharon's "roads led nowhere," but he should have added that the same is true for this settler's Israel where a new kind, the mainly American religious colonist-settlers, settle under the protection of the Israeli (and American) army; again a classical type of settler-activity.

623 Avishai Margalit, 2014, 14 from which the quotations are taken.

6.5 Profiles

The following comparison between the characteristics of Catholic and Protestant settlers and their colonial *Volk*-levels also implies comparative possibilities with the market-*oikos* elements.[624]

TABLE 2 Catholic and protestant settler profiles

Subjects	Catholic settlers	Protestant settlers
Cultural integration with indigenous people	+	–
Isolated from indigenous people	–	+
Intermarriage with ind. people	+	–
Spatially separated dwellings, etc.	+	+
Exclusive "racism"/ xenophobia	–	+
Inclusive "racism"/ xenophobia	+	–
Secular political start of settlement (monarch, etc.)	+	+
Religious political start (pope)	+	–
Religious theological start (God)	–	+
Conversion of ind. population	+	–
Language of conqueror is part of domination of indigenous people	+	–
Relation with mother country remains somehow intact	+	–
Political integration in wider context (continent, etc.)	+	–
Genocidal attacks on indigenous population	–	+
Gradual transfer of whole ind. population	–	+
Conquering activities at the start	+	–
Indigenous people as tourist attraction in the end	–	+

624 We are concerned here with not only relative, but also "more than average" characteristics.

The above analysis of the two models of the West's conquest of the "rest of the world" also reflects the main possibilities of Western involvement in the present political and ideological globalization.

Race, based on secular, civil, biological and social scientific theories, was not yet a concept in the early 19th century. People were only killed on theological-political grounds or as a consequence of primitive enmity or *xenophobia,* which cannot be perceived as an early form of racism.

All this became impossible (at least in theory or, eventually, as a consequence of new ethical principles). From about the middle of the 19th century, the newly invented race concepts and the practical racism did not refer to religious categories. colored people were segregated, exploited or eliminated based on "scientific arguments," and many kinds of (sub)races all over the world were documented, categorized and detested, particularly in the Western colonies.

However, after two World Wars some scientists made so much noise that *race* stopped existing, and UNESCO sanctioned this around 1950. Alas, enough other American scientists continued on this path, soon armed with the weapon of DNA. This was too often used as a blunt tool, even concerning a "Jewish Race."

It happens now only thanks to specific political and economic monopoly positions in the USA, accompanied by an inadequately equipped juridical apparatus, and not for true scientific reasons but for short-term profits. There are no political interests in the Empire-Volk chain, except police forces, which use these new weapons to extend their power positions. The new Trump-hype can bring some remarkable surprises in this regard.

Most settlers disappeared as such (not their heirs) with the decolonization movement; a few white colonizers refused to leave "their" land and started serious armed struggles with the relevant motherlands: Rhodesia (now Zimbabwe), South Africa, Algeria, Hong Kong.

The last settlers' colony still exists in the Middle East and refuses to surrender in order to decolonize like all the others.[625] This Biblical "stumbling stone" has a short future yet: if it is not transformed into a heap of rubble in the next wars like the largest part of the Middle East, or into a desert because of climate changes, it will lose its raison d'être to be "gatekeeper" for the oil-interests: the electricity revolution is an inevitable and irreversible fact.

625 Even in the USA people become impatient with "their colony" in the Middle East. See, for instance, the very polite Dov Waxman 2016, who did not arrive yet at the "chapter Trump" and its belligerent impact.

CHAPTER 7

On the Origin of Market Relations in (Asian) History

> Persian, I have never yet run from any man in fear and I am not doing so from you now. There is, for me, nothing unusual in what I have been doing: it is precisely the kind of life I always lead, even in times of peace. If you want to know why I will not fight, I will tell you. In our country there are no towns and no cultivated land; fear of losing which, or seeing it ravaged, might indeed provoke us to hasty battle. If however you are determined upon bloodshed … one thing there is for which we will fight—the tombs of our forefathers. Find those tombs and try to wreck them, and you will soon know whether or not we are willing to stand up to you.
>
> The Scythian chieftain Idanthyrsus to Darius, King of Persia.
>
> HERODOTUS, *The Histories.* iv, 125.

7.1 Stock Farmers Versus Peasants

Before I can explain why a nomad chief even dares to provoke a King of Kings, before we can understand why Max Weber's confrontation with Chinese life ends in failure, and before the heart of the historical matter of the market-*oikos* problem can be revealed by studying animal raising cultures, we have to go *back to basics* concerning stock-farmers and peasant life.

I had to create an opportunity to qualify "country" in the town-country relationship, while not forgetting the main subject of this book. The necessity of doing this is still not properly understood by most medievalists or classicists, while, around 1900 scholars like Weber had other things to do than care about a lifestyle that they supposed erroneously had largely disappeared from their countries. Only gypsies were sometimes discovered and mostly killed or chased away (like in today's Hungary and Romania), while people who were detested (like Jews) were often perceived as "nomads," even by intellectuals like Werner Sombart.

 | DOI:10.1163/9789004383913_008

It is, however, strange that most scholars did not discover the people accustomed to mobile life. Take, for instance, ancient Greek society, which is still seen as the *basis of Western European civilization*. Its fundamental dependence on nomadic and animal cultures disappeared in their extensive descriptions full of mythical aberrations.

This peculiar fact demands a thorough explanation.[626] Now the question must be answered first, what are those basic features of, for instance, the ancient Greek economy and society as "basis of not only Western civilization"? This has to be followed by incorporating it into elements of the market-*oikos* relations. The start seems very simple, but the consequences are very complicated.

Productive activities on the land can be divided into at least two main kinds, from which other can be derived., i.e. *cultures with plants* and *those with animals*. The former concern all *immobile a*ctivities of men with their plants, while the latter concern all *mobile* activities with their animals.

The criterion for defining a plant grower involves the way the plants are cultivated and not so much the soils. In the most extensive form, gathering, the soil (land) is a negligible factor. It is the same for the most intensive plantgrowing, greenhouse-cultivation.

Turning to animal breeding, something similar can be seen: in the most extensive form, hunting and fishing, the breeding aspect is reduced to taking into account the season and the age of the prey. In the most intensive form, the bio-technological one, this aspect has nearly disappeared. At this stage it is practically impossible to differentiate between a plant and an animal culture.

626 Material to do so could be the following. As mentioned earlier, Adorno reminded us of "the nomadism of Jews"; see start Chapter 5. Gilles Deleuze and Felix Guattari atttracted more publicity with the use of nomadism in their *Anti-Oedipus*, 1972. This French couple had apparently few things in common with Adorno. However, those were not unimportant elements: they knew about Freud's dubious theories, and they had not the faintest idea of nomadism, to which they referred so often, let alone its role in daily life or world-history. On the contrary! Deleuze himself hardly ever left Paris, rarely he travelled to another French city. About nomads he preferred to quote the historian Toynbee: "Nomads are people who do not move: they became nomads just because they disliked to leave home." Quoted by Antoine Verbij in *De Groene Amsterdammer*, 1991, 23-10-1991, 17. Deleuze and Guattari belong to the "magical Parisian scene" of the "1968 Movement" and to, what a peer reviewer of my book rightly indicates as, "an intramural European intellectual history." Their heirs continuously publish the same vague texts. See, for instance, Rosi Braidotti (since 1990 titles like *Nomadic Subjects*) or her Dutch supporters like the sympathetic Joke Hermsen (*Nomadic Narcism*, 1994); indeed a new brand of oikoidal products in the market of ideas is invented.

In antiquity around the Mediterranean region there were several kinds of animal breeders. An obvious criterion to differentiate among them is to look into the way *distances are covered* with the animals. If we leave aside hunters and fishermen, the following overview can be given.

In principle, *nomads continue tracking* with their animals. Large distances are covered with all of their possessions. Differences can be seen in the way the animals are followed (for instance, Sami following reindeer) or—the other way around (for instance, nomads leading camels). *Pastoralists* are already more bound to specific summer- and winter-pastures and the use of semi-permanent dwellings. They can cover large distances in the seasonal cycles, however. In the Mediterranean this form of animal breeding is given the slightly misleading name of *transhumance*.

Next we arrive at the *herdsmen and shepherds* (ranchers, gauchos, etc.) who are again more strictly bound to specific routes, pastures and more or less fixed settlements. In *animal-husbandry*, compared to all previous kinds, the breeders are nearly immobile, although the animals remain "movable goods"; the distances covered are largely fixed by the route between the stable and the neighboring pasture and the consumers of animal products.

Finally, there is bio-technological breeding in which the animal is transformed from a moveable into an immobile "plant": the life of a veal-calf is confined to *a way of no return* between box and butcher.

For the plant-cultures a similar overview is possible, but it must be clear by now that agriculture is only part of this culture. However, a specific kind of agriculture, the work in the fields aimed at *grain*-growing, received special paradigmatic attention. Grains like wheat, rye, barley and oats were very important in north-western European countries and elsewhere as well, because of the Western dominant position. The social, political and economic infra- and superstructures developed based on their production and consumption lead to the grain-paradigm, the model for all other countries.

But in Europe itself, its limits were clearly demonstrated in the southern countries bordering the Mediterranean Sea, where olive oil and wine-cultures existed with their very different production, consumption and marketing conditions. The European historians of the 19th and early 20th century assumed that in these southern countries, still the basis of a Western civilization, grain-growing cultures existed with all of their typical feudal relations, hierarchical structures and monarchies. That was a major fallacy. Its main consequence is that the differentiated animal cultures in the South were fully neglected.

When I reintroduced them, first in my thesis *Town and Country, Market and Oikos* (1986), and later in other publications, I was treated with serious disdain. My main inspiration was my doctorate supervisor, Bernhard Slicher van Bath, the famous agrarian historian and medievalist, who was the first to discover and describe the overriding importance of animal centered cultures in the Middle Ages of north-western Europe on the wet coastal lands with their strong attitudes of anti-feudalistic farmers' freedom.

That became the idea and model I tested for the southern Mediterranean countries, and they were confirmed. This lead to a fully new interpretation of, for instance, the famous debate about the so-called ancient economy (from Rodbertus to Moses Finley) and the course of history in Greek societies. In my interpretation, for instance, Sparta was perceived as a society with many customs inherited from a nomadic past.

My *Town and Country* presented a full reconstruction of Greek history from ca. 800–300 BCE as seen from an animal cultural angle, i.e. all kinds of husbandry from nomadism and pastoralism to stable-rearing of animals. This was seen from a production side rather than a consumption point of view.

The following very brief summary of the many antagonisms between a "plant-based" and an "animal-based" culture or society can be helpful in understanding my earlier studies and the subjects discussed in this chapter and, in particular, the worlds of difference between the two kinds of exploitation in pre-industrial and non-urban societies. See Table 3 below.

Whatever their highly important temporal or permanent *interrelations*, the "plant" and "animal" cultures and societies are diametrically opposed in principle. Historians, sociologists, economists or anthropologists have to treat them as such on penalty of losing all ties with realistic developments in these societies. It's impossible to neglect this by using empty "umbrella words" like *agriculture* which cannot mean more than "activities on the land or outside the city," etc.

Concerning the interrelations, it is important to point here to typical features as a consequence of the above basic characteristics. Animal-dung is sold to farmers to fertilize their lands (mutual interest); animal-products like wool, leather, meat, milk are sold to peasants and cities in exchange for money or urban products; the surplus of young men (B-2) "produces" warrior-mercenaries for the elite in the *oikos* (A) from which the typical medieval knights originate in my opinion (Ritter, chevalier); the same must be true for the fishermen-communities from which the sailors for the armadas originate.

One of the remarkable results of these studies was that it became clear why a *substantial* rise of small peasants hidden in a "closed world" could not be seen anywhere in ancient Greece, which was/is the basis of the Finleyan approach. Furthermore, it reveals how a main object of study, *property*, cannot be treated as a juridical property of arable land (as we know it today). We quickly learn that it is of crucial importance to differentiate strongly between *possession, usage* (temporal/ permanent), and *property* (as seen in custom, common

TABLE 3 Basic oikoïdal (A) and market (B) features

Arable farming and okoïdal socio-economic features (A)	**Animal husbandry and market features (B)**
1. Land is the main "means of production"; it is difficult to use it as "means of exchange" (immovable; succession rules, etc.).	1. Animals are the main "means of production"; they are simple to use as "means of exchange" (often legal means of payment).
2. Often intensively managed. Expulsion of labour power as a result of mainly *external* accidents like war or ecological changes, and conjunctural events like famines and poor harvests. "Risk-economy" is confined to leaving the land.	2. Extensively managed: always a labour-power surplus which has to work as merchant, mercenary, sailor, fisher, etc. Expulsion of these younger men and subsidiary business form a structural basis for a limited "risk economy."
3. Difficult relation with a money-economy except in times of surplus-production. Too often compulsory delivery of *products in natura* to religous and secular overlords.	3. Structural money-economy thanks to the "movable" animals, labour-surplus and animal-products. Compulsory deliverances unknown.
4. Too often the duty to render compulsory *services* for religious and secular overlords.	4. Feudal and state institutions cannot arise or gain only minor (temporary) influence as tribute-mongers, etc.
5. More or less exploitative classes and a hierarchical order ("the state") arise.	5. Make their own military and juridical organisations (self-government). Very inimical to (foreign) overlordship.

or Roman law, etc.) and then differentiate all this again for a "plant" and an "animal" culture. One may add the following for Greek history.

Greeks were well known as animal dealers, merchants and seafarers with cash products; as mercenaries or pirates, and as cultural intermediaries or money- and market-makers they were responsible for the rise of this "animal society." Nomads, pastoralists and, in general, all participants in an *animal culture* detested and fought every (state) power that tried to block or make them abandon their mobile way of (market-) life.

That is why Greeks had genuine democratic attitudes that, in most cases, ensured that no overarching power could be successful. Greek life was, *therefore*, a *stateless* life until Alexander the Great and the Romans with their legions of sturdy peasant-fighters put an end to this most inspiring epoch in world history.

Finally, and in contrast to conservative and some feminist opinions, it becomes plausible that the animal-tradition was also responsible for a basic *equality* between men and women *combined* with functional differences.

With all these characteristics, a vivid perception of a "democratic *market*-society" could be developed in opposition to the still dominant *Oikos* or *oikoïdal* ideology with their view of the hierarchical "closed" society of autarkic grain-growing peasants in a feudal setting with at best some market-activities on the fringe.

Now we can turn to the specific subject of this chapter, starting with a reminder of what the Scythian chief described, the permanent conflict in history—from old Persia to new China—between an Oikos as State, repressing all "uncontrollable moving things" like nomads, merchants and markets (whatever their wrong definitions).

7.2 Weber's Comparative World History

Soon after this legendary Scythian chief informed the King of Kings, Darius, about basic social and anthropological elements of nomadic life, this Persian conqueror like so many of his predecessors and imitators saw "his Waterloo."

Herodotus taught us another thing as well. The most important reasons for this failed clash of lifestyles were the substantial ignorance about "the enemy" and the inability to cope in a practical and peaceful way with alternative ways of life or social minorities. In our century there seems to be no change in these circumstances and attitudes as will be substantiated in this chapter.

The first part is devoted to the subject of the sociological ignorance about nomadism in the highly influential work of Max Weber; the main part sketches the practical difficulties Chinese and Russian states met in coping with their nomadic populations. Both parts together display the most important elements of the theory and practice of anti-nomadism in sedentary societies.

This is not only basic knowledge for understanding the next chapter. If one looks at the substantial clashes between Chinese and nomads in Xinjiang or at the implications of the far from secret war for Central Asian gas- and oil reserves in traditional nomadic areas or at the long-lasting Afghan drama, one knows how the chapter still concerns a topic of the day. Here, however, it's not the present but the past problems between sedentary and nomadic societies that have to come to the fore. In Max Weber's writings one can find a perception of the complexities of this subject in a world-historical context from which we can derive a specific part to discuss.

Interest in Max Weber increasingly shifts to his sociology of religion only,[627] but the Weber-literature remains historically an interesting part of sociological and other discourses. Weber's own writings—sometimes *nolens volens*—still help in tracing complicated historical and sociological problems. Even so, it is difficult to find articles or books about at least two important and mutually connected subjects however extensive the Weber-literature may be.

First, there are the (interrelations between) market and *oikos,* which formally cover only a very few pages of *Economy and Society* (*Wirtschaft und Gesellschaft*) as discussed in the first chapter. Second, there is the subject of the nomads or, in general, of mobile as opposed to sedentary peoples and societies.

The relationship between the two subjects can be found rather easily. Not only do the words of the Scythian chieftain above show the connections and contradictions, but also opinions relating mobile behavior to markets and a sedentary way of life to the agriculturally oriented *oikos* (as told, another word for a patriarchally ruled *latifundium*, household, manor, family, an estate as well as a state) demonstrate the relationship. Superficially, it looks as if Weber dealt with both subjects only sporadically. However, one can argue that they belong to the very heart of his thinking and oeuvre and, more important, that they belong to the center of intriguing and complex problems such as town-country contradictions.

In this chapter, I deal with the second theme as a consequence of the book's subject. Inevitably, the first subject will also be touched but analyses of *oikos*-market relations remain in the background. In the meantime, it is far from easy to discover Weber's opinions about nomads and related groups.[628] The *Economy and Society*-index does not help reveal traces of nomads or pastoralist people; in *Wirtschaft und Gesellschaft* there is one entry on Bedouins. In the essays on the sociology of religion there is a bit more and in the so-called *Wirtschaftsgeschichte* one can find also some interesting material.[629]

If the subject should be extended to all kinds of animal-breeding (*Viehaltung, Viehwirtschaft,* etc.) the yield on Weberian thoughts on the subject is

627 See Hans Derks, 1989, 282–297.

628 See first the excellent Tim Ingold, ed., 1997 with many relevant articles.

629 Wge, 39, 50–51.

again a bit larger.[630] So, all in all the result is rather meager. The same conclusion holds for the extensive Weber-literature: you will search in vain for an article on Weber and nomadism!

However, the following quotations will give a very different view of the priority Weber gave to the subject. We can also gain perspective of the problems that must be discussed. The following remarks are derived from the second version of his *Agrarverhältnisse im Altertum* (1898). In the introduction Weber states:

> The settlements of the West have in common a transition from nomadic animal husbandry to sedentary agriculture; East-Asian peoples, however, have in common a transition from shifting cultivation to sedentary agriculture.... The consequences are ... that in oriental villages, in so far they are not from modern origin, the western concepts of mark and allmende[631] are absent.... Also the "individualism" inherent in the property of herds and flocks with its sharp economic and social differentiation—in the West the primitive basis of feudalism—is absent in Asian cultures.... The East-Asians as well as the old American cultures seem to know feudalism in principle as group- or caste-feodalism: a strongly closed and locally organised warrior-group, often living in fortified settlements, is maintained in a *naturalwirtschaftlich*[632] way by a population who are considered as state-slaves or -servants. Also the Egyptian and Asian Orient is in their whole development, determined by the preponderance of a colossal Pharaohnic or imperial *Oikos*, i.e. the state-economy based on *Naturalwirtschaft*.[633]

630 In this case, in Wge more text is available and one can also consult GASW, 1–288 which is the article, "Agrarverhältnisse im Altertum" from the third edition of HdS.

631 "Mark" (or "merk") concerns "a boundary, or border region- and *markgenoten* came into use later to denote the wild pastures and the community that owned or used them." "Allmenden" were "commonly used plots" of pastures, woods etc. by village-, town- and city-peoples. See Bernard Slicher van Bath, 1963, 157–160 and Werner Rösener, 1997, 87, 103, 33.

632 Weber defined a "Naturalwirtschaft" in a highly nuanced way in WG, 53–58. Here: an economy without whatever exchange or without money but with exchange of goods.

633 Max Weber in HdS, 1898, 57, 58. Like the first edition of HdS, 1897, *Zweiter Supplementband*, 1–18 this second draft of Weber's *Agrarverhältnisse* is also never consulted. This is a serious mistake. One always uses the article in the third edition of the HdS, 1909. The English translator does not know of their existence as is shown in Max Weber, 1976, 29–30. Widow Marianne Weber, notorious for her dubious information about her Saint Max, did not mention the previous drafts either; see GASW, 1 note. In the *"Vorwort"* of GASW a much repeated remark is made about the short time Weber needed to write the lengthy third version. No wonder, the model was finished in the previous editions. Weber only had to fill in the details. The first version consisted only of chapters on Greece and Rome; the

So, here we deal with one of the broadest themes in comparative world history as well as a subject that can be tested in regional and local environments. This is also one of the most hotly debated subjects complicated by the changing opinions of participants during their lifetime.

Eleven years later for instance, Weber altered the first part of this fundamental statement in the following way:[634]

> The settlements of the European West have in common ... the transition ... from a dominant milk cattle-husbandry plus some agriculture to a dominant agriculture plus some cattle-husbandry in the definite sedentary constellation; the East-Asian peoples, however, have in common ... a transition from a shifting cultivation to a horticultural use of fields without any milk cattle-husbandry.

Which questions arise from these sweeping statements and what will be the "problem-definition" of this chapter?

First, there is the geographical expansion of Weber's argument. In the new edition Weber adds to the former that the given Northern European type of transition is also suitable for Southern Europe and the Near East. "East Asia" remains what it was: similar to "old American cultures," to Pharaohnic and other colossal imperial *Oikoi* with state-slaves and all the rest. Interesting is that here "Near East" spearheads the North European type of development right into a vast area with only "Eastern Despotism." In this way, the classic Greek and Hellenistic cultures get their space in time, let alone the Judaist phenomenon.

---

second added a chapter on Near Eastern developments and extended the Greek chapter considerably; as a new item, the third edition also contained a short (3% of the text) analysis of the Old Israelite situation.

634 GASW, 1. To understand Weber's opinions it is necessary to "translate" the content and not the form. I am, therefore, not fond of most of the available English translations, although they might demonstrate much better English! For example, Weber used the rather ambiguous "*nomadisierender Ackernutzung*" translated by R. Frank as "*nomadic agriculture.*" Perhaps Weber wanted to use a concept expressing a wandering way of collecting or growing fruits or grains by peasants. Wim Wertheim proposed to substitute for this the technical term *shifting cultivation or ladang*-cultivation, which was widely spread in Asian countries for a very long time. Western imperialists and developers wrongly opposed the burning of the (old) forest-land while looking elsewhere for cultivation opportunities as a very primitive and damaging way of food-production. If Wertheim's next proposition should be true that the typical western *three field system* is in principle a similar cultivation-technique, then already at the start Weber's thesis has to fall apart. However, "*nomadisierender Ackernutzung"* can be taken at face value as well: the use of the fields by animals *after* the harvests; they eat what is left and dung the area in the same time; everybody happy. One difficulty: Max Weber is seldom a simple scholar!

Next, it follows from both citations that Weber sees all histories ending in sedentary agriculture. Is this wishful thinking, already a reality or, for my part, a desirable perspective? These questions have to be posed against the background of the near impossibility to settle nomads. Only recently, after about 1870, nomads of the worlds' *Nomads Belt* were "settled" by force. Too often this kind of settlement meant nothing more than an attempted genocide.

In other cases world market prices in wool and other "nomadic" products were too low for a long period. Together with the usual hazards of nomadic life such as droughts and animal-pests, this depression meant the starvation of North African nomads at a large scale. Governments and development agencies experienced that their energetic efforts to *peasantize* nomads largely failed.[635] So, what is meant by Weber's "*transition from nomadic animal-husbandry to sedentary agriculture*"?

Furthermore, the *milk-question* as well as the *cattle-husbandry* phenomenon received pivotal importance. This problem is partly related to the far-reaching differences between a population's dominant milk-consumption and dominant meat-consumption. Partly it is related to the antagonism between the use of the animal's milk/meat and the use of animal-energy (horses, oxen, donkeys, etc.). At present, in industrial urban society *milk* seems to be one of the million consumer-products in a super-market. Sometimes, at the moment the so-called *milk-oceans* float the *European Economic Community* again, people awake but only for as long as headlines in the papers reach. Sometimes we are surprised by interesting anthropological studies about strange tribes, their bonds of blood and milk, their symbolic and medical use of milk, etc.[636]

Weber, however, even used the milk-item in a comparative world-historical perspective. But did he rightly understand that, as nearly no other product, milk is a metaphor for specific kinds of societies? Why did he give, for instance, East Asian peoples no access to milk cattle-husbandry? Is it not remarkable as well that, in fact, *nomadism* remains only a feature in Western history, whereas Asian history seems wholly occupied by peasants who later became horticulturalists?

The last element of this problem-definition concerns ideology. In all respects, one can say: Dealing with nomads is never value-free. Nomad-ideological problems concern, first, well-known discrimination-patterns that lead us to question their origin and to compare relevant histories.

Brent Shaw, for instance, began an important article, *Eaters of Flesh, Drinkers of Milk*, by offending the reader's "civilized sensibilities" to illustrate that

635 Philip Salzman, ed., 1980 provides an interesting introduction to the problem.

636 Marielouise Creyghton, 1981.

nomads, whether ancient or modern, have never had good press.[637] He quotes Hunter Thompson as follows:

> ...The Menace is loose again, the Hell's Angels, the hundred carat headline, running fast and loud on the early morning freeway, low in the saddle, nobody smiles, jamming crazy through traffic and ninety miles an hour down the center stripe, missing by inches ... like Genghis Khan on an iron horse, a monster steed with fiery anus, flat out through the eye of a beer can and up your daughter's leg with no quarter asked and none given...

Here, Shaw appeals to a string of prejudices commonly associated with mobile people. Immediately, he directs the reader's attention to the general effects of a "nomadic challenge." Shaw rightly complains about the "complete shortfall in recorded history of an entire sector of human community." In classical antiquity it is due to the lack of sympathy with the (pastoral) nomad in written accounts of historians, military men or administrators. Their perception of the world, their sedentarist outlook, determined to a large extent existing prejudices.

The ideological problems concerning nomadic peoples and societies can be also studied in all the three parts of Weber's sociology of religion. Indeed, it seems almost self-evident to develop the general argumentation of this chapter on the basis of these "economical ethical" (*wirtschaftsethische*) texts. Within his very incomplete *oeuvre*, they not only form a rather complete corpus but they also deal in a comparative way with regions most suitable for the study of nomadism i.e. the Chinese, Hinduistic or Palestinian societies/ histories.

It is well known that these analyses were of paramount importance for Weber to answer questions raised with the rise of modern capitalism in the West and the role of religion in that process. I cannot deal with that part of the problem here but by implication my analysis of Weber's view on nomadism etc. will affirm or criticize his capitalism-theory.

It is clear, then, that the given problem-definition displays a vast and complex field of research that must be kept in mind when looking into a specific corner of that field: Max Weber's views on the East-Asian, in particular Chinese, sedentarism-nomadism contradictions.

I put to the test, first, the Chinese and other Asian "milk and meat evidence" as a direct consequence of Weber's writings. It not only gives the opportunity to dive into Weber's thought but also to highlight some specific nomadic features.

637 Brent Shaw, 1982/'83, 5–31; Hans Derks, 1995, 27–40.

The second part of the chapter concerns the general characteristics of the sedentarism and agriculture versus nomadism and animal husbandry relationships. Much misunderstanding concerning nomadism throughout history can be discussed by means of a broad historical analysis so that a relevant insight is reached into a highly complex phenomenon such as "the (chance of) a transition from nomadic animal husbandry to sedentary agriculture."

I hope to show, at least, the main elements of this transition-problem in a Chinese and Central Asian context. In the end I can come back to the characteristics of Weber's nomadism-theory to be used as a stepping-stone for the next chapters.

7.3 Ideology

When Weber talked about the social basis of Chinese development in the 18th century, he pointed to the extraordinary intensity of the Chinese acquisitive drive.[638] Commercial organizations were very powerful as well as autonomous and the Chinese were very eager to work and perform well. In this respect nearly no one could compete with them. Weber supposed that the fast population-growth of the 18th century combined with an ever-increasing stock of strategic metals should have given China the best opportunity to become a capitalist country. But this did not happen. Why?

Weber summed up the following reasons: The large increase of the peasant population instead of a strong decrease as in England; the small-scale peasant-holdings instead of the agricultural large enterprises as in Prussia;[639] cattle-breeding was largely undeveloped and, subsequently, milk-drinking was absent and meat-consumption "something for the rich." This last item is even

638 See GAR, volume 1, 349–350. Weber used here "*Erwerbstrieb*" which is translated according WG, 371 and EC, 617, but "aquisitive drive," at least, does not remind to "*Haushalten*" as the unavoidable counter-concept to Weber's "*Erwerbstrieb*."

639 Mark Elvin, 1973, 268 gives the modern view. In the eighteenth and nineteenth centuries there was a fast increase of market towns: "...they grew up around temples, around the manors of great landlords and the country residences of important merchants, and even around industrial undertakings such as pottery works..." One development which can be compared to the Prussian situation (this occured at the same time but on a much larger scale!), was the penetration of the large agro-monasteries into the plains of Mongolia. In around 1825 "some 30% of the male population had taken vows. Monasteries increased in size and towns grew round them." Jack Gray, 1990, 94. Later, one got as much trouble with these monks as with the Junkers! But it is true, the small peasant economy prevailed, although their political-economy is hardly comparable to the European peasant economy which was Weber's frame of reference (see, for instance, Jack Gray, 1990, 8.).

seen as a "main contradiction" (*Hauptgegensatz*) between Europe and Asia. This could be expected given what was cited in the first paragraph.[640]

In trying to answer the question anew, Why all this? Weber apologized for *not* dealing with the case of the nomadic past of the Chinese. In a long note, however, he compensated this with a fundamental statement.[641]

He argued that nomadic invaders from Inner-Asia, who suppressed the population of the main Chinese valley's, showed up repeatedly. Weber went on to say that from time to time only the nomadic Mongols undertook serious efforts to sustain their power-positions against the higher farm-culture (by means of a prohibition to grow crops in a certain distance from the capital). However, the Chinese never drank milk and this fact is clearly more important than all histories about the continuity of the centuries old field cultivation and horticulture.

Besides this, the rituals of the Emperor prescribed the ceremonial use of the plow. Compared with these facts the nomadic descent of (part of) the old ruler-elite seems insignificant. The existence of "Men-houses" (*Männerhaus, -Bund,* etc.)[642] has nothing to do with "nomadism," but it shows that war and gaming were matters of concern in these communities, but that agriculture was a concern of the women. The absence of milk-consumption in China is seen as clearly very old and it contradicts the "Nomad Hypothesis." Large animals were used for work or sacrifice and small animals were used to satisfy the normal need for meat.

---

640 Wge, 39 note 1. In relation to his capitalism-thesis, he later—GAR, volume 1, 373–374—made the differentiation between the *political capitalism* of money-lenders and suppliers of patrimonial courts and *modern capitalism*. The first kind earned high profit-rates in their money-business and one knew how to exploit mines and commerce to accumulate wealth. "The development of the capitalism oriented to the market proper and free exchange remained, however, in statu nascendi." What developed in Western medieval cities was absent in China till today: there were "no legal and sociological bases for capitalist 'enterprises' with their rational *Versachlichung* of the economy ... the liability of the clans for their members was rudimentary developed ... commercial gains were invested immediately in land ... [it was] in particular an internal and political booty-capitalism which dominated the capital gains and ... land-accumulation," 374/ 375.

641 GAR, volume 1, 350, 351. The causal relationship in this note is highly blurred but that shall not be my first worry here.

642 Max Weber's reference to the "Männerhaus, Männerbund," etc. concerns a rather universal way of how men demonstrate their masculinity or their role as warrior. It was also one of the most beloved cultural items in German intellectual circles before 1945. Weber's famous concept of the charismatic authority is directly related to these debates, but also the fundamental way the German SS was organized. See the excellent and extensive publication of Gisela Völger and Karin Welck. Ed, 1990, volume 1, 99. This book has nearly 100 contributions from all over the world. For our market-*oikos* discussion it concerns many perfect illustrations of oikoidal characteristics.

Weber's views rest first and foremost on the typical European (sedentary!) prejudices about the always war-making and barbaric nomads; they not only kill and enslave poor peasants and threaten peaceful, god-fearing rulers, but they never accept any control or the authority of the State. As will be shown, the Weberian prejudices fit perfectly well with views within the Chinese *oikoïdal* (court) elite. But let me first give a short and rather unsystematic answer to the question of meat- and milk-consumption in Chinese history, which presupposes animal-breeding, pastures and so on.

7.4 Milk and Meat

It is said that the idea of the Chinese non-consumption of milk comes from Alexander von Humboldt, 1769–1859.[643] If he has stated this, his words must be hidden beyond his collected works. It would be interesting to know which sources, except his learned thumb, Humboldt used. In any case, the milk-statement must have been part of his general social evolution-theory in which everywhere sedentary agriculture had to come before nomadism and "hunterism."

Most scholars in the 19th century, however, adhered to the opposite theory, the so called *Dreistufentheorie* in which hunters are followed first by nomads and later by agriculturalists (*Ackerbauer*). Some even dared to expand this theory with "industrialism."

At the moment one can easily find supporters of both opinions but, in my view, they are both wrong starting-points. Apart from the fallacy of every *prime mover* thinking, at least, one has to consider all kinds of ecological, climatic or economical circumstances before posing relevant transitions. If this is done, one conclusion seems unavoidable: there have to be several developments for different regions thanks to combinations of possibilities. Second, the knowledge about the *mutual relations* or dependencies of agriculture, nomadism and the other forms has to be taken in serious consideration. So far, so good.

In Weber's Heidelberg the economic-geographer Eduard Hahn published numerous influential studies about this social evolution.[644] He was a rather

643 Eduard Hahn, 1909, 4, 5, 24.

644 Like *Die Entstehung der wirtschaftlichen Arbeit*, 1908 and *Das Alter der wirtschaftlichen Kultur der Menschheit*, 1905. The renewal of Humboldt's thesis was arrived by stating, for instance, the following stupidities: "Die Frau muß im wesentlichen dauernd die Nahrung beschaffen, und da sie fast nie zur Jägerin und selten zur Fischerin geworden ist…, so ist fast immer die wirtschaftliche Basis der Urstämme pflanzliche Nahrung." 1909, 5. Hahn became one of those forerunners of Fascism and Nazism with his opinion that "man's

aggressive conservative defender of "our agriculture" in science as well as in politics. Hahn renewed not only Humboldt's agricultural evolution-thesis but also his opinion about the Chinese milk-consumption. According to him, Humboldt said "that the consumption of milk—for us a self-evident matter—is detested by the Chinese as a people and that they have not done this for thousands of years." Hahn adds to this that Chinese at present never eat cheese: "From this food we received our bad smell, they think."[645]

Milk is a beloved subject of Hahn's book. Strange enough, he does not mention any reason why "the Chinese as a people" (!) should abhor this healthy white drink. Also in other respects Hahn used an equal development model as Weber: It is precisely milk consumption and animal husbandry in our culture that are strictly embedded within agriculture [*Ackerbau* or *Pflugkultur* for Hahn] and by this fact we received major elements of our identity. It is not difficult to prove that Weber is directly influenced by Hahn who does not discuss Chinese meat consumption or vegetarianism.[646]

Although early in the 20th century Chinese restaurants were not widespread, it remains strange how unfamiliar Weber was with Chinese food. At least, he would have known that pork always was (and is happily) a normal part of the common Chinese family-diet. By 5000 BCE, the Neolithic villagers' main meat animals were pigs and chickens. They also raised and ate sheep and

biological type was determined by domestication, which influences him in much the same manner as it influences animals." See ESS, volume 7, 244.; see also Friedrich Ratzel, 1909, volume 1, 322–325; first edition 1882. More important is the originally in 1897 written third chapter in Friedrich Ratzel, 1923, 33–59 about "Property and Domination" [*Besitz und Herrschaft*]. Here Ratzel formulated, in fact, the foundation for the influential and notorious *Deutsche Geopolitik* embedded in his description of the basic war between agriculture [*Ackerbau/ Boden-Kultur*] and nomadism. He used Hahn's *Ackerbau*—point of view in 49–50. For the very influential geographers "scene" see Gerhard Sandner, 1994 in: David Hooson, ed., 1994, 71–92. Lewis Mumford also accepted Hahn's perspective and at present feminists like Badinter still support his thesis! See Elisabeth Badinter, 1988, 54–56, 277.

645 Eduard Hahn, 1909, 24 see also 28; as a source he mentions E. Parker's *China, history*, London, 1901.

646 In GASW, 508–556 within a very principal discussion about some hot issues of the German historiography in his days like *Der Streit um den Charakter der altgermanischen Sozialverfassung*. Weber very positively referred to Hahn (524). Weber's affirmation is given although he strongly doubts Hahn's scholarship (note 1): in his perception Hahn has the "*überlieferten Vorstellungen über die 'Wirtschaftsstufen' zuerst einen eingehender begründeten Widerspruch entgegengesetzt…*" (H. criticized old-fashioned ideas about economic development in a highly appropriate way). It is informative how Weber here took the reverse position as in the Chinese case: here the old West-Germans as alleged nomads are not seen as consumers of milk, cheese and meat but first as "*Ackerbauer*," whereas the more eastern German tribes were (still) milk etc. consumers: 524–525. It is not possible to discuss this position here which must be seen in relation to Weber's East Asian views.

dogs. Soon afterwards the cow, water buffalo and duck were added and the Chinese meat roster was essentially complete.[647]

Since Weber thinks that the absence of milk-consumption in China is very old, then in the third century AD it was not necessary to come up with proposals for large-scale changes of pastures into arable lands. That occurred in specific parts of China, whereas elsewhere the extraordinary richness of many large estates could be reported where, for instance, "their horses, cattle, sheep and swine" were so numerous that "the upland valleys cannot hold" them.[648] Around 644, the emperor T'ai-tsung of the T'ang complained about the difficult food-situation and ordered:

> The situation is especially bad in the San-Wei, and yet grazing lands for pigs, sheep and horses are spread throughout this region. All of these should be done away with.... All the pasturages should be removed, so that the horses, cattle, pigs and sheep feed on the grass of the empty plains.[649]

647 Eugene Anderson, 1988, 143, 144, 164, 177. He also reports that in Sung China, as the "golden age of Chinese *sushi* making ... pork was the main meat eaten, but sheep, goat and even donkey were common...," 68. For the earliest milk and meat consumption in Central Asia now see the excellent Ahmad Dani and Vadim Masson, ed., 1992, 39, 225, 272, 432; David Christian, 1998 with numerous data on milk and meat consumption. Anderson tells about the traveller Robert Fortune who wrote in 1847: "The food of the people is of the simplest kind ... rice, vegetables, and a small portion of animal food, such as fish and pork."; 96. Hsiao-Tung Fei, 1980, 126–128 tells about the relative poor peasants diet in the thirties of the 20th century: "The only kind of meat eaten is pork..." and "During the period of agricultural work, the dinner is comparatively rich. They have meat and fish. But in ordinary times meat is not very often served. Pure vegetarianism is rare except for a few widows." In Kwantung there was even a tax on slaughtered animals in 1908. Such a tax is only appropriate if there is a large amount of meat-eaters. W. Yeh-chien, 1973, 79.

648 Mark Elvin, 1973, 33. In about 1100 when the Southern Sung introduced paper money a source reported that the bills were paid half in paper and half in cash: "A similar practice was followed among the common people for the mortgaging or sale of fields, houses, horses, cattle..."; 160.

649 See also Mark Elvin, 1973, 39 about the same time: "The importance of livestock in the farm economy of north-eastern China at this time is in marked contrast with the predominance of cereal crop cultivation, ...in the late traditional period and at the present." Other aspects of milk-drinking are given in Wolfgang Bauer's brilliant book, 1989. It is an analysis and description of most of the utopian visions and ideas about the best possible world in Chinese history from the beginning up to Mao Zedong's political-economical experiments. Bauer often reports about a most beautiful world "of milk and honey," a subterranean world with milk-resources about AD 825, see 275–277; a vision of a new world, Uttarakuru, still used in about 1650 in which there grew lotus-flowers with juice "which looks like milk, tastes sweet and delicious, smells like honey ... large, heavy clouds as big as the whole country ... wonderful rain ... like cow milk.... There is no egoism (wu wo), nor

One of Mark Elvin's relevant answers to the question also addressed by Weber as to why (Western) industrial capitalism did not develop in China from the 18th century onwards was: "There was a shortage of draught-animals, and possibly therefore of animal manures, as northern grazing-lands were turned into fields."[650]

Elvin's remark could mean that the government still failed to take announced measures, but also that over a very long period and well into modern times there were large areas with animal husbandry and, subsequently, milk-consumption. Elvin shows as well that, apart from milk, the *manure*-problem is of the utmost importance for the peasants and, in general, for the interdependence of agriculture and animal breeding. The large agricultural potential could only be exploited given an abundance of water and animal manure (see below).

In 1847 the traveller Robert Fortune "was surprised to find that in Foochow beef and milk were widely eaten."[651] At the end of the nineteenth century, Arthur H. Smith writes:

> In the northern parts of China the horse, the mule, the ox, and the donkey are in universal use, and in large districts the camel is made to do full duty ... it is the general practice to eat all of these animals as soon as they expire, no matter whether the cause of death be an accident, old age, or disease ... and this truth is recognized in the lower scale of prices asked for it, but it is all sold, and is all eaten.[652]

It is no surprise to read nowadays:

> The consumption of dairy products has increased markedly since World War II, but only in the northwestern pastoral regions are cattle widely used for meat or milk products.[653]

---

a ruler (wu chu) or police…" 235, etc. Another comment about Weber's meat-verdict can be seen in a Confucian story from the 13th century which shows the opposite: members of the sect of "Satans-friends and Vegetable-eaters" are forbidden to eat meat and to drink wine. Some of them became rich. This inspired the story-teller to complain about the naivety of the people "because it is selfevident that one becomes rich if one does not eat meat and drink wine."; 312.

650 Mark Elvin, 1973, 301.

651 Op cit. Eugene Anderson, 1988, 96. Foochow or F(o)uchou is located at the coast opposite Taiwan; a very remote place in relation to the pasture heartlands!

652 Arthur H. Smith, 1894, 21. The reverend Smith lived and worked for twenty-two years in China and also wrote books on Chinese village life.

653 Chiao-min Hsieh, 1973, 87, 88. This atlas is very helpful in discovering the many pitfalls and possibilities of the present Chinese climate, hydrology etc. and the resulting land use,

A comment on this very quick overview over the "milk-centuries" seems unnecessary.

This brings us to the following related "practical" points. If Weber looked into the matter of milk- and meat-consumption, he must have considered the densely populated eastern parts of China, the coastal-areas or the river-valleys (together about 50% of China's area and 75% of the population). The real Chinese pasture-provinces in the north, interior and (south)west are neglected. This must have seriously influenced his perception and that of many other scholars.

For all these people, the facts must come as a surprise: "Not only the Mongols, nomadic Turkic groups ... and Tibetans, but also the western Chinese eat yogurt, cheese, kumys ... and other fermented products."[654] But also elsewhere in China there were and are many opportunities for several kinds of pastoralism and animal breeding. A few statistics are sufficient to explain this point further.

In the 1930s a remarkable inquiry appeared from J. Lossing Buck et al.[655] This gave the first reliable possibility to compare Western and Eastern agricultural practices. Although Lossing Buck mainly studied the major agricultural areas, he could estimate that approximately one-fourth of all land was cultivated (between 12 to 45 per cent was the average in the world). One-half was in some kind of productive use consisting of trees, grass and reeds for fuel. One-fifth was occupied by forest and twelve per cent was real pasture. At the moment thirty-one per cent of the Chinese surface is qualified as pasture; it is an area as large as eighty per cent of Europe (excl. Russia) with a population of, at least, 200 million people![656]

If Lossing Buck only looks into the twenty-five per cent of cultivated land, he estimates that nearly ninety per cent is used for crops and about two per cent for pasture. In the United States this relation is forty-two per cent against

crops, etc. I don't know if this atlas may be accurate about the historical record. In that case Mongolia and many parts of Central Asia as Kazakhstan, Uzbekistan etc., which is an area nearly as great as Western Europe with 80% pastures, must also be considered.

654 Eugene Anderson, 1988, 145. For the present situation in Central Asia see C. van Leeuwen, ed., 1994.

655 John Lossing Buck, 1937/38. In the three volumes of this study the report is given from an eight years' field investigation of 17,000 farms involving 46,601 farm families in twenty-two out of China's twenty-eight provinces by over 3,000 experts.

656 This is not as remarkable as it seems because in scrutinizing Lossing Buck's data the gap can be diminished. Furthermore, one must always control the vital data used by the scholars at stake. Lossing Buck used, for instance, a total Chinese surface of about 1,400,000 sqare miles; the *Times Atlas of the World* gives a surface of 3,900,000 square miles (1959); the *Third World Guide* ('89/'90) uses 9,596,961 square kilometres, and so on.

forty-seven (and at the time in Europe—excl. Russia—it had to be about sixty-five and thirty per cent). Therefore, Lossing Buck concludes that there is limited animal industry in China and a consequent low food consumption of animal products, as compared with substantial animal industry and a high consumption of animal products in many of the Western countries.

In an optimistic mood, this could be seen as a first substantiation of Weber's thesis. However, the conclusion is drawn at the basis of only a *quarter* of the total Chinese surface. Notwithstanding this fact, Lossing Buck et al. concludes next:

> ...the density of animal population is, however, surprisingly high in China: 0.34 animal units per crop acre, as compared with 0.70 in Great Britain ... (it) means that over a large part of the country the farms are moderately to well-stocked. This is true in spite of the fact that 10 per cent of the farms have no animals. This degree of animal density is a large factor in the maintenance of the fertility of the land.[657]

The myths of a "vegetarian China" or of "China, the country of *only* small peasants" should come to an end. The same must happen with the related myth of "the Chinese or East Asian abstinence from dairy products." The classic Chinese explanation for this last myth is clear enough: "...prejudice against Central Asians and desire to avoid economic dependence on them."[658]

657 The American agriculturalist Lossing Buck and his team did a great job. It is, however, undeniable that he made only a typical agricultural investigation in the northern wheat- and southern rice-regions. Animal husbandry and its products in the broadest sense of the word got too less attention. Other sources like eye-witness accounts must be consulted awaiting new and relevant studies. See, for instance, Lossing Buck's colleague the important Frederick King, 1949. I thank Wim Wertheim for pointing to this study. This American agriculturalist made the following comparison about the animal density in Shantung, 206. Well-to-do farmers in this city are able to provide for eight people, two cows, two donkeys and about eight pigs. If taking the same density "an area of farm land equal to the state of Wisconsin would have 86,000,000 people; 21,500,000 cows; 21,500,000 donkeys and 86,000,000 swine.... It is clear, therefore, that either very effective agricultural methods are practiced or else extreme economy is exercised. Both are true." Elsewhere, 132, he tells about a cattle farm in Shanghai (!) with 40 cows, feeded with a.o. cotton seed cakes, which produced milk "far better than the Danish and New Zealand products served at the hotels." Still, even King cannot fully free himself from the vegetarian-myth in quoting an American colleague instead of looking around: 121.

658 Eugene Anderson, 1988, 145, 146. Of course, it is true that at the moment the majority of East Asians are poor milk- or dairy consumers. Buddhism, as another oikoïdal power, is effective by declaring cows as holy animals. It is also a typical oikoïdal argument to come up with a *biological* explanation for the alleged milk-abstinence in East Asia. Also in the

Here we arrive at the main point of the *Nomadic Challenge*. The given prejudice enlightens a most typical oikoïdal argument inspired by autarkic state-policies. "The Chinese State" (whatever this may be in Chinese history) had already become dependent on horse-imports from Central Asia: another dependence would have been "too costly and too humiliating"! After solving these fundamental practical problems, we can look into the Chinese Weber-case in more detail.

7.5 The Mutual Relationships

For a period of nearly two thousand years (200 BCE–AD 1700), "trade was the chief determinant of peace and war between the nomadic and Chinese peoples along China's northern borders."[659] The Turkic and Mongolian nomads needed and got particularly large quantities of rice, cloth, silk and lacquer ware for themselves and for trade with other (Near)Asian peoples. The grain was partly used as a supplement to their daily diet of milk and meat.

The Chinese agriculturalists needed and sometimes got slaves, but always got horses, cattle, sheep, wool, furs (sable and fox in particular), hides, tendons and horns, the famous jade or strategic metals as copper and iron in large quantities. From the Song Chinese, nomads bought rice etc. for large quantities of silver money, whereas in the Han-period the Chinese gave substantial amounts of money and gold as gifts.

---

case of milk-consumption one must be exact as possible because most nomads of Central Asia never drink *fresh* milk. It is first boiled and then fermented; butter and various kinds of cheese are made from fermented milk. Furthermore one has to understand the peculiarities of the various kinds of milk and their popularity for different reasons. Sheep and cow-milk are consumed the most but for special occasions the beestings (the first milk of cows, sheep and goats) or the fermented mare's milk (koumiss or kumys) are more popular. Camels do have a large milk production; it is said, however, that pregnant women do not drink this milk. See C. van Leeuwen, ed., 1994, 65.

659 For the following is most important Sechin Jagchid and Van Jay Symons, 1989. A general devastating critic of Weber's writings on China is Mark Elvin, 1983, 114–134. However, I can imagine that some think of Schluchter's, 1983, 11–55 very weak defence of Weber as even more devastating for Weber's "impressionistic" (Elvin) view. From both Elvin's article and Schluchter's defence, one can learn that Weber might have known better. First, the 18th century French writings (see Schluchter, 1983, 122) gave more differentiated information. Furthermore, the sinologist Arthur von Rosthorn (see Schluchter, 1983, 48 note 13 and 24), Weber's "club colleague" from Heidelberg, gave lectures on the subject. He could easily have informed Weber much better. Later he criticized Weber heavily in: Melchior Palyi, ed., 1923, vol. 2, 221–239.

In the 19th century, from a Central Asian perspective, the picture looks as follows.[660] In all nomadic societies along the Western Chinese borders there existed many bazaars. There livestock (sheep, camels, horses, etc.) and handicrafts (skins, leather, footwear, wool, carpets, etc.) were sold by nomads but nearly no food was sold. Dairy products normally were not used for trade or barter. The nomads bought agricultural products and products from city craftsmen like cotton, silk and pottery. Eventually, copperware, iron pots and so were also bought from city-merchants. Fundamental changes, however, did not occur before the collectivization programs from the thirties of the twentieth century onwards. Below I shall deal with that subject.

It would be an error to suppose that only pure nomadic products came to the Chinese farmers or that agricultural products went to the nomads. The Uyghur people, for instance, also traded white wheat, Tibetan wheat, yellow hemp, green onions and other vegetables to T'ang and later courts. In 48 AD, the Han court offered the Southern Xiongnu even 36,000 head of cattle, because they had to flee for the Northern Xiongnu without being able to save their herds. In the following years the court continued with these deliveries. Also in later sources, cattle and other animals appeared to be sold to nomads.

In the 19th century nomadic people in the west exchanged flour and other food products for Afghan and Arab wool. Also carpets and bags went from Arab countries into all the nomadic carpet-producing countries. In the spring the Afghans and Arabs even drove their rams through the southern regions of Tajikistan as far as Kokand near the Chinese border. No wonder that Emeljanenko could conclude: "The existence of these economic connections testified that the peoples and ethnic groups of Central Asia did not live an isolated life, limited within the framework of their natural economy."[661]

In this century, agriculture was also a somewhat larger share in the total economic and production activities of Central Asian countries. Several forms of sedentary life became more popular as urbanization increased. These kinds of mutual relations grew more intense as well. For some regions it seemed a reproduction of what had happened in the past.

From the earliest records of the Qin and Han periods until the seventeenth century both "parties" mostly accepted all the benefits of their mutual dependency. As such, this is a later development from the oldest records, the most famous Anyang oracle texts from Shang society (14th–12th century BCE). Here

660 T. Emeljanenko, 1994, 67–68.

661 T. Emeljanenko, 1994, 68. This implies a critique on Weber's ideas about *Naturalwirtschaft*.

in the middle and lower reaches of the Yellow River there emerged, from 2000 BCE onwards, proto-urban, rather democratic and women-friendly communities. They had well-developed agriculture as well as a prominent animal based economy (cattle, sheep, horses); the interdependence between the two economies, therefore, was an internal matter.

Conflicts with equally organized neighbors, however, were often caused by quarrels about grazing grounds.[662] In the Qin and Han periods, peaceful relations with nomads were ensured through certain ritualistic customs like intermarriages, bestowals etc. A market-urbanization along the frontiers and a market-infrastructure came into existence. There were nuclei of all sorts of economic or cultural interferences with effects felt deep into the hinterlands. During the 16th century there seems to have been a large-scale employment of Chinese peasants on Mongolian land, their labor demanded by Mongolian leaders to supplement their normal diet.[663] Still they needed grain shipped from the south of China, which demonstrates the extensiveness of their communication-lines.

Even this superficial profile shows the large degree of interdependence of nomads (pastoralists and other animal breeders) and agriculturalists. The very fact of this interdependence counteracts thoughts and policies exploitative in some way or other animosities and antagonisms between peoples.[664] What then can be said about the strongest form of animosity, war, between nomads and Chinese?

The *peacefulness* of the relations between the areas *was the norm and war the deviation or exception.* For historians and others familiar with the very bloody 19th and 20th centuries in Chinese history, this might be a rather utopian exclamation. But the very existence of the Great Wall, foreigner's main symbol for older Chinese society, also seems to be the main proof of the heavy antagonism between "barbarians" and "highly cultured" Chinese. (Contrary to popular belief, the Great Wall was not there in Mongol times).

662 T.V. Stepugina, 1991, 387–420.

663 That is a bit different from Weber's opinion that Mongolians prohibited the grows of crops.

664 Sechin Jagchid and Van Jay Symons, 1989, 191 note 37 in which Lattimore is quoted saying that the exchange of goods was important, but that "the steppe nomad can withdraw into the steppe, if he needs to, and remain completely out of contact with other societies." Jagchid also remarks that Lattimore did not study "the completely self-sufficient nomad, isolated in the remote vastness of the Central Eurasian steppe…" very well. Here the same complex problem arises as in the case of the autarkic peasant who has haunted ideological discussions in history, economy, sociology and philosophy for so long. See my, 1996–2 and Ole Bruun, 1996 about the herding household.

The first question is, therefore, why the peace was often violated, because the consequences were always rather far-reaching: no trade for years, poverty, devastation, and cruelties and, nearly always, the nomads gained the victories. For the Chinese, therefore, there was the near certainty that they had everything to lose with conflicts. They often knew this perfectly well.[665] Why then was war made against "the other"?

7.6 The Rulers and Their Wars

First, we have to remember what the Scythian nomadic chieftain Idanthyrsus told the Persian king Darius, himself an ideal-typical emperor from a Chinese perspective. From this speech one could derive the following thesis: The aggressive way Western ruling elites (who nearly always act on their own behalf) think about war is fundamentally different from the defensive attitudes of the Eastern competing leaders.

It is not necessary here to elaborate on this thesis, but keep it in mind.[666] To support this thesis, one could also refer to the *good savage* ideology or only (!) to practices of (semi-)democratic or non-oikoïdal leadership. Below some support for this will be given as well.[667] Here an analysis of internal Chinese constellations must be sufficient.

In the end Jagchid and Symons answer the question of why rulers made war in East Asia, as follows:

> (1) the prejudice and mistrust felt by nomad and also sedentarist toward the other; (2) the ineffectiveness of Chinese dynasties in implementing frontier trading policies and regulating unscrupulous frontier officials; and (3) the chaotic nature of the frontier, rife with unsavory characters and illicit trading activities.[668]

665 See the discussion at the court of the Chin dynasty, Jagchid and Van Jay Symons, 1989, 53, 54 and now as well Nicola Di Cosmo, 2006.

666 A substantiation of the thesis is given recently in my extensive study, 2012, in particular on 49–87; 189–227 or 512–529 and 711–735.

667 For the problem-definition of this part of the argumentation it should be appropriate to reproduce (part of) the famous debate about the so called *primitive warfare* (including Turney-High's dictum "True warfare is not primitive" written in 1942 !) which started a.o. by the social-darwinist Sebald R. Steinmetz, 1899 with his book and his article, 1914. Before World War II Steinmetz received the strongest opposition in the Netherlands from the ethnologist Theo van der Bij, 1929. Nowadays sociobiologists renewed Steinmetz' perspective; see for example William Divale, 1983.

668 Sechin Jagchid and Van Jay Symons, 1989, 165.

There could be more reasons to invade the land of "the other": famines, floods and other natural disasters made whole populations move in the wrong direction; for nomads, rinder- and other animal-pests were the worst dangers in life as direct attacks on their way of existence and, therefore, much more than Chinese armies, adventurous warlords or court-officials who wanted to gamble when in "the other" land impelled internal conflicts or raged civil war.[669]

What about the three points Jagchid and Symons raised? The last is clear enough. Smugglers, bandits, illicit trade in iron weapons etc. made the frontier-regions unsafe areas, apart from the fact, that the whole corridor was a *melting-pot of non-conformists* from both sides. It seems to me, however, to be exceptional that such groups should provoke parties to make war (probably the case of the Xianbei[670] in the Han-period). More important are the first two points.

The Chinese disdain for their northern and western neighbors in the first place originates from the court-located part of the Chinese elite. From here spread the stereotypical qualities assigned to all "barbarians" regardless of where they came from. One Chinese source qualifies the Xiongnu (about 50 BCE) as follows:

> The barbarians (*i ti*) are covetous for grain, they have long hair, they button their [clothes] on the left side, and are human faced [but] bestial hearted.[671]

This racism too frequently led Chinese rulers to see relations with nomads as deleterious to the Chinese state. Friendship or affection must be unknown to nomads, they supposed, and nomads know only greed; it is, therefore, wise to take aggressive measures against them. Also in this case, imperialism and racism were part and parcel of an (super)oikoïdal constellation. This is a

669 A typical example is also given in Sechin Jagchid and Van Jay Symons, 1989, 63 where court officials advised: "…the barbarians, both humans and animals, suffer disease and death. Drought and locusts have made their land turn red, and with their strength sapped by drought and disease they cannot even match a commandery.… How can we hang onto literary virtue and neglect military affairs?"

670 Under one of their tribal leaders, P'ien-ho, the Hsien-pei could be bribed to attack the other arch-enemy of the Han, the Wu-huan (about 50 AD). The initiative to render this service to the Han came from P'ien-ho c.s. in exchange for the vast sum of money of no less then 270 million coins each year. In the same period the Han also paid about 100 million coins to the Southern Hsiung-nu for the same kind of services. To *divide-and-rule* costed a lot of money those days. See Jagchid and Van Jay Symons, 1989, 32; Nicola Di Cosmo, 2006, 188–189.

671 Cited in Jagchid and Van Jay Symons, 1989, 174.

consequence of or legitimated by the ideological and abstract doctrine of the universal Chinese right of empire that is only comparable to the same doctrine of the Roman Catholic Church.

The nomadic rulers in their turn never accepted any kind of Chinese assertion of (cultural) superiority, which could be interpreted as an acceptance of a subordinate position. As the reason for this behavior Jagchid/Symons mention the preponderance of military power most frequently held by the nomadic peoples. More important to me is, that nomadic people do have a totally different way of treating rulers (including their own) as sedentary people.[672] This is seldom understood by sedentaries. They too easily believe in and accept hierarchies that are, by definition, based on (strong), often hereditary, forms of top-down discriminations.

The nomadic treatment of rulers and the general decision-making process rested, however, on a firm and basic kind of *practical democracy*. To put it bluntly: this was not a "top-down hierarchy" but a "bottom-up" constellation based on a strong mistrust for authority. For outsiders it seems difficult to discover the differences. In many cases that decision-making process consisted of (and often still has) the following elements.

Those who are powerful rulers in the eyes of outsiders do have internally (very) weak, non-hereditary and more or less ceremonial positions. For instance, the initiation-rituals for shamans are often equivalent to the "enthronement ceremonies" of the *qayan* (in the first Turk "State," 552–630) or other leader. A Turkish ancestral legend also points to the blacksmith as head, while in Shamanism there is a close relation between the shaman and the blacksmith. If the *qayan* comes from clan A, a consort is chosen from clan B as countervailing power (compare the two so-called "kings" in old Sparta).

These figures have to display for the outer world the might and glory of the confederation of clans or of the tribe, consisting of many clans. Clan elders (always *plural*) are, in fact, the first institutionalized rulers with real power. However, they too have to share this power with (extended) family-heads, who have to listen first and foremost to the meeting of experienced adult men and women of the families.

Most important is the even less known circumstance that the objects of the public decision-making processes in nomad circles are very different from

672 Hans Derks, 1995, Chapter I.1. For the following see M. Mori, Political Structure of the Ancient Nomadic State in Mongolia, in: *Proceedings 13th Int. Congres Hist. Sciences*. Moscow (1973), volume 1, 268–275. This is a good example of the desperation of fitting nomadic ruler-systems in "western" (in this case marxist class-) categories. Another example is Lawrence Krader, 1975, which was the subject of my Phd-study, 1978.

those in sedentarist environments. Here the complex *work* required through the year to breed, move and cater to the animals is the main object of political deliberations. In sedentary circles, however, the political deliberations nearly never concern work (of agriculturalists or other professions) or work organization. First and foremost, one deals with orders that heads of state or high ranked persons (fail to) give to lower echelons, the norms/laws involved or the status inside the hierarchy. Derived from these questions one probably worries about work proper and its organization.

Nomadic attitudes about foreigners were (and are) guided by the nearly unshakeable rules and rituals of hospitality. Sympathetic as this may be, this hospitality was also the "weak belly" in external relations of nomads and pastoralists. If they were confronted with foreigners or foreign institutions with hidden agendas, this hospitality was the open gate for all kinds of Trojan Horses. Generally speaking: People starting relationships with cheaters in an open mood of trust and friendship are, at least, one step behind. In the frontier-zones, in peace- and war-time, it became clear how frustrating mutual relations could be.

7.7 Imperial Oikoïdal Court Rules

The failure of Chinese dynasties to implement effective frontier trading policies, "left nomads vulnerable to unscrupulous Chinese officials and merchants, who often bilked them of their possessions."[673] Because these Chinese could cheat nomads rather easily (gadgets-for-worthwhile products, etc.), they regarded them as foolish. In their turn, nomads learned by bitter experience to see Chinese as mendacious and shrewd. Things went from bad to worse, when Chinese frontier-officials started all kinds of actions against nomads in the expectation to gain credits at the capital-courts.

An activist and provocative military approach (for instance by bribing Mongolian bandits) became part and parcel of a *courtly* career planning. In their turn, the high-ranking court-militaries suffered from the typical oikoïdal high rewards-heavy punishment policies. Their successes were proved "by counting the collected number of heads of enemy soldiers. This lead generals to order the slaying of non-belligerents to meet established quotas."[674] These massacres of nomadic peoples in the market-places often lead to counter-measures of the same cruel kind.

673 Jagchid and Van Jay Symons, 1989, 176.
674 Jagchid and Van Jay Symons, 1989, 178, 62.

The court-rule for failure was demotion or robbing of privileges or properties and sometimes execution. The inconsistencies of the rewards-punishment mechanism are seen where officials got rewards even if wars were lost, which was normally the case.

A striking example of alternative behavior is the famous nomad-leader Mao-tun (about 200 BCE) who once encircled a large Han-army. Instead of starting a slaughter as Chinese usually did, he opened the encirclement: "Fortunately, Mao-tun was more interested in economic than political or territorial gain."[675]

So, the general mental climate at the Chinese courts was, to say the least, not in favor of reasonable relations with nomads, their markets and cultures. This inevitably became one of the most important vehicles for anti-nomadic sentiments in the center as well as in the frontier-zones. It is worthwhile to consider these relations in more (historical and theoretical) detail, because they demonstrate in an extraordinarily clear way the contents of market-*oikos contradictions.*

Let's take the aforementioned complaint about the greed of nomads as a kind of excuse to take action against them. "Greed" for the Chinese must be an effect of the ineradicable attitude of nomads to make deals about everything and nothing and to get what they want for—what they consider—the lowest possible price. They are experts in selling and buying animals and related products. This market depends, to a large degree, on individual action and on the principle of *honesty is the best quality*.[676] Every participant learns this rather quickly through the given price-mechanisms (best quality, highest price) for which the norms are rather fixed.

Why does this rule exist? Because the price standard consists of animals from which already a nomad child knows the many (negative) qualities. During a long period also in European history it is well known that cows were widely valued as "legal means of payment" and as "walking wealth."[677] The source for the nomadic incessant drive to trade, in fact, *is the (ecological) necessity to look constantly for opportunities to get rid of more or less large parts of their flocks and flock-products.*

Furthermore, within nomad and pastoral ways of life, stress is laid on *individual achievement in their work and on the individual performance of*

675 Jagchid and Van Jay Symons, 1989, 57.

676 For a quite different use of this creed see WG, 383 and 723 or EC, 637 and 1206. It is quite revealing to study the oikoïdal way Weber perceives "the market" here in this unfinished text about the *Marktvergesellschaftung* (translated with "*The Market: Its Impersonality and Ethic*").

677 Hans Derks, 1995, 62–63.

work-skills. The permanent struggle to strike a balance between the drive for wealth and the crude laws of animal-health belongs to the very basis of nomadic or pastoralist life. All factors discussed so far (in a schematic way) are favorable for *open external relations*.

One of the consequences of these characteristics is, that nomads did not treat the Chinese in a racist and/ or disdaining way. They did not rush to accept Chinese culture either and viewed the Chinese as impolite and improperly raised. Typical nomadic advice from the eighth century after warning of the seduction of the bittersweet voices of the Chinese says:

> Thus, O Turk, when you go into that country you come to the edge of death, but when, on the other hand, you stay in your Otukan fastnesses, and only send caravans [for trade or tribute] you have no woes at all.[678]

It is not by accident that the Mongolian word for *merchant* was synonymous for a Chinese verb "to lie."

7.8 Market Behavior

The resulting market-behavior could become or be interpreted as naive if it is confronted with an alternative market-behavior from quite different origin. The frontier-zones gave this opportunity. The first is the confrontation with smugglers and illicit traders. Who receives these qualifications (according to topical criteria) is decided by both nomadic and sedentary norms that can seriously differ in this matter. Other alternatives that become apparent result from trade relations of common peoples in both cultures. As usual, sources are almost silent about the grassroots levels. The third kind of alternative comes here from sources that try to dominate fully, namely from the Chinese courts and related circles.

Their sedentary attitudes are first and foremost functional to a fixed hierarchical order based on the giving of orders by a few, the fulfilling of them by the (large) majority of a given population and their neglect by a (small) minority. (The hierarchy falls apart if the last two categories mutually alter their position). Market behavior of (high ranked) sedentarists compared to the normal sedentarist way of life is nonconformist. Compared to the normal nomadic way of market behavior it is also non-conformist. The grey area arising, in a socio-economic sense, corresponds to the frontier-area between two cultures.

678 Quoted in Jagchid and Van Jay Symons, 1989, 175.

It goes without saying that both nonconformist positions have to be valued by the norms in their cultures or lifestyles.

The nomads were (and still are!) very proud of their mobility and freedom and "their land was not denuded by the plow.... They disdained those who worked on their knees in mud and dirt..."[679] The Chinese autocratic leadership and government, however, derived their wealth mostly from immobile agricultural sources and showed little interest in mercantile activities, unless they derived from a sophisticated centralized government.[680] Also the agro-ideology it developed, thanks to many Confucian philosophers, stressed the high esteem of agriculture and, subsequently, the low esteem of merchants. They warned the governments involved in marketing activities that they

> entered into financial competition with the people, dissipating primordial candor and simplicity and sanctioning propensities to selfishness and greed. As a result, few among our people take up the fundamental pursuits of life, while many flock to the non-essential...[681]

This Confucian anti-marketing prejudice often led emperors to ignore or evade their responsibilities to regulate frontier markets. Those who took the initiative to open markets to all nomadic people were the exception to the rule;[682] too many even viewed trade with nomads as economically disadvantageous and in this way nurtured isolationism. Therefore, military action or the threat of attack was often the only vehicle open to nomads to force Chinese rulers to open markets. Normalization in an economic sense, however, never meant a substantial abolishment of ideological barriers on the side of the Chinese.

The nature of the Chinese bureaucracy also disfavored market-normalizations. The hierarchy at the top was small and too disciplined by the

679 Jagchid and Van Jay Symons, 1989, 175.

680 See Wang Hui about the qualities of the Song dynasty, 960–1279 in Viren Murthy, 2006, 149.

681 Quoted in Jagchid and Van Jay Symons, 1989, 177.

682 In around 1577, a large debate started about the need to continue the long peace and favorable market relations between Ming China and the Mongols. In defence of the markets, Fang Feng-shih, also gave a political argument: "When there are markets and tribute there is no war..." The relationship between war and agriculture, however, was set for the next centuries (or even millennia !?) by Shih Huang-ti, 247–210 BCE. He was a radical anti-market ruler and even hated "merchants who did not have any binding to the land and moved from town to town." Jan Duyvendak, 1948, 64. This author also wrote "Sje Hwang-ti strongly favored agriculture. In imposing heavy demands on manpower and services on the people, he tried to intensify agriculture in order to establish sufficient corn-supplies in wartime ... he gave peasants property rights on land and levied a tax related to the size of the plot."

courtly and imperial ritualistic rules. Active debate about market-frontier policies was restricted to a limited number of members of key ministries and a few individuals having direct access to the emperor. It is striking that court-officials who were in favor of peace and good commercial relations had to discuss their stand in terms of "peace to gain time to prepare the next military confrontation with the barbarians."[683] It is also striking that high Chinese court-officials thought to impress nomad leaders with the same kind of corruption as was usual at the court itself.

The case of the Mongolian leader Esen and the Ming court (about 1450 CE) is remarkable in this respect. When high court officials suddenly reduced prices offered to nomads for horses, they gave the nomads reason to invade China. This was not understood at the court because they gave Esen, personally, many gifts (silk rolls etc.). They looked at the highest person with which they made the deals as an absolute ruler, the type they knew the best.

In other words, these Chinese court-negotiators did not understand the nature of horse-prices, usually related to the income of at least all horse-breeders, nor did they understand the nature of honest trading (in this case even with a large part of a whole people), nor the true nature of the nomad decision-making process. This occurred despite the fact that Esen's bestowals were mistreated, cut or disfigured. This was a personal affront for a tribal leader, but as such an insult to the whole tribe.

Jagchid and Symons did not stop after they helped so well to undermine the myth of the barbarian nomads who constantly plundered, massacred or destroyed that beautiful, "agro-peaceful," imperial culture. The basic tenets of their thesis, in their view, fits perfectly well to the 19th and 20th centuries as nomads eventually were replaced by "white, mainly British barbarians."[684] Like the nomads, the British also failed to persuade the Qing court to grant them political and economic concessions during the first two centuries of their relationship. The British "discovered that the Chinese, and their Manchu overlords, were chauvinistic, arrogant, self-centered, and condescending towards them.... As was the case with the Turks and Mongols, the British also found it difficult to find goods to trade which the Chinese desired." They had to pay for silk and tea with hard currency (silver and gold bullion).

In the 19th century, however, the British started illegal trade to China (opium), which enabled them to purchase tea and silk without paying in bullion. The rest of this story is well known (the British-Chinese Opium War): "...as was

683 Jagchid and Van Jay Symons, 1989, 178.

684 Jagchid and Van Jay Symons, 1989, 185. A peer reviewer was not amused by Jagchid's parallel between nomads and British.

the case with nomadic peoples throughout Chinese history, war with China was undertaken to better secure goods the British felt were essential to the well-being of their country."[685]

In a bold futuristic forecasting, the authors could have envisaged a new trade-war between a strong market-oriented outer-world, that can recreate anew a typical wild-west frontier zone to do their Hong Kong-like business, and a still bureaucratized, old-fashioned court like centralized CP—headquarters. Realities are drastically changed, as we will see in the next chapters.

7.9 Ideological Historiography

Of course, in the scholarly literature used nowadays the strong reliance on court-sources makes sure that the "barbarians" are blamed for all anger and misery.[686] Unfounded are the suggestions that there is a permanent state of war at the (northern) borders during these 2000 years. The most negative consideration in this case is: Most of the time the Chinese power-elites may have been willing to destroy the "barbarians," but they did not have the resources to do this in such a vast area against such a powerful enemy. Their military activities, in fact, were restricted in all respects: in space, in time, in effect. Sometimes one even gets the impression of being confronted with fake-wars to sustain anti-nomadic sentiments and anti-market ideologies. It is an oikoïdal syndrome *par excellence* that gets too much attention.[687]

Historians and sinologists seldom tried to reverse this "central perspective" of what happened in its own right elsewhere in that very vast territory. Too often many scholars[688] tried to establish the false impression of an unchangeable China as an *Oriental* (*Palace*) *Despotism* that always sought to pose an *Asiatic Mode of Production* onto the most remote corners of this territory. One

685 Jagchid and Van Jay Symons, 1989, 186.

686 For the ideological interpretation of Chinese-Mongol history see Owen Lattimore, 1979, 479–491. Ten years later, David Morgan still writes about even the heyday of Asian nomadic history, Khubilai Khan's long hegemony (1260–1294): "Historians of China had previously tended to shun this period, preferring not to concern themselves with barbarian rule, but now their views on the impact of Mongol rule are shifting, and shifting in the Mongols favor." From the Chinese side another aspect of the ideological historiography is important whereas Morgan quotes: "...a biography [of Khubilai Khan] based merely on the Chinese records could not be written ... (because he is) portrayed ... as a typical Confucian ruler, not as a real human being." in: *Times Literary Supplement*, 5/8, 1988, 849.

687 In its most abstract way this happened in Lawrence Krader, 1979, 221–235.

688 A relevant overview provides Wim Wertheim, 1995, 17–29. Wim Wertheim, 1983, 57–133. See also Anatoly Khazanov, 1994, Chapter 5, Nomads and the state.

of the results is a very schematic "centrally guided" historiography, sociology, etc. One could better suppose as a rule a very differentiated development in time and in space.

Chinese old and new cities as "clear Western bourgeois" will be discovered along with purely residential/ oikoïdal cities and indigenous market-places; within the "real Chinese countries," there lived not only small peasants as the image prescribes, but also nomads, pastoralists or merchants; there were extensive trade-networks almost uninterrupted by "state"-influences.

Furthermore it is necessary to point to the substantial revolutionary potentials in large parts of the population in all periods of Chinese history. The target is directly or indirectly, nearly without exception the imperial authority and its representatives in some capital.[689] The result is often that the almighty emperor must be seen as a restricted power. In short: one could come nearer to the "truth" about China by supposing *normal* towns and countries with *normally reacting people* instead of imperial/ Confucian constructions and marionettes.

From the first Weber quotation in this Chapter 1 has to conclude that in the Weberian construction a "Chinese State" is seen as an *Oriental Despotism*. His *Oikos* is "colossal," all-embracing with subjects as "state-slaves." Wertheim rightly points to the fact that Weber, in *Economy and Society*, came up with the more specific perspective of the so-called "patrimonial-bureaucratic state."[690] This, however, cannot be seen as a kind of defense of Weber who rooted this kind of state in the princely *domain* (*oikos*) managed by means of the *Oikenwirtschaft*. This last domain-economy is based in the *manor*.

In this context Weber referred again to Pharaohnic Egypt, the Roman imperial domain, the Inca state, the Jesuit state in Paraguay, the Carolingian villas, the Near Eastern and Hellenistic states, etc. For instance:

> ...the actual political power of the Oriental sultans, the medieval princes and the Far Eastern rulers centered in these great patrimonial domains. In these latter cases the political realm as a whole is approximately identical with a huge princely manor.

It is important to understand the distinction Weber made here between the political (juridical and military) and economic realm of the prince. It seems nearly a matter of geography:

689 Hans Derks, De Taiping-opstand in China, 1850–1864, in: Hans Derks, ed., 1989, 153–159.
690 EC, 1013; WG, 585; Wim Wertheim, 1964, 106.

> We shall speak of a patrimonial state when the prince organizes his political power over extrapatrimonial areas and political subjects....[691] [About the economic impact of this state Weber did not talk, apart from the fundamental obligation of the subjects to maintain the ruler in a material sense] just as is the case in a patrimonial household.

Only for Pharaohnic Egypt did Weber postulates the extension of *both* the political and economic authority over the whole country. For this case one can easily substitute the *Oriental Despotism* concept, apart from the question whether Weber is right or wrong in the Egyptian case.

In the Chinese case, however, in my view we have to do with an isolated and rather autonomous super-*Oikos* that was and probably is in an economic sense of little or only negative value to the (rest of) Chinese society. In other words: here we cannot discover an *Oriental Despotism* but there existed a marked contradiction between the (imperial) *Oikos* and the market "extrapatrimonial economy." Through the nomadic part of this economy one can demonstrate the antagonisms at stake almost ideal-typically.

Which example could be more interesting than the recent collectivizations of the herding economies in Central and East Asia (Mongolia)?[692] As is well known, in these unique phenomena the Soviet (inspired) super-*Oikoi* ruthlessly tried to interfere with all aspects of agricultural and herding life.

In my view, however, these very powerful state-bureaucracies (inclusive of armies) did not succeed very well in their objective to eradicate (or industrialize) the nomadic way of life and all immanent market and mobile elements. Without going into much detail some of the main characteristics and effects of these collectivizations follow.[693]

7.10 Nomads and Oikoïdal Collectivizations

The imperialism of Tsarist Russia from the late 1500s to 1917 brought about an exceptionally broad contact among the peoples of Central Asia and newcomers. In the 19th century Russians introduced new agricultural techniques (iron plough) and settled peasants of divers origins in "Nomad's Land" including

---

691 EC, 1013.

692 For Central Asia see L. Popova, 1994, 69–83. For Mao's China see Veronika Veit, 1986, 155–183 and Owen Lattimore, 1980, 116–127.

693 For the general problem I only mention Peter Nolan, 1976, 192–219; Stefan Merl, 1990; Lynne Viola, 1996; Mark Tauger, 2010, 427.

Poles, Germans and Koreans. At the end of the century "Nomad's Land" of the cattle, camel and sheep breeders still existed.

However, it was clear that some areas' seasonal pastures, especially the winter ones, were reduced and that farmlands cut off nomadic routes and access to water reservoirs. Central Asia became gradually a grain and cotton belt for the Russians. Thirty years later it would become Krushchev's "virgin and long-fallow lands" that provided the first substantial increase in Soviet grain production above the pre-revolutionary level. Everywhere the urbanization was enhanced with its usual effects on the adjacent lands. These were serious but within those vast lands still the regional effects of Western imperialism were felt. It seemed that in 1914 almost a quarter of the Kyrgyz were leading some settled life.

According to Lattimore, the Russian soldiers and traders received much sympathy from the Siberian and Central Asian peoples during the 19th century. Usually Russian traders learned the indigenous languages. This good relationship was generally reproduced with Mongols who traditionally disliked Chinese with their economic monopolies. At Urga, the later Mongolian capital Ulan Bator ("Red Hero"), a substantial Russian and foreign population settled. From here the ideas of the October Revolution spread over the *yurtas* (nomadic tent-houses) and *auls* (nomadic villages). New Russian military technology (machine guns and artillery) and discipline was introduced.

Mongolian and Central Asian herdsmen fulfilled the preconditions for their own proletarian revolution *à la russe* against real class-enemies. The enemies were the Chinese bourgeoisie, the high priests, monasteries and some hereditary Mongolian "feudal nobles." In the tsarist Central Asian countries, the class enemies were different: the oikoïdal Tsarist bureaucracy inclusive of its Greek-Orthodox offshoot and the Russian backed Central Asian elite.

Peasants from all classes suffered the most from the atrocities accompanying the Russian collectivizations. There was never a comparable movement against the urban laborers or general urban population although they suffered as well by the side-effects of the collectivizations. Only one thing seemed clear for all levels of Soviet decision making: from 1929 onwards the *country*, as opposed to the *city*, definitely has to be re-modeled from the ground up in order to adjust to a rather unclear idea about a centralized, industrial urban society. In all corners of social and economic life a deep crisis undermined every possibility to have even a minimum existence in town and country.

The chaos, panic, wild massacres and deportations and the sharp contradictions between all levels of decision makers who reigned for years made the start of the collectivizations a nightmare. In my view, the most serious failure was that the power-interests of the super-*Oikos* always had to prevail over the technical, economical, agronomical etc., rationalities of country-life. In particular, the reproduction of the political idea of centralized decision making into the technical, economical, etc. realities created unsolvable disparities in the whole Soviet Union.

In the Central Asian republics, the peasants who had been settled in the 19th century by the Tsarist administration, had to pay the highest price. But a large number of nomads used an effective weapon unknown to their immobile "colleagues." In hindsight one can say that they demonstrated the irrationalities of the centralization-policies the first and make these abandoned the quickest. Many administrators in the new Soviet republics practiced centralization and concentration even in a much more vulgar and primitive way than in the West. Central Asia still had the image of a colony.

Their first ideal objective was crystal-clear: *peasantization* and settlement of these wild, uncivilized and uncontrollable peoples. At the same time these peoples had to cater to the enormous meat and wool needs of the fast-growing Western urban population. Sometimes hundreds of nomadic communities scattered in an enormous area were forcefully concentrated in only one place. Others interpreted the objective in the sense that all *yurtas* had to be arranged within the grid of an ideal square. Orders were given from behind the bureaucratic desks to shear millions of sheep in winter cold. The animals could not stand the weather and died.

Indeed, the breeders were faced with unprecedented casualties in the animal population while many lost their own lives in bitter fights. After the collectivization-campaigns and the terrible famine in 1931–33 in Kazakhstan only 1.3 out of 18.5 million sheep were left; the number of horses was reduced from 3.5 million to 855,000 in 1941; only 63,000 camels stayed alive of 1.04 million in 1935 (Popova).

Also the human population was decimated but not in the first place by the harsh repression and its by-effects. The nomads were not immune to certain diseases that came with the famine (typhoid). The nomads had a weapon that they used effectively: they knew how to flee with their animals and where to go. At least a million people from Kazakhstan (with 6.5 million people in 1920) and countless animals went to China, Mongolia, Afghanistan, Iran and Turkey. Later half of them came back.

After 1945 a certain *modus vivendi* between nomads and regime was found and between the indigenous livestock-breeding and the centralized *kolkhoz*- or *sovkhoz*-breeding that was often too large to handle. That was the sign the Soviets could not gain control over the Central Asian area's and had to stick to the approved methods of the Tsars to create and influence a dependent elite. As usual, in practice this "colonial elite" had only a restricted and relative influence in the country.

In the seventies and eighties the restrictions on establishing private farms etc. were weakened and they recently disappeared. A typical result of this process was the following: in 1989 a Kyrgyz *sovkhoz* state flock numbered 4,500 sheep, whereas 20,000 were privately owned. The same accounts for horned cattle. Another peculiarity is that the nomads, contrary to the peasants, still do not pay taxes which is a metaphor for their position *vis-à-vis* the state, the super-*Oikos*. Unchanged remained the hard-herding life as well.

So, generally speaking, one has to affirm the question whether the collectivizations in the Soviet nomadic countries were in vain. The effects of these collectivizations are, again metaphorically, that nowadays nomads even use helicopters for herding camels, cattle and sheep as well as the latest medical techniques for breeding and selection purposes. But still they favor living in the *yurts* and *auls* although their kids show the limits of these houses by buying ghetto-blasters and listening to house-music during their city-trips. Town-country contradictions take all kinds of forms!

The Mongolian collectivizations followed the Soviet model. After the Mongols gained their independence from China (1921), the state bureaucracy could come "closer" to the nomads as in the Soviet example. This resulted in some not insignificant differences from the Soviet *kolkhoz*-model. Still the most important economic activity in Mongolia remains animal breeding. The total number of animals is about 24 million (with 21 animals per person; the highest domesticated animal concentration in the world); 70% of the land surface is occupied by pasture and only 0.2% for agriculture (Veit). The camels, cattle, goats, horses and sheep still are herded all year long in a nomadic manner.

After 1948, however, the organizational framework gradually became the *cooperative* of herding-families (for 77% of all animals). In principle, this is a hierarchical way of organizing work that is alien to the nomadic ways of work organizations. The latter are based on the needs of the work to be done and not on the status and power of decision makers.

Probably, the practice corresponds still to the traditional and more democratic mode of organization but, at the moment, I do not have any information about this possibility. In any case, what was left from an oikoidal state-organization (outside the cities never more than 15%) was privatized in 1992. In short, also in the animal country *par excellence* the (Soviet) collectivizations did not work out as in peasant regions. Many Mongolians today—whether living within China's neighbourhood or in the former Soviet Union—

> ...look to Genghis Khan as their national hero.... Buddhist monasteries are being restored and reoccupied, the traditional Mongol script is

> replacing Cyrillic ... and statues of Lenin and Stalin are being torn down and replaced by those of Genghis Khan.[694]

Old oikoïdal forces of Mongolia are trying again to occupy the rooms at the top and reveal that the people did not forget the most classical oikoïdal tricks: To start a separation-movement in neighboring China's Inner Mongolia (with more Mongols than in their own country!) in order to gather "the whole Mongolian people" behind their ticket.

7.11 An Evaluation

In this chapter many details about the nomadic way of life in Central and East Asia are revealed to demonstrate how market-*oikos* relations work out on a large scale and over a long period. Of course, a demonstration like this (not with the practices involved!) could have been undertaken elsewhere in the many and vast parts of Chinese and Central Asian landscapes or from another point of view like that of the so-called "New Qing History" (if relevant).

A fruitful theoretical and practical discussion could follow after a confrontation with Philip Huang's research into peasant families and their markets in the Yangzi Delta. His research runs counter to the classical models of Adam Smith and Marx, but is indirectly highly dependent on "a Max Weber approach." He writes, for instance:

> ...the items that accounted for the bulk of the rural trade, grain and cloth, were produced on a small scale, by peasant farms and by peasant household handicrafts. Where this trading system parted company from the classical Marxist scheme is that it was not transitional to capitalist commodities exchange, as Marx assumed. ...This trade, of course, also differs from the two-way rural-urban trade of which Adam Smith made so much. For Smith, [this] exchange ... played a fundamental role in powering transformative economic development. Peasants purchased mainly subsistence goods produced by other peasants.... Even in the twentieth century, the inroads made by urban manufactures remained very limited...[695]

694 Lisa Husmann, "'National Unity' and National Identities in the People's Republic of China," in: David Hooson, ed., 1994, 149.

695 Philip C. Huang, 1990, 105.

Huang's alternative concerns the so-called substantivist approach.[696] As we have discussed earlier (Chapters 2 and 3) this approach has a long and interesting tradition starting with Rodbertus, Bücher, Weber, Chayanov before the war and Polanyi, Finley etc. after the war (*Oikos* controversy). The keyword in this approach is *autarkeia* or "self-sufficiency" (eventually "self-reliance") as the main anti-market concept. This very influential concept is, however, criticised as an ideological construction without practical relevance.[697] Further discussion about it must be reserved for another volume.

It is enough to conclude that even today in large parts of Asian countries, the way of life described in the main text prevails. Usually, the history of this corner of the world is told in terms of great nomadic conquerors or of barbarian nomadic Manchus who even became emperors of China.[698] The discriminating content of the *autarkeia*-concept is reproduced as well in such pejorative attitudes.

In my view, compared with the economic or cultural contradictions, continuities and interdependencies of nomads and sedentaries, these are mere political incidents that affected only a small elite. It is noteworthy that in the Mongolian history books, the "world-conquering" activities of some nomadic chieftains are not given much attention, while a "real political history" of these regions is still in its infancy.[699]

It is, therefore, a bit difficult to blame even famous scholars for a lack of knowledge. It may be that Max Weber was right in delineating the pivotal importance in history of the contradictions between sedentaries and nomads of different kinds and between agriculture and animal husbandry. It is, however, crystal clear that he failed to understand even the basic characteristics of the nomadic way of life and, consequently, failed to make the proper comparisons with his own sedentary way of life. He could have known from available sources that milk and meat in Central and East Asia were common consumer products and in many regions even the main ingredients of the daily diet. Also, within his own *Ackerbau*-stand, Weber could not differentiate between rice and wheat cultivation. By neglecting these large differences, some clues to a

696 Philip C. Huang, 1990, 6–7.

697 Hans Derks, "Autarkeia," 1996. This article demonstrates which false interpretation/translation of Aristotle's *oikos*-theory occurred in the Christian Middle Ages and its present reception; more important: that "autarkeia" has nothing to do with self-sufficiency but, on the contrary, that it represents the freedom of the market. This exactly concerns the source of the later "misunderstandings."

698 For this typical Western attitude to China see my 2012, Chapter 30, 593–627.

699 See the preface of the excellent Denis Sinor, ed. 1990.

capitalism discussion within a Chinese context remained hidden for him. In his time. much of that knowledge was available.

Weber, however, was highly biased by a complicated set of thoughts and norms that avoided the necessary change of paradigm. Therefore, the question of whether there is any empirical basis for Weber's Asian nomadic (pastoralist, non-sedentary, etc.) ideal type must be denied. Next, we can seriously question his broader approach to the theory of civilizations as stipulated in the first section.

The highly complex problem of the transition from nomadic animal husbandry to sedentary agriculture is a very basic feature in world history. It cannot be reduced to a practical affair, i.e. the eradication of tribal and other resources in the hope that nomads (a collective concept for many kinds of mobile people and groups) would disappear "automatically." First, it is necessary to start a fresh series of studies into the history of these social, economic or cultural transitions.

The above discussion should be compared to the Near Eastern nomads (Weber's perception of them) relative to the practicalities of the highly important role Bedouins, etc. have played in this part of the world and its dramatic history (see Chapter 5). With them we meet the most western nomads in Central Asia, trading partners along the Silk Road, the oldest and longest trading and cultural communication line, that shall be modernised now through a €100 billion investment by China.

CHAPTER 8

Town and Country in Chinese History: An Overview

8.1 Introduction

In his article about town-country contradictions in China, Wim Wertheim arrives at the subjectively right conclusion, that such a problem cannot be treated, let alone solved by a center-periphery approach.[700] Besides its being a metaphor, it could have remarked as well that it concerns here a uni-linear approach from the city/town in the direction of the country side, or from the Western metropolis through the non-Western city to the non-Western country.

Wertheim also points to another problem, that of the attempts to emancipate the peasant masses in the "Third World." Concerning the Chinese case and notwithstanding the above criticism, he ends his article with:

> For the center-periphery problematic the Chinese experiment is in so far of the highest importance, because the country side is not used as a periphery—at least not since 1958—but as the real center... The role of the urban industry remained a leading one... but still peripheral.[701]

With this reversal the metaphoric character of the center-periphery dichotomy is not negated, whatever the difficulty whether something can be leading and in the same time peripheral. Besides this conceptual problem Wertheim points to the overriding importance of the "peasant masses" in Chinese history and for a densely populated, large and often hungry stricken country as China.

What does emancipation of the peasants mean in this historical and geographical context? The answer must come in particular from a proper historical analysis. The sociologist Wertheim provides us, anyway, with a way to make this analysis through the following five phases in this history.

700 Wim Wertheim, 1972; see also his 1973, 34–35 and Hans Derks, 1986, 457. All left-wing scholars ("dependencia") at the time like Andre Gunder Frank, Galtung, Wallerstein, etc. used the center-periphery model. They arrived at the right conclusion that development problems concerned relations of exploitation and expropriation in town and country, but their "solutions" remained as "metaphoric" as their models, apart from their remarkable ignorance of agricultural and other practical problems.

701 Wim Wertheim, 1972, 102. For the next three quotations see same article.

 | DOI:10.1163/9789004383913_009

For imperial China he accepted practically the Max Weber and Wittfogel's *Oriental Despotism* (OD) interpretation: the "Eastern city" is first and foremost a "unit of consumption," the prince is living there and consumes the imported treasures; there is no exchange of services between town and country; the peasant is only object of exploitation; cities/towns are no centers of civil freedom as in Western history. It is the same position taken by Moses Finley in the 1970s and 1980s for the "ancient economy," again based on Max Weber.

In the 19th century, however, foreign capital penetrates into this imperial China. The harbor cities quickly change their character; Shanghai develops itself into a "primate city" with a one-sided orientation towards foreign trade:

> ... the relation to the countryside remained characterized by exploitation—but now a mutual exchange of large quantities of goods took place: resources from the country, end products from the city to the villages. Partly the latter were imported foreign goods...

In Shanghai itself there is the rise of a textile industry and a *Lumpenproletariat* develops. Until the establishment of the Peoples Republic the industrialization is seriously blocked thanks to the dominant foreign capital.

Contrary to the Russian Revolution "the Chinese one began in the country and ended in the city." The following period is characterized by the copying of the Soviet Russian model of urban industrialization and large-scale mechanization of agriculture. This failed. Reason:

> The unbelievable densities of the agrarian population, particularly in the southern rice producing regions... resulted in such a high growth figure, that it was totally impossible to develop an urban industry as quick as was needed in order to absorb the population surplus.

Next comes the period of *The Great Leap Forward*. In cities and towns there is an exorbitant increase of industrial production; also the women are employed at a large scale. In the countryside—"and this is really the success story of the Great Leap Forward"—there is full employment of human labor and not so much of modern mechanization. Numerous large hydraulic works are executed, the electrification of the countryside is enhanced.

A second derivation of the Soviet model is the establishment of the peoples' communes

> ...as units... in which an industrialization of the countryside could be organized... the spread of the industrial climate from the city to the

> countryside without a quick mechanization and based on an intensive use of the available labor force... that is the typical Chinese approach to the town-country relationship.

After 1970, again a new development can be registered as the light and middle-heavy industries in the countryside have been extended:

> The structure of the whole society becomes increasingly polycentrical... Also in the past the villages formed rather closed and autonomous units. Now this is in fact again the case when we read for village: peoples' commune. But this is accompanied with a substantial dynamism in every unit. There was the attempt to minimize the "scissor," the distance between the reward for urban industrial or bureaucratic work and the typical agrarian labor... On ideological grounds one tried to achieve a victory over the contradictions between head and hand labor, laborers and peasants, town and country... The result: urbanization of the countryside.

The history during and after Deng Xiaoping will be presented later. Wittfogel and Wertheim, both strongly influenced by the writings of Weber, gave me the tools to reconstruct this history in some detail despite disagreement in many respects with their analysis of Chinese history and society.

This reconstruction cannot be other than a superficial one, providing no more than a new outline for others' more detailed attempts. Although I have to go back for a while to the earlier history, I am not intending to centralize my story around emperors and their courts (see previous chapter), nor later around Mao or Deng and their circles, but as much as possible around the way people lived in cities, towns and villages. I also start following Wertheim's chronology as given above.

8.2 The Pre-Industrial Phase

In 20th-century historiography this phase covers a 3000-year period and ends at the end of the 19th-century or in 1912, the founding of the Republic of China in Nanjing; it is as such a good example of Western arrogance. If we try to avoid this attitude, then we still cannot make many generalizations about such a long history and such a vast country like China.

To generalize by means of concepts like "subsistence agriculture or subsistence livelihood" as typical for "Third World Countries" or of "thousands of years of world history" is irrational. Take, for instance, Philip Huang's conclusion after finishing a study of six hundred years of agricultural history in the Yangzi delta:

> Long before the coming of the Ming-Qing cotton revolution, the small-peasant economy of the Yangzi delta had reached an advanced state of growth with the perfecting of the yutian system of embanked we trice fields and the grid like system of rivers and canals under the "medieval" Tang and Song.[702]

But let's suppose that Wertheim's remarks concern the Ming (1368–1644) and Manchu (1644–1912) dynasties and then they are already absurd enough. There are two views.

Mark Elvin tells that in the 18th and 19th centuries there was a rapid increase of market towns, but this was largely thanks to a true oikoidal impulse (temples, manors of great feudal lords, although he also mentions pottery works).[703] Related to the rise of agro-monasteries in the Mongolian plains there was also some oikoidal urbanization.[704] The influence of the Max Weber interpretation is apparent here.

The second view is more concrete and convincing and will be described further in some details. This is largely based on Evelyn Rawski's comparative investigations for 16th century Fukien (today's Fujian province) and Han provinces in the 19th century that proved how *commercial* developments went far beyond existing town-country relations. This is demonstrated, for instance, in Fukien "where the expansion of foreign trade brought clear changes in the urban and rural economy."[705]

For the last 1000 years it is shown how in the agrarian economy, there exists a system of private property among a large number of free peasants with rather small landholdings. Even Wittfogel (OD) provides relevant data that undermines his central argument: 93% of the total land surface is private property, 3% crown domain and 4% "land of the state" (collective property) used for building schools and religious facilities.[706]

702 Philip Huang, 1990, 306. The *yutian* system of around 1000 concerned fields with built-up embankments, drainage and irrigation ditches. It is comparable with similar activities in the "Dutch" delta at the time. This should be added to Wang Hui's study of the Song, see Viren Murthy, 2006, 144–145.

703 Mark Elvin, 1973, 268.

704 John Gray, 1990, 94. "Oikoidal urbanization" concerns capitals and pure military, religious and government (administrative) centers. Cities and towns with, for instance, barracks or a church, only has an "oikoidal function."

705 Evelyne Sakakida-Rawski, 1972, 2; see also Philip Huang, 1990, 45.

706 Karl Wittfogel, 1962, 367 note 406. What is here "total land surface"?

Wittfogel acknowledges a bit earlier that his image of the unchanging hydraulic society does not quite fit China well.[707] Where it concerns such a dominant form of property, this is nearly lethal for his theory. Rawski adds to this, that whether the peasant works on his own property or rents the land, he is free to decide what to grow and how to deal with his products.[708] All this gave to the Chinese agrarian economy, to date, a large degree of flexibility, because there were neither institutional limits to grow new varieties or to develop new methods, nor were there bureaucratic obstacles to the spreading of the knowledge about new methods.

Based on sinologist Duyvendak Wertheim insists that in "imperial China" the internal cities were only administrative centers, where the peasants had nothing to do and were even left alone. This is the typical "oriental city as consumer city,"[709] seat of a prince with its court, in short a typical oikoidal settlement, without any exchange with the adjacent countryside.

To assess the town-country relations in the periods given above, one should make the following differentiation in the settlement pattern:

1. The relationship between the capital (of the whole country) and the surrounding environment. There is always one city for which eventually the above circumscription could be used.
2. The provincial capitals, of which there were about 20 in the Manchu period.
3. The numerous trading cities along the coasts and rivers, usually with developed crafts and industries.
4. The countless market settlements that are directly connected to the agrarian economy.
5. A limited number of cities far inland developed for specific purposes.

In a geographical sense one should also differentiate between the largely non-urbanized North and the highly urbanized South. At last is important how the interrelations between all these settlements and regions existed and changed.

707 Karl Wittfogel, 1962, 350. See also 155, 163, 168 for other examples of Chinese exceptions on his theory. See against Wittfogel Philip Huang, 1990, 144. See now Philip Ball, 2017, 100–104 how Wittfogel can inspire modern authors. This inspiration concerns the way water management ("hydraulics") is organized and dominates. Another example is the complicated system of dikes, polders and water technology in the coastal provinces of the Netherlands that exist many centuries.

708 E. Sakakida-Rawski, 1972, 3.

709 The idea of purely "consumer cities" is launched as early as Werner Sombart and belongs, for instance, also to the tools Moses Finley used in his analysis of the "ancient economy." See Hans Derks, 1995, 8, 11, 14 and in particular 194.

An indication of this can be found in the following remarks by Rawski:

> In Fukien as well as Hunan the expansion of the long distance trade brought about an increase of the periodic markets in the adjacent environment. This is one indication for the transmission of commercial influence of the market-town to the agrarian countryside. In different well-located regions one can see 'highly commercialized agriculture' and the periodic markets are used by the peasants/ farmers as "source for farming implements, credit and information about the condition of the larger markets outside his view."[710]

The main products in long distance trade were pottery, indigo, silk, cotton and ramie textile. Cities/towns and countrysides had their own specialities: ramie, for instance, was a typical byproduct of rural household labor, but the weaving of silk was dominated by urban craftsmen; cash crops and urban-rural crafts were, for a long time, the adequate answer to the commercial possibilities in Chien-ning.[711]

An important item is also the degree of exploitation and expropriation in this mode of production, because from this a class struggle was dependent. Together with many Japanese and Chinese scholars Rawski stresses that in each period there were poverty stricken peasants "of subsistence level," who could not pay their debts. She thinks, however, that the majority had a reasonable existence in the regions she investigated.[712]

This conclusion is based on the fact that the majority of the peasants were not only free to migrate, but did so. This seems a remarkable argument, because migration is too often due to poverty and repression (see below). The difficulty remains that even at the moment there are no reliable data about the magnitude of the different income groups or classes.

Indications of the reality are revealed in Rawski's research on property relations and the payments of taxes and leases. These were not disadvantageous for the peasant-leasers because they could get fixed rents and contracts for

710 E. Sakakida-Rawski, 1972, 8, 9. See also Philip C. Huang , 1990, 137–138.

711 E. Sakakida-Rawski, 1972, 64. Philip Huang, 1990, 48 writes: "Silk, cotton, and market rice powered a dramatic growth of towns and cities in the Yangzi delta in the Ming and Qing." See also appendix c with data about 457 towns (*zhen*), market towns (*shi*) and markets (*cunji*) of present day Shanghai municipality; 69 towns formed before 1850 with their major basis of formation (28 based on cotton goods; 14 administrative/military; 8 salt; 3 silk; etc. So that only about 20% were strict oikoidal settlements. Chien-ning was a rice prefecture of Fu-chien, South China.

712 E. Sakakida-Rawski, 1972, 193.

many years. Of course, in periods of crop failures they often could not pay the rent/taxes, but under other circumstances they could save rather easily.

In this system, the productive peasant/farmer had a much greater advantage than a non-productive one. Besides this the tenant was allowed to, or was not hindered from sub-lettingrent the land or selling the use rights. This resulted in a serious undermining of the power of the landlords: if the tenant had sub-let in bad times he could get his rent, but the sub-letter could not be expelled, even if he owed back rents. The lease contracts and the sub-lease contracts were, furthermore, independent of each other.[713] At last, there was the advantage that good soil was more rewarding for the tenant-farmer than for the proprietor.

To measure the degree of expropriation it is important to consider also the extra payments (hiring implements, etc.). It is shown that these payments were (very) low and to be paid at the conclusion of the contract or once a year in kind or with a silver coin. The degree of expropriation is also to demonstrate through the fluctuations in the rents. In a comparison between the years 1770 and 1823 it is shown how they were increased by 40%, but in the same period the rice prices increased 60%.[714] According to Rawski, here the landlords failed to stand up to inflation.

Another phenomenon to judge the position of the peasants vis-à-vis town-country relations is the prevalence of absentee landlordship, which is largely confined in the context of a commercialized economy. The landlords normally wanted to live in town, to invest in a lucrative trade, to receive a fixed payment for leasing and to not care about their land.

What happened in the countryside was largely unknown to them, even to a degree that could be reported: "When the tenant disappears, then disappears the rent and the landlord does not know the location of the land."[715] It is, therefore, largely a matter of prestige for the urban well-to-do to invest in this less profitable property.

All this gave the tenant good possibilities to apply coercive measures to the landlord, thanks to which the above mentioned migration argument becomes understandable. In the northern part of China, however, where there was much less possibilities to invest profitably outside agriculture, the position of the tenants was not as favorable whereas in the rice-growing regions their position was better as in the thee cultures.

713 E. Sakakida-Rawski, 1972, 20, 144 ff.

714 E. Sakakida-Rawski, 1972, 266 ff.

715 E. Sakakida-Rawski, 1972, 29.

Another famous subject in the *Asian Mode of Production* (AMP) and *Oriental Despotism* (OD) debates was the degree of power held by the state and its bureaucracy that, together with the landlords, was perceived as the heaviest burden for the peasants.[716]

Tenants paid rent, but no state taxes. Thanks to the given lease-sublease system some tax-pressure on land is further minimized. When the owner lived in the same village as the tenant, then it was easy for the tax collector to discover him; if he lived in town, then it was quite difficult. When the owner was found but the land was sub-let, than new difficulties for the tax officials were created. Therefore, the state was in pains to abandon this system, but largely in vain.[717]

Except during wars/revolts and in the neighborhood of state domains, where (oikoidal) urbanization was initiated by the state itself, the state was absent but for the periodic arrival of the tax collector and specific transport and communication tasks. Villages, however, sustained their own hydraulic works. If these were large, then they were executed and co-financed by the *local* aristocracy.[718] Therefore, the conclusion is that

> ...the state bureaucracy did not play an active role in the villages, but exercised only control from above... this passive control... aimed in the end to sustain the economic and social position of the state oriented elite.[719]

The Baojia or Pao-chia system, created for this aim, was a system of mutual responsibility and control in the village.[720] It developed, however, in the reverse direction to its purpose, i.e. a village organization to sustain order and security. Only in villages with one clan was there a certain degree of integration, but this was absent in multi-clan villages. The urban perception of the village as "a harmonic, eventually an organic unity," is also wrong in the Chinese case.

Clan associations had only a minor relation with production, that was nearly fully the concern of individual families. If there was a shortage of land, an endless reason for conflicts was given, because persons with less or no land had to lease themselves as wage worker. This concerns first and foremost the groups living at "subsistence level," however that is defined.

Add to all this the many relations with markets, towns and long-distance trade and the image of the closed, isolated village crumbles away. Anyway, this

716 J. Chesneaux, 1973, 10.

717 Philip Huang, 1990, 35 for the position of landlords which changed with "increased commercialization and the movement of landlords into towns and cities."

718 E. Sakakida-Rawski, 1972, 12; W. Franke, ed., 78.

719 Wilhelm Franke, ed., 1977, 78.

720 For more details see *Wikipedia* under "Baojia system."

image cannot lead to a truthful picture of what is going on in villages, although it remained true that villages in remote and infertile regions seemed to be closed to the outsider (which they sometimes were!):

> The image of patriarchal harmony was the idealistic conception of the wealthy, developed elite, and could be transmitted to the farmers/peasants only in a limited way.[721]

It remains remarkable that one immediately forgets how this same image is responsible for *our* perception of Chinese towns and cities and the relation with their countryside. They are only the first two of the above-mentioned types of towns that could reproduce in a reasonable way the material and cultural position of this elite in Chinese society. They are, thanks to Max Weber and many others mentioned above the standard image of the Chinese city/town.[722]

The things, so thoroughly criticized by Rawski return in the AMP and OD debates like the subject *feudalism*. What is Chinese compared to European feudalism? From the famous Chesneaux the following long quotation is given to show the (cognitive) problem arising from the European point of view:

> The agrarian society was not organized through large manors, like those of the Prussian Junkers or the English "squires," but the basic texture of society was the same. Even if the characteristic institutions of European feudalism, like serfdom, were absent, the concept of feudalism is not inadequate. Notwithstanding this, there was a serious difference between Chinese and European medieval feudalism. This did not concern the different kinds of dependency the peasants had to live with, but the role of the state. In European feudalism the state had only a limited influence, while essential public functions were delegated to the lord of the manor. In China, however, the state was "all powerful" and the peasant was exploited as thoroughly by the public demands of the state and bureaucracy as by the avarice of the landlords. Notwithstanding the early rise of private property of land, there remained this very stable social-political structure called by Joseph Needham... "bureaucratic feudalism."[723]

Simply because in the Chinese case there is no question of "fiefs" one cannot talk about feudalism. But there are other serious differences. As Chesneaux

721 Wilhelm Franke, ed., 1977, 80.

722 See, for example, for this image in the same W. Franke, ed., 323–324.

723 Jean Chesneaux, 1973, 11.

also acknowledged, the large landholdings found in Europe were nearly absent in most parts of this enormous country that was, itself, as large as the whole of Europe.

While the European system of fiefs is absent, the relation of (mutual) dependency between emperor or king and aristocracy was not present as well. These facts signify large differences in a juridical and economic sense.

Furthermore, the role played by the peasants seems similar in both cases: numerous peasant revolts can be registered. However, apart from the impression that quantitatively there were many more peasant revolts in China than in Europe (certainly in the 19th century), the Chinese revolts often led to the destruction of the governing regimes.

In many regions, where the repression of the peasants was stronger, revolts led to a real improvement in peasants' position; this was not so much so in the case of Western Europe, where the repression of the peasants was less severe. Thus, the Chinese peasants had a better position from which to negotiate than their European colleagues, even long before the Ming period.

Whether one can speak still *in abstracto* of "Chinese feudalism" seems to be a matter of intellectual taste; in my view, at least, there is no historical need to do so, other than for ideological reasons. For the relation peasant-state (bureaucracy), one can come to the following conclusions:

1. A comparison between the European Middle Ages and imperial China, in which specific phases must follow each other, is not correct in the chronological sense nor in a theoretical (let alone practical) sense. It is better to make a comparison, as Mousnier has, between absolutist France, tsarist Russia and imperial China in the Ming and Manchu periods.[724]
2. The aim and the results of peasant revolts in Europe and China was different: in the first case it concerned, in fact, an attack on the extreme exploitation and reduction of the pressure from above to a normal degree of exploitation; in the Chinese case it concerned a counter-attack directed above in an attempt to negate the distance between "them and us."
3. The relative "free space" that existed in China between state (bureaucracy) and the peasants allowed the latter to better organize their (conflicting) relation with the landlords with a greater chance of good results. This *class struggle* could be "disturbed" by the *status struggle* between peasant and state. In this case the peasant prefers the status struggle, because he has to fight groups that are not involved in the production.
4. Thanks to the existence of large landholdings in Europe, the relationship between lord and peasant was one of proprietors and landless folk (from

724 Roland Mousnier. 1972.

lessee to serf); in China, however, it mostly concerned a relationship between large and small proprietors or—as is explained above—between a(n absentee) landlord and a lessee who practically acts as if he is proprietor. These peasant positions allow for the accumulation of capital and, therefore, we can also conclude that

5. the class struggle in China rages between large and small (or potential) capitalists! In Europe the struggle concerns first and foremost freedom rights, while in China it concerns property rights or the right to accumulate (more) land.
6. The relations between town and country, in which the previous subjects are incorporated, seem to be not different from those in Europe. A full affirmation cannot be given before a further analysis is made, but the previously made differentiation between several kinds of cities must be followed: where these relations are determined by administrative, military centers and capitals the exploitation of the countryside is evident; where these relations concern trade and handicraft cities/towns, the exploitation is not absent, but not very sharp and mostly "bearable." Rawski discovered, for instance, in the southern Chinese cities, that as the distance between town and country increased the percentage of lease contracts increased as well and the duration of these contracts decreased.[725]

These remarks may be insufficient for broader conclusions about town-country relations in imperial China, but they already put many fixed opinions in a more realistic light.

8.3 The Roaring 19th Century[726]

To say that the history of the Chinese 19th century was very turbulent is certainly an understatement. In the 18th century there were several serious revolts, however, that were unmatched for several reasons, those of the 19th century.

From the *Heaven and Earth* revolt in 1787 or the *White Lotus* revolt in 1795 until the abdication of the last emperor (1911) here were some 6,600 large and smaller revolts! Half of them concern the years 1845–1865 and with them the name Taiping is identified. Geographically most revolts occurred in the plains of northern China (the provinces Shandong and Zhihli), central China (in the

725 E. Sakakida-Rawski, 1972, 148.

726 For the following paragraph I used Jean Chesneaux (1971) and (1973), my article on the Taiping in H. Derks, ed. 1989, 153–159. Now can be consulted Hans Derks, 2012 and in Dutch, 2015.

provinces Anhui and Jiangxi) and southern and southeast China (the provinces Guangdong, Guanxi and Jiangsu).

Many millions of victims suffered in mainly the district capitals and rural areas; in the Taiping period alone, it is thought that 4.5 million people died (there are no official figures). The largest slaughter occurred in the last act in this period, when at least 100,000 people were murdered in three days (they say) in Nanjing (1865).

The largest cities, including even Beijing, but also most provincial capitals remained relatively safe from all this turmoil. That is the reason why this era is usually spoken of as the century of the peasant revolts.

All these peasant revolts were, in fact, directed against a central government in the North. There was, however, a second reason for much of the lethal turbulence, Western imperialism, mainly introduced in China through the coastal regions in the south, via the opium wars.

There is no history so critical for the relationship between the West and the East (in our case: China) as the history of the opium monopolies, trade and wars. A still very imperial English historical atlas starts its description of the Chinese 19th century with:

> For much of the 19th century the Chinese failed to understand the challenge presented by Western powers. After a peak of prosperity under the Ch'ing in the 18th century, they regarded themselves as the center of world civilization and were slow to realize that Western power, with its superior technology, productivity and wealth, had overtaken them. Such attitudes informed their negative responses to British attempts to develop diplomatic relations from 1793. Matters came to a head when the Chinese tried to end the illicit trade in opium with its damaging economic effects. They were defeated by the British in the First Opium War and in 1842 forced to cede Hong Kong and five treaty ports in which foreigners were permitted to trade free from Chinese jurisdiction.[727]

Also a Second Opium War in 1856–1860 was provoked by the British. The historical website *The Victoria Web* writes now without any hesitation:

> The Anglo-Chinese Opium Wars were the direct result of China's isolationist and exclusionary trade policy with the West. Confucian China's

727 Richard Overy, ed., 2007, 256. See also his 193 for statistics of relation "export" of Chinese silver and "value of opium" until 1836. See for the narrative of the Opium Wars John Roberts, 2011, Chapter 14 and Jonathan Spence, 1990, Chapter 7.; Hans Derks, 2012, *passim*.

> attempts to exclude pernicious foreign ideas resulted in highly restricted trade.[728]

Even now the reasoning is deemed relevant: it is the fault of the Chinese that nearly the first relations between the West and the largest country of the East concerned drugs and two wars on drugs. Or: if the Chinese had traded with us, they would not have been killed. Or: if they had accepted being doped, we would not have made war.[729]

It seems as if there is not much difference between the blaming of the victims in the time of George Macartney or John Adams and today, between an earlier and present attitude *to punish the arrogance of those who resist our repression*. This apart from the ambiguous consideration of whether the British at that time had similar aspirations as the Chinese, what with their aim to convert the "rest of the world" into the Protestant Christian civilization after which so-called trade only for the benefit of the British could be organized smoothly. The large difference was, of course, that the British shot their Christian way through the world with their "superior arms technology" and the Chinese emperors with their abstract claim tried to impress only Chinese, an attempt that largely failed.

However, the main mistake in both quotations is that at least implicitly (and for the laymen directly) the impression is given that the Chinese were the bad guys spreading opium in the world, forming an assault on the innocent citizens of the West that had to be punished as severely as possible: a war on drugs was necessary to increase the profits of Western governments and traders, but also to restore the Christian moral standard of resisting on hallucinogenic drug (who wrote that religion was opium of/for the people?) And indeed, the hypocrisy of the colonial powers was so structured that they forbade opium use for their own "white citizens" only and never for the indigenous populations—on largely racist grounds.

Therefore, these wars were legalized by the recognition of a so-called foreign enemy, a false Western trick. The very truth, which had to be silenced as much as possible, was that the three most important Western imperialist

728 P.V. Allingham on "The Victorian Web," 2010 under "England and China: The Opium Wars, 1839–60."

729 As a reaction on my history of the opium problem an English reviewer defended even the thesis that it is the own choice of the Chinese that they consume opium and the British Empire cannot be blamed for this. J.B. Askew, 2013, 106–108. The source of this and related views—like "opium is largely harmless"—is the British historian R.K. Newman, probably also the teacher of Askew. In my 2012, 596–597, 634, 680 and passim I criticized these views.

powers in Asia (the Dutch, British and French) organized the production and trade of opium at the largest possible scale, with tremendous profits for them and terrible consequences for the indigenous peoples and societies.

What matters, of course, is the *monopoly* position in production and trade, the power of the arms with which this could be sustained and the scale of the consumption. No Chinese had such a monopoly position, only Western colonial governments did.[730] After 1900, the situation grew from bad to worse. All colonial governments were urged by their motherland states (which were attacked from all sides by anti-opium lobbies) of curbing opium consumption and related criminality. At the same time, however, the colonial governments wanted (and were urged by the motherlands) to increase the colony's profitability.

The moral wishes could be met and the greed of the colonial bureaucrats satisfied by increasing the opium prices at all levels and, therefore, negatively effecting "public" consumption. But if these bureaucrats were not personally involved in the smuggling, they had detailed knowledge about the smuggling they also stimulated. The bureaucrats' high monopoly prices stimulated the smuggler's lower prices, thereby increasing consumption and criminality. The strict oikoidal wish "to remove the private profit motive that had encouraged consumption and addiction"[731] had, therefore, the reversed effect: opium smuggling became never so much more widespread after 1900 and received such strong impulses that it evolved into a real scourge.

This criminality urged, in turn, new state measures, (secret) military and police organizations, more widespread corruption, stronger competition between the several colonial governments, all also influenced by World Wars I and II. Through this spiral the (colonial) state and its (expatriate) bureaucrats proved its (and their) necessity![732]

---

730 In particular Dutch sources with their extensive trade contacts with the (early) medieval Middle East and the Arab world could reveal how something like opium was used in Arab medicine and, probably, as an Arab luxury. The regions of the present Turkey and Iran were classical "opium" countries, but also several Balkan regions (Bulgaria, etc.). In China the use of opium was always forbidden, not in India. Alternative explanations are that the tobacco smoking Portuguese made smoking of opium, first added to tobacco, popular or that the Great Mogul had already an opium monopoly which was inherited by the British East India Company, etc.

731 E. van Luijk, J. van Ours, 1995, 1.

732 E. van Luijk, J. van Ours, 1995, 16–17 demonstrate how scholars can became ideologues of a specific state policy. They had no realistic view on the effects of state monopolies in this period but concluded "that the change in policy *per se* did indeed induce a substantial reduction in opium use. Apparently, by taking over the opium market the government removed the profit motive to stimulate consumption." (italics from authors.) Simply

The opium history demonstrates that one thing never can be left out of consideration: to question the role of the (colonial)state that covers its misdeeds with dubious Christian morality and policing or suggesting to its citizens that it can to save them from a bad outer world; it is a state that acts, *once out of sight of its citizens*, in (neo)colonies as the worst violator of everything it stands for in its own motherland.

The Chinese history shows how difficult it was to resist these attacks by the West, but China succeeded by *partly* copying the quasi-invincible and strongest weapons of the West, its technology and dubious imports of opium. It demonstrated, in economic terms, an effective case of import substitution, while half a century later a regime came to power that effectively eradicated opium production, consumption and trade. This example was not followed by the West and its dependencies in the East.

The result from these developments that could not be negated was the boost in the urbanization due to opium-smuggling, opium wars and the concomitant shipping, banking, militarization with its fleets and marine-harbors, influx of foreigners from all Western countries, migration from country to city, reconstruction of cities as a consequence of isolated urban quarters used as foreign concessions, and so on. This urbanization from the second half of the 19th century onward is a complex phenomenon with external and internal Chinese and foreign impulses.

One cannot forget, first, that around 1800 Beijing was the largest city *in the world* with its 1,100,000 inhabitants, slightly more than London with its 950,000 citizen, while Guangzhou (Canton) was the third largest with 800,000 people. China's overall population of about 400 million was, around 1850, highly unevenly spread over the eastern part of the country. Not only was China the most populous country in the world, but it was also very difficult to govern in a centralized way.[733]

Another feature concerns the impact of the imperialism of the 19th century. During the period of the opium wars, there existed in China about 300 cities with more than 10,000 residents, by no means the whole urban pattern. To this belonged, for instance, about 25,000 market towns with strong ties to the surrounding countryside and 3,277 "urban markets"; the oikoïdal part was

astonishing is the lesson they derive from their analysis "that the consumption of even addictive drugs is price-responsive, and a policy of socializing the hard-drug trade need not be as immoral as it sounds." What the state is doing cannot be immoral.

733 See for the following the article of W. Taubmann in: David Leese, ed., 2009, 140–143; T. Scharping in: David Leese, ed., 2009, 790–791; Jürgen Osterhammel in: David Leese, ed., 2009, 1009–1012 and Jürgen Osterhammel, 2014, 250–251.

formed by thousands of administrative centers, hundreds of "capitals," etc.[734] The settlement pattern was, therefore well divided between market and *oikos*.

Without a story these figures are rather meaningless. Osterhammel tells one:[735]

> These numerical impressions would suggest that... China... [belonged to]... the dominant urban cultures in the world... what was meant by "city" varied enormously. European visitors found the walled cities to which they were accustomed most often in China, but even there not all throughout the country; and travel reports repeatedly speak of Asia's shapeless, "nonurban" cities. Sometimes the distinction between city and country seemed to lose all of its sharpness... Nevertheless, *every* city was a sphere of dense communication and a consumer of surpluses produced in the country; it was in some way a nodal point of trade or migration. Each had to contend with supply and public order problems that were different from those in "the countryside" Asia's big cities somehow managed to solve these problems...

Their destiny was not very well fixed. Take, for instance, the 300 older cities mentioned above. Around 1850 their proportion in the total population was

734 In a contribution to a conference Kent Deng tried to answer with these and a mass of other relevant but mostly badly related figures the question "Why Was the Factor Market So Weak in pre-Opium War China?" (June 2005). See www.iisg.nl/hpw/factormarkets.php for the conference and other contributions: only with one eye on the population development in the 300 cities, he could have concluded that as such the marketing was not weak but the revoltionary pressures too strong. Mr. Deng is apparently a statistician with a specific ideological mission and not an historian who tried to reconstruct what really happened: if he 'proves' the "weakness of the Chinese market" by underplaying "a total of 2.8 million merchants (or 14 million including their families) for China's some 400 million citizens" (9) he does not realize that this means nearly 1 merchant on every 100 peoples (including children) or about 30 people on every merchant-family.

735 Jürgen Osterhammel, 2014, 252. In this citation he also points to Java, India and Japan and not only to China, but this text is symptomatic enough for China. For the walled cities see the remarkable book of David Bray, 2005, Chapter 2 in which this strict oikoidal plan became the model (archetype; ideal-type in the Weberian sense) of the *danwei*. This was, among others, the "workunit" in the or some industrial city(ies), which soon became a housing and living unit as well. As such it was an ideal construction used in city and other planning activities and a tool in the central planning of the state. Bray rightly compared its use with the rather utopian building plans and practices described by Anatole Kopp's, 1970 brillant analyses of the Sovjet architecture and city-panning in the revolutionary years 1917- 1935. For Bray it seems the proof that the Chinese socialist system belonged to century old Chinese traditions, which can be seen as a "meaningful overstatement."

not more than 3.7%: only twenty years *earlier* this was 12% and forty years *later* it was not more than 4.4% ! In this whole period these cities experienced a loss of about 8 million peoples due to the terrible impact of the many peasant revolts, the Taiping risings and the opium wars.

However, the latter were directly responsible for the establishment of the (unequal) *Treaty Ports.* Fifty to eighty of such locations were established in 1843–1917; they were located outside the given 300 cities or isolated within these cities (concessions). They attracted a lot of people; a few rich foreigners with substantial and lucrative privileges (extraterritoriality etc.) and many Chinese with only obligations. Half of these locations were the result of British-Chinese treaties, about ten were due to French-Chinese treaties, etc.[736] In addition China established another 35 cities with "treaty-facilities" on its own borders in the north.

This new combination *city-country with market-oikos* initiated a strong development mostly called "modernization" with a critical variable "industrialization." In the internal situation of cities and countries changed many things, but some remarkable reminiscences to earlier times (*walled cities*) and even Confucian traditions can be noted from the end of this roaring century onward.

These few remarks on one of the most important imperialist chapters, the opium history of East Asia, must suffice since an extensive history is now available.[737]

8.4 The Start of Industrialization

The story about the dominant influence of foreign capital, thanks to which the so-called Chinese isolation (and more specific: of rural China here contrary to coastal-urban China) is broken down and the city has gained the victory in which Western industrialization including proletarization developed, this story is seriously overdone.

In a comparison between India and China, Murphy studied the Western influence and criticized the euro-centric perception at issue.[738] For China he paid much attention to the "beach-heads of Western influence," the harbors. He poses the right question why contrary to South and Southeast Asia in China there was no Western colonial influencing (and settler's activity) of the hinterland.

736 See, for instance, Hans Derks, 2012, 411–414 about the French settlement in Shanghai.

737 Hans Derks, 2012.

738 Rh. Murphy, 1977.

In India the colonial domination is accepted and supported by loyal collaborators, who enriched themselves tremendously. The Chinese not only opposed Westernization, but they were not upset at all by the performance of those white Westerners in the so-called "concessions." The situation is best to compare with the minimal influence Hong Kong had on the People's Republic before the transfer of power.

Murphy describes how little the effectiveness and "staying power" of the Chinese production and exchange relations is influenced by the Western capitalistic mode of production. China did not like to buy foreign goods, because their quality—with some exceptions—was less or equal to Chinese products. The foreign-owned industry was practically only aimed at the foreign trade, while the Chinese import statistics mask the fact that these imports were largely destined to the treaty ports themselves.

In 1916 the first volume of *The Chinese Social and Political Science Review* was published in which Dakin K. Lieu described the attitudes concerning industrialization among "most publicists and students of economic science," as follows:

> We have enough to do with our foreign debt problem, our currency, taxation, and budgetary problems; we do not want to trouble ourselves any more with the question of industrial development. Let the business men look after that themselves, but let us devote our attention to those questions that more closely concern with our national economic policy.[739]

Here in an ideal-typical way the hard clash is documented between protagonists of a strict oikoidal economic state policy (eventually its renewal) and of the coming capitalist production, perceived even as a matter for business people only and not for engineers. In the definitions of Chapter 1: one tries to introduce capitalist production, while capitalism does not yet exist.

At this time Lieu argues, the industrial problem has become "a popular subject for empty talk" while it is in fact "a national food problem, plus the problems of clothing and shelter." For the "practical Occidental mind" this would be enough to take action, but the "over-idealized Chinese… will begin to observe ethical principles when their barns are full." Dakin Lieu does not know that he gave a perfect Chinese translation of a Western *materialist* dictum par excellence: *Der Mensch ist was er isst* [One is what one eats, Feuerbach].[740]

739 Dakin K. Lieu in: C.F. Remer, ed., 1933, 133.

740 See Iring Fetscher, 1973, 82–83.

By the efforts of all kinds of "over-idealized Western Christians" the materialist consequences of this dictum arae often fought in a lethal way, but here—let's be sure—it is a good characterization of the Chinese peasant's matter-of-fact mind formed by hard experience: first, security in the food situation, and later comes the moral component. It was too difficult for a Chinese peasant, if not for all Chinese, at the time to see whether this industrialization or capitalist production contributed to that security.

Dakin Lieu comes up with another surprise in order to support the industrialization of his country and "maintaining its existence and independence in the great international economic struggle." There are two options: making, in one's own territory, all kinds of industry, or only producing some specialties and securing the rest of the products through exchange with other nations. "In other words, it may exist either in a self-sufficient state, or in a state of international economic interdependence."

Both options lead to industrialization that is, however, a backward stage, whereupon Lieu asks: "... but what exactly is the nature of the stage, and how far back is it from the general degree of progress?"[741] To answer this question he, first defines the "backwardness" of the industrial system, which is

> ...about hundred and fifty years behind the pioneer industrial nations of Europe in industrial practices, and more than two hundred years in formative ideas... They have attained the stage of national economy while we are still in the stage of town economy.

Lieu, secondly, states that he defined "stage of economy" with the help of Karl Bücher's *Stufen* theory,[742] which we met in the form Max Weber gave it as an even more rigid variant of this typical oikoidal theory [*Evolution der Hauswirtschaft*]. He also refers to "another great German economist," Friedrich List, founder of a *National School of Political Economy* who speaks of

> national economy in contradistinction to cosmopolitan or universal economy... His system implies a self-sufficiency in the nation ... [whereas]... Bücher's system... does mean the breaking up of the self-sufficiency of towns.[743]

741 Dakin K. Lieu in: C.F. Remer, ed., 1933, 136.

742 In Lieu's wording: first stage (*Stufe*) of *Home Economy* with two periods (of domestic work and of wage work or custom work); second stage of *Town Economy* with two periods (of handicraft or price work and of commission work or house industry); third stage of *National Economy* with one period (of factory work).

743 Dakin K. Lieu in: C.F. Remer, ed., 1933, 140.

TABLE 4 Industrial establishments in China, 1913[a]

No. of employees	No of establishments
7 to 30	18 830
30 to 50	1 145
50 to 100	833
100 to 500	726
500 to 1000	145
1000 up	33
total	21 712

a Dakin K. Lieu in: C.F. Remer, ed., 1933, 142.

For Lieu List's "national system" becomes the model for the new China: it is indeed the very model of capital*ism* as defined earlier, the oikoidal state capitalism, here at the start of the Chinese industrialization circumscribed as follows:

> The organization of a large modern corporation is comparable only to that of a national government, comprising many territorial divisions, some of which are even located in foreign countries, like colonies in political organizations. This is even more important than the factory system...[744]

To demonstrate the backwardness of the industrial conditions of China, Lieu reproduced the latest statistics available to him related to the "industrial establishments" in the whole of China. Only 247 of them used electricity and only 904 had one hundred employees or more. In Tables 4–5 Lieu and others demonstrate the situation around World War I.

This table speaks for itself. The total number of modern corporations, including those involved in manufacturing as well as agricultural, commercial and transportation, was 415 in 1913 with a total capital of $64 million.

Then Lieu takes us for a walk through the streets of the larger cities like Shanghai, Hankou, Tianjin or Beijing and paints a very gloomy picture with only modern buildings "of Western type" on the Nanjing Road in Shanghai.

> The rest are workshops and commercial stores standing side by side, of nearly the same size and with nearly the same appearance. The premises

744 Dakin K. Lieu in: C.F. Remer, ed., 1933, 141.

> occupy a frontage of ten to fifteen feet; some have two stories but seldom more. The tools and the processes 'have remained the same as they were a few hundred years ago. They involve a good deal of manual labor, much of which is wasted... Accuracy in workmanship is not a quality that we can boast of... much improvement can be effected by a little change in the instruments used... and yet the poor workmen never think of that...[745]

This is a realistic picture, but to characterize the industrial climate in China in those days it is not enough as we will see. Only twenty years later, a city like Shanghai would be the most important for the Chinese internal relations as other older studies reveal, but is also a world economic and financial center, the bridgehead from which the British, Americans or French and Japanese tried to get a foothold in China.[746]

The city was perceived as an example of the New Industrial Era or, by Mao, as a purely capitalistic city that should be detested and attacked. Shanghai was also a haven of refuge for many rich, and for large masses of poor Chinese: the rich invested in factories and large pieces of urban land, while they had an important influence in banks. The poor formed, together with small minorities of foreigners like about 20,000 White Russians who fled for the Russian Revolution, or 2000 "half-caste Portuguese," a proletariat ready to make revolution.

In 1936 Shanghai already had 3,750,000 inhabitants including 68,000 foreigners, making it the 6th largest city in the world. Nearly the whole labor force had come from the hinterland. Shanghai had, therefore, an enormous consumer potential and was highly attractive for Chinese capital. It comess es no surprise that in 1936, from the 210 banks in the city there were 190 in Chinese hands.[747]

The English bank was the largest of all the banks, but it is thanks to "the clever Chinese banking policy" that the Chinese dollar was as stable as the English pound in the international monetary system. The Chinese owned porrtion of the Shanghai industry was also large: from the 2,700 factories there were 2,000 Chinese owned with, all together 250,000 laborers or 65% of the total labor force.[748]

In this city was concentrated a quarter of all factory laborers in China. This meant that only 150,000 Chinese laborers, about 10%, worked in foreign factories or under the command of foreign capital.

Another important aspect of the Chinese industrialization in the 19th and early 20th centuries is, that from around 1860 it had a state-capitalistic

745 Dakin K. Lieu in: C.F. Remer, ed., 1933, 143–145.

746 M. Pernitzsch, 1937. See below for the "Westernization of China."

747 M. Pernitzsch, 1937, 58, 59.

748 M. Pernitzsch, 1937, 81.

(oikoidal) character. It is not by accident that this first industrialization was a reaction to the numerous and very large peasant revolts of the 19th century. It concerns, therefore, the arms, textile and ship-buildings industries, while coal and iron mines were also opened.[749]

The state-capitalistic character is apparent from its organization and the initiators. The latter were (very) high-ranking bureaucrats who favored and established a "system of state control and management by merchants" (*Kuan-tu shang-pan*), or a 100% state venture (*Kuan-pan*). Attempts to establish a clear example of *capitalist production* (as defined in Chapter 1) with foreign capital participation were likely to fail because foreigners were nearly not interested in cooperating with Chinese entrepreneurs or in investing in Chinese industry. The Sino-Japanese war in 1895 strongly motivated the high-level bureaucrats to establish factories in the mining, smelting and textile sectors.

The foreign influence was largely confined to dominance in the trade markets. Thus the Chinese silk-industry (mainly in Shanghai) lost the competition with the Japanese on the American market because the Japanese of Shanghai had much more influence in the export of silk.[750]

The most modern industry in China was established by Japan in the chemical and metallurgical sector after Japan conquered northeastern China, an area with substantial coal and oil reserves. Of course, that industry was put fully in the service of Japanese war efforts.

The ratio of foreign to Chinese capital in the largest industry, the Shanghai textile industry, becomes clear in the following table.[751]

To make the comparison complete several other data points should be made available (output, profits, invested capitals, etc.), but these data are not available yet. Anyway, around 1900 the ratio is more or less equal, though this changes quickly in the advantage of the Chinese. After 1925, a definite breakthrough is arrived at the moment the foreign industry declines and the Chinese accelerates; an excellent example of import substitution.

Industrialization is not only introduced in the cities but also in the countryside. The research on this is beginning; a good example in the textile sector is given in a rural area about 110 kilometers north of Shanghai.[752]

749 Wilhelm Franke, ed., 1977, 142, 143; E. Köll in: Daniel Faure and T. Liu, ed., 2002, 107, 108; Gail Hershatter, 1986, Chapter 2.

750 L.K. Tao, S.H. Lin, ed., 1932, 89.

751 Derived from L.K. Tao, S.H. Lin, ed., 1932, 85. See also Jürgen Osterhammel in: A. Porter, ed., 1999, 162.

752 The following is based on E. Köll in: D. Faure and T. Liu, ed., 2002, 107–125. It should and could have been compared with the earlier "cotton revolution" as, for instance, described by Philip Huang (1990), *passim*.

TABLE 5 Shanghai textile industry, 1896–1930

Year	Number of factories		Number of spindles	
	Chinese	Foreign	Chinese	Foreign
1896	8	5	225 267	204 342
1906	17	5	426 767	214 347
1916	30	11	721 105	400 146
1925	76	37	1 600 000	890 000
1930	81	46	2 326 872	642 680

It concerns the Da Sheng No.1 Cotton Mill situated in Tangjiazha village in Nantong County, founded in 1895 by the famous scholar and retired official, Zjhang Jian, 1853–1926. Thirty years later the factory had 8,000, mainly unskilled, female workers with an administrative staff (including skilled workers, management and engineers) of 400. At that time every sixth person in the village area worked in the mill, while 62 % of the unskilled workers continued with farming during their employment in the mill.

The factory worked round the clock in two 12-hour shifts throughout the year starting at 05:30 in the morning. So, the fields were mostly cultivated by the women-workers outside their factory shift. In this way one earned an additional income. Köll thinks that farm work was marginalized in favor of factory work and regarded perhaps even as backward.

Apart from some linguistic problems here, in my view it is a matter of fact pointing to the distinction of town and country: a factory is something quite new coming from "abroad"; men are still higher rated than women in the countryside; the factory nurtured the distinction by hiring the peasant women as day workers through a middleman; the management commuted to the factory from the city; it is not in their interest to negate a male-female disparity since they mostly were in need of the cheap female labor. This perspective seems to be supported by the following.

Later the unskilled female workers would have entered the mill as children in the company of their mothers. Still, unskilled adult men received on average double the pay of the unskilled adult women. They all were day laborers but the skilled workers were paid per month and the managers were also entitled to a 15 per cent share in the company's annual net profit.[753]

753 A manager received a monthly income of about 80 yuan; compared to an income of an unskilled female worker the manager earned certainly ten times more exclusive his

Besides differences in payment, skilled workers and staff members could dwell on the site in non-village style houses with shops at the gate and a park prohibited for unskilled workers. The Chinese engineers were recruited in Shanghai, from the Nantong or other textile schools, but sometimes a foreign engineer (American or Englishmen) had to be hired for a short time.

With Max Weber's work ethic theory in mind, it can be seen that factory work discipline was so different from farm work, that was largely regulated by the seasonal cycles and was subject to the vagaries of the weather. The factory was ruled by a "factory agreement" designed by Zhang Jian himself.

It concerned "regulations that were among the most comprehensive regulations laid down for an industrial enterprise in China at the time." For the unskilled majority there were only commands, prohibitions and punishments (money fines were levied for the tiniest mistakes); there was a "neutral" (not from the village) factory police as guard of the compound and the work; for the skilled labor and management he emphasized attitudes and moral values besides money incentives. This model was important:

> The appeal to a moral code of conduct as a tool of management… reflected the shaping of a very sharp class distinction. Zhang Jian's regulations for his skilled and unskilled workers did not resemble English employers' attempts in the nineteenth century to prevent their workers from immoral behavior in- and outside the factory and to reform the whole man. He did not draw up regulations that attempted to improve the moral quality of his workers. However, the regulations for the management assumed that the managers were people of integrity even though, in a very practical way, bonuses were tied to performance. Despite Zhang Jian's personal Confucian commitments, the "factory agreement" of the Da Sheng No. 1 Mill was, as such, not a strikingly moralistic document.[754]

First, one cannot talk here about shaping class distinctions, because here new classes and class interests are not formed yet. In this case one has to deal with the introduction of a status hierarchy derived from the oikoidal view of society familiar within the higher bureaucratic elite of Zhang Jian.

He is anyhow a representative of the modernizing oikoidal power that is introducing capitalist industrialization within a traditionally formed setting

---

annual bonus. The assistant manager or members of the administrative staff started with 4 yuan monthly and could come to 40 yuan according to their responsibilities; engineers ranged between 24 and 33 yuan around 1910.

754 E. Köll in: D. Faure and T. Liu, ed., 2002, 114, 115.

(a kind of watch-tower at the gate, but with a Western style clock; a fenced compound and a park for the privileged, guarded by "foreign" hirelings, etc.): old money doing new things.

A really new industrialization organizes the work (hierarchy) according to the sequence, division and "value" of the work that is to be done to produce and market the products. If managers transform their profits into "castles," aristocratic titles, etc. one has to do with parvenue's: new money is doing old things. In these early Republican years facing the collapse of the Ming dynasty with all its consequences, Zhang Jian's regulations should be seen, as well, as a realistic accommodation to the new realities introduced by "Shanghai."

Based on what has been said so far, the following conclusions for China's industrialization before 1949 can be made:

1. The oikoidal, state-capitalist ventures aiming at the armament of the government or bureaucracy (including police and army) support these institutions in the internal war against the revolting peasants. It is, therefore, not the aim of this industrialization to produce goods for "the enormous Chinese market." In 1945, 68 percent of the industrial capital is still state-owned.
2. The localization of this industry in Shanghai and several coastal provinces makes it rather difficult to cater to "the enormous Chinese market," apart from the absence of enough or relevant transport roads to the rest of China.
3. The products at stake are nearly all consumption goods for the institutions mentioned in 1. Machines, for instance, necessary to enhance and differentiate production all over China are rarely made or distributed. The oikoidal approach is nearly ideal-typical in so far that it is a self-sustaining, autarkic approach.
4. The availability of foreign capital is evident but not imported and invested to conquer a Chinese market. It is exclusively available for the foreign concessions and for the foreign "motherlands."
5. The part of industrialization in the total Chinese economy is, in this period, still neglected, relative to their output and employment. In 1933 this part is not more than 3.4 %.[755]
6. The legitimation of this (limited) industrialization is given by the institutions mentioned in 1, but also by left-wing intellectuals from Shanghai and other large cities with modernization ideas like:

755 Wilhelm Franke, ed., 1977, 145.

> …in spite of all difficulties the Chinese have committed themselves definitely to industrialization to which there can be no alternative. The life and death of the nation… hangs entirely on the success or failure of industrialization… And in order to raise their living standard, it would be up to them to follow the trail modern industrial powers had blazed. An industrial regime for our people, whether on capitalistic or communistic lines, appears therefore to be inevitable.[756]

In short: the statements that there should be a dominant power of foreign capital, that there were large, organized streams of goods between town and country, or that Chinese industrialization was seriously limited by foreign capital, these statements cannot be supported by the facts.

8.5 The Shanghai Westernization

There are no books more widespread and as accurate relative to the relationship between China and the West in this period as the famous comic-strip album *The Blue Lotus,*1936. It is, of course, one of the spectacular adventures of the Belgian reporter Tintin written and designed by Hergé. As everybody knows *The Blue Lotus* is the name of a Shanghai opium den, meeting point for Tintin's criminal antagonists whom he could eliminate in defense of an opium-free world, but as well as an imperialist-free China.

The American businessman/gangster and racist bully Gibbons with his friend the corrupt British *police chief of the Shanghai International Settlement,* Dawson, both work together with the Japanese drugs dealer and spy, Mitsuhirato, to eliminate Tintin and to keep the poor Chinese doped, poisoned and repressed.

Thanks to the cooperation between the honest and brave Tintin and a Chinese secret society, *The Sons of the Dragon,* they succeed in unmasking Mitsuhirato as the organizer of the Mukden incident (blowing up of a railway; 18th of September 1931). It really happened and it became the excuse for the Japanese to accuse China of terrorist acts and occupy a part of China (invasion of Manchuria). A happy end: the boss of the opium cartel, the Greek Rastapopoulos and his Western friends from the Shanghai International Settlement are arrested, Mitsuhirato commits *seppuku* (ritual suicide) and Japan is kicked out of the League of Nations.

756 L.K. Tao, S.H. Lin, ed., 1932, 75.

The scenario provided by Hergé and the criminal Shanghai environment was quite realistic for a publication of 1936 and the prevailing view is, indeed, that Japan itself staged the Mukden incident in order to provide a pretext for war. This incident is not only followed by the creation of the puppet state Manchukuo (with Puyi as emperor), Japan's departure from the League of Nations, a Japanese attack on the northern part of Shanghai (1932), but also by the devastating Second Sino-Japanese war, 1937–1945.

Life in the Shanghai international concessions was only seriously influenced by this last effort of Japanese imperialism and its occupation of China. In every city guide of Shanghai one can now read the glorious story of *The Bund,* the architectural complex representative for the Westernization of Shanghai and China for which the construction started around 1870. In only the better stories can one find that the course of the first Opium War was decisive for the future of this major trading port for all of the lower Yangzi river region (1842, Treaty of Nanjing), for the entrance of Christian preachers (1848, first church built in Xujiahui).

In no single tourist guide is it told how a decade later a second Opium War started, how from Shanghai the British and French troops departed to show what imperialism really implied: the political and cultural destruction of the "guest country": Beijing was plundered, the Imperial Summer Palace destroyed and the most lucrative opium concession was extorted from the Chinese government.

In Shanghai, the new capital of the opium empire, opium could be collected and sold with so much profit that the first representational buildings of *the Bund* could be constructed with a splendid symbol of isolation found in its first park, Huangpu Garden, which was exclusively for foreigners, 1868. For those who had to bear the White Man's Burden, it was good to take a tea with your (Chinese) mistress here.

8.6 Town and Country in the Interbellum

Contrary to the Russian Revolution, the Chinese Revolution "began on the countryside and ended in the cities." Unless one uses peculiar definitions of "revolution," "countryside" or "city," this thesis affords a limited understanding of Mao and the Red Army driving the Kuomintang into the sea, after the People's Republic of China was formally declared on October 1, 1949.

It is well argued that the political Chinese Revolution began with the so-called "May 4th Movement" in Shanghai with strong influences from Beijing. The intellectuals from the two largest Chinese cities started an alliance with factory laborers, like their Russian colleagues in Petersburg did in 1917, in order to expand this alliance with peasants in and around these cities.

Also the Chinese Communist Party was established in Shanghai in 1921 under strong pressure from Moscow and the Comintern. The latter could, until 1958, propagate a perfect antagonistic view on town-country relations (see Chapter 9 about AMP) with a frequently changing Chinese leadership. This, in addition to the famous propaganda aim to overtake the large capitalist countries, implied by definition the domination of the countryside by the town.

The question is, of course, also in the light of present developments, whether China really left the Russian model of industrialization? But another question comes also to the fore in reference to a specific "Chinese Way" in which the Chinese tradition (whatever that means) delivered the model of development and, in particular, the supposed dominant role of the state in economic life.[757]

Wertheim posed another relevant question after he made a comparison between traditional village life, seen as relatively closed, autonomous and self sufficient, and the villages and people's communes around 1975: what is the real difference in village life between then and now?

What this tradition implied is discussed above sufficient for our purpose, so that we know that in earlier times villages seldom were isolated and autarkic and, therefore, a comparison is difficult to make with the communes. Whatever analogies can be drawn from the past, it is clear that in this transition period, indeed, a break in the Chinese history took place. Before we can exactly decide which were the real consequences, a further reflection on the *theory* of the Chinese Revolution is necessary.

A transition was envisaged from feudalism through capitalism towards socialism and communism. Characteristics of the Chines feudalism are mentioned above: this phase was, *at the top,* changed into a state-capitalism and, under Western influence in an relatively isolated part of China, a bourgeois capitalism can be seen. Officially the latter had only a very short existence from about 1900–1949. In this short period China was confronted with modernization through industrialization in the big cities and with a new industrial proletariat.

At the base of society, however, the "classical (dynastic) feudalism" disappeared in the 19th and beginning of the 20th centuries thanks to the "normal" endless peasant revolts or natural calamities, and "as usual" there followed a period of warlords fighting each other to become a new dynasty.

757 K. Buchanan, 1973, 105 through quoting Joseph Needham in this sense.

In most cases the peasants received the "normal" chance to get rid of their landlords and around 1925 they got the support of the latter-day victorious war-lord, Mao Zedong, who prophesied with his famous one-liner: "*A revolution is no dinner party*," which must be difficult to grasp for peasants who did not know dinner parties. This man with the urban, left-wing ideology had to fight his longest battle against the Kuomintang (KMT), the supporter of the landlords all of whom were concentrated in the cities.

The result of this *double contradiction between city and countryside,* the most typical characteristic of the Chinese *Interbellum,* is known: the peasants won again and their war-lord got the state power.

The next period is in fact also a classical one: at the base the position of the peasants vis-à-vis the landlords was substantially strengthened thanks to their own efforts and this meant that the poorer peasants increased their property at the cost of the earlier exploiters: therefore, the revolution did not bring about an end to private property.

On the contrary, for the many different regions and modes of production there were different regimes. The state power in Beijing moved in a strong yet ambivalent position: the ideology adopted at the top is first and foremost supportive for the urban industrial proletariat as the basis of the revolution, favoring urban industrialization, the negation of private property and the realization of a collectivist socialist economy, simply because urban factory laborers were not interested in landed property.

This policy is, in a most crucial sense, at variance with the needs and mode of production of the Chinese peasants. In addition, there are serious regional differences and disparities between areas with a dominant nomadic economy, sedentary agriculture and urban industrialism: one policy for this vast country, was asking for much trouble.

8.7 A Russian Lesson?

A comparison with the period directly after the Russian Revolution is obvious: there was also at that time an urban (theory) ideology at variance with the interests of the countryside, while the regional disparities in the whole vast area of European Russia and Siberia were as large as those in China. The difference is clear: in China the peasants were much more militant and experienced; in addition to this they were owner of their land and herds.

Also, in earlier centuries, peasant revolts were the ultimate menace for the rulers, but the 19th century was unprecedented in this respect and must have given the Chinese peasants very strong anti-state attitudes. In the 20th century's lethal struggle with the warlords these attitudes were not minimized and it is a special quality of the Chinese Communists that they got a strong peasant support. A small comparison with the Russian peasant population in the same revolutionary period shall give some perspective to this Chinese situation.[758]

Apart from the Russian civil war between the "Reds" and the "Whites" after 1917, there were also many peasant revolts and partisan groups mainly directed against the "White" movements. The largest peasant army was the Nestor Makhno movement in the Ukraine that fought with an army of 15,000 people at the disposal of the "Reds."

In Siberia the "White" commander Kolchak was forced to deal with numerous peasant revolts and guerrilla bands. "Red" activists in a united front with other left-wing groups often played a major role in the organization of the peasant movement.

The *First Peasant Congress,* in April 1919, tried to organize all groups and provide them with a common ideology: it proposed a peasant constitution; peasant government; communal taxes; it demanded the "distribution of the riches of the land among the toiling peasantry"; it even passed a peasant code against drunkenness, gambling and rape.

However, at the moment the "White" war-lords were defeated in the summer of 1920 several contradictory developments took place which ended in a total chaos: famine broke out in large parts of Russia and Siberia; small bands of "Whites" and hundreds of small-scale bandit armies terrorized various areas; brigades of the "Reds" started ruthless requisition of grain for the feeding of their urban sympathizers, which aggravated the terrible famine; corruption and despotism of local Soviet bureaucrats was widespread; in the Ukraine Makhno's peasant army did not want to cooperate with the "Reds" any more and started its own course; in the central Russian province of Tambov the Antonov rebellion and guerrilla warfare against the Soviets seemed invincible; and everywhere small and larger peasant revolts arose; unprecedented cruelties were executed as well by the peasants; thousands of Bolsheviks were brutally murdered. In short: a total break down of whatever power could be seen in 1920–1921.

Even Lenin was thrown into absolute panic: these peasant risings are "far more dangerous than all the Denikins, Iudeniches and Kolchaks put together." The Soviets changed their strategy from sending small detachments to regular elite troops:

758 For the following see J.N. Westwood, 1981, Chapters 12 and 13; Hans Derks, ed., 1989, 225–248; Orlando Figes in: E. Acton, ed., 370–381 and 457–468.

> … it was military might and ruthless terror that held the key to the suppression of the major peasant revolts, although in some places, such as the Volga famine region, hunger and exhaustion did the job instead.[759]

In the late summer of 1921, much of the countryside was struck down with famine and the peasant revolts had been defeated militarily. Makhno gave up the struggle in August 1921; in vast Siberia, peasant resistance remained at a small scale until 1923.

The aim and ideology of the peasants were largely uniform: to re-establish the peasant self-rule of 1917–1918. Embarrassing slogans like *Soviet Power without the Communists!* or *Long Live the Bolsheviks! Death to the Communists!* refer to the peasants' support of the Revolution of 1917, while Trotsky and his Communists had only brought about civil war, had confiscated the gentry's land to use it for collective farms, had stamped out free trade and usurped their local soviets.

In the following decade, a reversion to free trade in combination with the moderate New Economic Policy was a fully utopian wish as slowly the centralization of government, economy, planning and production was organized.

Now "collectivization" became the wonder-concept. In my view, the most serious failure was that the power-interests of the super-*Oikos* always had to prevail over the technical, economical, or agronomical logic of country-life. In particular, the reproduction of the political idea of centralized decision making into the technical and economical realities created unsolvable disparities in the whole of the Soviet Union. Anyway, not an example solving Chinese critical problems at the time.

8.8 The "New Democracy"

To embark on a rigorous extermination and collectivization policy in Stalinist style, was therefore, impossible in China, regardless of how much they may have wanted to follow this Soviet Russian line.

The Chinese leadership choose a piecemeal approach even relative to its own position: the pre-revolutionary state-capitalistic period was, in fact,

759 Orlando Figes in Idem, p. 378. In particular Tambov with the strongest peasant resistance the army was without much mercy. Figes: "It has been estimated that 100,000 people were imprisoned or deported and 15,000 people shot during the suppression of the revolt." But villages which condemned the "bandits" were rewarded with special deliveries; there were also amnesty rules and a lot of paper propaganda, from which one could not eat.

continued and even extended in the framework of what was called the "New Democracy."[760]

Within industry, capitalist owners could maintain their leadership; they were supported and industry was not nationalized. After about 1955, more private ventures were transformed in the above mentioned *Kuan-tu shang-pan* type (state control by merchants), as was the typical feature of the Chinese beginning of industrialization around 1900. Capitalists received the next twenty years' interest on their investments; the rich had no complaints and the laborers accepted their secure but low wages. Notwithstanding the anti-imperialist rhetoric, the foreign technicians and large foreign firms already in China were encouraged to stay.

A last important element concerned the position of the bourgeoisie from before 1949: it received a place of honor in the urban discussions and its members could develop themselves as far as possible. From them and from the class of landlords was derived the "technical intelligentsia" that came into power around 1975.

This whole policy allows us to understand, first, the urban-countryside concept as Spence indicates well:

> Countryside and city each had its own social rhythms and political priorities. To cement the revolution in the rural areas, it was essential to institute some variety of land reform and to maintain the wide basis of peasant support that had brought the CCP to power.[761]

After the debates in the 1930s, a *theory of transformations* was adopted and put into practice: the bourgeois-capitalist period of industrialization was too short in China to establish a proper urban industrialization; it had to be extended. The other side of this coin was, of course that the more urban industrialization was enhanced, the more laborers from the countryside had to urbanize.

Urbanization had to be made attractive, but the food situation could not be endangered by the departure of the peasants and, therefore, the agricultural productivity in the countryside in general, required serious enhancement and reorganization.

This created the next problem: to introduce a basically urban technology into a rural environment and society. Mechanization of agriculture was introduced in a strong drive to keep in touch with urban industrialization and

760 For the following see Wilhelm Franke, ed., 1977, 65–66, S. Andors, p. 38 ff, 45 ff for the existing contradictions between top and base and between town and country in this period. See also Jonathan Spence, 1990, 486–487. and 514 ff.; John Roberts, 2011, 418ß419.

761 Jonathan Spence, 1990, 515, 516.

secure its rural market. But the distances between urban industry and rural markets were too large and, therefore, the industrialization had to be planned in a rather decentralized way over the largest possible number of cities and towns in China.

This latter policy was already an aim of the Kuomintang,[762] but it was not very successful in introducing industry in the Chinese inland. Shanghai remained by far the largest industrial city and from here the industrialization of the rest of China was organized.

The transformation of China as envisaged in this theory is debated furiously following the AMP-OD lines. Once the idea to urbanize and industrialize a country as vast as China was accepted, the dynamics of the transformation as sketched were quite realistic and equaled, for instance, the urban-rural market model of Slicher van Bath as mentioned in the beginning.

The practice was, of course, highly unruly and following the rather spectacular events such as land reforms of the early 1950s, the later *Great Leap*, the *Cultural Revolution* in the second half of the 1960s, the Deng Xiaoping period of the 1970s and 1980s or the present leadership of the "technical intelligentsia" and its rise to world power, all these developments concern basically the urban-rural transformations of vast populous China.

What European nations did over a period of 200 years, and largely paid for by the resources and profits from imperialism and colonialism, China had to do in about 50 years and alone, while permanently being criticized or otherwise hindered by all former imperialist powers including the Soviet Union, who lost in their attempt to encapsulate China from 1850–1945.

The urban-country thesis, which is already supported by the previous text, can be further discussed as follows.

8.9 Land Reform, 1950–1952

The first attempt to reorganize the countryside in the style of so-called Chinese "communism" resulted in a series of mostly administrative changes.[763]

There came a rather fixed class differentiation between (very) large landlords, large farmers, middle class peasants, poor peasants and land laborers. For theory and practice this differentiation was adopted so the Party and the state could more easily organize their support in the class struggle. However, for the agricultural production this division had little effect, because everything had

762 Wilhelm Franke, ed. 1977, 65.

763 See K. Buchanan, 1973, 117; W. Geddes, 1963, 56; Wilhelm Franke, ed. 1977, 17–18; John Roberts, 2011, Chapter 23.

to be avoided to minimize the economic performance of the (very) large and middle class farmers.

Whether the distribution among the poor of the land belonging to the (very) large landlords, including that of religious institutions like the northern monasteries, happened on such large scale as the propaganda suggested, remains to be seen. The fact is, that officially throughout the whole country land laborers got land as private property.

In many cases the production surplus of the very large landlords was given to the lowest classes as capital, while also houses, draft-animals, tools, etc. were distributed among the poorest. A new marriage law gave unmarried, divorced, or widowed women the right to hold land in their own names. Those who were unemployed in the cities and wanted to return to their homes could get land. For all these aims, it has been estimated that about 40 percent of the cultivated land was seized from landlords and redistributed and about 60 percent of the population benefited from these measures.

Politically, therefore, the land-reform was highly successful because the regime gained the support of the two lowest classes, the largest part of the population. Economically the changes were minimal and in some sense aggravated the problem of the too-small scale of the agricultural production.

This problem remained, sometimes going from bad to worst thanks to the new distributions; the production relations inside the small family households did not change either. Theoretically an improvement was achieved, because as usual the planners in Beijing had "forgotten" something: the vast differences in soil quality were not accounted for.

Further "forgotten" was an investigation into the rather important problem of the peasants who had their main income from non-agrarian sources. In a vast and densely populated country like China, the treatment, let alone solving, of even minor problems asks for a tremendous input of energy, money, and labor.

The food and related ecological problem was and is not a minor problem, but is, rather the *overriding* one, also in an urban and industrial world (one cannot eat cars, nor drink oil): if it also changes substantially by an annual increase of millions of mouths, it is unprecedented that the Chinese regime succeeded in the end (in the 1980s) to solve their basic food problem and probably the related ecological problem for a population that, by that time, reached one billion people.

The other ecological problem is largely related to the urban-industrialized environment and that is not (yet) solved. Together they probably document the present most serious contradiction between town and countryside in Chinese history to which I return in the last chapter.

Here continues the history of the several phases in which blood, sweat and tears were shed before astonishing results could be gained. The outer world judge (and still judges) them in the harshest terms. Even scholars who saw the light and hailed the Chinese government's food and countryside strategies, like Wim Wertheim, were criticized for supporting mass executions, ridiculous utopian experiments from birds catching to garden furnaces and "Red Book" maxims.

The unorthodox mass measures of, for instance, the rather ridiculous sparrow catchings[764] were important as means for mass mobilization and creating homogeneity in the many regions and many kinds of peoples in China.

They were also means for the spreading of practical knowledge, apart from the messages of the Party or Chairman Mao. That these movements were bloodless does not convince anybody, but no Chinese or foreigner can prove how many victims they claimed for the simple reason that no one has count them or reliably estimated them as in other cases.[765]

8.10 City Reform, 1950–1955

Young urban cadres often joined work teams in the countryside and experienced for the first time the characteristics of this kind of life. Their diaries demonstrate a new enthusiasm and excitement. This demonstration of the "unity of town and country" could not hide the serious problems in the cities.

Here, it was necessary to first prevent violent class struggles so that industries could be (re)opened and workers retain their jobs. But also other struggles had to be fought: against old and new organized crime that tried to (re)gain power positions in the newly erected trade unions. To fight these, the Party needed urban cadres, "but the CCP was short of cadres with urban backgrounds, and was often forced to rely on cadres from peasant families with little or no experience of city life."[766]

764 There is a very well documented and illustrated Chinese blog entitled "People respond to Mao Zedong's call to eliminate sparrows." See Yancai He's blog: sina.com.cn/s/blog_767384c30102vwb.html; 2015-11-25.

765 Compared to the 19th century with its nearly permanent bloody peasant revolts it must have been a very quiet Mao-period! Another consideration is: as far as I know, there is no memory of massacres among the present Chinese comparable with the genocidal activities of the Japanese in Nanjing from December 1937-February 1938 with an estimated 300,000 dead victims apart from 20,000–80,000 rapes. Jonathan Spence, 1990, 517 rightly writes about "anecdotal figures," but still mention these for some reason or other.

766 Jonathan Spence, 1990, 517.

Also in the cities the Party first had to rely on existing city bureaucrats to whom they guaranteed their jobs, along with those of teachers, police, etc. Gradually it organized small study groups at every level of the cities (districts, wards and streets) to teach the new vocabulary, and other groups who were busy with cleaning, water supply, health care, neighborhood conflicts, children's bookstores, public security and so on.

Thanks to these group activities prostitution and opium addiction were soon "under control" and, a bit later, dramatically reduced with enforced methods of "cold turkey" withdrawal and by making the (former) addicts' families responsible for their staying clean. Together the trade and production of opium was radically attacked through execution of opium traffickers or uprooting of poppy fields.

Again representatives of peasant cadres executed all these measures by mixing Party ideology with strong anti-urban feelings by stating that

> ...old Shanghai [was fully dependent] on the imperialist economy [and that] Shanghai is a non-productive city. It is a parasitic city. It is a criminal city. It is a refugee city. It is a paradise of adventurers.[767]

A senior government figure in the region, the head of the Shanghai Municipal Committee, the powerful veteran Rao Shushi, even suggested abandoning the whole city and replacing it, including its schools, factories and population, into the countryside. There it only have to produce for the internal market. This concerns the same anti-urbanism as documented during and after the Russian Revolution. The CCP did not follow these suggestion but it was symptomatic enough that this could be contemplated publicly.

Other tensions between city and countryside concerned the languages spoken: Mandarin (in the northern cities) against dialects in the southern cities and the countryside. This led to stubborn tensions, that exist still at present. Resentments of the lower cadres, who felt discriminated against relative to the (northern) bourgeoisie they thought they were going to oust, mixed with the language tensions and motivated anti-urbanism.

8.11 To the Present

Between 1955 and the present lies a period of serious conflicts in China. Inside China with its experienced traditions of revolutionizing turmoil, this is

767 Quoted by Jonathan Spence, 1990, 518.

perceived totally differently than in foreign countries, let alone anti-Chinese regions of the West. The only antidote against false propaganda in this dossier is to accept only provable sources, writings and declarations.

What happened during the recent tribunal concerning the "Pol Pot genocide" should be a good lesson, first, to rely on these kinds of sources and second, to make a crucial difference between historical truth and juridical truth. For the latter, limited elements are enough like good lawyers, the availability of a limited number of relevant laws, and an overdose of spectacular pictures/ publicity. This is not relevant for the force of conviction on both sides.[768]

For what happened during the *Great Leap Forward* and the *Cultural Revolution,* the same problem exists. The data Frank Dikötter and others produced as evidence look superficially "better" than that used in the Cambodia Tribunal case, but still cannot be checked by independent scholars.[769]

It is beyond the scope of my study to comment on juridical cases about victims in this terrible period. In the search for the historical truth, the following elements are relevant. Let's take Ho-fung Hung's recapitulation of the Mao period:

> ... [which] showed how the Communist party-state managed to extract and concentrate scattered rural surplus and build up an extensive network of state-owned urban industrial capital through rural collectivization and the "price scissors" between agricultural and industrial products during the Mao period... Though the peasants were chained to their villages by the household registration system, which restricted migration from their birthplaces, their life expectancy and literacy rate improved significantly as a result of state investment in rural elementary education and public health ...[770]

Town-country antagonisms (urban versus rural industries, etc.) were closely connected to market-*oikos* contradictions (household-registration, fixed prices, central planning, etc.). In the mid-1970s the remarkable growth momentum

768 For the international Cambodia tribunal which recently produced its last reports, the Dutch lawyer Victor Koppe had to defend "The Second Man" of the Pol Pot regime. In a recent long TV interview, Koppe's own report was broadcast. It was devastating for the leadership of the tribunal which only wanted to facilitate the previous publicity about the cruel Pol Pot regime was not interested in Koppe's insistence coming up with the proper proofs and arguments and not the new evidence Koppe and his assistants could provide.

769 For Frank Dikötter see my 2012, *passim.*

770 Ho-fung Hung, 2017, 54.

was exhausted, "but it left China with a bulk of state capital and a vast pool of healthy and educated surplus laborers in the countryside."[771]

After these rigorous oikoidal reforms concentrated on the most important Chinese asset, the countryside, post-Mao China embarked on similar market reforms concentrated on the city, very logically starting again in the countryside itself with: decollectivization and reconstruction of the peasant economy. This was followed by an urban-state enterprise and price reform in the 1980s. The effects are given in the following table.

On this solid basis an acceleration of the whole economy could be realized in the next decade without much risk, so that enterprises could be transformed into *profit-oriented* corporations as *State-Owned Enterprises* (SOEs). They could *not* be defined as "capitalist" in the sense discussed in Chapter 1: they were not capitalist productions (c.p.'s), but they started to become "capitalist" in the sense that they were transformed from state-*subsidized* companies into (mainly urban) companies that had to survive on their *own profitable performance*. If that could happen, capital-*ism* was realized in a piecemeal process, as defined for the West European situation in Chapter 1.

As this phase developed successfully, the risk was taken to establish capitalist production (c.p.'s) in special areas, in the form of *privately owned* companies. It was a brilliant idea to allow first only foreign companies in this genre, and to later expand to include Chinese private owners. Currently, countrywide, there exists a mix of SOEs and capitalist production (c.p.'s, domestic and foreign) mostly concentrated in the cities, which "accelerated" into mega-cities with all attendant consequences.

TABLE 6 China's progress in poverty reduction[a]

Year	Millions	% of total
1981	840	84
1990	689	61
2002	359	28
2011	84	6
30-year reduction	– 756	– 78 pp

* number and percent of people living on $1.25 a day or less

SOURCE: WORLD BANK POVERTY AND EQUITY DATABANK

771 Ho-fung Hung, 2017, 54.

At last, a more detailed example can demonstrate what is going on in the urban real estate scene and what the previous overview meant in the practice of combining market-*oikos* with town-country relations or vice versa.[772]

In 1998 the government allowed people to buy a house; this was another fundamental switch from collective to private property and certainly as complicated. Apparently, it concerned an attempt to make available the very substantial capital Chinese had saved, for production purposes, to boost the building industry, to develop urbanization i.e. to stimulate the migration from the countryside to the cities and, eventually, to solve several men-women-children difficulties like the one-child system. Whether these aims had been forecast or not, the possibility to buy a house had these far-reaching consequences.

Until that year, the local state-*Oikos* built the houses through state-run industry or SOEs, and distributed them via the local-state bureaucracy. In 1998 this *Oikos* extended the already large building market (which could be called a SOM, State Organized Market) to include a brand new private real-estate market (which could be called a PREM) with all its consequences.

This PREM did not function differently from the markets in London, Paris or New York: a game of private investors (with risky overinvestments or unforeseen new government decisions), private owners (nearly always with large debts), private builders (with risky investors), private tenants (without legal guarantee against eviction from a rented house; with owners who might not maintain their property or who suddenly increase the rent).

This new mixed real-estate market resulted in massive new residential areas directly outside the cities, built on free agricultural land and connected to the cities with a large number of new roads and highways. The very ugly towering apartment blocks also started to appear in the inner cities in spaces cleared of architecturally interesting historical quarters.

In 2008 the worldwide economic crisis broke out. Although China had few debts abroad, internally the government itself became a "risky investor." This happened as well with the Chinese private investors who often had their enormous profits reinvested abroad. The result was that the general productivity in China decreased after 2008, and the government started to introduce massive new oikoidal investment programs: local communities were urged to provide as much agricultural land as possible to transform into urban building land; the banks started to provide huge building credits and mortgages, the building boom was accelerated and prices doubled. Whether this was the smartest

772 For the following I used the article of Qu Lei and Marisa Carmona, in: Marisa Carmona, ed. 2003, 95–119; Ho-fung Hung, 2017, passim and Mathias Bölinger in *Die Zeit*, 12 October 2017, 28.

policy remains to be seen (a drastic decrease in rents and private mortgages accompanied by a substantial debt-clearance could have been another option).

The big cities reacted with new demands: people who wanted to become private owners of a house had to provide at least half of the required capital from their own pocket; more than one house per family was disallowed; private investors reacted with strong increases of their prices: mortgages and rents; and large numbers of tenants and private owners disappeared to the countryside when they could not pay their debts anymore.

An investigation by the University of Economy and Finances in Chengdu (southwestern China) concluded two years ago that a "quarter of the housing stock" was empty; even in booming Beijing one-fifth of the available accommodation was not used, and the substantial incomes of the communities from selling building sites had seriously decreased. The PREM is now the most serious problem of the Oikos: nearly every intervention of the latter in the former will lead to serious repercussions.

Ho-fung Hung's book, *The Chinese Boom,* has a picture of a flattened balloon on the cover (and a text I shall comment on later), which is a logical image. In all probability, it is an overly pessimistic picture as well: in the past three-quarters of a century, the Chinese have proved convincingly that they understand the complications of socio-economic processes better than Western economists and are able to solve them: regardless of the costs!

PART 4

*Toward a Market–*Oikos *Theory*

CHAPTER 9

Old Market-*Oikos* Theories

9.1 An Old Debate About New Questions

In order to "hit" at the central theme of this book and the China-option, it is possible to consult a search engine. An alternative is to consult the China blogs available in most Western countries and find how, for instance, that the relationship China-capitalism is commented on vehemently.

Apart from the continuous astonishment about the Olympic Games (2008) or the spectacular urban building programs in Beijing, Shanghai and many other Chinese cities, it seems as if journalists, business people, bankers or politicians and diplomats write their impressions, profit and investment analysis, warnings and criticisms all on one subject: booming Chinese *capitalism* is the "awakening giant" taking over power from "the West" within a period of a decade or so. Nobody cares about proper definitions and most people think of capitalism as "something with/about huge amounts of money." This is probably the least important element now that money is threatened with being transformed into bitcoins!

Sometimes remarkable information is given in between the lines. Take for example the website *Beijing Made Easy!*[773] In between information for people looking for a Chinese hotel, or flight and travel data, it is possible to find something about one of our main concerns, the relationship between religion-capitalism.

Under the heading: "Chinese Religion and Philosophy" the traveler is first informed that "Chinese beliefs have always been Chinese more than they have been part of any one religion or philosophy." The implications of this ambiguous point of view are numerous, for instance, that the Chinese in town and country have not had a very close relation with one particular belief system (like Confucianism, Buddhism, Daoism, etc.) while looking first and foremost to the practical sides of Chinese daily life.

Or, a Chinese judges spirituality with criteria beyond this kind of thoughts. Or, in the shortest possible way: practicality and materialism rules over theory and spirituality. It is at least logical that this implies as well that the official state doctrine, socialism, is not a belief system but a set of practical rules about how to organize life in China; it would be a most interesting definition.

773 It is, alas, not to discover who or which institution acts as the publisher of this website, which has to make people automatically suspicious. In this case, it does not matter much.

 | DOI:10.1163/9789004383913_010

Pragmatically, therefore, one should judge the Chinese "religious" performance. If true, it is not a surprise that this website continues:

> This aspect will no doubt continue to be seen in the future as older beliefs adjust, and absorb the new ethos of capitalism and the growing influence of Christianity and Islam. Modern Chinese appear at first sight to have forgotten about religion and philosophy in the drive to get rich quick. Most of the traditional centers of religion—Confucian, Buddhist and Daoist temples—have either disappeared or turned into tourist attractions. Most Chinese are ... focusing on... how to create a stable society... This is unsurprising when you consider that the CCP has spent most of the past 50 years telling people that religion is mumbo-jumbo superstition and trying to supplant traditional beliefs with a philosophy combining Socialism and a great deal of patriotism... The government's switch to "Socialism with Chinese Characteristics" (code for naked capitalism, without the loss of face that dropping the socialist rhetoric would imply) has left a religious and spiritual vacuum that has yet to be filled.

Filled with what? According to official statistics Islam now has about 15 million adherents among the 1.3 billion Chinese, Christianity around 7 million; about the traditional belief systems I have no statistics; there seems also to be a few hundred Chinese Jews.

A first conclusion: quantitatively religion does not play a role of any significance in present day China. Indeed, a recent learned study about China by a well-known Marxist sociologist writes about a typical 18th century Scottisch calvinist economist, Adam Smith, as being like a "typical Chinese" of the 21st century and mentions "religion" not at all (and mentions Max Weber, the theorist of Calvinism and capitalism with stories about China, two times in passing).[774]

That cannot be the whole answer as, for instance, Max Weber's interesting analysis of Chinese religion reveals, or what history proves of the attempts of Christian religions, cultural expressions of Western civilization *and* its imperialism, to convert China. Below we have to return, albeit superficially, to this theme because it reveals much about the historical and present frictions between "China and the West."

But what about "capital*ism*" as the typical Weber feature: is there a relationship with this and Chinese "socialism" (let alone a non-existing communism)? The travelers' website even suggests that something like the present Chinese

774 Giovanni Arrighi, 2007; friends and foes describe this book in their reviews as "meager."

formula "socialism with Chinese characteristics" is simply a code for "naked capitalism"! Since the Chinese authorities allowed "Western capitalism" to settle, first, in industrial parks separated from ordinary society after Deng Xiaoping came in power, there seems some ground for this suggestion.

That seems only to be the case if one is prepared to define capitalism in the way it is done in Chapter 1, as the oikoidal variant of the combination state + private monopoly, but that is not the case with the authors of the travelers' website. If one should stick to the definition used there for capitalist production (c.p.) one arrives at highly difficult and much debated interpretations of Chinese history, and finds the start of the discussions to be about the so-called *Asian Mode of Production* (AMP) and the *Oriental Despotism* (OD). These debates have a long history as will be discussed and one can learn many interesting things of them, but one can question their relevance for a more or less sound assessment of the present Chinese situation versus "the West." Let's comment briefly on this last relation.

These remarks concerning religion-socialism-capitalism have much in common with classical left wing debates about the role of Zionism-socialism-Judaism. Thanks to a serious lack of historical studies among sociologists, political theorists and philosophers they too often defend defenseless matters like a left wing basis of Zionist nationalism or of Israel as a socialist democracy surrounded by feudal Arab potentates who had the backing of both reactionary European conservatives and the oil companies of monopoly capitalism.

It happened even that a "Marxist-Zionist" (whatever that may be) theorist like Shlomo Avineri combined Marx, Hegel and a critique of (colonial) capitalism to defend the Zionist settlers, using the framework of the Oriental Despotism and the Asiatic Mode of Production to criticize Arab feudalism and its role in creating a despotic state as in India or China, and as primitive compared to modern Zionism/ Israel. It was a replica of the older theory of "proletarian Zionism" (Borochov in the 1930s) and the ridiculous identification of Judaism with Zionism.

But also in the camp of the Zionists' enemies, too many intellectual groups used the same reasoning and sources to legitimate and support their case. Like the Zionists in the 1930s, the Pan-Arabist and other Arab nationalists in several corners of the Middle East also changed colors from support for the British or French to supporting their German enemy and competitor: they also adopted German romantic *Volk* and State/Nation ideologies ("organic nation-state"), adored Nazi-leaders and their performance.[775]

775 One of their main ideologues, Al-Husri, went so far that he "fused the German concept of the nation with the Arabic concept of 'group solidarity' (*asabiyya*), which he derived

Arab nationalism was first and foremost directed to the Turkish part of the Ottoman Empire, later to the Young Turks of Kemal Ataturk. This Ottoman Empire was, for all at the time the ideal-typical example of an Oriental Despotism.

In addition the concept of an Asiatic mode of production is, notwithstanding many reservations, accepted by Middle Eastern scholars like Ayubi as an ideal-type or abstract category of comparison (pointing mainly to socio-economic formations with "absence or weakness of private land-ownership and the powerful role of the state"). He, however, extended its scope strongly by "taking account of another mode of production that was never far away from any Arab society, the hydraulic or agricultural ones included: that is the 'nomadic' kin-ordered mode of production."[776] It is inevitable that Ayubi directly refers to the writings of Ibn Khaldun, his analysis of the contradictions between *bedu* and *badawa* (nomads and nomadism) versus *hadar* and *hadara* (urbanites and urbanity/civilization). This is important and not only because I analyzed this same contradiction in Chinese history.[777]

So, all the controversial subjects are mentioned above including the town-country relations that are of the utmost importance to understand the course of Chinese history at least as Mao Zedong himself understood in his alleged anti-urbanism,[778] mistrust of Soviet (read "city-centered") notions of how to build a socialist society, reliance on the peasant masses in several stages of the Maoist revolution or the famous foreign policy axiom of Lin Biao that the (Chinese) Country, in the end, will conquer the (Western) City. How important town-country relations are is also demonstrated on the micro-level of the life of village and factory women in present China.[779]

From Karl Marx, the most beloved wise man after Mao, many Chinese know (or at least knew) how important the town-country relationship is, that is, if the dazzling urbanization China experiences and the revaluation of the agrarian countryside does not impress them. Together with Indian urbanization

from Ibn Khaldun, and proceeded to develop his own 'pure' theory of nationalism." N. Ayubi, 1995, 139. The paradoxes in history are remarkable: it is this move which the Zionists Margalit and Buruma "mislead" to accuse Ibn Khaldun of making a pure Blood and Soil theory and to start ruffling the Holocaust drum to mobilize The West against the East and, of course, be silent about Zionist massacres or war crimes. See historian Benny Morris' writings about the *Nakba* and his conclusion that the Zionists missed the chance to murder all the Palestinians or see also the well spread opinions of the military historian and "father of the Israeli wall against the Palestinians," Martin van Creveld quoted in HA, 2004, 245, 246.

776 N. Ayubi, 1995, 48, 49.

777 Hans Derks, 1999.

778 R. Kirkby, 1985, 1–21.

779 Laurel Bossen, 2002; Anita Chan et al., 2009.

they are largely responsible for the situation that, a few month ago situated the world, for the first time in its long history, with 51% townspeople and 49% country dwellers.

It is in the European 19th century that all important political economists and other scholars pointed to this relationship as the most basic in society. Karl Marx, like his inspirations, Adam Smith and Hegel, wrote:

> The basis of all developed and through goods exchange connected division of labor is the separation of town and country. One can say, that the whole of the economic history of society is summarized in this movement...[780] [And twenty-two years earlier, in the *German Ideology*, he was more or less of the same opinion:]... The largest division of the material and spiritual labor is the separation of town and country. This contradiction between town and country starts with the transition from barbarism into civilization, from the tribal society into the state, from the locality into the nation...[781]

The important historian of the town-country relations, the agrarian historian Bernhard Slicher van Bath, turns us from our head back on our feet with the necessary details for at least European history like the following:

> There is an interaction between the birth and growth of towns and the degree of agricultural development in the country around them... In the vicinity of great towns and in thickly populated regions, "islands" are formed where agriculture stands at a higher level than in the surrounding countryside... The growth of a non-agrarian urban population means that farming in the vicinity of towns has begun to be commercialized. The peasants supply the townsfolk with all sorts of agricultural commodities, for which they receive money. With it they buy some of the town's industrial products such as cloth, linen, ironware, furniture, leather goods, etc. A local market for agricultural produce grows up. In this market, the price levels are of great significance; they are formed at the point where supply meets demand. As soon as imports from Eastern Europe are added, an international market is established...[782]

780 Karl Marx, 1971, 373.

781 Karl Marx, 1953, 379. It is remarkable that F. Braudel, vol. 1, p. 479 still support Marx but mixed both quotations!

782 Bernard Slicher van Bath, 1963, Chapter 2.

Compared to the Marx quotation, this is the one which provides the better indication of the complicated relations (peaceful interactions as well as conflicting contradictions) between town and country. Slicher van Bath develops this into a model, from the points of view of the agrarians, which we have to use and keep in mind when making below (a too short!) assessment of the role of town country relations in Chinese history. The old European theory or better, ideological fixation of an "urban-rural distinction as continuum," that we will meet as well in the interpretation of Chinese history,[783] is negated in the above quotation.

To cover a history of the relationship religion-capitalism-Chinese town/country is a complicated affair. Yet, it is unavoidable to highlight another very important background for the following history. Like the Zionist settlers' history, the following one fits perfectly in the expansion of Western imperialism because it is, in the most direct and shocking way, related to what was called, from about 1870 onwards, the *Far Eastern Problem.*

This existed long before: it was largely confined to attempts from all imperialist sides (mainly British, but with important roles for France, Germany, Japan and Soviet Russia) to knock down that most populated and nearly the biggest country in the world, China, and to the attempts of all these imperialists to knock each other down to get the largest slice of the Chinese cake. It is a problem that is, of course, closely related to all other imperialist, ethnic and class conflicts that show clear involvement of the highly belligerent Western elite.[784]

It is remarkable that in the present discussions about the role of China, there is nearly never any referrence to the serious *failures* of this Western imperialism to "open up" China and Japan for their products, policies, Christianity, culture, and so on in the 19th and first half of the 20th centuries. These two countries were perceived automatically as "closed," a term that became synonymous for backward, primitive and, of course, pagan.

783 See Daniel Faure and T. Liu, ed., 2002, 2.

784 For the endless and most cruel wars fought in the "glorious days" of imperialist policies (the 150 years after the Napoleonic Wars) also of other European countries everywhere in the world see Sandra Halperin, 2004, 136–145. From about 1795 to 1945 she provides the data of nearly hundred of these imperialist conflicts outside Europe (Extraregional Imperialist Conflicts Involving European Powers, 308) which is a conservative estimate. She also gives the data for imperialist conflicts *inside* Europe—about 46 cases—and rightly argues that both kinds of conflicts were closely related to the nearly 200 class conflicts and 125 ethnic conflicts inside Europe in the same period. All these are exclusive of the two world wars in this period! Together the Western elites in the 19th and early 20th centuries are responsible for an unbelievable continuous internal and external war. See also Hans Derks, 2012, 82–83, 208–209, 319–320, 414–415, 493, 559.

Anthony Pagden perfectly reproduces present ambiguous thinking. He tells that he does not write history in these terms, but still thinks he knows how to think globally without reference to China and India with their own histories that went in quite different directions. He still thinks that Western civilization "has now reached, almost, into the furthermost recesses of the world"[785] and is satisfied with it: the former barbarian from a remote time in which "his only concern has been war and its spoils" has later produced a civilization worthy enough to conquer the world!

In Pagden's perception Europeans had only two remaining competitors at the end of the 18th century, China and the Ottoman empire.[786] It is well-known how the *Eastern Question* lead to the destruction of this last empire, how this was divided up between the British and French intruders, the Zionist settler society was created and that afterwards a Middle Eastern region was left ploughed by the one war after the other, with Israel ever increasing in (re) armaments without any relevant material or cultural emancipation of its populations and an abortive Western enclave structured as an arsenal full of weapons of mass destruction guarded by an intransigent and aggressive military.[787]

For the "solving" of the *Far Eastern Problem* the same scenario was started as we will see and the relevant question arises: is the Western culture able to do something different than making endless wars in Europe and everywhere else in the world? Probably the confrontations between China and the Western powers in the past can give us a relevant hint for an answer.

This Chinese *Far Eastern problem* did not existed in the beginning of the 18th century as the Portuguese had only a trading post in Macao in the south of China and the Russians were permitted to send merchants to Beijing at regular intervals. The only ones who had secured their Asian place were the Dutch in the East Indies and the Spanish in the Philippines. After 1720 foreigners could trade directly with specific Chinese firms (*cohong*) in Canton only; about 250 years later a similar allowance was given to the Western capitalists to settle there with factories.

At the end of the 18th century, the Europeans, eager to extend their markets, became annoyed with the East and anxious "to open" it. The rising European competition between nations compelled the British to take the first hostile and aggressive steps against China. One of the first meetings between

785 Anthony Pagden, 2002, 176.

786 Anthony Pagden, 2002, 160.

787 How ruthless Zionist Israeli militaries are is perfectly documented *by themselves* in two movies. The first is called *The Gatekeepers*, 2012, directed by Dror Moreh (six interviews with heads of Israeli secret services) and *Zero Days*, 2016, directed by Alex Gibney, about the "digital need" to attack Iran.

the Chinese leadership, the emperor and his staff, and a representative of an European power, the British lord George Macartney (1793), was immediately "to the point" for

> ...his celebrated refusal to perform the traditional kowtow before the emperor... a measure of his conviction that what he looked upon as a suspicious, introverted civilization could not long resist the raw power of free trade—nor ultimately... the power of western technology.[788]

The answer of the Chinese emperor to the English king is worth repeating here as well:

> We have never valued ingenious articles, nor do we have the slightest need of your country's manufactures. Therefore, O king, as regards your request to send someone to remain at the capital, while it is not in harmony with the regulations of the Celestial Empire we also feel very much that it is of no advantage to your country.

What was to "celebrate" in Macartney's behavior was nothing but the arrogance of the stupid[789] and that not only in hindsight: in 1793 the British had nothing to offer to China but brutality, having lost, in those days, their largest colony in the Americas; the French Revolution definitely undermined their monarchy and aristocracyand a fierce industrial competition had started elsewhere in Europe.

And militarily? Well, during the 1790–1804 war of independence in Haiti, one of the largest English defeats ever, an army of 100,000 men and a large

788 Anthony Pagden, 2002, 161; for the answer of emperor Qianlong see Jonathan Spence, 1990, 200 and John Roberts, 2011, 243. The latter quoted, 253, also John Quincy Adams, former president of the USA, who pointed (December 1841) to this *kotow* as the cause of the Opium War: " ... the arrogant and insupportable pretensions of China that she will hold commercial intercourse with the rest of mankind, not upon terms of equal reciprocity, but upon the insulting and degrading forms of relation between lord and vassal."

789 The man, who had to negotiate with the Chinese emperor, wrote in his diary: "The Empire of China is an old, crazy, first rate man-of-war ... she may drift some time as a wreck, and will then be dashed to pieces on the shore ...." Quoted in John Roberts, 2011, 224. It was an opinion commonly expressed in many Western histories. Roberts still concludes: "The imperial system of government and the economy and culture which had developed under its aegis had come to the end of its effective life," 224. That there is debate about opinions like this (as he himself writes) is no reason to change this conclusion.

French fleet were crushed by the "Black Napoleon," Toussaint l'Ouverture, and other black leaders.[790]

It was the first time that the terrible repression of the West was avenged and even this event was not enough for the British aristocratic elite, here represented by a Lord Macartney to moderate itself or keep its big mouth shut: no, in the coming 19th and early 20th centuries the British and other imperialists demonstrated arrogance in a most exuberant way, the way of self-destruction.

Anyway, the advice of the Chinese emperor received a convincing empirical support: the mutual confrontation was in the end "of no advantage to your country" in the sense that the Chinese apparently did not need products made in Britain or elsewhere in Western Europe on some scale until Deng Xiaoping came to power! But did this first meeting lead to the advantage of the Chinese?[791]

After this first rather "innocent" diplomatic confrontation between the emperor and the lord came, however, a series of lethal events in the next and the 20th century in which the typical European imperial *claims culture* not only led to the one war after the other, or the settlement of expatriates in isolated corners of the East. Because opium was one of the most important trading products of the West, the first wars were opium-wars that resulted in the large scale doping of the indigenous populations in China, India and Southeast Asia mainly by the British, French and Dutch (colonial) governments.

No, these "foreign devils" were not very advantageous, to use an understatement, to the Asians, and they required an effective "exorcism." This happened in one country better than in an other, but the history under this perspective is not yet well known: what the historiography provides are, nearly without exception, products of a victorious Western culture, which leads to a dangerous unrealistic overestimation of its performance in the "Far Eastern problem" area.

The following historical reflection is, therefore, one *demonstrating the limits of Western capacities*, but in a very different way than in the horrible *Near Eastern problem:* when in about twenty years rather automatically the energy problem will be solved in the sense that "everybody drives on electricity" and the (oil) value of the Middle East will have been decreased near to nil. That is to say: many new ruins popular with future tourists and archeologists of the next

790 See my article on this revolution in Hans Derks, ed., 1989, 91–95.

791 Hans Derks, 2012, 82–86 and Part VI.

millennium have been created! I am afraid that this scenario remains impossible with the *Far Eastern problem,* as it was called around 1900.[792]

The superficial facts about the rise of Japan or the first imperialistic steps in Asia of both the young Soviet Union and the USA may be known[793] and reproduced in some relevant maps in *The Times* historical atlas, but in the details one has to look for the "foreign devils" as will be demonstrated later in the historical analysis of the most important part of the *Far Eastern problem,* the Chinese. Whatever its merits, it must remain brief.

Therefore, to systematize it I refer, first, to the most important intellectual debate concerning this *Far Eastern problem,* the more or less theoretical analysis of the AMP-OD discussions, after which we can better see how relevant the town-country relations in Chinese history are relative to the present interaction on global level between the "Western Capitalism" and the "Eastern Socialism/Communism."

9.2 A "Mode of Despotism"?

The best impression of the two main intellectual political economic perceptions of China in the West, the *Asiatic Mode of Production* (AMP) and the *Oriental Despotism* (OD), can be gotten from debates in the 1930s among many outspoken left-wing intellectuals, organizations and even countries, many of which became, after 1945, anti- left wing proponents and examples. Still Pagden referred to post-1949 China as "an example of 'Oriental despotism,' of all that was most damaging to the human spirit…"![794]

Most important among the first in this dossier is the sinologist and historian Karl August Wittfogel, 1896–1988, who not only changed his political position in a fundamental way, his substantial intellectual insights changed as well between the AMP and OD. He, furthermore, chose as his leading spirit in the first case, Karl Marx, and in the second, Max Weber. As a member of the German Communist Party of around 1925, he also participated in the most influential

792 Here older publications are much more interesting than the very few modern one's. It is symptomatic that if one "googles" the words "Far Eastern Problem" one gets first and foremost 1925 publications (Woodhead, Soyeshima), which are rather difficult to obtain. However, in old editions of well-known encyclopedias, much information can be found. Take, for instance the long article of N. Peffer with only references to literature of around 1900–1935, among others also Karl Wittfogel, 1931.

793 See N. Peffer, 95–97; Hans Derks, ed., 1989, 164–169 for Japan or 225–248 for Russia/Soviet Union.

794 Anthony Pagden, 2002, 162.

Institute of Social Research of Adorno and Horkheimer, while he later became a well-known proponent of the intellectual Cold War fighters and the historian of "hydraulic societies."

It is this among other elements in his biography and writings that made him, indeed, an "ideal-typical" representative of the schizophrenic positions taken by the West for or against China, a mindset with a long history and that continues to influence or haunt our present interpretations and ideological positions vis-à-vis China, its culture, dominant economic position and fears for its bright future.

Its main political background was given in the 1920s as Lenin painted a bright picture of the continuous global struggles in which "we" (Russia) could gain the first great victory thanks to the contradictions between the main imperialist powers of the West and those of the East, namely the United States and Japan. The answer to the next question, of whether "we" will get a second of such opportunity, was:

> This question should be answered, thus: that the outcome depends on too many circumstances and the end of the struggle, generally understood, can only be forecast in the sense that the enormous majority of the world's population will be made fit and educated for the struggle by capitalism itself. This last resort is decisive in the struggle, that in Russia, India, China, etc., the largest majority of the earth's population live. It is this majority which in recent years and very quickly, has become involved in its [own] liberation movement, so that in this perspective without any doubt, the end decision in the world struggle is determined. In this sense the victory of socialism shall be complete and definitive...[795]

As such it is a forecast that has historical value specifically today. Lenin's companions as well as his direct enemies are all dead and buried. Not long ago, however, in the course of the debates about Lenin's perspective up until today, Wittfogel and the concepts AMP and OD are vehemently discussed, criticized or thrown into the "dustbin of history" One cannot deny, therefore, that Wittfogel was a "good medium" and the concepts at issue are fascinating as was the case with, for instance, Max Weber's and Sombart's theories about the relationship religion-capitalism-double entry bookkeeping.

Time and again, Weber and Sombart were discussed by the AMP and OD debaters (see below). The relevant bibliography covers many hundreds of titles, but there are only a few who understand the dialectics of the factual, armed

795 Quoted in Iring Fetscher, ed., 1973, 735.

struggles (please read first André Malraux's *La Condition Humaine*, 1933) as well as the theoretical performance. A most remarkable fact is, that within these complicated debates and permanently changing struggles no one made the comparison between Wittfogel defending the AMP and Wittfogel defending the OD.[796] That is done below after a short impression of the dialectic of debates and bloody struggles.

In the USSR, the years after 1917 were filled with the bloody events of the civil war and later people were very busy to revolutionize, in theory and practice, the agrarian way of life in the direction of an urban, industrial one, Russian peasants had to be changed into Soviet laborers, rural communities had to be transformed into cities, rural handicrafts should be replaced by (urban) machine labor, and so on.

Serious theoretical problems had to be mastered as well concerning things like: why should it be evident that all historical developments are always directed to the negation of agricultural labor and communities in favor of urban, industrial social formations? Why should it be necessary that the urban proletariat should take the lead in the class struggles over the peasants here and abroad (this question directed very often to Asia, and China in particular)? Is historical development truly characterized by the sequence: primitive society, ancient slaveholders' society, feudalism, capitalism, socialism? How shall we understand "nature" in the context of an industrialized agriculture under socialist conditions? What means should be used to bring about the envisaged changes in society? And so on.

The first question was handled in European-wide debates about the "Agricultural Question" (*Agrarfrage*) and in so-called "Industrialization debates"; from a different point of view the same questions were discussed in the debates between the "urbanists and de-urbanists." The second question led to serious conflicts inside and outside the Comintern concerning how to wage an international class struggle and how to interpret several imperialism theories.

The next question led to substantial historical and economic debates about the nature of feudalism, the transformation problematic, new interpretations of Russian and Chinese history and the role of an urban proletariat in history; in short: the relevance of historical materialism was at stake. The "factor

796 See, for instance, N. Ayubi, 1995, 41. I must confess that the best example of this "misunderstanding" is regretfully my old friend Wim Wertheim, 1972, 32–35, who therefore largely inspired me to study Chinese history. See also 511 note 44 for an interpretation of Wittfogel which cannot be found in Karl Wittfogel, 1962, 171.

nature" was the focus of debate in the interpretations of dialectical materialism by its critics.[797]

At last the debates about the means that should be used to bring about the envisaged social and economic changes led to further debates and conflicts about revolution, the role of the state, bureaucracy, central planning, and so on.

The relevancy of the AMP debate is mainly that all those questions and their discussions became focused on "the development of Asia," making this debate highly complicated, but also intellectually much more important than all those separate debates. The AMP theory explicity concerned the above-mentioned second, third and last questions, while it implicitly concerned the debate about agrarianism versus industrialization. The "nature" debate remained at that time on the sidelines, but today it has probably come to the fore topic with debates about climatic change, environmental deterioration, etc. Let's give a short explication.

Trotsky has used the AMP theory in his criticism of Stalinism, the mushrooming bureaucracy and his reconstruction of Tsarist history, in the same way as later European student-leaders of the 1968s did (Dutschke, Bahro). The "eastern despotic" elements of this history are stressed, such as the absence of (real) medieval cities, in which handicrafts and civil freedom could flourish. By analogy of this history, Trotsky made far-reaching conclusions concerning Stalinist Russia.

This criticism did not have much practical consequences for Russian living conditions, though that cannot be gleaned from the debates in the Comintern. The choice of allies in the international class struggle was largely dependent on the interpretations of the AMP. In the next Table 6 the two positions are compared; it is important to mention that in the end, the AMP was negated by Stalin and the Chinese Communist Party in 1930. The practical political engagement determined to a large extent also the interpretation of European history. At last it should be remarked that in this period Wittfogel was one of the main advisors of the Comintern.

The table presents the "Asiatic structure" and the party that develops its argument from its interpretation of Asian history; "Feudal structure" develops its argument from an universal (but in fact European) theory of history.

797 Famous were debates between Deborin, Bucharin and others about the importance of biological knowledge and the environment for society: "Does society exist in an equilibrium with nature (*Gleichgewicht mit der Natur*)? Wich kind of balance: one that is static or dynamic: first a balance, next an undermining of this balance, followed by a restoration of the balance and this sequence as continuum? See Iring Fetscher, ed., 1973, 136–141.

TABLE 6 "Asiatic" and "Feudal" structures used in the debates around 1930

"Asiatic Structures"	"Feudal Structures"
1. supported by Trotsky, Rjazanof, Varga, e.o.	1. supported by Stalin, Mao, Bucharin, Comintern.
2. based on some Marx' theory of the AMP.	2. based on Marx'-Engels' theory of the transformation of feudalism into capitalism.
3. *interpretation of Chinese history*: a. absence of private property of the land; b. no feudal land owners; c. powerful aristocratic bureaucracy; d. weak urban development and, therefore, weak urban proletariat; e. autonomous urban bourgeoisie is absent. f. large hydraulic works made through an authoritarian state; g. strong community systems.	3. *interpretation of Chinese history*: a. private property of land is present; b. there are still (1930) "Pockets of Feudalism"; c. was not discussed; d. urban (industrial) proletariat has to cooperate with e. national bourgeoisie. f. is not true. g. "splintered," isolated village communities.
4. *political—strategic consequences:* a. the struggle must be waged *against* the alliance of bourgeoisie + imperialism + bureaucracy (incl. the crafts- and tradesmen who are working for these bureaucrats); b. the struggle must be waged *by* the alliance of urban proletariat + the "masses of peasants"; c. therefore there must come an alliance between town and country.	4. *political—strategic consequences:* a. the struggle must be waged *against* the alliance of foreign imperialists + "pockets of feudalism"; b. the struggle must be waged *by* an alliance of national bourgeoisie + urban proletariat (Kwo-mintang + CP China); c. therefore there must come a struggle of town against country.

For our discussion, one can conclude that for the 1930s, the theory of the AMP was used as a legitimation of political-strategic positions; that within "left-wing" circles there are at least two possible interpretations of the theory of the AMP; that the theory is used to support an urban, industrial political economy at the cost of agrarian social formations; and that, therefore, the theory of the AMP is in the end a modernization theory related to the town-country contradictions.

In China there was traditionally a substantial interest in economic matters as we will see below, but in the People's Republic after 1948, three broad areas received the most attention: "land tenure, foreign imperialism and 'the sprouts of capitalism.' In the post-Mao era, the 'Asiatic Mode of Production' was added to this list."[798]

Land tenure concerned issues of servitude among peasants; imperialism, of course, with the plundering of Chinese resources by foreigners; the third theme focused on the signs of development since the mid-sixteenth century (expansion handicraft, freeing peasant labor), while the new interest in the AMP in the 1980s

> …highlighted the dilemma of Chinese Marxist historians: how to fit Chinese history into the scheme of world history … it helped to legitimize China's recent economic policies, which may seem to transgress the stages of history normally posited in the Marxist scheme of history.[799]

It is, therefore, worthwhile to comment further on the history of AMP and OD, so that our own framework can become clearer.

9.3 The European Ancestors

Friend and foe referred to Karl Marx, but at the time his early writings (*Frühschriften*) had just been published (1932) and were not well studied; his *Foundations of the Critique of Political Economy* (*Grundrisse*), with major contributions to historical materialism, was published in 1939 but studied in the 1960s. The opening of his *Ethnological Notebooks*, with its many references to socio-economic circumstances in Asia, had even to wait another thirteen years (1973). The above table, therefore, belongs to Marx*ism* and only in a limited way to a Marx-tradition. What belonged to this tradition?

Historically, a theory of the AMP is derived from a series of prejudices, more or less founded on the opinions of travelers (Bernier) and scholars (Montesquieu, Adam Smith or Hegel) about non-Western peoples who, of course, were consequently qualified as barbarians, primitives, despotic, and

798 T. Rawski, L. Li, ed., 2.

799 T. Rawski, L. Li, ed., 3.

were considered as "racially less-valued" until Japanese began building better cars than Americans.

A largely misunderstood Aristotle is perceived to be the father of all these discriminating opinions, so detrimental to the images of Ottoman Turkey with Osmanli Sultan at his head (the "Grand Seignior" as Machiavelli, Bodin or Harrington called him).[800] Later Mughal India came into the orbit of an Oriental fixation of West European intellectual and political *juste milieus* until in the end also Japan and China are incorporated in this far from innocent play of words. Nobody cares about the sources but merely repeats a predecessor, who already wrongly quoted his ancestors.

Take a famous intellectual such as Perry Anderson who rightly referred to Aristotle, but could not mention the right source[801] and came up with a (in fact ideologically) distorted translation. Many of his predecessors did the same! Something must be said about this Aristotle. Is he really the bad guy who legitimated the West's lethal xenophobia or, with "the central canonical passage" (Anderson), is, therefore, also the source of the theory of Oriental Despotism?[802]

In his *Problems,* Aristotle poses several hundreds questions related to many kinds of disciplines or subjects (Why is it that some animals are prolific ..? Why are those who live in warm regions more cowardly or wiser than those who dwell in cold regions? Etc.) whereupon he *suggests* one or more answers that are clearly not meant as definite, but that are later often taken as such.[803] And it is not his purpose (nor of all normal Greeks) to use "barbarians" as primitive people, but only as *foreigners* (see the above discussion about *metics*).[804]

However, translators chose too often the "barbarian" alternative and wrote the much quoted sentence from the first book of *Politics* (1252b5-10) as:

800 For the following see Perry Anderson, 1974, 462.

801 Perry Anderson, 463 note 3, refers to Aristotle *Politics*, III, ix,3 but this has to be III, xiv, 20 ff. or 1285a, 19–25 . He, furthermore, produces a flawed text.

802 How Aristotle is also distorted by philosophical types like Martha Nussbaum see my, 1995–1, who did not discover the large differences between a christianized and a Greek Aristotle.

803 Aristotle, *Works,* edition Jonathan Barnes, 1984, volume 2, 1319–1528. The questions on "the effect of locality on temperament," 1412 ff. are the most popular. In my view they aim at provoking the pupils or listeners in his peripatetic school to think. It is to be hoped, anyway, that he did not believe the often nonsensical content of some suggested answers.

804 He once used, 1149a11, "some distant foreigners" to indicate that they could be foolish in case of epilepsy, etc. Therefore, "distant" should be better translated as "far away" in the meaning of "out of their mind."

> But among barbarians no distinction is made between women and slaves, because there is no natural ruler among them: they are a community of slaves, male and female. That is what the poets say: *It is meet that Hellenes should rule over barbarians*, as if they thought that the barbarian and the slave were by nature one.[805]

"Slave" in these and other Greek texts seldom meant "(Chattel)slave," who lived among the Romans but not in Greek societies. Aristotle points to servile, uncritical people concerning those who are in political power: they are absent in Greece, he thinks in an optimistic mood; a Greek is an "autonomous person" and opinionated, which is in fact the result of his (former) nomadic life.[806] When Aristotle is writing about the nature of tyranny he also tells us, for instance:

> There is another sort of monarchy not uncommon among foreigners, which nearly resembles tyranny. But this is both legal and hereditary. For foreigners, being more servile in character than Hellenes, and Asiatics [more so] than Europeans, do not rebel against a despotic government. Such kingships have the nature of tyrannies because the people are by nature slaves; but there is no danger of their being overthrown, for they are hereditary and legal. For the same reason, their guards are such as a king and not such as a tyrant would employ, that is to say, they are composed of citizens, whereas the guards of tyrants are mercenaries. For kings rule according to law over voluntary subjects, but tyrants over involuntary; and the one are guarded by their fellow-citizens, the other are guarded against them. (1285a, 19–28).

A few lines further, the necessary additional information is given (1295a10):

> Among barbarians there are elected monarchs who exercise a despotic power; despotic rulers were also elected in ancient Greece…[807]

805 How to understand this not in such an apodictic way as translated is made clear already in 1255a25–35: " … some are slaves everywhere, others nowhere …," etc.

806 For the subject "slavery in ancient Greece," see Hans Derks, 1986, 288–293 and for a healthy skeptical approach see Maxime Rodinson, 1974, 65. For Aristotle's *Politics* and the nomadic background, see Hans Derks, 1995, "A Note …."

807 These are B. Jowett translations of Aristotle's "Politics." Compare these with the most popular translation of Ernest Barker (respectively 138 and 179) and not only main differences in all respects become apparent, but also the pejorative use of "barbarian" as "uncivilized." Aristotle is not a supporter of tyranny ("No freeman willingly endures such a government," 1295a23), but he is no xenophobe.

Even from these few quotations it must be clear that Aristotle is a much more differentiated thinker than somebody who exclusively denounces foreigners as barbarian as equated to primitive, uncivilized or (later) racially inferior (*minderwertig*). It is largely due to the "compulsory conversion of a heathen as Aristotle" in medieval times that his criticisms of the powerful disappeared and the latter could become legitimated to repress "barbarians." Since the 18th century all data were gathered with this aim within a certain theoretical framework, that of *Oriental Despotism*.

Since Bernier (1625–1688) and Montesqieu (1689–1755), the government of Persia/Iran was the model for Oriental Despotism; Ottoman Turkey and Mughal India were soon added. Again an ancient Greek, an older one of their intellectual heroes, pointed at a fundamental element of the subject at hand. Herodotus, "father of history" and an "autonomous Greek" *par excellence*, who no doubt invented much of the dramatic dialogues in his story, tells about the Persian despot *par excellence*, Cyrus.

Once the great Cyrus was confronted with a Spartan envoy who warned him for the last time not "to harm any Greek city or they would take action."[808] Herodotus continues with:

> The story goes that when Cyrus heard what the herald said, he asked some Greeks who happened to be with him who the Lacedaemonians were, and what were their numbers that they dared to send him such a command. On being informed, he gave the following answer to the Spartan herald: "I have never yet been afraid of men who have a special meeting place in the center of their city, where they swear this and that and cheat each other…

This was intended by Cyrus as a criticism of the Greeks generally, because they have markets for buying and selling, unlike the Persians who never buy in open market, and indeed have not a single market-place in the whole country.

It is very doubtful whether Herodotus visited the capital of Persia, Ecbatana, which he depicts as a circular town ringed by no fewer than seven concentric walls (I, 98), which is seen as a purely mythical description. However, it has been rightly remarked about the Iranian cities that "the bazaar as an autonomous quarter within the town must go back to very ancient times."[809]

Through the most remarkable example of an oikoidal (autocratic) ruler Herodotus demonstrated, probably for the first time in history, to the

808 Herodotus, I, 153 also for the next quotation.

809 Xavier de Planhol, in: W.B. Fisher, ed., 1968, 436.

market-oikos contradiction as a fundamental difference between the free, autonomous Greek civilian bound to an urban market versus the autocratic conqueror, master over life and death of his subjects, who did not dare to protest against this fate. This case becomes rather complicated.

First, in all probability Herodotus was not right in supposing that there were no urban markets in Persia, but certainly right in posing the contradiction of free market Greek versus autocratic ruler. If he had known of the existence of the bazaars his story should have been different as well and related to the question of why Persian market-civilians had not (yet) protested/revolted against their autocratic ruler as Greek civilians must have done?

Next, the political philosophers and commentators like Bodin, Bernier or Montesquieu did describe "The Persian Ruler" as an oriental despot without referring to the counter-model of the market-bound civilian. Too often they detested all money-business.[810] These aristocrats pointed to different elements: the lack of private property and a hereditary nobility in an "Oriental Despotism." Their theory of OD rested on the "principle of fear" for the lethal deeds of a tyrant, that made all subjects equal. Montesquieu, therefore, stated in Anderson's writing:

> Men are all equal in a republican state; they are also equal in a despotic state; in the first, because they are everything; in the second, because they are nothing.[811]

Whatever Montesquieu's position at the time, as well as his weak argumentation and, of course, lack of sound data, he distorted the political views of the ancients and seriously influenced the image of "the Orient" as "Despotic": that life in "The East" never changed; the people are servile and lethargic under the permanent arbitrariness of tyrannical political powers; that only religion gives some principle of fixity; "... it is impossible to find a single trait that marks a free soul: only the heroism of slavery is to be seen."

810 Montesquieu, vol. 1, livre III, Chapitre III, 97–98 he attacked all money business which undermines the "vertu" and used many examples from the ancients, this time also of Athens' fight against the Persians during which they apparently bought thousands of slaves on the market.

811 Quoted by Perry Anderson, 1974, 464. I do not know which edition of *De L'Esprit des Lois* Anderson used, but in mine one cannot find the quote in vol. 1, book I, 81 but in Livre III, chapitre VIII, 105 something which is "nearly" similar: "Ce n'est point l'honneur qui est le principe des états despotiques: les hommes y étant tous égaux, on n'y peut se préférer aux autres; les hommes y étant tous esclaves, on n'y peut se préférer à rien." I have to refrain from some exegesis of Montesquieu's famous book.

From Aristotle's *Problems* Montesquieu did not learn how to pose questions, but to pose "truths" i.e. that the main grounds for the differences between West and East could be found in the geography (climate, topography, etc.). At the end of his first volume he not only denies the opinion of some missionaries who had rather favorable stories about China and its government, but he summarizes all the bad things he could find about China.[812]

Adam Smith, 1723–1790, seems to support his contemporary Montesquieu in his attack on "lying and stupid missionaries"[813] and apart from his much more convincing performance, he also added such elements as his exposé about the contradictions between town and country. Anderson quotes from him:[814]

> As the political economy of the nations of modern Europe has been more favourable to manufactures and foreign trade… The policy of China favors agriculture more than all other employments. In China, the condition of a laborer is said to be as much superior to that of an artificer, as in most parts of Europe… Reasons for this: a strong correlation between hydraulic works and the direct interest of the State in the public improvement of agriculture since it was proprietor of all land… In China, and in several other governments of Asia, the executive power charges itself both with the reparation of the high roads, and with the maintenance of the navigable canals… exceed very much everything of the same kind which is known in Europe.

Wittfogel was clearly inspired by Smith in (over)stressing the function of hydraulic works in OD, while Smith suggested that industry and trade was a typical European affair.

Marx, as the main ancestor in the AMP-OD debates, wrote in his earlier writings quite in tune with Smith, Montesquieu and others something that is easily to verify in lexicons with Marx's definitions.[815] In particular the Marx quote from his analysis of the British rule in India:

> The system of villages in the Asiatic mode of production is the solid basis of the oriental despotism.

812 Montesquieu, vol. 1, livre VIII, Chapitre XXI, 267–268.

813 Quoted in Perry Anderson, 1974, 467 note 11.

814 Perry Anderson, 1974, 466, 467.

815 Take, for instance, Konrad Lotter, ed., 1984, 51–52 lemma "Asiatische Produktionsweise" with five short Marx excerpts which are rather difficult to compare with what the table presents. The original quote is: "Das Dorfsystem ist in der asiatischen Produktionsweise die feste Grundlage des orientalischen Despotismus."

This should have disturbed many debates in the 1930s as every word of Marx still was sacrosanct. Marx, however, also had his ancestors.

Wittfogel even forged a close relationship between the *distorted* Aristotle and Marx when writing about what he called the "Rasse-moment" in Marxism.[816] He asked: Were those "barbarians" alien elements in an anthropological sense? The answer to his question he found in the following quote from Marx:

> Not all people (*Völker*) do have the same disposition (*Anlage*) for capitalist production. Some primitive people (*Urvölker*), like the Turks have no talent nor disposition for it. But… with the development of capitalist production an average level of the civil society will be created and with that also temperament and disposition [for capitalist production; c.p.] among the most different of people.

Possibly having as much influence as Marx, Weber wrote on the perception of the West-East contradictions in this same period. Since I discussed Weber's distortion of Chinese history at length in Chapter 7 only a few remarks and quotations will be sufficient. They are derived from the second version of his *The Agrarian Sociology of Ancient Civilizations*.[817] From its introduction the following summary can be given.

> The settlements of the West have in common a transition from nomadic animal husbandry to sedentary agriculture; East-Asian peoples, however, have in common a transition from shifting cultivation to sedentary agriculture… The consequences are… that in oriental villages, in so far they are not from modern origin, the western concepts of mark and *allmende* are absent… Also the "individualism" inherent in the property of herds and flocks with its sharp economic and social differentiation—in the West the primitive basis of feudalism—is absent in Asian cultures… The East-Asians as well as the old American cultures seem to know feudalism in principle as group- or caste- feudalism: a strongly closed and locally organized warrior-group, often living in fortified settlements, is maintained in a *naturalwirtschaftlich* way by a population who are considered as state-slaves or -serves. Also the Egyptian and Asian Orient is in their whole development determined by the preponderance of a

816 Karl Wittfogel, 1931, 9, 10.

817 This is the name of the not very reliable translation of GASWG, 1909, "Agrarverhältnisse im Altertum," 1–288. The long quotation is my summary of Weber's position at issue and a reminder to what is discussed in Chapter 7.

> colossal Pharaohnic or imperial "Oikos," i.e. the state-economy based on *Naturalwirtschaft*.[818]

Weber further argued that nomadic invaders from Inner-Asia who suppressed the population of the main Chinese valley's showed up repeatedly. In relation to his capitalism-thesis, he also made the differentiation between the *political capitalism* of money-lenders and suppliers of patrimonial courts and *modern capitalism*. The first kind earned high profit-rates in their money-business and one knew how to exploit mines and commerce to accumulate wealth.

> The development of the capitalism oriented to the market proper and free exchange remained, however, in statu nascendi. What developed in Western medieval cities was absent in China till nowadays: there were "no legal and sociological bases for capitalist enterprises" with their rational [*Versachlichung*] of the economy… the liability of the clans for their members' was rudimentary developed… commercial gains were invested immediately in land… it was in particular an internal and political booty-capitalism which dominated the capital gains and … land-accumulation.[819]

So far the ancestors, influencing the East-West perceptions in the debates of around 1930.

9.4 The Wittfogel Debates

Following Marx' lead, a full-fledged theory was developed in the 1930s by people like Wittfogel. After his emigration to the USA he changed his mind in a fundamental way and turned to the older OD framework, also in a highly erudite way. They represent two contradictory socio-historical theories that both belong to sophisticated Western perceptions of non-Western (in this case "Asian/Chinese") peoples.

In 1931, Wittfogel published a large and incomplete study, *Wirtschaft und Gesellschaft Chinas,* at the Institute of Social Research started by Adorno and Horkheimer. After his emigration he published about the same subject *Oriental Despotism,* 1957. Both publications are summarized in the following Table 7.[820]

818 See for the definitions of "Mark," "Allmende" and "Naturalwirtschaft" the notes 631 and 632 above.

819 GAR, 1934, vol. 1, 374, 375.

820 Karl Wittfogel, 1931 and also 1957, but I used the German translation from 1962. Most remarkable is that Arrighi, 2007 never mentions any Wittfogel publication.

TABLE 7 Two faces of one Wittfogel

"Wittfogel—AMP" (1931)	"Wittfogel—OD" (1962)
1. an interpretation of Asian societies by means of the Marxist dialectic of production relations/ production forces;	1. an interpretation of Asian societies by means of the role played by the state and bureaucracies;
2. perceives class struggle as possibility and necessity to transform agrarian societies into industrial one's;	2. stresses the near impossibility of change of Asian societies;
3. stresses in particular internal forces in the process of transformation;	3. only by means of external forces (internal) change can be achieved and arrived at;
4. in the methodology of the study W. sticks to the sequence: a. to study the production forces; b. historical development of production process; c. analysis production relations;	4. in the methodology of the study W. sticks to the sequence: a. society is taken, first, as a Whole, a Unit; b. in which the relationship center (state + bureaucracy) versus periphery (peasant societies) is analyzed in relation to large hydraulic works; c. the center—periphery relation is also used to give a typology of "hydraulic societies";
The categories used are derived from the "critique of the political economy";	The categories used are mostly derived from the political geography or geopolitics;
5. Karl Marx became the leading spirit;	5. at the level of ideas the sociologist Max Weber and cultural historian Alexander Rüstow became leading spirits;
6. Town-country contradictions were the basis of the analysis and, therefore, the history of the social divisions of labor became central;	6. town-country contradictions, production relations or -forces are not used or even mentioned any more. The social division of labor is only perceived for labor at a very large scale and on national level as division of a purely organizational nature.
7. The aim of the analysis is to contribute to the liberation of the (Chinese) society of all repression.	7. The aim of the analysis is to contribute to the struggle against despotic, totalitarian, socialist and bureaucratic regimes.
8. Basic to this analysis is the Marxist historical doctrine, characterized by a. the transition of primeval communities, slaveholders society, feudalism, etc.; b. class struggle.	8. Basic is a specific multilinear evolution theory, characterized by: a. the use of static "Whole" ("Ganzheit") concepts, which as such are caught in an evolutionary process; b. they are bound together by a "universalism"; c. changes are initiated by external forces or from above: by conquest or by actions from the top of the socio-political hierarchy.

The shortest way of characterizing these views is that both are political economic theories, but that in the 1931 version the economic element is dominant and in the other the state-political is dominant. The many criticisms were mainly directed to the last work; not seldom was it stated that both works were even similar (Henri Lefebvre, for instance)! The main topics here were the thesis of unchangeability and the exaggerated attention paid to large hydraulic works as proof of despotic regimes or powerful bureaucracies.

From the debates one can conclude, furthermore, that the stagnation argument is used too often to point to the lack of modernization of traditional societies compared to Western, industrial and capitalist one's and the reverse. This argument is, furthermore, used as a "proof" of Western superiority, always defined in capitalist and industrial terms. With these theories all kinds of political and economic aims, measures and actions can be legitimated from Eurocentrism and ethnocentrism to imperialist conquests.

The four theories in both tables can be verified internally by analyzing the (logical) qualities of the arguments, the use of the sources, concepts, and so on. In Chapter 8, I verified them in an external way by making first a concrete historical analysis of the main topic, the town-country antagonism.

Besides this there are many other links to this analysis. For instance, Wittfogel's OD is not only inspired by Max Weber, but without difficulties to characterize as a typical *oikoidal* theory since its focus is the state, its state-bureaucracy from which the economic performance of a rather belligerent society is derived. The fact that town-country contradictions are not treated in this theory directly implies that also they are viewed as something located "below the state," as part of a dominating state.

9.5 From Post-War Modernization to Shock Therapy

After the Second World War the Cold War aggravated contradictions that were from the perpetrators point of views, as different as given in the above tables, but for the victims of all the practical development activities in so-called Third World countries these differences were very difficult to discover.

For them the no-nonsense approach of the American modernizers and modernization theories must be the most recognizable in their own city slums, in which only Bollywood slumdog-millionaires can be created, or in eroded fields, where there is too little water and too much hunger. Shocking activities and therapies are not confined to Naomi Klein's world. Modernization theories of the 1960s were as clear and open concerning aims and methods and as shocking as the present practices.[821]

As an example, I chose the anthropologist George M. Foster's, 1913–2006, world-wide translated book how to deal with traditional societies in the world through a so-called "planned (culture) change."[822] This is the same as (the method of) "regime change" but in the socio-political realm. Foster uses six rules as follows.

1. *Cities are focal points of change.* Here the social and economic changes start in the higher circles and are spreading downward into the "traditionally inarticulate lower classes" and outward to the country. In particular Foster, Hoselitz and other point to Asian so-called "primate" cities with a supposed "intermediate position between East and West," where the elite has its headquarters, these cities are "eminently suitable vehicles for the introduction of new ideas and techniques." We will see whether this is true for the Chinese cities.
2. *Major shifts in the economic basis of livelihood* are nearly always followed by important changes in the nature of family relations. These changes are caused by the demands of urbanization, industrialization and a worldwide monetary economy. Family ties grow weaker and the trend is toward "individualization"; the nuclear family replaces the extended family as the dominant form in the cities.
3. *The introduction of cash crops and the increasing use of money* tend to destroy traditional rural cooperative work patterns. Apparently inspired by Max Weber, we are told that thanks to the attraction of the market a farmer or peasant normally becomes "rationa": he likes to hire laborers instead of buying food and drinks for conspicuous consuming friends; than this tradition belongs to the past and the farmer is "rational." The one who intends to plan a cultural change has to know the "process of syncretism," the method to pack an innovation in a traditional packing as the ancient Christians did with pagan customs (Christmas, etc.).
4. *Dietary deterioration frequently follows a shift from a subsistence to a monetary economy.* Primitive peoples mostly have balanced diets without knowing this. As soon they are obliged to buy their food serious difficulties arise: the consumption of sugar and other attractive elements increases; preserved and packaged food becomes a matter of prestige; food becomes too costly.

821 For a still no-nonsense description of the international aid flows after 1945, with all the fully remarkable figures, see the *World Bank* publication of I. Goldin, K. Reinert, 113–151.

822 For the following I used Chapter 2 of George Foster, 1966.

In short, these are the most important changes to the consumption side if a monetary, urban economy is introduced with the result being under-nourishment, previously unknown sicknesses (beriberi, for instance) and hunger. In this case the planner can adopt one of the following two policies:

If the area has not been saturated with industrial products, than one has to start a redevelopment of the environment and a fundamental immunization instead of improvement of the food menu; if, however, there are already cash crops, money lending, indigenous peoples adrift from their tribes and working in mines or factories then the learning of a Western dietetics is the most important. To come up with programs to remedy the causes of the undernourishment, hunger, etc. acts against planned culture change.

5. *Rapid acculturation frequently promotes village factionalism, and divisive tendencies become more apparent* than when tradition alone is the controlling factor in community cohesiveness. In these cases the foreign development technician has to emphasize impartiality and lack of favoritism so that development programs will not be threatened.
6. *Nationalistic movements may be thought of as one phase of the acculturation process*. There are different characteristics per phase that fit for nations as well as tribes: first phase with general discord with "the new," in particular caused by the elders; second phase with a head over heels acceptance of "the new" supported in particular by the youngsters and later by a local/national elite; the third phase is one of disillusionment caused by limiting measures put in place by those in power.

The planner of cultural change who knows these six things is able to avoid blunder, as well as capitalize on opportunities that would otherwise be missed. A specialist should know what people are proud of and understands why this is as it is, because only then he sees innumerable ways for using this knowledge to help him through the process of change.

These six notions are the one's used in all dominant modernization literature, but they also are practiced in organizations as the American Peace Corps, UNO, FAO, etc. They were/are also accepted in ethically guided opinions about culture change. The leading practical doctrine is:

> Modern primitives who have found themselves in contact with an industrial world in this century will never be peasants—an industrial civilization requires adjustments that do not include a peasantry.[823]

823 George Foster, 1966, 47.

At the moment Foster starts discussing the ethics of planned change he is defending "basic American national policy"; this is as clear as is possible when he answers the question what technical aid means for un(der)developed countries:

> It implies many things, such as potential modern imperialism, the danger of economic penetration, a shattering of traditional values, and it means also often-insensitive strangers taking the best houses and driving up the cost of living. Above all it says, in essence, "if you people will learn to do more things the way we do them, you will be better off." That is not a very flattering approach.[824]

This arrogance of "the stupid and powerful" belonged, indeed, to my own daily experience during a long stay as development planner in South America and Africa. It concerns 75% of all my former colleagues from all kinds of Western countries and 90% of those who had a leading role in the process.

They have/had to deal with bureaucrats at home and in the guest country, and with all kinds of private interests (consultants or contractors) which only come to earn a big living for as small a performance as possible. Some of them know their development literature and show you Foster's or Margaret Mead's demagogic advises about the conservatism and dirty way of the peasant life "which hinders them to participate in a world culture"[825] and which legitimate the social scientist and development planner to provide these peasants with "a large, cultural revision… which is the best that could happen to them in their life." Whereupon Foster adds:

> It is the height of irresponsibility to lead the culturally hungry people of newly developing countries to believe that they have complete freedom of self-determination… It is the task of the social scientist—the anthropologist and his colleagues in other fields… *to determine what the degree of latitude in choice may be…* industrialization leads to new societal patterns that *cannot be rejected.* The machine, perhaps regrettably, is an expensive investment and it cannot tolerate inefficient use; human labor in nonindustrial societies, on the other hand, is cheap. Willy-nilly, it will be molded to the machine's demands. (Foster's italics).[826]

These are the rather compulsory non-military terms in which "Western culture," whatever that means beyond Christianity, technical gadgets and military

824 George Foster, 1966, 261.
825 Margaret Mead quoted by Foster, 263, 264.
826 George Foster, 1966, 265.

bases, is transmitted. No one asks or asked to be converted to some Christian or American ideology or to be molded into a spare-part of a machine. That was not the case directly after the Second World War and it is still not the case.

The expatriates, who were and still are the messengers of these ridiculous ideas, come mostly from an "inarticulate" (Foster) middle class milieu in the Global City. However, as whites, well paid and politically influential in Third World countries they belong to the dominant upper class with all the problems of how to jump over their own shadow and mediocre civilized backgrounds. Their power is based on the development money they bring to the indigenous elite (all kinds of government-to-government investments) and, in ex-colonies, to the white settler population too often accompanied by foreign military.

Of the donor countries, the USA is the harshest, always anxious to sit on the front row for a dollar.[827] Besides that it has the most "military assistance" all over the world, pays the least for direct development (whatever the content), while the policy is: every dollar invested in these countries must bring us at least two in return.

The institutionalized Western hypocrisy is quantifiable where the huge investments in (or better: subsidy of) the agriculture of the USA (in particular the gen-technological reworked one) or the European Union is compared with the state of agriculture in so-called developing countries.

About the effects of this army of Western expatriates, nomadic successors of the extinct settled missionaries, nobody can have many illusions. About their context Wertheim, supporter of the policy "trade not aid," rightly concluded:

> The innovations introduced by the members of the urban or urbanizing elite normally do not support modernization, but only the impoverishment of the peasant masses.[828]

However, the the more relevant question is whether this impoverishment is not precondition for the encapsulating of this (local) elite and city into the Western Global City? In the latter the contribution of agriculture to the Gross National Product rapidly decreased in favor of industry, later services, and its food must come largely from elsewhere, which seems to be impossible if "elsewhere" is not transformed into an industrialized cash crop production for Western diets with Western investments/profits and, therefore, Western

827 Jeffrey Sachs, 2008, 234, 279–280; I. Goldin, K. Reinert, 122 provide the figures which show that the USA gives the lowest "official development assistance" (ODA) in the world as % of Gross National Income, which should be compared with the increasing debt crisis (140 ff.) and the support for the own farmers/ agriculture of the USA and European Union. This long before Trump jumped to his own protectionism.

828 Wim Wertheim, 1972, 104.

property rights, etc. These profits depend also on very low loans, very cheap labor (often of children and women), mineral resources, etc.

If one should accept the aims and consequences of Western aid, only the large differentiated programs executed over a long period of at least half a century can have relevant effects, i.e. an economic and social level more or less comparable to a constellation of a starting Western capitalism. They would be programs incorporating the *whole* chain of actions in favor of the indigenous population (from mining the resources to trade, production of end products, etc.). Undifferentiated large programs, like military and related "aid" to a country like Israel or Afghanistan, can only lead to fully distorted developments and further military colonization by a white or indigenous elite.

Geographically, Asian countries are the least vulnerable to the distorting effects of Western "aid"; the other extreme are the American countries in which the Westernization is completed and, therefore, the indigenous populations and their cultures nearly or wholly eliminated. Historically seen, the settlers' colonization with their lethal effects for indigenous people, cultures and environments fully replaced these cultures (in the North) or hegemonically repressed them (in the South).

After the year 2000, we experienced one global crisis after the other including subsequent accompanying literature, propagating the need for some "shock therapy." Hardt, Negri, Klein and others were their prophets, intellectually prepared by their ancestors like Anderson, Arrighi, Gunder Frank, Wallerstein and many others. About the start of this millennium Frank wrote:

> Capitalism shall recover itsself; the gap between North and South shall be deepened; and at the cost of enormous suffering a new capitalist world system shall be established around the year 2000.[829]

With two years still to come before the year 2000, this same "world system guru" started to see China as "a plausible new global leader in the twenty-first century."[830] His "capitalist world system" was (nearly) collapsed and it continued to collapse. The "shock-therapists" knew what happened. I quote what Hardt and Negri wrote in 2000:

> The geographical divisions among nation-states or even between central and peripheral, northern and southern clusters of nation states are no longer sufficient to grasp the global divisions and distributions of production, accumulation, and social forms. Through the decentralisation

829 I have to translate this from the Dutch: Andre Gunder Frank, "De criris van de wereldeconomie," in: *Komma*, 5-3-1985, 9.

830 See Ho-fung Hung, 2017, 116.

> of production and the consolidation of the world market, the international divisions and flows of labor and capital have fractured and multiplied so that it is no longer possible to demarcate large geographical zones as center and periphery, North and South ... all levels of production can exist simultaneously and side by side, from the highest levels of technology, productivity and accumulation to the lowest...[831]

If we view this with the "after Wittfogel" theories of modernization, dependency, revolution, liberation theological, we discover how their differences are largely a matter of semantics and jargon. Basic to all are notions about town-country antagonisms. Basic to all are the abundant use of strict dichotomies.[832]

"Modern" is related to the city/town but also to things like differentiated division of labor, high literacy, centralized and rather anonymous rule/government, high productivity, secularization and separation of church and state, industrial technology, etc. "Traditional" is then normally related to the countryside but also to other exact contradistinctions like simple division of labor, low literacy, local and personal rule, dogmatic religion, agrarian subsistence technology, etc.

Derived from all kinds of development literature the following Table 8 is made as a check-list for studying and interventions, for example, of and in the Chinese history of town-country relations.[833]

This "check-list" concerning town-country relations is given, because too many "Western sources" think (and thought) that the implied policy is founded on basic processes in history and society. This had to be falsified.

As a result of the theoretical analysis of Max Weber's and Werner Sombart's capitalism theories and some considerations on town-country antagonisms the given perception of market-*oikos* relations became a complicated affair. One by one I provided building blocks so that they can be used for a new theory of market-*oikos* combined with town-country relations.

Who (in the West) cannot wait until this theory is available, must be perfectly pleased by my newspaper that announced directly after the election of Donald Trump, that this

---

831 Michael Hardt, Antonio Negri, 2004, 334, 335.

832 A large amount of "traditional—modern" dichotomies can be found in H.-U. Wehler, 1975, 13–15.

833 The aim of the following table is strictly of a documentary nature: to gather at random several relevant *Western* opinions about the subject from many different sources. They are far from being a scientific systematic summary of basic town-country relations, which is given in Hans Derks, 1986, 51–94, 263–303, 456–507. They are often literally quotations from the literature used so far, from acknowledged development experts and some priests and politicians specialized in development policies. As such they are not derived from Chinese sources or of literature about China.

TABLE 8 Town and country parameters

City—town	Countryside
1. Christianity as a progressive belief system	1. Paganism "into religion transformed conservatism"
2. related to a higher Power with abstract rules;	2. related to higher powers "with which one has to deal according to specific irrational rules."
3. men makes nature slave of them which is the reason why they study the "laws of nature";	3. men is slave of nature;
4. de-sacralization of nature is based on the Bible;	4. de-sacralization of nature is needed in order to receive economic and social progression;
5. developed, civilized, rich, donor country, aid giver ...	5. under-developed, primitive, poor, blood-receiving country, helped ...
6. highly developed democracy;	6. the (folk-) community is despotic, absolutist, totalitarian and conservative;
7. it is an advantage for the economy if more wealthy trade (partners) are available;	7. "a certain labor obligation to produce products, to save in order to increase productivity and to arrive at an orderly society" is often unavoidable;
8. monetary economy transforms families into the direction of the "western biological nucleus family";	8. extended families are units of social and economic action;
9. centers of change by developed class structure;	9. unarticulated lowest classes;
10. independence, individualism;	10. guest friendship and help to relatives;
11. relations with "world culture";	11. primitive, isolated peasant life dirty, cruel, unhealthy...
12. aid must be given to avoid communism;	12. strong attraction to communism;
13. there is the obligation to missionary work and to exercise our culture mandate.	13. "undifferentiated culture."

> victory is one of the old over the young, of the country over the city, of white over black and of men over women.[834]

Isn't it a good summary of the subject of this study?!

834 *De Volkskrant*, 10-11-2016.

CHAPTER 10

A Sparring Partner for All Seasons

10.1 Introduction

In the previous chapter I finished the empirical part of this study about the market-oikos relationship. The content of that chapter may have reminded the reader of the adage that "there is nothing more practical than a good theory." However, are the theories discussed so far "good" or is it time now to develop a good theory after so many debatable, controversial or false theories and interpretations? As announced in the preface the last option reflects my intention and my conclusions the best.

However, this leads to the necessity of adding "a finishing touch" to Max Weber's theories that have accompanied the chapters in this book from the beginning to the end, like a *sparring partner*. Although, in all objectivity, an author like Karl Marx towers far above Weber's stature in many respects, he was not chosen to fulfill this function because Weber's historical scope was far broader and more attuned to a market-*oikos* discussion. In addition, there is hardly an element in his works that is not criticized vehemently. Therefore, it should have been logical to abandon him. I leave it up to the readers to judge whether it was a right decision to use him as sparring partner.

This last chapter is designed as both a tribute and a farewell, but it can also serve as an impulse to renew the debate about the highly complicated relationships of market-*oikos* and town-country. A new academic adventure is being planned along the lines given in the epilogue; it involves a hard confrontation with a rather grisly reality on a world scale. This demands relevant, adequate, comparable and multidisciplinary research fit to address much more complicated questions on that scale.

In Europe, the USA and elsewhere, this is not the best period for relevant scientific work outside propaganda programs, large media concerns or the widespread activities of secret services. In addition, the erosion in several disciplines is substantial thanks to the toll taken by the one crisis after the other.

The economists' toolkit, for instance, is empty and they mostly cannot compensate this with other kinds of knowledge: too often they are poor historians. American economists like Krugman or Stiglitz make a lot of noise as inventors of remedies for crises, but avoid writing about their silence before the crisis began. Their colleague, the Harvard economist Dani Rodrik, even complained:

 | DOI:10.1163/9789004383913_011

"Economists act as cheerleaders of hyper-globalization. What a distorted view the public receives from economic science...."[835] They are only "fine weather" experts, like Charles de Gaulle's claim about diplomats in his time: they were not around at the time of the Tulip Mania, and since then there have been crashes in the West every eight years (Kindleberger).

Noble Prize Winner Paul Krugman is more entertaining with his one-liners than with his mathematical models. He considers fully distorted market relations between China and the USA fair and balanced: the former sends us poisoned products, the latter returns treacherous securities. He could have made his case complete by remarking that some Chinese producers learned to poison products in a typically capitalist way by adding melamine and water to milk-powder or pet foods to increase profits. Their Western business partners used to inject meat with water to increase the weight and profit, etc. Apparently, Chinese "state-capitalists" attract the cheapest, cheating capitalist production partners and they copy too quickly from "the West."

But who is complaining? Dani Rodrik complains about his colleagues. He himself belongs to the "reasonable protectionists," and the enemies of social dumping and of dishonest competition. He would be happy with Weber's business advice to religious sectarians in the USA: "honesty is the best policy,"[836] or with my research-result about the centuries of peaceful trade in the East. His science cannot be saved by this and not by saying:

> Every economic question has two sides, from increasing of minimum wages to the maximizing of rent-increases. But in our contribution to the debate it looks like as if there is only one truth.[837]

---

835 In an interview in the Dutch paper *De Volkskrant*, 4–11-2017.

836 WG, 723 or ES, 1206.

837 WG, 723 or ES, 1206. See also *De Volkskrant*, 4–11-2017. The famous Dani Rodrik is a man who believes in one-liners and fairy tales like the one from Isaiah Berlin, who divided "thinkers" into hedgehogs and foxes. Berlin seemed to know that the former adheres only to great and grand ideas and that the latter acts pragmatically. The reader may decide for himself which kind Rodrirk belongs to when believing Berlin. He says to the "antiglobalistas," "Thanks to your anticapitalism, you do not understand how to use globalization and markets in an intelligent way. Think about the very quick economic development of China, Vietnam and earlier South Korea. That is just an enormous success." Whether this was a result of globalization and capitalism is debatable. Rodrik's English colleague, the famous Paul Collier, recently wrote about capitalism, " ... its performance has become manifestly unsatisfactorily ... It is time for 'The Future of Capitalism'. Unfortunately, nobody has yet successfully written that book." *Times Literary Supplement*, 27-1-2017, 3. He is right, although he could not have read my book.

As explained in the last part of Chapter 8, economic questions like "rent-increase" have more than two sides, but many will only be discovered when studying the historical problems rather than the juridical cases.

Max Weber could have been helpful to Americans to demonstrate what has to be their primary concern, but that advice applies to the Europeans and Chinese as well: indeed, Max Weber remains a sparring partner for all seasons, as will be demonstrated below again; not more, nor less.

10.2 Weber in the USA

Inspired by Upton Sinclair's novel *Oil!*, 1927, Paul Anderson made the breathtaking movie, *There Will Be Blood* in 2007, which explicitly addressed "the role of religion in the rise of industrial capitalism." This theme is further described in a more general way as a "conflict between religion and capitalism."[838] Apparently, this last perception "underestimates the subtlety of Anderson's argument." It is interesting to examine this argument, because it could bring us again to the heart of this book.

In an American Wild West setting of around 1900, the film shows the conflict between a typical sectarian local preacher (including his community, fully isolated from the world) and a misanthropic, overambitious oilman, searching and drilling for oil with his own hands and a bit of capital. The preacher extorts five thousand dollars out of the oilman to help him establish a church in exchange for permission to lay a pipeline over the land of his community. A most basic market-*oikos* deal!

At the moment the first oil derrick is to be dedicated, the oilman humiliates the preacher and is apparently unwilling to pay the money. The latter takes revenge in a dramatic way after a derrick fire occurs that seriously injures the oilman's adopted son: all this must be God's punishment on the oilman. It leads inevitably to his baptism; as a paralyzed victim of the screaming preacher, he has to creep literally through the dust. Not long after, the preacher leaves for bigger and more profitable evangelical pastures.

Many years later as the oilman lives a very fortunate but isolated and nearly insane life in his kitsch palace, the preacher arrives anew on the scene begging the oil baron to lease the land of his community for oil exploration. Remembering his humiliating baptism, the oil baron not only forces the preacher to

838 See the movie website http://coosacreek.org 15 Feb. 2008 *There Will Be Blood: Religion and Capitalism in America* with comments. The following three quotations come from this site.

scream out that he is a fraud, but afterwards he explains to him that he already siphoned the oil under the community's land dry ("I drink it up!"). Finally, he beats the preacher to death, speaking his last words, "I'm finished!"

It was obvious that Max Weber's famous study about Calvinism and capitalism was Anderson's intellectual role-model reproducing it as an ideal "ideal-type." Not only the present economic crisis in the capitalist West, but this cinematographic form also provided this well-known "ideal-type" with a brand-new image and impact. At the least, it inspired the casting of relevant older texts into that mold!

It is in some sense a risky affair but since my critical confrontations with Weber's writings and the mostly positive reactions to them, I decided to give it a new try. This was a particular challenge now that "western religions" are as dead as a doornail for many people and capitalism is caught in one of its worst crises. Additional considerations concerned my recent publication of a new kind of global history, which asks for a new reflection on the field of "Western morals" and "Western capitalism" effective on a global scale.

A critical discussion about the still relevant *basic concepts* at issue, namely religion in relation to capitalism, could be stimulated by looking whether something further can be learned from *There Will Be Blood.* Anderson's aim was apparently to show the *fraudulent relationship of capitalism and religion,* which has many aspects. He, however, dramatically demonstrates the *sectarianism,* pious irrationality and fundamental hypocrisy of Calvinist or puritan leadership and community. Regarding *capitalism,* its fundamental greed and lethal ambitions are stressed, its willingness to accept everything, even a conversion into a ridiculous sect, if it benefits business, while cheating sect and community at will after the goals have been achieved.

How a *relationship* between such stubborn phenomena can be twisted around in the US-perspective is revealed by the expert's analyses of the film. According to one, the film's message was that wealth is a sign of God's favor and, therefore, pursuing it is a God-given right. Another American analyst went even further:

> Conversely, if wealth is a sign of God's favor, the wealthy must be the most favored of God. Further, since America is (or was) the wealthiest of nations, we must also be the most favored; thus the "doctrine" of manifest destiny and our self-designation as the "New Jerusalem." Our progressivism has always been shored up by this very warped version of Christianity, and our sense that we are God's favorites.[839]

839 See previous note.

There Will Be Blood tries to demonstrate the main characteristics of this theology, but also how morally bankrupt it really is: the preacher is a financial failure and, therefore, no longer favored by God and ready to be eliminated; although the oil baron has won everything, he has lost all that matters: "he is an empty, used-up shell"; is this the end of the *American Dream* or the beginning of super-capitalist Trump's version of it, with his intention to make America "great again"?

Another commentator refers implicitly to Max Weber's capitalism theory and directly to the oilman. He perceives the latter as:

> ...the true face of "the protestant work ethic" and, like Christ who states "it is done," he states, "I am finished." We are presented with an honest man, who brutally and plainly shows the true face of a misguided theology.

The partisan reasoning seems to be here: that the preacher mixed up theology with business, and it is this amalgamation that leads to moral bankruptcy and blindness; the oilman was, in fact, right to kill the preacher. This is a direct hint about the influential, widespread and irrational activities of American sects and sectarian churches, even the American brand of the European Roman Catholicism; a large majority of its members voted for Trump because of the lethal "pro-life movement" that would be impossible to sustain in Europe.

It is logical that, for instance, this American brand of Roman Catholicism, so different from the European one with its empty churches, should be responsible for the globalization of this lethal fundamentalism: contrary to whatever sectarianism exists, Roman Catholicism has been a world church for centuries and still remains one to this day, the only one in the Western world. It is, however, now fully in decline thanks to its fundamental "otherworldly sexual principles" and attitudes and it is very doubtful whether McKinsey can sell it again.

Pentecostal sects or the Scientology movement now can jump into the empty US "global box" but do not rise above the most primitive "friend-enemy" dichotomies of the Tom Cruise films. Take, for instance, in this rich tree of good and evil sects, the so-called Christian Zionists, the inexplicable American adoration for Israel or the most aggressive and stubborn settlers transplanted from the center of New York to a caravan on so-called empty hills on Palestinian territory to spread a "Calvinist" sectarianism, repeating the tactic once used in The Wild West to commit a slow genocide of the indigenous people (see Chapter 6).[840]

---

840 John Mearsheimer and Stephen Walt, 2007, 132 and *passim*.

It is, however, a classical demonstration of the "white" sects at home that traditionally represent the main sources of American anti-Semitism,[841] while also claiming Israel as *their* "New Jerusalem" and its "Jewish population" as *their* guardians of the oil-wells until these wells "are siphoned dry." Sometimes USA-sects even nurture suppositions that the Holocaust took place in the USA for fundraising purposes![842]

More important is that the "siphoning dry of the oil-wells" will happen in the Middle East between 2025 and 2035, according to the experts now very busy with oil-scaling in the USA itself. They apparently expect that the electricity revolution of today shall stop at the oil polluted shores of the USA or the beach of Tel Aviv. In addition, there is a good chance that the climate change is leading to the "siphoning away" of water under Israel… The historian with a Jewish background, Tony Judt, called this whole constellation "an anachronism. And not just an anachronism but a dysfunctional one."[843]

These horror stories accompanying American and European settlers tell us much about the primitive reasoning and practices of religious sectarians and foreign colonial (military) rulers but less about capitalism and about the relationship religion-capitalism. It remains difficult to put the present phenomena in historical perspective or to ask if something can be learned from the past. It also remains too easy to twist the facts like "left-wing theologians" (Gollwitzer)

841 In the last decade there are as well "black" sects which could be accused of anti-Semitism since they stress the role of Jews in the introduction of slavery and/or carrying out slave trade; this is based on the reasoning that slavery and the slave trade together caused the "Black Holocaust." Here it is more a matter of semantics and arithmetic (every group its own Holocaust) or crying "anti-Semitism" if some undeniable facts could undermine a Zionist stand. And that "Jews" (not as group, of course!) were involved in whatever black American slave business or employment is certain and that the black slavery led to several times as many victims as the Jewish Shoah is possible as well. Anyway, these are facts which in present-day media-politics are too easily called a black "Holocaust." This 20th-century killing process is totally different from the slavery killings of the 16th–19th century. It is a good warning not to use the verdict "anti-Semitism" to silence enemies and correct criticism, to use "Holocaust" out of every historical context or to enrage a competition between minorities who suffered the most (not seldom in order to claim the right to open a huge guilt account or irrational support for some case). See the recent article Jeffrey Olick and Shannon Anderson, 2007, 494–498.

842 Interesting examples can be found in Hilene Flanzbaum, ed., 1999 or Peter Novick, 1999. For problems on the "theological front" see, for instance, Hector Avalos, 2007 and my review of it in *The European Legacy*, 14-3-2009. The latest on this "front" are "arguments" that anti-Semitism, anti-Zionism and anti-Americanism are perceived as one and the same thing.

843 See Tony Judt, Israel: the Alternative, in: *New York Review of Books,* October 2003; Jonathan Freedland, in: Idem, May 2015.

do by accusing capitalism (whatever definition) without any form of self-criticism. The obvious aim is to save the preachers and their churches from their age-old image of the strongest (ideological) supporters of the powerful.

To discover more about the religion-capitalism relationship, it should be obvious to combine both interpretations of the plot of *There Will Be Blood* if one wants to understand the motives guiding, for instance, the rather disastrous foreign policy of the USA after 1945. And does the clear reference to Max Weber's religion-capitalism relation in this intriguing Hollywood production bring us directly to the heart of the matter of my book?

Max Weber's sociology of religion, his famous theory about the connection between Calvinism (with its work ethic) and capitalism, was only indirectly the subject of the previous chapters. It may be true that history is a discussion without an end (Pieter Geyl), but happily many problems have been solved, and it is a waste of time and morally abject to continue to beat a dead horse.

I do not intend to reproduce this long *Protestant Ethic* debate.[844] However, before to start a new "sectarian massacre" one has to consider that one cannot rely on "the oilman": this man disappears definitely in a few years time!

10.3 Weber in Europe

A future Chinese government may be willing to combine its capitalism with its religious policy and create something like "capitalism as (a) religion." Among the members of the famous *Institute of Social Research* like Adorno, Horkheimer

844 In the very serious *British Journal of Sociology*, 43, 1992, 421–442 Christie Davis wrote a good compensation for this decision with her article: "The Protestant Ethic and the Comic Spirit of Capitalism." For definite answers to this question see already Richard Tawney, 1961 with the preface to the 1937 edition, X. For the German debate see Max Weber, 1968, volume 2, *Kritiken und Antikritiken.* It is very difficult to find true believers in this dossier, but they are still available. See several articles in the reader Victor Nee and Richard Swedberg, ed., 2007 also for other reasons a most disturbing book which is wholeheartedly recommended to learn why my own disciplines (sociology, history and economy) deteriorated so quickly in the last decade or so or how one can refrain in a nearly schizophrenic way from any historical analysis where this is most appropriate. Take, for example, Charles Stabel—305 ff. in this reader—who starts his contribution with: "Weber's *The Protestant Ethic and the Spirit of Capitalism,* now a century old, is surely the most brilliant and influential statement of the dominant, endowment explanation of economic development." Who writes this has never read Weber's text—not even in a critical mood—or never read the vitriolic commentaries of the relevant historians or never became suspicious about the remarkable support of many theologians, etc. Recently Peter Ghosh, 2008 and 2014 repeated the debate again through a clever biographical essay which fruitfully can be used along Joachim Radkau's biography, 2005.

or Marcuse it was Karl Wittfogel who could support or ridicule such a Chinese forecast. It was, however, his colleague Walter Benjamin, 1892–1940, probably the main Marxist spirit in this institute, who wrote a remarkable text titled *Kapitalismus als Religion.*

> Capitalism is to be seen as a religion, which means that capitalism satisfies the same worries, pains and unrests on which earlier the so-called religions gave an answer. This religious structure of capitalism is not, as Weber thought a religiously determined system [*Gebilde*], but a religious phenomenon as such. To prove this would take us into a boundless polemic [*Universalpolemik*].[845]

First, remarkable enough, Benjamin did not define capitalism. As discussed in the first chapter, this is of fundamental importance when one tries to assess texts like this. It should have been more appropriate if Benjamin had written about the *claim* of capitalism as being similar to an unfulfilled promise. In this case, the forecasted boundless polemic should have been focused on the question why this claim was always unfulfilled. That did not happen either. Therefore, the remaining possibilities to look at his texts are limited to the following. Some bold perspectives are, however, still given.

Benjamin produces four characteristics of this "religious capitalism": it is an extreme cult-religion (no dogmatics, no theology); it is a cult that lasts permanently; it does not bring reconciliation but indebtedness; and, last but not least, its god must be kept secret and only in the zenith of indebtedness can one talk to this god.

"It is this capitalism which is historically without precedent, namely that religion is no longer a reform of being [*Sein*] but its destruction." And after referring to Nietzsche's God-is-Dead philosophy and, more understandably, to Marx: "… the not returning capitalism becomes socialism with interest and

845 Walter Benjamin, 1991, volume 6, 100–103. It concerns a fragment of about 1921 which contains, in fact, only some loose notes and bibliographical data for a forthcoming article or book. In my view at least, he would never have reproduced its ambiguous argumentation. That is not the opinion in present-day Germany in which every scrap of Benjamin, including this one, is perceived as even a "berühmten Text." See Dirk Baecker, ed. or the use of it as basic credo for conservative Catholic theologians (2001, 2002) like Wolfgang Palaver, Kapitalismus als Religion, in: www.uibk.ac.at/theolog/leseraum/html/283.html of the Theological Faculty of the University of Innsbruck. He also published on the same website "Europe's Political Economy" with a first paragraph entitled "The Pagan Roots of Liberal Economic Theology" which demonstrates excellently why theology cannot be a science. See furthermore Charles Deutschmann, 2001, 32–56, which is translated in *Blätter für deutsche und internationale Politik,* 2007, 77–85.

interests-interest [*Zinseszins*], that is functional to the *Debt;* see the demonic ambiguity of this concept.[846]

A reasonable explanation of the four characteristics is not given, but speculations enough as ought to be to such a "secular theologian" as Benjamin. Capitalism is perceived as synonymous with a *permanent cult of indebtedness*, as a debt which never can be "redempted." This seems to me very close to the Calvinist's creed and it takes now only a few steps before Benjamin becomes a supporter of Weber's (and other's) *Protestant Ethic*-stand.

Before we have to blame Benjamin for this, it is worth considering "the demonic ambiguity" of Benjamin's fault ("Lord, forgive him his trespasses!"). A true double bookkeeping, DEB, only with the difference of a "t," appears on the intellectual horizon and then we have to end this book where we started. Indeed, a double meaning is at stake, *Debt and Guilt.* The former refers to "money," but the latter to mistake, fault or sin and, therefore, to "religion" or "law and punishment" To which of both refers Benjamin's "demonic ambiguity"? Not a small problem for Christians or monotheists, who want to do business and for Germans because in their language there is only one word, *Schuld*, for "everything." Therefore a "demon" or a god determines here the criteria and the punishment. (It must be the reason why in Germany there are and were so many "Dichter und Denker" and in the USA so many money-experts.)

Next, we speak in the English language of "national, public debt" and not "guilt" (and, of course, in Germany only "Staatsschuld"), because it concerns money. However, there is nothing so permanent as this kind of debt that now becomes a burden and everybody's guilt. As money it can be paid and in that case we can get rid of this debt. This is the *market* reasoning, while the "debt as guilt" is a strict *oikoidal* phenomenon and is as necessity because the state as, by definition, parasitic to the whole population, should be a non-productive and non-marketable quasi-permanent institution. This, since its invention as state (let's say: France 17th century) until now, notwithstanding the fact that hundreds of these institutions disappeared.

Another speculation is possible thanks to Benjamin's fragment. He speculates as well about how to get rid of capitalism if we may translate his

846 I am not very sure whether my translation is correct. So after referring to Nietzsche's *God-is-Dead* opinion Benjamin continues with: "Und ähnlich Marx: der nicht umkehrende Kapitalismus wird mit Zins und Zinseszins, als welche Funktion der *Schuld* (siehe die dämonische Zweideutigkeit dieses Begriffs) sind, Sozialismus." Benjamin's italics. For those who like to speculate about this theme or about Benjamin's position, see books like A. Knol, *Zins und Gnade,* 1967 and its source, K. von Vogelsang, *Zins und Wucher,* 1894, Roman Catholic theologians from which Palaver is the present successor. They are mentioned by Hellmuth Golllwitzer, 1974, 81 and 128.

Überwindung des Kapitalismus as such.[847] In any case, how he envisaged solving this problem is fully in line with a major subject of my book: *durch Wanderung*, by means of "roaming around," "migration" and the like: in short, forms of nomadism.

A last question for political theologians: Is it possible now to conclude that religion + capitalism evolves into socialism or that this is the consequence of Marx's theory? And leading to another speculation, that socialism becomes a religion when it "replaces" capitalism after other earlier "replacements," see below? Or: since he talks about religion and not anymore about Christianity, is his "theory" also applicable to Confucianism, Islam or any esoteric belief system as well? And so on, and so forth.

Some of Benjamin's questions are answered in a preliminary way by an acknowledged expert on the relation capitalism-Islam, Maxime Rodinson. He states:

> The precepts of Islam have not seriously hindered the capitalist orientation taken by the Muslim world during the last hundred years, and nothing in them is really opposed to a socialist orientation, either… the expansion of Islam was to an infinitely greater degree a function of sociological and purely circumstantial factors (of a political, military, etc., kind) than of ideological convictions. The fact is less obvious in the case of the expansion of religions that engage in vigorous missionary activity, like Christianity and Buddhism.[848]

In this case it seems impossible to develop something called "capitalism as Islam". Therefore, what urged Benjamin to write in this way remains obscure: to exploit a mere analogy (in fact, only a semantic joke as "satisfaction of needs" in both religion and capitalism) is far beyond his abilities. It is symptomatic that only reactionary German/Austrian theologians and orphaned left-wingers, always mesmerized by romantic pseudo-critical constructions, accept Benjamin's "solution" that capitalism can become a religion.

The demonic character Benjamin introduces is welcomed and reproduced by the former in a Manichean threat with Satan, while the others acknowledge this as support of their abstract anti-capitalism. Reading from their products, I did not get the impression that they worried about a proper definition of capitalism, nor about the historical realities of European Christianity or the economic characteristics of (some) capitalism.

847 Walter Benjamin, 1991, volume 6, 102.

848 Maxime Rodinson, 1974, 187–188.

Traditionally, it is also in these theological circles that Max Weber's capitalism theory is still accepted at face value within his sociology of religion.[849] Now, not even Tawney's solution is discussed, which says something about the connection between religion and capitalism:

> It had, obviously, two sides. Religion influenced, to a degree which today [1937. H.D.] is difficult to appreciate, men's outlook on society. Economic and social changes acted powerfully on religion. Weber, as was natural in view of his special interests, emphasized the first point. [And in view of the "solution" of *There Will Be Blood,* his additional paraphrase can lead to some speculation. H.D.] … Puritanism helped to mould the social order, but it was also itself increasingly moulded by it.[850]

In his dictum Benjamin further compares two phenomena ("Kingdoms," Tawney would say) that are focused on very different fields of attention: the one probably only satisfies spiritual needs and the other only concrete needs, while the risk of not doing this or the consequences of choosing a wrong direction are very different as well. Benjamin's characteristics perfectly fit a spoiled consumer society in Western capitals.

His references to the most controversial Europeans, Freud and Nietzsche, and to spiritual toys for the inhabitants of the residential areas in those capitals, are symptomatic: their thoughts are perceived as "great" types of capitalist religious thinking. Max Weber and Weber's theological friend, Ernst Troeltsch, is the main antagonist here, while the envisaged replacement of all Christian belief systems by the capitalist religion is not or only partially supported by them.

Benjamin, furthermore, presents a rather challenging historical insight:

> Capitalism has developed itself as a parasite of Christianity in Western Europe [*Abendland*]. This can be proven not only in Calvinism, but also in the other orthodox Christian denominations. This parasitic development has been formed in such a way that in the end basically its history

849 The person most at odds with Weber as well as with Benjamin's or the Roman Catholic stands is the American Weberian sociologist Randall Collins, who uses "religious capitalism" for monks who are making a deal with some of the products they grow or make. See his *Macrohistory*, 1999, introduction or 222–223. He apparently never read in Weber's oeuvre something about the *oikos*–market contradiction.

850 Richard Tawney, 1961, XII, XIII. Tawney is not even mentioned, for instance, in the reader of Victor Nee and Richard Swedberg, 2007 as necessary criticism of Weber's "Protestant Ethic."

> [of Christianity. H.D.] is the history of its parasite, capitalism. [Furthermore:] ... The Christianity of the Reformation period did not favor the rise of capitalism, but it transformed itself into capitalism.[851]

The first thesis fully contradicts the second: if the reformation of Christianity did not favor capitalism, how could it be a parasite of it? There is no place for some autonomous development à la Tawney, for example, whatever definition of capitalism is used.

Tawney's study was published in nearly the same year as Benjamin wrote his fragment. He clearly pointed to large differences between Luther(anism) and Calvin(ism) and their different influences on economic matters. That is one of the reasons why it is inappropriate to speak of "Christianity" which should "transform" itself into capitalism, if this should be the case at all.

The reason why I elaborate on this question is not just to search for the outlines of our subject but because time and again we will be confronted with the relationship religion-capitalism (or its history).

Without knowing of the existence of his fragment (and even of Walter Benjamin), I wrote a booklet long ago that had as its subtitle "A Critique of Religious Capitalism," 1970.[852] Apart from its obvious shortcomings, it did not defend a thesis about religious capitalism but pointed out the history of the mutual entanglement of capitalism and several European religions and how to deal with this. The confrontation of religion with capitalism was, therefore, my concern. The last sentence of the cover text demonstrated this in the spirit and capital letters of the 1970s: "Will GOD save us or CAPITAL? Or has, at last, the time come to do it OURSELVES?"

---

851 It cannot be coincidental that Benjamin has chosen to use the "*Abendland*" concept, which was the much heralded concept of the Roman Catholic radical conservative restoration in Germany. Directly after the First *and* Second World War it referred to the supposed medieval greatness of this church during the reign of Charlemagne, the center of which was located in Aix la Chapelle, the German Rheinland. After the loss of World War II the same revival was organized, of which the Catholic Konrad Adenauer was a staunch supporter. A strong anti-capitalism and nationalism were other characteristics of this movement. See Hans Derks, 2001, 208–216; "Abendland," in: *Wikipedia* (German). After 1945 the meaning of "*Abendland*" was extended as a concept in the Cold War rhetoric and identified with "The West" in its "eternal" struggle with "The East"; Charlemagne was already struggling against the Asian barbarians, you know.

852 Hans Derks, 1970. This youthful product of ca. 70 pages is a cultural-historical essay about the entanglement of Christian and capitalist interests which took shape (in my view at the time) in the European Enlightenment and about the subsequent erosion of this combination including the possibilities for further criticism.

These are probably still good questions, but they are reproduced here to indicate not only my long involvement personally with the problems at hand, but to show an alternative perspective for a Benjamin *and* a Tawney interpretation of the relationship religion-capitalism in European history. The differences concern the degree of integration in which Benjamin's "religious capitalism" represents a 100% integration of "religion" within "capitalism" and the reverse! We cannot know what would have been the outcome if Benjamin had elaborated on this relationship in a serious way. Whatever the merits of his other writings, "capitalism as religion" is not convincing; the study of both phenomena is seriously hindered by its further exploitation as happened in, for instance, Randall Collins's work.[853] Whatever the outcome of a new thorough historical and sociological investigation, let's stick for the time being to the "Tawney rule": "They cannot collide, for they can never meet."[854]

Even this is a truth that is difficult to swallow in Benjamin's country of birth, Germany, where now a new wave of radical conservatives (*Alte Kameraden*) disturbes people's patience with history. Happily, other youngsters like Ingo Haar and Michael Fahlbusch rightly rebelled against the old guard during the *Frankfurter Historikertag* of 1998; now they have created interesting publications accompanied by the *Handbuch völkischen Wissenschaften,* 2008 with a second and enlarged issue in 2017.

Apparently, it is not accidental that this book ends by pointing not to an encyclopedia for *Staatswissenschaften* (HdS) as in the preface, but for *Völkischen Wissenschaften*. What was cut out of the memory of the established post-war research on the Second World War came to the fore, because the motivation to do this work derived from criticism of the strong collaboration between Nazis and their own teachers and the shameful silence about the real backgrounds and enigmas.

This *Handbuch* discusses previously unknown details about persons, institutions, research programs and foundations that played important roles or had crucial functions in the Nazi-regime. In his introduction Paul Weindling rightly starts at the historical beginning:

853 In particular chapter seven, "An Asian Route to Capitalism," of Randall Collins, 1999, gives a distorted view on the Indian, Chinese and Japanese economic histories. At all costs he tries to mold them into a Weberian "Protestant Ethic" framework and uses inappropriate concepts like "religious economy," etc. He, furthermore, only refers to Wittfogel's study *Oriental Despotism* as a universal adjustable concept without knowing of Wittfogel's other intellectual life. See now how to deal with Chinese, Indonesian or Japanese societies under the pressure of colonialism en imperialism in Hans Derks, 2012.

854 Richard Tawney, 1961, 274.

> Notwithstanding the central importance of concepts like *Rasse* and *Volk* in German science in the 20th century, the postwar German academics avoided, for a long time, criticism of the heritage of these *völkischen* concepts... Adolf Hitler... and the *Machtstaat*... were the reasons for all troubles... not scientists, let alone the civil scene in which people debated about the meaning of *Rasse* and *Volk* [see Chapter 4. H.D.][855]

A final example is appropriate now to demonstrate the Weindling quote in connection with the subject of *The Market and the Oikos* and Max Weber's role in its study. Wolfgang Mommsen, one of the best German Max Weber-experts once wrote an essay about "The City and Culture in the German Kaiserreich" in which he acted as a good civil mythmaker:

> This form of a practical-rational way of life has, as Max Weber demonstrated, its true basis in the Protestant asceticism. It produces the large social energies without which the existence and the quick development of the modern, market-oriented capitalism would not be possible. The ideal of a civil life in a profession was—in the first instance—directed to an increase in profit and wealth, but was at the same time strongly bound to ethical components: honesty, sense of duty [*Pflichterfüllung*], economy [*Sparsamkeit*], a sober lifestyle... They were perceived as obliging virtues. In this way the love of gain [*Erwerbstrieb*] as the definite motivation for economic activities under the preconditions of the development of capitalism, could be tamed as well as ideologically legitimated.[856]

It is a remarkable sentence for a German historian, heir of a famous historian's dynasty, and Weber expert: the rather sectarian "Protestant asceticism," so explicitly bound to puritanism/Calvinism, simply could not be found in Europe at the time, except in remote corners like the coastal parts of the Netherlands or Scotland and other tiny spots: it had no influence whatsoever, let alone on capital*ism*, which can be connected only to cooperation with a Lutheran or Catholic state! Weber himself was an a-religious Lutheran, just like the elite in the whole northern part of Germany, northern Europe and England; and this Lutheranism (or Anglicanism) was socially, economically or culturally

855 Paul Weindling in: Ingo Haar and Michael Fahlbusch, ed., 2008, 13.

856 Wolfgang Mommsen in: Tilo Schabert, ed., 1990, 87, 88. My italics. "Erwerbstrieb" has connotations like "commercial ability," "greed," "profitmaking." They concern all negative attitudes of the market in contrast to the honest oikoïdal "satisfaction of needs" (*Bedarfsdeckung*).

the same as Catholicism but without a pope, the religious leader of the rest of Europe. After the war *all* those northern states even stuck to secular, monarchical, oikoïdal constructions (and if that were not possible, a Soraya adoration could provide solace).

What happened after the era from the 1870s to 1918 was not only the *end* of the European empires like Germany, Austria-Hungary, Russia and France and the definite defeat of liberalism as the last supporter of capitalist production (c.p.), it was the *start* of capital*ism* as the close cooperation of state and monopoly capital, and the enormous rise of popular "-isms" that *all* told the masses to attack "market-capitalism" without a proper definition: fascism, nazism, socialism, communism, anarchism and their nationalistic derivatives like Zionism. The result was that they *all* strengthened, in their way the oikoïdal state-apparatus with *its* capital*ism*. The staunch nationalist Max Weber became its "rational prophet."

The "sober lifestyle" was nothing but a necessity of life for a large middle class caught between the rich elite with their conspicuous consumption and the more serious poverty of the proletariat. What is called *Erwerbstrieb* is part of the elite-ideology and *Wunschdenken* (wishful thinking): *all* who are below them should be non- or contra-revolutionary, pious, obedient and hardworking; after that life only the poor could acquire heaven.

In short, if what Mommsen wrote was indeed Max Weber's opinion, then this is more wrong than demonstrated in Chapter 1; if it concerns Wolfgang Mommsen's opinion, he did not really understand Weber's theories.

Both, in a way, refrained from studying the realities of the enigmas, but Max Weber was quite honest about it. Exactly at the time when he should have started an in-depth investigation of *Volk* and *Volksgemeinschaft,* he confessed that a concept like "ethnic" is completely useless, but continued with:

> We are not busy with sociology for its own sake but want to show briefly which very complicated problems are hidden behind an allegedly quite simple phenomenon.[857]

The remark is located in *Wirtschaft und Gesellschaft* directly after the short *oikos*-section and the subsequent very short chapter concerning the related concepts of race, tribe, ethnic community and nation. Weber never did renew the discussion about the *combination* of these concepts.

---

857 WG, 242; see also ES, 395; "Wir aber treiben nicht Soziologie um ihrer selbst willen und begnügen uns daher, in Kürze aufzuzeigen, welche sehr verzweigten Problemen sich hinter dem vermeintlich ganz einheitlichen Phänomen verbergen." I prefer my translation.

This combination was appropriate for Weber as well as Mommsen because *Volksgemeinschaft* was "one of the most important dictums in the political rhetoric of the Weimar Republic."[858] It is the period in which the German enigmas were created that still haunt us today.

10.4 Weber in China

I referred above to an "inevitable conflict" between the USA and China. The newest book I could consult about China published in the USA has a disturbing title: *The China Boom. Why China Will Not Rule the World;* it was published in 2017 by the experienced scholar Ho-fung Hung, an associate professor of political economy at Johns Hopkins University.[859]

As a symbol of the title-message a flattened balloon with the Chinese flag is given on the cover; the "boom" was apparently so heavy that the balloon collapsed. The message is clear: "So, readers, US politicians, military, journalists or bankers, do not be afraid anymore: the universal struggle of Capitalism versus Communism shall be won by us"; and if a Chinese professor in Amerika launches this message, it must be the very truth. Let's suppose that all this concerns "sales tactics" because the content of the book is not so overdone.

Like every good scholar, Ho-Fung Hung is also a myth-hunter. According to the cover text, he even challenges four myths at once:

> ...that China could offer an alternative model of growth; that China is radically altering power relations between the East and the West; that China is capable of diminishing the global power of the United States; and that the Chinese economy would restore the world's wealth after the 2008 financial crisis.

To "hunt" these myths, the author uses Max Weber's *The Protestant Ethic and the Spirit of Capitalism* from which he derives his definition, his idea of capitalism or the "capitalist spirit."

This idea is not more developed than what Weber wrote in his treatise: "Man is dominated by the making of money, by acquisition as the ultimate purpose

858 Michael Wildt, "Anmerkungen zur 'Volksgemeinschaft,'" in: *Zeiträume Potsdamer Almanach, 2009* (Potsdam: Zentrum für Zeithistorische Forschung), 201–211. See also the article by Norbert Götz, "Volksgemeinschaft" in the Ingo Haar and Michael Fahlbusch, ed., 713–721.

859 Ho-fung Hung, 2017.

of his life," which is of course practically and historically utter nonsense. The author tries to upgrade this by referring to "theorists of capitalism" like Wallerstein and Arrighi, which is not surprising since he teaches at the *Arrighi Center for Global Studies*.

As explained in my Chapter 1, however, capital-*ism* is a *combination* of strong state-power (bureaucracy, military, police) and monopolizing economic interests in which banks play an important role relative to, for instance, the *national debt* problem. As such, these combinations form the most powerful oikoidal systems. This shall be explained at the end of this section.

Ho-fung Hung wrote an interesting book with useful data and analyses about China, but its general scope and his reception of Weber's writings should be revised. The article by Po-Fang Tsai about the reception of Weber's sociology in China and Taiwan could be helpful in this regard.[860]

Before the war, two of Weber's books were already translated into Chinese: the *Protestant Ethic* (1930, 1940) and *General Economic History* (1936). They seem to have played a not unimportant role in the modernization debates and the discussions of the "cultural philosophers" of the New Confucianism; details are not available.

It is possible that German sociologists like Tönnies, Simmel, Max and Alfred Weber or Werner Sombart were perceived at the time as a good alternative to the British and French sociologies of the main colonial powers. Their practical use was limited, and in the ideological discussions, writers like the Germans Spengler and Nietzsche were preferred. In the 1930s the debates among Chinese intellectuals changed from the pros and cons of westernization to "modernization Chinese style."

It took about five decades before a new Weber reception occurred; in Taiwan, there was even a true "Weber Fever" in the 1980s:

> It was in these circumstances that Weber took center stage as a prophet who seemed to foresee the relationship between economic development and ethical orientation, but failed to apprehend some key characteristics of Chinese culture… [and]… was replaced by more advanced interpretations of Weber from Taiwan and China.[861]

860 Po-Fang Tsai, 2016, 118–133. The author works at the *Graduate Institute of Humanities in Medicine*, Taipei Medical University, Taiwan. The article has a useful bibliography with many Chinese "Weber"- articles.

861 Po-Fang Tsai, 2016, 122.

This "replacement" was done under the direct influence of the American Gary Hamilton and the German Wolfgang Schluchter, one of the most important Weber-promoters in the West.

They also introduced the "Weber as anti-Marx" approach to support the activities of Cheng-Shu Kao and collaborators (supervised by Hamilton) and Chung-Hwa Ku and Duan Lin (both supervised by Schluchter). Kao further introduced the works of Schütz, Marcuse and Habermas in the 1990s.

Po-Fang Tsai also provides an overview of the Weber-translations (*Economy and Society*, ES, in Taiwan 1985–99 and in China 1997–2010, etc.) and also of translations of Weber-interpreters like Bendix, Giddens or Schluchter. In China the journal *Guowai Shehuixue* (Foreign Sociology) started to appear in 1988, a product of the very active Guo-Xun Su, who also published a Weber monograph in which he pointed out, for instance,

> ...that Weber's deliberative attitude toward western capitalism would be invaluable for Chinese intellectuals seeking to develop a non-Marxist sociology in the context of heated debates about the sinification of the social sciences in post-reform-era China... Su's (2007, 2011) criticisms were aimed at Weber's treatment of Taoism rather than Confucianism...[862]

From Po-Fang Tsai's overview, we get the impression that Weber studies have been emancipated now from Western interpretations in both China and Taiwan. However, in their development to the present, different end-results have come to the fore. This could be due to the Western visiting scholars like Hamilton or Schluchter who propagated "Weber as anti-Marx," while an approach of "Marx as anti-Weber" would be at least as relevant.[863] If the former approach had some function in the Cold War policy at the time, it has not been explained.

An adequate follow up to Po-Fang Tsai's overview is Don Zang's dramatic article in a relevant journal, the *Max Weber Studies*.[864] Zang divides the Weber reception in China into two periods. The first from 1985–1992, is covered by Po-Fang Tsai and is judged positive (a "Weber Fever"!) by Don Zang. This

862 Po-Fang Tsai, 2016, 129.

863 If these Western teachers used in their lectures the only reasonable attempt of making a Weber-Marx comparison, the "operations in Taiwan and China" must have been rather satisfactory: Veit Bader, ed. 1976, 2 volumes.

864 Don S. Zang, 2014, 1–33. The author is an Associate professor of Law at the University of Washington.

changes drastically from 1993 onward. Zang even laments in the name of Max Weber personally, as if the man has not been dead for a century! Zang writes:

> But the real tragedy *for* Weber, or *his* nightmare... when China's legal theorists turned against *him* by treating him as an icon for Eurocentrism... the second period is essentially an anti-modern project camouflaged in postmodernist terms... the real tragedy, or the nightmare, is that *if Weber were to wake up in China today,* he might find what's going on in China looks rather familiar. (my italics, H.D.)

These last three words could be perceived as the self-criticism *of Max Weber!* What is wrong with throwing-away inadequate (theoretical) products from the West? Weber's theories were criticized time and again during the past century in the West. Notwithstanding this, it was decided to export them as still good enough for the ex-colonies (Schluchter, Hamilton). Not only did right-wing Westernizers do this as a contribution to the Cold War; left-wingers were not less stubborn.

Take, for instance, a typical left-wing Dutch philosophy professor, Lolle Nauta (known as "ideologue of the socialist party"), who ca. 1975 started teaching Hegel's theories in Zimbabwe as money for agricultural projects was not available there and the hungry students had only Hegel's *Phänomenologie* to swallow; the imported professor has been paid a higher income for this service from the Dutch development-funds than two presidents of Zimbabwe.

Thanks to Ho-fung Hung's Arrighi-function we can now also remember Arrighi's Pavlovian reaction concerning an early-modern Chinese admiral: it was impossible that this Chinese man could conduct large-scale business in South Asia; he must have been on a mission to "conquer the whole world" as one of his pupils again suggests on the cover of his new book. Or concerning the Weber reception, this author remarks in 2017:

> Though many scholars have rejected Weber's cultural explanation of the rise of capitalism, his definition of capitalism as a system with the "ceaseless accumulation of capital" as its modus operandi can be found in many works by contemporary theorists of capitalism, including Immanuel Wallerstein and Giovanni Arrighi.[865]

865 Ho-fung Hung, 2017, 6.

In a recent, ordinary, empirical research project, Weber-reception receives another function. Take the one found in the regions of the "Overseas Chinese" by Swee Hoon Chuah and others.[866]

They wanted to study something like *The Spirit of Overseas Chinese Capitalism* inspired by Max Weber's *Protestant Work Ethic*. The Chinese in Southeast Asia make up less than 5% of a population of 600 million, but they contribute many times their share to the regional economy. Most of them settled in Southeast Asia in the beginning of the 20th century as the political and economic turmoil in China became too dangerous and widespread. They were not settlers in the sense defined in Chapter 6. Half a century later, "ethnic Chinese" controlled between one-quarter and three-quarters of private business activity in Southeast Asia, an economic miracle that attracted a great deal of research. Had they read Weber's famous treatise?

By adopting an irrational expectation about how helpful Weber's "spirit" could be, they could not discover the "mystery" of how these Chinese immigrants became so successful in a relatively short time. I did not receive the impression that the research-team contains people with a relevant historical background of the region, nor of Weber's work.[867] This use of Weber is, therefore, nothing but innocent namedropping.

Last but not least a few remarks about a really serious scholar, Wang Hui and his emancipated and critical Chinese reception of Max Weber. Viren Murthy's long introduction to Wang Hui's "magisterial four-volume book *The Rise of Modern Chinese Thought*" (Chinese language; 2004) made me anxious to study this, but it has not been translated. Murthy's introduction made clear how rich his works are in historical subjects, methodological discussions and highly relevant criticisms of European "holy spirits." It is impossible, therefore, to comment here in a relevant way on Wang Hui's ideas.

In English he recently published a book entitled *The Politics of Imagining Asia* (2011) that attracted good attention.[868] It can be characterized as "typically Chinese" because it analyzes "nationalism" and its application in Japan with all possible consequences. This nationalism, with its European sources, is historically and topically a highly controversial phenomenon in a Chinese context. It is closely connected to the discussion reproduced in Chapter 9.

His book also contains a chapter on Max Weber in which Wang critiques Max Weber's *Confucianism and Taoism*:

866 Swee Hoon Chuah, ed., 2016, 1095–1118.

867 I wrote extensively about the "Overseas Chinese" in my 2012, Chapter 25, 459–485.

868 Wang Hui, 2011.

> "Weber and the Question of Chinese Modernity" discusses some basic issues concerning how to reflect critically on the categories that we use to understand China. In particular, Wang warns against using a transhistorical concept of "rationalization" and encourages scholars to focus on the intricate politics of translation when categories such as "science" and "revolution" were introduced into the Chinese lexicon.

Weber's equation of a "worldwide phenomenon of modernity" with his view on the continual refinement of this "Western rationalization" is rightly criticized and, as I understand it, counteracted by his own Chinese work and the attempt to develop a native Chinese "modernity" (with Chinese concepts).

Wang Hui must be glad with the subject and text of this book: the word "rationalization" is not mentioned at all, while from beginning to end the main categories used by Weber and Weber-supporters are "translated." This means: redefining and/or confronting with their historical (Chinese) basis the concepts like "capitalism," "market," "tradition," "town/city," "oikos," "racism," "the West," "the East," and so on and so forth and in particular with the *combination/relationships* in which they are effective, known or negated.

The several reviewers of his book comment that "Wang interrogates how we should understand pre-modern spaces and times in a way that both reveals their otherness and helps us to rethink our own present."[869] We are confronted with a scholar who brings case-studies to the fore in order to define and understand long-term developments of social, political or historical problems. It's a method that can be only applauded.

When Viren Murthy remarks that "Wang's concepts of socialism and capitalism need to be articulated more completely before we can assess the legacies of Sun Yat-sen, Mao and Lenin"[870] or analyze the "logic of global capitalism," then I can only invite him to do this along the lines and criticisms demonstrated in this book. For instance, something like "capitalist modernity" is in need of rephrasing or complete negation in the light of the given market-*oikos* history.

One form of the "rephrasing" attempted in my book can now be summarized (and simplified!), while negating previous suggestions à la Ho-fung Hung and

869 Viren Murthy, 2006, 137–165. See also the review by Viren Murthy of *The Politics of Imagining Asia* by Hui Wang and Huters in: *The China Journal,* 67 (2012), 178–180 and reviews of this book in *Asian Studies Review* 36–33, 2012, 435–436 by Joel Wing-Lun; *China Perspectives* 4, 2012, 77–78 and *National Identities*, 18, 2016, 430–433 by Susanne Weigelin-Schwiedrzik. However, the book was not available in Amsterdam university libraries.

870 Viren Murthy, 2012, 181.

adjusting his message: both the "USA" and "China" can be defined as "(super-) Oikoi"; there are two kinds of those *Oikoi*: in the one *combination* dominates the economic interest, and in the other, the political-bureaucratic interest; the USA is at the moment the best example of the former and China of the latter. Whether one calls the first capitalist and the second socialist or both capitalist, does not matter at all in the light of the following basic characteristics.

They both negate internal and external market-forces, -activities, etc., and, therefore, the frequently heard slogans of opposition groups concerning technological change, climate change, refugees, navigating contemporary globalization, and so on, like "active state policies are required!" or "The free market fetish is a dead-end!" They seem to be utter nonsense: from before the two world-wars, what was already available of a "free market" was effectively eliminated as oikoidal capital-*ism* was established with its world-wide impact. Opposition groups have to retune their slogans.

The USA-*Oikos* is not only *technically* the largest and most sophisticated military *oikos*, but is also strongly bound to the European-Christian *perpetrator-traditions* (war, imperialism, genocides, colonialism, "friend-enemy" thoughts-including those of Max Weber- and related longstanding perpetrator practices). The "economic interest"- part of this *combination* erodes, is negated or gradually disappears thanks to the perpetrator interests and a new cycle starts in its conjuncture; indeed, it seems to be a waste of time and energy to copy this professional loser's "manifest destiny" (it is not realised enough that the USA has lost *every* war after 1945, except against the tiny island Grenada in the Caribbean in 1981).

The Chinese *Oikos*, whatever its present economic, military and political power is not only in several respects *technically* still a kind of "third world" country (unbalanced town-country antagonisms, etc.), but is also strongly bound to the European-Christian *victims-traditions* (thanks to opium- and other wars, imperialism, and colonialism) and to the subsequent *liberation-and development-traditions* (thanks to liberation from European and other occupiers, etc. and lessons like the "Great Leap Forward").

The Chinese "political-bureaucratic"-interest part of its *combination* is affected by both traditions, but it is too difficult to assess whether this is leading to erosion of this interest (in concrete terms: of the power of the party) because several kinds of "unforeseen" foreign economic or political compensations, losses or gains can happen or the continuous—and rather inevitable—internal tensions between centralizing and de-centralizing interests. Modern technology probably allows it to make a relevant and adequate communication network: not only "clever cities" but a "clever country" as well.

It is straightforward to predict that if such an "erosion" + foreign gains occur, the oikoidal interest is negated in favor of "the market" (whatever its topical definition). In particular, both traditions can contribute to an active policy to counteract the negative consequences: an aggressive *peace*-policy against the traditional *perpetrator*-policies of the West can benefit the current historical Chinese strong traditions of external rather than global *market* activities.

The necessity to apply, for instance, the historical method of Wang Hui to investigate the complicated Chinese past in order to build up the present Chinese positions, once combined with many others in a pool of experiments, demands great flexibility to yield a profitable way to learn the "lessons from both traditions" aimed at developing an "aggressive *peace* policy" synonymous with an ultimate market destiny.

CHAPTER 11

Epilogue

In the previous chapters, many basic theoretical and practical elements of market-*oikos* relations were discussed, using the works of Max Weber to accompany this research. The task ahead is obvious: combine them and possibly add new elements into a sound market-*oikos*/ town-country theory, helpful for complicated and controversial future research. Which difficulties arise when combining the discussed elements? Which new elements could or should be added? What should be the subject and method of such operations and the subsequent studies? Not all questions can be properly answered but the following belongs to the necessary attempts.

11.1 A Favorite Method

We should avoid developing apriori theories and laws, applying old sociological or economic models, or using mathematical models for non-quantifiable items. We should also avoid as much deductive thinking/work as possible.

First and foremost, a kind of "map" should be prepared from the problem(s) to be investigated or analyzed: this should be done from all possible points of view, so that the endresult is a basic "map of the problem" we intend to study. This can be a rather superficial but interdisciplinary exercise or a more detailed one like that given in the first chapter of this book or in the first part of my previous study, *History of the Opium Problem*.

A handy tool in this procedure is an etymological analysis of specific items that pop up during this "mapmaking." Take for example "hands" and "feet," which I have analyzed before.[871] The comparison between an animal and a plant culture (Chapter 7 above) directly points to the importance of a comparison of mobility and immobility, respectively, in which the use of "feet" and "hands" is of pivotal importance (the hand as even "the main tool of the evolution" in Marx's and Engels's theory).

From this, we can derive the way(s) to proceed: alone or together with representatives of other disciplines; along empirical and/or theoretical investigations; always following both temporal (diachronical) and "spatial" (synchronical) directions. And we can derive specific theses for use as

871 Hans Derks, 1986, 101–120.

 | DOI:10.1163/9789004383913_012

guidelines in the investigations: like the ones that follow here as a result of this book. Although an attempt is made to formulated them in a non-eurocentric way, it is evident that thanks to Max Weber's major influence on the composition of this book, Eurocentric thoughts prevail.

11.2 The Theses

In the previous chapters a significant amount of data and their combinations or theories are discussed about the market-*oikos* and town-country relations. The task ahead is to formulate a new (interdisciplinary) theory about these relations. The following theses could be perceived as stepping stones to that aim.

1. From time immemorial there has been an asymmetrical relationship between human *oikoi* and their environment in the sense that nature/environment is "doing what it does" and oikoi are by definition obliged "to get what they need by all means" and if "it" is not there, one has to look for "it" elsewhere. Human history, therefore, continues to change by improving the "getting," the "means," the "looking" and "the ability to cover distances." This produces a good definition of market-*oikos* relations, while "the place in which one (temporarly) lives" and its direct environment must be the beginning of what much later becomes "town" versus "country." This combination is fundamental to what follows (see Chapters 2 and 3).
2. What has to become the "market" (equivalent to "what is available") is fully indifferent to *oikoi*. This may be a basic idea, but to become a true market, the *oikoi*'s *selection out of what is available* is no less basic after the improvement as described under number 1, above, has taken place: the main selection is between the sedentary and the mobile, the plant and the animal cultures (see introduction to Chapter 7), forget the Darwinian selection-stories.
3. Thanks to the basic asymmetrical relations in (1) and (2), an appropriate definition of "market" is also: the space in which a communication system of the several *oikoi* has to take place, aiming at the exchange of what is considered as surpluses of productions and services, which is usually a rather peaceful communication between mutually foreign *oikoi*.
4. If this communication is an exception and a warlike or inimical venture, the market is directly negated (after one directly has to suffer from the problematic "autarchy"), which happens only from the oikoïdal side and, in history, particularly by the large "units" of *oikoi* like states (-as-Oikos); see Chapter 6.

5. In the majority of the history of this communication, barter-exchange is the only way of dealing; money has been used to a certain extent rather recently (as such a limitation to the whole market process for a long time), while barter always remains available and possible until today along with the money-distribution. The most recent development, the typical bank-policy of the negation of cash money and the use of virtual money (bitcoins, etc.) are in reality the most far-reaching negation of existing market-means. The *oikoi* that organize this "secret" communication negate the market as a public institution.[872]
6. Money cannot be identified with capital*ism*; it is an abstract value *tool* and not an object of property in situations in which no interchange of goods is possible or desirable (see Chapter 1.2). To exchange abstract tools for tools has nothing to do with a market communication system.
7. A market cannot be identified with capital*ism*; it is by definition a peaceful communication system in which something is interchanged between interests with an asymmetric value and property behavior concerning supply and demand. Participants in a market are by definition *potentially* at an equal information level (not necessarily topically).
8. An oikos as an extended family of fathers, mothers, children and other "members" system with its own value-system is the most reasonable interest-constellation on a human scale if it is constantly directed towards interchange and communication between supply and demand in every aspect of life. Every oikos is a combination of social, economical, political and spatial aspects, whatever the different "colors" of this combination among oikoi. The most important historical differences are the ones between sedentary and agriculturally oriented *oikoi* and mobile, animal-oriented *oikoi* (see Chapters 2 and 7).
9. If they meet each other in a market-based communication deals must be made on pragmatic grounds, which can lead to more permanent peaceful relations, and not only in local environments (see Silk Road market). The developed xenophobic, moral, religious and other resentments have to be negated (for the time being) because they are limitations to market behavior (see Chapters 1.3, 3, 4, 5).
10. Agricultural *oikoi* are internally hierarchically structured much more sharply then non-sedentary ones (see Chapters 3, 7 and the beginning of 8); anti-market sentiments are always available. If they are part of a larger hierarchical and sedentary constellation (see feudalism, aristocracy,

872 It seems that Russia has introduced or plans to introduce its own bitcoin ("cryptorubel"): *Volkskrant* 17-10-2017.

religious institutions; Chapter 9) the given resentment characteristics are articulated more sharply through ideological and religious features and thanks to economic interests of the larger "unit": the stronger the pressure from "above," the more difficult it is for market-communication to develop and the greater the chance that the "larger unit" will impose its own market-relations inimical to those of the "lower-units."[873]

11. A state is an *oikos* (-like) system on an inhuman scale, which by definition undermines the functioning of markets and of *oikoi* on a human scale and capitalist production-consumption relations. See Chapter 4. A still non-existent "ideal state" should be a non-ideological and non-moral tool of the communication system caring for the functioning of the market communication, nothing more and nothing less; see Chapter 6.
12. Double-entry bookkeeping and cameralist bookkeeping were/are tools of the state to organize its income system and to intervene in and control market-participants and their gains/losses as an important source of state-income. Renaissance states started with it with the help of religious institutions, for internal use and armies used it for external activities. See Chapter 1.4. The later, larger, absolutist states-*oikoi* rationalized it and made its typical (parasitical) *balance* system into a general principle of political economy and philosophy: this type of *oikoi* can only create costs (court, army+ police and bureaucracy). Payments of all these costs became the subject of a large command-structure that created all possible new *oikos versus market* conflicts concerning taxation of people, capitalist production and distribution, creation of eternal state-debts or simply by robbing internal and external interests and competitors in oikoïdal dynastic wars.
13. When thanks to the Enlightenment and French Revolution, this monarchical-aristocratic state-*oikos* (strongly backed by the Catholic and Protestant religions) developed into the civil nation-state (strongly backed by the new modern science), nationalism inherited and modernized notions of *race-nation-Volk-language* that became the main elements of the new oikoïdal state; see Chapters 1.5, 9.
14. Capital*ism* undermines the proper functioning of markets and of capitalist production thanks to its inherent monopolistic drive and its unavoidable

873 A most spectacular historical example is the monarchical-aristocratic transformation of a rather peaceful global commerce of private commercial *oikoi* into a fighting and conquering organization under a centralized heading, the VOC (Dutch East India Company) around 1600. See my 2015, 24–35.

cooperation with an *oikos*-as-state in national, foreign or colonial settings; see Chapters 1.4, 6 and 8.

15. The framework in which 1–14 have mainly existed, acted and developed during a large part of history consists of the antagonistic relations of town and country: a few months ago we arrived at the situation that 51% of the world population was dwelling in towns and cities; see Chapters 1–10.

11.3 The Follow-up

Indeed, towards a Market-*Oikos*, Town-Country theory.

Bibliography

Achtemeier, Paul, ed. *The HarperCollins Bible Dictionary.* New York: HarperCollins, 1996.

Adorno, Theodor. *Kritik: Kleine Schriften zur Gesellschaft.* Frankfurt a.M.: Suhrkamp, 1971.

Adorno, Theodor. *Studien zum autoritären Charakter.* Frankfurt a.M.: Suhrkamp, 1976.

Aho, James. *Confession and Bookkeeping: The Religious, Moral, and Rhetorical Roots of Modern Accounting.* New York: SUNY Press, 2005.

Al-Wardi, Ali. *Soziologie des Nomadentums: Studie über die iraqische Gesellschaft.* Neuwied: Luchterhand, 1972.

Aly, Götz and Susanne Heim. *Vordenker der Vernichtung: Auschwitz und die deutschen Pläne für eine neue osteuropäische Ordnung.* Frankfurt a.M.: Fischer, 1993.

Anderson, Eugene. *The Food of China.* New Haven/London: Yale University Press, 1988.

Anderson, Perry. *Lineages of the Absolutist State.* London: New Left Books, 1974.

Anderson, Perry. *The New Old World.* London: Verso, 2011.

Andors, Stephen. *China's Industrial Revolution. Politics, Planning and Management, 1949 to the Present.* London: Robertson, 1977.

Anonymous. *Antisemiten-Spiegel: Die Antisemiten im Lichte des Christenthums, des Rechts und der Wissenschaft.* Danzig: Verlag A.W. Kafemann, 1900.

Archer, Robin. *Why is there no Labor Party in the United States?* Princeton, NJ: Princeton University Press, 2007.

Arrighi, Giovanni. *Adam Smith in Beijing: Lineages of the Twenty-First Century.* London; Verso, 2007.

Arrighi, Giovanni. *The Long Twentieth Century: Money, Power, and the Origins of Our Times.* London: Verso, 1994.

Askew, James. "Review of Hans Derks' 'History of the Opium Problem.'" *Social History of Alcohol and Drugs* 27 (2013): 106–108.

Augstein, Rudolf, ed. *"Historikerstreit." Die Dokumentation der Kontroverse um die Einzigartigkeit der nationalsozialistischen Judenvernichtung.* München: Piper, 1987.

Austin, Martin and Pierre, Vidal-Naquet. *Economic and Social History of Ancient Greece: an introduction.* London: Batsford, 1977.

Avalos, Hector. *The End of Biblical Studies.* Amherst: Prometheus Books, 2007.

Ayubi, Nazih. *Over-stating the Arab State. Politics and Society in the Middle East.* London: Tauris, 1995.

Bachararch, Zwi. "Ignaz Zollschans Rassentheorie." In *Jüdische Integration und Identität in Deutschland und Österreich, 1848–1918*, 179–199. Edited by Walter Grab. Tel-Aviv: Universität Tel-Aviv, Fakultät für Geisteswissenschaften, 1984 (ed., 1984).

Bader, Veit, ed. *Einführung in die Gesellschaftstheorie. Gesellschaft, Wirtschaft und Staat bei Marx und Weber.* Frankfurt a.M.: Campus Verlag, 1976.

Badinter, Elisabeth, *De een is de ander.* Amsterdam: Contact, 1988. Translation of *L'un est l'autre*, 1987 by Rosalie Siblesz.

Baecker, Dirk, ed. *Kapitalismus als Religion.* Berlin: Kadmos, 2003.

Baillie, Harold W. and Casey, Timothy K. eds. *Is Human Nature Obsolete? Genetics, Bioengineering, and the Future of the Human Condition.* Cambridge, MA: MIT Press, 2004.

Ball, Philip. *The Water Kingdom. A Secret History of China.* London: Vintage, 2017.

Bannock, Graham, ed. *The Penguin Dictionary of Economics.* Harmondsworth: Penguin, 1978.

Barkan, Elazar. "Mobilizing Scientists against Nazi Racism, 1933–1939." In *Bones, Bodies, Behavior: Essays on biological* Anthropology, 180–206. Edited by George W. Stocking jr. Madison: University of Wisconsin Press, 1988.

Bates, Daniel. *Nomads and Farmers: A Study of the Yörük of Southeastern Turkey.* Ann Arbor: University of Michigan Press, 1973.

Bauer, Wolfgang. *China und die Hoffnung auf Glück.* München: DTV, 1989.

Baum, Rainer. *The Holocaust and the German Elite. Genocide and National Suicide in Germany, 1871–1945.* Totowa NJ: Rowman, 1981.

Beattie, Alan. *False Economy. A Surprising Economic History of the World.* New York: Riverhead/Penguin, 2009.

Beck, Rainer. *Unterfinning: Ländliche Welt vor Anbruch der Moderne.* München: Beck, 1993.

Beck, Ulrich. *Was ist Globalisierung?* Frankfurt a.M.: Suhrkamp, 1997.

Belich, James. *Replenishing the Earth: The Settler Revolution and the Rise of the Anglo-World, 1783–1939.* Oxford: Oxford University Press, 2011.

Bendix, Reinhard. *Max Weber: An Intellectual Portrait.* London: University of California Press, 1977.

Benjamin, Walter. "Kapitalismus als Religion." In *Gesammelte Schriften*, Vol. 6. Edited by Walter Benjamin. Frankfurt a.M.: Suhrkamp, 1991.

Bentmann, Reinhard and Müller, Michael. *Die Villa als Herrschaftsarchitektur: Versuch einer kunst- und sozialgeschichtlichen Analyse.* Frankfurt a.M.: Suhrkamp, 1970.

Benvenisti, Meron. *Sacred Landscape. The Buried History of the Holy Land since 1948.* Berkeley: University of California Press, 2000.

Bergier, Jean-François. "From the Fifteenth Century in Italy to the Sixteenth Century in Germany." In *The Dawn of Modern Banking*, 105–131. Edited by the Center for Mediaeval and Renaissance Studies. New Haven and London: Yale University Press, 1979.

Berman, Harold. *Law and Revolution: The Formation of the Western Legal Tradition.* Cambridge, MA: Harvard University Press, 1983.

Bernard, Jacques. "Trade and Finance in the Middle Ages, 900–1500." In *The Fontana Economic History of Europe*, Volume 1, 274–339. Edited by Carlo Cipolla. London: Collins, 1973.

Bij, Theo van der. *Ontstaan en eerste ontwikkeling van den oorlog.* Groningen: Wolters, 1929.

Bintliff, John. "Regional Survey, Demography, and the Rise of Complex Societies in the Ancient Aegean." In *Journal of Field Archaeology* 24 (1997a): 1–38.

Bintliff, John, ed. *Recent Developments in the History and Archaeology of Central Greece.* Oxford: BAR Int. Series 666, 1997b.

Blänkner, Reinhard. "Spät-Alteuropa oder Früh-Neuzeit?" *Geschichte und Gesellschaft* 13 (1987): 559–564.

Boardman, John, ed. *The Cambridge Ancient History.* Cambridge: Cambridge University Press, 1992, vol. 5, The Fifth Century B.C.

Boardman, John, Jasper, Griffin and Oswyn, Murray, eds. *The Oxford History of Greece and the Hellenistic World.* Oxford: Oxford University Press, 1991.

Boehlich, Walter, ed. *Der Berlinder Antisemitismusstreit.* Frankfurt a.M.: Insel Verlag, 1988.

Boldt, Hans. *Deutsche Verfassungsgeschichte: Politische Strukturen und ihr Wandel.* München: DTV, 1990, 2 volumes.

Boltanski, Luc and Eve Chiapello. *The New Spirit of Capitalism.* London/New York: Verso, 2005.

Bosl, Karl. *Die Gesellschaft in der Geschichte des Mittelalters.* Göttingen: Vandenhoeck-Ruprecht, 1966.

Bossen, Laurel. *Chinese Women and Rural Development: Sixty Years of Change in Lu Village, Yunnan.* Lanham/New York: Rowman & Littlefield, 2002.

Braudel, Fernand. *Ecrits sur l'histoire.* Paris: Flammarion, 1969.

Braudel, Fernand. *Civilization and Capitalism, 15th–18th Century.* London: Collins, 1983, 3 volumes.

Bray, David. *Social Space and Governance in Urban China. The* Danwei *System from Origins to Reform.* Stanford: Stanford University Press, 2005.

Bright, John. *A History of Israel.* London: SCM Press, 1979.

Brunner, Otto. "Zum Problem der Sozial- und Wirtschaftsgeschichte." *Zeitschrift für Nationalökonomie* 7 (1936): 671–685.

Brunner, Otto. "Moderner Verfassungsbegriff und mittelalterliche Verfassungsgeschichte." *Mitteilungen des Österreichischen Instituts für Geschichtsforschung,* 14, Ergänzungsband (1939): 513–528.

Brunner, Otto. *Land und Herrschaft: Grundfragen der territorialen Verfassungsgeschichte Südostdeutschlands im Mittelalter.* Brünn/ München: Rohrer Verlag, 1943. Expurgated USA-translation by Howard Kaminsky and James Van Horn Melton, 1992.

Brunner, Otto. *Neue Wege der Sozialgeschichte.* Göttingen: Vandenhoeck und Ruprecht, 1956.

Brunner, Otto. *Das Fach "Geschichte" und die historischen Wissenschaften.* Hamburg: Selbstverlag der Universität, 1959; Rektoratsrede from 11.11.1959.

Brunner, Otto. *Neue Wege der Verfassungs- und Sozialgeschichte.* Göttingen: Vandenhoeck und Ruprecht, 1968.

Bruun, Ole. "The Herding Household: Economy and Organization." In *Mongolia in Transition: Old Patterns, New* Challenges, 65–90. Edited by Ole Bruun and Ole Odgaard. Richmond, Surrey: Curzon Press, 1996.

Bruun, Ole and Odgaard, Ole, eds. *Mongolia in Transition: Old Patterns, New Challenges.* Richmond, Surrey: Curzon Press, 1996.

Bryer, R.A. "The History of Accounting and the Transition to Capitalism in England. Part One: Theory." *Accounting, Organizations and Society* 25 (2000a): 131–162.

Bryer, R.A. "The History of Accounting and the Transition to Capitalism in England. Part Two: Evidence." *Accounting, Organizations and Society* 25 (2000b): 327–381.

Buchanan, K. *The Transformation of the Chinese Earth.* London: Bell, 1973.

Budde, Karl. "Das nomadische Ideal im Alten Testament." *Preußische Jahrbücher* 85 (1896): 57–79; earlier published in *The New World,* Boston, 1895.

Buisson, L. *Zum Gedenken an Otto Brunner, 1898–1982.* broch. Hamburg: Universität, 1983.

Bullock, Alan, Trombley, Stephen and Lawrie Alf, eds. *The New Fontana Dictionary of Modern Thought.* London: HarperCollins, 1999.

Burleigh, Michael. *Germany turns Eastwards. A Study of "Ostforschung" in the Third Reich.* Cambridge: Cambridge University Press, 1989.

Buruma, Ian and Avishai, Margalit. *Occidentalism: The West in the Eyes of Its Enemies.* New York: Penguin Press, 2004.

Busolt, Georg, Bauer, Adolf and Müller, Iwan. *Die griechischen Staats-, Kriegs-, und Privataltertümer.* Nördlingen: Beck, 1887.

Campbell, John K. *Honour, Family and Patronage.* Oxford: Oxford University Press, 1964.

Carmona, Marisa, ed. *Globalization and the Return of the Big Plans.* Delft: Delft University Press, 2003.

Carrier, James, ed. *Meanings of the Market. The Free Market in Western Culture.* Oxford/New York: Berg, 1997.

Cartledge, Paul. *The Spartans: An Epic History.* London: Channel Four, 2002.

Cashmore, Ellis, ed. *Dictionary of Race and Ethnic Relations.* London: Routledge, 1994.

Casson, Lionel. *Reisen in der Alten Welt.* München: Prestel, 1978.

Center for Mediaeval and Renaissance Studies. *The Dawn of Modern Banking.* New Haven/London: Yale University Press, 1979.

Chan, Anita, Madsen, Richard and Unger, Jonathan. *Chen Village: Revolution to Globalization.* Berkeley: University of California Press, 2009.

Chandler, Alfred. "The United States: Evolution of Enterprise." In *The Cambridge Economic History of Europe,* Vol. 7–2, 70–134. Edited by Mathias, Peter and Michael Postan. Cambridge: Cambridge University Press, 1978.

Charyn, Jerome. "Amerikas Totenmaske" in: *Die Zeit,* 14 Aug 2008.

Chatty, Dawn, ed. *Nomadic Societies in the Middle East and North Africa: Entering the 21st century.* Leiden/Boston: Brill, 2006.

Chesneau, Jean. *Peasant Revolts in China 1840–1940.* London: Thames and Hudson, 1973.

Chiapello, Eve. "Accounting and the Birth of the Notion of Capitalism." *Critical Perspectives on Accounting* 18 (2007): 263–296.

Ching-Wah Yip, Francis. *Capitalism as Religion? A Study of Paul Tillich's Interpretation of Modernity.* Cambridge, MA: Harvard University Press, 2005.

Christian, David. *A History of Russia, Central Asia and Mongolia.* Oxford: Blackwell, 1998, vol. 1.

Chuah, Swee Hoon ed. "Is There a Spirit of Overseas Chinese Capitalism?" *Small Business Economics* 47 (2016): 1095–1118.

Cipolla, Carlo, ed. *The Fontana Economic History of Europe.* London: Collins/Fontana Books, 1973, 9 volumes.

Cohen, Edward. *Athenian Economy and Society: A Banking Perspective.* Princeton: Princeton University Press, 1992.

Cohen, Hillel. *Army of Shadows: Palestinian Collaboration with Zionism, 1917–1948.* Berkeley: University of California Press, 2008.

Cohen Stuart, Geert. *The Struggle in Man between Good and Evil: An Inquiry into the Origin of the Rabbinic Concept of Yeser Hara.* Kampen: Kok, 1984.

Coldstream, John Nicolas. "The Formation of the Greek Polis: Aristotle and Archaeology." In *Vorträge/Rheinisch-Westfälische Akademie der Wissenschaften: Geisteswissenschaften; G. 272.* Opladen: Westdeutscher Verlag, 1984.

Collins, Randall. *Macrohistory.* Stanford: Stanford University Press, 1999.

Connolly, Peter and Dodge, Hazel. *The Ancient City: Life in Classical Athens and Rome.* Oxford: Oxford University Press, 1998.

Creveld, Martin van. *The Rise and Decline of the State.* Cambridge: Cambridge University Press, 1999.

Creyghton, Marielouise. *Bad Milk: Perceptions and Healing of a Children's Illness in a North African Society.* Amsterdam: University of Amsterdam, 1981.

Dale, Gareth. *Karl Polanyi: A Life on the Left.* New York: Columbia University Press, 2017.

Dani, Ahmad Hasan and Masson, Vadim, eds. *History of Civilizations of Central Asia* (Paris: Unesco, 1992), Vol. 1: The Dawn of Civilization: Earliest Times to 700 B.C.

Davis, Christie. "The Protestant Ethic and the Comic Spirit of Capitalism." *British Journal of Sociology* 43 (1992): 421–442.

Delumeau, Jean. *Sin and Fear. The Emergence of a Western Guilt Culture 13th–18th Centuries.* New York: St. Martin's Press, 1990.

Derks, Hans. *Tussen hemel en aarde, stad en land: Kritiek van het religieuse kapitalisme.* Groningen: Wolters-Noordhoff/ Eurosboekje, 1970.

Derks, Hans. *De Armoede van het Ekologisme.* Utrecht: University of Utrecht Press/ Werkgroep Milieukunde, 2e ed., 1975.

Derks, Hans. *Karl Marx en Lawrence Krader over de zgn. Aziatische Productiewijze.* Amsterdam: University of Amsterdam, 1978; Phd. study.

Derks, Hans. *Stad en Land, Markt en Oikos.* Amsterdam: University of Amsterdam, 1986; Doctoral dissertation.

Derks, Hans. "Das Ende eines einmaligen Phänomens? Die Max Weber Literatur, 1920–1988." *Zeitschrift für Soziologie* 18 (1989a): 282–297.

Derks, Hans, ed. *Kroniek van drie eeuwen revoluties.* Groningen: Wolters-Noordhoff, 1989b.

Derks, Hans. *De Koe van Troje: De mythe van de Griekse Oudheid.* Hilversum: Verloren, 1995a.

Derks, Hans. "A Note on 'Homogalaktes' in Aristotle's POLITIKA." *Dialogues d'histoire ancienne* (CNRS) 21 (1995b): 27–40.

Derks, Hans. "Über die Faszination des Haus-Konzeptes." *Geschichte und Gesellschaft* 22 (1996a): 221–243.

Derks, Hans. "Autarkeia in Greek Theory and Practice." *The European Legacy* 1 (1996b): 1915–1933.

Derks, Hans. *Deutsche Westforschung. Ideologie und Praxis im 20. Jahrhundert.* Leipzig: Akademische Verlagsanstalt, 2001a.

Derks, Hans. "Un Mal Splendide: hommes et femmes dans une 'antiquité postféministe.'" *Dialogues d'histoire ancienne* (CNRS) 27 (2001b): 7–43.

Derks, Hans. "The Ancient Economy: the Problem and the Fraud." *The European Legacy* 7 (2002): 701–735.

Derks, Hans. *Jew, Nomad or Pariah. Studies on Hannah Arendt's Choice.* Amsterdam: Aksant/Transaction Publisher, 2004.

Derks, Hans. "Religion, Capitalism and the Rise of Double-entry Bookkeeping." *Accounting, Business and Financial History* 18 (2008a): 187–213.

Derks, Hans. "New Political Economy of Ancient Greece?" *The European Legacy* 13 (2008b): 743– 745.

Derks, Hans. *The History of the Opium Problem. The Assault on the East, ca. 1600–1950.* Leiden/ Boston: Brill, 2012.

Derks, Hans. *Victims and Perpetrators. Dutch Shoa, 1900–1945 and Beyond.* Paderborn: Brill-Schoeningh, 2018.

Deutschmann, Charles. "The Promise of Absolute Wealth: Capitalism as a Religion," *Thesis Eleven* 66 (2001): 32–56.

Diakonoff, Iwan, ed. *Early Antiquity.* Chicago: University of Chicago Press, 1991.

Di Cosmo, Nicola. *Ancient China and its Enemies: The Rise of Nomadic Power in East Asian History.* Cambridge: Cambridge University Press, 2006.

Divale, William. *Warfare in Primitive Societies: A Bibliography*. Santa Barbara: Clio Press, 1983.

Doering, Detmar. *Mythos Manchestertum: Ein Versuch über Richard Cobden und die Freihandelsbewegung.* Berlin: Friedrich Naumann Stiftung, 2004.

Doren, Alfred. *Italienische Wirtschaftsgeschichte.* Jena: Fischer, 1934.

Drukker, Jan. *The Revolution that Bit its own Tail: How Economic History Changed our Ideas on Economic Growth.* Amsterdam: Aksant, 2006.

Duby, George. *Rural Economy and Country Life in the Medieval West.* London: Edward Arnold, 1968.

Duby, George. *The Early Growth of the European Economy: Warriors and Peasants from the Seventh to the Twelfth Century.* New York: Cornell University Press, 1974.

Duyvendak, Jan. *Wegen en gestalten der Chineesche geschiedenis.* Amsterdam: Elsevier, 1948.

Eberhard, Wilhelm. *Conquerors and Rulers: Social Forces in Medieval China.* Leiden: Brill, 1970.

Edwards, John R. *A History of Financial Accounting.* London: Routledge, 1989.

Efron, John. *Defenders of the Race: Jewish Doctors and Race Science in Fin de Siècle Europe.* New Haven/London: Yale University Press, 1994.

Eich, Armin. *Die politische Ökonomie des antiken Griechenland, 6—3. Jahrhundert v. Chr.* Köln: Böhlau Verlag, 2006.

Eisenstadt, S.N. ed. *The Protestant Ethic and Modernization. A Comparative View.* New York: Basic Books, 1968.

Elvin, Mark. *The Pattern of the Chinese Past.* Stanford: Stanford University Press, 1973.

Elvin, Mark. "Warum hat das vormoderne China keinen industriellen Kapitalismus entwickelt? Eine Auseinandersetzung mit Max Webers Ansatz." In *Max Webers Studie über Konfuzianismus und Taoismus*, 114–134. Edited by Wolfgang Schluchter. Frankfurt a.M.: Suhrkamp, 1983.

Emeljanenko, T. "Nomadic Year Cycles and Cultural Life of Central Asian Livestock-Breeders Before the 20th Century." In *Nomads in Central Asia: Animal Husbandry and Culture in Transition, 19th–20th Century*, 67 ff. Edited by Cornelis van Leeuwen. Amsterdam: Royal Tropical Institute, 1994.

Evans, Richard and Lee, William, eds. *The German Family.* London: Croom Helm, 1981.

Fanfani, Amintore. *Catholicism, Protestantism and Capitalism.* London: Sheed & Ward, 1939.

Faure, David and Liu, Tao Tao, eds. *Town and Country in China.* New York: Palgrave, 2002.

Favier, Jean. *In Naam van God en des Gwins: De wording van de zakenman.* Amsterdam: Contact, 1990, Dutch translation of *De l'or et des épices,* 1987, by Borsboom, Floor and Fonderie, Josine.

Fei, Hsiao-Tung. *Peasant Life in China: A Field Study of Country Life in the Yangtze Valley.* London: Routledge & Kegan Paul, 1980.

Fetscher, Iring, ed. *Der Marxismus: Seine Geschichte in Dokumenten.* München: Piper Verlag, 1973.

Finkelstein, Israel. *The Archaeology of the Israelite Settlement.* Jerusalem: Israel Exploration Society, 1988.

Finley, Moses. *The Ancient Economy.* London: Chatto and Windus, 1975.

Finley, Moses. *Economy and Society in Ancient Greece.* London: Chatto and Windus, 1981.

Finley, Moses. *Ancient History: Evidence and Models.* London: Chatto and Windus, 1985.

Fischer, David. *The Great Wave: Price Revolutions and the Rhythm of History.* Oxford: Oxford University Press, 1996.

Fischer, S. "In Defense of Double Entry Accounting." *The National Public Accountant* (Mai 1997).

Fishberg, Maurice. *The Jews: A Study of Race and Environment.* London: Walter Scott Publishing Co, 1911.

Fisher, William, ed. *The Cambridge History of Iran.* Cambridge: Cambridge University Press, 1968, vol. 1.

Flanzbaum, Hilene, ed. *The Americanization of the Holocaust.* Baltimore: Johns Hopkins University Press, 1999.

Flight, John. "The Nomadic Idea and the Ideal in the Old Testament." *Journal of Biblical Literature* XLII (1923): 158–226.

Forte, Juan Manuel. "Religion and Capitalism: Weber, Marx and the Materialist Controversy." *Philosophy & Social Criticism* 34 (2008): 427–448.

Foster, George, *Oude culturen in een technische wereld.* Utrecht: Spectrum, 1966.

Fourquin, George. Histoire économique de l'Occident médiéval. Paris: Colin, 1969.

Foxhall, Lin. "The Control of the Attic Landscape." In *Agriculture in Ancient Greece*, 156 ff. Edited by Bernhard Wells. Stockholm: Swedisch Institute at Athens, 1992.

Franke, Wilhelm, ed. *China Handbuch: Gesellschaft, Politik, Staat, Wirtschaft.* Reinbek b/H.: Rowohlt, 1977.

Freedland, Jonathan. "The Liberal Zionists." *The New York Review of Books* (August 14, 2014).

Frühsorge, Gotthardt. "Die Einheit aller Geschäfte: Tradition und Veränderung des 'Hausmutter'-Bildes," *Wolfenbütteler Studien zur Aufklärung* 3 (1976): 137–157.

Fuchs-Heinritz, Werner, ed. *Lexikon zur Soziologie.* Opladen: Westdeutscher Verlag, 1995.

Gawantka, Wilfried. *Die sogenannte Polis: Entstehung, Geschichte und Kritik der modernen althistorischen Grundbegriffe der griechische Staat, die griechische Staatsidee, die Polis.* Stuttgart: Franz Steiner, 1985.

Geddes, William. *Peasant Life in Communist China.* Ithaca, N.Y.: Cornell University Monographs, no 6, 1963.

Geijsbeek, John B. *Ancient Double-entry Bookkeeping.* Houston: Scholars, 1914.

Geismann, Georg. "Der Berliner Antisemitismusstreit und die Abdankung der rechtlich-praktischen Vernunft." *Archives Européennes de Sociologie* 34 (1993): 3–16.

Geremek, Bronislaw. *La Stirpe di Caino. L'immagine dei vagabondi e dei poveri nella letterature europee dal xv al xvii secolo.* Milano: Mondadori, 1988.

Geulen, Christoph. *Wahlverwandte: Rassendiskurs und Nationalismus im späten 19. Jahrhundert.* Hamburg: Hamburger Institut d. Sozialgeschichte, 2004.

Ghosh, Peter. *A Historian Reads Max Weber: Essays on the Protestant Ethic.* Wiesbaden: Harrassowitz, 2008.

Ghosh, Peter. *Max Weber and "The Protestant Ethic": Twin Histories.* Oxford: Oxford University Press, 2014.

Gilman, Sander. Smart Jews: The Construction of the Image of Jewish Superior Intelligence. Lincoln/London: University of Nebraska Press, 1996.

Ginat, Joseph. *Blood Disputes among Bedouin and Rural Arabs in Israel: Revenge, Mediation, Outcasting and Family Honor.* London: University of Pittsburgh Press, 1987.

Goetz, Hans-Werner. *Leben im Mittelalter. Vom 7. bis zum 13. Jahrhundert.* München: Beck, 1987.

Goetz, Hans-Werner. *Moderne Mediävistik: Stand und Perspektiven der Mittelalterforschung.* Darmstadt: Wissenschaftliche Buchgesellschaft, 1999.

Goldthwaite, Richard. *The Economy of Renaissance Florence.* Baltimore: The Johns Hopkins University Press, 2009.

Gollwitzer, Helmuth. *Die kapitalistische Revolution.* Münich: Kaiser, 1974.

Gottwald, Norman. *The Tribes of Yahweh: A Sociology of the Religion of Liberated Israel, 1250–1050 BCE.* New York: Orbis Books, 1979.

Grab, Walter, ed. *Jüdische Integration und Identität in Deutschland und Österreich, 1848–1918.* Tel-Aviv: Universität Tel-Aviv, 1984.

Granovetter, Mark and Swedberg, Richard, eds. *The Sociology of Economic Life.* Cambridge, MA: Westview Press, 2001.

Gray, Jack. *Rebellions and Revolutions: China from the 1800s to the 1980s.* Oxford: Oxford University Press, 1990.

Haar, Ingo and Fahlbusch, Michael, eds. *Handbuch der völkischen Wissenschaften: Personen, Institutionen, Forschungsprogramme, Stiftungen.* München: K.G. Saur, 2008; 2017 second edition in 2 volumes.

Hahn, Eduard. *Die Entstehung der Pflugkultur.* Heidelberg: Carl Winter's Universitäts Buchhandlung, 1909.

Hall, Jonathan. "Polis, Community, and Ethnic Identity." In *The Cambridge Companion to Archaic Greece*, 40–61. Edited by H.A. Shapiro. Cambridge: Cambridge University Press, 2007.

Hall-Matthews, David. "Inaccurate Conceptions: Disputed Measures of Nutritional Needs and Famine Deaths in Colonial India." *Modern Asian Studies* (2007) E-journal.

Halper, Jeff. *Between Redemption and Revival: the Jewish Yishuv in Jerusalem in the Nineteenth Century.* Boulder: Westview Press, 1991.

Halperin, Sandra. *War and Social Change in Modern Europe: The Great Transformation Revisited.* Cambridge: Cambridge University Press, 2004.

Hamilton, Gary. "Why No Capitalism in China? Negative Questions in Historical Comparative Research." *Journal of Developing Societies* 1 (1985): 187–211.

Hamilton, Gary. "Max Weber and the Analysis of East Asian Industrialisation." *International Sociology* 2 (1987): 289–300.

Hansen, Mogens. *The Athenian Democracy in the Age of Demosthenes: Structure, Principles, and Ideology.* Oxford: Blackwell Publishers, 2001.

Hansen, Mogens, ed. *The Return of the Polis: The Use and Meanings of the Word Polis in Archaic and Classical Sources.* Stuttgart: Franz Steiner Verlag, 2007.

Hazlitt, William. *The Classical Gazetteer: A Dictionary of Ancient Geography, Sacred and Profane.* London: Whittaker, 1851.

Herberg, Will. *Protestant, Catholic, Jew. An Essay in American Religious Sociology*. New York: Anchor Books, 1960.

Hernandez-Esteve, Esteban. *Preliminary Accounting Thought in Spain, 13th to 16th Centuries*. Paper presented to 11th World Congress of Accounting Historians. Nantes, 2006.

Hershatter, Gail. *The Workers of Tianjin, 1900–1949.* Stanford: Stanford University Press, 1986.

Hilberg, Raul. *Unerbetene Erinnerung: Der Weg eines Holocaust-Forschers.* Frankfurt a.M.: Fischer, 1994.

Himadeh, Sa'id, ed. *Economic Organization of Palestine.* Beirut: American University of Beirut, 1938.

Hodkinson, Stephen. "Animal Husbandry in the Greek Polis." In *Pastoral Economies in Classical Antiquity*, 35–75. Edited by C.R. Whittaker. Cambridge: The Cambridge Philological Society, 1988.

Hodkinson, Stephen. *Property and Wealth in Classical Sparta.* London: Duckworth, 2000.

Ho-fung Hung. *The China Boom: Why China Will Not Rule the World.* New York: Columbia University Press, 2017.

Hooson, David, ed. *Geography and National Identity.* Oxford: Blackwell, 1994.

Horkheimer, Max. *Gesammelte Schriften. Briefwechsel 1913–1973.* Frankfurt a/M.: Fischer, 1995, vol.15–vol. 18.

Horkheimer, Max and Adorno, Theodor. *Dialektik der Aufklärung.* Amsterdam: Querido, 1944.

Hourani, Albert. *A History of the Arab People.* London: Faber & Faber, 1991.

Hsieh, Chiao-min. *Atlas of China.* New York: McGraw Hill, 1973.

Huang, Philip. *The Peasant Family and Rural Development in the Yangzi Delta, 1350–1988.* Stanford: Stanford University Press, 1990.

Humphreys, Sally. *Anthropology and the Greeks.* London: Routledge/Kegan Paul, 1978.

Husman, Lisa. "National Unity and National Identities in the People's Republic of China." In *Geography and National Identity*, 149 ff. Edited by David Hooson. Oxford: Blackwell, 1994.

Hutton, Will. *Describing Greece: Landscape and Literature in the* Periegesis *of Pausanias.* Cambridge: Cambridge University Press, 2005.

Hutton, Will and Giddens, Anthony, eds. *Global Capitalism.* New York: New Press, 2000.

Hyam, Ronald. *Empire and Sexuality: The British Experience.* Manchester: Manchester University Press, 1990.

Infield, Henrik F. *Co-Operative Living in Palestine.* London: Kegan Paul, 1946. International Library of Sociology and Social Reconstruction. ed. Mannheim, Karl.

Ingold, Tim, ed. *Companion Encyclopedia of Anthropology.* London: Routledge, 1997.

Israel, Jonathan. *The Dutch Republic: Its Rise, Greatness, and Fall, 1477–1806.* Oxford: Clarendon Press, 1995.

Jagchid, Sechin and Van Jay, Symons. *Peace, War, and Trade along the Great Wall: Nomadic—Chinese Interaction through two Millennia.* Bloomington: Indiana University Press, 1989.

Jäger, E.L. *Beiträge zur Geschichte der Doppelbuchhaltung.* Stuttgart: Kröner, 1874.

Jew Daniel, Osborne, Robin and Scott, Michael, eds. *M.I. Finley. An Ancient Historian and his Impact.* Cambridge: Cambridge University Press, 2017.

Judis, John. *Genesis. Truman, American Jews, and the Origins of the Arab/Israeli Conflict.* New York: Farrar, Straus and Giroux, 2015.

Jütte, Robert. "Zwischen Ständestaat und Austrofaschismus: Der Beitrag Otto Brunners zur Geschichtsschreibung." *Jahrbuch d. Instituts für Deutsche Geschichte der Universität Tel Aviv* 13 (1984): 237–262.

Kamen, Henry. *Empire.* New York: HarperCollins, 2003.

Kaube, Jürgen. *Max Weber: Ein Leben zwischen den Epochen.* Berlin: Rowohlt, 2014.

Kaye, Joel. *Economy and Nature in the Fourteenth Century: Money, Market Exchange, and the Emergence of Scientific Thought.* Cambridge: Cambridge University Press, 1998.

Kellenbenz, Hermann. *Deutsche Wirtschaftsgeschichte.* München: Beck, 1977–1981, 2 volumes.

Kellenbenz, Hermann, ed. *Handbuch der europäischen Wirtschafts- und Sozialgeschichte.* Stuttgart: Klett-Cotta, 1980 ff, 6 volumes.

Keller, Wolfgang. *Und die Bibel hat doch recht.* Hamburg: Rowohlt, 1964.

Kerber, Harald and Arnold, Schmieder, ed. *Handbuch Soziologie.* Reinbek b.H.: Rowohlt, 1984.

Khaldūn, Ibn. *The Muqaddimah: An Introduction to History.* Edited and translated by Franz Rosenthal. Princeton: Princeton University Press, 1967, 3 volumes.

Khazanov, Anatoly. *Nomads and the Outside World.* London: The University of Wisconsin Press, 1994.

Kiepert, Heinrich. *Lehrbuch der alten Geographie.* Berlin: Reimer, 1878.

King, Frederick. *Farmers of Forty Centuries or Permanent Agriculture in China, Korea and Japan.* London: Cape, 1949.

Kirkby, R.J. *Urbanisation in China: Town and Country in a Developing Economy, 1949–2000 AD*. London: Croom Helm, 1985.

Kirshner, Julius and de Roover, Raymond, eds. *Business, Banking and Economic thought in Late Medieval and Early Modern Europe*. Chicago: University of Chicago Press, 1976.

Kirsten, Ernst. *Die griechische Polis als historisch-geographisches Problem des Mittelmeerraumes*. Bonn: Dümmlers Verlag, 1956.

Kirsten, Ernst. *Landschaft und Geschichte in der antiken Welt*. Bonn: Habelt, 1984.

Kirsten, Ernst and Kraiker, Wilhelm. *Griechenlandkunde: Ein Führer zu klassischen Stätten*. Heidelberg: Winter, 1967, 2 volumes.

Klein, Naomi. *The Shock Doctrine: The Rise of Disaster Capitalism*. London: Allen Lane, 2007.

Kocka, Jürgen. "Entepreneurs and Managers in German Industrialization." In *The Cambridge Economic History of Europe*, 492–590. Edited by Peter Mathias and Michael Postan. Cambridge: Cambridge University Press, 1978, vol. 7.

Köll, Elisabeth. "Factories in the Countryside: The Industrial Workforce and Social Division in Nantong County, 1895–1937." In *Town and Country in China*, 107–125. Edited by David Faure and Tao Tao Liu. New York: Palgrave, 2002.

Kopp, Anatole. *Town and Revolution: Soviet Architecture and City Planning 1917–1935*. London: Thames and Hudson, 1970.

Kornemann, Ernst. *Staaten, Völker, Männer: Aus der Geschichte des Altertums*. Leipzig: Dietrich'sche Verlagsbuchhandlung, 1934.

Krader, Lawrence. *The Asiatic Mode of Production*. Assen: Gorkum, 1975.

Krader, Lawrence. "The Origin of the State among the Nomads of Asia." In *Pastoral Production and Society/Production pastorale et société*, 221–235. Proceedings of the International Meeting on Nomadic Pastoralism in Paris 1–3 December 1976. Cambridge: Cambridge University Press, 1979.

Kriedte, Peter. *Taufgesinnte und großes Kapital: Die niederrheinisch-bergischen Mennoniten und der Aufstieg des Krefelder Seidengewerbes*. Göttingen: Vandenhoeck und Ruprecht, 2007.

Krieger, Karsten, ed. *Der Berliner Antisemitismusstreit 1879–1881: Eine Kontroverse um die Zugehörigkeit der deutschen Juden zur Nation*. München: Saur, 2003, 2 volumes.

Kroeschel, Karl. *Haus und Herrschaft im frühen deutschen Recht*. Göttingen: Vandenhoeck und Ruprecht, 1968.

Kroeschel, Karl. *Deutsche Rechtsgeschichte*. Westdeutscher Verlag: Opladen, 1983a/1986, 2 volumes.

Kroeschel, Karl. "Verfassungsgeschichte und Rechtsgeschichte des Mittelalters." In "Gegenstand und Begriffe der Verfassungsgeschichtsschreibung." In *Der Staat* Beiheft 6 (1983b): 47–77. Quaritsch, Helmut, ed.

Kühl, Stefan. *Die Internationale der Rassisten: Aufstieg und Niedergang der internationalen Bewegung für Eugenik und Rassenhygiene im 20.Jahrhundert*. Frankfurt/New York: Campus Verlag, 1997.

Kuklick, Henrika, ed. *New History of Anthropology.* Chichester, West Sussex: Wiley, 2009.

Kulischer, Josef. *Allgemeine Wirtschaftsgeschichte des Mittelalters und der Neuzeit.* München: Oldenborg, 1971, reprint from 1928 edition, 2 volumes.

Kumar, Dharma, ed. *The Cambridge Economic History of India.* Hyderabad: Cambridge University Press, 1984, 4 volumes.

Kuper, Adam and Kuper, Jessica, eds. *The Social Science Encyclopedia.* London: Routledge, 1999.

Labrie, Arnold. "IJkpunten in het theoretische en historiografische debat." In *Nationalisme, naties en staten. Europa vanaf circa 1800 tot heden*, 50–104. Edited by Leo Wessels and Toon Bosch. Nijmegen: Vantilt, 2015.

Lachin, Mauriche. *La Chine Capitaliste.* Paris: Gallimard, 1938.

Landmann, Salcia. *Der ewige Jude.* München: Piper, 1974.

Lange, Matthew. *Anti-Semitic Elements in the Critique of Capitalism in German Culture, 1850–1933.* Bern: Peter Lang, 2007.

Lattimore, Owen. "Herdsmen, Farmers, Urban Culture." In *Pastoral Production and Society/Production pastorale et société.* Proceedings of the International Meeting on Nomadic Pastoralism in Paris 1–3 December 1976. Cambridge: Cambridge University Press, 1979, 479–491.

Lattimore, Owen. "The Collectivization of the Mongolian Herding Economy." In *Marxist Perspectives* 3.1 (1980): 116–127.

Le Goff, Jacques, ed. *La Nouvelle Histoire.* Paris: Retz-CEPL, 1978.

Le Goff, Jacques. *Money and the Middle Ages: An Essay in Historical Anthropology.* Cambridge: Polity Press, 2012.

Le Goff, Jacques and Schmitt, Jean-Claude, eds. *Dictionnaire raisonné de l'Occident Médiéval.* Paris: Fayard, 1999.

Leake, William. *Travels in Northern Greece.* London: John Rodwell, 1835.

Leese, Daniel, ed. *Brill's Encyclopedia of China.* Leiden/Boston: Brill, 2009.

Leeuwen, C. van, ed. *Nomads in Central Asia. Animal Husbandry and Culture in Transition, 19th–20th Century.* Amsterdam: Royal Tropical Institute, 1994.

Leibowitz, Yeshayahu. *Het geweten van Israel.* Amsterdam: uitgeverij Arena, 1993.

Leland, Jamison A., ed. *Tradition and Change in Jewish Experience.* New York: Syracuse University Press, 1978.

Léon-Dufour, Xavier, ed. *Vocabulaire de Théologie Biblique* (Paris: Cerf 1962).

Lévy, Eduard. *Sparte: Histoire politique et sociale jusqu'à la conquête romaine.* Paris: Edition Du Seuil, 2003.

Lieu, Dakin K. "The Social Transformation of China." *The Chinese Social and Political Science Review* 1 (1917): 66–80.

Lieu, Dakin K. "The Industrial Transformation of China." *The Chinese Social and Political Science Review* 1 (1916): 133–153.

Lindenfeld, David. *The Practical Imagination: The German Sciences of State in the Nineteenth Century.* Chicago: University of Chicago Press, 1997.

Lindquist, Sven. *The Skull Measurer's Mistake.* New York: The New Press, 1997.

Lipphardt, Veronika. *Biologie der Juden: Jüdische Wissenschaftler über "Rasse" und Vererbung, 1900–1935.* Göttingen: Vandenhoeck und Ruprecht, 2008.

Little, Lester K. *Religious Poverty and the Profit Economy in Medieval Europe.* London: Elek, 1978.

Littleton, Ananias C. *Essays on Accountancy.* Urbana: University of Illinois Press, 1961.

Lopez, Roberto. "Italien: die Stadtwirtschaft vom 11. bis 14. Jahrhundert." In *Handbuch der europäischen Wirtschafts- und Sozialgeschichte,* 451–471. Edited by Hermann Kellenbenz. Stuttgart: Klett-Cotta, 1980, vol. 2.

Lossing Buck, John. *Land Utilization in China.* Shanghai: 1937/38, 3 volumes.

Lotter, Konrad, ed. *Marx-Engels Begriffslexikon.* München: Verlag Beck, 1984.

Lucassen, Leo, ed. *Gypsies and Other Itinerant Groups: A Socio-Historical Approach.* London: Macmillan, 1998.

Luijk, Eric van and Jan van Ours. "The Effect of Government Policy on Drug Use: Java 1875–1904." *The Journal of Economic History* 61 (1995): 1–17.

Lustick, Ian. "Abandoning the Iron Wall: Israel and 'the Middle Eastern Muck.'" *Middle East Policy* XV (2008): 30–52.

Maccoby, Hyam. *A Pariah People: The Anthropology of Anti-Semitism.* London: Constable, 1996.

MacMullen, Ramsay. *Christianity & Paganism in the Fourth to Eighth Centuries.* New Haven: Yale University Press, 1997.

Mann, Michael. *The Sources of Social Power.* Cambridge: Cambridge University Press, 1987.

Margalit, Avishai. "In the Shadow of Sharon." *The New York Review of Books* (20 February, 2014).

Marramao, Giacomo. *The Passage West: Philosophy After the Age of the Nation State.* London: Verso, 2012.

Marshall, Richard. *The Local Merchants of Prato: Small Entrepreneurs in the Late Medieval Economy.* Baltimore/London: Johns Hopkins University Press, 1999.

Marx, Karl. *Das Kapital: Kritik der politischen Ökonomie.* Berlin: Dietz, 1971, 3 volumes.

Marx, Karl. *Frühschriften,* edition S. Landshut. Stuttgart: Kröner, 1953.

Marx, Karl. *Grundrisse der Kritik der politischen Ökonomie.* Frankfurt a.M: EVA, w.y.

Marx, Karl. *Grundrisse.* London: Penguin Books, 1973.

Marx, Karl and Engels Friedrich. *Ausgewählte Briefe.* Berlin: Dietz, 1953.

Massin, Benoit. "From Virchow to Fischer: Physical Anthropology and Modern Race Theories in Wilhelmine Germany." In *Volksgeist as Method and Ethic: Essays on Boasian Ethnography and the German Anthropological Tradition,* 79–155. Edited by George Stocking jr. Madison: University of Wisconsin Press, 1996.

Mathias, Peter and Michael Postan, eds. *The Cambridge Economic History of Europe.* Cambridge: Cambridge University Press, 1978., vol. 7–1 and 7–2.

Mauss, Marcel. *Die Gabe.* Frankfurt a.M.: Suhrkamp, 1968.

Mayer, Jane. *The Dark Side: The Inside Story of How the War on Terror Turned Into a War on American Ideals.* New York: Doubleday, 2008.

McKeon, Michael. *The Secret History of Domesticity: Public, Private, and the Division of Knowledge.* Baltimore/London: Johns Hopkins University Press, 2005.

Mearsheimer, John J. and Stephen M. Walt. *The Israel Lobby and US Foreign Policy.* London: Allen Lane, 2007.

Medick, Hans, ed. *Industrialization before Industrialization.* Cambridge: Cambridge University Press, 1981.

Mendenhall, George. "The Hebrew Conquest of Palestine." *The Biblical Archaeologist* XXV (1962): 62–121.

Merl, Stefan. *Bauern unter Stalin: Die Formierung des sowjetischen Kolchossystems 1930–1941.* Berlin: Duncker & Humblot, 1990.

Meyer, John W. *Weltkultur: Wie die westlichen Prinzipien die Welt durchdringen.* Frankfurt a/M.: Suhrkamp, 2005.

Meyer, Konrad, ed. *Gefüge und Ordnung der Deutschen Landwirtschaft.* Berlin: Reichsnährstand Verlag, 1939.

Meyer, Eduard and Bernhard Luther. *Die Israeliten und ihre Nachbarstämme: Alttestamentliche Untersuchungen.* Halle: Niemeyer, 1906.

Mielants, Eric. *The Origins of Capitalism and the "Rise of the West".* Philadelphia: Temple University Press, 2007.

Millett, Paul. *Lending and Borrowing in Ancient Athens.* Cambridge: Cambridge University Press, 1991.

Minaud, Gérard. *La Comptabilité à Rome: Essai d'histoire économique sur la pensée comptable commerciale et privée dans le monde antique romain.* Lausanne: Presses Polytechniques, 2005.

Minogue, Kenneth. "State." In *The Social Science Encyclopedia,* 835–837. Edited by Adam Kuper and Jessica Kuper. London: Routledge, 1999.

Mitterauer, Michael and Sieder Reinhard, eds. *Historische Familienforschung.* Frankfurt a.M.: Suhrkamp, 1982.

Mokyr, Joel. *The Gifts of Athena: Historical Origins of the Knowledge Economy.* Princeton: Princeton University Press, 2002.

Mokyr, Joel, ed. *The Oxford Encyclopedia of Economic History.* Oxford: Oxford University Press, 2003, 4 volumes.

Mokyr, Joel. *A Culture of Growth: The Origins of the Modern Economy.* Princeton: Princeton University Press, 2017.

Monteil, Victor. *Les tribus du Fârs et la sédentarisation des nomades.* Paris: Mouton, 1956.

Morris, Ian. "The Early Polis as City and State." In *City and Country in the Ancient World,* 25–57. Edited by John Rich and Andrew Wallace-Hadrill. London: Routledge, 1991.

Morris, Sarah and John Papadopulos. "Greek Towers and Slaves: An Archaeology of Exploitation." *American Journal of Archaeology* 109 (2005): 155–225.

Mousnier, Roland. *Peasant Uprisings in Seventeenth-century France, Russia and China.* New York: Harper, 1972.

Muchembled, Robert. *L'invention de l'homme moderne: sensibilités, moeurs et comportements collectifs sous l'Ancien Régime.* Paris: Fayard, 1988.

Mukherjee, Prabhat. "The Orissa Famine of 1866." *Orissa Historical Research Journal* 6:1 (1958 for 1957): 69–95.

Muller, Jerzy. *The Mind and the Market: Capitalism in Modern European Thought.* New York: Knopf, 2002.

Müller, Klaus E. *Geschichte der antiken Ethnologie.* Reinbek: Rowohlt, 1997.

Murphy, Rhoads. *The Outsiders: The Western Experience in India and China.* Ann Arbor: University of Michigan Press, 1977.

Murray, Oswyn and Simon, Price, ed. *The Greek City. From Homer to Alexander.* Oxford: Clarendon Press, 1990.

Murray, Oswin. "Life and Society in Classical Greece." In *The Oxford History of Greece and the Hellenistic World*, 256 ff. Edited by John Boardmann.Oxford: Oxford University Press, 1991.

Murthy, Viren. "Review of Wang Hui 'The Politics of Imagining Asia'." *The China Journal* 67 (2012): 178–180.

Murthy, Viren. "Modernity Against Modernity: Wang Hui's critical history of Chinese Thought." *Modern Intellectual History* 3 (2006): 137–165.

Nafissi, Mohammad. *Ancient Athens & Modern Ideology: Value, Theory & Evidence in Historical Sciences. Max Weber, Karl Polanyi & Moses Finley.* London: Institute of Classical Studies, 2005.

Nee, Victor and Richard Swedberg, eds. *On Capitalism.* Stanford: Stanford University Press, 2007.

Needham, Joseph. *The Grand Titration: Science and Society in East and West.* London: George Allen & Unwin, 1969.

Nixon, Lucia and Price, Simon. "The Size and Resources of Greek Cities." In *The Greek City: From Homer to Alexander*, 137–171. Edited by Oswyn Murray and Simon Price. Oxford: Clarendon Press, 1990.

Nolan, Peter. "Collectivization in China: Some Comparisons with the USSR." *Journal of Peasant Studies* 3.2 (1976): 192–219.

Nolte, Paul. "Der Markt und seine Kultur: ein neues Paradigma der amerikanischen Geschichte?" *Historische Zeitschrift* 264 (1997): 329–360.

Noordman, Dirk. *Economie en filosofie in de Vroege Middeleeuwen, 750–1250.* Hilversum: Verloren, 1996.

Northrup, David. "Migration from Africa, Asia and the South Pacific." In *The Oxford History of the British Empire. The Nineteenth Century*, 88–101. Edited by Andrew Porter. Oxford: Oxford University Press, 1999.

Noth, Martin. *Geschichte Israels.* Göttingen: Vandenhoeck und Ruprecht, 1966.

Novak, Michael. *The Catholic Ethic and the Spirit of Capitalism.* London: Macmillan, 1993.

Novick, Peter. *The Holocaust and Collective Memory: The American Experience.* London: Bloomsbury, 1999.

Oberling, Pierre. *The Qashq'i Nomads of Fars.* The Hague/Paris: Mouton, 1974.

Oexle, Otto. "Sozialgeschichte—Begriffsgeschichte—Wissenschaftsgeschichte: Anmerkungen zum Werk Otto Brunners." *Vierteljahrschrift für Sozial- und Wirtschaftsgeschichte* 71 (1984): 304–342.

Ogilvie, Sheilagh. *State Corporatism and Proto-industry: The Württemberg Black Forest, 1580–1797.* Cambridge: Cambridge University Press, 1997.

Olick, Jeffrey and Shannon Anderson. "The Holocaust." In *International Encyclopedia of the Social Sciences.* New York: Macmillan, 2007, vol. 3.

Origo, Iris. *The Merchant of Prato: Francesco di Marco Datini.* Harmondsworth: Penguin, 1986.

Osborne, Robin. *Demos: The Discovery of Classical Attika.* Cambridge: Cambridge University Press, 1985.

Osborne, Robin. *Classical Landscape with Figures: The Ancient Greek City and its Countryside.* London: George Philip, 1987.

Osterhammel, Jürgen. *The Transformation of the World: A Global History of the Nineteenth Century.* Princeton: Princeton University Press, 2014.

Osterhammel, Jürgen. "Britain and China, 1842–1914." In *The Oxford History of the British Empire. The Nineteenth Century*, 146–170. Edited by Andrew Potter. Oxford: Oxford University Press, 2007.

Overy, Richard, ed. *The Times Complete History of the World.* London: Times Books, 2007.

Pagden, Anthony. *Peoples and Empires: Europeans and the Rest of the World.* London: Phoenix Press, 2002.

Pagels, Elaine. *Adam, Eve and the Serpent: Sex and Politics in Early Christianity.* New York: Vintage Books, 1988.

Palyi, Melchior, ed. *Erinnerungsgabe für Max Weber.* München: Duncker und Humblot, 1923, 2 volumes.

Pappe, Ilan. *Ten Myths about Israel.* London: Verso, 2017.

Parks, Tim. *Medici Money: Banking, Metaphysics and Art in Fifteenth-Century Florence.* New York: Norton, 2005.

Passow, Richard. *"Kapitalismus": Eine begrifflich-terminologische Studie.* Jena: Fischer, 1927.

Pastoral Production and Society/Production pastorale et société. Proceedings of the International Meeting on Nomadic Pastoralism in Paris 1–3 December 1976. Cambridge: Cambridge University Press, 1979.

Patai, Raphael and Jennifer Patai-Wing. *The Myth of the Jewish Race.* New York: Scribner, 1975.

Peffer, Nathaniel. "Far Eastern Problems." In *Encyclopaedia of the Social Sciences*, 92–100. New York: Macmillan, 1949, vol. 6.

Perelman, M. *The Natural Instability of Markets: Expectations, Increasing Returns and the Collapse of Markets.* London: Palgrave/Macmillan, 1999.

Perkins, Dwight, ed. *Agricultural Development in China, 1368–1968.* Chicago: Aldine Publishing Company, 1969.

Pernitzsch, M.G. "Shanghai." *Mitteilungen der Ausland-Hochschule an der Universität Berlin* XL (1937, Ostasiatische Studien): 37–92.

Planhol, Xavier de. "Geography of Settlement." In *The Cambridge History of Iran*, 409–468. Edited by W.B. Fisher. Cambridge: Cambridge University Press, 1968.

Pomeranz, Kenneth. *The Great Divergence: China, Europe, and the Making of the Modern Economy.* Princeton: Princeton University Press, 2000.

Pomeroy, Sarah, ed. *Ancient Greece: A Political, Social and Cultural History.* New York, Oxford: Oxford University Press, 1999.

Pompen, Erik, "Begrotingscontrole [National Budget Control]," in: www.trends.be, 2007.

Popova, L. "Modern Animal Husbandry in Central Asia: A Call for Research." In *Nomads in Central Asia: Animal Husbandry and Culture in Transition, 19th–20th Century*, 69–83. Edited by Cornelis van Leeuwen. Amsterdam: Royal Tropical Institute, 1994.

Porter, Andrew, ed. *The Oxford History of the British Empire. The Nineteenth Century.* Oxford: Oxford University Press, 1999, vol. 3.

Postan, Michael, ed. *The Cambridge Economic History of Europe.* Cambridge: Cambridge University Press, 1971ff., second edition, 8 volumes.

Pounds, Norman. *An Historical Geography of Europe 450 BC–AD 1330.* Cambridge: Cambridge University Press, 1973, 3 volumes.

Powers, Samantha. "The Democrats & National Security." *The New York Review of Books* (14 August 2008).

Pribram, Karl. *Geschichte des ökonomischen Denkens.* Frankfurt a.M.: Suhrkamp, 1998, 2 volumes.

Proctor, Robert. "From Anthropologie to Rassenkunde in the German Anthropological Tradition." In *Bones, Bodies, Behavior: Essays on Biological Anthropology*, 138–180. Edited by George W. Stocking Jr. Madison: University of Wisconsin Press, 1988.

Proctor, Robert. "Temporality as Artifact in Paleoanthropology: How New Ideas of Race ... Affected Conceptions of Human Origins." In *New History of Anthropology*, 259–275. Edited by Henrika Kuklick. Chichester, West Sussex: Wiley, 2009.

Proctor, Robert. "Human Recency and Race: Molecular Anthropology, the Refigured Acheulean, and the UNESCO Response to Auschwitz." In *Is Human Nature Obsolete? Genetics, Bioengineering, and the Future of the Human Condition*, 235–269. Edited by Harold Baillie and Timothy K. Casey. Cambridge, MA: MIT Press, 2004.

Quaritsch, Helmut, ed. "Gegenstand und Begriffe der Verfassungsgeschichtsschreibung." *Der Staat* Beiheft 6 (1983).

Quaritsch, Helmut, ed. *Positionen und Begriffe Carl Schmitts.* Berlin: Duncker and Humblot, 1991.

Qu, Lei and Marisa Carmona. "Beijing Courtyard Houses as Cultural Recourses." In *Globalization and the Return of the Big Plans*, 95–119. Edited by Marisa Carmona. Delft: Delft University Press, 2003.

Rabe, Hannah."Haus." In *Historisches Wörterbuch der Philosophie*, 1007–1019. Stuttgart: Schwabe Co, 1974, vol. 3.

Rabe, Hannah. "Das Problem Leibeigenschaft: Eine Untersuchung über die Anfänge einer Ideologisierung." *Vierteljahrschrift für Sozial- und Wirtschaftsgeschichte* Beiheft 64 (1977).

Radkau, Joachim. *Max Weber: Die Leidenschaft des Denkens.* München: Hanser Verlag, 2005.

Ratzel, Friedrich. *Anthropogeographie.* Stuttgart: Engelhorn Verlag, 1909.

Ratzel, Friedrich. *Politische Geographie.* München/Berlin: Oldenbourg, 1923.

Rawski-Sakakida, Evelyn. *Agricultural Change and the Peasant Economy of South China.* Cambridge, MA: Harvard University Press, 1972.

Redford, Donald. *Egypt, Canaan, and Israel in Ancient Times.* Princeton: Princeton University Press, 1993.

Reifer, Tom. "Capital's Cartographer. Giovanni Arrighi: 1937–2009." *New Left Review* 60 (2009) 119–131.

Reinharz, Jehuda, ed. *Dokumente zur Geschichte des deutschen Zionismus, 1882–1933.* Tübingen: Mohr, 1981.

Remer, Charles Frederick, ed. *Readings in Economics for China.* New York: Garland Publishing, 1980; reprint of original 1933, Commercial Press, Shanghai.

Remer, Charles Frederick. *A Study of Chinese Boycotts with Special Reference to Their Economic Effectiveness.* Baltimore: The Johns Hopkins Press, 1933.

Renton, James. *The Zionist Masquerade: The Birth of the Anglo-Zionist Alliance, 1914–1918.* London: Palgrave Macmillan, 2007.

Rhodes, Peter J. *The Greek City States: A Source Book.* Cambridge: Cambridge University Press, 2007.

Rich, John and Andrew Wallace-Hadrill, eds. *City and Country in the Ancient World.* London: Routledge, 1991.

Roberts, John. *A History of China.* London: Palgrave, 2011.

Rodinson, Maxime. *Islam and Capitalism.* London: Allen Lane, 1974.

Roover, Raymond de. "The Organization of Trade," In *The Cambridge Economic History of Europe*, Vol. 3, 42–119. Edited by Michael Postan. Cambridge: Cambridge University Press, 1971.

Roover, Raymond de. *Business, Banking, and Economic Thought in Late Medieval and Early Modern Europe.* Chicago/London: University of Chicago Press, 1976.

Rosenbaum, Heidi, ed. *Seminar: Familie und Gesellschaftsstruktur. Materialien zu den sozioökonomischen Bedingungen von Familienformen.* Frankfurt a.M.: Suhrkamp, 1978.

Rosenbaum, Heidi. *Formen der Familie. Untersuchungen zum Zusammenhang von Familienverhältnissen, Sozialstruktur und sozialen Wandel in der deutschen Gesellschaft des 19. Jahrhunderts.* Frankfurt a.M.: Suhrkamp, 1982.

Rosenberg, Nathan, and L. Birdzell *How the West Grew Rich: The Economic Transformation of the Industrial World.* London: Tauris, 1986.

Rösener, Werner. *Einführung in die Agrargeschichte.* Darmstadt: Wissenschaftliche Buchgesellschaft, 1997.

Rosthorn, Arthur von. "Religion und Wirtschaft in China." In *Erinnerungsgabe für Max Weber*, Vol. 2, 221–239. Edited by Melchior Palyi. München: Duncker und Humblot, 1923.

Rousseau, Jean Jaques. *The Social Contract and The Discourses.* New York/Toronto: Everyman's Library, 1993; translated by G.D.H. Cole, introduction by Alan Ryan.

Runciman, W.G. "Doomed to Extinction: The *Polis* as an Evolutionary Dead-End." In *The Greek City: From Homer to Alexander*, 347–369. Edited by Oswin Murray and Simon Price. Oxford: Clarendon Press, 1990.

Rupnow, Dirk. *Judenforschung im Dritten Reich: Wissenschaft zwischen Politik, Propaganda und Ideologie.* Baden–Baden: Nomos, 2011.

Ruppin, Arthur. *Soziologie der Juden. Bnd. 1. Die soziale Struktur der Juden; Bnd. 2. Der Kampf der Juden um ihre Zukunft.* Berlin: Jüdischer Verlag, 1930–1931.

Ruschenbusch, Eberhard. "Zum letzten Mal: Die Bürgerzahl Athens in 4. Jh. v. Chr." *Zeitschrift für Papyrologie und Epigraphik* 54 (1984a): 253–269.

Ruschenbusch, Eberhard. "Die Bevölkerungszahl Griechenlands im 5. und 4. Jh. v. Chr." *Zeitschrift für Papyrologie und Epigraphik* 56 (1984b): 55–57.

Ruschenbusch, Eberhard. "Die Zahl der griechischen Staaten und Arealgrösse und Bürgerzahl der 'Normalpolis'." *Zeitschrift für Papyrologie und Epigraphik* 59 (1985): 253–263.

Sabean, David. *Property, Production and Family in Neckarhausen 1700–1870.* Cambridge: Cambridge University Press, 1990.

Sachs, Jeffrey. *Common Wealth: Economics for the Crowded Planet.* London: Penguin/Allen Lane, 2008.

Salzman, Philip, ed. *When Nomads settle: Processes of Sedentarization as Adaptation and Response.* New York: Praeger, 1980.

Sand, Shlomo. *The Invention of the Jewish People.* London: Verso, 2009.

Sand, Shlomo. *On the Nation and the "Jewish People".* London: Verso, 2010.

Sand, Shlomo. *How I Stopped being a Jew.* London: Verso, 2014.

Sandner, Gerhard. "In Search of Identity: German Nationalism and Geography 1871–1910." In *Geography and National Identity*, 71–92. Edited by David Hooson. Oxford: Blackwell, 1994.

Schabert, Tilo, ed. *Die Welt der Stadt.* München: Piper, 1990.

Schäfer-Lichtenberger, Christa. *Stadt und Eidgenossenschaft im Alten Testament: Eine Auseinandersetzung mit Max Webers Studie 'Das Antike Judentum'.* Berlin/New York: de Gruyter, 1983.

Schäfers, Bernhard, ed. *Grundbegriffe der Soziologie*. Opladen: Leske, 1998.

Scheidel, Walter, ed. *The Cambridge Economic History of the Greco-Roman World.* Cambridge: Cambridge University Press, 2007.

Schlimmer, Johan. *Oude Aardrijkskunde.* Groningen: Wolters, 1879.

Schluchter, Wolfgang, ed. *Max Webers Studie über das antike Judentum.* Frankfurt a.M.: Suhrkamp, 1981.

Schluchter, Wolfgang, ed. *Max Webers Studie über Konfuzianismus und Taoismus: Interpretation und Kritik.* Frankfurt a.M.: Suhrkamp, 1983.

Schluchter, Wolfgang, ed. *Max Webers Sicht des Islams.* Frankfurt a.M.: Suhrkamp, 1987.

Schluchter, Wolfgang and Fr Graf. *Asketischer Protestantismus und "Geist des modernen Kapitalismus": Max Weber und Ernst Troeltsch.* Tübingen: Mohr, 2005.

Schmitz, Wilhelm. *Haus und Familie im antiken Griechenland.* München: Oldenbourg, 2007.

Schmitz-Berning, Cornelia. *Vokabular des National-Sozialismus.* Berlin/New York: Walter de Gruyter, 2000.

Schubert, Eric. "Innovations, Debts, and Bubbles: International Integration of Financial Markets in Western Europe, 1688–1720." *The Journal of Economic History* 48 (1988): 299–307.

Schulz, Hans-Dietrich. "Land–Volk–Staat: Der geographische Anteil an der Erfindung der Nation." *Geschichte in Wissenschaft und Unterricht* 1 (2000): 4–17.

Schulze, Hans K. *Grundstrukturen der Verfassung im Mittelalter.* Stuttgart: Kohlhammer, 1985, 2 volumes.

Schwab, Dieter. "Familie." In *Geschichtliche Grundbegriffe*, vol. 2, 264. Edited by Otto Brunner. Stuttgart: Klett-Cotta, 1975.

Segev, Tom. *The Seventh Million. The Israelis and the Holocaust.* New York: Hill and Wang, 1993.

Seraphim, Peter. "Die Wanderungsbewegung des jüdischen Volkes." *Schriften zur Geopolitik* Heft 18 (1940).

Shapiro, H.A., ed. *The Cambridge Companion to Archaic Greece.* Cambridge: Cambridge University Press, 2007.

Shaw, Brent. "Eaters of Flesh, Drinkers of Milk: the Ancient Mediterranean Ideology of the Pastoral Nomad." *Ancient Society* 13/14 (1982/'83): 5–31.

Shipton, Kirsty. *Leasing and Lending: The Cash Economy in Fourth-Century BC Athens.* London: Institute of Classical Studies, 2000.

Sinor, Denis, ed. *The Cambridge History of Early Inner Asia.* Cambridge: Cambridge University Press, 1990.

Sirks, Boudewijn. *Qui annonae urbis serviunt. De juridische regelingen in het Romeinse Rijk inzake het vervoer van onus fiscale, met name voor de annona, over zee en over de Tiber.* Amsterdam: University of Amsterdam, diss., 1984.

Slicher van Bath, Bernard. *Mensch en Land in de Middeleeuwen.* Assen: Van Gorkum, 1944, 2 volumes.

Slicher van Bath, Bernard. *The Agrarian History of Western Europe A.D. 500–1850.* London: Arnold, 1963.

Slicher van Bath, Bernard. "Agriculture in the Vital Revolution." In *The Cambridge Economic History of Europe,* vol. 5, 42–134. Edward Rich and Charles Wilson, ed. Cambridge: Cambridge University Press, 1977.

Slicher van Bath, Bernard. "Robert Loder en Rienck Hemmema." In *Bijdragen tot de agrarische geschiedenis,* 52–81. Edited by Bernhard Slicher van Bath. Utrecht: Het Spectrum, 1978.

Smith, Arthur. *Chinese Characteristics.* New York: Revell Company, 1894.

Smith, George. *The Historical Geography of the Holy Land.* New York: Harper Torchbooks, 1966.

Smith, Vincent. *The Oxford History of India.* Oxford: Clarendon Press, 1928.

Snodgrass, Anthony. "Survey Archaeology and the Rural Landscape of the Greek City." In *The Greek City: From Homer to Alexander,* 113–137. Edited by Oswyn Murray and Simon Price. Oxford: Clarendon Press, 1990.

Snodgrass, Anthony. "Archaeology and the Study of the Greek City." In *City and Country in the Ancient World,* 1–25. Edited by John Rich and Andrew Wallace-Hadrill. London: Routledge, 1991.

Sofri, Guido. *Über asiatische Produktionsweise.* Frankfurt a.M.: EVA, 1969.

Sombart, Werner. *Die Juden und das Wirtschaftsleben.* Leipzig: Duncker und Humblot, 1911.

Sombart, Werner. *Händler und Helden: Patriotische Besinnungen.* München/ Leipzig: Duncker und Humblot, 1915.

Sombart, Werner. *Der moderne Kapitalismus: Historisch-systematische Darstellung des gesamteuropäischen Wirtschaftsleben von seinen Anfängen bis zur Gegenwart.* München/Leipzig: Duncker und Humblot, 1919.

Sombart, Werner. *Deutscher Sozialismus.* Berlin: Buchholz und Weisswange, 1934.

Soto, Hernando de. *The Mystery of Capital: Why Capitalism Triumphs in the West and Fails Everywhere Else.* New York: Basic Books, 2000.

Spence, Jonathan. *The Search for Modern China.* New York: Norton, 1990.

Spufford, Peter. *Power and Profit: The Merchant in Medieval Europe.* London: Thames & Hudson, 2002.

Stark, Rodney. *Victory of Reason: How Christianity Led to Freedom, Capitalism, and Western Success.* New York: Random House, 2006.

Ste. Croix, Geoffrey de. The Class Struggle in the Ancient Greek World from the Archaic Age to the Arab Conquests. London: Duckworth, 1981.

Stearns, Peter, ed. *Encyclopedia of Social History.* New York/London: Garland, 1994.

Steinmetz, Sebald. *Der Krieg als sociologisches Problem.* Amsterdam: Versluys, 1899.

Steinmetz, Sebald. "Die Bedeutung des Krieges bei den Kulturvölkern," *Zeitschrift für Socialwissenschaft*, NF 5 (1914): 295 ff. and 386 ff.

Stephanson, Anders. *Manifest Destiny: American Expansionism and the Empire of Right.* New York: Hill and Wang, 1995.

Stepugina, T.V. "The First States in China," In *Early Antiquity*, 387–420. Edited by Iwan Diakonoff. Chicago: University of Chicago Press, 1991.

Stewart, Frank Henderson, ed. *Texts in Sinai Bedouin Law.* Wiesbaden: Harrassowitz, 1988–1990, 2 volumes.

Stocking, George W. Jr., ed. *Bones, Bodies, Behavior: Essays on biological Anthropology.* Madison: University of Wisconsin Press, 1988.

Stocking, George W. Jr., ed. *Volksgeist as Method and Ethic: Essays on Boasian Ethnography and the German Anthropological Tradition.* Madison: University of Wisconsin Press, 1996.

Stocking, George W. Jr. *Delimiting Anthropology. Occasional Essays and Reflections.* Madison: University of Wisconsin Press, 2001.

Supple, Barry. "The Nature of Enterprise." In *The Cambridge Economic History of Europe*, vol. 5, 394–462. Edited by Eduard Rich and Charles H. Wilson. Cambridge: Cambridge University Press, 1977.

Swanson, Robert, ed. *Promissory Notes on the Treasury of Merits: Indulgences in Late Medieval Europe.* Leiden: Brill, 2006.

Swedberg, Richard. "Max Weber's Vision of Economic Sociology," In *The Sociology of Economic Life*, 77–96. Edited by Mark Granovetter and Richard Swedberg, ed. Cambridge, MA: Westview Press, 2001.

Takebayashi, Shiro. *Die Entstehung der Kapitalismustheorie in der Gründungsphase der deutschen Soziologie: Von der historischen Nationalökonomie zur historischen Soziologie Werner Sombarts und Max Webers.* Berlin: Ducker & Humblot, 2003.

Talmon, Jacob. *The Unique and the Universal: Some Historical Reflections.* London: Secker & Warburg, 1965.

Tanimoto, Masayuki, ed. *The Role of Tradition in Japan's Industrialization: Another Path to Industrialization.* Oxford: Oxford University Press, 2006.

Tao, L.K. and S.H. Lin "Industry and Labor in China." In *International Unemployment: A Study of Fluctuations in Employment and Unemployment in Several Countries, 1910–1930.* The Hague: International Industry Relations Institute, 1932.

Tauger, Mark. "Soviet Peasants and Collectivization, 1930–1939: Resistance and Adaption." *The Journal of Pasant Studies* 3 (2010): 427–445.

Tawney, Richard H. *Religion and the Rise of Capitalism.* Harmondsworth: Pelican, 1961.

Tchernia, André. *Le vin de l'Italie romaine: essai d'histoire économique d'après les amphores.* Paris: École Française de Rome, 1986.

Thanh-Hung, N. *Zur Theorie der vorkapitalistischen Produktionsweisen bei K.Marx und F.Engels.* Gaiganz: Politladen Verlag, 1975.

Thurow, Lester. *The Future of Capitalism: How Today's Economic Forces Shape Tomorrow's World.* New York: William Morrow, 1996.

Tomlinson, Richard. *From Mycenae to Constantinople. The Evolution of the Ancient City.* London: Routledge, 1992.

Toorn, Karel van der. *Sin and Sanction in Israel and Mesopotamia: A Comparative Study.* Assen: Van Gorcum, 1985.

van der Toorn, Karel. *Scribal Culture and the Making of the Hebrew Bible.* Cambridge, MA: Harvard University Press, 2007.

Toynbee, Arnold. *A Study of History.* Oxford: Oxford University Press, 1957; Somervell Abridgement.

Tribe, Keith. "Review of Shiro Takebayashi." *Max Weber Studies* Beiheft (2006): 135–139.

Tschajanow, Alexander. *Die Lehre von der bäuerlichen Wirtschaft. Versuch einer Theorie der Familienwirtschaft im Landbau.* Berlin: Paul Parey, 1923; translated from the Russian by Friedrich Schlömer.

Tsetskhladze, Gocha, ed. *Greek Colonisation: An Account of Greek Colonies and Other Settlements Overseas.* Leiden: Brill, 2006.

Tsai, Po-Fang. "The Introduction and Reception of Max Weber's Sociology in Taiwan and China." *Journal of Sociology* 52 (2016): 118–133.

Turda, Marius and Paul Weindling ed. *"Blood and Homeland": Eugenics and Racial Nationalism in Central and Southeast Europe, 1900–1940.* Budapest/New York: CEU Press, 2007.

Vaux, Roland de. *Ancient Israel: Its Life and Institutions.* London: Darton/Longman, 1961.

Veblen, Thornstein. *The Portable Veblen.* New York: Viking, 1948, edited by Max Lerner.

Veit, Veronika. "Die Mongolen: Von der Clanföderation zur Volksrepublik." In *Die Mongolen. Beiträge zu ihrer Geschichte und Kultur,* 155–183. Edited by Michael Weiers. Darmstadt: Wissenschaftliche Buchgesellschaft, 1986.

Verlinden, Charles. "Markets and Fairs." In *The Cambridge Economic History of Europe,* vol. 3, 119–57. Edited by Michael Postan. Cambridge: Cambridge University Press, 1971.

Vidal-Naquet, Pierre. *The Jews: History, Memory and the Present.* New York: Columbia University Press, 1996.

Viola, Lynne. *Peasant Rebels under Stalin: Collectivization and the Culture of Peasant Resistance.* New York: Oxford University Press, 1996.

Völger, Gisela and Karin Welck v., eds. *Männerbande, Männerbünde. Zur Rolle des Mannes im Kulturvergleich.* Köln: Rautenstrauch-Joest Museum. (Ethnologica NF, Band 15), 1990. 2 volumes.

Voltaire. *Dictionnaire Philosophique.* Paris: Pierre Didot, 1816; édition stéréotype.

Vooys, Adriaan de. *Griekenland: Het heden van Hellas.* Meppel: Boom, 1962.

Waal, Pieter de. *De leer van het boekhouden in de Nederlanden in de zestiende eeuw.* Roermond: Romen, 1927.

Waibel, Alois A. *Moraltheologie nach dem Geiste des heiligen Alphons M. Liguori.* Regensburg: Joseph Manz, 1839–1844, 8 volumes.

Walkenhorst, Peter. *Nation—Volk—Rasse. Radikaler Nationalismus im Deutschen Kaiserreich 1890–1914.* Göttingen: Vandenhoeck & Ruprecht, 2007. Kritische Studien zur Geschichtswissenschaft 176.

Wang Hui. "The Liberation of the Object and the Interrogation of Modernity." *Modern China* 34 (2008): 114–140.

Wang Hui. "Weber and the Question of Chinese Modernity." In *The Politics of Imagining Asia,* 264–308. Edited by Wang Hui and Theodore Huters. Cambridge, MA: Harvard UP, 2011.

Warnke, Martin, ed. *Politische Architektur in Europa vom Mittelalter bis heute.* Köln: DuMont, 1984.

Waterfield, Robin. *Athens: From Ancient Ideal to Modern City.* New York: Basic Books, 2004.

Waxman, Dov. *Trouble in the Tribe: The American Jewish Conflict over Israel.* Princeton: Princeton University Press, 2016.

Weber, Max. *Zur Geschichte der Handelsgesellschaften im Mittelalter nach südeuropäischen Quellen.* Amsterdam: Bonset, 1970, reprint from the original 1889.

Weber, Max. "Agrarverhältnisse im Altertum." In *Handwörterbuch der Staatswissenschaften,* 2nd edition, vol. 1, 57–85. Edited by Joseph Conrad. Jena: Fischer, 1898.

Weber, Max. *Wirtschaftsgeschichte: Abriss der universalen Sozial- und Wirtschaftsgeschichte.* S. Hellmann, S. and Melchior Palyi, ed. München/ Leipzig: Duncker–Humblot, 1924a. Abbreviated: Wg.

Weber, Max. *Gesammelte Aufsätze zur Sozial- und Wirtschaftsgeschichte.* Tübingen: Mohr, 1924b. Abbreviated: GASW.

Weber, Max. *Gesammelte Aufsätze zur Religionssoziologie.* Tübingen: Mohr, 1934, 3 volumes. Abbreviated: GARS.

Weber, Max. *Die protestantische Ethik.* München/Hamburg: Siebenstern, 1968, 2 volumes.

Weber, Max. *Wirtschaft und Gesellschaft: Grundriss der verstehenden Soziologie.* Tübingen: Mohr, 1976a, 5th edition. Abbreviated: WG.

Weber, Max. *Economy and Society: An Outline of Interpretive Sociology.* Berkeley: University of California Press, 1978, translated by Guenther Roth and Claus Wittich. Abbreviated: ES.

Weber, Max. *The Agrarian Sociology of Ancient Civilizations.* London: New Left Books, 1976b, translated by R.I. Frank.

Wee, Herman van der. "Monetary, Credit and Banking Systems." In *The Cambridge Economic History of Europe*, vol. 5, 290–394. Edited by Edward Rich and Charles Wilson. Cambridge: Cambridge University Press, 1977.

Wehler, Hans-Ulrich. *Modernisierungstheorie und Geschichte.* Göttingen: Vandenhoeck & Ruprecht, 1975.

Wehler, Hans-Ulrich. *Aus der Geschichte lernen?: Essays.* München: Beck, 1988.

Wehler, Hans-Ulrich. *Deutsche Gesellschaftsgeschichte, 1700–1990.* München: Beck, 1989–2008, 5 volumes.

Weiers, Michael, ed. *Die Mongolen. Beiträge zu ihrer Geschichte und Kultur.* Darmstadt: Wissenschaftliche Buchgesellschaft, 1986.

Weigelin-Schwiedrzik, Susanne. "Review of Wang-Hui 'The Politics of Imagining Asia'." *National Identities* 18 (2016): 430–433.

Weindling, Paul J. "Central Europe Confronts German Racial Hygiene: Friedrich Hertz, Hugo Iltis and Ignaz Zollschan as Critics of Racial Hygiene." In *"Blood and Homeland": Eugenics and Racial Nationalism in Central and Southeast Europe, 1900–1940*, 263–283. Edited by Marius Turda and Paul Weindling. Budapest/New York: CEU Press, 2007.

Wells, B., ed. *Agriculture in Ancient Greece.* Stockholm: Swedisch Institute at Athens, 1992.

Welskopf, Elisabeth, ed. *Hellenische Poleis. Krise–Wandlung–Wirkung.* Berlin: Akademie Verlag, 1974, 4 volumes.

Wertheim, Wim. *East-West Parallels: Sociological Approaches to Modern Asia.* The Hague: Mouton, 1964.

Wertheim, Wim. "De integratie van stad en platteland in China." *Sociologische Gids* 19 (1972): 92–102.

Wertheim, Wim. *Evolutie en Revolutie.* Amsterdam: Van Gennep, 1973.

Wertheim, Wim. *Emancipation in Asia: Positive and Negative Lessons from China.* Rotterdam: CASP, 1983.

Wertheim, Wim. "The Contribution of Weberian Sociology to Studies of Southeast Asia." *Journal of Southeast Asian Studies* 26.1 (1995): 17–29.

Westermarck, Eduard. *Ursprung und Entwicklung der Moralbegriffe.* Leipzig: Verlag Klinkhardt, 1907, 2 volumes.

Westwood, John N. *Endurance and Endeavour. Russian History, 1812–1980.* Oxford: Oxford University Press, 1981.

Weulersse, Jean. *Paysans de Syrie et due Proche-Orient.* Paris: Gallimard, 1946.

Whittaker, C.R., ed. *Pastoral Economies in Classical Antiquity.* Cambridge: The Cambridge Philological Society, 1988.

Wildt, Michael. "Anmerkungen zur 'Volksgemeinschaft'." In *Zeiträume Potsdamer Almanach,* 201–211. Potsdam: Zentrum für Zeithistorische Forschung, 2009.

Will, Eduard. "Trois quart de siècle de recherches sur l'économie grecque antique." *Annales* 9 (1954): 7–22.

Wills, Garry. *A Necessary Evil: A History of American Distrust of Government.* New York: Simon and Schuster, 1999.

Wilson, Charles. "Trade, Society and the State." In *The Cambridge Economic History of Europe*, vol. 4, 487–577. Edited by Eduard Rich and Charles Wilson. Cambridge: Cambridge University Press, 1977.

Wing-Lun, Joel. "Review of Wang Hui 'The Politics of Imagining Asia'." *Asian Studies Review* 36 (2012): 435–436.

Wippermann, Wolfgang. *"Wie die Zigeuner": Antisemitismus und Antiziganismus im Vergleich.* Berlin: Elefanten Press, 1997.

Wittfogel, Karl August. *Geschichte der bürgerlichen Gesellschaft.* Wien: Malik Verlag, 1924.

Wittfogel, Karl August. *Wirtschadt und Gesellschaft Chinas: Versuch der wissenschaftlichen Analyse einer grossen asiatischen Agrargesellschaft.* Leipzig: Hirschfeld, 1931. *Erster Teil, Produktivkräfte, Produktions- und Zirkulationsprozess.* Schriften des Instituts für Sozialforschung an der Universtät Frankfurt a.M., 3.

Wittfogel, Karl August. *Oriental Despotism. A Comparative Study of Total Power.* New York: Vintage Books, 1981; orig. 1957; German edition, 1962.

Wortmann, Johan C. *Na de E.I.S.—tijd.* Eindhoven: Technische Universiteit Eindhoven, 2003.

Wycherley, R.E. "Classical Cities and Sanctuaries." In *The Cambridge Ancient History*, vol. 5, The Fifth Century B.C., 184–205. Edited by John Boardman. Cambridge: Cambridge University Press, 1992.

Wyrwa, Ulrich. "Review of M.Lange." In *H-Soz-u-Kult* (22–12-2008).

Yamey, Basil. "Scientific Bookkeeping and the Rise of Capitalism." *The Economic History Review* 1 (1949): 99–113.

Yamey, Basil. "Early Views on the Origins and Development of Book-Keeping and Accounting." *Accounting and Business Research* 10, 37A, Special Issue (1980): 81–92.

Yamey, Basil. "Some Reflections on the Writing of a General History of Accounting." *Accounting and Business Research* 11 (1981): 127–135.

Yamey, Basil. *Further Essays on the History of Accounting.* New York/London: Garland, 1982.

Yamey, Basil. "Double-entry Bookkeeping." In *The New Palgrave. A Dictionary of Economics*, vol. 1, 917–920. Edited by John Eatwell, Murray Milgate and Peter Newman. London: Macmillan, 1987

Yamey, Basil. "The Historical Significance of Double-Entry Bookkeeping: Some Non-Sombartian Claims." *Accounting, Business & Financial History* 15 (2005): 77–88.

Yeh-chien, W. *Land Taxation in Imperial China, 1750–1911.* Cambridge, MA: Harvard University Press, 1973.

Young-Bruehl, Elisabeth. *Hannah Arendt: For Love of the World.* New Haven: Yale University Press, 1982.

Zalashik, Rakefet. *Das unselige Erbe: Die Geschichte der Psychiatrie in Palästina und Israel.* Frankfurt a.M.: Campus, 2012.

Zang, Don S. "The West in the East: Max Weber's Nightmare in 'Post-modern China'." *Max Weber Studies* 14 (2014): 33 ff.

Zertal, Idith. *From Catastrophe to Power. Holocaust Survivors and the Emergence of Israel.* Berkeley: University of California Press, 1998.

Zollschan, Ignaz. *Das Rassenproblem unter besonderer Berücksichtigung der theoretischen Grundlagen der jüdischen Rassenfrage.* Wien-Leipzig: Wilhelm Braumüller, 1912; dritte, verbesserte und vermehrte Auflage.

Zollschan, Ignaz. *Revision des jüdischen Nationalismus.* Wien-Berlin: Löwit Verlag, 1919.

Zollschan, Ignaz. *The Significance of the Racial Factor as a Basis in Cultural Development.* London: Le Play House Press, 1934.

Name and Subject Index

Abel and Cain 187, 188, 189, 190, 191, 192, 193, 195, 196, 197, 198, 199, 200, 201, 203, 205, 206, 208, 209, 210, 211, 213, 214
Adorno, Theodor 179, 180, 181, 182, 184, 185, 213, 237, 327, 338, 354, 377
Africa 41, 138, 216, 223, 225, 229n, 235, 245, 343
agriculture XVI, XXIV, 18, 19, 65, 88, 89n, 95, 98, 99, 105, 186, 198, 199, 203, 221, 222, 238, 239, 243, 244, 244n, 245, 247, 248, 249, 250n, 252, 256, 257, 264n, 271, 273, 274, 276, 277, 280, 303, 306, 321, 328, 336, 337, 344 *See*: peasants
Aho, James 5n, 6, 29, 30, 30n, 31, 33, 34, 35, 36, 37n, 38, 39, 40, 41, 51, 52, 57n, 62, 68n
Alberti, Leonardo XIX, 20, 36, 37n, 68, 105
Amalek(ites) 187, 187n, 188, 195, 196, 197, 198, 210, 217
Anderson, Eugene 251n, 252n, 253n
Anderson, Paul 350, 351
Anderson, Perry 5n, 332, 335, 336, 345
Anderson, Shannon 353n
animal breeding (husbandry) 19, 90, 95, 96, 98, 99, 101, 106, 111n, 124, 185, 197, 204, 237, 238, 242, 243, 245, 247, 249, 250, 253, 254n, 257, 271, 273, 337
animal culture 89n, 97, 101n, 110, 111n, 112, 130, 163, 185, 191, 193, 198, 202, 209, 236, 237, 239, 240, 244n, 245, 248, 252, 254, 256, 263, 270, 308, 372, 373
animal products 112, 238, 239, 245, 251n, 254, 262
anthropology, cultural 105
anthropology, physical 129, 137, 142
antisemitism (anti-semitism) 28, 126, 139, 140, 141, 142, 150, 151, 154, 157, 165, 167, 168, 173, 179, 181, 185, 212, 214, 353
Aquinas, Thomas 32, 56, 57, 109
Arabs 4, 148, 149, 158, 160, 164, 169n, 170, 171, 172, 186n, 211, 231n, 233, 256
Arendt, Hannah XXVII, 136, 173, 215, 233
aristocracy 10, 11, 18, 33, 48, 68, 154, 230, 282, 284, 324, 373
arithmetic 38, 41, 54, 55, 56, 59, 60, 68, 353n
Aristotle XII, XIV, XIX, 17, 19, 22, 23, 32, 35, 55, 56, 57, 72, 74, 76, 91, 99, 100, 105, 108, 109, 113, 114, 119, 120, 125, 156n, 227, 273n, 332, 333, 334, 336, 337
Arrighi, Giovanni 5n, 223, 224n, 318n, 338n, 345, 364, 366
Ashkenazim 138, 171, 172
Asiatic Mode of Production XXII, XXVI, 266, 319, 320, 326, 329, 330, 331, 336
astu – *agros* 83, 85, 93, 95, 99, 100, 101
astu – city 17, 84, 88, 93, 96, 98, 102
Athens 71, 73, 74, 83, 84n, 86n, 87, 88, 90, 93, 94, 95, 96, 97, 98, 100, 102, 111, 222, 335n
Attica 74, 83, 84n, 86, 88, 94, 96, 98, 99, 101, 102
autarky XIII, 17, 63, 73n, 108, 112, 120

balance XX, 27n, 43, 44, 46, 47, 49, 50, 51, 53, 56, 59, 60, 262, 329n, 349, 374
banks 10, 13n, 20, 31, 32, 33, 35, 38, 40, 44, 46, 48, 54, 57, 58, 62, 65, 96, 111, 150, 154, 289, 295, 313, 317, 364, 373
barter 24, 65, 206, 256, 373
Bedarfsdeckung XVIII, 18, 21, 27, 64, 108, 113n, 120, 184, 361n
Bedouin 133n, 185, 186, 187, 188, 189, 193, 194, 195, 196, 197, 203, 205n, 209, 242, 274
Beijing 222, 286, 289, 294, 301, 303, 308, 314, 317, 323
Benjamin, Walter XVIII, 355, 356, 357, 358, 359n, 360
Ben Gurion 141, 162n, 166, 170, 216
Berman, Harold 37n, 39, 40
Bintliff, John 72, 77, 78, 86n, 87, 88, 89n
bookkeeping (DEB) XVIII, XXVI, 4, 5, 22, 29, 34, 35, 36, 39, 40, 41, 42, 43, 45, 47n, 52, 54, 58, 65, 77, 225, 327, 356, 374
Braudel, Fernand 5n, 32n, 41, 50n, 116, 117, 118, 119n, 321n
Bray, David 290n
Brunner, Otto XXIII, 104, 105, 106, 111n, 114, 115, 116, 117, 118, 119, 121, 122, 125
Bücher, Karl XXI, 17, 19n, 21, 110, 113, 273, 293
budget, state 22, 23, 45, 52, 65, 114n, 292
bureaucracy XIV, 11, 16, 18, 35, 66, 114, 148, 264, 269, 271, 282, 283, 284, 299, 313, 329, 330, 339, 340, 364, 374

Cain and Abel (*see*: Abel and Cain)
Calvinism XVII, XVIII, XXV, 5, 30, 36, 53, 61n, 63, 318, 351354, 358, 361
capital (city) 73, 108, 155, 248, 261, 267, 269, 278n, 279, 285, 286, 295, 301, 324, 334
capital (money, etc.) 4, 7, 9, 9n, 15, 16, 18, 24, 27, 29, 39, 43, 47n, 51, 52, 4, 56, 58, 67, 101, 208, 221, 276, 285, 291, 294, 296, 308, 311, 313, 346, 350
capitalist production (cp) 4, 7, 9, 10, 11, 12, 13, 15, 16, 18, 31, 40, 43, 61, 62, 64, 68, 114, 272, 292, 296, 298, 312, 319, 337, 349, 362, 374
capitalism XV, XVI, XVII, XVIII, XXII, XXIV, 4, 5, 5n, 6, 8, 9, 12, 13, 14, 17, 20n, 27, 30, 36, 41, 44, 60, 62, 64, 66, 68, 121, 126, 131, 162, 173n, 175, 177, 179, 217, 246, 248n, 293, 300, 302, 312, 317, 318, 326, 328, 330, 338, 345, 349n, 350, 352, 354, 357, 359, 361, 364, 366, 373, 374
catholicism 5, 49n, 12, 14, 30, 31, 36, 37, 38, 53, 62, 63, 227, 352, 362
cattle XII, 25, 90, 96, 103, 185, 187n, 194, 205, 244, 245, 247, 251, 252, 254n, 256, 257, 269, 271
Chamberlain, Houston 141, 142, 143, 168
China IX, XVII, XXII, 4, 15, 16, 48, 241, 247, 250, 253, 260, 266, 277, 284, 289, 310, 317, 323, 328, 369
  agriculture 221, 250, 253, 255, 256, 279, 307, 336
  capitalism 252, 274, 306, 318, 319, 322, 349, 354, 363
  colony IX, 225, 286, 291, 295
  bourgeoisie (elite) 249, 269, 283, 302, 310, 324, 344
  history (historiography) XXIV, 224, 250n, 251n, 258, 266, 272, 277, 283, 289, 302, 305, 308, 314, 320, 327, 330, 368
  industrialization 291, 292, 294, 295, 296, 299, 306
    market-*oikos* XXII, 249, 257, 263, 268, 280n, 290n, 291, 296, 299, 306, 312, 313, 349, 365, 372, 373
  modernity XVIIn, XXII, XXVI, 291, 294, 295, 312, 341, 346, 367
  nomads in/and 241, 246, 248, 255, 257n, 259, 261, 264, 268
  revolts, revolution 284, 285, 301, 302, 303, 309n, 324
  state 259, 260, 261, 264, 265, 267, 268, 283, 301, 302, 345
  town-country IX, XXV, 252n, 267, 275, 277, 279, 283, 285, 289, 301, 306, 307, 309, 320, 322, 346, 347
  trade with IX, 28n, 177, 224n, 265, 274, 323
  war with XXVI, 224n, 241, 257, 258n, 266, 286
  Weber about/in XXII, XXV, 15, 215, 236, 247, 250, 255n, 276, 298, 318, 326, 337, 363, 364
  West, comparison/ relation with XXVI, 248n, 273n, 284, 286, 289, 292, 300, 317, 322
  See also Asiatic Mode of Production, Beijing, feudalism, husbandry, Mao Zedong, milk, Mongols, opium, Oriental Despotism, pastoralism, peasants. Shanghai, village
chrematistic 35, 108, 114
Christianity XXV, 30n, 61, 108, 152, 175, 201, 202, 318, 322, 343, 347, 351, 357, 358, 359
Chuah, Swee Hoon 367
church 10, 11, 12, 18, 31, 32, 33, 34, 37, 40, 46, 48, 52, 55, 60, 65, 67, 68, 105, 109, 124, 131, 151, 153, 158, 167, 167n, 202, 217, 225n, 228, 278n, 346, 350, 352, 354
city XVI, 16, 21, 46, 57, 64, 71, 72, 73, 75, 76, 77, 78, 82, 83, 85, 89, 91, 93, 99, 108, 111, 129, 176, 186, 203, 265, 289, 290n, 295, 307, 309, 310, 340, 347, 361
city – country IX, 72, 76, 95, 96, 101, 102, 209, 223, 239, 243n, 254, 254n, 271, 275, 276, 279, 290, 291, 301, 303, 306, 309, 310, 347
city – state 17, 48, 57, 71, 72, 73, 74, 75n, 77, 78, 87, 88, 89n, 99
Colbert XIV, 44
collectivization 256, 268, 269, 270, 271, 305, 311, 312
colonialism XXV, 127, 157, 223, 224, 227, 229, 307, 360n, 369
colonist XXV, 135, 157, 167, 168, 172, 227, 229, 230, 231, 233
commenda 32, 37, 38, 39
common law 37, 38, 39, 40
Conrad, Joseph XVIII

Confucianism XXV, 317, 357, 364, 365, 367
court 20, 35, 40, 48, 151, 208, 232, 248n, 249, 256, 258n, 259, 261, 262, 263, 265, 277, 279, 338, 374

Darius 236, 241, 258
Darwin 130, 131, 140, 142, 143, 145, 162, 258n, 372
Datini 34, 34n, 36, 38, 39, 46, 54
demand XII, XVI, XVIII, XX, 8, 13, 16, 18, 23, 28, 32, 42, 44, 50, 52, 53, 57, 63, 64, 66, 68, 90, 101, 108, 153, 154, 160, 161, 162, 232, 257, 264n, 283, 304, 314, 321, 341, 373
Dreistufen – theory 249
double-entry bookkeeping (DEB). *See*: bookkeeping

Edwards, John XXVII, 3n
Eisenstadt, Shmuel 173, 217n
Elvin, Mark 247n, 251n, 252, 255n, 278
empire 19, 61, 76, 109, 112, 167, 171, 201, 222, 223, 228, 229, 230, 231, 233, 235, 260, 287n, 320n, 323, 324n, 362
England (UK) XIV, 7, 9, 10, 11, 13n, 19, 35, 181, 207, 224, 225, 247, 361
equality 50, 56, 57, 59, 121, 241
equilibrium XX, XXI, 42, 50, 51, 58, 59, 329
ethnos 74, 74n
Europe(an) IX, XII, XIV, XVII, XVIII, XIX, XXI, XXII, XXIV, XXV, 3n, 4, 13, 14, 19, 29, 35, 41, 44, 52, 54, 61, 71, 75, 83, 105, 117, 119, 127, 130, 138, 148, 158, 162, 164n, 169, 172, 180, 217, 222, 228, 237n, 248, 262, 283, 284, 307, 321, 325, 329, 331, 350, 353, 355, 362, 369
exchange XV, XVI, XX 19, 23, 24, 25, 28, 33, 35, 55, 56, 57, 65, 66, 86, 108, 119, 124, 127, 239, 240, 243n, 256, 272, 276, 279, 321, 338, 372, 373

Fahlbusch, Michael 360, 363n
family XI, XIII, XVI, XX, 17, 18, 19, 20, 21n, 23, 37, 38, 63, 79, 96, 106, 107, 113, 117, 119, 120, 121, 122, 123, 151, 182, 190, 191, 202n, 204, 211, 233, 242, 250, 260, 290n, 308, 314, 341, 347, 373
feudalism 243, 283, 284, 302, 319, 328, 330, 337, 339, 373
Finley, Moses XXI, XXIV, 19n, 72, 73, 74n, 77, 78n, 79, 91n, 92, 95, 96n, 99, 100, 108, 110, 111, 112, 239, 273, 276, 279n
Fishberg, Maurice 133, 144, 145, 146, 156, 173n, 177
Florence 34n, 35, 46
France XXVI, 8, 9, 10, 11, 19, 44, 45, 50, 118, 284, 322, 356, 362
Franciscans 54, 55, 56, 57, 228
Franklin, Benjamin XVIII, 20n, 36

Gawantka, Wilfried 78, 111n
Geny, Eveline XXVI
geometry, political 20, 54, 58
gerim 209, 210, 211, 212
Germany XVI, XVIII, 8, 10, 11, 12n, 13n, 14, 20, 34, 44, 45, 50, 62, 104, 111n, 115, 116, 117, 126, 129, 131, 140, 141, 148, 149n, 152, 153, 155, 157, 169, 170, 172, 216, 225, 355n, 356, 359n, 360, 362
Gilman, Sander 137, 156n, 173, 176, 177, 178
Gottwald, Norman 192n, 194, 196, 203
Greece 19, 71, 72, 83, 85, 92, 111n, 124, 239, 333
Grenznutzen 18, 27
gypsy 185

Haar, Ingo 300, 363n
Hahn, Eduard 249, 250
Hamilton, Gary XVII, 365, 366
Hansen, Mogens 76, 94, 96
Hausgemeinschaft XIV, XIX, 18, 21, 25, 26, 64
Haushalt 20, 21, 21n, 22, 22n, 23, 24, 27, 30n, 63, 113, 247n
Hausvaterliteratur 20, 105
Herodotos 236, 241, 334, 335
Hesiodos 85, 105
hinduism 183
Historische Schule XIX, 127n
Holocaust 116, 137, 148, 149, 159n, 212n, 214, 217, 320n, 353n
Horkheimer, Max 179, 180, 181, 182, 327, 338, 354
house-oikos X, XI, XII, XIII, XIX, XX, 17, 22, 23, 35, 37, 84, 93, 104, 105, 106, 107, 108, 109, 110, 112, 113, 114, 115, 120, 121, 123, 124, 125, 186, 187n, 192, 204, 205, 248, 269, 271, 293n, 298, 308, 313, 314, 343
household IX, XI, XII, XIII, XIV, XIX, XX, 14, 17, 18, 20, 21, 22, 24, 25, 26, 27, 31, 37, 38,

household (cont.) 43, 44, 48, 51, 54, 58, 61, 63, 65, 67, 79, 86n, 94, 95n, 96, 97, 105, 108, 109, 113, 114, 115n, 122, 124, 242, 257n, 268, 272, 280, 308, 311
Humboldt, Alexander von 249, 250
Ho-fung Hung 311, 312, 314, 345n, 363, 364, 366, 368
hunters 196, 221, 238, 249
husbandry 19, 88, 90, 95, 98, 99, 106, 111n, 112, 124, 185, 204, 238, 239, 240, 243, 244, 245, 247, 250, 252, 254n, 273, 274, 337

industry XX, 10, 18, 60, 65, 108, 125n, 154, 254, 275, 276, 292, 293, 295, 296, 297, 299, 306, 307, 313, 336, 344
imperialism XXV, 131, 223, 227, 231, 233, 259, 268, 269, 286, 289, 301, 307, 318, 322, 328, 330, 331, 343, 360n, 365, 369
information system 14, 15, 42, 43, 44, 66, 67
India IX, 4, 16, 48, 183, 210, 226, 288n, 290n, 291, 292, 319, 320, 323, 325, 327, 332, 334, 336, 360n
Islam XXV, 4, 167, 168, 194, 199, 318, 357
Italy 6, 11, 13n, 26, 36, 40, 41, 46, 48, 50, 59, 116

Jabotinsky, Ze'ev 141, 158n, 162n, 166
Jagchid, Sechin 255n, 257n, 258, 259, 260, 264n, 265
Japan 14, 280, 290n, 295, 296, 300, 301, 309n, 322, 326, 327, 332, 360n, 367
jews XXV, 5, 12, 29, 32, 54, 127, 133, 135, 138, 138n, 146, 150, 153, 155, 156, 162, 166, 170, 173, 180, 184, 199, 203n, 205, 212, 230, 23
Jewish Question 129, 131, 133n, 136, 140, 150, 152, 155, 182, 184 (*see*: antisemitism)
Jewish Rasse 129, 132, 133, 137, 139, 141, 143, 145, 146, 156, 157, 163, 164, 171, 214
judaism XXV, 28, 61, 63, 126, 133, 134, 135, 151, 153, 159, 162, 167, 175, 182, 190, 194, 206, 214, 217, 315

Kameralistik XVIII
Kapitalismus XVII, 8, 9, 12, 13n, 24, 29, 30, 62, 355, 356, 357
Kapitalrechnung 27, 28, 50, 113n
Kroeschell, Karl 104n, 106n, 115, 115n, 123
Krugman, Paul 348, 349

Lamarck, Jean-Baptiste 142, 143, 145, 155, 156, 162, 165
language XXV, 22, 49, 67, 91n, 113, 127, 128, 130, 132, 134, 158, 159, 160, 161, 163, 175, 216, 229, 234, 269, 310, 374
Lebensraum 107, 130
Leibowitz, Yeshayahu 134, 135, 167, 215, 216n, 218
Lipphardt, Veronika 138n, 139, 140, 141n, 144, 145n, 156n, 157n, 173n
Lossing Buck, John 253, 254
lutheranism XXV, 12, 14, 62, 105, 150, 151, 173n, 200, 225n, 359, 361

Maccoby, Hyam 212, 213, 214, 215
Mao Zedong 251n, 303, 309n, 320
market IX, XII, XIII, XIV, XV, XVI, XVII, XVIII, XIX, XX, XXI, XXIII, XXV, 8, 9, 15, 19, 23, 28, 39, 43, 57, 63, 64, 67, 95, 102, 108, 120, 124, 198, 268, 299, 370, 372, 373
  market, accounting 65
  market competition 16, 18
  market economy 7, 18, 19, 22, 24, 28, 29, 38, 58, 64, 95, 102, 112, 225, 240, 245, 280n, 296, 299, 313, 321, 362
  market, evolution of 65, 111, 114, 223, 264n, 317, 334, 361
  market, financial (capital) 23, 26, 32, 39, 108, 111n, 114, 240, 356 (*see*: money)
  market, free (open) 8, 13, 68, 248n, 264, 338, 369
  marketing XX, XXII, 112, 238, 264, 290n
  market, labor 39, 68, 112, 335n, 346
  market language 22, 262, 356
  market, monopoly 68
  market – *oikos* (theory) IX, XIV, XVI, XVII, XVIII, XXI, XXII, XXIII, XXIV, XXV, XXVI, 3, 4, 6, 14, 15, 16, 17, 17n, 27, 33, 37, 41, 43, 44, 58, 63, 64, 71, 79n, 114, 190, 207, 221, 234, 236, 242, 262, 268, 272, 290, 291, 311, 335, 372, 373
  market places 47, 63, 71, 80, 186, 199, 247n, 257, 261, 264, 265, 267, 279, 280, 282, 289, 307, 335, 341, 346, 347
  market, power (politics) 68, 217, 312, 313, 369
  market science 20, 224n, 239, 240, 273, 317, 321, 339, 340, 348, 349n, 371

market society XXII, 16, 26, 61, 63, 95, 206, 213, 225, 240, 241, 242, 262, 263, 299, 335
market system 8, 10, 56, 57, 63, 64, 67
market war 290n, 296, 323
Marx, Karl (Marxism) XIV, XV, XVII, XXVI, 6, 7, 8, 9, 10, 12, 13n, 25, 64, 67, 76, 97n, 110, 127n, 133n, 177, 181n, 192, 225n, 226, 260, 272, 318, 319, 320, 321, 326, 330, 331, 336, 337, 338, 339, 348, 355, 356n, 357, 365, 371
meat 239, 245, 246, 247, 248, 249, 250, 252n, 253, 255, 270, 273, 349
Mendenhall, George 194
mercantilism XII, XIV, XVIII, 21
metics 95n, 96, 97n, 98, 102, 204, 205, 208, 209, 332
Meyer, Eduard 77, 110, 168, 188n, 195n, 197, 198n, 210n, 212n
Meyer, Hajo 149
Middle East (Near East) 11, 129n, 130, 132, 136, 137n, 146n, 231, 233, 235, 288n, 319, 320, 323, 325, 353
milk 180, 181, 186, 239, 244, 245, 247, 248, 249, 250, 252, 254n, 273, 349
monarchy XIII, 10, 18, 20, 33, 48, 61, 67, 180, 198, 199, 204, 324, 33
money XIV, XV, XVI, XVIII, 4, 7, 9, 14, 18, 19, 23, 24, 25, 27, 28, 31, 32, 35, 37, 39, 43, 49, 50, 52, 53, 55, 56, 62, 63, 65, 66, 86n, 102, 108, 111, 124, 138, 162, 168, 174, 189, 201, 214, 216, 228, 239, 240, 248n, 255, 298, 321, 335, 338, 341, 344, 356, 363, 373
Mongols 247n, 248, 253, 255, 257, 260n, 261, 263, 264n, 265, 266n, 269, 271, 272, 278
Monopol der Gewalt 13, 75n
monopoly XXII, 10, 12, 13, 14, 60, 61, 62, 68, 183, 217, 226, 235, 269, 286, 288, 319, 362, 364, 374
Murthy, Viren XXII, XXIIIn, 264n, 278n, 367, 368n
Mussolini, Benito 207

nation XIII, XIX, XXIV, XXV, 49, 50, 73, 80n, 117, 128, 130, 132, 135, 136n, 144, 150n, 152, 153, 157, 158, 159, 162, 167, 177, 222, 230, 231, 233, 293, 300, 307, 321, 336, 351, 362
national(ism) XVI, XXIII, XXIV, XXV, 11, 12, 14, 45, 48, 49, 110, 126, 127, 129, 130, 131, 132, 139, 140, 141, 153, 157, 159, 160, 162, 207, 223, 230, 271, 292, 294, 319, 330, 342, 362, 367, 374
National Socialism 12, 105, 108, 115, 116, 126, 131, 132, 141, 145, 184, 216n
Naturalwirtschaft 18, 243, 256n, 337
Nomadic Question 182, 183, 184, 185, 186, 188, 195, 199, 200, 213, 236, 237n, 242, 248, 255, 268
nomadism XXIV, 19, 48, 79, 92, 106, 112, 179, 180, 181, 182, 184, 186, 189n, 194, 204, 211, 213, 236, 240, 241, 243, 245, 247, 260, 274, 320, 337, 357
nomads XIX, XXV, 65, 67, 68, 75, 84, 133, 180, 184, 185, 186, 187, 190, 191, 192, 193, 194, 196, 197, 198, 202n, 205, 209, 238, 257, 262, 270

Oikenwirtschaft XIX, XXI, 17, 109, 112, 267
oikoïdal economy 17, 36, 67, 68, 108, 198
oikos X, XI, XII, XIII, XIX, XX *See*: family, house, household, state
oikos – market. *See* market-*oikos*
oikos – market controversy XXI, XXIV, 19n, 104, 109, 110, 111, 112, 123, 273
Olivi, Peter 56, 57
opium (wars) IX, XII, XXII, XXVI, 224, 265, 286, 287, 288, 289, 290, 291, 300, 301, 310, 324n, 325, 369, 371
Oresme, Nicolas 32, 35, 57
Osborne, Robin XXI, 77n, 78, 89, 90, 97, 99n, 100, 101, 111n

Pacioli, Luca 32, 34, 36, 41, 42, 44, 45, 46, 48, 49, 52, 54, 55, 56, 57, 58, 59
Palestine XXV, 136, 137, 138n, 144, 147, 148, 157, 158, 161, 162, 166, 167, 168, 169, 170, 171, 172, 185, 186, 187n, 198n, 214, 224, 226, 230, 231, 232
pariah complex 183, 184, 185, 193, 200, 204, 205, 206, 209, 210, 211, 212, 213, 214, 215
Parsons, Talcott 12, 22, 25, 27n, 114n
pastoralism 106, 111n, 112, 239, 253
pasture 84, 238, 243n, 249, 251, 252n, 253, 269, 271, 350
Patai, Raphael 133, 138n, 145, 146, 147, 173
patriarch 107, 108, 114, 120, 122, 180, 182, 193, 204, 205, 206, 209, 211, 213, 214, 215, 228, 242, 283
Pausanias 79, 80, 81, 82, 92, 93

peasants 3, 71, 74n, 95, 112, 121, 149, 185, 186, 187n, 190, 195, 197, 198, 199, 200, 209, 222, 236, 239, 241, 244n, 245, 249, 251, 252, 254, 257, 264n, 267, 268, 269, 270, 271, 272, 275, 278, 279, 280, 281, 282, 283, 284, 299, 302, 303, 304, 305, 306, 307, 308, 321, 328, 330, 331, 342, 343
Po-Fang Tsai XVIIn, 364, 365
Polanyi, Karl XXIn, XXI, XXII, XXIV, 19n, 110, 124n, 273
polis (poleis) 71, 72, 73, 75, 76, 78, 82, 84, 87n, 89, 90, 92, 93, 126, 186
polis – city(state) 17, 71, 72n, 74, 76, 77, 79, 80n, 82, 86n, 99
polis – *oikos* 17, 63, 79, 83, 101
political economy XII, XIII, XX, 21, 105, 247n, 293, 331, 336, 339, 355n, 363, 374
protestantism 10n, 30, 31, 60, 61, 225, 226n

Rachfahl, Felix XVIII
race concept XVI, XXIV, XXV, 11, 126, 128, 132, 134, 135n, 136, 137, 137n, 140, 141, 142, 143, 145, 146, 152, 159, 173n, 176, 178, 187, 193, 207, 216, 235, 362, 374
Rasse XVI, XXIV, 126, 130, 132, 139, 142, 145, 177, 216n
Redford, Donald 190, 195n, 199, 206, 207n, 210
religion XVII, XVIII, XXIV, XXV, 4, 5, 10n, 15, 29, 38, 41, 48, 60, 66, 129, 134, 167, 175, 183, 198, 206, 216n, 217, 225, 228, 287, 317, 347, 350, 351, 354, 355, 357, 358, 374
Rodbertus, Carl XIX, XXI, 8, 17, 19, 109, 113, 120, 239, 273
Rodinson, Maxime 333, 357
Rome 71, 112, 153, 223, 243n
Roman Empire 19, 61, 109, 201, 223
Roover, Raymond de 6, 31, 35n, 38n, 39, 47, 57
Roth, Günther 12n, 22, 25, 30n, 114n
Ruppin, Arthur 133, 140, 144, 166, 167, 169, 174
Ruschenbusch, Eberhard 77, 86n, 87, 89, 91
Russia, Soviet XXII, 11, 138n, 159n, 170, 171, 177, 241, 268, 269, 276, 284, 295, 301, 302, 303, 304, 305, 310, 322, 323, 327, 328, 362, 373n

Sabean, David 123, 124
Sand, Shlomo 132, 135n, 136n, 137, 160n
Schmitt, Carl 116, 117, 119
Schmoller, Gustav von XIX, 19
Segev, Tom 148, 149n, 231
Seligman, Edwin XX
Sephardim 138, 138n, 163, 171, 172
Shanghai 254n, 276, 280n, 291, 294, 295, 296, 297, 298, 299, 300, 301, 307, 310, 317
Shaw, Brent 245, 246
slaves (slavery) XII, 10, 73, 94, 96, 97, 98, 112, 113, 120, 127, 147, 191, 205, 211, 222, 223, 224, 225, 226n, 227, 228n, 229n, 243, 244, 249, 255, 267, 328, 333, 335, 337, 339, 347, 353n
Slicher van Bath, Bernhard XXVII, 65n, 111n, 112, 238, 243n, 307, 321, 322
Sombart, Werner 4, 5, 6, 7, 8, 11, 19, 20, 22, 25, 29, 30, 38, 41, 49, 60, 61, 66, 108, 111, 131, 141, 168, 172, 173, 174, 175, 176, 207, 236, 279, 327, 346, 364
Soto, Hernando de 15, 16, 43, 62
Soviet Union. *See*: Russia
Sparta 75, 76, 77n, 83, 88, 90, 91, 92, 93, 102, 212, 222, 239, 260, 334
Staatswissenschaft XVIII, XIX, XX, 7, 20, 105, 130n, 360
state XII, XIII, XIV, XIX, XX, XXIV, 11, 13, 14, 16, 21, 58, 61, 72, 74, 75n, 83, 86n, 107, 108, 109, 117, 119, 123, 134, 154, 158, 167, 186, 211, 222, 223, 225, 230, 240, 241, 260n, 266n, 267, 278, 282, 283, 288, 289, 296, 306, 319, 321, 329, 330, 339, 356, 361, 374
  state (as *oikos*) XIII, XIX, XXX, 12, 19, 20, 62, 106, 110, 120, 124, 132, 241, 271, 294, 313, 372, 374, 375
  state-bureaucracy. *See*: bureaucracy)
  state – church 12, 33, 67, 134, 228, 346
  state, city. *See*: city-state
  state-household 20, 24, 63n, 79, 108
  state, management. *See*: budget
  state, nation. *See*: nation
  state, patrimonial 20, 202, 267, 268
Stevin, Simon 37n, 52, 54, 58, 59, 60
Strabo 80, 83, 84n

Talmor, Ezra and Sacha XXVI
Tawney, Richard 354n, 358, 359, 360
Thucydides 84, 87, 90, 91, 102, 209

town-country XV, XVI, XXII, XXIII, XXIV, XXV, 64, 67, 83, 94, 98, 100, 101, 102, 108, 112, 221, 236, 271, 275, 277, 278, 279, 285, 302, 311, 313, 320, 321, 326, 339, 340, 346, 348, 369, 371, 372, 375
trade IX, XII, XV, XXII, 9, 13n, 24, 32, 39, 49, 66, 67, 88, 95, 96, 101, 111, 112, 120, 168, 177, 183, 187, 217, 221, 226, 255, 256, 262, 264, 266, 272, 280, 285, 296, 305, 324, 330, 336, 344, 347 *See*: exchange, market
transhumance 185, 238
Treitschke, Heinrich von 150, 151, 152, 154, 155

Unesco 128, 146, 235
United States 7, 110, 145, 231, 253, 327, 363
usury verdict 32, 48, 49

Varro, Terentius XIX
Vaux, Ronald de 188n, 189, 192n, 194, 195, 198, 203n, 211, 212
Veblen, Thorstein 127, 128
Vidal-Naquet, Pierre 74, 77, 110n
village XX, 16, 72, 73, 74, 82, 84, 86n, 88, 90, 92, 99, 124, 183, 243, 269, 277, 282, 297, 302, 311, 330, 336, 342
Virchow, Rudolf 129, 151
Volk (*Völker*) XVI, XX, XXIV, 117, 127, 128, 130, 132, 136, 145, 150n, 158, 159, 162, 167, 170, 176, 216, 222, 230, 234, 361, 374
völkische Wissenschaft 130, 131, 139, 141, 159, 319, 337, 360, 361
Volksgemeinschaft 129, 130, 145, 160, 175, 214, 362, 363
Volkswirtschaft XIX, XX, 110, 126

Wang, Hui XVIIn, XXII, XXIII, 264n, 278n, 367, 368, 370
Weber, Max IX, XVII, XXIV, XXV, 3, 6, 8, 12, 13, 16, 17, 28, 31, 36, 38, 44, 62, 63, 66, 71, 78, 104, 113, 116, 120, 126, 126n,131, 203n, 206, 241, 249, 254, 339, 340, 341, 348, 361, 366XIX, 71, 243, 244, 245, 249, 268, 273, 337
  Agrarian Sociology XIX, 71, 243, 244, 245, 249, 268, 273, 337
  Antike Judentum 183, 184, 185, 186, 205, 208, 210, 215
  Economy and Society 14n, 17, 18, 20, 21, 22, 23, 25, 26, 27, 114n, 242, 362, 365
  Protestantische Ethik (Weber Thesis) XVII, XVIII, XXII, XXIV, 5, 20n, 29, 30, 36, 126, 351, 354n, 360n, 367
  Sociology of Religion 15, 173n, 188, 193, 205, 210, 212, 246, 354, 355, 367 (*see*: Abel and Cain, Amalek)
  Wirtschaftsgeschichte 21, 26, 38, 64, 182, 242, 247, 249, 262
  Wirtschaft und Gesellschaft 14n, 17, 18, 20, 21, 24, 25, 27, 37, 50, 63, 67, 71, 113, 114, 221, 242, 362
Wehler, Hans-Ulrich XXVII, 116, 120, 121, 150, 155n, 346n
Weizmann, Chaim 141, 148, 161, 166, 216
Wertheim, Wim XXVII, 244n, 254n, 266n, 267, 275, 277, 278, 279, 302, 309, 328n, 344
Westforschung 116n
Wing-Lun, Joel 368n

Xenophon XIX, 96n, 103 105

Yamey, Basil 5n, 6, 26, 29n, 30n, 41, 47, 49n, 51

Zalashik, Rakefet 147, 148, 149n, 166, 169, 170, 171n, 172n
Zertal, Idith 148, 149n
zionism 131, 134, 136, 137, 138, 139, 140, 144, 157, 160, 161, 172n, 174, 216, 231n, 319, 353n, 362
Zollschan, Ignaz XXIII, XXIV, 133, 137, 138, 139, 140, 141, 143, 144, 147, 149, 155, 156, 157, 158, 160, 162, 164, 166n, 174, 175, 177

Printed in the United States
By Bookmasters